Mary R. Murrie

Xmas 1930

LIVES OF THE
ROMAN EMPRESSES

, *After the painting by J. L. Gerome*

Cleopatra Obtains an Interview with Cæsar

LIVES OF THE ROMAN EMPRESSES

THE HISTORY OF THE LIVES AND SECRET
INTRIGUES OF THE WIVES, SISTERS AND
MOTHERS OF THE CAESARS

By

JACQUES BOERGAS DE SERVIEZ

With An Introduction by

ROBERT GRAVES

Author of "I, Claudius," "Claudius the God," etc.

Illustrated

NEW YORK
WM. H. WISE & CO.
1935

CONTENTS

iii

CONTENTS

LIST OF ILLUSTRATIONS

INTRODUCTION TO THE
LIVES OF THE ROMAN EMPRESSES

By Robert Graves

The lives of the Roman Empresses up to the reign of Constantine make an excellent dramatic sequence, and it is easy to see why this should be so. In the first place, the Imperial office was not hereditary in the modern European sense, nor yet was it a presidency conferred by popular balloting. It fell to the man who was most strongly placed at the time of the reigning Emperor's death, or who could create the vacancy by conspiracy. Sometimes a son succeeded his father because nobody was bold enough to present himself as a rival candidate for the Empire, but far more often the new Emperor was a powerful general or a more resolute member of the Imperial family than the natural heir. Of the first twelve Cæsars only one, Titus, immediately succeeded his father; of the next twelve again, only one, Caracalla; of the next twelve again, only one, Gallienus. And in the intrigues for the possession of the throne women played a most important part, especially the wives, sisters, or daughters of the reigning Emperor. The custom of inheritance by direct succession in the male line was followed in Roman times by Parthia, Armenia, Commagene and other eastern powers; and with this custom went, as now, that of alliance with neighbouring royal houses by intermarriage. Attempts were sometimes made to draw Rome into this system, as when Caracalla demanded in marriage the daughter of the king of Parthia; but they came to nothing because this oriental routine did not appeal to the Roman political temper.

Intermarriage between neighbouring dynasties has on the whole a steadying effect on international politics, but does not make for great historical variety. One head of an ancient ruling house, unless he happens to be demented or feeble-minded, is very much like his predecessors and monarchical contemporaries, and the queens or Empresses seem equally lacking in individuality. In-breeding and

vii

regal monotony tend to produce a rather dull or else degenerate royal type. The lives of dynastic queens make, as a rule, pretty wearisome reading: each has been a 'princess,' and has undergone the stultifying education reserved for princesses—has been brought up from infancy in a strict Court code of maidenly deportment, the only release from which comes with an arranged marriage to some distant relative, the crowned head of a foreign country. Her new life means scarcely more than adaptation to a not so very different Court code. She can have little hope of sharing in the government of her new country. All that is expected of her is to supply male heirs and more princesses.

At Rome things were very different. In reading the history of this period one is constantly interested to see what odd sort of Emperor the times will throw up next, and whether he will have got his throne by the help of his predecessor's mother, sister, wife or daughter, or, if he manages without such assistance, what new striking face will be added to the portrait gallery of Empresses. Roman women of all stations had greater independence than the women of any other historical age except the present. The Empress was often a person of outstanding political energy who had put the Emperor on the throne and ruled through him. Such was the terrible Livia, Augustus's wife, with whom rests the main responsibility for the conversion of the Republic into an Empire. Her rule lasted for an extraordinarily long time. Fifty-one years of it were covered by the reign of Augustus whom she kept constantly at work at her side in the imperial business; but he grew feeble and querulous in the end and she removed him, it was whispered, by poison. She then put on the throne Tiberius, her own son by a previous marriage, and continued for another fourteen years to control affairs through him; and this in spite of the keen humiliation he felt in being beholden to his mother for a position to which his signal services to the State properly entitled him. Livia's great-granddaughter, Agrippina the Younger, the wife of Claudius, though she did not marry him until he had been Emperor for some years, was an Empress of the same type. She poisoned Claudius when he seemed to be getting somewhat senile and put her son Nero on the throne. Until Nero realized his own powers and, chafing at her domination, had her murdered, she continued to be the virtual ruler of Rome, as she had been during the last years of Claudius's reign. Plotina, Trajan's wife, to whom he owed as much as Augustus owed Livia, was the person who suggested his adoption of Hadrian: Hadrian succeeded and Plotina continued in power.

The word 'Empress' is misleading. Roman Empresses were not styled 'Imperatrix' (the Latin word from which 'Empress' is derived.) 'Imperatrix' would have meant that they commanded armies, which they did not. Their title was 'Augusta' (the sacrosanct), and it carried no executive powers with it, but merely denoted that the woman who bore it was deserving of national respect. It did not even mean, necessarily, that she was the Emperor's wife. The first three women to win the title were Livia, as Augustus's wife, Octavia as his sister, and Antonia as Caligula's grandmother. It meant something like 'The First Lady of the Land,' with this difference, that unless the Senate chose to take away the title from her, she remained Augusta for life: she did not disappear into obscurity after a short period of glory like the wife of an American President. There might be more than one Augusta living at the same time, but as a rule the senior continued to exercise her old influence—like a Dowager Empress of China—long after the Emperor through whom she had won her title was dead. Her sphere of influence was defined by custom rather than by legal enactment, but Rome came to look on her as an indispensable character in the Imperial system. She set the general political tone and was a symbol of social stability. Some Empresses, of course, were not gifted politically, being the dull wives of energetic husbands, or women interested only in having a good time. Among the latter sort were several obvious adventuresses, such as Poppæa, Nero's wife in succession to the unfortunate Octavia. Still others were unwilling victims of imperial caprice, like Severa, the Vestal Virgin, one of Heliogabalus's wives. Thus, although a woman might, as Augusta, exercise a powerful control of affairs through an Emperor, she could not issue orders in her own name. Nor, in a military campaign, could the soldiers' oath of allegiance be properly sworn to her personally as Imperatrix. Only Zenobia broke this military convention: but she was not in the regular line of Empresses. She was the widow of a King of Palmyra who had been rewarded for his services to Rome by being made a colleague in the Empire. Her gifted Roman contemporary, Victoria, had to choose a shadow-Emperor as nominal commander of the forces whom she led to victory.

As soon as the Empire hardened into an autocracy, there was no limit to the fantastic excesses in which an Emperor might indulge if he chose. The one solid basis on which his power rested was the good will of the Army, and especially that of the Prætorian guards. So long as he was willing and able to purchase their support he had complete liberty of action. He could be as virtuous or as wicked as he pleased—behaving either like the ideal man in a philosophical treatise or like a criminal lunatic in a melodrama. This power deranged the minds of a number of Emperors, as for instance Caligula, Commodus and Caracalla; they took an imbecilic delight in the consciousness of being above all human law. Once at a banquet Caligula burst into laughter at the notion that he had only to give the word to one of the Guards, and off would come the head of the Consul reclining so peacefully at his side. Such Emperors made very difficult sons and husbands, and their women had to be constantly on the alert. Cæsonia, Caligula's last wife, did what she could to restrain his violent caprices; and he seemed to accept her right to do so, (jestingly attributing her influence over him to some love-charm, the secret of which he would one day fetch out of her by the fiddle-string torture). But against the self-will of an Emperor the title 'Augusta' was little protection. If the Empress was not quick to realize her danger and find a resolute new candidate for the Empire, she was destroyed.

The absolutism of the Czars of Russia—the word Czar, of course, is a Russianization of Cæsar, for the Czars faked their pedigree absurdly back to Augustus—has provided annalists with some very queer stories. But even in Russia there was a check on the Czar's exercise of his powers: namely, the orthodox Church and the conscience of Christendom. The Czar might quarrel with the bishops and patriarchs, but he could not at pleasure, as a Roman Emperor could, impose on his subjects a religious cult of his own choosing. Caligula was the first Roman Emperor to build a temple in his own honour at Rome, but he was not so daring in this matter as some of his successors. Heliogabalus, for example, gave his own divinity, or rather that of a Syrian Sun-God with whom he identified himself, precedence over all the gods in the Pantheon and amused himself by arranging marriages in Heaven not only between this Elagabalus and Urania, an African moon-goddess, but also between other unmarried gods of ancient standing. He even had children of illustrious families offered on his altars as sacrificial victims. Such megalomania was often accompanied by its opposite, micromania. Heliogabalus, dressed as a woman, allowed himself to be married to a favourite slave and in the capacity of a wife performed the usual household drudgeries of spinning and carding wool. Other crazy Emperors, such as Nero and Commodus, degraded themselves equally, according to Roman standards, by taking part in gladiatorial sports and singing-contests on the stage. But Nero always arranged that the judges should award him the first prize for singing, though his voice was thin and reedy, and as for Commodus (to quote William Ramsay):

In the arena he slew thousands and tens of thousands of wild beasts, but his arrows were shot and his darts were hurled from behind a screen of network which protected his person from the possibility of risk. He butchered hundreds of his fellow men in gladiatorial combats; but while he was clad in the impenetrable armour and wielded the heavy blade of a *secutor,* his antagonists had no defences except weapons of lead or tin; and when, dressed as Hercules, he crushed with his club the unhappy creatures dressed up to resemble the monstrous progeny of Earth, the rocks which they hurled at their assailant were formed of sponge.

Rome as a whole accepted this extraordinary sort of behaviour as just what one might expect from an autocrat. But behind the scenes the Empresses were always at work. When things had gone a little too far they usually contrived to have the Royal Clown removed by a Palace conspiracy. It is not too much to say that while the Empire as a whole was kept from falling to pieces by the discipline and professional conscience of the legionary soldier on the frontier, the dangerous effects of imperialistic caprice at Rome itself were counteracted by the conservatism and common sense of the Empresses. Heliogabalus was brought to book in the end by his grandmother Mæsa; Commodus by Marcia, not an Empress but the reigning favourite—an attempt on his life by his sister Lucilla having been unsuccessful. Strong-minded Empresses, if they happened to enjoy sexual dissipation, were able, as the Empress tradition strengthened, to indulge themselves as freely as the Emperors. Though in the reign of Augustus his favourite daughter Julia and her daughter of the same name were banished to prison-islands and never forgiven for disgracing the Imperial family by their indiscreet adulteries, by the time of Marcus Aurelius we find the Empress Faustina going down to the quays at a sea-side resort and making the sailors march past her naked so that she could single out the one whose physique pleased her best. Marcus Aurelius knew all about Faustina's practises, but honourably refused to divorce her as his counsellors urged: for it was through her influence that he had become Emperor.

To De Serviez, who published this work in 1728, the idea of such openly unchaste behaviour on the part of a woman of rank was shocking and repellent; as was, equally, such a presumption as that of the Empress Mæsa's in actually daring, in defiance of all precedent, to take part in a debate of the Senate and vote like a man. Modern readers, though perhaps pitying his outraged sense of propriety, will be unable to recapture his mood of indignant bewilderment. Famous actresses and women of title whose sexual vagaries are no secret are nowadays not socially ostracized; women cabinet-ministers and ambassadors are a political fact. There has been a remarkable change in emotional values, too, since De Serviez wrote. For example, when we read how Agrippinilla examined the severed head of Lollia Paulina, her rival, to make sure that the executioner had not tried to pass off on her some other woman's head, and remarked, 'yes, I recognise the teeth; it's hers, all right,' the modern reaction is less one of horror than of sophisticated admiration for her lack of squeamishness. Whereas when we read of Empresses who were extremely virtuous and allowed themselves to be grossly put upon by their husbands—their virtue is usually attributed by later historians to Christian influences—the modern reaction is less one of admiration and pity than of pity and scorn. It is curious that the modern temper should be nearer that of nineteen hundred years ago than that of even ninety years ago.

Our grandparents were peculiarly shocked by the terrible extravagance of the Empress Poppæa who kept five hundred she-asses to

provide her with milk for her daily bath. Apart from the fact that
it was asses' milk, not cow's milk, there seems nothing particularly
out of order to us in this daily bath of a few score gallons of milk—
as we do not writhe morally when we hear of Beverly Hills bathing-
pool facilities. Milk is now recognised as an excellent emollient
for the skin, and if the milk that is constantly being poured away
by the dairy-combines to keep up market prices were canalized for
the toilet uses of film princesses or World's Richest Heiresses, adverse
publicity would not result. Cleopatra's action, imitated by Caligula,
of dissolving a pearl in vinegar and drinking it, would rather appeal
to our cocktail sense of humour, not to mention our love of carefree
gestures. And since the discovery of the Japanese culture pearl any
action taken to relieve the glutted pearl-market is in accordance with
the best principles of economy—like patriotically burning national
bonds.

From a modern point of view, indeed, the Roman Empresses do
not seem nearly so bad a class as old-fashioned historians have made
them out to be. One or two, unfortunately, found it necessary to
keep power by committing incest with a son or brother, but apart
from this nothing so very shocking is recorded of them. They do
not even seem to have been notably cruel. One of the later Empresses
was once cheated by a jeweller who sold her paste diamonds for
true ones. An Emperor would have had the man thrown to the
lions or flayed alive. The Empress merely paid him back in his
own coin. She did indeed threaten him with lions and put him into
the arena, but when the door of the beast-house was opened, out
flew not a lion but a game-cock which darted at his face and pecked
him severely. Then she asked him how he liked being cheated.

De Serviez appropriately concludes his story with an account of
Constantia, the sister of the Emperor Constantine—in whose reign
Christianity was finally established as the state religion, and the
seat of Empire moved from Rome to Constantinople. Christianity
marked the end of the power of the old-style Empress. Christian
authority was reserved strictly for men. A woman might on rare
occasions lead armies or sway the Senate, but ecclesiastical law prevented her from participating in Church affairs. When the Church
became the official conscience of the State, the Empress, who had

filled this role unofficially for some three hundred years, was out of employment. Thus De Serviez, though he has shown that it was largely through the influence of the Empresses—two of whom were martyrs to the Faith—that the Cross triumphed, feels obliged to commemorate the victory with a general reproof to all women who attempt to meddle with religion:

Nothing is generally attended with worse consequences than a woman's pretending to superior wisdom and talents in point of religion; for as their want of learning and erudition does not admit of their penetrating those mysteries that are so much beyond their capacity, it is very easy for them to be mistaken. The obstinacy with which they maintain their opinions is apt to make them deaf to all the arguments that would be capable of undeceiving them; and if they happen to be persons of authority, what evils and mischiefs may not be committed in pursuance of a passion which they falsely call a true zeal for the Church? We have a sad example of this in Constantia, a princess of uncommon merit, exempt from most of the weaknesses of her sex, who added to an extraordinary beauty the greatest perfection of mind. She had a masculine courage, a large share of discretion and prudence, and solid virtue. She was distinguished by the force of her genius, a penetrating judgment in the most intricate affairs and a surprising eloquence. . . . She was, however, obstinately attached to her own ideas, even in religious matters, which occasioned great inconveniences and disadvantages to the Church.

To read De Serviez therefore is doubly interesting. Not only are we given a highly coloured picture of the pagan era, but we see it through the eyes of a writer of the succeeding Christian era whose moral comments are sometimes more startling even than the events to which they refer.

AUTHOR'S PREFACE

WHILST the republic of Rome maintained her liberties, the Roman ladies were not distinguished one from another but by their beauty and wit, their virtue and their courage. As they were excluded from dignities, it was only by their personal merit that they made themselves considerable, and acquired glory. Lucretia got herself a great name by her chastity in giving her husband, at the expense of her life, an heroic instance of her innocence; and, in the vengeance which she took on herself for the crime of Tarquin's son, she left the ladies a model of conjugal fidelity, which we do not find that many have afterwards copied.

Cloelia and her companions made themselves famous for their courage, boldness, and love for their country, as did Porcia, Cato's daughter, by swallowing burning coals, in order to procure to herself that death which her friends would have hindered her from; but she deceived the vigilance of those who watched her, by that action which has made so much noise in history. But, from the time that the Emperors made themselves absolute masters of the republic, their wives shared with them their grandeur, their glory, and their power; the Roman people, being then given up to flattery as much as they had formerly been jealous of their liberty, strove to give the Empresses pompous and magnificent titles, and to decree them extraordinary and excessive honours. One might then see the Emperors' wives honoured with the titles of August and Mothers of their Country. Some of them had a seat in the senate, governed Rome and the empire, gave audience to the ambassadors, and disposed of posts and employments; others were consecrated priestesses, and even exalted to the rank of goddesses.

It is of these Empresses that this book treats; and particular care has been taken to distinguish those who were of, or who were married into, Augustus's family, because they were the most remarkable. All the facts here reported are taken from original authors; and, for our justification, as much care as possible has been taken throughout, to quote our authorities.

In speaking of the Empresses, it would to be sure have been very difficult to be quite silent as to the Emperors; we have even enlarged upon some of these princes, because we do not doubt but many, who may peruse this book, will not be at all sorry to find in it a part of their history. If I have not mentioned all that might have been said of these Empresses, I believe I have, at least, reported as much as was necessary to make them known. To say the truth, I have been sometimes almost tempted to suppress a great many things which I have, nevertheless, been obliged to touch upon, but yet with all the regard to decency a man can have, who would be extremely sorry to offend against the rules of good manners. But I hope that nobody will have any great reason to blame me upon that subject, since, even in the most shameful passages of these Empresses' lives, I have carefully avoided making use of any shocking expressions.

HISTORICAL NOTE

THE RULERS OF IMPERIAL ROME

From Julius Cæsar to Constantine the Great

AFTER the assassination of Julius Cæsar (44 B.C.), his power
passed into the hands of his nephew Octavius, who became lord
of the Roman world, the most important addition to which made
by himself was the kingdom of Egypt. The undivided rule of
Octavius dates from 30 B.C., when he assumed the title of
Augustus, by which he has ever since been known. His reign
lasted until A.D. 14, and he was succeeded by Tiberius, his
adopted son, in whose reign disappeared the last remnants of the
old Roman constitution. Tiberius was succeeded by Caligula,
who was a great grandson of Augustus in the female line. After
him reigned Claudius I. and then Nero. Tyranny and shameless
corruption and licentiousness reached their height under these
three emperors. Next in order came Galba, Otho, and Vitellius,
who followed each other in rapid succession, each reigning only a
few months. The reign of their successor, Vespasian, extended
from A.D. 70-79. Vespasian was followed by his son Titus,
whose successor was his brother Domitian. On this tyrant's
assassination, the humane Nerva was made emperor, and reigned
two years. His successor, Trajan, added Dacia (modern Ru-
mania and Transylvania) to the empire, and carried the Roman
arms to the Persian gulf, conquering many countries of the East.
These conquests were abandoned by the next Emperor, Hadrian,
who restored the Euphrates as the eastern boundary of the empire. Following Hadrian came Antoninus Pius, whose heir was

Marcus Aurelius Antoninus. The 84 years (A.D. 96-180) of the reigns of Nerva, Trajan, Hadrian, and the two Antonines are considered the most glorious period in Roman history. It is from the year of the accession to the throne of Commodus, son of Marcus Aurelius, A.D. 180, that Gibbon dates the commencement of that empire's decline. At that time the empire consisted of Italy, Spain, Gaul, Britain, Rhætia, Noricum and Pannonia, Dalmatia, Mœsia and Dacia, Thrace, Macedonia, and Greece; Asia, Syria, Phœnicia, and Palestine; Egypt, Africa, and the Mediterranean with its islands. The population is estimated at 120,000,000. The emperor Commodus, who became one of the worst of tyrants, was assassinated, and his successor, Pertinax, was murdered by the Prætorians, who sold the empire at auction to Didius Julianus, who after a brief reign of three months was in turn murdered by the prætorian guards as the price of the favour of Septimius Severus. Severus's son Caracalla, and Heliogabalus, first cousin of the latter, rivalled Caligula and Nero in infamy. The conduct of these two, and most of the emperors who subsequently ruled, accelerated the decline of the empire. Alexander Severus, Decius, Aurelian, and Probus are the principal exceptions. Aurelian conquered Zenobia and destroyed Palmyra (A.D. 273), and Probus is regarded as one of the best as well as ablest of the Roman emperors. Under the rule of Diocletian (A.D. 285-305) the empire experienced some revival of its power. But as the emperors had mostly abandoned the old city, and the constitution of the empire was assuming an oriental character, the greatness of Rome of the Cæsars scarcely belongs to that age. Constantine the Great, the first of the Christian emperors, formally transferred the capital to Byzantium, thenceforth called Constantinople, though its founder meant it should be called New Rome. From that time, A.D. 330, should be dated the cessation of the Roman ascendency, though the remains of the empire continued to influence the world down to the middle of the fifteenth century, when Constantinople fell into the hands of the Turks.

For the purpose of enabling readers of "The Roman Empresses" to conveniently fix the dates of events described in its pages, the following Chronological Table will be found of advantage:

CHRONOLOGICAL TABLE

SHOWING THE PERIODS COVERED BY THE RESPECTIVE REIGNS OF THE ROMAN RULERS FROM CÆSAR TO CONSTANTINE THE GREAT

Born   Died

100 B. C.—44   —Cæsar, Caius Julius. Dictator, 49 B. C.—44.

63 B. C.—A. D. 14   —Augustus, Caius Octavius Cæsar. First Roman Emperor, 30 B. C.—A. D. 14.

    Under Augustus, Roman literature reached its highest point. He so adorned the capital, that it was commonly said of him, that he found Rome "brick, and left it marble." The birth of Jesus Christ occurred in his reign.

42 B. C.—A. D. 37 —Tiberius (Tiberius Claudius Nero Cæsar). Emperor, 14 A. D.—37.

12 A. D.—41   —Caligula, Caius Cæsar. Emperor, 37 A. D.—41.

10 B. C.—A. D. 54 —Claudius I. (Tiberius Claudius Drusus Nero Germanicus). Emperor, 41 A. D.—54.

37 A. D.—68   —Nero, Lucius Domitius Ahenobarbus. Emperor, 54 A. D.—68.

3 B. C.—A. D. 69   —Galba, Servius Sulspicius. Emperor, 68 A. D.—69.

32 A. D.—69   —Otho, Marcus Salvius. Emperor, January-April, 69.

15 A. D.—69   —Vitellius, Aulus. Emperor, July-November, 69.

9 A. D.—79   —Vespasian (Titus Flavius Sabinus Vespasianus). Emperor, 70-79.

Born　　　*Died*

40 A. D.—81　　　—Titus (Titus Flavius Sabinus Vespasianus). Emperor, 79-81.

Called "the delight of mankind." Accomplished the capture of Jerusalem and the dispersion of the Jews. His reign was marked by the destruction of Herculaneum, Stabiæ, and Pompeii by the eruption of Vesuvius. He finished the Colosseum, begun by his father Vespasian, and completed the subjugation of Britain.

51 A. D.—96　　　—Domitian (Titus Flavius Domitianus Augustus). Emperor, 81-96.

32 A. D.—98　　　—Nerva, Marcus Cocceius. Emperor, 96-98.

52 A. D.—117　　　—Trajan (Marcus Ulpius Trajanus). Emperor, 98-117.

Under Trajan the Roman arms were carried further than ever before or after, and rarely suffered defeat. For many generations afterward his reign was looked upon as the most brilliant in imperial annals. His memory was long cherished by the Romans, and 200 years later the senators were in the habit of saluting the emperor with the acclamation: "Be happier than Augustus and better than Trajan."

76 A. D.—138　　　—Hadrian (Publius Ælius Hadrianus). Emperor, 117-138.

86 A. D.—161　　　—Antoninus Pius, Titus Aurelius Fulvius. Emperor, 138-161.

121 A. D.—180　　　—Marcus Aurelius (Marcus Aurelius Antoninus). Emperor, 161-180.

No monarch ever lived more beloved, or died more regretted, than Marcus Aurelius, whose whole life was a practical example of his own philosophic doctrines of mildness and toleration, which he so eloquently advocates in his famous "Meditations." These breathe the very spirit of the Christian religion which he persecuted, so that it cannot be doubted that he either wholly misunderstood the system of Christianity, and believed its followers, as many in that age did, to be a political sect devoted to the promulgation of pacifism, and averse to all forms of government, or that he was misled by ill-advisers. This pagan philosopher was the last of "The Adoptive Emperors," which included his four predecessors, Nerva, Trajan, Hadrian, and Antoninus Pius; so called because each was the adopted son of his predecessor. They constitute the greatest and noblest group of Roman Emperors, and, according to the historian Gibbon, the period of their reigns is the happiest in the history of the world.

Born	Died	
(?) A. D.—169		—Verus, Lucius. Colleague of the Emperor Marcus Aurelius, 161-169.
161 A. D.—192		—Commodus, Lucius Ælius Aurelius. Emperor, 180-192.
126 A. D.—193		—Pertinax, Helvius. Emperor, 192-February, 193.
132 A. D.—193		—Didius Julianus (Marcus Didius Commodus Severus Julianus). Emperor, March-June, 193.
146 A. D.—211		—Severus, Lucius Septimius. Emperor, 193-211.
188 A. D.—217		—Caracalla, Marcus Aurelius Antoninus. Emperor, 211-217.
164 A. D.—218		—Macrinus, Marcus Ophelius. Emperor, 217-218.
205 A. D.—222		—Heliogabalus, Varius Avitus Bassianus. Emperor, 218-222.
205 A. D.—235		—Alexander Severus, Marcus Aurelius. Emperor, 222-235.
(?) A. D.—238		—Maximinus, Caius Julius Verus. Emperor, 235-238.

Born	Died	
158 A. D.	238	—Gordianus I. ("The Elder"), Marcus Antoninus. Emperor, six weeks (238).
(?) A. D.	238	—Pupienus Maximus, M. Clodius. Emperor, 3 months (238).
224 A. D.	244	—Gordianus III., Marcus Antoninus Pius. Emperor, 238-244.
204 A. D.	249	—Philip (Marcus Julius Philippus), "The Arabian." Emperor, 244-249.
199 A. D.	251	—Decius, Caius Messius Quintus Trajanus. Emperor, 249-251.
(?) A. D.	253	—Gallus, Caius Vibius Trebonianus. Emperor, 251-253.
(?) A. D.	269	—Valerianus, Publius Aurelius Licinius. Emperor, 254-260.
235 A. D.	268	—Gallienus, Publius Licinius Egnatius. Emperor, 260-268.
214 A. D.	270	—Claudius II. (Marcus Aurelius Claudius). Emperor, 268-270.
212 A. D.	275	—Aurelian, Lucius Domitius. Emperor, 270-275.
200 A. D.	276	—Tacitus, Marcus Claudius. Emperor, 275-276.

After the assassination of the emperor Aurelian in March, 275, there was for six months a period of what Gibbon calls a "tranquil anarchy," during which the army and the senate mutually solicited each other to select a successor to the throne. Tacitus was unanimously elected emperor by the latter body September, 275, but died within little more than half a year from the commencement of his reign.

232 A. D.	282	—Probus, Marcus Aurelius. Emperor, 276-282.
222 A. D.	283	—Carus, Marcus Aurelius. Emperor, 282-283.
(?) A. D.	285	—Carinus, Marcus Aurelius. Emperor, 283-285.
245 A. D.	313	—Diocletian, Valerius. Emperor, 285-305.

According to Gibbon, Diocletian, like Augustus the adopted son of Cæsar and the first Roman emperor, may be considered as the founder of a new empire. Diocletian inaugurated the period of the "Partnership Emperors," by associating with him in the labours of government three colleagues—Maximian (Hercules), Galerius, and Constantius. These four princes distributed among themselves the wide extent of the Roman empire. Each was sovereign within his jurisdiction; but their united authority extended over the whole monarchy, and each of them was prepared to assist his

Born	Died	
		colleagues with his counsels or presence.
(?) A. D.—	311	—Galerius (Galerius Valerius Maximinus). Emperor of the East, 305-311.
(?) A. D.—	310	—Hercules: Maximian, Marcus Aurelius Valerius, surnamed Herculius. Emperor with Diocletian, 286-305 and 306-308.
(?) A. D.—	313	—Maximinus, or Maximin, Galerius Valerius. Emperor, 308-313.
(?) A. D.—	324	—Licinius (Caius Flavius Valerius Licinianus). Emperor, 313-323.
274 A. D.—	337	—Constantine I. (Flavius Valerius Aurelius Constantinus), surnamed "The Great." Emperor, 323-337.

LIVES OF THE
ROMAN EMPRESSES

THE ROMAN EMPRESSES

CALPURNIA

WIFE OF JULIUS CÆSAR.

ULIUS CÆSAR had four wives. The first was Cossutia, daughter of a Roman knight, and extremely rich. He was very young when he married her, and as his inclinations were not much consulted in this match, he put her away before he had cohabited with her, in order to espouse Cornelia, daughter of Cinna, who was distinguished by having been four times consul. This alliance drew upon him the jealousy of Sulla, whose power was very formidable at Rome, where everything was governed according to his will and pleasure.

This dictator, who was Cinna's mortal enemy, used all his endeavours to induce Cæsar to put away Cornelia, but in vain; Cæsar was not a man capable of yielding easily to another, and, having been brought up by his aunt Julia (Marius's wife), was, from his infancy, taught that invincible aversion that all Marius's relations had to Sulla, for they had opposed themselves as a barrier against the tyrannical power of this dictator. On the other hand, Cæsar loved Cornelia; but if he could have prevailed upon himself to put her away, especially to please Sulla, his father-in-law Cinna was powerful enough to make him repent it.

Sulla was then possessed of a power little less than absolute, and, imagining that everything ought to give way to him, was extremely exasperated at the resistance which he met with from Cæsar; and, to punish him, stripped him of the priesthood, seized everything belonging to him and his wife, deprived him of all right of succession, and would probably have carried his resentment further, if he had not been taken up with getting rid of some other enemies whom he thought more considerable, and if the vestal virgins,[1] and many other persons of importance, had not interested themselves for Cæsar.

[1] Numa Pompilius, second King of Rome, caused a temple to be built in honour of the goddess Vesta, in which was preserved the fire called sacred and eternal, because it was never suffered to go out; and he instituted religious women (a sort of nuns) whose business it was to take care of it, and who were named vestals from the goddess Vesta, to whom they were dedicated. The oldest of these virgins was styled the great vestal, and she had a supreme authority over the rest. They vowed to preserve their virginity for thirty years, after which they were permitted to quit that state, and to marry, or pass the remainder of their lives as they thought proper; but few made use of this liberty, for it was observed that, as many of them as had quitted their profession to marry or live in the world, were afflicted in the latter end of their lives with perpetual sickness, disorders, and a thousand misfortunes, which were looked upon as a just punishment for their desertion. This had possessed people's minds with superstition and fear, so that there were scarce any of the vestals that had courage enough to quit their condition. As for those who broke their vows before the expiration of the thirty years, and were guilty of any breach of chastity, they were condemned to death in the following manner:—They were buried alive in a deep dungeon, which was dug on purpose in a place called the accursed field. They were let down with their faces covered, as being unworthy to see the light, and nothing allowed them but a lighted lamp, a little bread and water, some milk, and some oil. And the day whereon they were thus interred, all the town was in mourning, the shops shut up, and nothing to be seen on every side but the deepest melancholy. Her sacrilegious accomplice had also his share in the punishment as he had in the crime, for he was whipped to death. As the most essential part of the vestals' duty consisted in their maintaining the sacred fire day and night, they were

Sulla, who was extremely penetrating and well acquainted with the enterprising genius of that ambitious Roman, foresaw the misfortunes that he would one day bring upon the Republic; he, therefore, not only opposed

continually upon the watch; but if any of them were so negligent as to let it go out (which was reckoned the forerunner of some dreadful calamity) the offender was chastised very rigorously, for she was scourged quite naked by the chief priest in a dark place behind a curtain. This severity was the reason that nobody cared to make their daughters vestals; on the contrary, everyone sought pretences to avoid it, whence it happened that they were afterwards obliged to take them by force. The Emperors sometimes recompensed the generosity of those who offered their daughters with a good grace. And we read that Tiberius, after the death of Occia, the chief vestal, being under some difficulties about filling up her place, and Fonteius Agrippa having presented his daughter (who, nevertheless, was not received), rewarded the good intention of that Senator, by making the young lady a present of a sum amounting to fifty thousand livres. It is to be observed, that it was not every girl that could be admitted into this order, for she was not to be less than six years old, nor more than ten; she was to have no defect in her speech or limbs, nor subject to any disorder. Her parents were to have been exempt from a state of servitude, and such as had never followed any low occupation. They even gave the preference to the daughters of such women as had been but once married. When none offered themselves voluntarily, the great Pontiff singled out twenty girls, who drew lots, and he selected her on whom the lot fell. She was carried immediately to the temple of Vesta, shaved, and clad in the proper habit, for it would have been a very immodest and scandalous thing if one of these virgins had made use of any dress or ornaments that were not suitable to the sanctity of her profession; and Titus Livius tells us, that the vestal Minucia was extremely blamed for having dressed in a manner not conformable to her condition. The accusation was not without grounds, as the event proved; for soon after, Minucia was condemned to undergo the punishment appointed for those who lost their virginity. The vestals had a right to several privileges, and had revenues assigned them by the public. When they walked abroad, they were preceded by lictors, like the magistrates; and if they met any criminal going to execution, he was pardoned, provided the vestal made oath that her meeting him was mere chance, and that there was no design in it. Their persons were sacred; and at public assemblies they were entitled to the chief places. In short, the Romans had the greatest respect for them. They reconciled the nobles when they had any quarrel among them, and nobody durst refuse them anything they asked, so much were they esteemed. This was the reason that Cæsar's friends, in order to obtain his pardon from Sulla, had recourse to the vestals. Their number was limited to six by King Servius, but afterwards they were increased to twenty.

We must not forget to take notice that, if the holy fire happened to go out, it was not to be rekindled but by lightning or the rays of the sun.

Cæsar's friends by all the reasons he was master of, but disguising his private resentment under the mask of the public interest, endeavoured to persuade them that they ought to be so far from interceding for Cæsar, that they should contribute all they could to his destruction, since, if he were suffered to live, he would, some time or other, ruin the party of the nobility, which they themselves had defended with so much zeal and courage. Fortune, however, rescued Cæsar from the hatred of Sulla. The Dictator, being at last overcome by the importunity of those whom he could not well refuse, was obliged to pardon him; but, to show them how unwillingly he complied with their request, "I grant you," says he, "what you ask, but remember that more than one Marius is concealed in the person of Cæsar."

Cæsar was quæstor [1] when he lost his wife Cornelia; and, as he loved her beyond measure, he was excessively afflicted at her death. He gave public tokens of his grief in the pompous eulogy which he pronounced upon that

[1] The office of quæstor was one of the most ancient posts in Rome, and was reckoned an introduction into affairs of the greatest importance. Nobody could enjoy it who was not twenty-seven years of age. At the beginning there were but two of them, who had the charge of the public treasure and ensigns of war; but Italy having been all made tributary, and the revenues of the Republic being considerably increased, six more were added, and Sulla augmented them to twenty; but Cæsar made them still more numerous. Of all these quæstors no more than two resided at Rome, who kept registers of all the receipts and payments of the Republic, and the rest were sent into the provinces to keep an account of the revenues ordinary, extraordinary, and casual; as, for example, the spoils taken in war, or at the surrender of towns, the sale of prisoners, and other like occasions. The employment of quæstor became more honourable under the Emperors, for when the Prince could not, or would not, go to the Senate, he sent thither his orders by the quæstors. They took cognisance of all causes relating to the public debts, a power which Nero deprived them of, to give it to the intendant or commissary of the city. The Emperor Claudius added several new honours to this employ; but on the other hand he disgraced it by rendering it venal, by Dolabella's advice.

The assassination of Cæsar in the Senate

occasion from the Tribunal of Harangues;[1] and, certainly, he had all the reason in the world to lament his loss, for Pompeia, whom he married soon after, caused him a great deal of vexation.

She was daughter of Pompeius Rufus, and niece to Sulla. This lady was young, handsome, lively, and of so amorous a disposition, that she did not value herself upon an over-strict fidelity to her husband, whom she married, perhaps, much more through policy[2] than inclination. She carried her complaisance very far for Publius Clodius.[3] This person was of an illustrious family, whose antiquity surpassed that of Rome itself. He[4] was then in the flower of his age, very handsome in his person, and possessed of vast riches, which he did not always make the best use of. He had a great deal of very agreeable wit, and a cheerful humour, always dis-

---

[1] Or, "orators' tribunals." In the middle of the square called Forum Romanum was a temple dedicated to Fortune, adorned with the iron and copper belonging to the ships of Antium which were taken by the Romans. Of the beaks of those ships was made a sort of tribunal or pulpit raised very high, upon which the magistrates mounted when they were disposed to harangue the people. Round this tribunal were ranged the statues of many great men of the Republic. It was also from this place that funeral orations were pronounced; and it was there that Cicero so frequently thundered out his eloquence. It was afterwards disgraced, by fixing upon it the heads of the greatest men of the Republic. Marius caused to be put there the head of Mark Antony the orator (who formerly had adorned it with triumphal spoils). He also placed young Marius's head there; and Mark Antony the triumvir exposed in that place the head and right hand of Cicero.

[2] Sueton. vit. Jul. Cæs.

[3] Publius Clodius was descended from the noble house of the Clodians, who always maintained the interests of the Senate and patricians against the people; and Clodius, of whom we are now speaking, was the first of his name that took part with the people against the Senate. He caused himself to be adopted by a plebeian, that he might be capable of being chosen Tribune of the people; and we shall see what use he made of the authority which that employment furnished him with. Clodius's wife was named Fulvia, by whom he had his daughter Clodia, who was married to Augustus, and divorced soon after.

[4] Plutar. vit. Cæs. vit. Cicer.

posed to mirth and pleasure; but he was rash in his
enterprises, irregular in his desires, furious in his hatred,
impudent in his manners, neither respecting laws nor
magistrates; showing in his countenance that air of assurance which independence is apt to give; inclined to the
most infamous actions, witness his abominations with his
own sisters; in short, ready to hazard everything to
gratify those appetites which are generally the unfortunate attendants of giddy youth, and in which he was
encouraged by the bad example of many of the most
illustrious citizens of Rome, now grown weary of being
virtuous.

Clodius, being the person I have described him, insinuated himself into the good graces of Cæsar's wife, and
presently discovered that he was not indifferent to her.
Aurelia, Cæsar's mother,[1] a lady of great penetration,
and of the strictest virtue, was not the last that perceived
it. She therefore narrowly watched the conduct of her
daughter-in-law, whose behaviour seemed very suspicious: Aurelia was an Argus not easily to be lulled
asleep.

Clodius put in practice all his cunning and stratagems
to see Cæsar's wife, but to no purpose; for Pompeia
could not move a step without being guarded by her
mother-in-law. Wherever she went, she was still accompanied by this severe spy, who saw into her very
thoughts, and watched her so closely, that it was impossible for her to steal one favourable glance.

Aurelia was, however, imposed upon at last by the two
lovers, in spite of all her vigilance. Love took a pleasure
in deceiving her, by inspiring Clodius with a secret way

[1] Plutar. vit. Cæs. and in Regum Apophthegm.

of seeing his mistress. Every year a solemn sacrifice was
performed at Rome in honour of the Good Goddess [1] in
one of the consuls' houses, and, in their absence, in one
of the prætors.[2]   Amongst other very odd ceremonies

[1] The Good Goddess had many names, but Fauna was the true one.
She was the wife of one Faunus, and was so prudent, modest, and chaste,
that it is reported no man but her husband so much as knew her name,
and that none else had ever seen her face. A misfortune that happened
to this rare woman occasioned her being made a goddess. Her husband
being one day absent, she found, by chance, a bottle of wine, which she
tasted, and finding it good, made so free of it as to be drunk, being quite
ignorant of its nature, and never having met with it before. Faunus
happened to come in just then, and finding her in this condition, in the
heat of his passion seized some twigs of myrtle, of which he made a
whip, and gave her so many strokes that she died of it. This cruel cor-
rection was followed by a bitter repentance; he was ashamed of his
violence, and the merit of his wife, whom he had treated with so much
injustice and inhumanity, greatly added to his grief. The evil being
however past remedy, and not having it in his power to restore her to
life, he was resolved to make her a goddess by procuring her immortality.

[2] After the Kings of Rome were banished, two consuls were created,
who had the administration of affairs. But when it happened that the
consuls were obliged to quit the town to command the armies, they
created a prætor to administer justice in Rome, and he was to supply the
place of the consuls, for when they were absent, his power was very
considerable; he had then authority to assemble the Senate, in which he
presided; to abolish some laws, and to make new ones. It was also at
his house that the sacrifice to the Good Goddess was celebrated. In
short, all the power of the consuls was then vested in him. At first the
prætor was chosen out of the order of patricians, but afterwards the
plebeians were also admitted to that office. And because one prætor was
not sufficient for the town, on account of the great number of strangers
who flocked thither upon business, they created another, whose duty it was
to dispatch the affairs of these strangers, called Prætor Peregrinus.
Afterwards they were increased to six; two of whom were to decide the
differences and disputes of private persons, and the others took cognisance of such crimes as were of a public nature. At last all the provinces being become tributary, and fallen under the yoke and government
of the Romans, other prætors were ordained, and sent into the provinces.
They had a right to wear the robe called Prætexta, and to be preceded
by lictors, and even to command the troops that were in their respective
provinces. The town prætor lodged in the palace that formerly belonged
to the Kings. His tribunal was called the Prætorium, and from thence
came the name of the guards called the Prætorian Cohorts, because they
were appointed to attend the prætor, and waited upon him in the hall of
justice during his stay there. The prætors were not to be absent from
Rome above ten days. When the prætor condemned any person to death,
he quitted his purple robe and appeared in deep mourning.

essentially necessary upon this occasion, that of never celebrating them but by night was most scrupulously observed, and no man whatsoever was to be admitted, not even the consul or prætor at whose house they were solemnized. The wife or mother of the consul or prætor presided, and was assisted by the vestal virgins. Nothing could gain admittance that had the least appearance of the male sex. The ladies took so much care to be exempt from all suspicion of gallantry,[1] that they were not permitted to have so much as a sprig of myrtle in their nosegays, because that shrub was dedicated to Venus.

In spite of the danger the transgression of these laws was attended with, and against which nobody till then had ever dared to offend, Clodius, hurried on by the impetuosity of his headstrong, unthinking youth, was incapable of making reflections; and, therefore, without the least scruple, he resolved to profane these solemnities, and lay hold on that opportunity of seeing Cæsar's wife. The sacrifice was to be celebrated that year at her house, and that night was intended to be for her a night of triumph; she was to appear in the assembly with all her graces and charms. Much would have been wanting to her satisfaction, if her lover was not to have seen her in her beauty, and Clodius could never have survived the grief of such a disappointment.

They agreed, then, to see each other in the very place of the sacrifice, without troubling themselves about the danger to which they were exposed, nor the difficulties that lay in their way. The enterprise was hazardous, but love is more than ever desirous to triumph upon such occasions; so the design was thus concerted. It was

[1] Plutar. Quæst. Rer. Rom.

determined that Clodius should be dressed in woman's clothes, that he should enter Cæsar's house in the crowd, and that Abra, one of Pompeia's women who was in the secret, should introduce the disguised lover into her chamber, where Pompeia was to meet him. This girl was mistress of all the address that was necessary to conduct an intrigue, and Clodius had made her entirely his friend. He knew that in affairs of gallantry, it was impossible not to have some confidant, and a chambermaid has a natural right to a trust of that nature.

These measures being taken, and the hour of sacrifice come, Clodius, without fear or foresight, gives himself up to his fortune; takes a woman's habit, and being young, his countenance did not betray him; he joins those who were going into Cæsar's house, and, being favoured by the darkness of the night and his disguise, goes in with them to assist at the sacrifice. Abra took care to be punctually at the door to receive him, and, having very cunningly conducted him into her chamber, ran to give Pompeia notice that her lover waited for her.

Time, which seems very tedious upon these occasions, appeared much so to Clodius, and the more so, since Abra (by some of those unlucky accidents which often happen in adventures of this kind) was employed about other matters (probably by order of Aurelia), and could not, for a long time, carry an answer to the metamorphosed lover, who was all this while very uneasy, and, being naturally of a restless temper, was extremely fretted by these delays, which he accounted for by a thousand reasons, without hitting upon the true one; and, his uneasiness increasing every moment, he foolishly quitted the chamber, and wandered about the house. This impatience quite spoiled all the measures he had settled with Pompeia; for, not knowing what to do, and affecting to hide his face by avoiding the light and the company, he gave room for suspicion. A servant maid of the house, taking him for a woman, asked him who he was and what he looked for? This abrupt question disconcerted him; he seemed in confusion, but at last answered that he wanted Abra. The concern he showed, together with the sound of his voice, which did not agree with his dress, discovered the mystery; the maid found out the cheat, and began to cry out as loud as she could, that there was in the house a man in woman's clothes.

This uproar ruined the two lovers and their schemes, and struck all the assembly with astonishment. The lady rambled about the house without knowing whither, and had trouble enough to find Clodius, whom she hid again in the same chamber, after rating him severely for his imprudence. This unfortunate accident, which was enough to put to a nonplus the greatest presence of mind and quickest invention, embarrassed her beyond description. In the meantime, the sacrifice and all the ceremonies are interrupted, Aurelia commands all the doors to be shut and lighted torches to be brought, and, after a diligent search in every corner, finds Clodius in the confidant's chamber, and turns him out.

This scandalous affair happening among a company of women it cannot be supposed it could remain a secret. The ladies longed to be at home to communicate it to their husbands, and, consequently, it was all over the town the next morning. Pompeia and Clodius became the subjects of all the conversation; and nothing was spoken of but this rash undertaking. Cæsar, being thoroughly persuaded that Clodius did not proceed in this affair unknown to Pompeia, put her away.

One of the tribunes,[1] in the meantime, takes cognisance of this sacrilegious affair, and Clodius is cited to his trial; but, finding that the best thing he could do was to deny the whole charge, he protested that he was falsely accused, and that he was absent from Rome the night of this sacrifice, which he offered to prove. The examination was not favourable to him. A great many witnesses deposed against him, and, among the rest, Cicero declared that Clodius had consulted him at Rome that very day.[2] This evidence was of so much weight as to leave no room for doubt, and amounted to a demonstration, in a place where the honesty and uprightness of Cicero were held in the highest veneration.[3]

[1] The people being quite wearied out with the tyranny of usurers and the oppressions they suffered under the great men of Rome, retired into one quarter of the town and mutinied. Agrippa, a most prudent and much esteemed senator, was deputed to quell this sedition, and knew so well how to manage them, that he was so lucky as to succeed upon certain conditions, the principal of which was, that the people should have their own magistrates, that they should be chosen from their own community, and that their persons should be safe and inviolable. They were called Tribunes of the People. At first only two were created, but afterwards they were increased to twenty, and were designed, at the beginning, only to defend the people against the power of the nobility, but in time became so formidable as to counterbalance the authority of the consuls; for the tribunes had a right to convoke the people as often as they thought proper, without interruption from any person whatsoever. They had power to establish laws which should bind the three orders, and took under their protection all such as had recourse to them, and by those means sheltered them against the proceedings of all other magistrates, excepting the dictator. They had also a right to oppose the decrees of the Senate, which they examined into. They could even imprison the consuls; for as their persons were in a manner sacred, nobody had courage enough to oppose them. Sulla indeed lessened their power considerably, and the Emperors afterwards abolished entirely this dignity, as being opposite to the tyranny they assumed.

[2] Valer. Max. lib. 8. c. 5.

[3] It is well known that Cicero was one of the greatest men that ever Rome produced. His name is derived from the Latin word Cicer or vetch, because the first man that gave some reputation to the family had

Clodius little expected that Cicero, upon whom he had conferred great obligations, would have appeared against him; he had sheltered and protected Cicero from Catiline's resentment, who, many a time, would have attempted to kill him, if Clodius had not perpetually stood

on his nose a wart that resembled a pea. Cicero, however, would never change his name; and when his friends attempted to persuade him to it, he answered, that he would make his name so famous that few should surpass it. His merit raised him to the highest dignities of the Republic, of whose liberties he was always a most generous and zealous defender. He discovered Catiline's conspiracy, and caused the authors and accomplices to be punished as they deserved, which procured him the love and esteem of all the Romans. Cicero was the greatest orator that ever was born; and it may be affirmed, that his conclusions were a sort of law to the Senate. He had frequent quarrels with Clodius and Mark Antony. It is reported that he was one of those who conspired against Julius Cæsar, and that Brutus, after that prince had been assassinated in the Senate House, looking about for Cicero, showed him his sword yet smoking with the blood of Cæsar, and cried out to him, that Rome had at last recovered its liberty. Cicero was reproached with being of a very timid and cowardly disposition. He had also a large share of vanity, and never spoke a quarter of an hour without running into praises of himself, and putting the Senate in mind of the public services he had done. He married Terentia, by whom he had a daughter, who was married to Piso, and afterwards to Lentulus; also another who survived him, and a son called Marcus Cicero. Towards the latter end of his life he put away Terentia, because he imagined she despised him, and that during his absence she had dissipated his substance and contracted debts. But when he married a young girl soon after, whom he was much in love with, people were apt to attribute that divorce to other reasons. He also put away his second wife, after the death of his daughter, who died in child-bed, because he fancied she rejoiced at his loss, which was very great, for he loved her with the utmost tenderness. Terentia lived one hundred and seventeen years. It is said that Cicero's mother at his birth felt no pain. He was called Marcus Tullius Cicero. In the beginning of the sixteenth century, a tomb was discovered in the high-road near Terracina, which was called by the Romans Via Appia, and in it was found the body of a young girl swimming in a certain unknown liquor. The corpse had fair hair turned up with a gold buckle, and as fresh as if alive. At the feet of the body was a lamp burning, which went out as soon as the air came to it. By the inscriptions it appeared that it had been buried in that place fifteen hundred years, and it was supposed to be the body of Tullia, Cicero's daughter. It was carried to Rome, and exposed in the Capitol, where great crowds of people came to view it; but as the credulous multitude would needs have it to be the body of a saint, because it was not corrupted, the Pope ordered it to be thrown by night into the Tiber.

between him and danger, and he was not a man to see his friend insulted. So considerable a piece of service added to the intimate friendship that had always subsisted between them was the reason that Clodius could never forgive this deposition of Cicero, which he thought the highest ingratitude, and felt ever after an implacable hatred of him.[1]

It is certain that Cicero was more to be pitied than blamed. He did not give his evidence willingly, nor appear against Clodius till he was compelled to it by an

[1] Clodius being full of resentment against Cicero, got himself chosen tribune of the people, on purpose to be revenged. In fact, he banished him from the city, set his country house on fire as well as that which he had at Rome, caused all his goods to be sold by auction, and vexed him by all possible means. Cicero retired to Dyrrachium, whose inhabitants received him with the utmost respect, and he stayed there till Milo, who was chosen tribune, recalled him, and openly espoused his interests, by declaring himself for Cicero against Clodius; for Milo, who was a man of spirit and great quality, despised a person that could with so much spite and cruelty persecute the most zealous and faithful citizen of Rome. This occasioned a falling out between Clodius and Milo, which came to the greatest degree of hatred, and from that time they sought for nothing but opportunities of plaguing each other. Clodius was the first that declared war; for perceiving that Milo strove for the consulship, he did all he could to oppose him, and to that purpose assisted Scipio and Hypsæus, the other competitors. The two parties were extremely irritated, and almost came to blows. During this dispute, Clodius, returning from Aricia, met Milo on the Appian Way as he was going to Lanuvium. Their servants began the fray, and the masters at last engaged with great fury, till Clodius was killed. The accident put all the town in an uproar; and the Senate, to prevent greater disorders, created Pompey consul, and ordered him to enquire into the murder. Pompey named commissaries out of every order of the town; and Milo recommended his cause to Cicero, whom he prayed to defend him. The orator, who was under great obligations to Milo, exerted the whole force of his eloquence, and composed that admirable speech (Orat. pro Milone) which anybody that pleases may see; but his manner of uttering it was not of a piece with the composition; for Pompey having posted some soldiers about the place to prevent disorders, Cicero was intimidated so much, that in pleading, he did not pronounce half the excellent things he had prepared, so that Milo was condemned to a severe banishment to Marseilles. It is reported, that reading one day the oration of Cicero which was composed for that occasion, he said, that if Cicero had spoken it as it was written, Milo would not then be employed in catching oysters at Marseilles.

authority more to be feared than the tribune. Terentia, his wife, a most obstinate and furious woman, obliged him to act thus. She was provoked against Clodius, because his sister Claudia had attempted to steal from her her husband's affections. This lady, being very beautiful, was much taken with the merit of Cicero (who had exalted himself to the consulship through all the degrees of honour, and was in the highest esteem at Rome), and would have been very well pleased to have married him. As this could not be brought about but by Cicero divorcing his wife, Claudia secretly employed one named Tullus in the affair, an intimate friend of Cicero, who visited him every day, and who was very familiar with Clodius, to whose house he had also free access.

As soon as Terentia had discovered this secret negotiation, she became furiously jealous, which made her the scourge of her family. As she was not a woman to swallow her grief silently, she made an uproar that would have wearied out the patience of a Stoic. Never were Cicero's virtue and philosophy put to so severe a trial; his wife made the house ring again with her continual brawling, and, as Claudia was out of her reach, she discharged her rage upon everybody about her. She desired nothing so much as an opportunity of showing her hatred, and greedily seized that which this affair of Clodius furnished her with; so, making use of the absolute authority she had assumed over her husband, she forced him to depose against the brother of her rival. No doubt but it was committing a great violence upon him, who was very sensible of the favours he had received from Clodius, but obey he must, and esteemed himself happy enough to make peace in his family upon those terms.

Cicero, however, was not the only person that accused Clodius; for people of all sorts witnessed against him, and charged him with numerous crimes; even Lucullus, his brother-in-law, produced a servant-maid, who deposed that Clodius, by a horrible incest, had rendered his sister unfaithful to her husband.[1]

It is certain that nobody thought him innocent, and he never would have been acquitted, if the severity of the laws had been put in force; but his high birth and great connections, which took in all the nobility of Rome, together with the protection of the people, who unanimously declared for him, outweighed his crime.

Thus did favour take the place of justice, and he escaped the punishment he deserved, how glaring soever his fault was.

It is true that the Senate, to save appearances, had recourse to expedients.[2] The majority of the judges gave their opinion in a confused sort of manner; and the sentence was couched in such unintelligible terms, that they were forced to explain it by another; which affected obscurity brought him off.

The most remarkable circumstance in this affair was, that whilst Cæsar's friends were extremely zealous for his honour, he himself was quite indifferent. He was too well acquainted with his wife's gallantries to imagine that this was the first instance of her transgression. He

---

[1] Clodius had three sisters whom he brutally abused; the eldest, called Terentia, was married to Marcius Rex, and Claudia, the second, to Metellus Celer. She was called in derision Quadrantaria; for, not being reckoned very cruel, she had been played a scurvy trick by her lover, who instead of money which he had promised her, sent her a purse full of Quadrantes, a sort of small coin of base metal. The youngest was wife to Lucullus.

[2] Plutar. Vita Cæsar. Vita Cicer.

had taken some pains to examine into the matter, and probably found out more than he had a mind to know. He was, however, cited to be heard, but did not think proper to complain much. So unseasonable a tranquillity surprised everybody. He was interrogated as to his wife's adultery, but answered that he knew nothing of it. He had indeed put her away, which was a tacit acknowledgment of her guilt; but, being asked why he did so, answered that Cæsar's wife ought to be exempt, not only from crime, but from suspicion.

He met with one of that character in Calpurnia, Piso's daughter.[1] As Cæsar was already grown very powerful, he destined his new father-in-law to succeed him in the consulship, that sublime [2] dignity which was then so much sought after.[3]

Cato, that severe censurer of all those that had more

[1] See note on p. 27.

[2] After the Romans had shaken off Tarquin's yoke, they created other magistrates, to whose hands the government of the Republic was intrusted. They were called consuls, from the Latin word consulere, which signifies to take care of anything, to the end that their name might continually put them in mind of their duty. There were but two of them: they continued a year in their employ, and were absolute in their authority as long as it lasted. They could not obtain it till they were forty-three years of age. The consuls were chiefs of the council. They had a sovereign command in the town, the armies, and the provinces. They were also at first called prætors, but afterwards another officer was created and distinguished by that name, the consuls being known by no other title than that of consul. They were always chosen in the field of Mars, and taken from among the patricians, till the Licinian law, which ordained that one of them should be a plebeian. The consuls were preceded by twelve lictors, who carried bundles of rods with hatchets tied up in them, to scourge or behead upon the spot, if necessary. The chief of them was called the great consul, and the other was his partner in the consulship. Nobody was superior to them, for their power was absolute, which the law of the Twelve Tables sufficiently shows, viz. "Regio imperio duo sunto, iique præeundo, judicando, con- "sulendo, Prætores, judices, Consules appellentur; militiæ summum jus "habento; nemini parento; ollis salus Populi Romani suprema lex esto."

[3] Sueton. vit. Jul. Cæs.

than ordinary ambition, could not see with patience this sort of traffic, but openly declaimed against such an encroachment on the public liberty, and said it was a shame that the command of the armies, the government of provinces, and the principal dignities of the Republic should be prostituted at that rate, and depend upon marriages. This, however, was the last fault of that nature that Cæsar was guilty of; for he found, in Calpurnia, every quality that could deserve his esteem.

She was of an illustrious family, descended from Numa Pompilius, second King of Rome. Her beauty was accompanied with a consummate prudence, penetrating wit, a degree of eloquence that did not yield to that of the greatest orators, and a true Roman generosity; she was, in short, such a woman as Cæsar's wife ought to be, who, having formed the vastest and most audacious project that the mind of man was capable of, aspired to no less than the conquest of the world.

In all degrees and vicissitudes of fortune, she preserved an evenness of temper that nothing could alter; for, however high a condition Cæsar had exalted himself to by his victories and triumphs, she never became the more haughty or proud; every day of her life was the same.

It certainly was a rare thing to meet with so much modesty in such a glorious station; and was the more commendable in Calpurnia, because everything seemed to flatter her ambition and vanity. Her fortune could not but be extraordinary, since it was the same with Cæsar's, who, from a plain Roman Senator, was, by his superior genius and prodigious courage, become master of the Romans. His arms, which so many conquests had rendered terrible to all the world, were also formidable to Rome; and this Republic, so jealous of her liberty; this Republic, who had given laws to so many nations, and brought so many people under the yoke, was obliged to suffer that of one of her own citizens. The Senate, that most venerable body, master of all the kings of the earth, became a slave to Cæsar. One might see all those great men of which it was composed striving to outdo each other in respect and submission, and decreeing to the tyrant of their liberties the most pompous and most sacred honours.

They styled him Father of his Country, made him perpetual Dictator,[1] that sovereign dignity which Sulla, with all his power and authority, never dared to keep possession of, because it aroused odium the moment any person attempted to do so.

Cæsar had a distinguished place in the Senate. They caused a temple to be erected to his honour before his palace; and raised a superb cupola on the roof, putting

[1] The dictatorship was an extraordinary office, which the Romans never had recourse to, but upon the most pressing occasions, and when the Republic was threatened with some imminent danger. The dictator was chosen by the consuls; and the election was never made but by night. He had an absolute power of life and death over the citizens; his sentence was without appeal, except one example to the contrary, which Titus Livius takes notice of, where we read, that M. Fabius appealed from the judgment of the dictator Papirius, to the tribunes of the people. "Tribunos Plebis appello et provoco ad Populum." The dictator was styled the master of the people, Magister Populi. All the other magistrates were subordinate to him; his commands were respected as so many oracles, and the consuls themselves were entirely submissive to them. He was preceded by twenty-four lictors, and was bound by no law. He named whom he pleased for general of the horse (Magister Equitum), who was an officer next to himself in command, and who never fought but on foot. The dictator's commission was in force but six months, as they would not give so exorbitant a power for a longer time, for fear the person in whom it was vested should thereby make himself the tyrant of the Republic.

it, by that, on a level with the temple of the gods.[1] They
also gave his name to one of the months [2] of the year,[3]
placed his statue among those of the gods, and carried
their impious and sacrilegious flattery so far as to grant
him immortality, even during his life.[4]

Among these excessive honours, Calpurnia was not forgotten, and the Senate, so liberal towards Cæsar, did not
show themselves niggardly with regard to her. For,
besides those conferred upon her husband, and which,
of course, reflected back upon her, they invented particu-

---

[1] No person was permitted to erect a dome on his house, which was
an honour peculiar to the sacred temples.

[2] Romulus, first King of Rome, made the year consist of ten months,
and began it by the month of March, so called after the god Mars,
whose son he pretended to be. Numa Pompilius added two more, but
the year still began by the month of March. July being the fifth month,
they called it Quinctilis, till, in order to do honour to Cæsar, they changed
its name to Julius, as they afterwards did the sixth to Augustus, in
honour of that Emperor.

[3] Suet. Plutar. vita Jul. Cæs. Florus. lib 4. c. 2.

[4] The apotheosis, or conferring divinity, was a ceremony observed
among the Romans, when they had a mind to place an Emperor, Empress, hero, or any other illustrious person in the ranks of the gods.
The principal things to be observed in this consecration were these:
They made an image of wax, resembling the person to whom they
were about to grant the divinity; this was placed upon a bed of parade,
and the senators and other persons of distinction, of both sexes, went to
pay their respects to it for seven days. The image was afterwards
carried with great pomp into the Roman Forum, where the praises of the
deceased were sung, and from thence to the field of Mars without the
town, where the eulogy was pronounced. The pontiffs or priests, in
the meantime, placed the image on the second step of the funeral pile,
which was five degrees or stories high, and shaped like a pyramid, the
inside of which was filled with small dry wood, and a great quantity
of perfumes. At .ast the Emperor, assisted by the consuls and other
magistrates, set fire to it, and as soon as it was kindled, they let fly
from it an eagle, if the person was a man; and if a woman, a pea-
cock. The bird, frighted by the flames, flew off, and the people
imagined that it carried away with it the soul of the deceased among the
gods. After the ceremony they caused a temple to be built in honour
of the new divinity. At first this extraordinary honour was not easily
granted; it was the reward of great exploits and superior merit, and
never conferred till after the death of the person; but afterwards
flattery came to such a pitch, that it was given to living people.

lar honours for her. No sort of praises or pompous
titles were omitted; for, after the Senate had, by a most
servile complaisance, granted divinity to Cæsar, what
might not his wife aspire to?

But, notwithstanding all this, which, one would think,
was enough to corrupt the sentiments of any person, it
made no impression on Calpurnia. Never was the least
symptom of pride seen in her, nor did her elevation
get the better of her modesty. No difference was to be
seen between Calpurnia, wife of Cæsar, the plain senator, and of Cæsar, master of the world. Her manners
were always the same; that is, they were always courteous
and affable. Her goodness and sweetness of temper, in
the most elevated station, were as much admired, as
was afterwards that firmness of soul which she showed at
the unfortunate death of her husband.

However moderate Cæsar's government was [1] (who
piqued himself upon his clemency and generosity), it yet
became insupportable to a people accustomed to liberty,
who did not know what it was to be slaves, having never
obeyed any laws but those which they themselves had
made, and therefore looked upon his prodigious power
and elevation to be, not so much the reward of his merit,
as a mark of their weakness and indolence. The Senate
was composed of an infinite number of great men, several
of whom had commanded Cæsar, and could not bear to
yield to an absolute authority, and be forced to obey him
who, but a little before, had been obliged to execute
their orders. They could not bring themselves to be dependent upon a man they thought no way superior to
them, but by an unlimited ambition. They therefore

[1] Plutar. Suet. vita Jul. Cæs.

united, and, under the specious name of defenders of the public liberty (but rather through envy and private resentment), resolved to shake off this unsupportable yoke, and put a speedy conclusion to Cæsar's power, together with his life.

It was in the hearts of Brutus and Cassius that this treason was hatched; they gained over to their party a great many of the most illustrious senators; and waited only for an opportunity to put it into execution. They pitched upon a day whereon Cæsar was to assemble the Senate, in order to propose affairs of the greatest importance. Calpurnia had secret foretellings of the misfortune that threatened her. She dreamt that the dome (which, by a solemn decree of the Senate, had been raised on the top of her house) fell down, and that Cæsar was murdered in her arms. This frightful dream awakened her, and scarce had she opened her eyes, but the doors of her chamber flew open of themselves, with a great noise, which exceedingly surprised her, little superstitious as she was. Her affection for her husband made her apprehensive that this could portend no less than some dreadful misfortune to him; and her alarms redoubled when she found him obstinately determined to go to the Senate, in spite of all these presages, which gave him notice of the impending mischief and notwithstanding all the warnings he had, that his life was in the utmost danger, that the Ides of March would be productive of some direful event, that that very day would be fatal to him.

Calpurnia added to her prayers and tears the entreaties of Cæsar's friends, and it was thought all this made some impression on the Emperor, for he seemed to hesitate whether he should meet the Senate that day, or put off to another the proposal he had to make to them about carrying on the war against the Parthians. Being at last resolved not to go, because, besides all this, he was not well, he was sending Mark Antony to break up the assembly, when Decimus Brutus came in, and told him that the Senate waited only for him, and that, being met by his order, they were determined to honour him with the title of King of all the Provinces, and to prevail on him to wear the regal ornaments; that it would argue an unbecoming weakness to mind a woman's dreams, and that it would be too haughty a behaviour to send back the senators without saluting them, and returning them thanks, at least, for their good intention.

These persuasions determined the wavering mind of Cæsar. He suffered himself to be prevailed upon; and so much the more easily, because Brutus lay under the greatest obligations to him, and upon him he thought that he might safely depend. He went then to the Senate, accompanied by these false friends. He was but a little distance from his house, when a slave was very importunate to speak with him; but, not being able to penetrate the crowd that surrounded him, he went to Calpurnia, and begged her to keep him at her house, till the Emperor returned, having, as he said, matters of the greatest importance to communicate.

Another man, more able, or more fortunate, than the first, made his way through the crowd, and, coming up to Cæsar, presented him a memorial containing the whole secret of the conspiracy, entreating him to read it immediately, because he would find in it affairs of the utmost consequence. But Cæsar, though he often attempted to look into it, was still prevented by the people, who talked to him about other matters.

Thus he, being destined to destruction, entered the Senate, attended by those who did not conduct him thither but in order to sacrifice him to the public liberty (which they said he had overthrown), or, rather, to their own private jealously.

It was certainly a great misfortune to him that Mark Antony did not go into the Senate with the rest, for he was not of the number of those assassins, but on the contrary, very much attached to his interest, so would certainly have defended him.[1] Brutus had foreseen this, and, therefore, contrived to have him stopped at the door, pretending earnest business, though in reality it was only to give the conspirators time to finish what they were about, and the artifice succeeded.

Cæsar was scarce sat down, when the conspirators came about him, as if to do him honour. Cimber began to lay hold of his robe. At this signal, which they had agreed upon, Casca gave him a stab with his poniard, and the rest of them surrounded him with their swords drawn.

Cæsar defended himself for some time, till, taking notice of Brutus amongst his enemies, with his naked sword, whom he had always assisted to the utmost, loaded with benefits, and loved above all men, for more reasons than one;[2] he then covered himself with his

---

[1] Many are of opinion that Mark Antony knew of the whole affair, which they say Trebonius imparted to him as they went together to meet Cæsar; and add that Mark Anthony, though he refused to be one of the conspirators, yet was faithful enough to them not to reveal the secret.

[2] Servilia, Brutus's mother, was the most beloved of all Cæsar's mistresses. He made her a present of a pearl that cost him one hundred and fifty thousand crowns; there was nobody at Rome that did not look upon Brutus as the fruits of their amours, and yet he made no

sword, saying: "What, my dear Brutus, art thou also in the number of these murderers?" These were his last words, after which he expired in the Senate House, having received twenty-three wounds.

Thus, as an historian remarks, he who had filled the world with the blood of others, filled the Senate House with his own.[1]

This murder, which threw all the town into confusion, filled the heart of Calpurnia with inconsolable grief. She paid to the memory of her husband that tribute of tears and affliction which she owed to the merit of so great a man; and, not content with that, she was resolved to give public marks of her esteem for him, in making his funeral oration, at the tribunal of harangues, which she did with an eloquence that surprised all the world. She did not, indeed, attempt to destroy herself, true tenderness and affection not requiring such violent proceedings. Her behaviour was not like that of a woman out of her senses, but her sincere love and esteem were none the less conspicuous. She sufficiently showed, by her manner of bewailing him, that she was convinced that nothing could ever make her amends for her irreparable loss. She said adieu to all the pleasures of life, and passed the remainder of her days in mourning and sorrow, at Mark

scruple to conspire against Cæsar. Some there are who excuse him on account of his great zeal for the liberties of his country, which Cæsar had encroached upon; but this has not been able to justify him to all the world. And the author of the distich, that is to be seen under a bust of Brutus in the great Duke's Gallery at Florence, did not approve of that action. This bust is the workmanship of the famous Michael Angelo, who did not live to finish it, which gave occasion to a poet to put these two verses:

"Dum Bruti effigiem sculptor de marmore ducit
"In mentem sceleris venit, et abstinuit."

[1] Florus. lib. 4. c. 2.

Antony's house, with whom she generously divided her
treasures, that he might be enabled to revenge the death
of her illustrious spouse.[1]

[1] Calpurnia's family was exceeding noble and ancient. Most people
reckon Calpus, son of Numa Pompilius, among her ancestors. Ovid
affirms it,

> "—— nam quid memorare necesse est,
> "Ut domus a Calpo nomen Calpurnia ducat."

It was divided into two branches, one of which was distinguished
with the glorious name of Frugi, which is as much as to say, worthy
people. As for the surname of Piso, it was common to both. Calpurnius
Piso, father to Calpurnia, was consul in the seven hundred and fifty-
third year of Rome. Calpurnia delivered up to Mark Anthony all
Cæsar's papers and effects. This Calpurnia is different from a Roman
lady of the same name, who once pleaded her cause with so much anger
and fury that she gave occasion for an edict that none of her sex
should ever plead after.

LIVIA

WIFE OF AUGUSTUS

F all the Roman Empresses, Livia may be said to have done the greatest honour to her dignity, and to have best supported the character of it. Augustus owed a considerable part of his glory to her, and not only consulted her in the most important and difficult affairs, but generally took her advice.[1] She was the daughter of Livius Drusus Calidianus, who, being of the number of the proscribed persons during the furious proceedings of the Triumvirate, joined the party of Brutus and Cassius,[2] and killed himself after the battle of Philippi, that he might not fall into the hands of Mark Antony and Augustus.

Livia's family was, without contradiction, one of the most illustrious of Rome,[3] for her ancestral stock was more ancient than Rome itself, and there are none that have made more noise in history, whether we consider the great men it has produced,[4] or the inclination of all the Claudian family (Publius excepted) to take part with the people against the Senate, which people were

[1] Senec. de Clemen. lib. 1. c. 9.
[2] Dio. lib. 48. Vel. Pater. Hist. lib. 2.
[3] Plutar. vit. Publicol.   [4] Sueton. vit. Tiber. c. 1. and 2.

always treated by the patricians [1] with haughtiness, contempt, and insolence.

Calidianus was descended from this Claudian family, for it was only by adoption [2] that he belonged to that of the Livians, from whence he took the name of Livius, and his daughter that of Livia.

To her high quality, Livia joined [3] a beauty which surpassed that of all the other ladies in Rome. Her mind was vast, elevated, cultivated with a prodigious stock of learning, and capable of the greatest things. She discerned justly, [4] had a gaiety of temper that was charming and lively, and a profound penetration, which, in the most intricate affairs, gave her so happy a facility in choosing the best method, that, afterwards, [5] Augustus never had any serious discourse with her that he did not insert in his journal. But then, she was haughty, [6] proud, ambitious, and had, in short, that disdainful air so natural to the Claudian family. She had not, for all that, a forbidding way; and, though she prided herself upon the ancient severity of manner, she knew how to soften it [7] by an affable behaviour, and a certain liberty that would not have been permitted to the women of Rome at the beginning.

[1] For the better comprehending what is meant by patricians, it must be observed that Romulus singled out those of the best fashion at Rome, and separated them from the others. As they were the most considerable in point of riches, prudence, and wisdom, he distinguished them with the venerable name of fathers, and the rest were only called the people. The posterity of these fathers were called patricians; and Romulus chose one hundred of them, whereof he formed the Senate. From among the other families, patricians as well as plebeians, he took three hundred more, of which he composed a body of citizens between the patricians and the people, which was styled the order of knights; so that every Roman was either a senator, a knight, or a plebeian.

[2] Tacit. Ann. 5. c. 1.   [5] Senec. de Clement. lib. 1. c. 9.
[3] Vell. Pater. Histor. lib. 2.   [6] Sueton. vit. Aug.
[4] Macrob. lib. 2. c. 1.   [7] Tacit. Ann. 5. c. 1.

Such was Livia, who was married to Tiberius Claudius Nero (also of the Claudian family), a man of extraordinary experience, and so brave, that Julius Cæsar, who knew how to distinguish true merit, honoured [1] Tiberius with the pontificate; [2] he also committed to his conduct the colonies which he sent to Arelate, Narbo,[3] and other towns of Gaul, to reward the important services,[4] he had done the Republic when he commanded the fleet in the war of Alexandria, which was concluded by the important victory that Cæsar gained, and to which Tiberius Nero did not a little contribute.

This marriage was soon fruitful. Livia became with child, which gave her a joy that nothing could equal but the fear she was in of not having a son, which she wished for with that ardent passion so natural to young married women. There was nothing which she did not do to be informed whether her desires should be accomplished. This curiosity was pardonable at her age; and it is reported that she took it in her head to have an egg from under a sitting hen,[5] and that by dint of holding it close in her hand, or in her bosom, she warmed it so as to hatch

---

[1] Vell. Pater. Hist. lib. 2.

[2] The pontificate was one of the finest employments at Rome. The pontiffs were established by King Numa Pompilius to preside at the public ceremonies; they took cognisance of everything that regarded religion and the worship of the gods, as well as the safety, liberty, and fortune of the citizens. At the beginning of their institution they were but four, and were taken out of the order of patricians. Afterwards four others were added, and chosen from among the knights; and Sulla, at last, increased the number to fifteen, which body was called the College of Pontiffs, over which the chief presided, and was styled the sovereign pontiff. As many and great privileges were annexed to this dignity, great pains were taken to obtain it. The Emperors did not think it below them to take possession, and even to be proud of this employment; but Theodosius thought proper to abolish it.

[3] Arles and Narbonne.   [4] Suet. vit. Tiber. c. 4.

[5] Plin. lib. 10. c. 55. Suet. vit. Tiber.

it, and it produced a chicken with a remarkable comb, which she looked upon as ominous, and foretelling a son. The event answered her expectations. She was delivered of Tiberius Claudius Nero, who, in his childhood, was exposed to many hardships and misfortunes. As this part of the history is necessary to explain that of Livia, it will not be amiss to be as particular in it as possible.

After Julius Cæsar was assassinated in full Senate, as we have related, people flattered themselves that Rome [1] would find the end of her slavery in the death of her tyrant, and that the Republic would see her liberty spring up again after the destruction of her oppressors. But this murder proved, on the contrary, only the seed of endless discords and divisions, and the occasion of the most cruel civil wars. Empires have, without doubt, their fates and periods, as well as men. Rome had attained her utmost pitch of glory and grandeur; and, according to the vicissitudes of all human affairs, could not but fall back again to her primitive condition, and be again fettered with those chains which she imagined she had so happily shaken off. Mark Antony (general of the army under Julius Cæsar) and Octavius Cæsar, Julius's nephew and adopted son (since known by the name of Augustus), were both resolved to revenge his death, but each from different motives in appearance, though tending to the same end, viz., the gratifying of their ambition. Mark Antony was then consul, which gave him an absolute authority. His family were possessed of the most important employments; and his two brothers were, the one tribune, and the other prætor. Puffed up with this exorbitant power, he thought he had a right to aspire to

[1] Florus. lib. 4.

everything; and, in consequence of this boundless presumption, he demanded the government of [1] Cisalpine Gaul, which had been given by Cæsar to Decimus Brutus, who was afterwards one of his murderers.

Antony did not find it so easy a matter to obtain as he imagined. The Senate dreaded his ambition, and did not care to increase it by giving him so important an employ; besides, Brutus was looked upon as one of the defenders of the public liberty. It was not forgotten that the ancient freedom of Rome was in a great measure owing to some of his ancestors,[2] and that an ardent love

[1] Cisalpine Gaul was what we now call Lombardy, a part of Italy between the Alps and the Apennine Mountains, on both sides of the River Po.

[2] Junius Brutus, son of Tarquinia, sister to Tarquin the proud, perceiving that this cruel prince put to death the principal persons of Rome, from whom he imagined he had a great deal to fear, pretended to be mad, to make himself contemptible, and that he might not give jealousy to that suspicious tyrant. It soon appeared, however, that Junius, under this pretended disorder of the brain, concealed the most profound prudence. Titus and Aruns, the King's sons, consulting the oracle at Delphi, by order of their father, on account of a prodigy that had lately happened at Rome, would needs take their cousin Junius with them to make sport of. After they had made their demand of the oracle about the prodigy, they asked which of them should rule after Tarquin? The oracle answered that it should be the first among them that should give a kiss to his mother. The two princes imagining that this could only regard them, agreed to cast lots which of them should first kiss their mother. Brutus had more sense than to interpret the oracle literally, and soon comprehended that there was something mysterious in it; so pretending to fall, he kissed the earth, which is the common mother of all men. The oracle was verified. Sextus Tarquinius, another of the King's sons, having brutally attempted to defile the bed of the senator Collatinus, in endeavouring to ravish his wife Lucretia, this scandalous enterprise so provoked the Romans that they took arms, under the conduct of Brutus, who encouraged them to revenge the outrage, and made them take an oath that they would be no longer subject to kings. And, in fact, they drove Tarquin and his family out of Rome, and placed the sovereign power in the hands of two magistrates, whom they called consuls. Brutus was the first they selected to fill this high dignity, and showed, by his behaviour, that they were not deceived in the choice they had made; and that nobody could be more fitted than he to defend that liberty which he was the author of. He sustained the interests of the Republic with so much zeal, made the people so sensible of the

for the Republic was, in a manner, hereditary in his family; it was not, therefore, reasonable to strip Brutus of his government, in order to give it to Antony. This was done, notwithstanding; but it was at the request of Augustus, whom the Senate had no mind to disoblige by the refusal of the first favour he asked.

Mark Antony lying under such obligations, it might be supposed that he would express all possible marks of gratitude to Augustus, his benefactor, but other considerations took place; for,[1] being full of resentment that Julius Cæsar had made Augustus his principal heir to his prejudice, he was resolved to thwart him in all his projects; to give a malicious turn to his designs, in order to make his actions suspected;[2] and, the more effectually to make him odious, and ruin him with the Senate, he accused him of heinous crimes; and went so far as to affirm that Augustus had a mind to assassinate him.[3]

These bad practices of Antony were too notorious to be hid from Augustus, who, though very young, knew that it behoved him to stand continually on his guard against a man he had so much reason to mistrust; and, not doubting but Antony was the person in the world he had the most reason to dread and be apprehensive of, he broke off all commerce with him; and, that he might not be in a capacity to hurt him, he was determined to ruin

advantages and sweetness of independence, and gave so many proofs of his affection to his country, that after his death the Roman ladies went into deep mourning for a year, and a statue was erected to his honour in the Capitol. His memory was always held in veneration at Rome, and the origin of the Republic was looked upon as his work; for which reason, when Julius Cæsar had made himself absolute, they found one day written under Brutus's statue these words, viz.: "O, that it were the will of the gods that thou were alive!"

[1] Florus, lib. 4.
[2] Vell. Pater. Hist. lib. 2.   [3] Sueton. vit. Aug.

his party. To this purpose, considering that the government of Cisalpine Gaul furnished great power and advantages to whoever should be in possession of it, and that
it was of the greatest importance to him to disappoint
Antony in that respect (though it was he who procured
him the employment), he resolved to make Brutus his
friend, who was yet in his government; he sent him word
then not to quit or yield it up to Antony; and, that Brutus
might put an entire confidence in him, he sent him provisions and ammunition to Modena, whither he was
retired, and also assisted him with men and money,
deferring, till another opportunity, the revenging of
Cæsar's murder.

Mark Antony's year of consulship being over, the
Senate assembled to create new consuls, and to deliberate
about the precautions that were thought necessary to be
taken against the boundless ambition of this man, with
whom they were not at all satisfied, no more than with
Dolabella his colleague. The famous orator, Cicero,
who, without doubt, was the first in reputation and
authority in the Senate, having lately quarrelled with
Antony, declaimed vehemently against him. Never was
his eloquence employed with more art or success. Being
supported by the friendship of Augustus, who had committed his interests to his care, and whose arms and influence gave him courage, he drew Antony's [1] picture
with so much artifice, and so cunningly exaggerated his
vices and ambition, that the Senate imagined they saw in
him a mixture of all sorts of crimes. Never did Cicero
so advantageously make use of his art of persuading;
for, after having censured the life, and exposed all the

---

[1] Philippic. 2.

actions, of Antony, he clearly convinced the Senate that the [1] bad effects and consequences already produced by his ambition were but forerunners of what was to be expected; so that Antony was declared an enemy to the State by a decree that frightened him so much, that he was obliged to get away from Rome, where he thought he could no longer remain in safety.

Antony did not lack friends who endeavoured to justify him of the faults he was accused of, but their efforts were in vain. The eloquence of Cicero was victorious.[2] The Senate, prejudiced against Antony, commanded him to lay down his arms;[3] and, upon his refusing, Augustus, together with the consuls Hirtius and Pansa, had orders to go and fight him before Modena, which he had besieged. The good cause triumphed. Antony's army was beaten, and he was obliged to depend on a shameful flight for his safety. The siege was raised, and the Senate had nothing to regret but the loss of the two consuls, who were snatched out of the arms of victory, and, after having well performed their duty, both perished in the battle. The manner of their death was variously reported.[4]

Augustus did not reap from this victory all the fruit that he expected. The partisans of Pompey, who were

---

[1] Eutrop. de gestis Roman.
[2] Vell. Pater. Dio.   [3] Appian. Flor. Sueton.
[4] After the battle of Modena it was said at Rome that Augustus caused the two consuls to be killed, that he might be sole master of the armies. Pansa's death especially looked so suspicious that Glycon, the physician, was arrested by order of the Senate, it being supposed that he had poisoned the consul's wounds to please Augustus. Several were of opinion that Augustus himself killed Hirtius in the heat of the fight; and if there were some who maintained that Augustus was incapable of so infamous an action, there were not wanting others who affirmed that everything was to be feared from so ambitious a man, and one who had such vast designs.

very numerous, took fresh courage upon Antony's being worsted; they hated Antony, because he had much contributed to the ruin of Pompey the Great; but Augustus was not less odious to them, for as he was adopted son and heir to Julius Cæsar, they saw plainly that he could not choose but be an enemy to Pompey's posterity. They therefore united to make him lose the reward of his labours, and found many specious reasons for so doing; especially their seeming zeal for the public welfare served to cloak their private resentment. They showed the danger of exalting too high a man who might one day make himself master of the Republic; that Augustus, under pretence of defending Rome, aimed at nothing but arbitrary power; and that, if the Senate knew its own true interests, it would be always upon its guard against him, as he was not less heir to Cæsar's ambition, than to his wealth. These remonstrances had such an effect, that the honour of a triumph was decreed to Brutus, without mentioning Augustus, to whom they also refused the consulship, though he afterwards obtained it by Cicero's assistance.

Augustus was very much surprised to find the high expectations that his victory had given him so cruelly disappointed. He accused the Senate of ingratitude, and said that Brutus had been only a calm spectator of the battle, whilst he, on the contrary, had exposed his life as much as the meanest soldier, and yet they had thought proper to rob him of the honour that was due to him, to bestow it upon Brutus. These proceedings filled him with indignation against the Senate, and he was resolved to be revenged for so cruel a piece of injustice.

He was in this situation, when Lepidus (into whose army Antony had retired after the above-mentioned battle), being desirous to take advantage of the humour he saw Augustus was in, insinuated to him that he ought not to put too much confidence in the Senate, who were entirely devoted to Pompey's friends, and whose memory was yet very dear to them; that he ought, rather, to think of revenging the death of his father, than favouring those who had assassinated him; and, seeing that these arguments made an impression upon him, he proposed that he should be [1] friends with Antony, and that they three might be closely united together, in order to be revenged on their respective enemies.

Augustus found his advantage and satisfaction in this proposal. Lepidus (distinguished by his birth, his victories, and his immense riches, which had made him formidable in the Senate) had the command of a great army, and could turn the scale in favour of whatever party he espoused. Augustus perceived that, by making peace, he might have the use of that general's forces, as well as of those of Antony, to mortify the Senate, who, he said, had used him so ill; in short, he was not master of either troops or authority enough to compass his designs alone, and, therefore, could not avoid having recourse to the assistance of others. He accommodated himself, then, to the times and to his own necessity; and, pretending to bury in oblivion the ill-treatment he had received from Antony, he offered to make up matters with him; and the conditions were soon agreed upon. Lepidus, Mark Antony, and Augustus, met in an island between

[1] Vell. Pater. Hist. lib. 2.

Perusia and Bononia; [1] they embraced, and making each
other the strongest protestations of a sincere friendship,
they formed that famous triumvirate that filled Rome
with blood. Every sentence of this fatal agreement carried death and destruction along with it. It was resolved
that they three should take upon them the government of
the Republic with sovereign authority; that there should
be no more consuls; that they alone should dispose of
everything; that they should divide among them the
provinces and the legions; that they should make war
against Cassius and Brutus; and that they should deliver
up to each other their respective enemies, in order to take
a cruel vengeance on all such as they imagined had injured them. And, to make this reconciliation more sincere, and the union more durable, it was determined that
Augustus should marry Claudia, Antony's daughter-in-
law, whom Fulvia had by Clodius, her first husband.

This monstrous project being thus concerted, the
bloody catalogue of persons who were condemned to

[1] The river Lavinius, in the Modenese, between Perusia and Bononia,
forms a little island, which Lepidus pitched upon for the interview
between Antony and Augustus. When they three approached the island,
Lepidus, who was the mediator, and in whose probity the others had
great confidence, went alone to visit the island, and examine whether
there might not be some soldiers concealed, that there might be no room
for suspicion, Antony keeping on one side of the river and Augustus on
the other, each being accompanied by five legions under arms. Lepidus,
having strictly searched every corner of the island, made a signal to the
two generals that they might safely pass, by lifting up his robe, which
was the sign agreed on. Immediately Augustus and Antony, leaving
their followers at the end of the bridge made for the communication,
advanced singly, and with an equal pace, to the middle of the island,
where they met; and that there might be no jealously between them,
they searched each other, for fear of arms being concealed; and after
having embraced, they three sat down in an open place, where they
might be seen by their people. Augustus, being consul, placed himself
in the middle between Lepidus and Antony. Their conference continued
three days, and the triumvirate was the dreadful result of it.

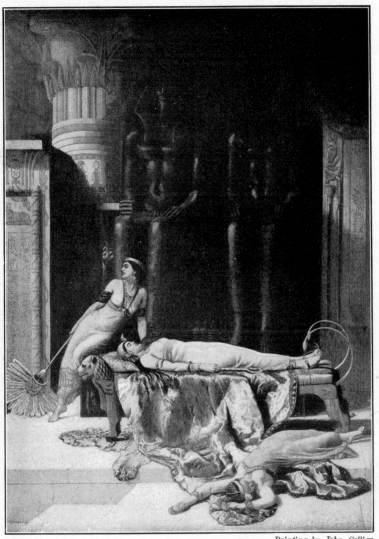

The Death of Cleopatra

death was fixed up at Rome, in large characters, the number of which increased every day; and those who thought themselves very lucky, when they found no mention made of their names in the list, learned next day by their death, that they had been added. Everybody's life depended on the whims and caprice of these barbarians; and those dignities, which till then had been sacred and inviolable, were no protection at all to the possessors of them. Consuls, prætors, and tribunes, might be seen upon their knees at the feet of their slaves, supplicating them not to disclose the places where they might hide themselves. It was forbidden on pain of death to give protection to any that were condemned, or even to mourn for them. It was a capital crime to show the least signs of pity; for a sigh or a tear was an offence not to be forgiven. In short, things were come to that degree of misery, that it was looked upon as a miracle of good fortune to escape the fury of these three tyrants.

Never was the appearance of Rome so horrible; nothing was to be seen but trouble and confusion; and nothing was spoken of but punishments, death, and bloody executions, of the like of which, till then, Rome had never been the theatre, except during the horrible proscriptions of Sulla and Marius. Above one hundred and forty senators, and two thousand knights were massacred. Neither age, relationship, innocence, virtue, nor friendship, were spared. No state or condition was exempt from the fury of these three monsters. The ties of blood were of no weight with those, whose insatiable desire of revenge got the better of nature and all other considerations; witness the proscription of Lucius Cæsar, uncle to Mark Antony; of Lucius Paulus, brother to Lepidus; and of

Toranius, Augustus's tutor; and if they were not put to death, it was solely owing to the respect which the instruments of these cruelties (employed by the triumvirate) had for these great men. Never had Rome more just or more melancholy cause of affliction. The streets were choked up with the dead bodies of the most illustrious citizens; nor was there any family of distinction on which these tyrants had not stamped their hatred and cruelty in characters of blood. Every day the orators' tribunal was loaded with the heads of the most distinguished Romans.

But the most moving and deplorable spectacle of all was to see, in the same place, the head of Cicero,[1] the most eloquent orator that ever was, and the most zealous defender of the public liberties. He fell a sacrifice to the hatred of Antony,[2] against whom he had so often declaimed in the Senate with irresistible force: and this triumvir was not ashamed to purchase the death of his enemy, at the expense of his own kith and kin; for he sacrificed his uncle to Augustus's resentment, and exchanged his head for that of Cicero. Never did a man shed the blood of an enemy with so much pleasure; for Antony would have returned from the gaining of the most important victory with less pride and satisfaction than he felt upon this occasion; and he could not possibly have expressed the joy he conceived at the death of this formidable adversary more than by the pleasure he took in earnestly contemplating the head, which he caused to be brought to him for that purpose, that he might be sure of its being the head of Cicero. Never would Fulvia be deprived of the pleasure of feasting her eyes upon this

[1] Vell. Paterc. Histor. lib. 2.   [2] Florus, lib. 4.

dismal sight. As this was the first opportunity she ever had of being revenged upon the man, whose vehement invectives had so often provoked her, she took into her hands this head, so venerable even in death, and after having poured forth against it a torrent of insulting words, she allowed herself the base and malicious satisfaction of piercing, with the bodkin of her hair, that tongue which had so often thundered in the Senate against her husband, and sometimes against her [1] brutal

---

[1] Cicero's proscription was the point that was most of all contested among the triumvirs. Antony would hear of no arrangement, if the death of this orator was not granted him. Lepidus was well enough pleased, but Augustus would by no means consent to it; he even held out the first two days; but on the third he demanded in return the head of Lucius Cæsar, uncle to Antony, taking it for granted that Antony would no longer insist upon the destruction of Cicero; but Antony took him at his word, and gave up his uncle, so as to procure himself that inestimable pleasure. Lucius, who was with his brother Quintus Cicero at his country house near Tusculum, being informed of this, set out for Macedonia, to visit Brutus, and took his brother with him. But as they departed in great haste, they forgot to take money for their journey, so that, Cicero having but little about him, and Quintus none at all, the latter went home to get some; but being betrayed by his own servants, he was killed, together with his son. Cicero embarked on his voyage, and was some days at sea; but whether that element did not agree with him, or that he always hoped Augustus, to whom he had rendered such great services, would never abandon him, he caused himself to be put on shore, and travelled towards Rome, hesitating what to do with himself; for sometimes he had thoughts of going privately to Cæsar, and of killing himself at his feet; but afterwards changing his mind, he went again on board the ship, in order to go to another country-house which he had near Gaeta. He stayed there but one night, because his domestics, not thinking him safe, prevailed on him to leave that place, and embark again. His litter had not proceeded two miles from the house, when people, who were sent by Antony, arrived there, conducted by Herennius, and Popilius Lena the centurion, whom Cicero had defended in a prosecution for a murder, which would have cost him his life, if it had not been for the eloquence and protection of that orator. None of the servants could tell where Cicero was; and the assassins might not have found him, if Philologus, Quintus's freedman, and whom Cicero himself had taught, had not betrayed his benefactor, by disclosing the secret of his journey, and the road he had taken. These wretches had not far to go before they overtook him. Cicero hearing the noise of their horses, stopped his servants, and when he put his head out of the litter, Herennius had the

pleasure, an insult which was afterwards practised in like manner [1] by an incestuous princess upon the tongue of the greatest among the children of men.[2] These bloody proceedings dispeopled Rome, for everybody fled as fast as they could, and, among the rest, Calidianus, Livia's father, who went to join Brutus and Cassius; but this proved no place of safety to him, for the triumvirs attacked them in the provinces whither they had retired, and were so fortunate as to defeat them beyond all possibility of recovery at the famous battle of Philippi: these two were called the last of the Romans.

This victory might be reckoned the expiration of the Republic, for all hope of liberty vanished with the two generals, who had undertaken to defend it; and the last day of Brutus might be reckoned the first of Rome's slavery. Augustus proceeded to the city as soon as he had made a new division with Antony, for Lepidus, with whom they had fallen out, had no part in it; and Antony went into Asia to keep the provinces in subjection and punish the kings who had taken part with the enemies of Rome.

Being now separated by so many seas and nations, it might be supposed they were in no danger of giving each other any reasons for jealousy and discontent; but peace can never long continue between two ambitious persons. The ardent desire they both had to govern without a rival, presently gave occasion for a fresh rupture. Augustus, who was very ambitious, could brook no rival;

cruelty to cut it off, as also both his hands, whilst the rest of the assassins shut their eyes, that they might not be witnesses of so horrible an execution. As soon as Antony saw Cicero's head, he said that he had done with proscriptions, for that his vengeance was fully satisfied.

[1] Hieron. adversus Rufinum.　　　[2] St. John the Baptist.

while Antony wished to be sole master, as if the whole
world were too little to satisfy the desires of two men.
Their jealousy increased with their ambition; it soon
degenerated into hatred, and they only waited for a fair
opportunity to declare war.

Fulvia, Mark Antony's wife, was the firebrand that
soon kindled it. She was perfectly aware of the violent
passion her husband had conceived for Clèopatra, Queen
of Egypt,[1] whose wonderful beauty was so much extolled,
and this caused her such jealousy as soon deprived her of
sleep, and afterwards of her reason. She was not a
woman to suffer patiently an affront of that nature, and
therefore, without the least hesitation, resolved to punish
her husband by being as unfaithful to him as she imagined
he was to her. This was indeed carrying her resentment
a great way; but Fulvia, the most proud and impetuous
of women, was a stranger to moderation in hatred and
revenge.

Augustus, then, was the person she selected from whom
to exact reprisals, and, without reflecting on the consequences, she let him know the whole violence of her
passion; and, that her revenge might not sleep any longer,
she thought proper to spare him the trouble of taking
such steps as decency seemed to require. But what shame
and mortification was it for the wife of Antony to find

[1] Cleopatra Queen of Egypt was reckoned one of the most accomplished beauties in the world; she had a wonderful talent for making
herself beloved, when she had a mind to exercise it. Julius Cæsar was
smitten with her irresistible charms, and had a son by her, whom he
called Cæsarion. The eldest son of Pompey the Great was also proud to
wear her chains. Mark Antony was rather bewitched than in love with
her, and it may well be said, that it cost him the Empire and his life.
It is reported that Cleopatra never really loved any of these great men,
and that she never had a sincere affection for any but Dellius, who was
Antony's confidant. Cleopatra had a son and a daughter by Antony;
the former was called the Sun, and the latter the Moon.

herself despised by Augustus (who, without doubt, was otherwise employed), and who was not content with that, but added the most provoking insults and railleries, so that she became the subject of everybody's malicious wit. Further, that she might not imagine his slighting her proceeded from any scruples on account of his having married Claudia, her daughter, he sent her back to her mother, protesting that she was as much a virgin as when he first saw her; and soon after married Scribonia, daughter of Scribonius Libo, and widow of two consuls.

It is easy to conceive the rage Fulvia was in when she reflected upon the steps she had taken, and the disagreeable consequences of them. Her love gave way to her fury, and she breathed nothing but revenge. She swore the destruction of Augustus, and longed for nothing so much as an opportunity to accomplish it. She knew Antony was plunged in the delights and pleasures of Egypt, and thought there could be no surer method of tearing him from the arms of Cleopatra than by promoting a war between him and Augustus. It was not long before Augustus furnished her with a pretence for it. He had, some time before, intended to distribute among his legions, by way of reward for their services, certain lands that he had promised them; Fulvia opposed it, for fear this bounty should alienate the soldiers from Antony,[1] pretending that this distribution could not be made without her husband's consent, and that they ought to wait for his return. Augustus, whether it was that he would not be the cause of their falling out, or on account of his eagerness to oblige Fulvia,[2] left things as they were, and put off the troops with fair words; but when

---

[1] Sueton. vit. Aug.   [2] Vell. Pater. Histor. lib. 2.

once he had broken with Fulvia, he no longer kept faith with her, but, on the contrary, gave immediate satisfaction to the legions.

This was the signal for war. Fulvia, whose pride, obstinacy and passion were excessive, and who was in the highest degree exasperated against Augustus,[1] filled Rome with trouble and confusion.[2] She obliged Lucius Antonius, her brother-in-law, and all her husband's friends, to take up arms; everything was in tumult, and the city divided into factions; and because Augustus's party was the strongest (its head being present), Antony's friends quitted Rome, and joined themselves to Lucius Antonius, who had retired to Perusia. Tiberius Nero went thither with the rest; but, seeing that Augustus carried terror throughout Italy, he left it suddenly, and went to join Antony near Sicily.

His wife Livia accompanied him on his journey, or rather his flight, which was attended with many dangers and misfortunes; for Augustus's troops, being dispersed throughout all the neighbourhood of Rome, and being informed of Tiberius's escape, searched for him with the utmost diligence, to sacrifice him to the wrath of their general. And they pursued him so closely, that they could not have failed to overtake him near Naples, had it not been for the darkness of the night, and his quitting the high road, with his wife and their little son Tiberius, and travelling in ways that were unknown and difficult. This was not the only risk they ran in their hasty and troublesome flight, for, after having been in great danger at sea, and wandering about in Sicily and Achaia, they carried their child into Lacedaemonia [3] (which was under

[1] Dio. lib. 48.   [2] Sueton. vit. Aug.   [3] Sueton. vit. Tib.

the protection of some of the Clodian family). This, however, they were forced to leave very suddenly in the night, passing through dreadful and dangerous forests, out of which flames issued in abundance, and so enveloped the little fugitive band, that the fire caught hold of Livia's hair and robe, but did not damage either her or the child she had in her arms.[1] This passage has caused historians to make many reflections on the vicissitudes of Fortune, whose surprising turns and changes are such as should prevent us from being surprised when matters happen quite contrary to our schemes and designs; for Livia was obliged to travel over all these countries, and undergo all these dangers and hardships, to avoid him who was soon to be her husband, and the soldiers were indefatigable in their efforts to discover and to take away the life of him who was one day to be the absolute master of their own.

In the meantime, Fulvia died in the East, whither she had gone, like one of the Furies, to rouse Antony from his lethargy; and, as she had been the occasion of the war, the friends of Cæsar and Antony had no great difficulty in making peace between them, when she was no longer in the way.[2] To make this peace more solid-

[1] Vell. Paterc. Hist. lib. 2. Dio. lib. 18.

[2] When Fulvia was dead, the breach between Cæsar and Antony was made up by the mediation of Mæcenas on the one side, and of Cocceius Nerva and Fonteius on the other. The rendezvous of these mediators was at Terracina; the famous poet Horace, who was going to Brundisium, happened to be there at that time;[a] we shall take an opportunity of mentioning who Mæcenas was. As for Cocceius (surnamed Nerva), he was a famous lawyer, of very noble family, for it is said that Nerva, who was Emperor after Domitian, was descended from him. He was always much esteemed by Augustus. Fonteius Capito was Antony's greatest friend: he was reckoned the most accomplished Roman of his time. Both of them were men of so great probity, that they were frequently employed as mediators to reconcile differences.

[a] Horace, Sat. 5. lib. 1. Aversos soliti componere amicos.

and durable, the interests of young Pompey were taken
into consideration at the same time, and everything
arranged to the satisfaction of all parties. This reconciliation was cemented by the marriage of Octavia (sister
of Augustus, and widow of Marcellus) to Antony, which
was celebrated at Rome with great pomp and magnificence. Nothing was omitted that could induce the people
to forget their past calamities. All sorts of shows, feasts,
and diversions, were the consequences of this peace. All
those who had fled from Rome returned thither in safety,
and Tiberius Nero also brought back his wife Livia.

She was then in the height of her beauty, to which was
added a wit and vivacity, that made her the very life
and soul of all company in which she happened to be.
She had also the most winning and insinuating manner
in the world, which was natural to her. One might see
in her a noble sort of haughtiness, which she knew how
to tone down and soften upon occasion, and could adapt
to the character of the person she conversed with. All
these qualities, which were not to be met with but in
Livia, soon made Augustus very sensible of her merit.
This was very soon perceived, by the attachment and complaisance he showed for her, and the famous entertainment,[1] which he gave his friends the first time he was
shaved, was attributed to this new passion of his; he was,
ever after, very careful to keep himself close-shaved, in
order to be more agreeable to his new mistress.[2]

[1] Dio. lib. 58.
[2] The Romans were accustomed to give a great feast the first time
they shaved themselves. These feasts were called Barbatoria, and
were solemnized by a sumptuous dinner, which they gave to their
friends: they preserved with a great deal of superstition this first beard.
We read that Nero preserved his very carefully in a golden box, and
dedicated it to Jupiter in the Capitol. Most commonly they caused them-

It is very probable that Livia did not long suffer
Augustus to languish, whatever a certain historian has
been pleased to say on that subject.[1] It is even reported
that she soon gave him undoubted marks of her affection.
She was extremely ambitious, and the indifferent circumstances of Tiberius were not capable of gratifying her
vanity. Cæsar Augustus, on the contrary, saw nothing
above him, and did not despair of getting rid of his only
rival one way or other, and so increasing and establishing
his power, which was already little less than absolute.[2]
Besides, Cæsar had accomplishments that were not easy
to be resisted.[3] He was extraordinarily handsome, of
middle height, indeed, but so well proportioned that he
did not seem short,[4] except when compared to a taller
man.[5] He was then in the prime of his youth, his
hair was fair and naturally curly; he had a Roman nose,
and eyes so brilliant and sparkling, that it was very
difficult to bear the lustre of them, or look earnestly at
him without being dazzled, as a soldier told him one day;
in his countenance shone a certain majesty, mixed with
sweetness, which called forth the respect of all that
saw him; the beauties of his mind were equal to those
of his person; he was of a delightful and affable temper,
lively in conversation, polite in his manners and discourse, and constant in his friendships. With all these
advantages, it was not possible for Livia to remain long
in doubt whether she should be favourable to him or not.
She accordingly listened to Cæsar; and the charms which

selves to be shaved for the first time the day they put on their manly
robe (toga virilis), but sometimes later; uno atque eodem die togam
sumpsit, barbamque deposuit. (Suet. vit. Cai.)

[1] Tacit. Ann. 5. c. 1.   [2] Sueton. vit. Aug.   [3] Eutrop. de gestis Rom.
[4] Aurel. Victor. Epitome.   [5] Dio. lib. 48.

he found in her made the odd and gloomy temper of
Scribonia appear insupportable to him, for he was already
very much disgusted with her, on account of her passions
and jealousies. He put her away on the very day she
was brought to bed of Julia, and, making use of his power
to second his inclinations, entreated Tiberius Nero to
yield him his wife.

It is not known whether this was done with Livia's
consent, but it may easily be supposed that this ambitious
woman was not long deliberating between her duty and
her fortune, between Cæsar and Tiberius.

She was then six months gone with child, not without
well-grounded suspicions of being so by Augustus. Now,
by the laws,[1] women were forbidden to marry again, till
their husbands had been dead ten months, and were
obliged to stay the same time after being divorced, to
prevent the confusion [2] which would otherwise be caused
in families by the uncertainty of birth. Augustus pretended to be mighty scrupulous upon this point, for he
affected to have great respect for the laws.[3] He assembled the College of Priests, to consult them about this
important point, whether he might marry a woman with
child; and, pretending to be anxious to have nothing to
reproach himself with, he caused Apollo and the other
divinities to be consulted. The oracles of the gods and
the decision of the pontiffs were favourable to his inclinations. Thus, being cured of his scruples, and his doubts
being removed, he married Livia, to whom he had lately
been a bitter enemy, and obliged Tiberius Nero not only
to consent to it, but even to give her away, as if he had
been her father. His nuptials were celebrated with a

[1] Dio. lib. 48.   [2] Seneca. de consolatione.   [3] Prudent.

grand entertainment, to which Tiberius was one of the first invited.

A comical remark of one of those agreeable little prattling boys, whom the Roman ladies were so fond of, made the company laugh heartily.[1] The guests being placed at table, the child took notice of Livia's being seated next to Augustus, and Tiberius Nero at the other side of the table. "Is that your place, madam," said he; "ought you not to sit near your own husband?" This served to divert them a great deal. When they rose from table, Augustus took Livia home with him.

Three months after, she was brought to bed of a son, who was called Claudius Drusus Nero. Augustus sent the child to Tiberius Nero, being unwilling to keep it at his own house, lest he might be suspected of being its father; and he caused it to be inserted in his journal,[2] that, his wife Livia having been delivered of a son at his house, he had sent the child to Tiberius Nero, its father. But these precautions did not dissipate the suspicions of the public, for it was generally believed that the young Drusus was his; and amongst other railleries, it was said that everything prospered with fortunate people, for they could have children in three months.[3]

This marriage of Augustus with Livia (though big with child) was not, however, without precedent. [4] Pompey married Æmilia, daughter of Æmilius Scaurus, already the wife of another man, and with child. [5] Cato of Utica, after having had children by Marcia, his wife, made no difficulty about yielding her up to his friend Hortensius, who had requested that favour of him, and

---

[1] Dio. lib. 48.   [2] Sueton. vit. Aug.   [3] Dio. lib. 48.
[4] Plutarch. vit. Pom.   [5] Vit. Caton.

taking her back after the death of that orator. Cato was reproached with having parted with his wife when she was poor, and taken her back when she was become rich. And even Octavia, sister to Augustus, was with child by Marcellus, when Mark Antony married her.

Matters were in this situation at Rome, when [1] Pompey and Augustus, quarrelling about trifles, plunged the Republic into fresh troubles and a new war, which Augustus [2] conducted with a good deal of imprudence, and was therefore not always successful. His fleet was twice very severely handled, and he was obliged to refit it with great difficulty and expense. Lepidus, whom he had called in to his assistance, gave him cause to suspect some treason, and in attempting to guard against it, he was twice very near falling into the hands of Pompey's lieutenants. His misfortunes did not end there, for he was defeated at sea, near Sicily, and, after seeing half his fleet perish, for a long time he did not know where to shelter himself, so that he would have been utterly ruined, if the rash and headstrong courage of Pompey (intoxicated by this success) had suffered him to make the most of this advantage.

This bad news threw Livia into great perplexities, and furnished her with matter for the most serious reflections. She knew that the issues of war are always doubtful and precarious; that Pompey, to whom Fortune appeared to be reconciled, was much respected at Rome, and in the armies; that Augustus could place no dependence upon the promises of Antony, who was entirely governed by his caprice and amours, and not by his interest and his reason; that Fortune, which hitherto had smiled upon

[1] Eutrop. de gest. Rom. lib. 7.　　[2] Dio. lib. 48.

Augustus, might at last turn her back upon him; all these considerations caused her many a disagreeable moment. Besides, people's minds were disquieted at Rome by several prodigies and extraordinary presages that had happened lately, so that Livia stood in great need of the consolation she received from a curious incident that took place at a country-house she possessed near Rome. An eagle, that had snatched up a chicken with a little branch of laurel in its beak, let it drop softly near her. Everybody that imagined they had any skill in fore-telling events, agreed that this promised Livia nothing less than the sovereign power; and that the laurel plainly signified the great glory and honour which her prosperity should enjoy. This was too flattering a prognostic not to be heeded;[1] on the contrary, Livia took all possible care of these two objects of her hopes. The chicken became so prolific, that the village where it was reared was called the village of hens; and the laurel, which she caused to be planted, was cultivated so successfully, that in a few years it was big enough to furnish laurel branches to crown the conquerors on the occasion of their triumphs.

Livia in a little time had the pleasure of seeing the beginning of the fulfilment of this prediction, in the victory that Augustus gained over Pompey. For the two fleets met, and the most bloody battle ensued that had ever been known. Each fleet was composed of almost four hundred sail, and these ships, all together, resembled a floating city. Agrippa, Augustus's admiral, employed all his industry, skill and courage to conquer; and Demo-chares, Pompey's admiral (a most experienced officer),

[1] Sueton. vit. Galb.

exhausted his whole stock of knowledge and bravery, to force victory to declare on his side. They fought for a long time with equal success, and with so much obstinacy and fury, that the armies who were on shore perceived the sea to change colour, tinged with the blood of an enormous number of soldiers, some of whom were swimming about among the waves, and others floating, dead, upon the water, together with fragments of the broken vessels.

It seemed as if Fortune was in doubt which side to declare for, or else that she hesitated on purpose, to give the two generals an opportunity of displaying their valour and abilities, and to make them dispute the victory with one another.

Augustus and Pompey were with their armies on shore, anxious spectators of the battle, the result of which was to decide their fortune, and waited with the utmost impatience to see the issue of this important action. A profound silence was observed on both sides, as long as the victory was doubtful; but Agrippa having had the good fortune to sink some of Pompey's ships, Augustus's soldiers were so encouraged by the success, that they made the air ring with their shouts, and so terrified Pompey's men, that they began to waver. In fact, this accident caused such an alteration in the fight, that Pompey's fleet was defeated. Demochares killed himself through despair, and Pompey only survived him to perish soon after by the hands of an infamous assassin, and thus Augustus was delivered from this formidable enemy.

Never did a conqueror use his victory more cruelly. As this war had kept him in a state of continual alarm and the utmost uneasiness, he suffered himself to be hurried on by his resentment against all such senators and knights as had taken part with Pompey. He punished them with death, and sullied his triumph with the blood of the most illustrious men in the Republic. He afterwards gave his troops some tokens of his generosity. Of all the honours which were decreed him by the Senate, he would only accept the privilege which they granted to his wife Livia, and his sister Octavia, to dispose of their effects as they thought proper, and that their persons should be sacred and inviolable, like those of the tribunes. After having settled certain affairs in Rome, he went to give battle to Mark Antony, with whom [1] he had lately fallen out again, and entirely defeated him at the famous battle of Actium, which drove Antony into such despair, that he killed himself, in which Cleopatra, who was the principal cause of his destruction, imitated him soon after.[2]

[1] Sueton. Dio.

[2] Cleopatra, seeing that Fortune was favourable to Augustus, was the first to betray Mark Antony, though she was the only cause of his misfortune. She secretly gave up the town of Pelusium to the conqueror, and made a great many of Antony's ships pass over to his side. Antony knew that she was betraying him, but was too much in love to wish her any harm, and so fell into the snare that was laid for him. For Cleopatra, flattering herself that she could make Augustus sensible of her charms, gave out that she had killed herself, imagining that Antony would never survive her, and by that stratagem hoped to deliver Augustus from his formidable rival. Her artifice succeeded: Antony, who was bewitched by Cleopatra, notwithstanding her treachery and perfidy, had no sooner heard of her death, than he ran himself through the body with his sword. But a moment after, being informed that she was in good health, he repented of this rash and fatal action, which was to separate him from the object of his passion. He caused himself to be put into a basket and drawn up into the tower where Cleopatra was, and expired in her arms. Cleopatra, however, being informed that Augustus's fair words and courteous treatment showed that her life was to be spared, only that she might grace his triumph (which she dreaded more than death), resolved to live no longer. She dressed herself in her most magnificent apparel, and laid herself down upon a sumptuous bed, where she was found breathless. On her arm were

This victory restored peace to the Republic, and gave Augustus the sovereignty of the world. He returned to Rome, preceded by the report of his victory, and followed by the loud acclamations of the people, loaded with glory and honour. He was received everywhere, and especially at Rome, with the respect that was due to the lord of the whole earth;[1] and his triumph, the most superb that, till then, had ever been seen, lasted three days successively, which were passed in amusements, feasts, shows and rejoicings, which at last succeeded the rivers of tears that had been shed during so many civil wars. The Senate was at a loss to invent titles of honour and dignities in any way proportionate to the greatness of Cæsar and his family. He was created consul, tribune, censor, proclaimed father of his country, and chief pontiff. They honoured him [2] with a new name, and called him Augustus, as if he partook of the nature of the gods; which the poets did not scruple to attribute to him in their verses, which are so many shameful monuments of their flattery and impiety.

Augustus's empire may be said to commence from that time.[3] The city assumed a new appearance, and the state quite another form. The Republic was changed into a monarchy. All yielded to the new yoke, and those people who, of all others, were most jealous of their liberties, were reduced to the most submissive servitude. Those very Romans, who, at the beginning of their Republic, had, in their barbarous zeal, sacrificed their own children

perceived little marks, apparently due to the bite of an asp, or else she had made them herself with the bodkin of her hair, which she had previously dipped in some malignant poison.

[1] Sueton. Flor. Dio. and others.
[2] Horat. Od. 3. lib. 2.　　　　　[3] Tacit. Ann. 1.

to its interests,[1] were now offering vows for the preservation of those who had deprived them of that liberty, the
defence of which had induced them to become parricides.[2]

The Senate, whose decrees had been till then so greatly
respected, now acted only according to the will of the
prince, for the past miseries and calamities had destroyed
all such senators as had any zeal for the public welfare;
and none remained but some timid magistrates, who had
not courage enough to swim against the stream. The
Senate was, for the most part, composed of young men,
who, never having experienced the sweets of liberty, were
not sensible of the yoke they were bringing themselves
under; and, consequently, neither freedom in their votes,
nor honesty in their deliberations, were any longer to be
met with. Justice was crushed by fear; the laws lost
their force; the prince was the only oracle consulted;
and the mercenary votes of those self-interested magistrates were sure to be always conformable to the will
of the sovereign, who purchased them by rewards, which
the senators basely preferred to their honour.

The provinces regulated their conduct by that of Rome,
being thoroughly fatigued with so many civil wars, and
by the rapine and extortions of the governors, who, to
enrich themselves, were continually plundering them.
In short, they chose rather to obey one Emperor than the
greedy viceroys, which were sent them by the Senate.

[1] Liv. Florus.
[2] Junius Brutus, of whom we have already made mention, after
having driven Tarquin the Proud from Rome, was informed that this
prince had a secret understanding with some persons in the city, who
were endeavouring to re-establish him on the throne, among whom the
most zealous were Titus and Tiberius, his own sons. He caused them to
be arrested, cruelly whipped, and afterwards beheaded in his presence,
to show the people that the love of his country was stronger than
nature in him.

Thus, all submitted to the new order of things, without the least resistance; and distant kings strove who should show the greatest marks of their respect for Augustus, and endeavoured to win his favour, by putting themselves as soon as possible under his protection.

They erected triumphal arches in his honour, built noble cities, which they dedicated to him, and omitted nothing that could testify their profound veneration and dependence. Herod, King of Judæa,[1] was one of the foremost in displaying his magnificence, and in complimenting Cæsar. This prince (the greatest politician of his time) had been the most zealous of all Antony's friends; and when he was defeated, it was generally thought that Herod's ruin would have followed of course, because Augustus was extremely irritated against all those who had taken part with his enemy; but the Jewish monarch, who, on the most pressing occasions, had always the greatest presence of mind, knew very well how to extricate himself from this difficulty and remedy the bad state of his affairs, which his attachment to the interests of Antony had, to all appearance, ruined. He went to Rhodes,[2] where Augustus then was, and, laying aside his crown and royal robes, and everything that savoured of majesty, except his greatness of soul, he threw himself at

[1] This was Herod the Great, famous for his cruel massacre of the Bethlehemite children, which he had ordered, hoping to include amongst them the Saviour of the world, whom the magi searched for under the title of the new-born King of the Jews. It is credibly reported that this inhuman prince sacrificed his own son among the rest; and that Augustus, hearing of this butchery, said that he would rather be Herod's hog than his son. This was not the only action of Herod's that Augustus disapproved of; for we read that this tyrant having one day done something that did not please Augustus, the latter wrote to him that hitherto he had treated him as a friend, but for the future he would treat him as a subject.

[2] Joseph. Antiq. Judaic. lib. 15.

the Emperor's feet, and then ingenuously admitted that he had assisted Antony with men, money, and counsel, and would have served him in person, if he had not then been engaged in other wars. "I did not," said he, " abandon him after his defeat, neither did the love I had " for him change with his fortune; on the contrary, ever " true to his interests, I did my utmost to prevent his ruin, " by the most prudent and zealous advice I could give, " which, in all probability, would have succeeded, if it " had been followed; for I would have had him by all " means abandon his Cleopatra, who, I told him, was the " greatest and most dangerous enemy he had, rally his " forces, and endeavour to repair his loss. If," continued he, " my firm attachment to Mark Antony (who " honoured me with his friendship and loaded me with " benefits) is to be reckoned a crime, I own myself guilty; " every well disposed heart would have done the same; " for can one possibly be ungrateful to one's benefactor? " At least, it is not in my power to be so, for I am too well " acquainted with the laws of gratitude. Your Majesty " may try, if you please, to put yourself in Antony's place; " and you will find in Herod the same zeal, the same " fidelity and affection for you, that he had hitherto for " your enemy."

These noble sentiments pleased Augustus; he not only pardoned Herod, but confirmed him in the Kingdom of Judæa, to which he added several very considerable towns; [1] and, admiring the greatness of his courage and resolution, at a time when he had everything to fear, he conceived so great an esteem for him, that, next to Agrippa and Mæcenas, he honoured him most with his

[1] Nicephor. Calist. lib. i. c. 6 & 9.

friendship. Herod, like a subtle courtier, cultivated it as much as possible; he built, in honour of Cæsar, a fine city, which he called Cæsarea, in which were two magnificent temples. He instituted to the glory of this Emperor [1] solemn games and sports, and gave great rewards to the conquerors. Livia, also, being desirous to contribute her share in these rewards, sent about five hundred talents to Judæa for that purpose.

It was not on Augustus only that all these excessive honours were conferred. Not only did Livia share them, but others also were invented particularly for her. A town,[2] which was called Liviada, was built in her honour. The Senate exhausted all their ingenuity in finding out the most delicate and most studied praises. They gave her the most pompous titles; among others, the superb name of Augusta, and mother of her country. The poets [3] celebrated her in their verses; and, by a sacrilegious excess, made her a goddess; they erected temples to her, and made a divinity of the most ambitious of women: shameful baseness! which occasioned this reflection, that if divine honours were thus prostituted to women, what worship could be thought of which could be deemed appropriate for the gods?

Augustus also desired to give proofs of his esteem and tenderness for Livia, by displaying his magnificence in her favour.[4] He caused a house, which had been Pollio's, to be pulled down. This house was situated in the Sacred Way, and took up so much ground, that it resembled a town. After removing from it [5] all the costly

---

[1] Joseph. Antiq. Jud. lib. 16. c. 19.   [2] Gaulter. Monum. Sicil.
[3] Horat. Od. lib. 314. Ovid. de Pont. Eleg. 1. Prudent. lib. 1. in Symmach. Tacit. Ann. 1.
[4] Dio. lib. 54.   [5] Ovid. Fast. 1.

furniture, with which the Princess Julia had adorned it, he erected on its ruins a most superb portico, which he dedicated to Livia;[1] and, not content with giving her public marks of his esteem, he also added many special and domestic favours, putting the greatest confidence in her and anticipating all her desires, by contributing as much as he possibly could to her pleasure and satisfaction. In short, her authority was not less absolute than his own.

To tell the truth, Augustus could not well do less for her, considering the great regard and tenderness she always had for him; though it cannot be denied that there was a great deal of art and cunning in her manner of proceeding, which the Emperor did not find out till it was too late.[2] She never gave herself any trouble about his amours and gallantries, and was so far from thwarting him in his pleasures by a disagreeable jealousy, that she was very well pleased when he was so engaged. She even carried her complaisance so far as to be extremely civil to Terentia, Mæcenas's wife, who was passionately beloved by Augustus; and though, in her heart, she felt nothing but hatred and envy towards this rival of hers, who had robbed her of her husband's affections (notwith-

---

[1] Disce tamen, veniens ætas, ubi Livia nunc est
Porticus, immensæ tecta fuisse domus.

Pollio was a freedman of Augustus, and had the honour of being raised to the order of knighthood. They tell of him that, at a dinner to which he had invited the Emperor, one of his own slaves happened by chance to break a fine vase of crystal: Pollio being extremely provoked at this accident, ordered the poor creature to be thrown into a fishpond. The slave cast himself at Augustus's feet, and begged he would intercede for him, which he did; but Pollio not only refused his request, but would not even change the manner of his death, although the Emperor earnestly desired it. This disobliging and brutal behaviour displeased Augustus so much, that he ordered every crystal vessel that Pollio had to be broken to pieces in his presence.

[2] Xiphil. in Aug. Dio. lib. 48.

standing his outward behaviour), yet she exhibited so
much evenness of temper in all those disputes which their
emulation stirred up between them, that it sufficiently
proved the respect she had for him. She did not affect
that sort of austere virtue that makes people inaccessible,
but, on the contrary, indulged herself in all those innocent
pleasures which became her rank and condition, partak-
ing of all the parties of pleasure and amusements which
were then in vogue at Rome, and were promoted by
Augustus, as well as the other grandees of the town, who
had the art of introducing infinite variety into them;
sometimes games and sports, sometimes races and shows
of different kinds, at which all the better sort and people
of quality were sure to attend, and never failed to pay
their court to the Empress, who always behaved upon
those occasions with the greatest modesty and reserve,
managing her reputation with so much skill and prudence,
that, though people had not the same opinion of her
virtue that they had of Lucretia's, yet she took care that
nobody should have any cause of reproach against her.
She was far from being as scrupulous as she pretended
to be (witness the great regard [1] she had for some particular persons), but was always desirous it should pass for
esteem only. She was often heard to say that a prudent
woman always finds in herself wherewithal to preserve
her virtue; and, one day, when some young gentlemen,
who had been so imprudent as to put themselves in her
way, quite naked, were to be put to death for it, she
pardoned them, saying that a naked man made no more
impression upon the imagination of a virtuous woman
than a statue.

[1] Dio. lib. 48.

Policy was the very soul of her actions and conduct, and history furnishes but few examples of women who practised it with more skill and good fortune. Those who were most keen-witted could never discover her real sentiments; not even Augustus, with all his art and skill, could avoid being deceived by her. She knew well how to take full advantage of his weakness, and acquired such an ascendency over him that nothing could resist it; and Cæsar, master of the world, might very properly be said to be slave to Livia. This was the origin of the excessive authority of this Empress, which was so much revered, and to which sacrilegious and extravagant homage was paid; and yet this, however much it might flatter her vanity, was not capable of entirely satisfying her ambition.

The throne, which was the most elevated of all stations, could not limit her desires. Her joint occupation of it with Augustus was reckoned as nothing, so eagerly did she desire that her posterity should also be raised to that exalted rank, and that was the goal which all her projects held in view. She caused the most important and most distinguished posts to be given to Tiberius and Drusus (her two sons by her former husband). They had the conduct of the armies, and the command of the legions, the authority of the Emperor being always vested in them; and, however inconsiderable the services they rendered to the State were in themselves, Livia extolled them to the skies by the most pompous reports that she caused her emissaries to make of them, and so ordered matters that triumphs were decreed them upon every trifling occasion.

Justice, however, should be done to everybody, and it

must be confessed that Tiberius and Drusus were great captains. The first was not only brave, but possessed a vast genius, equal to anything he undertook. He understood perfectly the art of war,[1] and was so prompt in determining what he was about, that it is reported he never deliberated twice about the same thing. Very severe in military discipline, he was the first in all dangers and hardships, encouraging the soldiers by his example, and surmounting by his constancy and perseverance all difficulties. He was generally successful in war, which was owing to his great abilities, not to chance or fortune. But, on the other hand, what vices sullied and tarnished his good qualities![2] He was cruel, arrogant, jealous of other people's merit, of a dark and gloomy temper,[3] incapable of tenderness or friendship, affecting, even towards his nearest relations, a brutal sort of pride, which made people afraid to approach him. He was deceitful and dangerous, never acting but with artifice and cunning. A thick veil was always drawn over his feelings. His words were wrapped up in obscurity and equivocation, so that it was almost impossible to unriddle them, or find out his real meaning; and if it was difficult to comprehend it, there was no less danger in letting him know that one understood him. People had great reason to apprehend his dark mistrustfulness, which made him sacrifice to his suspicions all those whom he hated on account of their merit or virtue. Besides, he was addicted to great excess in wine, which he carried to such a pitch, that people, in raillery, called him Biberius, instead

[1] Plutarch. Sueton. vit. Tib. [3] Eutrop. 2. Aurel. Vict. Epit.
[2] Tacit. Ann. 1.

of Tiberius.[1] But, above all, he was given to the most shameful debaucheries, which he continued to an extreme old age in the island of Capreæ, where, in an old and worn-out body, he abandoned himself to the most unruly and depraved passions of youth. Horrible impieties! which have noted and marked that island with an infamy that ages have not been able to wash out. These vices of Tiberius were no secret, nor were they unknown to Augustus, who, in speaking of him, told his friends one day, that the Roman people would be very unfortunate in being governed by a man who would make them suffer incredible misery.

Drusus, on the contrary, was more polite, humane, and honest than his brother, but no less brave, nor less experienced. He had acquired immortal honour by a great number of victories, which had prepossessed everybody in his favour. He was affable and sincere, and so great an enemy of dissimulation, that it is generally thought he would have restored to the Republic its ancient glory and liberty, if he had succeeded Augustus. Never was there a prince with better dispositions. He loved virtue,[2] and what was to be wondered at in him is, that, in the most corrupted court, at an age the most liable to criminal pleasures, and enjoying a rank that would have furnished him with opportunities enough of gratifying all the passions, he still continued innocent, and as blameless as his wife Antonia, so much commended for her chastity. With all this merit, he could not but gain the esteem of everybody, and especially of Augustus, who, it is

[1] Some of Tiberius's courtiers having suggested to him one day that he should punish the impudence of these people, he answered, that in a free city the tongue ought to be free.

[2] Valer. Maxim. Suet. vit. Tiber. Tacit. Ann. 1. c. 3.

reported, would have named him for his successor, if
he had not apprehended that by so doing he would confirm the suspicions people already had of his being his
son; or else he had a mind to set off his own reign the
more, by having so unworthy a successor. But what
most probably induced him to select Tiberius was his
being absolutely unable to refuse the Empress anything.

Such were the two sons of Livia, who, notwithstanding
their merit, fell far short of the Prince Marcellus, who,
besides being possessed of all the good qualities in the
world, was nephew and son-in-law to Augustus, which
were glorious advantages, and caused him to be looked
upon as presumptive heir. This was a powerful obstacle
to the ambitious views of the Empress, and always inspired her with a secret design of destroying him. In
fact, he did at last fall a victim to her ambition, for he
died in the flower of his age; and we shall see, in another
place, that Livia was thought not to be innocent in the
affair. Augustus was extremely afflicted at this loss, and
had no sooner begun to get over it than he had fresh
matter for grief, occasioned by a dangerous conspiracy
against his life. The chief·person concerned in it was
Cinna, grandson of Pompey the Great, who had drawn
into it the principal persons of the city. This would
have been fatal to the Emperor, if one of the conspirators had not revealed the plot. Augustus, being informed
of the danger to which he was exposed, was never in so
melancholy a situation, nor more sensibly alarmed.[1] He
was in doubt whether he should employ severity or
clemency. On the one hand, he apprehended that, if he
should pardon the guilty, it might encourage others to at-

[1] Dio. lib. 55.

tempts of a similar nature; and, on the other, he was
afraid that, by punishing some of them, the rest might
be the more exasperated, especially considering that his
having put to death Caepio and Murena for a similar
enterprise had not prevented Cinna and his accomplices
from conspiring against his person.

These cruel perplexities and agitations had such an
effect on him that he could not sleep, but was full of
anxiety and fear, which made him incapable of taking
any rest. Thus, one may see that there is no condition
of life exempt from trouble; no good fortune or pleasure
that is not mixed with secret bitterness. This incident in
Augustus's history shows us that the throne is far from
being the seat of peace and tranquillity, since it generally
happens that sovereign power is nothing but slavery, and
brings with it innumerable cares and solicitudes.

Livia, who shared her husband's anxieties as much as
his pleasures, earnestly enquired the cause of his melancholy; on the Emperor having told her the occasion of it,
she endeavoured to encourage him by saying [1] that he
ought not to be surprised that some people, jealous of
his glory, had declared against him, because, let a prince
be never so moderate and equitable, it was not possible
for him to please everybody. " Great men," said she,
" think they have a right to ask everything, and to ob-
" tain everything; those who are in a lower station think
" themselves despised if they do not get what they re-
" quire. From thence proceed cabals, conspiracies, and
" rebellions against the government; for discontented
" people hope to find their advantage in any change. You
" have nothing to do but to double your guard, and cause

[1] Dio. ibid.

" the palace to be surrounded with the soldiers who are
" most faithful to you, which will effectually hinder the
" traitors from attempting your life." " This precau-
" tion," replied Augustus, " would be to no purpose; for
" the sword of those who ought to guard the prince is
" often more to be dreaded than that of declared enemies.
" The most zealous courtier in appearance is often the
" most formidable enemy, and the more to be appre-
" hended, as he conceals his real nature under the deceit-
" ful mask of friendship, and has the more opportunities
" of gratifying his malice and hatred, the less he is mis-
" trusted. If foreign enemies made war against us, we
" have officers, generals, and friends to oppose them; but
" if those pretended friends become our enemies, what
" remedy have we? Nothing, then, remains but rigorous
" punishments, to prevent their wicked designs; and that,
" without doubt, is the only method we have to determine
" upon."

When Livia perceived that the Emperor was resolved
to put the conspirators to death, she undertook to prevail
on him to change his mind, and spoke to him as follows:
" The honour I have, sire, of being your wife, and of
" sharing all your fortunes, whether good or bad, permits
" me also to declare my mind freely and without disguise,
" which I take the liberty to do with all sincerity. You
" will please to consider that all bad people are not of the
" same character; some have, naturally, bad dispositions;
" others fall into wickedness, for want of judgment and
" discretion. I do not say that all those should be par-
" doned who attempt your life (for that would be at-
" tended with the worst results), but, in my opinion, less
" rigour might be shown to those whose indiscreet youth

" may prompt them to actions which they would not com-
" mit, if they were capable of reflection. It very seldom
" happens that many guilty persons are punished, with-
" out several innocent people being made to suffer. If
" you are so merciful as to pardon these criminals, your
" clemency will cause their sincere repentance and
" acknowledgments. Cinna, illustrious by his birth, his
" name, and his exploits, will return to his senses, and
" sincerely repent of these violences. An enemy who has
" been generously pardoned, when one has had an oppor-
" tunity of punishing him, has no longer the power to
" hurt his benefactor."

Livia possessed the art of persuasion to such a degree,
that it was impossible for Augustus to resist it. Her
advice was as fortunate as it was prudent. The Emperor, who had been very attentive, thought her reasoning so just, that he could not help being of her opinion.[1]
He sent for Cinna, and gave him a full account of the
conspiracy, reproached him tenderly with his ingratitude,
and reminded him of all the favours he had conferred
upon him; and, after having forced this conspirator to
own his crime, he not only pardoned, but named him
consul for the following year and, for his sake, forgave
all his accomplices.

This extraordinary clemency of Augustus exercised an
irresistible charm; and Cæsar's kind remonstrances had a
better effect than his utmost severity could have had.
This generosity not only extinguished the conspiracy, but
entirely gained him the hearts of all the Romans.
Everybody praised Livia, to whose counsel this noble
action was attributed, and not a word more was to be

[1] Senec. de Clement.

heard of revolt. Augustus looked upon himself as indebted to her for all the glory that he acquired by this moderation, and, consequently, regulated all his future conduct by her advice.

The Empress did not fail to make the most of the happy frame of mind Augustus was in with regard to her, and did not let slip this opportunity of advancing the fortunes of her sons; for, as this was the most important point to which all her actions tended, she could not bear the least obstacle to it; which, without doubt, was the reason of her making away with Marcellus, in order to pave the way to the throne for Tiberius. But the births of Gaius Cæsar, and Lucius Cæsar, his brother (sons of Julia, Augustus's daughter, whom he had married to Agrippa, after the death of his nephew), were a terrible disappointment, disconcerted all her projects, and prepared for her other subjects of jealousy, as well as material for new crimes. Her policy caused her to adopt all possible methods to obtain her ends. She then laboured with all her might to procure her sons the highest and most important posts; and, although Tiberius had already been made tribune, and Drusus consul, Livia was preparing new honours for them, when Providence, which often confounds our best-contrived designs, partly overthrew those of the Empress, by one of the most afflicting events that could possibly happen—the death of her son Drusus.

Tiberius, after having conquered Illyria,[1] and reduced the Germans (who were become insolent upon Varus's signal defeat) to submission to Augustus, came to Rome

---

[1] Sueton. vit. Tiber.

to receive the honour of a triumph,[1] which was one of
the most magnificent that had ever been known, owing to
Livia's attention and lavish expenditure. Tiberius gave
a most magnificent entertainment to the senators, the
knights, and the people; and the Empress, together with
the Princess Julia, did the same to the ladies. Livia did
not stop there. She caused a magnificent temple [2] to be
built, to perpetuate the memory of his victories, and dedicated it to the goddess of Concord, near the Capitol. She
had an altar erected in it to the honour of Augustus;
and, among other rare and rich presents with which she
adorned it,[3] people most of all admired a piece of crystal
of fifty pounds weight, and a small tree of the true cinna-
mon, which she consecrated herself, and placed in a large
basin of massive gold, from which distilled a certain
liquor in drops, which became extremely hard and
precious.

After Livia had procured all these honours for Tiberius, she set about doing the same for Drusus, when the
news of his death arrived at Rome, almost as soon as that
of his victory; so that the pompous preparations which
were made for his triumph served as melancholy trophies
for his funeral. This excellent prince had subdued the
Sicambrians and other neighbouring nations (ancient
Germans, from whom were descended the inhabitants in
the territories of Hesse Cassel and Gueldres), and had
made himself very formidable to all Germany, where,
notwithstanding the vigorous resistance he everywhere
met with, he had extended his conquests as far as the
banks of the Rhine. He was about to pass this river,

---

[1] Dio. lib. 55.   [2] Ovid. Fast. 1.
[3] Plin. Hist. Nat. lib. 37. c. 2. lib. 12. c. 15.

when he was arrested by death, in the midst of his
glorious career; for, when he was one day on the brink
of the river,[1] a spirit appeared to him, under the appearance of a beautiful woman, and said to him, in a menac-
ing tone: "Whither does your ambition hurry you?
"Retire; you are come to the utmost limit of your con-
"quests, and of your life," and vanished. This fatal
prediction was soon verified. Drusus [2] died as he was
just going to Rome to receive the reward of his victories.
This melancholy news, which was soon brought to Court,
turned the public rejoicings into the deepest mourning.
Livia's affliction was so great [3] that the philosophers
were sent for to give her what consolation they could;
and the Senate, in order to contribute what lay in its
power to mitigate her grief, granted her the privileges
which the laws give to women who have three children.
Poor comfort in her unspeakable loss!

Certainly, Drusus was worthy of the tears that were
shed for him. His merit was so great, that, if it could
be said there was true virtue among pagans, nobody
would have a better claim to it than he. Livia was not
the only mourner upon this occasion; for Augustus, to
whom Drusus was very dear, for more reasons than one,
was extremely affected by this loss. But, above all,
Antonia, his wife, was afflicted beyond measure. She was
daughter to Mark Antony, the triumvir, wonderfully
beautiful, and every author bears witness to her prudence
and discretion. She always lived with her husband in
such harmony and love, that they were both of them
patterns of virtue and conjugal fidelity, in a court where
gallantry and debauchery were become the fashion. The

[1] Dio. lib. 55.   [2] Sueton. vit. Tib.   [3] Senec. Consol. ad. Marc.

irregular conduct of so many ladies, who indulged themselves without scruple in all the pleasures and vices of the times, and which were authorised and established by custom, made no impression upon Antonia. Those maxims which were most capable of corrupting the heart found that of the Princess Antonia always protected by wisdom and virtue. Her reputation was so clear and free from the least suspicion, that no lady in Rome was in higher esteem. Drusus was the only object of her inclinations, for which reason [1] she would never hear of a second marriage. She resolved to consecrate the rest of her life to the memory of Drusus, and passed it [2] chiefly at her country-house, of which she was very fond, and where, among other innocent amusements, she [3] took great pleasure in taking care of and playing with a fish, which she loved mightily, and made it wear ear-rings. This curious thing drew an infinite number of people to her house, who flocked thither to see it.[4]

Drusus being dead, Livia employed all her care and diligence in favour of Tiberius; and seeing that Augustus was advancing in years, she thought it was of the utmost importance to remove every obstacle that stood between her son and the throne, and especially to get rid of all those who were next in succession. She could safely do whatever she thought proper, for the Emperor was entirely governed by her, without reflecting that, by giving her so absolute a power, he betrayed himself; besides, Livia was, in a manner, adored at Rome, where her authority was more respected than that of the Emperor; everybody submitted to her orders, and that

[1] Joseph. Antiq. Judaic. lib. 18. c. 8.
[2] Valer. Max. lib. 4.   [3] Plin. lib. 7. c. 19.   [4] Plin. lib. 7. c. 55.

which would have been impossible to another was perfectly easy to her; for, in order to compass her designs, she knew how to proceed silently, without force or violence.[1] Her policy and ambition caused her to adopt measures that were impenetrable, even to those who were most clear-sighted; and it was not without reason that Caligula afterwards called her [2] Ulysses in woman's apparel.

It was to some secret influence of her deep and dangerous policy, that the tragical and sudden deaths of Gaius and Lucius (sons of Julia and Agrippa) were attributed. [3] These two princes, so nearly related to Augustus, possessed merit equal to their birth. The eyes of all the world were upon them, as immediate heirs to the Empire; for there was no sort of reason to suppose that Cæsar would go out of his own family for successors; and Livia had no doubt that they were intended to succeed, since Augustus had sufficiently declared his design, by adopting his two grandsons, and bestowing upon them the most honourable posts; for he had named them " princes of the Roman youth," and was resolved to appoint them consuls as soon as they had reached man's estate, so that it might be said they had already their foot upon the throne; but that was the utmost limit of their fortunes. Lucius died suddenly at Marseilles; and Gaius, his brother, in Lycia, as he was returning from the Armenian war, during which he received a wound, which, no doubt, was purposely prepared for him.

Augustus, seeing none of his kindred now left, except

[1] Tacit. Xiphilin. [2] Sueton. vit. Cai. Caligula.
[3] Tacit. Ann. i. c. 3.

Agrippa, youngest son of Julia, adopted him, together
with the son of Livia. This step, which divided the Empire between Tiberius and Cæsar's grandson, might have
been thought sufficient to satisfy this ambitious Empress;
nevertheless, she was not able to bear this partnership
in sovereignty, nor could she endure that her son should
have a colleague in a dignity which had cost her so much
anxiety and so many crimes. She did not long hesitate
whether she should free herself of this grievance or not.
She practised all her artifices to make Agrippa suspected
by the Emperor, whose mind she so poisoned with malicious reports, and put so ill a construction upon all the
actions of this poor prince, that the Emperor, taking all
for granted that she was pleased to suggest, banished his
grandson to the island of Planasia.

This banishment was thought very cruel, because it
was very unjust. Agrippa did not, indeed, possess that
politeness and affability with which Lucius and Gaius, his
brothers, were endowed; on the contrary, he was somewhat boorish, a defect which the polished manners of
the Court had not been able to remove, and was very indifferently educated; but, on the other hand, this was the
only crime with which he could be reproached, except
that of being too nearly related to Augustus.

Thus, the blind deference which this Emperor showed
to the will and pleasure of Livia made him the tyrant of
his family, and the principal instrument of the ambition
of her who aimed at nothing but to destroy that family,
and who, concealing her perfidious designs under a false
show of zeal for Cæsar's glory, laid the foundation of
her son's grandeur in the ruin of those who might either
thwart or defer it. Augustus himself knew it at last,

but too late to apply any remedy. He often complained to his friends of his cruel destiny in thus losing all his relations in so short a time (though they were very numerous), which laid him under the necessity of calling in as successor his wife's son, to the prejudice of the only grandson he had left, whom he had condemned to a rigorous banishment, without so much as knowing for what. He called to mind the miserable end of his nephew Marcellus, and of Lucius and Gaius, his grandsons, who had perished in their youth, and in whose death it seemed as if there had been something extraordinary. These reflections, which moved him extremely, also set him thinking of Prince Agrippa's misfortunes, against whom he had been so cruelly and unjustly irritated; and, fancying that he had found out the true cause of it, he formed a resolution to go and pay him a visit in his place of exile. He did not communicate his design to anybody but Fabius Maximus, not thinking it proper to confide in a number of people; and, after [1] having taken all the necessary precautions to keep this journey secret, he went thither, accompanied only by the above-mentioned senator. The interview was tender and affecting. Cæsar's heart melted at the sight of his grandson; many tears were shed on both sides, and those of the Emperor made people think that the fortune of this poor young prince might one day change, much to his advantage.

This excursion, however, was not so much a secret as Augustus imagined. Maximus had not been able to conceal it from his wife Martia, and she had the weakness or imprudence to mention it to Livia. This produced in the mind of the Empress a mistrust that was fatal both

[1] Tacit. Ann. i.

to the Emperor and his grandson, and even Livia, in spite of all her cunning, could not help revealing her vexation to Augustus. She told him, with a certain air of pride and indignation, "that there had been no occa-"sion for all this secrecy, nor was his visit to Planasia of "such vast importance that it required so much mystery; "and that she could not but take this want of confidence "very ill, as it would render her very odious to his suc-"cessor, who would always look upon her as a person he "ought to suspect, since Augustus did so."

The Emperor, who had confided the matter to no one but Maximus, was at a loss to find out the person that revealed it; and this imprudence stirred up in Cæsar's heart a resentment of which he could not forbear giving Maximus evident tokens, by one of those terrible glances of the eye which he was perfect master of upon occasion, and which threw Maximus into such despair, that he immediately resolved to destroy himself. He communicated his design to his wife, telling her that, since he had had the misfortune to displease the Emperor by betraying his secret, he could not think of living any longer. Martia owned herself guilty.[1] "It is I," said she, "that "am the cause of your misfortune; and since I am be-"come unworthy of your confidence, by having revealed "a secret of such importance, it is but just that I should "punish myself for my unpardonable indiscretion." Scarce had she finished these words, than she plunged a poniard into her breast,[2] and Maximus immediately followed her example. [3] Tacitus will not allow this, since

[1] Just. Lips. in Tacit.   [2] Plutarchus.
[3] Auditos in funere ejus Martiæ gemitus semet incusantis quod causa exitii marito fuisset.

he reports that Martia lamented the death of her husband, taking the blame of it upon herself.

Be that as it may, Augustus never had an opportunity of bringing about any change in Agrippa's fortunes. The Emperor died soon after, and nobody doubted but it was due to Livia, who is said to have given him figs that were poisoned, to prevent the reinstatement of Agrippa in his favour and the consequent frustration of all her expectations.

Augustus died at Nola, in the very chamber where his father, Octavius, had died.[1] His last words were in favour of Livia; for, after having asked his friends [2] whether he had acted his part well on the stage of the world, he addressed himself to his wife,[3] charged her to be mindful of their marriage as long as she lived, and then expired, bestowing upon her marks of his tenderness and affection.

His death drew sighs and tears from all Rome; for, since it was fated to have a master, the Republic could not possibly have had a more worthy one. His magnificence and generosity had brought the greatest and most powerful men of the city to submit to the yoke. His moderation made it plainly appear that, in all the violent acts of the triumvirate, he had acted contrary to his natural kindliness, and that he was an enemy to blood. His excellent virtues caused it to be said of him that either he should never have died, or should never have been born.

His death was kept secret for some time, because it was apprehended that Tiberius's absence might be prejudicial to his interests; but as soon as he arrived, Augus-

[1] Aur. Victor. Epit.   [2] Dio. lib. 56.   [3] Suet. vit. Aug.

tus's death was announced at the same moment as Tiberius was proclaimed his successor. Livia, upon this occasion, did not forget her usual policy; she affected an inconsolable grief, and shed tears in abundance. The first thing she did was to cause all imaginable honours to be paid to his memory. She had him immortalised, and endeavoured to persuade everybody that there was something superhuman in him, which Senator Atticus confirmed, by swearing (in order to ingratiate himself with Livia) that he had seen Augustus's soul mounting up into heaven; and the Empress, who knew very well that he had not sworn for nothing, made him a considerable present, to reward this mercenary oath.[1] Superb temples were erected in honour of this new god. Altars and priests were dedicated to him, and the Empress herself desired to be one of the number. Augustus, by his will, left her the third part of all his riches, and adopted her into the Julian family, whence she took the name of Julia. Thus, by an odd coincidence, Livia was, at the same time, widow, daughter and priestess of Augustus.

The new reign was signalised by the murder of poor Agrippa. Livia was resolved to be revenged upon that unfortunate prince for the mistrust of Augustus; and, to remove the odium of that inhuman action, she gave out

[1] Atticus did, through complaisance and flattery for Livia, what the Senator Proculus had done formerly through policy: for Romulus having been assassinated by the senators, whom he began to treat with haughtiness, one day after he had been haranguing the troops, and the people being greatly disturbed by his sudden disappearance, Proculus swore that he saw the King mounting up to the skies with a venerable countenance like that with which the gods are represented. The people gave credit to this, and more so because just at that time there was a most violent storm, which furnished the senators with an opportunity of getting rid of their King, without notice being taken of it.

that Augustus had so ordered it in his will. But everybody knew that this was only another crime added to all
the rest she had been guilty of, in order to establish
her own power and that of her son, which increased
daily, by the base and abject submission of the Romans,
whose flattery caused them to seek out fresh titles and
honours to be conferred on the Empress. That of
" mother of her country " was solemnly confirmed, and it
was ordered that to Tiberius's titles should be added
that of son of Livia, as much as to say that the honour
he enjoyed of having her for his mother gave an additional lustre to all the rest. They even voted that she
should enjoy the singular privilege of an altar of adoption, but Tiberius, who did not much approve of gratifying his mother's ambition to such a degree, rejected these
flattering propositions of the Senate. He looked upon
the excessive honours and authority which were given
to his mother as a diminution of his own. He remon-
strated with these servile magistrates, that honours
should not be heaped upon women out of all bounds and
measure; that, as for himself, he would never consent
to their decreeing him any that were extraordinary;
and, covering with the mask of moderation his jealousy
of his mother's greatness, he would never permit that her
household should be augmented by the addition of a
single officer.

This behaviour of Tiberius was very mortifying to
Livia, who had an inexhaustible fund of ambition. As
she regarded the elevation of her son as the result of
her labours, and had raised him to that pitch of grandeur
in order to perpetuate her own, she never ceased to din
this into his ears. and to tell him perpetually that he held

the Empire from her, in order to give him to understand that his acknowledgments ought to bear a proportion to the favours he had received. Tiberius, however, often failed in that respect; and, whether it was owing to his bad disposition, or that he could not endure his mother's making the authority of the laws give place to her, he seized every opportunity of curbing her ambition.

The affair of Urgulania, the Empress's favourite, furnished him with one, and also afforded Piso an opportunity of showing a great deal of firmness and resolution, at a time when submission and flattery held the place of virtue. This senator had lent money to Urgulania, and to recover it, he was obliged to have recourse to the prætor, who cited her to appear before his tribunal. She was under Livia's protection, and, consequently, very powerful at Court, which [1] made her so proud and haughty, that, in contempt of the most ancient and severe laws, she haughtily refused to go before the Senate, or [2] any magistrate, when cited. Encouraged by Livia's authority, she went to the palace at the very time when she ought to have been at the court of justice; for the Empress, who set no more limits to her power than to her ambition, had made a great deal of noise about this discourtesy of Piso, and openly complained that she thought herself affronted in the person of her favourite.

Tiberius could not well avoid interesting himself in an affair which his mother had so much at heart, and thought that decency obliged him to intercede with the prætor in favour of Urgulania, against whom the impolite creditor was very persistent. He set out for the prætor's house, affecting a calm and serene countenance;

[1] Tacit. Ann. 2. cap. 14.   [2] Ibid. Ann. 4. c. 21.

but, that the magistrate might have time to decide the affair before his arrival, he stopped so often in the streets, talking to one or other, that he plainly showed he was not very solicitous about the matter. Livia was not the last that perceived it; and, not being willing to expose herself to the vexation of finding the case go against her, she called for money, and paid Piso the debt herself.

It was not only upon this occasion that the Emperor showed himself indifferent to his mother; at another time he gave evident proofs of it, and in a more brutal manner, when her honour was directly attacked.[1] Farilla, grand-daughter of Augustus's sister, having spoken some words that were very insulting to Tiberius and Livia, at a full assembly, she was accused of this crime; and, to make her still more in fault, they alleged that she had been guilty of a horrible adultery, and had sullied the blood of the Cæsars by an infamous prostitution.

All looked upon Farilla as lost. The accusation was no trifling affair, as it concerned both the Emperor and his mother; it was accordingly expected that there would be some dreadful punishment inflicted on the delinquent; and it was probably the fear of pronouncing too mild a sentence, that induced the Senate to consult Tiberius. But the Emperor did not gratify the expectations of the accusers or the public, much less those of Livia. His answer was, that the Julian law had sufficiently regulated the punishment for adultery; and, as to what regarded himself, he did not desire that Farilla should suffer for having spoken ill of him; so there remained nothing to

[1] Tacit. Ann. 2.

consider but the offence against Livia, upon which the consul asked Tiberius's opinion. The Emperor did not at first give any answer, but it was easy to perceive his thoughts from his looks; and, accordingly, he went the next morning to the Senate, and, as if he had spoken his mother's sentiments, declared that (however provoking the lady had been), the Empress did not desire any notice should be taken of it.

Such was the recompense that Livia received for all the crimes she had committed to raise her son to the throne. The ingratitude she met with from him did not, however, discourage her from taking every step that was necessary to leave him in quiet possession of that Empire which she had procured for him at the expense of so much blood; and, to remove everything that might give him the least room for jealousy, she persecuted all those of Augustus's family that were of importance by their birth or merit. As Prince Germanicus and his wife, Agrippina, were certainly the principal persons, and most esteemed at Rome, she took care to single them out for destruction.

Germanicus was the son of Drusus and Antonia, of whose great merit we have already made mention. He was in so high a degree [1] possessed of every good quality —military, civil, or political—that it was said he might be compared to Alexander as to his virtues, without the least tincture of his faults. He was brave without rashness, discreet, mild, honest, affable, liberal, of inviolable fidelity, prudent, an enemy to vice, a man of a noble and great soul, tempering the majesty of his elevated station with sweetness and courtesy. His mind corresponded to

[1] Tacit. Ann. 2. c. 74.

his birth. He had no sentiments but what were great and exalted, was perfect master of the art of speaking well, and, in short, was ignorant of nothing that a great prince ought to know. By all these virtues and extraordinary qualifications, Germanicus well deserved the praises that were given him and the esteem in which he was held, not only at Rome, but all over the world. Never was general so much beloved by the troops as this excellent prince by his; they frequently offered him the throne, which he as often refused, and thereby showed himself worthy of it.

Agrippina, his wife, was in no way inferior to him. She was grand-daughter of Augustus, and deserved the most lofty eulogies. Her charity was so universally acknowledged, that it was not in the power of the most envenomed calumny to injure her reputation; and this was the more commendable in her, as her mother set her but a very bad example. She was endowed with an extraordinary courage and greatness of soul, and it might be said that she was superior to the weaknesses of her sex. She had, however, some faults, which pass for noble ones in persons of her rank. She was not without a share of haughtiness and ambition, incapable of yielding, and exhibited in all emergencies a heart inflexible against all the vicissitudes of fortune. She was an enemy to dissimulation and flattery, and upon all occasions gave proofs of her sincerity, showing by her words, in her person, and in all her conduct, that noble kind of pride with which her birth, as well as the innocence of her life, and a generally admired character inspired her.

Livia,[1] whose reputation was by no means so well es-

[1] Tacit. Ann. lib. 2. c. 43.

tablished, although to all appearance her conduct was beyond reproach, could not bear to hear Agrippina's virtue and goodness continually extolled, which, at the same time, she could not help esteeming, though she could not prevail upon herself to imitate her. Besides, having been always accustomed to receive the homage of the most important persons, who were very assiduous in bestowing upon her the honours she expected, it was insupportable to her that Agrippina should be the only one that affected not to show her that servile complaisance and refused to bend under the yoke that the rest of the world submitted to. The resistance seemed to lessen her power; and she was the more sensible of it, as she laid it down as a rule that nobody whatever should dare to contend with her. This was the first cause of the rivalry which afterwards divided these two princesses, and of that implacable hatred that Livia ever after felt towards Agrippina.

Tiberius himself was not exempt from this jealousy with regard to Germanicus; and his dislike was so much the more dangerous, as it was secret. He could not endure to see in this prince virtues to which he had no pretensions himself. The triumphs of Germanicus, which were echoed all over the Empire by the applause which was bestowed upon them, and which were so many undeniable proofs of his merit, produced in the heart of Tiberius the most bitter envy. This was the origin of the indefatigable endeavours of him and his mother to thwart all the designs and undertakings of this prince; but this was but poor satisfaction, and not at all proportionate to their malice and hatred. They appeased it, therefore, at last, by the death of this great man, who

was poisoned by the treachery of Piso and Plancina, his
wife, who were sent on purpose into Syria, where Germanicus was in command of the army.

When the news of his death was brought to Tiberius,
he pretended to be extremely afflicted, but it was impossible for him to make people believe him innocent; for
the secret orders that he had given concerning Germanicus were seen in the hands of Piso, who was even ready
to produce them in full Senate for his own justification,
and to throw upon the Emperor the shame and horror
of this murder, as well as of all the other wrongs that
had been perpetrated in Syria. Agrippina left that
country, in order to bring to Rome the urn and ashes
of her husband. All classes in the city then honoured,
with their unfeigned tears, the arrival of that precious
pledge, which brought fresh into everybody's mind the
remembrance of Germanicus's virtues. They all left the
city, and went to meet the procession in deep mourning,
that they might offer the shade of that beloved prince
the most profound and substantial tokens of their grief.
Never was there seen so great a concourse of people together. All the houses in Rome were deserted. The
Senate, knights, plebeians, women, and children, in short,
everybody was gone to meet the urn, which was received
with as much respect as if it had been a god.

Neither Livia [1] nor Tiberius were present, not thinking proper to show themselves in public, for fear their
looks should be observed, and people should see in their
countenances the joy of their hearts upon this occasion.
Livia, however, could not help giving proofs of her satisfaction, by openly defending Plancina, and protecting

[1] Tacit. Ann. 3.

her by her intrigues and authority against the punishment she deserved.

After the Empress had sacrificed to her jealousy and ambition all the victims that were necessary, she thought she had nothing more to do but to enjoy, without care or trouble, the fruits of her labours. Her grandeur and power were become idols, that were more worshipped at Rome than the gods. The Senate exhausted their whole store of praise and submission, being very ingenious at finding out new methods of pleasing her, and inventing new honours to gratify her vanity; they even carried their flattery so far as to grant her the privilege of sitting among the vestal virgins at the theatre, placing among those who made profession of religion the woman in the world who had the least, though she wore the mask of it. As to her making magnificent presents to the temples of the gods, that was only done to impose upon the public. She was not, indeed, covetous in such matters; for, not only did those at Rome feel marks of her liberality, but in all the provinces she was careful to display her magnificence in that respect, especially at the Temple of Jerusalem. She sent thither vases of gold and other precious materials of very great value, as so many monuments of her piety, or, rather, her hypocrisy.

Tiberius, however, could not endure the unbounded ambition of his mother; for, though he himself had as great a share of it as anybody, yet he esteemed only the solid and substantial part, not regarding the show or outside, so that the pomp and magnificence that Livia so much insisted upon was insupportable to him. He dissembled, notwithstanding, as long as the Empress was content with titles and honours; but as soon as he perceived that she was carrying matters further, he could no longer forbear letting her know that her behaviour was not at all to his taste, especially with regard to an inscription that was to be put upon an image dedicated to Augustus, in which she had her own name placed before that of the Emperor. He did not fail to look upon this preference as a manifest attack upon his rights; but, not being willing to expose himself to all the quarrels he foresaw would occur between himself and his mother, he made a pretence of quitting Rome, and retired to [1] Capreæ, where he passed the rest of his life in those abominations that cannot be read without horror; and, in the meantime, Livia reigned absolute at Rome, where her authority was more fully established by the absence of the Emperor. She even enjoyed for a long time the pleasure of governing, and lived to an extreme old age, owing to her excellent constitution, the use of Pucinum wine, and perpetually chewing a certain sweetmeat composed of a root which Pliny calls [2] Inula Campana. But at last she was obliged to yield, and pay the tribute due to Nature. She fell sick, and the news of it was soon carried to Capreæ to Tiberius.

Though filial duty was not strong enough in Tiberius

---

[1] Capreæ was an island near Naples, where there was no port or harbour that could admit of large ships. There was only a little creek for the entrance of boats and small frigates, and they were discovered before they could come near the place by the sentinels, who were continually upon the watch. The air was very moderate and mild, even in winter, because the neighbouring mountains which sheltered it broke the force of the winds; and in summer the heat was not excessive, it being always fanned by the sea breeze. This was the place Tiberius selected to make the scene of such obscenities as cannot be mentioned. Formerly in this island were two towns; at present there is but one, called Capri, which is a bishop's see, where John Gloria, inventor of the mariners' compass, was born.

[2] Plin. lib. 14 c. 8.

to rouse him out of his disgraceful lethargy, yet one
would have imagined that gratitude and decency would
have obliged him, at least, to visit his mother, who had
given him the Empire; but Tiberius was not influenced
by either one or the other. Whether it was that in
reality he did not care for seeing her, or that he was
ashamed to show at Rome a head that was grown grey
in the most odious debaucheries; or, lastly, whether it
was owing to his not being able to refuse anything to his
favorite, [1] Sejanus, who chose rather to keep him in
Capreæ, that he himself might have the conduct of
affairs,—he excused himself from visiting her on various
pretexts, and, in the meantime, Livia died,[2] being eighty
years of age. Her body [3] was placed in the mausoleum
of Augustus, and Gaius Caligula, grandson of this Empress, pronounced her funeral oration.

The Senate decreed to the memory of Livia as great
honours as they had done to her person during her lifetime. But Tiberius, always affecting a great deal of
moderation, forbade them, and would not suffer her to
be immortalised. And, for fear they should think he
was wanting in respect for his mother, he gave out that
she herself had so ordered it.

---

[1] Ælius Sejanus was præfect of the prætorian guards. He raised
himself by his cunning and artifice to the highest degree of favour that
it was possible for man to arrive at. He entirely possessed all the confidence of Tiberius. He was so inordinately ambitious that he aspired
to no less than the Empire. He caused Drusus, son of Livia, to be
poisoned, and persecuted Agrippina and all her family beyond measure.
He was the author of countless deeds of violence that the Emperor committed. Tiberius at last became acquainted with the perfidious designs
of Sejanus, and caused him to be condemned by the Senate at the very
time when this insolent favourite thought that the Emperor was going
to raise him still higher.

[2] Dio. lib. 58.   [3] Tacit. Ann. 5.

JULIA

WIFE OF TIBERIUS

HERE is nothing perfect in this world. The most exalted fortune and rank do not make their possessors so happy but that something is still wanting to perfect their happiness. This was the saying of a poet [1] who lived in Augustus's time, and I do not know whethe1 anybody ever verified it more clearly than that Emperor. He had made himself master of the world by his valour and the good fortune of his arms; the mildness of his temper, the gentleness of his rule, and the prudence of his conduct had quite obliterated all the horrors of the triumvirate, wherein he was but too much concerned, and bent to the yoke even those who were most stubborn. He was feared by his enemies, respected by the inhabitants of the remotest corners of the world, adored by his subjects, esteemed by everybody.[2] He gave the world a taste of the delights of that peace which was so much wished for, and which was the fruit of the victories he had gained over those who were more envious of his glory and fortune than zealous for the public freedom. In short, the limits of his Empire were no other than those of the whole earth; so that, if one might judge of

[1] Horat. Od. 2. 18.   [2] Suet. vit. Aug.

things by appearances, Augustus could not but have been the happiest of mortals. However, if people do not suffer themselves to be dazzled by the lustre of his grandeur, but will take a nearer view of him, examine his domestic affairs, and look into his heart, they will find that his cares, fears, perplexities, and afflictions more than counterbalanced the sweets of empire. For that supreme power was never free from anxiety of every kind, not to mention the untimely death of his nephew Marcellus, which almost broke his heart; nor the conspiracies [1] which were continually being formed against him, and kept him in cruel and perpetual alarms; not to mention the defeat of Lollius, or the total overthrow of Varus,[2] events which had such an effect upon him as to make him show signs of affliction that were unbecoming a great prince. If we only consider the unspeakable vexation that the enormous irregularities of his only daughter Julia caused him, we shall reckon this prince the most

[1] Sueton. vit. Aug. Aurel. Victor. Epitome in Aug.

[2] Quintilius Varus was of a family more illustrious than noble. He had been governor of Syria, and it was said of him that he entered a rich province poor, and left a poor one rich. He was afterwards sent into Cisalpine Gaul, where he caused to be restored to Virgil all his goods, which the troops had plundered him of, and which piece of generosity that poet has so highly eulogised in one of his eclogues. Augustus after that gave him the command of the army which he sent against the Germans; but Varus, suffering himself to be surprised by Arminius, general of those barbarians, was entirely defeated. Three legions and all the auxiliary troops were cut to pieces, and almost all the officers killed. Varus, ashamed to survive this shameful disgrace, destroyed himself, as his father and grandfather had done before him upon similar occasions. The dismal news of the loss of the troops and destruction of the army no sooner reached Rome, than Augustus was seized with the most violent grief that man was capable of. He tore his robe to pieces, groaned piteously, and dashed his head against the wall, crying out every moment, "Varus, give me back my legions." He let his beard grow, and in short, showed all the signs of inexpressible sorrow. This was looked upon as the greatest loss the Romans had ever sustained in a foreign country since the death and defeat of Crassus, in the Parthian campaign.

unfortunate of men in the most exalted station. Shame, confusion, anger and sorrow were the implacable enemies that tore his heart. He reckoned Scipio, Gracchus, Crispinus and Julia's other admirers [1] his mortal foes. In short, Julia seemed only to have been born to poison her father's happiness by the bitter mortifications that she caused him.

Cæsar Augustus's daughter Julia was born to him by Scribonia, his third wife, and he took such particular care of her education, that the crimes with which she dishonoured herself can be attributed to nothing but the extraordinary depravity of her mind; for the Emperor kept so strict an eye over her conduct, that his vigilance extended even to the minutest of her actions. He made her employ herself continually in needlework, in order to leave her no idle moments, which are generally passed in occupations less commendable.[2] He forbade her to say or do anything except in public, that the fear of being censured might put her always on her guard, and that her words and actions might be such as should deserve a place in the diary which he intended to keep. Besides, all commerce with strangers was absolutely prohibited, and Tucinius, a handsome young man of rank, drew upon him Augustus's indignation, for having paid his respects to the princess at Baiæ. The Emperor wrote him a very sharp letter upon that subject, and highly blamed his indiscretion.

But how could the strictest education operate upon a subject, which Nature might be said to have turned out of her hands ruined and spoiled? The violent bias that Julia had to libertinism baffled all her father's precau-

[1] Senec. de brevit. vit.   [2] Sueton. vit. Aug.

tions, and Augustus's vigilance proved too slight a barrier to stem the furious torrent of such a temperament. The Emperor, who was fond of her to excess, could not forbear treating her with greater leniency than he should have done. Fatal indulgence, which was the cause of her irregularities, and the reason for her afterwards giving full scope to her vicious inclinations!

Julia had great beauty, which a noble negligence in her apparel rather set off than otherwise. She was of a cheerful and most agreeable temper, and her conversation had something in it so lively and charming, that all who approached her were delighted with it. To the fire and vivacity of the most insinuating and ready wit was joined so large a store of learning, that she was able, with a great deal of judgment, to give her opinion of and even criticise books. A graceful person, a smiling countenance, and irresistible charms accompanied her grand and majestic air, which was without affectation or study; on the contrary, her behaviour and all her actions were softened and embellished by that easy and free carriage, which is peculiar to such as have been brought up in high life. Her eyes made as many conquests as they cast glances, so dangerous were they to those who would preserve their liberty; and over her whole person was diffused something so bewitching, that it was impossible to resist her. In short, one might venture to affirm that Julia was, beyond contradiction, the most charming lady in the Empire.

She was but very young when Augustus thought of procuring her a husband, and he did not long hesitate as to the person; he selected young Marcellus, son of Marcus Claudius Marcellus and his sister Otavia; and,

certainly, he could not have made a more worthy choice,
for Marcellus possessed all the good qualities that can
render a prince accomplished. His name sufficiently denoted the illustrious family from which he had sprung,
for he was descended from that famous Marcellus,[1]
who showed the world that Hannibal was not invincible;
and who, after having killed, with his own hand, Viri-
domarus, King of the Gauls, had the glory of being the
third, after Romulus,[2] who consecrated to the gods the
arms of the enemies of the Republic—glorious monuments, which demonstrated that, in the family of Marcellus, valour and nobility were of the same date! This
young prince had an excellent address, a winning air,
was humane and affable, popular and amiable, and gained
the love and esteem of all who approached him; and
people, above all,[3] admired in him that growing merit
which proved him to be the true descendant of his worthy
ancestors, whose virtues and extraordinary qualities he
possessed in an eminent degree. Such was Marcellus,
whom his uncle Augustus was resolved to draw still
nearer to him by marrying him to his only daughter Julia.
The Emperor, who was detained at Tarragona by indisposition, could not be present at the wedding, but, for all
that, would not defer it. He charged his favorite,

---

[1] Tit. Liv. Florus lib. 2. Plutarch vit. Marcel.

[2] Romulus, the first King of Rome, was the first who offered to the
gods the spoils of his enemies; for, having in battle killed Acron, King
of Cænina, he dedicated his arms to Jupiter, in a temple which he
caused to be built near the Capitol, where the Cordeliers' Church, called
Ara Cœli, now stands. This was called the temple of Jupiter Feretrius,
from the Latin word, *fero,* which signifies to carry, because the triumpher
himself carried the spoils he was to consecrate.
"Sed quia victa suis humeris hæc arma ferebant,
"Hinc Feretri dicta est ara superba Jovis.

[3] Horat. Od. 12. lib. 3.

Agrippa, with the care and management of the nuptials, and he showed himself worthy of that honour, and acquitted himself in such a manner as fully answered the Emperor's expectations.

The ceremony was performed at Rome with the utmost magnificence, corresponding to the birth and high rank of the Prince and Princess. Agrippa had, luckily, an opportunity of adding very much to the grandeur of it,[1] for it happened that, just at that time, he finished that famous temple, which he dedicated to Jupiter and all the gods, by the name of the Pantheon;[2] and the solemnity of this consecration was so grand and superb that it contributed greatly to the sumptuousness of Julia's marriage. Agrippa, being resolved to do all possible honour to the daughter and nephew of Cæsar, and that nothing should be wanting to show his gratitude to his great benefactor, opened his treasure house, and displayed all his magnificence upon this occasion. Nothing was to be seen at Rome but races, sports, shows, and amusements of all sorts, in which the Senate, knights and everybody partook and expressed their satisfaction in every possible manner. The Empress Livia was the only person who, in the midst of these rejoicings, had secret grief and sorrow at heart, for her sentiments in regard to Marcellus were very different from those of the rest of the world; she looked upon that young Prince as a

[1] Dio. lib. 55.

[2] The Pantheon is a famous temple built by Agrippa, and by him consecrated to all the gods. It is now the finest piece of antiquity of that kind at Rome. It is of a circular form, which Agrippa chose in preference to any other, to imitate the sky, and that there might be no jealously among the gods in point of precedence. There is no window in this temple, so that the light is admitted only through an opening at the top. Pope Urban the Fourth dedicated it to the Virgin Mary and all the saints.

powerful obstacle to the advancement of her son Tiberius, in favour of whom she had formed vast designs. She thought of nothing less than procuring the Empire for him, and in order to compass that great result, made no scruple about cutting off all those who stood in her way.

Marcellus was the first victim that was sacrificed to Tiberius, because the great advantage he had of being nephew, son-in-law, and presumptive heir to Augustus, kept the son of Livia at a vast distance from the throne. The Empress thought proper (before Marcellus could have children) to shorten his days, in order to pave the way for Tiberius. It is not very well known what method she took to accomplish her design, for never did woman know better how to conceal her intentions; she had the cunning to throw over this horrid crime a veil which eighteen centuries have not been able to remove.

When Augustus returned to Rome, he found Marcellus much nearer related to him than he was before, and saw, with great pleasure, that everybody's heart was as much inclined to the Prince as his own. The Senators, in order to pay court to Augustus, received Marcellus into their number, and gave him the rank of those who had been prætors. He was allowed to be a candidate for the consulship ten years earlier than he ought, according to the laws; and, to these great and valuable honours, the Emperor added such others as made all the world take it for granted that he intended him for his successor. But, however charming and amiable were the good qualities of this Prince, they were not enough to win the heart of Julia, who was not sensible of that transcendent merit which was so much admired by everyone else; and Marcellus, who so much deserved to be universally esteemed, was the person she loved least of all. As she was born with an amorous temperament, or, rather, an ungovernable inclination to vice and debauchery, she listened with attention and complaisance to all those who were presumptuous enough to make declarations of their passion. She was constantly surrounded with such of the courtiers as were reckoned the most gallant and polite, who never ceased to make their offerings of the most delicate praise and flattery, which was so much malignant poison, and with which her susceptible heart was soon infected. Numbers of her lovers were rewarded for this constant attention, and it is credibly reported [1] that Tiberius, among the rest, received from her at that time the most evident proofs of her affection.

Affairs were in this situation, when Augustus was attacked by a complaint, that made everybody despair of his recovery,[2] till Antonius Musa,[3] a famous physician, was called in, and he was so happy in the choice of his medicines, that in a little time the Emperor recovered.

[1] Suet. vit. Tib.
[2] Sueton. vit. Aug. Plin. lib. 19. cap. 8. Horat.
[3] Antonius Musa was the greatest physician in Augustus's time, and had been emancipated by the Emperor. His brother was physician to King Juba. Musa cured Augustus of a most dangerous disease by ordering him a cold bath. This brought him into the highest esteem at Rome, where his prescriptions were regarded as so many oracles, and cold baths were afterwards very much in fashion. Horace, who intended to make use of the hot baths at Baiæ, by the advice of Musa altered his mind in favour of the cold; which greatly enraged the inhabitants of Baiæ against Musa, who had made their town deserted, by persuading all the world to go to Gabii or Clusium, places famous for cold baths. Musa, besides the glory of having restored to Cæsar his health, received from this prince magnificent presents, and was permitted to wear a gold ring as the knights did. The Senate erected a statue in his honour, and placed it close by that of the god Æsculapius: upon his account great privileges were also granted to those of his profession.

This sickness of Augustus was the occasion of a misunderstanding between Marcellus and Agrippa, which
in all probability would have ended in a downright
quarrel, if Augustus had not by his prudence prevented it.

The Emperor, as soon as he found himself taken ill,
deposited in the hands of Agrippa the ring he was accustomed to make use of as a seal. This great mark of
confidence produced in the heart of Marcellus a gloomy
jealousy, which quite overcame him. He thought it a
preference as mortifying as it was unjust, and from that
time looked upon Agrippa as his rival in Cæsar's favor;
nor could he hinder himself from showing evident tokens
of his displeasure and resentment. This was reported to
Augustus, and, as, on the one hand, he loved his nephew,[1]
so, on the other, he had a perfect esteem and affection
for Agrippa; he therefore resolved to take a middle
course to satisfy both parties.[2] He sent away his favourite for some time into Syria, with the honourable
title of governor, and raised Marcellus to the dignity of
the Pontificate and the Ædileship.[3] He acquitted himself
so well in both these offices, that the Romans were delighted with him; but, in the midst of the applause that

[1] Tacit. Ann. 1.   [2] Vell. Paterc. Hist. lib. 2.
[3] The ædiles were officers, who were entrusted with the government
of the city. They had charge of the public and sacred buildings, the
solemn games, and the management of the theatres. The duties of
their office also obliged them to take care that the streets were kept
neat and clean. This was so rigorously exacted of them, that Vespasian,
when he was ædile, having neglected to have a street cleaned, through
which Caligula was to pass, the latter, finding a heap of dirt, ordered
it to be gathered and thrown upon the magistrate for his negligence.
None but the ædiles were permitted to have ivory seats in their carriages.
None under twenty-seven years of age were capable of enjoying this
dignity. But, though great respect was paid to their persons, yet they
were not inviolable, for a magistrate invested with greater authority
had power to imprison them.

was given him on all sides, he was attacked by a disorder
that no one at first thought dangerous. Musa had the
care of him,[1] for he enjoyed the highest reputation on
account of his having cured Augustus by ordering him
the cold bath. He adopted the same method with Marcellus; but, whether his distemper was different from
that of the Emperor, and required other remedies, or
whether Livia [2] (as was generally believed) had given
secret orders, Marcellus died in the twenty-fourth year
of his age, exceedingly regretted by Augustus, the Court,
and all the Empire, leaving Julia a childless widow.

His death filled Rome with sorrow. The Princess
Octavia, his mother, was inconsolable. The Emperor
was exceedingly afflicted, and the tears [3] he shed upon
that occasion were glorious demonstrations of the esteem
he had for him and of Marcellus's merit. It was certainly impossible for Augustus to find so worthy a successor. Julia endeavoured to behave in such a manner
as custom and the rules of decency required, but they
seemed insufferably tedious to her; for, as she was then
in the flower of her age and height of her beauty, and of
all things hated restraint, she was much rejoiced to enter
into that state of independence which Marcellus's death
procured her. She was not then bound to a strict observance of that decorum which her marriage imposed
upon her, but was at liberty to encourage all the gay and
polite young men of quality and distinction, who paid
their court to her very assiduously. Thus she easily
comforted herself for the loss of a husband, who had
been forced upon her without her heart having been
consulted.

[1] Hor. Epod.   [2] Dio. lib. 54.   [3] Vell. Paterc. Hist. lib. 2.

It is well known that the age in which Augustus lived
might be called the golden age, and the most productive
of great men. There never was any but that of Louis
the Great that could be compared to it. The horrors
of a war, during which Rome had seen the purest and
noblest blood of her citizens spilt, were at last succeeded
by a lasting peace, the delights of which the whole world
enjoyed. The whole earth obeyed Augustus, and all
the men of the Empire, who were distinguished by their
illustrious birth, the importance of their posts and dignities, the politeness of their manners, the greatness of
their genius, or the reputation of their great exploits,
composed the Emperor's court, where gallantry reigned
with sovereign authority, Augustus himself being the
great encourager of it. And, though his amours were
never allowed to interfere with his duty, it must be confessed that his love for women was more owing to his
natural inclinations than policy, whatever some have been
pleased to assert. His principal courtiers were
Mæcenas,[1] a person of great importance, on account of

[1] Mæcenas, who was descended from the Kings of Tuscany, had
very great influence at the court of Augustus. He was possessed of
every good quality, but his moderation especially was so great, that he
refused all preferment, and would never accept of any higher dignity
than that of a knight. Augustus had the greatest esteem for him, consulted him in his most important affairs, and had so high an opinion
of him, that if at any time he was obliged to quit Rome and Italy, he
entrusted Mæcenas with the government. This favourite never made
use of his influence, except to do all the good that lay in his power;
and above all, he was the most zealous protector of learned men. He
used to speak his mind to the Emperor with great freedom, and it is
reported that one day, when Augustus was seated on his tribunal
administering justice, and seemed inclined to condemn a number of
people, Mæcenas, who perceived it, not being near enough to speak
to him, threw the Emperor his notebook, in which were written these
words, " Rise, hangman, and leave the court "; which bold words saved
the lives of all the prisoners. Augustus permitted him to say what he
pleased, and never took it amiss; on the contrary, he was very glad to

his great influence with the Emperor, and justly celebrated for his love of learning, and his encouragement
of the muses; Agrippa, Augustus's favorite, famous for
his victories and his wisdom; Tiberius and Drusus, sons
of the Empress, who, being honoured with the most
important posts, held the first rank; Julius Antonius, son
of Mark Antony, a very considerable person; Cinna,
grandson of Pompey; Murena, brother-in-law of
Mæcenas; Julius Florus, a near relation of Augustus;
Varus, once illustrious for his exploits, and since remarkable for his being defeated; Lollius, much esteemed by
Cæsar; Silanus, another of the Emperor's near relations;
Crispinus, the Consul; Sestius,[1] highly esteemed by
Augustus; Gracchus, of a most noble family; Cicero,[2]

be corrected by a man he greatly loved. It is true that Cæsar's regard
for Terentia, Mæcenas's wife, occasioned a coolness between them,
which was the reason that Cæsar did not place so much confidence in
him as formerly. After all, Mæcenas would have been more to be
pitied, if he had been more faithful to his wife, but it is well known
that he was extremely in love with the wife of Sulpicius Galba, whom he
visited every afternoon, when her husband went to sleep. Galba was
resolved to let Mæcenas know that he knew of this intrigue; so, having
one day invited Mæcenas to dine with him, he pretended to sleep after
dinner, but perceiving that a servant, who had also a mind to take the
advantage of his master's drowsiness, was filching a bottle of excellent
wine, at the very time when Mæcenas was paying his addresses to the
lady, Galba cried out, "You rogue, do you imagine that I sleep for
everybody?" (Puer, non omnibus dormio).

[1] Lucius Sestius, a Roman senator, was so firm a friend to Brutus,
that, after having followed his fortunes in all his wars, he had the
boldness and generosity, after his death, publicly to honour his memory,
and to keep a staute of him in his house, without fearing to draw upon
himself the anger of Augustus. And the Emperor, admiring the inviolable loyalty which Sestius showed towards his ancient friend, even
after his death, conceived so high an esteem for him, that he gave him
numerous marks of his benevolence, and made him consul.

[2] Marcus Cicero, son of the orator, escaped by a sort of miracle from
the fury of the triumvirate. He had neither the learning nor the
merit of his father; on the contrary, he was subject to many failings,
being especially given to wine, which made him often guilty of unworthy actions, as witness the heinous affront he offered to Agrippa,
Augustus's son-in-law; for when they happened to be at table together,

son of the famous orator; Asprenas, and a large number of others who were exceedingly distinguished at Court.

The Muses were cultivated by such skilful masters that none could ever be compared to them. Ovid, the most gallant of all the Romans, and such a master in the art of loving, was the pride and delight of the Court, by reason of his happy genius, and his facility in composing verses. Virgil [1] was in the highest esteem for his exten-

Marcus Cicero, getting drunk, threw his wine in Agrippa's face. As Augustus had not without great regret sacrificed Cicero to the resentment of Antony, he thought himself obliged to repair the injury, as much as in him lay, by extraordinary kindnesses to his son. In fact, as soon as the Emperor had overcome all obstacles, he restored to Cicero his estate, and did him the honour to make him his colleague in the consulship. Cicero made use of the power and influence which this high office afforded him to blacken the memory of Mark Antony, in revenge for the ill usage with which the triumvir had persecuted his family. He caused his statutes to be broken to pieces, prevailed on the Senate to publish an edict, that not only should no sort of honour be done to his memory, but that no one of that family should be suffered to take the name of Mark, to show his hatred to the triumvir; which obliged the young Mark Antony to take the name of Julius. Augustus permitted the consul to gratify his resentment in these trifles, because he had always a great esteem for Cicero's family. It is reported that when Cæsar went one day to visit one of his nephews and found him with one of Cicero's books in his hand, the young prince endeavoured to hide it, being afraid that Augustus would be angry at his reading the works of a person to whose death the Emperor had contributed: but Augustus, having taken the book, read it for a considerable time, returned it, and said, "My nephew, this was a man of prodigious learning, and a true "lover of his country."

[1] It is not necessary to say anything by way of commendation of Virgil; his works have acquired him such glory and reputation as must last for ever. He was born at Mantua, or rather at a village near that place. His mother was on a journey, and her pains came upon her so suddenly, that having no better convenience, she was delivered of him under a tree, and it is reported that this child did not cry when he was born. Virgil was well known to Mæcenas, who was the great protector and patron of learning; and it was through his interest that he was introduced to Augustus's Court, and received into the Emperor's favour, who made him considerable presents, which the poet did not fail to acknowledge, and took care to proclaim in his poems the virtues and great actions of that prince. Virgil died at Brindisi in the fifty-first year of his age, just when he was intending to correct and revise his works. His body was carried to Naples, according to his own

sive knowledge and the nobility of his thoughts and expressions; Horace was remarkable for his excellent poetry and most agreeable humour.[1]   At that time also lived Propertius, Varius, Tibullus, Catullus, Cornelius Gallus, Quintilius, a Roman knight, Asinius Pollio, and a multitude of other great men, illustrious for their learning and birth; some of whom celebrated the exploits of Cæsar, others composed works of learning and wit, while

request, and a monument was erected for him on the high road to Pozzuoli. Monsieur de Guise, in his memoirs, says it is of white marble, and that it has the form of a dome. Virgil was a man of good presence, but sickly and asthmatic. On his tomb were engraven these two lines composed by himself.

> Mantua me genuit; Calabri rapuere, tenet nunc
>   Parthenope. Cecini pascua, rura, duces.

[1] Horace is no less famous than Virgil. He was born at Venusium, a town situated on the confines of Apulia and Lucania; his father, who is said to have been the son of a freedman, having acquired some riches by fingering the public money, carried Horace to Rome, where he gave him a liberal education, which was not thrown away upon him, for Horace learnt everything that children of the highest rank ought to learn. In order to add philosophy to his other accomplishments, he went to Athens, but the civil wars soon interrupted his studies. Julius Cæsar having been killed, and Brutus having retired to Macedonia, Horace, who had put himself under his protection, followed the fortunes of that Senator, who gave him employment in his army; but, as he had little taste for a military life, he quitted Brutus at the battle of Philippi, and returned to Rome, where, finding himself destitute of money and friends, he was forced to compose verses for a livelihood, some of which falling accidentally into the hands of Virgil and Varius (who were then in great esteem at Rome), they showed them to Mæcenas, who was so taken with them, that he expressed a great desire to be acquainted with the author. He sent for him, and finding in this young poet an extraordinary wit and vivacity, presented him to Augustus. Horace employed his surprising talents in poetry in celebrating the Emperor's victories and great actions, and composing panegyrics upon Mæcenas, Agrippa, and all those who were in power, whose friendship he secured by those means; and when he had gained that point, he set himself to write his satires, in which he does not spare such as he thought deserved censure. Horace was low of stature, and was bleareyed; in one of his eyes he had a fistula, which occasioned Augustus to say that when he had Horace and Virgil near him, he might be said to be between sighs and tears, alluding to the fistula of one and the asthma of the other. Horace died in his fifty-seventh year.

there were not a few who sang their amours under feigned names, or censured the manners of the times.

, On the other hand, the Empress Livia; Octavia, Augustus's sister; his two nieces, sisters to Marcellus; Antonia, wife of Drusus; and the other Antonia, wife of Domitius Ahenobarbus, daughter of Mark Antony, the Triumvir; Scribonia, whom Augustus had divorced; Servilia, who also had been wife of Augustus; Claudia, daughter of Claudia and Fulvia; Agrippina, daughter of Agrippa; Terentia, wife of Mæcenas, and Cæsar's mistress; Vipsania, Urgulania, and Prisca, the Empress's favorites; Farillia, Augustus's near relation; Hortensia, famous for her eloquence;[1] Cornelia, and a very large number of other ladies of the most distinguished merit, were the shining ornaments of Augustus's Court. But none of them was to be compared to Julia. She was then surprisingly beautiful; so it was no wonder that everybody paid court to her, which they did with the greatest assiduity, some because they were smitten with her charms, others out of respect to the Emperor, and large numbers in order to obtain some favour by her interest.

Augustus,[2] as soon as he conveniently could, thought about a fitting husband for her, and, after a little hesita-

---

[1] Hortensia, daughter of the celebrated orator Hortensius, together with his name, inherited her father's eloquence, of which she one day gave proof before the triumvirs, who had imposed a heavy tax upon the Roman ladies, which they were very desirous to have abolished. They applied to several famous advocates to plead their cause, but they all declined it, not daring to appear before those three tyrants upon such an occasion. Hortensia showed more courage and nobility of mind than those orators; for, after having prepared a fine speech, she demanded an audience, which was granted; and she pleaded her own and the other ladies' cause with such irresistible eloquence and politeness, that if she had not the glory of getting the tax totally abolished, she succeeded so far as to have it reduced to a mere trifle.

[2] Sueton. vit. Aug.

tion, acting upon the advice of Mæcenas,[1] selected his favourite, Agrippa. That wise and good friend always spoke his mind to Augustus sincerely and without reserve, sometimes, indeed, a little disrespectfully, but the Emperor did not mind it, knowing that he was quite disinterested and was solicitous for nothing but the honour and welfare of his master. As they were discoursing together one day, Augustus turned the conversation upon Agrippa, and begged Mæcenas to give his real opinion of him. Mæcenas (taking into consideration the numerous offices that Cæsar had heaped upon Agrippa, the latter's great victories, and the prodigious esteem and influence he enjoyed in the Empire) answered Cæsar, that he had raised Agrippa to such an extraordinary eminence, that he must either put him to death or make him his son-in-law. This was a rare example of generosity, seldom practised amongst courtiers, who are generally as eager to hinder the preferment of others as they are to advance their own fortunes, always imagining that the exaltation of others is a disadvantage to themselves.

Marcus Vipsanius Agrippa [2] was not very illustrious by birth, but he made ample amends for the obscurity of his family, by being possessed of every virtue, civil and military, whereby he attained the highest power and influence that a favourite could possibly reach, which furnished him with [3] innumerable opportunities of showing his capacity, as well as his uprightness and integrity. He was a most experienced general, valiant and fortunate, an excellent soldier, an able counsellor, a disinterested courtier, and a great politician. Besides the requisites

---

[1] Dio. lib. 54.   [2] Tacit. Ann. 1. c. 3.
[3] Vel. Paterc. Histor. lib. 2.

that go to form a great man, he had all those that are
necessary to make an honest one. He was an enemy
to dissimulation, a sincere friend, a strict observer of his
promises, free from jealousy, and of a most winning behaviour, never proud of his grandeur and power (however great his influence was with the Emperor), humble,
easy of access, and ever ready to do good offices. He
was, consequently, never envied in his exalted station,
but, on the contrary, universally esteemed and beloved.
In short, there was nobody who did not rejoice when
Augustus bestowed his daughter's hand upon him.

Agrippa was already, in a manner, one of Augustus's
family, for [1] he had actually married Marcella, daughter
of Octavia, the Emperor's sister, for which reason
Augustus, before he gave his daughter to Agrippa, paid
the compliment to his sister Octavia of intreating her to
yield him her son-in-law and to consent that he should
become his. After which, Agrippa put away Marcella,
and married the Princess Julia. The issue of this marriage were Gaius Cæsar and Lucius Cæsar, whom Augustus adopted; besides Julia, who was married to Lucius
Paulus, and Agrippina, who was married to Germanicus.

Agrippa was too far advanced in years to match with
Julia, who was in the prime of her youth and charming,
as we have described her. Neither did she pride herself
upon her fidelity, for, as she regarded not her reputation,
she gave encouragement to all the passionate declarations
of as many as pleased to introduce themselves into her
presence, and gratified her lovers to the utmost of her
power. Gracchus was one of those who had most reason
to boast of his good fortune.[2] The nobility of his family,

[1] Sueton. vit. Aug.   [2] Tacit. Ann. 1.

the gracefulness of his person, and the gift of well
expressing his sentiments, procured him from Julia substantial marks of her esteem, for which he afterwards
paid very dear.   Crispinus,[1] who had been consul, and
who, also, under a grave and severe exterior, concealed
a large store of villainy and perfidiousness, was also one
of her favourites.   Julius Antonius was another of her
gallants; Scipio, Appius Claudius, and a great many
others, shared in her good graces.   In short, there was
no man (however low and mean) who dared not form
designs against the honour of the Princess.

Such notorious and scandalous behaviour could not but
be known by all the town.   Julia became the common
topic of raillery and ridicule.   Those to whom she prostituted herself with so little reserve made her the sport of
their conversation, and she herself, not caring what
people said of her, published her own infamy, and was
the first to make a jest of her debaucheries.   Some of
her lovers asking her one day how it came to pass that
her children were so like Agrippa, who, in all probability,
was not their father, she answered, laughing, that she
never took a passenger [2] except when her vessel was full;
thus making a jest of that which ought to have caused
her the greatest shame and confusion!

I know not whether any credit may be given to the
report of Augustus's having had too much complaisance
for his daughter.   The extraordinary indulgence that he
showed her gave occasion to censures that were not much
to his honour,[3] and the banishment of Ovid corroborated
these suspicions.   It is credibly affirmed that this poet,

[1] Vell. Paterc. Hist. lib. 2.
[2] Numquam, nisi plena navi, tollo vectorem.   Macrob. lib. ii. c. 5.
[3] Aurel. Victor, Epitom. in Aug.

who was so long the ornament of Rome, was deeply in
love with Julia, and was far from being hated by her.
It is said that he one day surprised the Emperor taking
liberties with Julia, which were not very usual between a
father and his daughter; an unlucky accident for Ovid,
whose curiosity was severely punished by a rigorous exile,
which, nevertheless, was given out to be due to quite
another sort of crime! Be this true or not, it is certain
that Caligula afterwards [1] did not scruple to say that his
mother, Agrippina, was the fruit of the incestuous
amours of Augustus and Julia.

She was a second time set free by the death of
Agrippa, who was regretted by all the world, and especially by Augustus, who chiefly owed his fortune to the
wisdom and bravery of that great man. Julia was then
with child, and soon after was delivered of a son, who
was called Agrippa Postumus. It may be imagined that
she was easily comforted for the loss of a husband, who
was too well acquainted with her behavior not to have a
very bad opinion of her. Her mourning was, accordingly, ceremonious, and not sincere; for he was scarce
dead, when, finding herself once more at liberty, and
not much restrained by the presence of her father, who
was often [2] obliged to leave Rome on account of dis-
turbances in one or other of the provinces, she was resolved to deny herself nothing, but to gratify her vicious
passions without bounds.

This irregular conduct of hers was well enough known
to Tiberius, who, in Marcellus's lifetime, had sufficient
proofs of her not being of an unkind disposition. It was
to him, however, that Augustus married his daughter,

[1] Sueton. vit. Cai.   [2] Vell. Paterc. Histor. lib. 2.

after having hesitated some time whether he should give her to a senator or a knight.[1]   It was no small affliction to Tiberius to be forced to part with his wife Agrippina (by whom he had had his son Drusus, and whom he loved infinitely), to marry Julia, with whose character he was so well acquainted; but it was the Emperor that spoke, and, besides, as he knew it could not but be a considerable step to the throne, his ambition got the better of all other considerations; he divorced Agrippina and married Julia. It was soon observed that his having parted with his first wife was a great grief to him; for, meeting her once by chance, he changed countenance so much that the company soon perceived how far he was from being cured of his affection for her, and that she was by no means indifferent to him, for which reason Agrippina was requested to avoid him as much as possible, for fear that Tiberius's dislike to Julia should increase in proportion to his love for the other.

These precautions being taken, there seemed to be a tolerable understanding between the newly married pair, and people even thought that they were more or less fond of each other; but, alas! this state of things was only of short duration.   Tiberius was well informed of the life she led; and for her part, she despised him as being her inferior, and because his gloomy and surly humour was not at all agreeable to her gay and wanton disposition. In short, the wedding bonds became insupportable chains to both of them, and their mutual hatred went so far (especially after the death of a son they had), that, a historian tells us, they did not cohabit together.[2]

Then it was that Julia, no longer exercising any

---

[1] Sueton. vit. Aug. 63. vit. Tib. 7.   [2] Sueton. vit. Tib. c. 7.

restraint, gave herself up entirely to all manner of excesses. Those considerations, which one would imagine
were capable of making an impression on the most dissolute and abandoned, had no sort of effect upon her,
whose ungovernable appetites hurried her away in spite
of duty and all obstacles. Neither the shame she
brought upon herself, nor the reflection upon her birth,
which she so much dishonoured, nor the indignation of
her father, with which she was threatened, were able to
keep her within the bounds of decency. All those who
attempted to advise her she reckoned intolerably impertinent, and listened only to the poisonous and tainted lessons of her paramours, who were a set of the most debauched wretches, and easily infused their detestable and
corrupted maxims into a heart that offered no resistance.

Tiberius, who could not remain an unconcerned spectator of all these disorders, determined to leave Rome,
under pretence of being weary of fatigues and business.
It cost him a great deal of trouble to get leave, for
Livia, his mother,[1] besought him, with tears and entreaties, to stay; and the Emperor made bitter and very
moving complaints to the Senate that Tiberius persisted
in his resolution to forsake him; but he was inflexible,
so they were forced to consent at last,[2] when they saw
him so obstinate in his design, that, upon their continuing
to oppose him, he abstained from eating during four
days.[3] He then quitted Rome in a fury; went to Ostia
without speaking to or saluting anybody, and landed at
Rhodes, where he passed many a tedious and melancholy
hour.

[1] Vell. Paterc. Hist. lib. 2.   [2] Tacit. Ann. 1.
[3] Sueton. vit. Tib. c. 10.

It is said that Tiberius had many reasons for this retirement. He was apprehensive that the young Princes Lucius and Gaius might be jealous of him, or rather, he was jealous of them; for he could not endure to see them preferred to the highest dignities, and looked upon them as the apparent heirs of the Empire. He also imagined that his absence would add to his importance, as he would thereby become more necessary; for, as he knew he had done the Republic great services, he took it for granted that they would not be able to do without him. But it is certain that his chief reason for leaving Rome was the vexation that the horrible irregularities of his wife caused him, the more so because he dared not put her away, nor so much as reprimand her, for fear of provoking Augustus. He knew that she took a good deal of pains to give the Emperor a bad impression of him, by the letters which she continually wrote to him with that intent, which were full of invectives and complaints; these letters were supposed to be the work of one of her gallants, and in them nothing was omitted that could make him appear in the blackest colours.

Tiberius's absence furnished Julia with an opportunity to ruin herself entirely; for there was then nobody to be a check upon her, and, consequently, no bounds were set to her vicious appetites, which a long practice of gratifying had rendered so habitual, that the miserable woman found it impossible to act otherwise. Senators, knights, consuls, all were welcome. She was not one of those nice, scrupulous ladies who make a secret of their amours, and conceal them under a grave and demure exterior; so much precaution would have been an insufferable restraint to her. She received her lovers by

troops,[1] and ran wild with them about the streets of
Rome in the night, and afterwards went and partook of
suppers and entertainments that they had prepared for
her, which she only quitted to dishonour [2] every corner
of the town with her prostitutions, which she had the
impudence to practise even on the Orators' tribunal,
where her father had caused to be published such severe
edicts against adultery,[3] without observing any restraint
or considering anything but the gratification of her furious appetites. All this was not sufficient; but, as if it
had been her whole study how she could possibly carry
her excesses further still, she took it in her head to have
placed every day on the statue of Marsyas [4] as many
crowns as she had committed crimes during the night.[5]

If all this were not attested by authors whose veracity
has never been called in question, nobody would give
credit to it. In fact, how inexpressibly shameful was it
for the daughter of the master of the world to divest
herself of all modesty and decency, and even to glory in
her abominations! The Emperor was afterwards thoroughly informed of them, but too late to apply any
remedy. It is a fatal misfortune attending princes, that

---

[1] Admissos gregatim adulteros.   [3] Vell. Paterc. Hist. lib. 2.
[2] Dio. lib. 54. Xiph. in. Aug.   [4] Plin. lib. 21. c. 11. Senec. de Benef.
[5] Marsyas was a famous player on the flute in Phrygia, who was
so conceited as to challenge Apollo. The god (as may well be imagined)
came off conqueror, and in order to punish the insolence and presumption of his rival, he had him flayed alive. Others say that Marsyas
was a priest of Bacchus. His statue was erected in every free town,
as a mark of its liberty, because Bacchus was also called Liber, which
is as much as to say, "free." Be that as it may, there was at Rome a
statue of Marsyas in the square called Forum Romanum, which was
looked upon either as a monument of liberty, or of Appollo's victory.
It afterwards became a custom for the lawyers to place, upon this
statue, as many crowns as they had gained cases; and it was in imitation of them that Julia eam coronari iubebat ab iis quos in illa nocturna
palæstra valentissimos collucatores experta erat. Muretus on Seneca.

they are the last who are acquainted with the affairs of
their own family, and, at the same time, they know
everything which passes elsewhere.

It is, however, very true that Augustus was not quite
ignorant of his daughter's. licentious conduct, for there
were not wanting persons to give him hints of it; but,
whether he was loth to believe these reports, or that his
journeys and the multiplicity of his affairs diverted his
thoughts from examining into those matters, he left her
entirely at liberty, till, being fully informed of those scandalous proceedings, he gave himself up to grief beyond
what he had ever felt upon other occasions.

At first nothing would satisfy him but treating Julia
with the utmost severity. Sometimes he had a mind to
put her to death, and, soon after, changing his mind, was
resolved to banish her into some desolate island. When
he reflected on her prostitutions and most shameful behaviour, he was so overwhelmed with confusion, that he
hid himself for a great while, and would receive no
visits; and then it was that, being in the greatest degree
sensible of all the affliction a father is capable of feeling
on such an occasion, his rage against Julia was carried
to its utmost extent. He wrote a long letter to the
Senate, containing all the details of his misfortune, and
in terms so pathetic and moving, that his excess of grief
and affliction appeared in every line of his epistle.

When he had time to cool a little, natural affection
took the place of anger, and he repented that he had
published his daughter's crimes, which, unfortunately,
he had been ignorant of till then, or else had neglected
to take the proper measures concerning them. After
that, he cursed his daughter who was the cause of them,

and bewailed the loss of Agrippa and Mæcenas, who
would either have prevented these evils by their good
advice, or at least have comforted him under them. So
true it is, that nothing can make one amends for the loss
of a sincere and disinterested friend. Augustus, among
so many millions of subjects, was not able to find two
who could take the place of Mæcenas and Agrippa.

The Emperor, in the meantime, was determined not
to allow the corrupters of Julia to go unpunished. He
made a strict search for them, but yet did not chastise
them all equally. In the first transports of his rage, he fell
upon one of these miserable delinquents, and, forgetting
his own dignity, stooped so low as to beat him severely
with his fist, till the criminal reproached him with the
breach of his own law as to the penalties in cases of
adultery, whereat he was so much ashamed,[1] that he did
not appear in public for a long time. Sempronius Gracchus was banished to Cercina, an island in the African
sea, where Tiberius afterwards, to avenge the affront he
had received, put him to death. Crispinus, Claudius and
Scipio were also condemned to banishment, which was
thought a milder punishment than they deserved.

Julius Antonius, the most illustrious of all her lovers,
did not come off so well. He fell a sacrifice to Cæsar's
resentment; and, to say the truth, he was the most
blamable, being under infinite obligations to the Emperor; for, after the battle of Actium and the death
of Mark Antony, Augustus gave a singular instance of
his moderation and clemency, not only pardoning the son
of his enemy, but giving him [2] the pontificate, the consul-

[1] Plut. Tacit. Ann. 1. Vell. Paterc. Senec. de Clement.
[2] Vell. Paterc. Hist. lib. 2.

ship, and several governments. He did not stop there,
but honoured him by becoming a connection of his by
giving him a daughter of Octavia, his sister, to wife.
Julius Antonius, notwithstanding all these favours, being bewitched by the beauty of Julia, and having the
misfortune to be agreeable to her, forgot all this, and
rushed headlong to the gratification of his passions.
He became the seducer of his benefactor's daughter,
which ingratitude cost him his life. Some say that he
killed himself, to avoid a worse death that was preparing for him; others affirm that he was formally condemned and executed in consequence of the sentence pronounced against him for the crimes of adultery and
treason. Be that as it may, it is certain that his amours
with Julia were the occasion of his death, and that he
owed his ruin to love, as his father had done.

The Princess had her share in the punishment, for
Augustus banished her to the island of Pandateria; and,
being apprehensive that her gallants might visit her, he
expressly forbade that anybody should presume to go
thither without his permission; and, when any man asked
his leave to do so, Augustus [1] would examine, with great
strictness and attention, their size, age, colour of their
hair, their features, the blemishes or particular marks
on their body, in order, by these precautions, to hinder [2]
anyone from seeing her in disguise, imagining that, in
case he should be deceived, in spite of his vigilance, and
any lover should venture to transgress his orders, he
might be able to find him out by these marks and tokens.

Phœbe, who had been given her freedom by Julia, and
was her associate and confidante in all her prostitutions,

---

[1] Dio. lib. 54.   [2] Sueton. vit. Aug.

anticipated the punishment she deserved by hanging herself; and Augustus asserted that it would have rejoiced
him if his daughter had imitated her. Nobody doubted
but he spoke sincerely, for he did not feel the death of
those who belonged to him so keenly as their dishonour;
and it was observed that he lamented his condition whenever he thought of his daughter, the other Julia, his
grand-daughter, who was as debauched as her mother,
and of Agrippa Postumus.

Tiberius was all this while at Rhodes, where he was
impatiently indulging his spleen and ill humour, when he
was informed of what had taken place at Rome, and
how the Emperor had punished Julia. He was extremely glad to be revenged upon her for the affronts he
had received; but, as he was master of the art of dissimulation, he affected a false compassion for her, and
wrote an artful letter to the Emperor, whom he entreated to have pity on her, and to excuse her weakness,
which, perhaps, had been represented in too unfavourable a light; to make some allowances for the liveliness
of her temper, and to abate somewhat of his severity for
his sake. Thus he pretended to have a great affection
for his wife, and to feel her misfortunes very keenly,
when, at the same time, nothing could have given him
greater pleasure than her sufferings.

The people were touched with compassion for her, and
begged for her return and forgiveness with more sincerity, but with no better success. Augustus was implacable, and swore that fire and water should sooner
agree together than he would consent to her return.
Cæsar's obstinacy in this respect increased the people's
desire to obtain their request; they redoubled their ef-

forts, and, in order that the Emperor might be disengaged from his oath, and have it in his power to recall her without being guilty of perjury, they threw into the Tiber a large number of lighted torches, that the ridiculous prodigy of a union of fire and water might thereby be bought about. But Augustus was not to be prevailed on to alter his mind, and, hearing that there was a design to carry her off by force, he changed the place of her banishment, and sent her to Rhegium in Calabria, where she was treated with a little less rigour; but he first dissolved the marriage that he had obliged Tiberius to contract with her.

Augustus died, and it was generally supposed that Julia's exile would end with her father's life, and that Tiberius would recall her, since he had interested himself so much in her behalf. But the new Emperor soon showed that his conduct had been dictated by policy, not by love; he had suffered too much annoyance from Julia's behaviour to pardon her, so that he no sooner grasped the reins of government, than he forgot all he had written to Augustus in her favour. He immediately forbade her to stir out of her house, and deprived her of the little money that her father had allowed her, under pretence that there was no mention made of it in Cæsar's will. In short, he so contrived matters, that she perished in hunger and misery. It cannot be said that this Princess was much to be pitied, since it is certain that her crimes did not deserve a less punishment.

LIVIA ORESTILLA, LOLLIA PAULINA AND CÆSONIA

WIVES OF CALIGULA

THE Emperor Gaius was son of Germanicus and Agrippina.[1] He was also called Caligula, from the little boots which he wore, after the manner of the soldiers, among whom he was bred,[2] and this bringing up gained him the affection of the troops.[3] He passed some of his youth with Tiberius in the island of Capreæ, where he was a witness of all those abominations into which that Emperor plunged himself, and which he afterwards imitated. He also learned there the art of dissimulation (so necessary in Courts), and had an opportunity of acquiring and practising that great degree of cunning which enabled him to accommodate himself to the odd and dangerous humour of Tiberius, from whom he found means to conceal all his vices by most profound and matchless artifice; he contrived to

[1] Tacit. Ann. 1.
[2] Gaius Cæsar Caligula was born on the last day of August, during the consulship of his father and of C. Fonteius Capito, at the time when the legions, commanded by Germanicus, were in their winter quarters; which the Romans looked upon as an omen of his future grandeur. And as soon as he became Emperor these two lines, to the same purport, were published:

In castris genitus, patriis nutritus in armis,
    Jam designati principis omen erat.

[3] Sueton. vit. Cai.

117

insinuate himself into the good graces, and preserve the
esteem, of the Emperor, in spite of the many snares that
were laid for him by his enemies, who did their utmost
to make him complain, that they might have it in their
power to ruin him. By thus wearing a mask, he deceived
even Tiberius, who, of all men living, was the most impenetrable in his designs and words. His being perpetually obliged to act such a part as this could not but
have been extremely disagreeable to him, but it was absolutely necessary to his designs. He was naturally
haughty, proud, cruel and insolent, and altogether so
different from what he pretended to be when in awe of
Tiberius, that it afterwards occasioned people to say
that there never was a better servant, nor a worse
master.[1]

His first wife was Junia Claudia, daughter of Junius
Silanus, remarkable for the antiquity of his family. He
married her by the orders of Tiberius, for which he
pretended to have the greatest respect; and, though he
did not like his wife, he took care to treat her with great
kindness. She died in child-bed, which he was rather
glad of than otherwise, especially as she was not a person
who could contribute much to the accomplishment of his
vast designs. For this reason, he looked about for one
that was more for his purpose, and at last pitched upon
Ennia, wife of Macro, præfect of the prætorian guards,[2]

---

[1] Sueton. vit. Cai. c. 20.
[2] After the Emperors had entirely destroyed the liberty of Rome,
these prætorian cohorts were appointed guards to the Emperor and
to the city. They had a camp in the middle of Rome, and became so
powerful, or rather so insolent, that, when any of the Emperors were
killed, they took upon themselves to choose another, and the Senate was
often obliged to confirm their choice. Augustus made two of them
captains of his guard. Whoever were possessed of those posts, became

who succeeded Sejanus in his post and in the favour of the
Emperor, though he was as unworthy a man as the other.
This woman had an inexhaustible fund of ambition, and,
as her vanity had been fully gratified by the vast degree
of influence and almost absolute power that her husband
had exercised under Tiberius (who was drawing fast
towards his end), there were no ways or means, however
bad, that she was not capable of putting in practice to
perpetuate her authority.

Caligula had no great trouble to gain over a woman
of such a disposition; nor was it any wonder that he
found her so ready to listen to his proposals. She had
been always at the top of Fortune's ladder, and was
extremely anxious to maintain her position, by securing,
in her interests, the person who, very shortly, was to be
master of the world. Caligula promised to marry her as
soon as he was in possession of the sovereign authority,
if she would make use of her power with Tiberius in his
favour, and prevail upon Macro to do the same; and, to
convince her of his sincerity, he added to his protestations a promise in writing, signed by his own hand, and
confirmed it with such oaths as were capable of over-
coming the most obstinate credulity; but it afterwards
cost him no more trouble to forget than it had done to
make them.

These artifices of Gaius had their desired effect.
Ennia,[1] dazzled by the lustre of the throne, was not able
to resist these seductive and flattering hopes, though
she had not better security for them than the promise of

afterwards very influential, so that from Constantine's time they were
reckoned the first officers of the Empire. The prætorian soldiers had
better pay than the other troops.

[1] Sueton. vit. Cai.

the basest and most dissembling of princes, whose affection she endeavoured to purchase beforehand,[1] by
granting him all the favours in her power, and shamefully prostituting herself to him, whose pretended love
was only a masterpiece of policy, foolishly believing that
Caligula would keep his word with her, and that, when
he came to the throne, he would strictly carry out what he
had promised when he stood in need of her assistance.
The most scandalous thing in this infamous business was,
that Macro, who was intoxicated with his power and
influence (the diminution of which by the approaching
change of government he dreaded above all things), was
himself the chief instrument in assisting Caligula to
corrupt his wife; for he imagined that he could not but
be always dear to a prince who was under such obligations to him, and, consequently, that he ought to stick
at nothing to humour him. Fatal blindness of the man
that is devoured by ambition, who is not ashamed to
bring upon himself a real and present disgrace for a
bare prospect of future grandeur, though his hopes are
uncertain and deceitful! The interested solicitations of
this flattering courtier betrayed his designs, and were too
easily seen through to escape the penetration of Tiberius,
who was not readily imposed upon, and who was resolved
to show that he had found out the design. One day the
artful Macro, having cunningly turned the discourse upon
Gaius, whom he praised excessively, the Emperor interrupted him,[2] and told him coldly that he perceived he
was turning his back on the setting, and his face to the
rising sun.

Caligula, however, recompensed very ill the substantial

[1] Tacit.   [2] Tacit. Ann. 6. cap. 46. Dio. lib. 58.

favours conferred upon him by Macro, who, besides,[1]
was very useful to him in governing the Empire; for, not
remembering that he was indebted to Macro and his wife
for it, he never omitted an opportunity of using them ill.
Hatred and ingratitude soon took the place of his pretended friendship,[2] for he sacrificed them both to his
brutal fury. A melancholy instance of the little dependence one ought to place on the favours of princes that
have been purchased by wickedness!

Tiberius, having, by his death, set Caligula at liberty,
delivered him from the insupportable yoke of subjection
and dependence.[3] It may be said that he mounted the
throne amidst universal approbation, for everybody
offered up their vows for his prosperity. The Senate, the
legions, and the people, gave evident tokens of the joy
they felt at his elevation. The people conceived the
highest satisfaction at seeing on the throne the son of
Germanicus, whose memory was so dear to them, and
whose virtue seemed to revive in this young Prince. The
legions had desired nothing so ardently as the pleasure
of obeying an Emperor who was born among them, and
who had passed his youth in the camp and army. The
Senate that had been so humbled by Tiberius and so terrified by his repeated acts of tyranny, who were almost
continually in deep mourning for the death of some of
their most illustrious members (sacrificed to his jealousy
and cruelty), hoped to find in the young Gaius a wise
and mild Emperor. They therefore, to show the extraordinary joy and satisfaction he caused them, unanimously
decreed him the Empire absolutely, without a partner,

[1] Philo. Leg. ad Cai.   [2] Sueton. vit. Cai.
[3] Aurel. Victor. Epitom. in Calig. Philo. Leg. ad Cai.

contrary to Tiberius's will, who had ordered that his
grandson should be joined with him in the government.
In short, as the first beginnings of liberty always seem
sweet after a reign of slavery, everybody hoped to find,[1]
under this young Prince, a happy change in his fortune,
and each promised himself some advantage or other, so
that the day of his elevation was called Rome's second
birth.

Caligula, at first, justified the high opinion that everyone had of him by a few pretended shows of virtue and
justice. He paid very punctually the legacies of Tiberius
and Livia; and to their bounties he added some of his
own. He caused the documents [2] which he found, in-
criminating those who had persecuted his mother and his
family, to be publicly burnt, to show that he was ready to
sacrifice his own private resentment to the good of the
public, and even of his enemies. He punished the misbehaviour of the governors of provinces, among whom was
Pontius Pilate,[3] procurator of Judæa, who, being convicted of bribery, extortion, and other crimes, was
banished to Vienne,[4] where he became his own executioner, and killed himself in despair.[5] Caligula also drove
out of Rome those corrupt and effeminate wretches who
had been instruments of Tiberius's monstrous abominations. He degraded as many of the knights as had dishonoured their dignity by any notorious crime. Lastly,
he set at liberty all those who had been imprisoned by
the cruelty of his predecessor, and, in addition, made
some of them very considerable presents.

[1] Sueton. vit. Calig. c. 16.   [2] Dio. lib. 59.   [3] Luc. 3.
[4] Colonia Julia Vienna, Vienna Allobrogum. Not the capital of
Austria.
[5] Niceph. Callist. lib. 1. c. 1. 16.

The happy beginnings of the new reign buried in oblivion all the horrors of the last; and there seemed to be little doubt but that an Emperor, who, in his youth, could give such tokens of solid wisdom, would be a pattern of consummate prudence, as soon as he should have attained to a riper age. All the actions of Caligula proclaimed his merit and eminent virtues, and increased the high idea that everyone had formed of the new government. But these serene days were soon changed into frightful storms, for they were not the natural effects of real goodness, but a wicked and malicious disguise that he had put on, the better to deceive mankind and to establish himself upon the throne, upon which he was no sooner firmly seated than he threw off the mask. By degrees he showed himself in his true colours; and, at last, weary of this restraint, he gave himself up entirely to those passions that had long been curbed and checked by a tedious and distasteful dissimulation. They broke loose like an impetuous torrent [1] that had undermined its banks, and bore down all before them. He showed himself such as he really was,[2] that is to say, cruel, wicked, and furious—the tyrant,[3] and not the father of the Republic. In short, he verified the prediction of the late Emperor concerning him, who discovered enough of his natural temper, notwithstanding his childhood and the thick cloud of dissimulation in which he wrapped himself. Tiberius said, that in Gaius he was nourishing a serpent for the Republic,[4] and a Phæthon for all the earth.

Gaius Caligula verified this prophecy. The death of Tiberius broke the bonds that held in check his depraved

---

[1] Sueton. vit. Cai.
[2] Dio. lib. 59.
[3] Aurel. Vict. in Epit. in Calig.
[4] Sueton. vit. Cai.

inclinations, which were as shameful as they were violent; so that this Prince, though but a youth, was thoroughly acquainted with all those vices, which one would imagine required a long life of iniquity for a man to have made himself so perfect a master of. After having debauched his sisters by horrible incest, he exposed them to be treated after the same manner by other young men as wicked as himself, and afterwards confined them in islands for having committed the very crimes that he had compelled them to commit; telling them, with a brutal and threatening air, that he had, not only islands, but knives. He forced his sister Drusilla from her husband, Cassius Longinus (a person of high rank, who had been consul, and to whom she was lately married), and kept her publicly in his house as his wife, showing such a furious passion for her, that, when she died, he ran into the most shameful and ridiculous extravagances, by way of demonstrating his grief. In short, he was guilty of the greatest of all brutalities, and what was the most unnatural thing that can be conceived—he debauched a daughter he had by one of his sisters [1] before he became Emperor.

These infamous practices were not confined to his own house. There was hardly an illustrious family in Rome, nor any lady of quality in the city, whom he did not dishonour; this he generally chose should take place before their own husbands, who were obliged to be witnesses of their misfortune,[2] after which he added the most provoking insults and affronts he could think of.[3]

He scandalously maintained in his house the courtesan Pyrallis, who was the most famous concubine of her time. At last, after having glutted all his detestable appetites

[1] Eutrop. in Cai. Calig.   [2] Sueton. vit. Cai. 36.   [3] Dio. lib. 59.

in ordinary vices, he prostituted his own person by a brutality that would scarce be credible, if there had been anything too bad for him to be capable of.   He had practised all sorts of crimes from his cradle, and set out, as we have observed, with abusing, most abominably, his own sisters.

LIVIA ORESTILLA

WIFE OF CALIGULA

ALIGULA'S passion for his sister Drusilla had been so violent, that it was supposed he would have been incapable of engaging in any new amour; but he, who, by the natural levity of his temper, was extremely given to change, could not remain long in the same mind. Livia Orestilla was the person who innocently inspired him with a new passion. She belonged to one of the most ancient and most illustrious families of Rome; and Calpurnius Piso, to whom she had lately been betrothed, set no less value on her birth than on her beauty. This nobleman, who was of the highest rank [1] and immensely rich, was resolved to celebrate his nuptials by a magnificent entertainment, to which all the people of distinction were invited. The bridegroom, in order to make it still more grand and pompous, entreated the Emperor to honour him with his presence, for which he paid very dearly, for it cost him no less than his quiet and his liberty.

Orestilla was very young, and very beautiful, the Emperor very susceptible of love, and possessed of absolute power; it is often dangerous to be too courteous

[1] Dio. lib. 59. Sueton. vit. Cai.

to guests of that kind. Everything was carried out on a
most lavish scale; nor were the most delicate meats, wines,
and the richest furniture wanting, to gratify the sight
and taste even of those who were the most difficult to
please. Orestilla, the chief ornament of the assembly,
appeared in all her charms, which were set off to the
utmost with jewels, rich clothes, and everything that was
rare and costly. All this could not fail to make the
greatest impression on the Emperor, nor was it at all
improbable that Orestilla entertained some design of that
nature; for that flattering superiority of power, which
raises one so much above other people, is so extremely
tempting, that few have moderation and humility enough
to resist it. Be that as it may, the mirth and pleasure of
the banquet concluded in a way very mortifying for Piso,
the more so because he was far from expecting any such
thing; for he little imagined that the bride was to fall
to the share of another person, after he had been at all
the expense of the wedding. Caligula, whilst at table,
fell in love with Orestilla, and not being overburdened
with the gift of self-denial, carried her off without any
ceremony, conducted her to the palace, and married her; [1]
he afterwards confirmed the marriage by an edict, declaring that he had married Orestilla, though the wife of
another man, after the example of Romulus and Augustus. But he was not so constant as either of those two
princes, for he soon after put her away; so true is it that
the most violent passions are the easiest extinguished,
and that love, which is so sudden, often ends the same
way. But what was most of all unjust in Gaius was, that,

[1] Dio. lib. 59.

after he had divorced Orestilla, he would not suffer Piso to have her;[1] and, suspecting that they might see each other, notwithstanding the prohibition, he banished them both to separate islands.

[1] Sueton. lib. Cai.

LOLLIA PAULINA

SECOND WIFE OF CALIGULA

OLLIA PAULINA was not happier than her predecessor. She was grand-daughter of Marcus Lollius, remarkable for nothing [1] but possessing in perfection the art of concealing the worst vices under the appearance of modesty and wisdom. In fact, he disguised himself so well, that, keen-sighted as Augustus was, he was deceived by him, and took the mask of virtue for virtue itself, which he thought he was rewarding, when he honoured Lollius with the highest offices; for he made him governor of Galatia, with the rank of proconsul, when that kingdom, after the death of Amyntas, was reduced to a province. He afterwards made him consul, and gave him the command of the armies in several expeditions, in which he was not always successful; and at last, in order to show him the highest mark of his esteem, he entrusted him with the guardianship of his grandson, Gaius Cæsar, when he sent him into the East;[2] in which honourable employment Lollius acquitted himself very ill, for he gave the young prince very bad advice,[3] and, by false reports and fabrications, inspired him with an implacable

[1] Vell. Paterc. Histor. lib. 2.   [3] Dio. lib. 59.
[2] Tacit. Ann. 3. c. 48.

hatred against Tiberius.[1]   He also frustrated, by his
underhand practices,[2] whatever conquests Gaius might
have made, thus basely betraying the trust that was reposed in him, to satisfy his insatiable avarice, though a
great poet has been pleased, in one of his flattering odes,
to praise his disinterestedness.[3]   For Phraates, King of
the Parthians, at an interview which he had with the
young prince Gaius Cæsar, on one of the islands of the
Euphrates, discovered to him the infidelity of Lollius,
his governor, who, being dazzled with the gold of those
Oriental kings, and, not being able to resist their presents, sold them the secrets that had been communicated
to him, and informed them of everything that had been
resolved upon in the Roman council.   This base and unworthy behaviour obliged Gaius to deprive him of his
confidence and friendship.   Lollius, finding his reputation
ruined, and not being able to say anything in his own
justification, poisoned himself, that he might not survive
his disgrace.   Such is generally the miserable end of
traitors.   They meet, sooner or later, with the punishment due to their perfidiousness, either in a violent death,
or in dragging on a wretched life loaded with shame and
infamy, hated by those whom they have betrayed, and
despised by those to whom they have sold their honour
and probity.

Lollia had all the advantages that could be desired.
Her birth was illustrious, her beauty remarkable, and her
character very high.   To all these good qualities were
added immense riches,[4] which furnished her with the
means of making a very considerable figure at Rome.

---

[1] Vell. Paterc. Histor. lib. 2.   [3] Horat. Od. 4. 9.
[2] Sueton. vit. Tib.   [4] Plin. lib. 9. c. 35.

She was even remarkable for making a good use of that
wealth, which had been the fruit of her father's horrid
extortions and treasons.

Memmius Regulus, consul and governor of Macedonia
and Achaia, married her, and soon after took her with
him to his government. Their unlucky stars, or rather
the brutality of Caligula, in a little time brought them
back to Rome.[1] The Emperor, having one day heard it
said that Lollia's grandmother had been a lady of extraordinary beauty, was seized with a great desire [2] to
see the grand-daughter of so remarkable a person. He
did not long hesitate whether he should gratify his
curiosity or not. Memmius, who was then at the head
of the army, had orders to hasten as soon as possible
to Court, together with Lollia Paulina, his wife.

She no sooner made her appearance, than Caligula
was deeply in love, and, being hurried on by his furious
passion, obliged Memmius to yield her to him. He even
compelled him to act the part of her father upon this
occasion, and to give her away. He then married her
with all the usual formalities, much in the same manner
as Augustus had married Livia.

Lollia was very sensible of the advantages that this
great change of fortune afforded her, and was, no doubt,
rejoiced to have her vanity thus gratified; but her satisfaction was of as short continuance as the Emperor's
passion, for Caligula (as ready to hate as he was to
love) was soon as much disgusted with this lady as he
had been with the others, so that, with all her beauty and
rich apparel, she was not capable of fixing the heart of
this fickle and capricious prince,[3] who divorced her with-

[1] Sueton. vit. Cai.   [2] Dio. lib. 58.   [3] Dio. Sueton. vit. Cai.

out giving any reason for it, and very coldly sent her away, strictly charging her never to marry anyone else.

Lollia Paulina, who had been with so much rapidity exalted to the sovereign power, was as suddenly reduced to her former condition, and became an example of the instability of Fortune, and how little it is to be reckoned upon. She supported it, however, with a great deal of firmness and resolution, comforting herself with her riches. She partook of all amusements, but was very careful of her conduct, so as to give no room for censure. She shone at all assemblies,[1] as well by her captivating beauty, as by the pearls, rubies, and most valuable diamonds, with which she might be said to be rather covered than adorned, for which she was not indebted to the generosity of Caligula, but to Lollius, who had accumulated all this weath by the plunder of whole provinces.

She lived in this manner during the rest of Caligula's reign and the beginning of Claudius's; but, after Messalina's death, Paulina, who had by no means lost her taste for power and authority, began to conceive hopes of remounting that throne, which she had lost by the inconstancy of Gaius. She might reasonably have aspired to this exalted degree of honour, if there had not been a great many competitors; but the throne has too many charms not to make more than one person sigh for it.[2] Every lady of beauty and distinction at Rome flattered herself with having as good pretensions to the sovereignty as Paulina; but there were two especially who disputed with her the heart of Cæsar. Ælia Pætina and Agrippina were these two dangerous rivals. These ladies, as

[1] Plin. lib. 9. c. 35.   [2] Tacit. Ann. 12. c. 1.

may well be imagined, made the most of their beauty, and neglected nothing that could possibly set themselves off to advantage. They had almost an equal degree of favour and interest, being each of them supported by one of the three favourites who governed the Emperor. Claudius, the most stupid and irresolute of men, hesitated a great while before he could come to any resolution; and, before he determined, was resolved to know the opinions of Pallas, Callistus, and Narcissus, his three masters; for Claudius had vested the sovereign authority and entire government of the Empire in the hands of these unworthy wretches, who ruled the world according to their own humour and caprice.

Narcissus proposed Ælia Pætina, who had already been married to Claudius and divorced without any crime being imputed to her. Callistus, who supported Lollia's interests, represented to the Emperor that, though it was true that Pætina had been divorced without any reason, it would be dangerous to expose himself and his children to her vengeance, since she was full of resentment for the affront that had been put upon her, and that she would never be other than a cruel step-mother to his children; that his marrying her a second time would make her only more haughty and imperious; that nothing of all this was to be feared from Lollia, who was remarkable for her illustrious birth, and for her beauty, in which respect but few could be compared to her, and for such a reputation, as was proof against the utmost that malice could invent. He added, that the particular interest of Britannicus and Octavia (who were Claudius's children by his wife Messalina) required Lollia in preference to any other, because, as she had never had children, she would look upon her husband's as her own.

Pallas, speaking on behalf of Agrippina (to whose interests he was particularly attached, for reasons that were far from being innocent), proclaimed aloud her extraordinary qualifications, and laid great stress upon the nobility of her birth; for she was descended from the family of the Claudians, just as the Emperor was. He extolled to the skies her beauty and merit; and Agrippina herself had the art of fortifying his reasons in such a manner, by her cunning and bewitching caresses, which were not at all consistent with modesty, that Claudius decided in her favour by a false and ill-judged decision, of which he had very soon reason to repent.

This choice confounded all the hopes of Paulina, who now saw her pretensions vanish, and all her ambitious projects come to nothing; but that was not her only misfortune, for the revengeful spirit and jealousy of Agrippina were the occasion of others, which were fatal to her.[1] This princess, who had extremely dreaded the power of her rivals, conceived an implacable hatred towards Paulina, and resolved to punish her assurance in asking to marry the Emperor, which she looked upon as an attack upon her rights. She thought proper, indeed, to conceal her resentment for some time, but as soon as she had secured her fortune, she indulged her rage to the utmost.

The speediest and most cruel effects of her fury fell upon Lollia, because her beauty was the most formidable. Agrippina, whilst her power was but yet in its infancy, did not care to proceed in a violent manner, and would

[1] Tacit. Ann. 12. cap. 22.

not venture to put Lollia to death without some pretence, which it was no easy matter to find, because the conduct of this lady had always been such as gave her enemies no handle against her; but the Empress, not being longer able to deny herself the satisfaction of sacrificing this victim to her malice, suborned someone, who accused her to Claudius of the crime of superstition.

In order to render it more plausible, the charge was embellished with many specious circumstances, which were artfully invented. She was reproached with having [1] given credit to the predictions of the Chaldæans, and said to have sacrilegiously searched into the dark secrets of futurity, to discover whether the Emperor's marriage would be fortunate or not, and to have consulted the oracles of the gods, to satisfy this criminal curiosity. All these charges were very grave, but they were all false, and it would have been very easy for Lollia to have shown the contrary (for they were supported by no proofs), if she had been permitted to justify herself. But care was taken that she should have no such opportunity. That would have brought too much confusion upon the authors of this calumny, and the innocence of the accused could not have been proved without publishing the infernal malice of the accuser.

As soon as this accusation had been trumped up against Lollia, the Emperor proceeded to inform the Senate of it. At first he spoke very highly of Lollia, mentioning her great nobility, and how much she was to be respected for being the daughter of Lucius Volusius, and niece of Cotta Messalinus. He spoke of her marriage with Memmius, who was illustrious by his high offices, but was maliciously

[1] Tacit. Ann. 12. c. 22.

silent as to her having been the wife of Caligula, for fear that it would put them in mind of the manner in which he was treating the wife of an Emperor, who ought not to be put on a level with ordinary people. At last, after having tried the Senate with a very tedious discourse, he told them that Lollia had thought fit to disturb the State with her dark practices, and, that it might not be in her power to put her mischievous projects into execution, he sacrificed her to the public weal, and immediately banished her from all parts of Italy, and confiscated her estate, leaving her but a very small portion of her immense riches.

This unjust exile, one would think, was a punishment severe enough for an imaginary crime, and one that ought to have satisfied Agrippina; but it seldom happens that malicious people can prevail on themselves to set bounds to their revenge, when they have in their hands the power to gratify that diabolical passion. Agrippina mortally hated Lollia, and it was not possible that the fire of her implacable wrath could be extinguished by anything less than the blood of her enemy. A tribune was at once despatched to the place of her banishment, with orders to put her to death; and it is very probable that the Empress took care to chose a proper person to perform this infamous commission. She was not deceived in her choice, for this unjust order was executed with the same cruelty with which it had been given; and Lollia expiated by her death the unpardonable crime of having endeavoured to marry Claudius. Agrippina's vengeance was not yet entirely glutted; she was determined to carry it beyond the death of her rival, and therefore commanded her head to be brought to her, in order to feast her eyes upon so agreeable a spectacle. She enjoyed this poor satisfaction,[1] for the head was brought to Rome. She contemplated and examined it very narrowly; and, being afraid that some other head might have been brought instead of Lollia's, she had [2] the cruel curiosity to convince herself of the truth, by brutally opening her mouth, which she did with her own hands, to see by her teeth, which it seems had some peculiar formation, whether it was really the head of Lollia.

[1] Dio. lib. 60.   [2] Xiphilin. in Claud.

CÆSONIA

THE LAST WIFE OF CALIGULA

FTER Caligula had divorced Lollia, as has been related, Cæsonia made her appearance.[1] She was the daughter of Orfitus and Vestilla. When Gaius espoused her, Cæsonia was married to another man [2] who had three daughters by her. She possessed neither the beauty nor the prudence of Gaius's other wives,[3] notwithstanding which he loved her the best, and was always faithful to her. He could not possibly have made a choice more worthy of himself, nor selected one who would enter more cordially into all his ways and humours. She was impudent, bold, and haughty to the last degree.[4] Her lewdness and cruelty were equal to his, and she contributed not a little to those tragical executions that filled Rome with blood and tears during the reign of this tyrant.

The Emperor had loved her long before he married her; and it is reported she employed other arts besides her beauty to gain his affections; for we read that she prepared him a potion (of the ingredients of which a poet pretends to give us an account [5]), which, having had

---

[1] Sueton. vit. Cai.
[2] Plin. lib. 9. c. 7.
[3] Dio. lib. 59. Suet. in Cai. cap. 25.
[4] Joseph. Ant. Judaic. lib. 20.
[5] Juvenal. Sat. 6. 610.

a greater effect than she intended, disturbed his brain, and was the occasion of that fury which made him commit so many extravagances and cruelties.

Caligula, being quite mad with love for his Cæsonia, dressed her up sometimes like a soldier, showed her to the troops in this dress, forced her to ride on horseback by his side, and often exposed her quite naked to his friends, telling them that, by speaking a single word, he could make that pretty head of hers leap from her shoulders, with which polite compliment he generally concluded his brutal caresses.

His passion for her increased after the birth of a daughter he had by her. He was so overjoyed to see himself a father, that he committed a thousand ridiculous extravagances. He then, in the most formal and solemn manner, declared himself husband of Cæsonia, and father to the young princess. She was called Julia Drusilla, and the mother was honoured with the title of August. He obliged everybody to make him presents upon this occasion,[1] and most basely received the money that was brought him from all parts for the maintenance of the child. He had her carried into the temple of all the goddesses, and placed in the arms of Minerva, to whom he entrusted her education, asserting that Jupiter and he were equally fathers of Drusilla, and that he left the people to judge which she would have most reason to be proud of. It is certain that nobody had the least reason to doubt whether Caligula was her father or not. The signs of cruelty which soon appeared in this girl were a sufficient proof of it. Never was there seen so ill-disposed a child; a devilish sort of malice was soon per-

[1] Josephus. Suetonius. Dio.

ceived in her, and such an inclination to cruelty, that it was dangerous to let any children come near her; so much did she delight in scratching them, pulling out their eyes, and doing them all the mischief in her power.

As everybody knew that Caligula's love was nothing but caprice, and finished as brutally as it began, it was expected that his inclination for Cæsonia would soon give place to some other passion, and that he would get rid of her as he had done of her predecessors. But he was always constant to her, which made it generally believed that she had given him love potions; for he carried his love so far that he was not able to live a moment without her.[1] He gave her leave to distribute as she pleased the spoils of the Germans, whom Galba had defeated. He frequently spoke himself of the violent love he had for her, declaring that he was surprised at it; and in some of his fits of passion he was heard to say, that, rather than not draw the secret from her, he was determined to put her to the torture.

If Gaius's unaccountable passion for Cæsonia made it generally believed that he was out of his mind, nobody could have the least doubt of it, when they saw him commit such other follies, that the historians, who give us an account of them, would scarce be believed, if it was not well known that men are capable of all that is bad, when the Almighty abandons and leaves them to themselves. For, not content with being superior to the rest of mankind, he was resolved that nothing in heaven or earth should be above him; therefore he insolently determined to make himself a god, though guilty of actions that savoured less of the man than of the devil. This

[1] Pers. Sat. 6. 47.

foolish and wicked fancy gave the finishing stroke to his senses, and quite put an end to the little reason he had left. He commanded that he should be respected as a divinity, that everybody should prostrate themselves before him, and pay him adoration. Nor had he much difficulty in obtaining that from a people as much given to flattery as he himself was to pride and vanity. He often amused himself with sitting in the temples among the statues of the gods, and receiving the homage that was paid to him with the same deference as to the gods themselves; which impiety was no less dishonourable in the infamous courtiers who paid it him, than it was in him who required it. Sometimes he appeared with the ornaments belonging to the gods of fable; with wings, for example, on his feet and the wand in his hand, like Mercury; at other times, with a crown like the rays of the Sun, in imitation of Apollo; and often with a sword and buckler, like Mars. He frequently affected to whisper to the statue of Jupiter, and then pretended to listen to it, as if the god had been speaking to him, to show that the gods themselves looked upon him as their equal.

This mad and unaccountable pride inspired him with a violent desire to have his statue placed in the Temple of Jerusalem. He imagined that it would greatly contribute to his deification, and, knowing that the Jews would by no means suffer any image in their temple, he decided to use stratagem, and then to employ his authority to the utmost, but neither the one nor the other succeeded; he always met with in the Jews a resistance, which zeal for their religion rendered so invincibly obstinate, that neither threats nor promises could prevail upon them to admit of a novelty so monstrous, and so contrary to their law. All these difficulties did not discourage him: but, still persisting in the resolution of being a god, he called Jupiter his brother, and invited the Moon, when it was at the full, to come and lie with him, declaring that she was his wife. Sometimes he would threaten Jupiter, saying, "Either kill me, or I will kill thee." At last, being persuaded that he was a god, he caused a magnificent temple to be built in honour of himself, in which the victims that were offered up to him consisted of the most rare and costly birds. Priests were instituted to him on purpose, amongst whom Cæsonia was consecrated a priestess. He was resolved to increase the number of them, and, by the most ridiculous imagination in the world, he caused his horse Incitatus to be also made a priest; a worthy pontiff to such a divinity! This, however, was not the only honour that he conferred upon him; he often invited him to supper, and commanded his oats to be given him in a golden manger. He fitted up a house for him with the richest furniture, and appointed officers of his household, assigning him revenues wherewithal to entertain splendidly the guests that should be invited to eat at his house; and, that his Incitatus might pass through all the grades of office,[1] he determined to make him consul, degrading, by this contempt, the highest dignity of the Empire.

His cruelty carried him to excesses so great and barbarous, that Tiberius, in comparison with him, might pass for a mild and merciful prince. After having put to death Macro and Ennia, his wife, by way of recompense for having procured him the Empire, he sacrificed to his brutal fury Silanus, whose daughter he had married in

[1] Sueton. vit. Cai.

Tiberius's reign, and so, by an almost unprecedented inhumanity, he became the butcher of his father-in-law.
He compelled fathers to be present and look upon the
execution of their children, without permitting them to
shut their eyes, that they might be spared so dismal a
spectacle; and, as if he took a particular pleasure in violating the laws of nature, when one of those miserable
fathers, who had been ordered to see his son put to
death, excused himself on account of an indisposition, the
tyrant had the cruelty to send him a litter.

The greatest potentates were as liable to the effects of
his fury as the meanest people. Ptolemy, son of King
Juba, and cousin-german to his father, Germanicus, was
most cruelly and unjustly murdered. Mithridates, King
of Armenia, was thought to be very fortunate, when Caligula contented himself with only condemning him to a
rigorous banishment. All those who had been exiled
were put out of their pain by being speedily executed,
because, when the Emperor happened by chance to ask
one of the persons that had been long banished and recalled at the beginning of his reign, how he had employed
his time during his exile, the other imprudently answered,
that he had continually prayed for the death of Tiberius
and the accession of Caligula. Gaius immediately took
it for granted that all those whom he had sent into banishment were of the same mind, and wished for *his* death;
upon which ridiculous notion, he commanded them all to
be massacred. Cannius, the philosopher, was so bold as
to speak to the Emperor with a little more liberty than
ordinary, for which he was ordered to prepare for death,
and was accordingly put to the sword; for Caligula was
never known to break his word upon such occasions.

The centurion, who came to conduct him to his execution, found him playing at chess, with all the calmness imaginable, and such as was worthy of his profession.

We should never have done, if we were to go into the particulars of his cruelties, which filled Rome with murders. But, though they were monstrous of their kind, and infinite in number, they could not satisfy his insatiable thirst after blood. He was frequently heard to say that he wished the Roman people had but one head, that he might have the pleasure of destroying them at one stroke. As to his abominable lewdness, it is not to be read or mentioned without horror, but what else could be expected from a prince that was born with the most vicious and depraved appetites? We can only add that a government, exercised with such insupportable insolence and barbarity, could not but give occasion to innumerable discontents and murmurings; nor were there wanting people enough who were resolved, at all hazards, to get rid of this monster, who was abandoned by those gods, whom he pretended to equal, and detested by all mankind, whom he ruled with tyranny and oppression. Many conspiracies were formed against him, which, being either premature or ill-concerted, were discovered, and expiated by the death of their authors; but Cassius Chœrea and Cornelius Sabinus conducted theirs with so much cunning and secrecy, that Caligula received at their hands the just reward of his wickedness.

The news of his assassination filled Rome with joy, but people were apprehensive that it might not be true. To put the matter beyond all doubt, the centurion Lupus hastened to the palace, where he found Cæsonia and the princess Drusilla, her daughter, weeping over the bleeding corpse of Caligula. Cæsonia showed the excess of her grief by abundant sighs and tears, and by deploring the misfortune of her husband; she bitterly lamented his obstinacy in not taking the advice which she said she had often given him.

These words were variously interpreted. Some imagined [1] that she had advised the Emperor to shed no more blood, but to affect, at least, some sentiments of humanity for the future. Others, on the contrary, were of opinion that [2] she had got some intelligence of the plot, and had told the Emperor that there was no way of preventing its consequences, but by putting all the conspirators to death. Be that as it may, on Lupus [3] making his appearance before Cæsonia, bathed in tears, she entreated him to come near and assist her in paying the last duty to the Emperor's body. But, being conscious at the same time that Lupus was come with another design, she at once altered her tone, and, putting on a firm and bold countenance, prepared herself for death, entreating him to deprive her of a life that was already odious to her. Lupus, who came with no other intention, did not keep her long in pain. He ran her through the body with his sword; and afterwards seizing the young princess, dashed out her brains against the wall, with a barbarity that agreed very well with his name.

[1] Joseph. Antiq. Judaic. lib. 19.   [2] Sueton. vit. Calig.
[3] Dio. lib. 59.

VALERIA MESSALINA

WIFE OF CLAUDIUS

HERE are vices as well as virtues that seem hereditary in families; and the bad examples of parents have sometimes a sort of contagious effect upon their children. A lady, whose works have been much admired by the public, has very justly observed that a coquettish mother seldom has daughters who are remarkable for their virtue. Valeria Messalina is an unfortunate example that sufficiently justifies the truth of this maxim. She was the daughter of a vicious woman, whom she not only imitated, but surpassed in all manner of debaucheries. Her whole life was one continued series of crimes and most shameful impurities. Her prostitutions were infamous, public, and detestable. The most brutal pleasures were what she most delighted in, and the most horrible vices showed themselves to her under the most charming and delightful forms. Virtue was the only object she looked upon with horror, and her reputation was the thing in the world she set the least value upon. She forgot her dignity, her birth, and the natural modesty of her sex, as well as the fidelity she owed her husband, in order to abandon herself to brutal passions, without the least regard to decency, without fearing to

incur the punishment of such of her predecessors as had pursued the like courses, without dreading either the censure of the world, or the anger of Claudius the Emperor. Never was seen such an utter contempt for shame and modesty as in her.

She was the daughter of Valerius Messala Barbatus and of Lepida, who was accused of magic as well as prostitutions, and of having had incestuous intercourse with Ahenobarbus, her brother. From this impure source sprang Messalina, who was married to her cousin Claudius, who had had four wives before, namely, Æmilia Lepida, whom he divorced without cohabiting with her: Livia Medullina, who died the very day of her marriage: Plautina, by whom he had Drusus, who, a few days after his betrothal to the daughter of Sejanus, was choked by an accident; for, as he was amusing himself with tossing up a pear and catching it in his mouth, it got so far down his throat, that he died before any relief could be had; he had, besides Drusus, a daughter called Claudia, whom he exposed quite naked before her mother's door, upon a well-grounded suspicion that he was not her father: for much the same reason, he put away Plautina, in order to marry Ælia Pætina by whom he had Antonia; her he also divorced, that he might marry Messalina, his relation, who was by much the worst of them all. He was then only a private person; he had by her a daughter called Octavia, afterwards married to Nero, and a son called Britannicus, who was born on the twentieth day of his reign.

Messalina had naturally such a violent passion for gallantry, that it was a very difficult matter for her to keep within the narrow bounds of marriage. She had beauty enough to procure gallants, and too little virtue to let them suffer long; so that she was guilty of innumerable transgressions of that sort, besides cruelty and avarice, to which she was as much inclined. Her power was equally fatal to all that were chaste and rich. The depravation and corruption of her heart excited the one, and her insatiable love of money caused her to practise all manner of cruelty against the possessors of it in order to gratify the other. Debauchery and avarice were, then, the two centres round which all the desires and actions of this Empress turned. It is hard to conceive the miserable conditions of an Empire that is governed by a woman, who has nothing at heart but the gratification of her appetites, whose violence, meeting with no resistance, spreads their indiscriminately fatal influence upon all those whom her caprice inclines her to persecute. For Messalina could not have carried her impudence and tyranny to such lengths, if they had been opposed at first; but, her crimes being in a manner permitted, she was encouraged to go on in the same course. So true it is, that there is nothing so bad but a wicked heart is capable of it, when suffered to proceed without control.

Claudius was made Emperor in a tumultuous manner by a body of soldiers, who thought proper, of their own authority, to advance him to the throne. He was seized with a panic at the sight of this confused multitude, which he imagined was come to kill him. He was heavy and stupid, too thoughtless to mind his wife's conduct, and too timid to punish her irregularities; of an easy, indolent temper, and entirely taken up with the pleasures of the table and gaming,[1] never troubling his head about his domestic affairs nor those of the Empire, which seemed to him an insupportable burden, and which he chose rather to lay upon his freedmen, a gang of base, artful, and self-interested wretches, to whom he entirely abandoned himself, and who, having infinitely more at heart their own private advantage than the honour of their master, made him do whatever they pleased, in such a manner that Claudius was less their sovereign than their slave.

This stupid indolence was the occasion of all Messalina's debaucheries. From hence proceeded all those horrible prostitutions and tyrannical cruelties, that made her so formidable to those who were rich or virtuous. At first she pretended to keep within certain bounds, and to be a little secret in her amours; but finding that nobody offered the least opposition, and that she might undertake everything without fear or reserve, she shook off shame and constraint, and indulged to the utmost her

[1] Gluttony was Claudius's predominant passion. He gave, almost every day, sumptuous entertainments in public, to which a vast number of guests were invited, frequently six hundred at a time. A story is told of Titus Vinius, of very noble family, who being one day invited to dine with the Emperor, got an opportunity of stealing a gold cup from the sideboard. Claudius was informed of this, and being resolved to mortify him for the theft, invited him to dinner again the next day with the same company, but gave orders that only earthenware vessels should be put near Vinius. This insulting distinction was taken notice of by all the guests, who were informed of the affair, upon which a great laugh was set up at poor Vinius's expense, and all eyes were fixed upon him. This was a greater mortification than any corporal punishment. It is reported that Claudius was so fond of lengthening out these entertainments, that, for fear any of his guests should be injured by the restraint they might be under in his presence, he resolved to publish an edict, by which everybody was permitted to break wind at table, having been informed that one of those who had been invited and had been detained a great while at table had been made very ill by not having that liberty.

infamous passions, which by degrees became quite familiar to her. This miserable habit rendered her mind impervious to all the reasons that might have persuaded her to observe some rules of decency; she therefore plunged into the most scandalous behaviour, which she carried to such a degree,[1] that the historians who have transmitted these facts to us own that posterity will hardly ever be brought to believe them.

She began her cruelties by the murder of the princess Julia, daughter of Germanicus and wife of Vinicius.[2] This lady, together with her sister Agrippina, had been banished to the island of Pontia by order of their brother Caligula, who deprived them of their liberty after having robbed them of their honour.

Claudius, their uncle, being touched by their misfortune, recalled them from exile, and restored to them their estates and all their former splendour. These illustrious persons appeared again at Court, where they held the rank that was due to their birth, their beauty, and their merit. The Emperor seemed to have a great regard for Julia, and it was observed that he did not dislike to be alone with her, and that they passed a considerable share of their time together. Messalina took these marks of the Emperor's complaisance for love, and was forthwith alarmed at it.[3] Claudius was weak and fickle; Julia handsome, and perhaps ambitious, and her charms were powerful enough to inspire the Emperor with an inclination to marry her. Messalina was apprehensive of this, and consequently looked upon Julia as her rival. She had also another reason to hate this princess. She was

[1] Tacit. Ann. 11. Sueton. vit. Claud. c. 22.
[2] Sueton. vit. Claud.   [3] Dio. lib. 60.

descended from the family of the Cæsars, and inherited
a sort of noble haughtiness,[1] which would not suffer her
to stoop to those base, unworthy flatteries that the Empress required (the ordinary steps by which people
climb up to favour), but which she never could submit
to. These were the true provocations; but the Empress
did not fail to accuse her of many crimes which could
not possibly be proved, for which, notwithstanding, Julia
was banished; and, soon after, her life was sacrificed to
Messalina's jealousy.

Seneca had also his share in the disgrace,[2] being accused of not having always behaved with the wisdom of
a philosopher with respect to the princess Julia, upon
which account Claudius banished him to the island of
Corsica. Seneca (Stoic as he was [3]) felt very sensibly
the shame and suffering of this exile, of which he preserved a bitter remembrance, which broke out into satires
and invectives against Claudius, as soon as the Emperor's
death had secured him from further mischief. Agrippina
very narrowly escaped the same punishment as her sister.
Messalina could not pardon her beauty and merit, but, on
the contrary, was resolved that her death should expiate
those heinous crimes; but that of Drusus's daughter seeming the more necessary of the two, she turned her
thoughts entirely to that.[4] This princess, who was called
Julia, and was also niece to Claudius, had the misfortune
not to be agreeable to Messalina, for which crime she was
soon put to death. It was this Julia who had contracted
so intimate a friendship with Pomponia Græcina, wife of
Plautius, who, seeing Julia treated with so much cruelty,

[1] Sueton. vit. Claud. [2] Tacit. Ann. 12. [3] Senec. Lud. in Claud.
[4] Sueton. vit. Claud. Dio. lib. 60. Tacit. Ann. 13.

broke her heart with grief, after passing her whole life in mourning and affliction, nourishing her melancholy in solitude, far removed from all pleasures and diversions, even the most innocent. This Pomponia was a lady of very great merit. Her conduct was always so regular and unblamable, that it was generally supposed she had embraced the Christian religion,[1] which the apostles St. Peter and St. Paul had already preached at Rome. In fact, she was accused of being inclined to the new and foreign superstitions, as they called the Christian faith.

Messalina, having thus cured her jealousy by the death of her that caused it, thought of nothing but how to satisfy her appetites. All those who had virtue enough to resist her infamous pursuits soon felt the effects of her cruelty; for she made no scruple to accuse them of treason or some horrid crime, upon which they were put to death without mercy. Appius Silanus was one of the first who died a martyr to his virtue. Claudius had married him to Domitia Lepida, his mother-in-law, and honoured him with his friendship and particular esteem; it must be acknowledged he was worthy of it, as well on account of his birth as his extraordinary merit, which had procured him the honour of having for his first wife Æmilia Lepida, grand-daughter of Augustus. Silanus, who was universally esteemed, had the misfortune to be agreeable to Messalina, who, regarding nothing but her brutal passion, was not ashamed to make him advances to which he had the greatest aversion.

He represented to her that, being so nearly related to her as he was, he could not comply with her unlawful desires, without being guilty of the greatest crime; but

[1] Baron. ad Ann. Ner. 3.

this had no effect upon Messalina. The most powerful considerations are of no weight, when nature and temperament are to be forced. The Empress, whose violent desires were increased by difficulties, redoubled her efforts in proportion to the resistance she met with. Silanus was victorious in this conflict, and Messalina had the mortification of having employed all her threats and promises to no purpose. This was sufficient to enrage the Empress beyond all bounds. She could not be so keenly disappointed and affronted without being full of indignation. She swore to destroy Silanus, and thereby make herself amends for the scandalous steps she had taken without success. She took care not to appear in this affair herself, but committed the management of it to Narcissus, who was entirely devoted to her, and who was full of expedients when a piece of work of that sort was in hand.

This freedman, who was become exceedingly powerful by his immense riches, which he had amassed by theft and rapine, and by being the scourge of all those that had money, whether at Rome or in the provinces, readily fell in with Messalina's design of ruining Silanus, whose virtue she had not been able to overcome; and because no crime could justly be laid to his charge, they were forced to have recourse to calumny and artifice. Narcissus came one morning very early into the Emperor's chamber, with a melancholy countenance, which he well know how to put on, and after a good deal of sighing and lamenting the evil things he had to foretell, declared to Claudius that he had dreamt he saw the traitor Silanus plunge his dagger into the Emperor's heart.

Messalina, upon this, pretended to be extremely terrified, and protested that she had frequently dreamt the same thing of late. Claudius, who was very weak and foolish, fell at once into the snare that was laid for him. He was immediately seized with a panic, the more so because, at the very time when Messalina and Narcissus were acting their part so well,[1] a person came to inform the Emperor that Silanus was at the door. This was true, for by a diabolical stratagem, orders were sent him the night before to be at the palace early in the morning, which command Silanus was obliged to obey. Claudius no sooner heard of his being there, than (being already frightened at what had been told him) he was convinced of the truth of it, and no longer doubted of his being come to put his wicked designs into execution. Fear would not permit him to weigh and consider the matter, nor to examine whether Silanus was really guilty or not; for he ordered him to be killed that moment. This stupid prince imagined he owed his life to Narcissus, and expressed great indebtedness to him, for that he was (sleeping as well as waking) solicitous for his safety and welfare. He was not ashamed to go afterwards to the Senate, and give them a tedious account of the whole affair.

Silanus's murder served as a sad warning to all honest and good people, how precarious their lives were under this phantom of an Emperor, who served only as the instrument of which Messalina and his wretched freedmen made use; and the misfortune of Silanus gave them sufficient warning of what they were to expect. To prevent this, they determined to deprive Claudius of the throne which he filled so unworthily, and formed themselves into a conspiracy, wherein many senators and

[1] Sueton. vit. Claud.

people of distinction were concerned; and, that a person
of weight and consideration might be at the head of
them,[1] they chose Furius Camillus Scribonianus, governor
of Dalmatia, who had a considerable army under his
command. This general, flattering himself with vain
hopes and expectations of nothing less than the throne,
permitted the troops to salute him as Emperor, the
grandeur of this high dignity concealing from him the
danger to which he exposed himself.

As this hazardous affair was undertaken with precipitation, and conducted without prudence, it came to nothing.[2] Camillus and his accomplices, knowing Claudius to
be extremely timid, contented themselves with writing
him a letter, full of threats and reproaches, insolently
ordering him to quit the throne which he was totally unfit
for, and re-assume his private capacity. This ill-con-
sidered design was fatal to all those who were concerned
in it, so that Camillus's joy was as short as Claudius's
fear; for, just as he was deliberating with the Senate
whether he should submit to Camillus, the news arrived
of the conspiracy having broken up of itself, the soldiers,
from religious scruples, refusing to obey their comman-
ders, though they had taken the oath to the new Emperor;
for, when they attempted to take the colours from the
place where they were fixed in the ground, nobody was
able to remove them. As they were very superstitious,
this intimidated the legions,[3] and they immediately concluded that the gods were adverse to their acknowledging
the usurped authority of Camillus, and so they abandoned
him. He immediately fled to an island, where he was

---

[1] Tacit. Ann. 12.   [3] Tacit.
[2] Dio. lib. 60. Sueton. vit. Claud. 35.

killed in the arms of his wife Junia, and expiated his rashness by a tragical end; which may serve as a lesson to
ambitious people, to teach them that reason ought to
banish from their minds those false notions of grandeur,
which vanity and pride are apt to encourage, and that an
untimely end is generally the fate of those, whose foolish
ambition leads them to rebel against the lawful authority.

In the meantime the conspirators were diligently
sought after; and this plot furnished Messalina and Narcissus with an opportunity of gratifying their greed and
cruelty; for, affecting an extraordinary zeal for Claudius,
they filled Rome with murder and destruction, so that the
town had never groaned under so cruel a scourge. Riches
became fatal to all those that were possessed of them;
witnesses were suborned to prove them guilty of treason,
their estates were confiscated, and very often they were
put to death. Nothing was heard of but horrible torments and bloody executions, so that none were safe but
the poorest class of people. All the families of distinction were reduced to the most shameful misery; for the
extortions and rapines of Messalina and Narcissus were
a flame that could never be extinguished but by a shower
of gold. One might then see Roman knights [1] and Senators put to the torture, notwithstanding their rank and
dignity. In short, matters were come to such a pitch of
misery, that great numbers preferred to kill themselves
than continue to live in such a condition. Cæcina Pætus
was one of that number, being encouraged thereto by the
example of Arria, his wife, who, seeing him hesitate
about it, plunged a poniard into her own breast before his

---

[1] Dio. lib. 60.

face, with such a firmness of soul, as was much admired in those days, and still makes a great noise in history.[1]

Messalina, rendered more insolent by the failure of the conspiracy, and by the full liberty she had of practising her wickedness, indulged still more her vicious appetites, which were now carried to the utmost excess. Being intoxicated with her power, which was formidable to all the world, she imagined that everything ought to give way to her, so that she thought the least resistance intolerable. In the number of her paramours were Proculus, Urbicus, Trogus, Calpurnianus, captain of the guards, Rufus, the senator Vergilianus, Montanus a Roman knight, Cæsonius, and multitudes of others, whom a poet calls the rivals of gods.[2]

Plautius Lateranus was one of her gallants, as also the physician Valens, who prided himself much upon his eloquence. Vinicius was one of the few that did not carry his complaisance so far. He was of an illustrious family, which had given several consuls to the republic. He possessed all the qualities that were necessary to make an honest man,[3] enhanced by a politeness and affability that gained him the esteem of all the world. Tiberius, who had honoured him with his alliance by marriage, also gave him many important offices; and

---

[1] Cæcina Pætus, a man of Consular rank, being implicated in the conspiracy of Scribonianus, was apprehended and brought to Rome, whither his wife also hastened after him, to try if it was possible to save his life; but finding that there was no probability of succeeding, she endeavoured to persuade her husband to prevent the torments that were preparing for him by a voluntary death. But perceiving that he had not the courage to deprive himself of a life which he was not, however, long to enjoy, she took a dagger and plunged it into her own bosom; then drawing it out, presented it to her husband, saying, very calmly, Pætus, it is not very painful. (Pæte, non dolet.)

[2] Juvenal. Sat. 6.   [3] Dio. lib. 60. Tacit. Ann. 15.

Caligula (whose odd and capricious temper it was no easy matter to please) could never find any fault with him, so judicious and blameless had his conduct always been. Nobody but Messalina was capable of depriving the Senate of one of its most illustrious members. This Empress, who put no limits to her pleasures or desires, being hurried on by her brutal passions, made advances of gallantry to Vinicius, which were not received as she wished and expected. She found in this worthy senator that goodness which she had divested herself of. He was too virtuous to defile the bed of his Emperor, and therefore constantly resisted her attempts, and nobly despised her threats; but it cost him very dear.

A woman who has had the weakness to offer favours which have not been accepted, is extremely to be feared. She is capable of all the cruelties with which the desire of vengeance can inspire her. As she cannot bear the sight of the man to whom she would have prostituted her honour and her person, she thinks of nothing so much as of ruining one who she imagines eternally reproaches her with her infamous behaviour. Both sacred and profane history furnish us with abundance of examples of what a woman thus disappointed is capable of. Joseph lost his liberty for having preserved his chastity inviolable. He was deprived of his offices, and shut up in a frightful dungeon, for having virtuously opposed the impudent and earnest solicitations of Potiphar's wife. And the Empress [1] Mary of Arragon, wife of Otto III., caused a young count of her Court to be cruelly put to death for having been more faithful to his prince than she was to her husband. He would never commit the crime to which

---

[1] Crispin in Othon. 3 Sigon.

she had long solicited him, which provoked her so much, that she herself accused him to the Emperor of having attempted to seduce her. That over-credulous prince condemned him, too hastily, to have his head cut off; but, soon after that was convinced of the injustice he had done him.

Such was the fate of Vinicius; he survived his victory but a very little time. Messalina, to whose power every thing yielded, not at all ashamed of having taken such scandalous measures, but enraged at their having been unsuccessful, and not being able to endure that her impudent behaviour should be continually reproached by his virtue, had him put to death. He was poisoned by her order, and was a tragic instance of the danger there was in disobeying her.

All that has been said of this Empress is but a sketch of her abominations, which were without number. She was not content with being plunged in the grossest and most infamous debaucheries (such as prostituting herself to all comers,[1] without being ever able to satisfy her insatiable desires), but she must needs have companions in her lewdness; and because example is of great force, and seems to authorise wickedness, she imagined that, if there were any other women who could be prevailed on to imitate her, it might in a great measure diminish the scandal. She tried persuasion, but finding that would not do,[2] compelled ladies of the highest quality in Rome to live with her in that shameful state of libertinism; and, because that was not sufficient, she determined to carry her brutality as far as it would go, and therefore obliged these ladies to prostitute themselves to the greatest de-

[1] Xiphilin. in Claud.   [2] Aurelius Victor; Epitome in Claud.

bauchees that could be found, and that in the presence
of their husbands, who had to be spectators of their own
infamy, and very often accomplices and consenters to it,[1]
for she heaped favours and rewards upon all such as
approved of these abominable prostitutions; while, on the
contrary, those who refused to be witnesses of their
shame, were sure to die martyrs to their bashfulness and
modesty. At last this monster of impurity, being weary
of all sorts of vices of the ordinary kind, for which she
had no longer any relish, resolved to invent something
new, to gratify, if possible, her unbounded lewdness. To
this end she ordered a chamber in the palace to be fitted
up on purpose to be the scene of these abominable prostitutions, where the chastity of the most distinguished
ladies in Rome was to be violated. On the door of this
infamous place she caused to be written the name of the
most notorious courtesan of the town, whom she person-
ated, and was the first to prostitute herself promiscuously
to every man that pleased to come, and that every night,
making a most shameful profit of her crimes, and brutally
exacting the price of those favours she granted so easily,
never retiring till morning.[2]

Here amazement seems to be exhausted; for it cannot
be conceived how these things (which were so notorious
and public that the most distant nations were not ignorant
of them) should have been unknown to Claudius only,
and that the Emperor had nobody about him sufficiently
devoted to him to inform him of the horrible debaucheries
of his wife. It is true that he was so stupid and weak,
that Messalina made him believe whatever she had a

---

[1] Juvenal. Sat. 6.
[2] Et lassata viris, nondum satiata, recessit. (Juvenal. ibid.)

mind to, easily destroying the effect of what any body told him to her prejudice. She had gained such an ascendency over him, that nobody durst trust him with a secret upon which his life depended, being assured that, as she governed him so absolutely, she would soon extort it from him; for she had the secret of making him approve of everything that she did, even of her prostitutions.

This was evident in the affairs of Mnester, the most famous dancer of his time. Messalina, who had long since acquired a front of brass, not knowing what it was to blush, and always running after new pleasures, was so furiously in love with him, that she erected statues in honour of him at the Emperor's expense, which were so many monuments of her impudence as well as of the Emperor's weakness.

But, however ardently and earnestly she solicited Mnester to show the same complaisance to her that so many others had, she always met with a resistance that was not to be overcome, which did not proceed from his virtue, but from his fear of being one day punished for his rashness. Messalina was not discouraged; she pressed the comedian, caressed him, threatened him, and in short, attacked him in so many forms that, being at last conquered by her importunities, he promised to do whatever she pleased, if the Emperor consented.

To insist upon such terms as those was (one would imagine) to require impossibilities, because one must be out of their wits to suppose an Empress could carry her impudence so far as to hope for her husband's consent in such a case. But these conditions, however extravagant and difficult in appearance, cost Messalina no trouble at all. She went directly to Claudius; and after a thousand deceitful caresses which she bestowed upon him, complained that, having sent for Mnester upon some trifling business, he had refused to obey her: she dwelt much upon the contempt people showed for her orders, and pretended to be much afflicted at it, beseeching the Emperor to give directions that more respect should be paid her for the future. Claudius, who was stupid and foolish in the highest degree, was immediately convinced of the reasonableness of her words; he sent for Mnester, and commanded him to obey the Empress in every particular. Such a positive order cured Mnester of his scruples, and dissipated all his fears. He became Messalina's gallant with the approbation of Claudius, which approbation he did not fail to take advantage of afterwards.

This dancer, however, was not over faithful to Messalina, for he was also beloved by Poppæa. The Empress, being desirous to keep her gallant to herself, was no sooner informed of this intrigue, than she made up her mind to destroy her rival. This lady was remarkable for her extraordinary beauty, to which none could be compared but that of Sabina Poppæa, her daughter, who was much handsomer, and at least as debauched as the mother, as if it had been decreed that all of that name were to be lewd and beautiful.[1] She was accused of living in criminal intimacy with Valerius Asiaticus, a senator of great distinction, who had been twice consul. This was the crime with which Messalina reproached Poppæa, and she was the more zealous in this affair, because, in the same accusation, she contrived to involve Asiaticus,[2] that she might have an opportunity of seizing on the famous gardens of Lucullus, which he was in possession of, and

[1] Dio. lib. 60.   [2] Tacit. Ann. 11.

which she had long coveted. Thus her jealousy and
avarice were both concerned in the destruction of Poppæa
and Asiaticus.

Suilius and Sosibius, tutors of Prince Britannicus,
joined with her in this piece of iniquity. Those venal
wretches accused Asiaticus of having committed adultery
with Poppæa; and, because Messalina was ashamed to
punish in others what she had been so often guilty of
herself, this accusation was corroborated by another of
greater importance. Asiaticus was charged with having
persuaded the garrisons of Germany to revolt, and with
promising to put himself at the head of them. The
calumny was carried yet further; it was said that Asiaticus had been the author of Caligula's murder, and that he
had boasted of that horrid assassination. Messalina
could not possibly have been better served, nor could her
wicked agents find out a more plausible pretence for
Messalina's vengeance and persecution, than that of
bringing to justice a person who had murdered an
Emperor.

Asiaticus, upon this, was arrested at Baiæ; he was
loaded with chains, brought to Rome, and conducted to
the Emperor's palace to be tried. As he was innocent of
all these crimes, he appeared before the Emperor with
such an assurance as always accompanies a good conscience. He vindicated himself so effectually, by proving
the falsehood of this charge, and putting to confusion
one of his accusers, by reproaching him with the heinous
crimes he had been guilty of, that the Emperor, being
convinced of his innocence, showed a great disposition
to pardon him. Messalina herself (cruel and implacable
as she was) could not forbear showing some signs of hu-

manity upon this occasion, and was not able to hear him justify himself with so much strength and eloquence, without shedding tears. But her compassion soon gave place to her covetousness; and, as she was not a person to be wicked by halves, especially when the question was to gratify her darling passions, she charged Vitellius (as she went out of the Emperor's chamber, where this farce was acted) to be sure not to let the pretended criminal escape. Messalina could not have given this commission to a man more capable of executing it; she was well acquainted with his character, for he had frequently given her sufficient proofs of his abilities in cases where baseness and perfidy were necessary. This corrupt and flattering courtier, seeing that Claudius hesitated whether he should condemn or acquit Asiaticus, approached the Emperor, and with diabolical malice affected a false compassion for the prisoner, with whom he said he had always lived in the closest friendship. He mentioned everything in his favour that he thought capable of touching the Emperor, and dwelt upon the many considerable services he had rendered to the state, particularly to Claudius's family, and afterwards, shedding some artificial tears, entreated the Emperor, in the name of Asiaticus, to give him leave to choose what kind of death he liked best, since he desired no other favour.

Claudius, believing that Vitellius spoke thus at the instigation of Asiaticus, granted his request. The unfortunate senator, being thus condemned, chose to be bled to death, and so had all his veins opened, after protesting that it would not have grieved him so much to have lost his life by some of Tiberius's artifices, or the cruelty of

Caligula, as by the cunning stratagems of a wicked woman, and a number of vile mercenary sycophants.

Poppæa did not long survive Asiaticus, for Messalina so terrified her with threats, that she chose rather to die once for all by her own hand than remain in continual fear and apprehension. The accusers of Asiaticus, who had not prosecuted him for nothing, were amply rewarded for their pains. Crispinus, captain of the guards, received a great sum of money, together with the insignia and privileges of the prætors, for having arrested him at Baiæ. Messalina made Sosibius a very considerable present, and the best posts in the Empire were bestowed upon Vitellius, who preserved them by the same methods by which he had acquired them, that is to say, by all sorts of baseness and wickedness, and especially flattery, which he carried so far as to carry always about him [1] one of Messalina's shoes, which he was not ashamed to kiss continually in public, as if it had been something sacred.

After all that we have said of Messalina, it might have been thought impossible for her to go to greater lengths in wickedness than she had hitherto done, and that there was no crime left for her to commit; but we have yet one to speak of, which was without example. She took it in her head to marry publicly Gaius Silius, with whom she was excessively in love, and so to have two husbands at once. Silius belonged to one of the most illustrious families of Rome, and never was there seen a handsomer man. He was appointed consul for the next year. His wife was Junia Silana, a lady of great distinction and merit, and Messalina, in pursuance of her ridiculous

[1] Sueton. vit. Vitell.

scheme, obliged him to put her away, in order to supply her place.

Though this shameless Empress had long since bid adieu to every pretence of decency, yet she could not but foresee that this monstrous marriage must needs make a great noise throughout all the Empire. This reflection induced her to prepare people's minds for a thing so extraordinary, by introducing [1] the custom of women having several husbands. She imagined that, however strange it might appear at first, example would soon authorise and make it familiar, and that nobody could reasonably blame her for doing what many others did as well as she. But afterwards, considering that people would never be reconciled to such a novelty, because of the great and many inconveniences it must be attended with, and being weary of ordinary pleasures, which were become insipid by being so easily obtained, she was resolved not to deny herself any longer the satisfaction she hoped for from this marriage, but to carry it out, let what would happen, without giving herself any trouble about the consequences, not doubting but she should get over it as she had done in the case of innumerable crimes of which she had been guilty. Taking it therefore for granted that there was nothing too difficult for her to perform, she heaped all sorts of favours, riches and honours upon her new husband that was to be. The servants of the Emperor, as well as the most magnificent and costly furniture in the palace, were all sent to Silius's house, and nothing was wanting but the title of Emperor.

Silius, however, in the midst of all this pomp and splendour, was far from being easy in his mind; he foresaw the

[1] Tacit. Ann. 11. Xiphilin. Suet. vit. Claud.

Roman Courtesans

From the painting by Georges Rochegrosse

peril to which he exposed himself by this rash and hazardous enterprise. Fear of punishment made him even hesitate for some time between duty and ambition; but at last he shut his eyes against all danger, whether it was that he hoped, by some means or other, to escape the chastisement he deserved, or that he was apprehensive of being ruined if he should disoblige Messalina, or, in short, that, being weary of a private life, he was resolved to obtain the throne if possible. Be this as it may, he was the first to press Messalina to conclude the marriage, and to celebrate it publicly.

All the usual solemnities were strictly observed. The contract was drawn up in due form.[1] Witnesses were called in to sign it; the solemn clause (that they were married to have children) was not forgotten; but the miracle of all was, that Claudius signed the contract himself, Messalina making him believe that all this was being done only to avert from him certain misfortunes with which he was threatened (and which were foretold would befall him) in order to make them fall upon Silius. A visit paid by Claudius into the country a few days after gave them an opportunity of celebrating their nuptials with great magnificence; Messalina appeared dressed like a bride and sacrificed to the gods for the prosperity of her marriage; and, after a superb entertainment which she gave the guests, at which she was placed (according to the custom of the ceremony) next to Silius, to whom she showed all the marks of tenderness and affection that she could have done if he had been her real husband, she retired to her new husband's house, and lived with him as intimately as if she had been with Claudius.

[1] Tacit. Ann. 11.

This story would certainly pass for a fable, if the veracity of those who have transmitted it to us could be called in question; and Tacitus, who is one of them, says he is persuaded that posterity will not easily give credit to it. But what is most wonderful is, that Claudius, who was then at Ostia (whither Messalina excused herself from going on pretence of some indisposition) knew nothing of what had taken place, though everything was done in presence of the three orders; and in all probability this piece of unprecedented assurance would have passed unnoticed as the rest had done, if Narcissus had not taken care to inform the Emperor of it.

This favourite, as well as many of the other freedmen, had abandoned the interests of Messalina, after she had put to death one of their fraternity named Polybius, whom she had formerly loved but too well. This was looked upon by them as a specimen of what they had to fear, and united them against the Empress, upon whose friendship they saw plainly they could never depend. They therefore resolved to ruin her, and waited only for a fair opportunity of doing it effectually. Callistus, Pallas and Narcissus in particular thought it incumbent on them to inform the Emperor of this marriage of Messalina with Silius, for fear he should come to know of it by some other means, and then they would have been liable to punishment for so criminal a silence; besides, they plainly saw their lives were not in safety if Silius should succeed in his enterprise. Pallas and Callistus, however, soon changed their opinion, and were determined to try if it was not possible to prevail on Messalina to return to her duty, and break off her infamous commerce with Silius. This resolution was as soon

abandoned as taken, and another was adopted. On the
one hand, they were convinced of the absolute power the
Empress had over Claudius, and that she could make him
believe what she pleased, if she could but be admitted to
speak to him a moment; and on the other hand, being
persuaded that, as she had been accustomed all her life
to such unbounded libertinism, it was absolutely impossible for her to break herself of it, they resolved not to
meddle in it one way or the other: Pallas, because he was
afraid of undoing himself in endeavouring to ruin the
Empress; and Callistus, because he knew, by the long
experience he had gained in the preceding reigns, that the
sure way of maintaining one's power and influence in
Courts is by practising the arts of dissimulation, and not
presuming to give advice. Thus these self-interested
and base favourites preferred their safety to their duty;
the fear of losing their fortune quite silenced them, and
they thought it the best way to leave the management of
this affair to Narcissus.

As for him, he persisted in his design of informing the
Emperor of the marriage of his wife with Silius; and his
only care was, how to keep it secret from Messalina.[1]
Claudius had two concubines, who were more in his good
graces than most other people, who, being flattered and
caressed and promised great rewards by Narcissus, undertook to disclose the affair to Claudius. They went to him
at Ostia, and throwing themselves at his feet, told him,
with seeming fear and consternation, that Silius, who
was become husband to Messalina by a monstrous and
treasonable impudence, thought of nothing less than de-
throning him; that at Rome everything was in confusion,

[1] Tacit. Ann. 11.

and that Silius was practically Emperor; to which they added, that Narcissus had charged them with this commission. Claudius, struck with astonishment and fear, sent for Narcissus, who was also at Ostia, and interrogated him as to this marriage. This was what he expected; so, affecting a melancholy countenance and voice, he confessed that hitherto indeed he had concealed from him the horrible adulteries and prostitutions of his wife with Valens, Plautius, and innumerable others, to whom she had entirely abandoned herself, thereby affronting her husband and her Emperor in the most insulting and outrageous manner; he had been unwilling to acquaint the whole Empire with the shame and disgrace which this abominable and scandalous behaviour brought upon Cæsar's family; and besides, he had still entertained hopes that Messalina would repent of her wickedness; but, since the dishonour was now public, and Messalina showed no signs of repentance, and he himself desired to be acquainted with his wife's conduct, he was no longer at liberty to disguise the truth, nor to conceal the Empress's marriage with Silius, which had been celebrated in the most solemn manner before the whole city. Geta, captain of the guards, and Turranus, superintendent of the corn supplies, confirmed what Narcissus had said; and in short, everybody advised the Emperor to provide for his safety. The Emperor was at first so terrified, that he thought himself ruined beyond redemption. He made what haste he could to camp, but, not thinking himself safe there, enquired every moment whether Silius was yet Emperor.

In the meantime Messalina, being intoxicated with her wild and disorderly pleasures, was in the house of Silius, her new husband, with whom, in spite of all the crimes she was guilty of, she enjoyed herself as calmly as if she had nothing to fear. She had assembled a troop of favourites and women as debauched as herself at a masquerade. They celebrated the feast of Bacchus with all the impure ceremonies and infamous gestures which were practised at the Bacchanalia. Valens was one of this disgraceful party; and this vicious physician, having climbed to the top of a high tree, cried out that he foresaw some dreadful calamity that was to happen to them from Ostia. This was literally verified, for, soon after, the people came from all parts to give them notice that Claudius, being fully informed how matters were, was coming from Ostia to punish the horrid behaviour of his wife as well as that of her wicked accomplices. Cæsar's approach struck this insolent company with such panic, that they all fled different ways. Messalina retired into the gardens of Lucullus, of which she had robbed Asiaticus; and Silius, affecting a false security, went to the council to perform the functions of his office, though in reality his apprehensions were as great as the danger that threatened him.

As for Messalina, she was indeed terribly alarmed, but yet did not despair of extricating herself, if she could but speak a few words to Claudius, so much did she rely on his stupidity. This would not be the first time she had got out of danger by making notorious lies pass for truths. She had the secret of lulling him to sleep by her artful caresses, which seldom failed of producing the designed effect.

In order to move him to compassion, she sent Britannicus and Octavia to meet him, and entreated the great

vestal Vibidia to accompany them.[1] She herself followed
on foot from one end of Rome to the other, abandoned
by everybody, for none were touched with her misfortunes, on account of the abominable life she had led. At
last finding, at the farthest gate of the town, a gardener's
cart, she got into it, and went to meet the Emperor, whom
she hoped to mollify if she could possibly secure an audience. Narcissus, who knew very well of what importance it was that she should not see Claudius (who in that
case would certainly have pardoned her) very cunningly
contrived that they should not meet. He took care to
accompany the Emperor in his coach, and talked of
nothing all the way but Messalina's prostitutions.
Vitellius and Cæcina, who were also in the coach, kept a
profound silence, and spoke not a word either for or
against her, that they might not incur her displeasure if
she came off victorious, and also that it might not be said
they approved of her debaucheries, if they undertook to
justify her.

At last Messalina appeared, and loudly insisted that
the mother of Britannicus and Octavia should have an
opportunity of speaking to the Emperor. This was a
critical moment for Narcissus, and it is certain that his
fate and that of Messalina depended on that instant.
This subtle courtier, who knew the importance of it, did
all he could to hinder the Emperor from hearing her,
and amused him with reading memoirs which contained
the history of Messalina's conduct, until she and her
children were left far behind. Vibidia, however, notwithstanding all Narcissus's endeavours, found means to
speak to Claudius. She represented to him with great

[1] Tacit. Ann. 11.

freedom, that he ought not to take for granted all that had been told him of Messalina; that these reports were so many impostures which her enemies had invented to blacken her in his opinion, and ruin her. That at least it was but reasonable she should be heard before she was condemned. Narcissus, who was afraid this vestal might change the Emperor's mind, which he knew was irresolute enough, interrupted her abruptly, and told her that Messalina would be heard, but that a vestal as she was should mind her own business.

Claudius was all this while quite dumb, and, to see him, one would have imagined that he was in no way interested in what passed. But as soon as he arrived at Rome, Narcissus very cunningly conducted him to Silius's house, which he found magnificently adorned with the most sumptuous furniture of his palace, which had belonged to the Drususes and Neros, his ancestors. He then fell into a rage proportionate to his shame, and immediately ordered Silius, and some of the other seducers of Messalina, to be put to death. Lateranus owed his safety to the merit and services of his uncle, and Cæsonius was pardoned for reasons that modesty will not permit us to mention, and for which he deserved, long ago, to have lost his life.

Mnester pleaded the absolute command of Claudius to obey Messalina in every particular; and protested that he should never have been guilty, if he had not been so by order of the Emperor; that, being forced to obey, he became a criminal with regret and by necessity, far from having those ambitious and self-interested views which Messalina's other lovers had, who only dishonoured the

Emperor with an intent to aggrandize their own families, or to gratify their passions.

Claudius was a little staggered by these reasons, and without doubt would have pardoned Mnester, if all the freedmen had not represented to him, that he ought not to forgive a crime in him that had cost so many others their lives, and that death ought to expiate his assurance in having defiled the Emperor's bed; since, in fact, he had committed adultery with Messalina, whether it was by his consent or by force; so he underwent the same fate as the rest.

While all this was going on, Messalina, who had retired to the gardens of Lucullus, was in terrible agitation. Sometimes she despaired of being ever able to obtain her pardon, and at other times flattered herself that she might probably obtain forgiveness by the help of those caresses that had so often re-established her in the good graces of Claudius. It is certain that, if Narcissus had not hastened the death of the Empress, and thereby put it out of Claudius's power to forgive her, he would have done it; for having returned to his palace, and finding a good supper served up, he forgot, over his cups, all he had been told of Messalina, and commanded that somebody should go and tell that miserable wretch (that was the term he made use of) to come and justify herself the next morning.

The Empress's vindication of herself would infallibly have brought about her acquittal and the ruin of her accusers. Narcissus was persuaded that his life depended on the death of Messalina, and that he should be undone if she was admitted to an audience of the Emperor, because he knew that Claudius would never have the resolution to condemn her if she made her appearance before him, in which case she would have found no difficulty in making him believe whatever she pleased; he therefore resolved to risk everything. He went out of the Emperor's chamber, and meeting some centurions, ordered them in the Emperor's name, to go and put Messalina to death; and Euodus, a freedman belonging to Claudius, was commanded to assist at the execution. They went immediately to the gardens of Lucullus, where they found Messalina lying upon the ground in such circumstances as would naturally have excited pity. Lepida, her mother, was with her, not being willing to quit her in her misfortunes, though the Empress had behaved very undutifully to her in her prosperity. Her mother, knowing how many and heinous her crimes had been, exhorted her to anticipate, by a voluntary death, the cruel one, which no doubt was preparing for her. But Messalina, who had been so long accustomed to pleasure and vice as to be utterly incapable of any sentiments of honour (for suicide was so accounted among the Romans), could do nothing but shed tears, and bewail her miserable condition.

In the meantime the soldiers broke open the doors of the garden, and the captain presented himself before her without speaking a word. Euodus, who had been a slave, did not show her the same respect, but on the contrary, affronted her in the most outrageous manner, brutally reproaching her [1] with all the shameful actions of her life, and insulted her with a rudeness that was worthy of his former condition. This treatment soon gave the Empress to understand that there was no hope left for

[1] Tacit. Ann. ii.

her. She attempted to kill herself with a poniard, which her trembling hand frequently applied to her bosom, but as often refused to do its office; but the centurion, without waiting any longer, spared her the trouble, and ran his sword through her body.

Claudius was at supper when the account of her death was brought him. The messenger did not inform him whether she had died by her own hand or another person's, nor did he give himself the trouble to ask any questions about it; on the contrary, as if they had told him the most indifferent news in the world, he called for some wine, and continued to eat and drink very heartily. The next day he showed no tokens either of joy or grief; nay, so great was his stupidity, and so little did he remember what had happened, that one day being at table, he asked why the Empress did not come.[1]

Such was the miserable end of Messalina, whose life was one continued series of monstrous crimes. And here it must be observed, that she was massacred in the gardens of Lucullus, which she had violently taken away from Asiaticus, and in order to obtain them, had most barbarously murdered him.

[1] Sueton. vit. Claud.

AGRIPPINA

SECOND WIFE OF CLAUDIUS

OT one of the Empresses has made more noise than Agrippina. Everything connected with her was remarkable; her birth, her beauty, her faults, her good qualities, and her misfortunes. She was daughter of Germanicus,[1] the delight of the Roman people, and of Agrippina, granddaughter of Augustus, who was delivered of her in a town which was afterwards called the colony of Agrippina, and now Cologne. She was observed to have a double tooth on the right side, which Pliny looked upon as a certain presage of great fortune.[2]

Agrippina had received from nature all the advantages of body and mind, that would have rendered her a most accomplished princess, if she had not degraded them by making a very bad use of them. Her beauty [3] yielded to none in Rome. She had a majestic air, noble manners, and a lively and enterprising intellect, capable of the greatest undertakings, which she gave proof of in the refined vigour of those curious memoirs, which she composed upon her own adventures,[4] and which were of no small service to Tacitus, the historian, when he wrote

[1] Tacit. Ann. 12.
[2] Plin. hist. nat. cap. 8.
[3] Xiphil. in Claud.
[4] Voss. de Hist. Lat. I. 1.

his Annals. But, on the other hand, her avarice was insatiable,[1] her jealousy such as made her capable of the most cruel revenge; and especially, her ambition was without bounds, which was the principal, and perhaps the only cause, of all her crimes and misfortunes. Daughter, sister, niece, wife and mother, of Emperors or Cæsars,[2] from her cradle she had so violent a desire to rule, that she could set no limits to it. This vice was so ingrained in her very nature, that it corrupted all her actions, and produced in great abundance all sorts of crimes.

Agrippina was brought up with her grandmother, Antonia, who, by her irreproachable conduct, might have served her as a model of virtue; but this excellent[3] princess, who educated the children of her son Germanicus along with her own, and endeavoured to inspire them with sentiments of honour and goodness, soon perceived that all her labour was in vain. She had the mortification of finding her granddaughters capable of the most infamous actions, at an age when they could not be thought susceptible of any passions; but vice made its appearance before their reason began to dawn,[4] and they sullied their tender years by committing the most horrible incest with their brother, Caligula; so true it is, that modesty, prudence, and virtue, are not always the fruits of birth, good example, or instruction; it is too often seen that these virtues are more owing to constitution than anything else.

Agrippina was very young when her mother brought

---

[1] Plin. lib. 7. c. 8.

[2] Agrippina was a great granddaughter of Augustus, granddaughter of Agrippa, daughter of Germanicus, wife of Claudius, sister of Caligula, and mother of Nero.

[3] Eutrop. Suet. vit. Cai.   [4] Dio. lib. 59.

to Rome the ashes of Germanicus, which melancholy
sight opened afresh the wound which the death of that
accomplished prince had made in the hearts of the Romans, and did not a little contribute to the extraordinary
affection which they had, and always preserved, for his
children.   Tiberius, jealous as he was of the merit of
this great man (and of whose death he was not innocent) yet affected a deep sorrow for his death, which he
pretended to regret as much as possible, and, taking upon
himself the care of his children, invited Gaius Caligula
to live with him, and, as soon as Agrippina was of a
proper age, married [1] her to Domitius Ahenobarbus.

This nobleman, besides his illustrious birth, had the
honour of being related to Cæsar's family, and therein
consisted all his merit; for, excepting that, the sun never
shone upon a more wicked man.   He was perfidious,
brutal, cruel, stained with murders, adulteries, and even
the most horrible incest with his sister Lepida, in short
he was loaded with all sorts of crimes.[2]   He owned,
himself, that from his marriage with Agrippina, nothing
could ever spring but what would be pernicious to the
republic; and, in fact, no good was to be expected from
the union of so detestable a man and a woman,[3] whose
vice and lewdness might be dated almost from her cradle.

This prediction was but too well verified by the birth
of Nero, who was born at Antium, and came into the
world feet foremost.   He was the cruellest scourge that
could afflict the Empire.   His parents deliberated a great
while what they should call him, and Agrippina having
desired Caligula, who reigned at that time, to give him a
name, the Emperor, out of derision, would needs have

[1] Tacit. Ann. 4.   [2] Sueton. vit. Ner.   [3] Plin.

him called Claudius, because he was then the sport of
the Court.[1]   This vexed Agrippina extremely, and she
had him named Domitius after his father.

As Agrippina had started with committing incest, nobody could expect that she would prove an example of
chastity; neither did she belie the bad opinion that
everybody had of her, for she lived with her brother
Gaius in disgraceful intimacy.[2]   Tigellinus was banished
for having carried on an amour with her, and Lepidus,
her cousin-german and brother-in-law, was, according to
Dion, put to death for having received criminal favours
from her.

Lepidus, without doubt, did not deserve less punishment, for he was bound to Agrippina by so many ties,
that he ought to have behaved more honourably towards
her; this, however, was not the fault that made him so
blamable in the eyes of Caligula; for the Emperor, in
putting him to death, intended to punish his ambition
more than his debaucheries; since Lepidus designed to
pave himself a way to the throne through Agrippina's
means,[3] and she endeavoured to make Lepidus her friend
with the same view.   This design cost those who were
engaged in it very dear, for Lepidus lost his head,[4] and
Agrippina had the mortification of being forced to carry
the urn, wherein were enclosed the ashes of her lover,
upon her shoulders, from the place of execution to Rome.
This was not the only suffering she underwent; Gaius, being disgusted at her and her other sister, railed at them
most bitterly, reproached them with their shameful and
scandalous crimes, published their love letters, which

[1] Suet. vit. Ner.
[2] Tacit. Ann. 14.
[3] Rutil. in itiner. Lepid.
[4] Dio. lib. 59.

informed the whole city of their intrigues, and banished
them to the island of Pontia, after having consecrated,
to Jupiter the Avenger, three poniards, which he pretended they had prepared in order to assassinate him.

The death of Caligula put an end to Agrippina's exile.
Her uncle Claudius recalled her and her sisters, and restored to them all that their father (who was dead) had
bequeathed them, and which Caligula had seized upon.
It did not appear that Agrippina's banishment had in the
least diminished her ambition, which was still predominant; on the contrary, the magnificence and splendour
of the Court increased her thirst after power to such a
degree, that she set no bounds to it. This devouring
passion extinguished the few sentiments of honour she
had left, so that she resolved to employ all sorts of
means to advance her fortune. The first project thought
of was to try all possible arts to make the Emperor, her
uncle, in love with her. With this view, she took care to
display all her charms, which this weak prince was the
more susceptible to, as she did not fail to heighten them
by such artful and engaging ways, as few people would
have been able to resist, and of which she was perfect
mistress. Claudius had not penetration enough to see
into her intentions, being too stupid to comprehend that
all this was practised to further some deep design. This,
however, was not the only method Agrippina took to
obtain her ends, for her policy soon suggested other
ways. She was apprehensive that she might not be able
of herself to gain her point, for which reason she thought
it necessary to look out for a husband capable of giving
her all the assistance she stood in need of, and who had
ambition and courage to seize the Empire in case of

Claudius's death. Galba seemed a very fit person for
this purpose; the important offices he held, his high
birth, and great reputation, made him of importance at
Court, and in the whole Empire. But, as he responded
but indifferently to her advances, she turned her thoughts
in the direction of Crispus Passienus. He had neither
the nobility nor the power of Galba; but, to make
amends, he was extremely rich, and she did not doubt
but this treasure would be of great service to her in her
chief scheme; for at all times money has been the chief
motive in important undertakings. She married him, but
knew how to get rid of him, as soon as she had possessed
herself of his wealth. This furnished her, very opportunely, with the means of gratifying her taste for luxury
and appearing everywhere with distinction, which, till
then, she had not been able to do, because she inherited
but the third part of her first husband's estate, which was
but small. The figure she now made brought her into
great repute at Court; but on the other hand it alarmed
Messalina, and it was not very safe to provoke her.
Agrippina, who had too much sense not to be aware of
what she was exposing herself to, chose rather to dissemble than risk her life. She accordingly decided to
affect great reserve and circumspection, when she was
with the Emperor, and before witnesses, reserving her
flatteries and caresses, which were scarcely ever innocent, for private opportunities.

It was not only with regard to Claudius that she was
prodigal of her favours, for she bestowed them very
liberally upon all who could be of any service to her in
her projects, and was not long before she reaped the
fruits of them; for, after Messalina's death, Callistus,

Narcissus and Pallas were each of them determined to have the honour of procuring the Emperor another wife. The three favourites had so completely got over Claudius, that he had neither power nor resolution to oppose the will and pleasure of these insolent ministers, who, having the sovereign authority thus vested in them, ordered everything as they pleased, without respecting the laws of the Emperor, who blindly gave in to them in all sorts of affairs; and they took care to keep him in this state of indolence, that they might have the sole direction and management of everything. Pallas was his steward, Narcissus his secretary, and Callistus gave answers to the petitions that were presented to him. In these three important posts, they became a scourge to the whole Empire, for, as they had raised themselves by all sorts of base actions, they performed the duties of their respective offices with the greatest insolence. People were obliged to pay them, with all possible deference and respect, that homage which was not given to the Emperors themselves without great regret. It was to them that the most considerable of the senators, as well as all others of the highest quality, paid their court assiduously, and in the most servile manner, to preserve their substance and their lives; for they were become the arbiters of everyone's fortunes. Children did not enjoy the inheritance of their parents, except when they were pleased to permit it. All the provinces groaned under the weight of the taxes they laid on them, only the least part of which was brought into the Emperor's coffers. Their houses were filled to overflowing with the wealth which they had acquired by rapine and oppression. In short, they knew so well how to fatten themselves at the expense of others, that they were each of them richer than Crœsus.

After Narcissus and Callistus had recommended to Claudius, the one Petina, and the other Lollia, Pallas spoke for Agrippina. We have already noticed the reasons he alleged in her favour; they were such as determined Cladius to prefer her to the other two; but there remained one obstacle, and that was the near relationship that existed between them, for it was quite a new thing among the Romans for an uncle to marry his niece; such an alliance was always reckoned the forerunner of some misfortune to the Empire; for which reason it would never have been agreed to by Claudius, if Vitellius, the most servile wretch in the world, had not helped him to get over all scruples, with his usual artifice and cunning.

This flattering courtier, perceiving that the Emperor hesitated about concluding his marriage with Agrippina, because of the nearness of their relationship, represented to him that there was no need of all these difficulties, for that sovereign princes had nothing to do with the laws that were made for private persons; and that, for reasons of State, the ordinary rules and customs were frequently to be dispensed with; if he still persisted in these scruples, he advised him to leave the matter with the senate, the proper interpreters of the law, and if they decided in favour of the marriage, there could no longer be any room for doubts. Claudius consented to this proposal, and the senate was assembled for that purpose. Vitellius did not fail to hasten thither, and as soon as the affair was brought forward, exaggerated the necessity of the Emperor's taking another wife to assist him in his domes-

tic affairs,[1] that so he might be more at leisure to attend
to those of the Empire. He added, that in his opinion
there was no occasion to deliberate a moment upon the
choice of a proper person, since Agrippina was the only
one that could reasonably be proposed to him, because
of the great qualities that Cæsar's wife ought to be possessed of, and which were not to be met with but in her.
As to her being the Emperor's niece, no great stress
ought to be laid upon that, the marriage being necessary
for the good of the State, to which the laws should always give place. It would not be the only case in which
things of that nature had been permitted, since formerly
the marriage of cousin-germans was forbidden, and yet
at present nothing was more common. The senate
passed a decree conformable to the advice of Vitellius
and the inclinations of Agrippina, who now became the
wife of Claudius, and was advanced to that throne, which
she had so ardently wished for. She signalised the beginning of her reign by an action that was agreeable to
all the orders of the city; this was the recall of Seneca,
the philosopher, from the banishment to which Claudius
had condemned him (for a crime which was not very
consistent with the gravity of his profession) and his
appointment as tutor of Domitius. This was highly approved of by all, for Seneca was in great reputation at
Rome; and everybody was in hopes that the young prince
(being formed by so skilful a master) would have no
other sentiments than those of honour and moderation.

Agrippina's advancement obtained for her no less than
absolute power, and she thought of nothing but the
means of preserving it; the methods, however, which she

[1] Tacit. Ann. 12.

adopted, were always either cruel or shameful. She
kept all those in a servile and dependent state who were
not important on account of their influence or their
offices. She persecuted those whom she imagined she had
any reason to be afraid of, and who could not be prevailed upon to espouse her interests. She won over (by
granting the most criminal favours) such as by their
power and authority at Court might be any hindrance to
her vast projects; those who had resolution enough not
to regard her threats, had very seldom virtue enough to
resist her charms,[1] so that, between her power and her
beauty, she gained all her points.

This success only served to make her more haughty,
and the Emperor, after becoming her husband, became
her slave. She governed this weak prince so completely,
that she disposed of everything according to her own will
and pleasure. If she had favours to confer, she neither
minded birth nor merit, nor anything but the attachment
that people had to her person; the result of which was,
that the highest offices were bestowed upon upstarts, who
had never been known or heard of before, except for
having been guilty of some notorious crime, which had
procured them her esteem. As for virtue, it remained
in obscurity, because it was sure to meet with no recompense. People were admitted into the senate who possessed neither honour, nobility, nor merit, and at the
same time the descendants of those patriots and senators
who had been the ornaments of Rome, were languishing
in misery and contempt; so that the most honourable
governments and offices of the Empire were disgraced
by the meanness and baseness of those who were exalted

---

[1] Xiphilin. in Claud.

to them; and those glorious ornaments, which formerly were never granted but to the greatest and worthiest of men, were now prostituted to the vilest wretches and such as had been slaves.

To render service to the State was no longer the way to advance one's fortune; nor was the conquest of provinces, the winning of battles, or any such like exploits, the road to preferment in these miserable reigns; but it was by committing the blackest crimes that men attained to the dignity of prætor, censor, or consul, which glorious and honourable posts could now only be obtained by treasons, calumnies, murders and perjury.

But the most deplorable circumstance was, that the senate, being chiefly composed of low, servile people, approved (by shameful decrees) of all that the Emperors, or rather their minions, were pleased to do. What they did in favour of Pallas will be sufficient to show to what a miserable state of servitude this venerable body was reduced, which was formerly so respected and so jealous of its liberties, that it was not able to endure the least encroachments of the first Emperors, but was now obliged to yield to every honour and caprice of a shameless woman, and the vilest wretches in the Empire.

Thus Rome, after having groaned under the tyrannical government of Messalina, fell under that of Agrippina,[1] who was not less cruel, nor less covetous, nor perhaps much less shameless. There was indeed this difference between them, that, whereas the former dishonoured her husband and the Empire by prostitutions, to which she was hurried by an invincible inclination to lib-

[1] Xiphilin. in Ner.

ertinism, the other was only guilty when her interest made it necessary.   Messalina boasted of her debaucheries; Agrippina, on the contrary, disguised hers under the veil of a grave and demure countenance.   In short, Messalina was bad through her natural disposition, the other through policy; for she only bestowed her favours upon those who could forward her ambitious views and promote the advancement of her son, which was the favourite project that employed all her thoughts, and for the success of which she took infinite pains, though it was foretold her that he would repay them with horrible ingratitude; for, having one day consulted the Chaldæans as to the fate of her son, the soothsayers answered that he would be Emperor, but that he would put her to death.   The unfavourable part of this prediction certainly counterbalanced, at least, what was agreeable, and Agrippina had no reason to be overpleased with it; however,[1] the joy of having her ambition gratified would not permit her to reflect upon the evil which threatened her, but turned her thoughts entirely upon that which indulged her vanity; she was so transported that she cried out, "O, let my son kill me, provided he reigns."

As soon as Agrippina imagined her authority and power were sufficiently established, she turned all her thoughts to satisfying her vengeance.[2]   Lollia Paulina was the first victim that was sacrificed to it; and we have already seen that the jealousy of this Empress was only appeased by the death of her rival.   Calpurnia, a very illustrious lady, and of the highest quality, paid for the praises that Claudius one day bestowed upon her

[1] Dio. Tacit. Ann. 14. Sueton.   [2] Xiphil. in Claud.

beauty at the expense of her life; and all those whom
Agrippina found amiable enough to please the Emperor
became the objects of her hatred and persecution.

Her covetousness was also the occasion of her committing great cruelties: she suborned false witnesses
against those whose riches she could not obtain by other
means; and, however innocent people were, they were
soon thought criminal enough, if possessed of great
wealth; nor was it possible for anybody to save their
life, but by relinquishing their estates to the greediness
of Agrippina. Statilius Taurus [1] incurred the implacable
hatred of this Empress by refusing to give up all his
fortune to her. He was the son of that Taurus who had
the honour of being twice consul, and who so remark-
ably displayed his magnificence in the noble amphitheatre,
which he built at an enormous expense in Augustus's
reign. He owned gardens which he reckoned the finest
in Rome, and which he kept in excellent order. Agrippina had long earnestly coveted these gardens, but not
having a lawful pretence to seize them, she had recourse
to her ordinary means, calumny and oppression.

The Court was full of those venal mercenary wretches,
who were capable of all manner of wickedness, when it
became necessary to advance their fortunes, so that there
was no need of Agrippina giving herself much trouble
to send a man for her purpose: Tarquinius Priscus soon
relieved her of all anxiety upon that score. This villain
had been lieutenant to Taurus, when he was proconsul of
Africa; and, though he had been a constant witness of
Taurus's mildness and integrity in the exercise of his

[1] Tacit. Ann. 12.

government, he did not scruple to accuse him falsely of corruption and even of magic.

Taurus, who was perfectly innocent, was so astonished to find that the very person was become his accuser, who was best able to justify him, if he had been attacked by another, that he was not able to bear such an instance of perfidiousness and ingratitude: he chose therefore to anticipate what he took for granted would be the judgment of the senate, and in a fit of despair deprived himself of that life, which in all probability they would have spared; for they were so firmly persuaded of his innocence, that, notwithstanding all the influence and interest of the Empress, Priscus was deprived of his office, and ignominiously expelled from the senate. This was not the only punishment he underwent, for, soon after, being himself convicted of rapine, extortion, and other crimes,[1] he was condemned to suffer the penalty of the law in cases of that nature; and the remembrance of his conduct towards Taurus made all the world rejoice at his execution.

Agrippina was extremely piqued and mortified at the misfortune that had befallen this man, who had only turned false accuser at her request, and to do her pleasure; but what happened to Vitellius, her chief favourite, affected her still more. He was accused by Junius Lupus of having dared to carry his ambition so far as to look at the throne with a wishful eye, and to entertain hopes of seizing the Empire. Claudius, who was timid, jealous, and suspicious, listened very attentively to this accusation: but the Empress, who had her own reasons for protecting Vitellius, very warmly espoused his interests.

[1] Tacit. Ann. 14.

She at first had recourse to tears and entreaties, but proceeded at last to threats, to oblige the Emperor to pardon him. She succeeded in her undertaking: Claudius believed everything that she had a mind he should believe, and Vitellius was acquitted. Junius, his accuser, was banished; for Vitellius, out of his good nature and compassion, desired that no other punishment should be inflicted on him.

All these successes encouraged Agrippina to carry her schemes still further; and that her son Domitius might be as nearly related as possible to Claudius, she formed a design to get him adopted by the Emperor, though he had his son Britannicus, a young prince of great promise. Pallas employed his influence to bring this about; and in order to gain his point, he had only to speak the word. Domitius then became Cæsar's adopted son, and was called Nero. The people, who approved of this piece of injustice, applauded it heartily, saying that the Emperor had done very well to associate with himself a partner in the government, who might share its fatigues with him. Praises in abundance were bestowed upon Nero, and Agrippina was honoured with the title of August.

Claudius soon contrived that his favourite Pallas should be rewarded for the step he had made him take; and this deserves to be related, because it shows what a pitch the stupidity of the Emperor, the insolence of his freedmen, and the senility of the senate had reached. A decree had been passed against those women who prostituted themselves to slaves. Claudius gave out that this salutary law had been made at the instigation of Pallas. Borea Soranus and all the other senators proposed that Pallas (by way of recompense for the extraor-

dinary services he had rendered the State) should be
entreated to accept the prætorian insignia,[1] that he
should have the privilege of wearing the gold ring, which
belonged to the knights, and that he should be presented
with a sum amounting to about seven hundred and fifty
thousand livres. This modest slave, as Pliny calls him,[2]
accepted the honours, but refused the money. Claudius
went to thank the senate for their liberality; and told
them, that Pallas, with great gratitude, accepted the
honour of the ring and the prætorian insignia, but desired to be excused as to the money, being resolved to
continue in his ancient poverty. This consisted in being
possessed of only fifteen millions of livres.

Such commendable moderation procured him new
honours. Scipio proposed that he should publicly receive
the thanks of the senate, for that, being descended from
the kings of Arcadia, he should forget the grandeur
of his extraction, and stoop so low as to sacrifice himself
to the welfare of the public, and condescend so far as to
accept office under the Emperor. Pallas, in order to
transmit to posterity this instance of his extraordinary
modesty, ordered that, in his epitaph, it should be inserted that, the senate being inclined to make him a
present of a considerable sum of money, he was content
with having deserved it. It is difficult to say, which is the
more capable of arousing the indignation of the reader,
the provoking insolence of this rapacious villain, or the
shameful baseness and senility of the senate, reduced to
the miserable and hard necessity of prostituting to a ras-
cal that deserved to be hanged such honours and praises
as would have been too glorious even for the most vir-

[1] Tacit. Ann. 12.   [2] Plin. lib. 2. epist.

tuous and illustrious Romans. To this poor and despicable condition must all those expect to be reduced, who
sacrifice their honour and duty to their fortune and
ambition.

That of Agrippina [1] was not yet satisfied, neither by
the magnificent titles which were heaped upon her, the
exalted station to which she was raised, nor the extraordinary advancement of her son, who was now within
measurable distance of the throne. On the contrary, all
this only served to augment her pride. She now resolved to omit no opportunity of showing to all the
world what a pitch of grandeur she had attained. She
went to the Capitol in a superb triumphal chariot, which
till then had been a privilege belonging only to things
sacred. She never honoured the public assemblies or
temples with her presence except in a rich and most
magnificent coach, passing through the streets with a
pompous and numerous equipage, loaded with jewels, and
clad in a robe of cloth of gold, the sumptuousness and
splendour of which wonderfully set off her beauty: never
had there been seen such pride and haughtiness.

She was not content with displaying all this magnificence before the inhabitants of Rome, but also resolved
to give strangers and foreign kings an exalted idea of her
splendour and authority. She commanded that the capital of the Ubians should be called after her name, and
sent a colony thither. She showed herself one day,
seated upon an elevated throne, between the Roman
standards and the eagles, where she received the
homage [2] and submission of Caractacus, general of the
troops of Britain, who, accompanied by his wife and

[1] Xiphilin. in Ner.   [2] Tacit. Ann. 12. c. 37.

brothers, came to return her thanks for his liberty. And, to make it appear that her interest and power did not consist only in a brilliant exterior, but in a real and solid authority, she opposed the Emperor's favourites in the affair of the Jews against the Samaritans. And, though Claudius had issued a decree in favour of the latter, Agrippina, who espoused the cause of king Agrippa, who interested himself for the Jews, had it revoked, and obliged the Emperor to issue one in favour of the Jews, on purpose to show that her solicitation was not to be resisted.

The report of the absolute power that Agrippina had acquired over the Emperor (of which she gave such manifest tokens), soon reached the most distant nations; and all countries strove with each other, which should pay her the most profound respect; so that not only the great men of Rome, but those of the whole world, endeavoured to give her all possible tokens of their entire submission. The most curious and magnificent presents were sent her from every corner of the earth; and among the rest, a nightingale as white as snow, which cost an immense sum, and a blackbird,[1] that spoke as distinctly as a man; a rarity that had never been seen before. Claudius, who did not know all that Agrippina was capable of, gave encouragement to her enterprises by his indolence and blind condescension to her will and pleasure, without reflecting that he acted against his own interests; and she depended so much on his stupidity, that there was nothing so difficult that she did not hope to succeed in it. She procured her son the privilege of wearing the *toga virilis,* long before the time allowed

[1] Plin. Hist. Nat. lib. 10. cap. 59.

by the laws, and also that of standing for the consulship
in the twentieth year of his age: she prevailed upon
Claudius to give him leave to exercise the power of pro-
consul outside the city. She caused to be distributed
(in the name of this young prince) a largess or present
of money to the soldiers and people, in order, by means
of this generosity, to diminish the affection which they
had for Britannicus and prejudice them in favour of
Nero. In short, she caused him to be declared prince of
the Roman youth. And, that the magnificence of his
apparel might be of a piece with his pompous titles and
all the rest of his grandeur, when the ceremonial games
in the Circus were performed, Nero appeared most sump-
tuously adorned with a triumphal robe, whilst Britannicus, on the contrary, was only clothed in his prætexta, a
distinction that was thought very unjust, and caused
many officers to reflect upon the hard usage which the
Emperor's son met with. This compassion proved fatal
to them; for all those who showed any tenderness for
Britannicus were dismissed from their employments, and
others, more devoted to Agrippina, put in their places.
Geta and Crispinus were the first who were punished for
showing some tokens of pity and affection for that poor
prince. The Empress took from them their commissions
as captains of the guard, and those two offices were com-
bined in one and disposed of in favour of Burrus,[1] who,
indeed, was perfectly skilled in the art of war, but knew
very well from whom he received it, and upon what conditions it was given him.

Thus Agrippina, with great cunning and art, greedily
seized upon every opportunity of showing her son to

[1] Tacit. Ann. 12. cap. 42.

advantage, in order to make him acceptable to the legions
and the people; but nothing could have happened more
luckily for him than a great scarcity of provisions, which
afflicted Rome at that time. Agrippina, to make the
evil appear greater than it was in reality,[1] stirred up, by
her emissaries, a sort of sedition, to intimidate the Emperor, who was then indisposed, and not able to apply
any remedy to this grievance. The people clamoured
importunately for bread, and assembled in great multitudes, the noise of which soon reached the ears of
Claudius, who being frightened by the bawling of the
mob, declared by a decree, which Agrippina dictated, that
they should address themselves to Nero, who was quite
capable of governing; and that, his own indisposition
not permitting him to take the necessary steps at this
juncture, he had reposed that trust in Agrippina's son.
Nero did not fail to make the most of the lessons his
mother gave him. He caused a great quantity of corn
to be distributed to the people, which he knew how to
find without much trouble, and afterwards went to the
Capitol, accompanied by the senators, to offer vows for
the Emperor's recovery, which was certainly the thing in
the world he least desired. Narcissus knew better than
anybody that this was only a trick of Agrippina. He
had thoroughly studied the Empress's temper, and consequently was not ignorant of the object of all her
schemes and designs. He had more than once hinted
them to the Emperor; for, being his secretary, he had
frequent opportunities of speaking to him in private.
For this reason Agrippina mortally hated this favourite,
whom she continually found in her way, and always

[2] Zonar. Tacit. Ann. 12.

inflexible; but not daring to attack him openly, because
of the power he had over the Emperor (which he sufficiently demonstrated in the affair of Messalina), she
was very anxious to find means of destroying him
secretly; and, for that purpose, endeavoured as much as
possible to give the Emperor a bad impression of him,
not directly, but with all the art and cunning she was
mistress of. This made her eagerly embrace the opportunity of prejudicing Narcissus, which offered itself in
the shame fight that was to be represented on the lake
Fucinus, and for which Claudius had prepared and armed
a hundred galleys. The borders of the lake and all the
neighbouring hills and mountains were covered with an
infinite number of people, that were come from Rome
and all the towns thereabouts, to be present at this
magnificent show. The Emperor,[1] clad in his coat of
arms, was seated upon a splendid throne that was erected
for him on an eminence, and Agrippina, most sumptu-
ously apparelled, upon another just by him. The battle
was fought without any bad consequences, but afterwards, the Emperor must needs have another performed
by people on foot, for which purpose bridges had been
thrown over the lake; Claudius had ordered a grand entertainment to be prepared, to amuse the whole Court, in
a place fitted up for that purpose, just at the mouth of
the lake, and on the very spot through which the water
was to run when let go; but the expected enjoyment
was changed into fear and dread; for, the bank being
cut to give the water of the lake a passage into a canal
that was dug to receive it, the water rushed out with such
violence, that it bore down all before it, so that numbers

[1] Dio. lib. 60. Tacit. Ann. 12. Sueton. vit. Claud.

of people were drowned; and such a panic seized the whole multitude, that those who were nearest the water side, in order to save themselves from the danger, crowded upon those that were next to them, and they again upon the next, with such terrible cries, added to the horrible noise of the water, that even those who were most distant were terrified beyond expression: never had there been known so dreadful a disaster.

Claudius, who was naturally fearful, was more alarmed than other people, and Agrippina, seeing him in this situation, laid hold of the opportunity to irritate him against Narcissus, upon whom she threw all the blame, because he was the person the Emperor had made choice of to manage the whole affair. She told Claudius that nobody was at fault but he, whose sordid avarice had prompted him to put into his own coffers the money that was destined for this representation; that, under an appearance of fidelity and extraordinary attachment to his prince, he was guilty of the most notorious rapine and extortion; that the provinces groaned under his oppressions, and that, though his riches were prodigious, yet they were not able to satisfy his insatiable covetousness.

Narcissus defended himself with a great deal of resolution. He accused Agrippina of being insupportably proud and ambitious. He plainly showed the Emperor that, if she hated him, it was not because he was rich, but because he would not join with her in her wicked designs, being too faithful to his master. Narcissus was certainly in the right, and was well persuaded that the aversion Agrippina had to him was due to that. He did not scruple to explain himself very freely upon that subject, whenever he was in the company of his intimate

From the painting by Georges Rochegrosse

A typical street scene in ancient Rome. The populace were not slow in following the example of some of the Empresses who set no bounds to the indulgence of their taste for flirtation

friends; and used to tell them that, whether Britannicus
or Nero was Emperor after Claudius, he was sure neither
one nor the other of them would suffer him to live long:
Britannicus would put him to death, to revenge that of
his mother; and Nero, because he would sacrifice him to
Agrippina's resentment; but that, whatever happened,
he thought the obligations he was under to the Emperor
would never permit him to betray his interests; that it
was from this motive that he had brought about the
death of Messalina, who dishonoured her husband by
her prostitutions, and for the same reason, he gave
Claudius notice of Agrippina's bad intentions in other
respects, adding that she did not lead an over chaste life.
He declared that it would have been safer for the Emperor to have let Messalina live, because, as she was
entirely taken up with her debaucheries, she had never
been guilty of forming any designs against her husband's
life; whereas Agrippina had already exterminated most
of Cæsar's family, and aimed at nothing less than advancing her posterity to the throne.

Claudius himself had formerly thought something of
the kind, and had been informed that Agrippina did not
conduct herself very prudently, for he had heard of
some of her gallantries and ambitious projects.   He
even one day in his cups ventured to say, that he suffered
the wickedness of his wives for a time, but that it would
fall heavily upon them at last.   These words were told
to Agrippina, who being apprehensive of undergoing
Messalina's fate, resolved to be beforehand with
Claudius, and get rid of him as soon as she could.   But
before she proceeded to this bold undertaking, she was

determined to sacrifice Domitia Lepida,[1] Nero's aunt, to her vengeance, whom she accused of practising magic, in order to compass the death of the Emperor's wife by her enchantments, and of having stirred up a revolt in Calabria to indulge her treasonable designs against the State.

Narcissus openly undertook to justify Domitia against these imaginary crimes, but Agrippina's authority prevailed against his solicitations, and Domitia was condemned to death. The interest that the Empress had in the destruction of this lady was soon discovered, and it was found out that Domitia, who was rich, had made Nero considerable presents from time to time, which so won his affections, that he expressed great love for his aunt, and at the same time kept away from his mother, who treated him rudely. This exasperated Agrippina against Domitia, of whose grandeur and beauty she was already jealous.

The Emperor, however, was afterwards informed, that Domitia had been condemned unjustly, and had perished through the artifice of Agrippina. He examined the behaviour of his wife, and reflected upon all that Narcissus had told him, which gave him so much uneasiness, that he imagined his health was much impaired by it, and went to Sinuessa to use the baths of that place; but he met with his death where he hoped to find his recovery, for Agrippina made use of that opportunity to poison him,[2] because she had not so many eyes upon her in that place, as she would have had at Rome. For this purpose, she made use of the famous Locusta,[3] and gave her orders to prepare a very active poison. This was

---

[1] Tacit. Ann. 12.   [2] Tacit. Ibid.   [3] Sueton. vit. Claud.

put into [1] a ragout of mushrooms, which Claudius was
very fond of; but because it operated but slowly, and the
Emperor was seized with vomiting, they were afraid it
would have no effect, so Xenophon, a physician, [2] who
had no scruples, and was entirely devoted to Agrippina,
pretending to assist the Emperor and facilitate his vomiting, put a feather down his throat, that was dipped in
so subtle a poison that he expired a few moments after.

Agrippina kept his death secret, until she had made
all arrangements in favour of her son. She assembled
the senate and the consuls, and ordered them to offer
vows for the Emperor's recovery; she heaped clothes
upon him, as if it were to keep him warm; and, carrying
her artifice further still, sent for the comedians to divert
him, pretending it was by the directions of the Emperor;
and, that nobody might inform Britannicus and Octavia
of the death of their father, she kept them shut up in a
room, where she pretended to make much of them, and
heaped upon them the feigned caresses of a tender
mother.

However, the report of Claudius's death was soon
spread about the city, and Nero, accompanied by Burrus,
showed himself to the soldiers, to whom he promised
great rewards, and they, hearing nothing of Britannicus,
proclaimed Agrippina's son Emperor. This hasty election was presently confirmed by a decree of the senate,
who issued another soon after, by which Claudius was
placed in the number of the gods. Nero, who knew that
Claudius had been poisoned with mushrooms, ever after
called them food for gods. [3]

[1] Dio. Xiphilin. in Claud.   [2] Aurel. Victor.
[3] Sueton. in Ner. 33.

Agrippina, seeing her wishes accomplished, thought of nothing but how to gratify her revenge; she fell furiously upon all those who had thwarted her designs, and from whom she apprehended she had anything to fear. Junius Silanus [1] was the first victim of her hatred. This prince, whom Caligula called the golden sheep, because of the sweetness of his temper, was great grandson to Augustus, and had been made proconsul of Asia. Agrippina dreaded him, on account of his high birth and the great love the people had for him; for they openly declared that he ought to be Emperor, that he deserved it, and was more capable of it than Nero, a young man without experience, who had obtained the reins of government by means of innumerable crimes that his mother had committed. Another reason induced Agrippina to destroy Silanus, which was the fear she was in lest he should revenge the death of his brother Lucius Silanus, whom she had put to death. These were his crimes, for which Agrippina had him poisoned, and was consequently delivered from her apprehensions.

Narcissus was the second person condemned. Agrippina hated him mortally, because she had always found in him a fidelity, that neither her threats nor her promises had ever been able to corrupt: a very scarce virtue, in an age when perfidiousness and treason never went unrewarded. Accordingly, as soon as Claudius was dead, Narcissus was arrested and kept in close confinement, where he languished in such extreme misery, that he was forced to put an end to his own life, though Nero had desired that he should be spared. A memorable example of the viscissitudes of fortune, who smiles only upon

[1] Tacit. Ann. 13. c. 1.

us for a time in order to humble and mortify us more
cruelly afterwards: or rather, a terrible lesson for those
bloodsuckers, who drain the people by their extortions,
and who are permitted by divine Providence to fall into
their original poverty! It is certain, that Narcissus did
not deserve a more happy end; and it was but just [1] that
he should die in poverty and misery, who had acquired
immense riches by robbing the whole world, and who,
by one continued series of rapine and extortion, had
heaped up more riches than Crœsus and the kings of
Persia.[2]

Agrippina had promised her resentment a great many
more sacrifices, but Burrus and Seneca did not always
approve of these violent measures, but opposed them as
much as was in their power. They were Nero's tutors,
and had an equal authority; and though they were of
different characters (Burrus being severe and Seneca very
mild) yet they were good friends, and acted in concert to
infuse good notions into his mind, and put some check
upon the Empress's ambitious career. Pallas was Agrippina's prime minister, who influenced her in all sorts of
affairs; and he who had so much abused the absolute
power that he had assumed in Claudius's reign, aspired
to the same degree of authority under Nero; but this
prince was not of a temper to be treated in such a
manner by one that had been a slave, and who was
insupportable to him from the arrogance and severity he
affected; besides, Burrus and Seneca could not bear that
anybody should claim to govern the Emperor but themselves. They looked upon the lessons that other people

---

[1] Dio. lib. 60. Sueton. vit. Claud.
[2] Juvenal. Sat. 14.

presumed to give him as an attack upon their privilege, for which reason they omitted nothing that could give Nero a bad opinion of him, and also resolved to humble the Empress, and to mortify upon every occasion as much as possible the woman who, in the name of her son, governed the Empire absolutely.

The first opportunity they had of doing this was the audience which Nero gave to the Armenian ambassadors, who were come to Rome, to discuss certain affairs of their country. The day being come when this ceremony was to take place,[1] Nero was seated on his throne for that purpose; and Agrippina, who looked upon her son's elevation as a work of her contrivance, expected precedence everywhere as formerly, and intended to sit upon the same throne with the Emperor. It would certainly have been a strange and unheard-of thing, if a woman had presided upon so remarkable and solemn an occasion; and the ambassadors, who had the highest idea of the majesty and grandeur of the Roman Empire, could not have been witnesses of the despicable state of slavery to which the people were reduced, without abating very much of the respect they had for the Romans, and forming notions very different from those they had conceived. Nero himself, whatever deference he had at that time for his mother, did not approve of this innovation. In the meantime, Agrippina advanced and nobody said a word: but Seneca,[2] seeing the scandal that the Empress's pride would bring upon the Roman Empire, advised Nero to come down from the throne, as if it were to receive his mother and do her honour: Nero did so, and, paying

[1] Xiphilin. in Ner.   [2] Tacit. Ann. 13.

her a great many compliments, found some pretence to
put off the audience to another day.

Burrus and Seneca, after this attempt of Agrippina's,
no longer doubted that she intended to govern the
Empire; they therefore united themselves more closely
together against her, and determined to take such
measures as should put a stop to her career; but they
did not exhibit good judgment, for they tolerated an
amour that Nero was carrying on [1] with Acte, who had
been a slave, in order to set this girl in opposition to the
haughty proceedings of the Empress, and by this ill-
judged complaisance, they caused a disastrous result, for
Nero was so captivated with her charms, that nothing
would serve him but marrying her, thereby trampling
under foot all manner of order and decency.

Agrippina felt that her influence and interest were very
much weakened by the favour this girl enjoyed; and
not being able to bear that her power should be diminished by a miserable concubine, broke out into the utmost
fury and rage against her son, which had not the effects
she had hoped; for, instead of lessening his affection
for Acte, it inflamed him the more; and, because Agrippina became every day more jealous in proportion to her
son's attachment to Acte, she carried her resentment so
far as to make use of the most abusive language to the
Emperor, which exasperated him to that degree, that
he quite lost all respect for her; and, that he might
render her odious to the people,[2] he pretended to have
a mind to quit the Empire, and retire to Rhodes, where
he said he could be quiet.   The quarrel between Nero

---

[1] Dio. lib. 61.   [2] Sueton. vit. Ner.

and Agrippina [1] furnished matter of laughter and mirth
to all Rome; for, in their wrath, they reproached each
other with certain truths that ought not to have been
mentioned, but with which the public was perfectly
acquainted.

As Nero, however, considered that for many reasons
it was incumbent on him to be upon tolerable terms with
his mother; he pretended to have nothing more to say
to Acte, and when he designed to make her any presents,
he desired his favourite Serenus to give them as from
himself. Agrippina, who was continually upon the watch
as to her son's conduct, was so far deceived that she
took this change in his behaviour to be owing to his
repentance, or the effect of a dislike he had taken to
his mistress; and, that she might cure him entirely of his
passion for her, did not spare either caresses or the most
shameful complaisance. She went further still, for, laying aside her usual pride and haughtiness, she condemned
her past conduct, and to show her son that she was determined to live with him for the future upon friendly
terms, she offered to serve him herself in his pleasures
and intrigues. But the Emperor, who could not trust to
her fair promises, was always upon his guard against
them, and knew that some deep design lay at the bottom;
so that, though he strove all he could to disguise his
real sentiments, it was not possible for him to wear a
mask continually, but now and then the truth would
break out; and Agrippina, who had a great deal of
penetration, soon perceived it, and could not forbear
complaining. This revived their first disagreement, and
the breach became wider than ever.

[1] Tacit. Ann. Dio. lib. 61.

Agrippina was the first who caused it to break out; for, Nero having sent her one day the most precious and costly furniture of the palace, as well as the magnificent robes and jewels that had belonged to the preceding Empresses, she looked upon it as a great affront, and said with an air of haughtiness and contempt, that she did not accept these things as a gift, but as a small portion of what he had received from her, since in reality he was beholden to her for everything he possessed.[1] These words were soon reported to Nero, and even represented worse than they really were. He was offended in the highest degree, and by way of being revenged, without directly attacking his mother, he dismissed Pallas from his office of treasurer.

This disgrace of this favourite of Agrippina (with whom she had a most intimate and shameful intercourse) wrought her up to the greatest pitch of rage and fury, so that she no longer kept any bounds. Nothing was to be heard but bitter complaints, which she thundered out continually in the palace, and threatened Nero that she would cause Britannicus to be brought into the camp and shown to the legions as lawful heir to Claudius, and then declared Emperor. She protested that she would reveal to the whole world the wicked means that had been made use of to place upon the throne her husband's adopted son, to the prejudice of him whose right it was; that she was well assured the troops would have more regard for Germanicus's daughter, than for Burrus, that man of yesterday, or Seneca, that infamous and venal wretch who had been banished, and who intended to usurp the government between them. After these

[1] Tacit. Ann. 13.

threats, she poured forth against Nero all the insulting and provoking language she could think of; she took it into her head to invoke the deified Claudius, and the ghost of Silanus; and, suffering herself to be transported with fury beyond all bounds, she laid hold upon the Emperor, and could scarcely keep from striking him.

Nero had never been in so much perplexity before. He was alarmed at the terrible threats of his mother, with whose temper he was too well acquainted to doubt whether she was capable of being as good as her word; he reflected upon all that she had said of Britannicus, who was already old enough to be very formidable, and to be well enough acquainted with his right to the throne which he had been robbed of. In fact, that young prince had given people to understand, that he was by no means ignorant of his claims,[1] for, as he and his companions were one day diverting themselves at a game in which a king was to be chosen to command the rest, when the lot had fallen upon Nero, he commanded Britannicus to sing a song, with a design of turning him into ridicule. Britannicus obeyed immediately and sang one much to the point, in which he said that by treasonable practices they had deprived him of his father's throne. This song, which seemed as if it had been premeditated, moved all the company, and particularly disconcerted Nero so much that, not doubting that Britannicus would soon carry these considerations much further, he resolved to put this dangerous rival out of the way.

Nero had another reason (such as it was) for being jealous of Britannicus,[2] which was as weak and unjust as it was ridiculous. The latter happened unfortunately

[1] Tacit. Ann. 13. c. 15.   [2] Sueton. vit. Ner.

to have a very good voice; and Nero, who must needs
pass for the best singer in the world, could not bear to
be outdone by Britannicus; so this poor young prince,
having become odious to the Emperor by his merit and
nearness to the throne, was poisoned.

Agrippina (to do her justice) was never suspected of
having had any hand in this horrid crime. The astonishment she was struck with, and the terror that seized
her when Britannicus dropped down dead suddenly, sufficiently justified her in that respect; and, to say the truth,
she had but too much reason for her apprehensions; for,
in losing Britannicus, she lost her best support, and the
only person by whose means she hoped to maintain her
authority, which was already declining.

Being destitute of this resource, she thought it expedient to show favour to such people as she hoped had
any friendship for her, and to enter into private cabals
with them. She was very affable to the captains, centurions, and all such as had any influence or authority,
as if she had determined to make herself the head of
a party, and become formidable to Nero; but he, who
no longed kept any restraint in regard to her, soon penetrated her designs; and, in order to render them abortive,
deprived her of the usual guard that had always attended her, as mother and wife of the Emperor. He
caused her to be lodged in Antonia's house, where he
visited her but very seldom, and always with a considerable escort. He carried his severity further still, for
he obliged her to quit Rome,[1] and gave her a very indifferent house outside the city, whither he sent people

[1] Sueton. vit. Ner. 24.

on purpose to insult her brutally, and who affronted her in every shape they could think.

From this moment the scene was quite changed with Agrippina;[1] all her grandeur vanished; her influence and authority sank to nothing. This idol, that had been worshipped by all the world, received no more homage or flattery; there did not remain the least trace of her dignity and magnificence, nor the least shadow of that extravagant power, which she had exercised with so much pride and haughtiness; and this Empress, before whom every knee had formerly bent, was all on a sudden so utterly abandoned, that of the innumerable crowd of adorers,[2] who a little before had worshipped at her shrine, none came near her but a few women, who visited her much less from friendship than a desire to hear her complaints, to observe maliciously the minutest of her actions, and to keep a sort of register of every word that escaped her, in order to report them afterwards to Nero. Thus it frequently happens, that people's affections alter as fortune changes, and examples are very numerous of those turning most against us, who in our prosperity seemed our greatest friends. Agrippina sadly experienced the truth of this, for Silana, who had been her most intimate friend, was the most forward to persecute her, and caused her to be accused by Paris of having a design to seize the Empire. It is true that Silana had reason to be not over fond of Agrippina, but she did not succeed in her revenge as she expected.

Silana was a lady of illustrious family and very handsome, but her beauty was of that sort in which might be perceived a good deal of studied affectation; and besides

[1] Dio. lib. 60. [2] Tacit. Ann. 13.

this, she was very rich. There was a great intimacy between Agrippina and her, which the former cultivated as much as possible, because, Silana having no children, the Empress was in hopes of coming in for a good share of her large possessions. All Agrippina's pretended love and kindness were founded upon these interested views; for it plainly appeared, notwithstanding her dissimulation, that she loved the lady's estates more than her person; for Sextus Africanus, a Roman knight, being resolved to marry this lady, Agrippina, who saw that all her hopes would be destroyed and her greed disappointed by this marriage, did her utmost to hinder it; sometimes by giving Africanus a very bad character of the lady, and arousing suspicions in him with regard to her reputation. Sometimes, again, she would insinuate, that it would be ridiculous for a young man like him to marry a woman so much older than himself, whose beauty was much upon the decline. In short, she made use of so many methods to give him a bad opinion of his mistress, that he no longer felt any affection for her.

The lady presently discovered that this change in her lover was owing to Agrippina's good offices, which she resented so much, that she eagerly seized the opportunity of avenging her disgrace; and, in order to compass her design with the less danger, she employed two of her confidantes to persuade Paris, the comedian, to be her accuser. Paris could not choose but acquit himself well in acting a part so conformable to his profession. He went to Nero one night when he was indulging in dissipation, and appearing before him with a melancholy countenance, which seemed to denote the greatness of the

danger he came to inform him of, told him, sighing, that
he had discovered the most deep laid conspiracy against
him, and that the author of it was no other than his own
mother, who, not being able to endure that any person
should reign but herself, had entered into a solemn com-
pact with Rubellius Plautus, whom she was to marry and
make Emperor; and by this marriage the government of
the Empire was to be vested in her; that what chiefly
induced her to select Plautus for carrying out this ambitious project was his high birth, he being great grandson of Augustus, for he did not doubt that that consideration would gain him a prodigious number of
friends. This news terrified Nero to such a degree, that
he had a great mind to put both his mother and Plautus
to death on the spot; but Burrus, whose advice was
always listened to, moderated the violence of his temper,
by representing to him that, a criminal, however guilty,
ought always to be heard, and especially a mother; that
Agrippina had but one accuser, who laid a crime to her
charge that was hardly credible; that this story, coming
from such a person as a comedian, was not to be taken
for granted; and in short, that so rash and hasty a
resolution, formed in the night, and in the midst of a
debauch, could not but be much blamed by all the world.
He added, that he did not take upon him to vindicate
Agrippina, but on the contrary, if upon a strict examination it should prove true, he would not scruple himself
to be both her judge and executioner.

Nero yielded to these arguments, and sent Burrus the
next morning to his mother, accompanied by Seneca and
some others, to be witnesses of what she should say in
her defence. Burrus interrogated the Empress as to

the crime she was accused of,[1] and affected a certain
threatening air, that would have much disconcerted anybody but herself. But Agrippina did not upon this occasion forget either her courage or her pride. She answered him with a disdainful sort of contempt, that she
was not at all surprised that Silana, who had never had
a child, should be ignorant of the maternal tenderness
a mother has for her offspring; but that she would have
her know that it was not so easy for a mother to destroy
her son, as it was for a courtesan to change her lovers;
that her enemies, she supposed, by suborning the infamous Atimetus and a vile comedian against her, had a
mind to entertain people with a farce; that an accusation
brought by such wretches ought to be of no weight; and
that she defied her bitterest enemy to produce one witness, worthy of credit, to prove that she had ever
solicited the cohorts of the town, or endeavoured to corrupt the provinces, or tampered with the slaves or freedmen to induce them to revolt against her son. She then
showed that the crime she was accused of was absolutely
inconsistent with her own interest, because, if Britannicus
was Emperor, she might flatter herself with the hopes of
living out of danger, which she could never do if Plautus
or any other had the sovereign command; because she
would never, in that case, want enemies to accuse her of
such crimes as would admit of no pardon except from a
son to a mother.

The Empress's manner of justifying herself greatly
affected those that were present. They did all they could
to appease her; but she insisted upon speaking to her son,
and accordingly was brought before him. She disdained

[1] Tacit. Ann. 13.

to say a word in her defence, thinking it inconsistent with her dignity to clear up or contradict all the falsehoods and calumnies that had been alleged against her. She also affected to be quite silent as to the favours she had heaped upon him, that she might not seem to reproach him with them, but peremptorily demanded that he should punish her adversaries for their malice, and enable her to reward her friends. Both demands were granted. Silana was banished, Atimetus, one of her accusers, was put to death, and the employments of chief commissary of provinces, the government of Egypt, and other important posts, were bestowed upon the Empress's friends.

Agrippina, having thus dexterously made use of the artifice that her enemies had employed to ruin her to re-establish her authority, left nothing undone that could confirm it; but the laws of modesty will not permit us to state the means she employed for that purpose. As she perceived her influence was diminished by that of Sabina Poppæa, with whom Nero at that time began to be enamoured, she made use of all her charms in order to oppose them to those of Poppæa; for she knew that her son was very susceptible to love, and that he stuck at nothing, when the question was to gratify his inclinations. She therefore formed the detestable resolution of exerting her utmost endeavours to create in her son such sentiments as are shocking to nature, by making him all the seductive and shameful advances in her power, hoping that by means of these infamous caresses she might be able to erase from his mind those feelings of regard he was beginning to conceive for Poppæa. Sometimes she would go to him when he was elated with wine [1] and took care to make her appearance in such a dress as was most capable of exciting desire. At other times she affected to display her beauty before him, with the same assurance and impudence that a courtesan practises before a gallant. When she went with him in his litter,[2] she caressed him in the most shameful manner, to tempt him to commit abomination with her; nor was there wanting evident demonstration that these incestuous flames of Agrippina met with a suitable return in Nero.

She did not however by this crime reap all the satisfaction she hoped for, because Nero was soon disgusted with it, and gave himself up entirely to his passion for Poppæa, which tormented the Empress with the most cruel jealousy. Poppæa, on her side, was not idle, but, taking advantage of the favourable sentiments the Emperor exhibited towards her, never ceased [3] to irritate him against his mother, by telling him that she could not endure that anybody should govern but herself; that any power superior to her own gave her offence, and consequently, that he ought to be always suspicious of such unbounded ambition, for that the Empress would omit nothing to get rid of those who presumed to put themselves into rivalry with her. Nero, therefore, who of himself was sufficiently inclined to believe everything that was bad of his mother, gave credit to all this, and resolved to put to death her who had given him life and the Empire, and to deliver himself at once from one whom he no longer looked upon but as the declared

---

[1] Tacit. Ann. 14. c. 2. [2] Sueton. vit. Ner. 28. Aurel. Vict.
[3] Xiph. in. Ner. Dio. lib. 61.

enemy to his pleasures, and the only obstacle to his happiness.

He had designed this long ago, and nothing troubled him but how to remove from himself the suspicion of it; for this reason he would not have recourse to any violent means, because that would have made too much noise. He tried several times to poison her,[1] and, in particular at an entertainment,[2] which, by agreement between him and Otho, the latter gave to the Emperor and his mother, at which there was no want of magnificence, gallantry, and good cheer, to take away from Agrippina all mistrust by these false tokens of friendship and respect. But these attempts were always in vain, because the Empress was always upon her guard against any snares of that sort that her son might lay for her, and had provided the most powerful antidotes, which she never failed to make use of as often as she thought there was occasion; this decided the Emperor to despatch her at all hazards.

It is reported that Seneca did not endeavour to dissuade [3] him from this horrible design, though this is scarcely credible. It is even affirmed that the philisopher, perceiving that his lessons produced no fruit, but that the devilish inclinations of Nero were infinitely stronger than all his maxims, encouraged him to commit this parricide, which he was already guilty of in his heart, that so execrable a crime might draw down upon him the hatred of the gods and men. Be it as it may, Nero, having fortified his mind against all that could happen,

[1] Tacit. Ann. 14.   [3] Xiphilin. in. Ner.
[2] Sueton. vit. Othon.

thought of nothing but how to bring it about. At first [1]
he had recourse to a plank so contrived, that it was to
fall upon her in the night and crush her to pieces; but
this design having been discovered, Anicetus, one of his
freedmen, who had looked after him when he was a
child (a person fertile in expedients of this nature),
offered to find out a method of putting her to death,
without suspicion falling upon anyone. He was then
commander of the galleys in the port of Misenum, and
hated Agrippina as much as she did him. Nero did not
believe he could possibly find out a fitter man for his
purpose than this infamous officer, who was capable of
any wicked action. In fact, he undertook to have a
galley made in such a manner that the bottom should
open, and, at the same moment, the upper part should fall
of itself, so that Agrippina could not fail to be either
crushed to death or drowned, without giving the least
room for suspicion, since it would pass for one of these
unfortunate accidents that happen frequently at sea.
The Emperor was to carry out the farce, by erecting
temples to his mother's memory, which were to be looked
upon as undeniable demonstrations of his grief, respect,
and affection, and would infallibly remove all grounds of
suspicion.

Nero approved of this scheme; and, the better to put
it into execution, it was resolved that it should be done
at Baiæ,[2] in the Campagna of Rome, when the feast of

[1] Sueton. Vit. Ner. Tacit. Ann. 14. Dio. lib. 62.
[2] Baiæ was a very agreeable town in the Campagna of Rome. There
were hot baths, to which people resorted as much for pleasure as
health. The country about it was extremely fertile, and the neighbourhood of the town abounded with magnificent palaces, and delicious

Minerva was to be celebrated. The ceremony served
Nero for a pretence to leave Rome, and he invited his
mother to be of the party. He was already reconciled
to her in appearance, and pretended to be very sorry
he had ever failed in point of respect to her. He blamed
his past conduct, and protested that for the future she
should never have the least reason to complain of him,
for he said it was only reasonable that children should
bear with the humours of their parents, to whom they
owed their life and being. Thus this unnatural and cruel
prince disguised the most horrible perfidiousness that
could enter into the heart of man, under the specious
show of filial tenderness and affection. He was persuaded that his mother would the more easily fall into
this snare, as women are always apt to believe what
they ardently desire. The plot being thus laid, and all
his measures taken, Nero left Rome, together with his
mother, in a galley, which they had taken care to adorn
magnificently. They arrived at Antium, where the Emperor left Agrippina, and proceeded to Baiæ. After having passed a few days there, he wrote his mother a
letter full of kindness and respect, and entreated her to
come and pass some time with him. She parted from
Antium and landed at Bauli, a pleasant country-house
between Misenum and Baiæ, by the sea-side. Nero was
there ready to receive her, conducted her to the castle
that she might rest herself, and then returned to Baiæ.

gardens, so that the Romans used to flock thither in great numbers.
Horace in one of his poems sets forth its praises,

> Nullus in orbe locus Baiis prælucet amœnis.

Martial says also, that Baiæ surpasses all description,

> Laudabo digne, non satis tamen Baïas.

This town was destroyed by earthquakes.

Notwithstanding all the precautions that were taken to keep this matter secret, Agrippina was informed of it; somebody had informed her of the plot against her, and she was at a loss what to believe. In this state of uncertainty she would not venture herself at sea again, but was carried to Baiæ in a chair. She was there received by her son with all possible demonstrations of tenderness and affection, and treated in the most sumptuous manner. The Emperor, to remove all grounds of suspicion, even consulted her about some serious affairs, granted her several favours without her asking them, invented all sorts of amusements for her, and made her always sit above him, which mark of respect pleased her infinitely.

This extraordinary fit of good humour in the Emperor deceived Agrippina. She took this cunning outside appearance for true affection and duty, for never was artifice better carried out. When Agrippina was to return to Bauli, Nero embraced her in the kindest and most affectionate manner imaginable, whether in order to conceal his design the better, or because nature was working for the last time upon the heart of this barbarian; he escorted her to the sea-side, and the galley in which she had come being damaged as by accident (though by Nero's secret orders) he desired her to embark on board of that which Anicetus had prepared, commanding that officer to escort, or rather to destroy her.

The weather was as fine and the sea as calm as possible,[1] as if Providence had so ordered it, that Nero might have no excuse for his crime, nor attribute his mother's misfortune to the darkness of the night or a

[1] Tacit. Ann. 14.

tempestuous sea. Agrippina had none of her retinue
with her but Crepereius Gallus, who stood under the
helm, and a lady named Acerronia Polla, who sat at the
Empress's feet, and was congratulating her on the happy
reconciliation between her and the Emperor. The galley
had proceeded but a little way, when, at a signal given
by Anicetus, the floor of the cabin where Agrippina was,
being loaded with lead, gave way. Crepereius was
crushed to pieces by it,[1] and consequently died upon the
spot; but the place, where Agrippina was, held out some
time longer, because that part of the floor was too strong
to yield immediately under the weight. The confusion
that this occasioned was so great, that the sailors who
were in the plot were vexed beyond measure at the disappointment, and did not know what to do. The springs,
which were to occasion the opening of the vessel at
the instant when the floor was to fall, did not perform
their office, because the sailors who were not in the secret
hindered the others in such a manner that, in order to
sink the galley, they were forced to overset her; but this
was not to be done without great difficulty, because those
who were innocent undid all that the others performed,
by working in the opposite direction.

During this terrible fright and hurry, Agrippina and
Acerronia fell into the sea. Acerronia, who suspected
no treason, called out for help; and, that it might come
as speedily as possible, never ceased bawling that they
should save the Empress-mother. This zeal for Agrippina was the cause of Acerronia's death, for, as it was
their intention to murder the Empress, they dashed

[1] Dio. lib. 62. Sueton. vit. Ner.

Acerronia's brains out with their oars, taking her for Agrippina.

The Empress, on the contrary, said not a word, but had the good fortune to keep herself above water till she was assisted by some boats that were at a little distance, and received no other damage than a blow on the shoulder. She was immediately carried to a neighbouring house, not far from where Nero was, and as soon as she had a little recovered from her fright and fatigue, Acerronia's being knocked on the head, the pains the sailors took to wreck the galley and many other circumstances crowded into her mind, and overwhelmed her with melancholy reflections.

She had too much penetration not to see into this mystery, and soon came to the conclusion that the affair did not look like chance or accident; but, on the other hand, she was too politic not to pretend that she had no manner of suspicion. She immediately sent off her freedman Agerinus, to inform Nero of the risk she had run and the escape she had had, and to desire him not to take the trouble of coming to see her, since in her present condition she required nothing but rest. Her avarice, however, did not forsake her in the midst of her terrors and apprehensions, for she caused Acerronia's last will to be looked for, and sealed up all her effects very carefully; in this she did not in the least dissemble.

Nero had waited with the utmost impatience for the conclusion of this business, and was in the greatest uneasiness and perplexity, when he heard that his mother was saved, which he did not at all expect, for he thought the matter had been too well contrived to fail; and perceiving, by what was reported to him, that she could be in

no sort of doubt but that it was a designed thing, he was
afraid that she would certainly stir up against him the
senate, the army, the people, and even the slaves.   In
this dilemma he sent for Burrus and Seneca, to tell them
his opinion, and to consult them as to what was fit to
be done.

They continued some time silent, but at last Seneca,
who generally spoke first, looked at Burrus, as if it were
to learn his sentiments, whether it would not be right that
soldiers should be commanded to go and kill her.   Burrus
answered, that the prætorian guards had too much respect for Cæsar's family and the memory of Germanicus,
to do any such thing; but that it was Anicetus's business
to finish what he had undertaken.   Anicetus did not require to be long entreated, but undertook the business
very willingly; and Nero, in the transports of joy that
he felt upon this occasion (having found a man ready
to oblige him so greatly) cried out, that at last he might
say he was really Emperor, and would always acknowledge himself beholden to Anicetus for it.

Just then a messenger came in to tell Nero that the
Empress had sent Agerinus to him, who prayed to be
admitted; he was brought in, and while he was speaking,
a poniard was slily conveyed between his feet, to make it
be believed that he had brought it under his robe, and
dropped it by chance.   The Emperor sent him immediately to prison, as if he had come to assissinate him, and
this rumour was industriously reported, that when the
death of Agrippina should be known, people might
imagine she had killed herself from vexation that she had
missed the opportunity of destroying her son.

While all this was passing at Baiæ, the noise of the

accident that had happened to the Empress was spread about the country, as a misfortune that had happened merely by chance; and the people flocked [1] from all parts of the sea-side, to give what assistance was in their power. Some threw themselves into the first boats they could meet with, others waded into the water as far as they were able, and great numbers, holding up their hands towards heaven, made the air echo with their cries and supplications for the Empress's safety. Multitudes came with torches to enquire if she was safe, and as soon as they knew that she was so, and had retired, they all hastened to see her, and to congratulate her on her escape, returning thanks to the gods for having saved her from so terrible and surprising an accident.

Agrippina, however, could not help being in a cruel state of uneasiness; the dread she was in of the misfortunes that threatened her put her in a miserable condition. No kind message came from her son to cheer her heart, nor did Agerinus, whom she had sent, return to give her any comfort, so that she had a secret presentiment that her fatal hour was approaching. At last Anicetus came in, accompanied by soldiers, at the sight of whom all the company were terrified. The soldiers, by order of their chief, surrounded the house, and after having broken open the outward door, and seized upon all the domestics that he could find, Anicetus came to the chamber whither the Empress had retired; the room had not much light in it, and the Empress had nobody with her but one of her women, who, hearing the noise that the soldiers made, was seized with a panic and fled, as most of the rest had done; then the unfortunate

[1] Tacit. Ann. 14.

Agrippina, seeing herself abandoned by all the world, said to her woman as she was going, "What! dost thou quit me too?" Anicetus was the first that came in, attended by two officers of the marines, and as soon as Agrippina perceived him, she told him with a great deal of resolution, that, if he came to see her, she begged he would go and tell Nero that she was better; but, if he had any design upon her life, she could not believe that her son had any hand in it, or was capable of commanding a parricide like this. These words did not in the least move the ruffians; for, while she was speaking, they surrounded her bed, and one of the officers who came with Anicetus, and was not less brutal than he, gave her a violent blow on the head [1] with a stick, and a centurion immediately drew his sword to kill her; then Agrippina, who could no longer doubt but her son was the author of her death, presented herself to the murderers, and told them they should begin by piercing that belly that had produced such a monster as Nero; and that instant she was run through the body in several places.

Nero's unnatural barbarity was not yet satisfied; for, after having murdered his mother, he added insults that were rather more cruel than the former action. When he was sure she was dead, he had the abominable curiosity to see her body quite naked, and brutally point out her faults and perfections; and then, with a smiling and pleased countenance, turned round to those about him, and told them, in a jocose manner, that he did not think he had so beautiful a mother. Some there are who deny this, but when we consider his character in general, and especially that he kept a concubine a great while, merely

[1] Dio. Tacit. Sueton.

because she happened to resemble his mother,[1] without much difficulty we may believe him capable of it.

This detestable Emperor did not peaceably enjoy the fruits of this horrid murder; for, though the sovereign authority with which he was invested, and which he so much abused, screened him against human justice, it could not protect him against the divine vengeance, from which nobody can hide themselves. He was tormented with the intolerable pangs of conscience,[2] which gave him no rest day or night. He was frequently heard to cry out, that the ghost of Agrippina pursued him wherever he went, and that furies and devils surrounded him. He sought to hide himself in dark and desolate places, and immediately after, was impatient to quit them. Thus, those places where he hoped to find most rest and quiet only served to fill his mind with horror, dread and despair, the just reward of his crimes.

[1] Xiphilin. in Ner.
[2] Tacit. Ann. 14. c. 10. Dio. lib. 61.

OCTAVIA

WIFE OF NERO

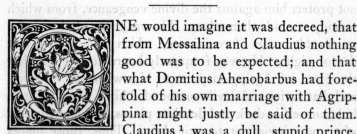NE would imagine it was decreed, that from Messalina and Claudius nothing good was to be expected; and that what Domitius Ahenobarbus had foretold of his own marriage with Agrippina might justly be said of them. Claudius [1] was a dull, stupid prince, nearer of kin to a beast than a man (as Seneca observes), and Messalina a woman quite destitute of decency or modesty. Notwithstanding which, Octavia, whose wisdom, prudence, and virtue were as remarkable as her high birth, was the offspring of that union which promised so little benefit to mankind. She was eminently good in a most wicked and depraved age, and in a corrupt court where vice reigned triumphant. Her conduct was always irreproachable, and the bad example of her mother failed to corrupt her. To her beauty, which was incomparable, was united that noble simplicity and amiable modesty, that never fails to captivate the hearts of all who are witnesses of it. She had the greatest sweetness of temper, without the least tincture of affectation. In short, she possessed all those virtues and good qualities that were worthy of a better reign. Never did princess more deserve to be happy, and yet [2] there never was any who

[1] Lud. in Claud. [2] Senec. in Octav.

suffered more, nor whose patience was more put to the
test; for she did not know what it was to enjoy one
quiet day, nor could her whole life be reckoned anything
but one continued series of bitterness and vexation; so
that it may truly be affirmed of Octavia, that she died
without ever having tasted the least pleasure.

She was but very young when the Emperor, her father,
thought of finding out a suitable husband for her; and
of all the men of distinction and high quality at Rome,
who might have aspired to that extraordinary honour,
Lucius Silanus was thought the most worthy. He was
remarkable for his illustrious birth and great merit, being
great grandson [1] to Augustus; but these, advantageous
and honourable as they were, did not recommend him to
the love and esteem of all mankind so much as the
virtues he was endued with. He had the sweetest temper,
together with the most beneficent disposition, a noble air,
a mind well formed, and a great soul; there was nothing,
in short, that one would have wished to have altered in
his whole person or conduct. The Emperor had the
greatest regard for him, and therefore made choice of
him for his son-in-law; in consequence of which, he was
solemnly betrothed to Octavia, and, in order to render
him more worthy of her, the Emperor granted him [2]
several marks of honour that had never been given [3]
except to those who had triumphed, together with several
other privileges, that made him very important at Rome,
where all those that were descended from the Cæsars
were respected in an extraordinary manner.

This marriage would certainly have been brought

[1] Tacit. Ann. 12. c. 3.   [3] Sueton. vit. Claud. 27.
[2] Tacit. Ann. 13. c. 1.

about if Messalina had lived a little longer, but her immodesty and cruelty had occasioned her being put to death; and Agrippina, the proudest and most ambitious of women, being substituted in her place, prevailed upon the Emperor to take other resolutions more conformable to her views. This Empress, whose love of power and authority was boundless, only married her uncle Claudius with a design to ruin his family, and cause the Empire to come into her own. This was the aim of all her grand schemes. She considered that, if Nero her son married the Emperor's daughter, it would be a great step towards the throne; and, to bring about his marriage, she had nothing to do but break off that which was agreed upon between Silanus and Octavia. To this end it was necessary to prove Silanus guilty of some crime that would make him unworthy of being so nearly allied to the Emperor.

Vitellius, who was censor at that time, undertook this infamous commission. This unworthy magistrate (who by art as well as nature [1] was perfectly well qualified for insinuating himself into the good graces of people in authority) was ever ready to advance his fortune at the expense of his honour and integrity. He thought he could not possibly do Agrippina a greater piece of service than by ruining Silanus, whom she hated; and in order to succeed, he had recourse to falsehood and imposture. He accused him of imaginary crimes, since he could lay no real ones to his charge. At first he very cunningly spread reports that were calculated to tarnish his character and reputation, and which Agrippina's emissaries took care to propagate and encourage. He himself also,

[1] Tacit. Ann. 12. c. 4.

as censor, reproached him with too great an intimacy with
his sister Junia; pretexts were found for this infamous
aspersion, and it was asserted that Silanus's love and
affection for his sister ought to be construed in a criminal
sense. Upon this false accusation, which was without the
least proof, the corrupt censor declared him unworthy to
hold his offices, so that Silanus, who was prætor, and
performed the functions of his office with the greatest
honour and integrity, found his name expunged from the
list of senators, and was obliged to resign the prætorship
without knowing for what reason.

Claudius suffered himself to be imposed upon by this
artful accusation; and the more easily because, as he
loved his daughter extremely, he would not give her a
husband who had fixed his affections elsewhere; he therefore broke off the intended marriage between Silanus and
Octavia; [1] and the pretended criminal, knowing full well
that his enemies would not stop there, and that Agrippina,
whose deep designs he easily penetrated, would never be
satisfied until she was revenged on a man who stood
between her and her ambitious projects, either in despair,
or being compelled to do so, killed himself, and thereby
avoided the persecution that was preparing for him.

Nothing could have been a greater disappointment to
Octavia than the breaking off of this marriage; for no
sooner was it accomplished, than Agrippina set about promoting the other between her son Nero and Octavia,
which she had so much at heart. Pollio, who was to be
consul the next year, being gained over by Agrippina,
proposed this matter to Claudius; and he, who never
acted but according as he was influenced by other people,

[1] Tacit. Ann. 12. Senec. in Oct. Sueton. vit. Claud.

agreed to it at once; so they were betrothed, and Nero, by that means, paved himself a way to the throne. There were others who had a hand in this work besides Pollio; for all those who were concerned in Messalina's death favoured the advancement of Nero, for fear that, if Britannicus should become Emperor, he would revenge the death of his mother.

The success that Agrippina had hitherto met with in all her enterprises continually encouraged her to take up new ones; for, besides the absolute power she had acquired over her husband, whom she kept in a complete state of slavery, she had also the assistance of all that stupid Emperor's favourites, for he was entirely governed by them, and was by no means capable of penetrating the deep and ambitious designs of his wife, as it plainly appeared, when they so easily prevailed on him to adopt Nero. Pallas, who was attached to the Empress by a criminal intercourse, took upon himself the management of that piece of work, and it did not cost him much trouble to bring it about. The necessities of the State, the youth of Britannicus, the precarious state of health the Emperor was in, and the reasonableness of giving him an assistant upon that account, were the arguments he made use of to that purpose; to which he added the example of Augustus, who had adopted [1] the son of his wife Livia. All these reasons convinced Claudius, that not a moment ought to be lost in so necessary a work; so Domitius (as he was always called before) was admitted into the family of Claudius, and named Nero, by an adoption that was without precedent in the patrician family of the Claudians.

[1] Tacit. Ann. 12.

This adoption, which put Nero on a level with Britannicus, was authorised by the senate (ever ready to subscribe to the Empress's will and pleasure) and ratified by the most fulsome and flattering decrees; but all honest well-meaning people disapproved of them in the highest degree, and commiserated a poor prince, whose interests were basely deserted, in order to build up the fortunes of a stranger upon his ruin. Heaven seemed to be provoked at this piece of injustice,[1] for the sky was all on fire the day it was done, as if to represent the character and violent temper of Nero, and it seemed to be a prediction of the flame that this wicked prince would one day kindle in Rome.

Octavia foresaw all the consequences of this unjust adoption, which caused her to shed many a bitter tear; she could not help bewailing the condition of a brother so soon to fall a victim to the ambition of a cruel stepmother, whose principal aim was the destruction of all her family. In fact, all the necessary preparations previous to this marriage of Nero and Octavia were at once made; and that there might remain no obstacle in the way,[2] the princess was taken into another family, by a similar adoption, that a brother might not appear to marry a sister.

The nuptials were celebrated with more precipitation than pomp, but Nero was full of joy and satisfaction; not that he cared for Octavia, but because it gave him a near prospect of the throne. Octavia, on the contrary, who was sacrificed to the ambition of Agrippina, was overwhelmed with melancholy. Agrippina's wishes were now accomplished; and having taken such measures as could

[1] Dio. lib. 60. Xiphilin. in Ner.   [2] Dio. lib. 61.

scarce fail of securing the Empire to her son, she then thought of nothing but how to strike the important blow that she had long meditated in her heart.

Claudius's imprudence hastened his own destruction; for one day at table he happened (when heated by wine, which was no rare occurrence) to say, that his marriages had been unfortunate, but that sooner or later he would find a way to be revenged on those who affronted him. This was enough for Agrippina, who thought it high time to prevent the effects of these threats. Locusta,[1] who was very skilful in the art of shortening life,[2] was immediately set to work; and Claudius, a few days after, having eaten some mushrooms, found the end of his life in that ragout, of which he was very fond. He was afterwards deified, and Nero was saluted Emperor, to the prejudice of Britannicus, who was the lawful heir.

It is easy to imagine what must have been Octavia's grief upon this occasion; for, young as she was,[3] she knew both the cause and the author of the Emperor's death. But the art of dissembling is of very great use in courts. Octavia looked upon herself as a stranger in her father's palace, and was taught, by so many misfortunes, to conceal her true sentiments. She found it of the greatest importance to her to seem ignorant of many things, and had often occasion to put this in practice. As Nero only married her to make use of her as a stepping-stone to the throne, he never showed the least inclination for her; so, as soon as he was become Em-

[1] Locusta was a famous poisoner, who did great mischief in Rome, for which she had been put in prison, but Nero gave her her liberty, in order to make use of her for poisoning Prince Britannicus. The Emperor Galba put her to death.

[2] Tacit. Ann. 12. Sueton. vit. Claud. Dio. Eutrop.

[3] Tacit. Ann. 13.

peror, he placed his affections elsewhere, and entirely
despised and slighted his wife, whose chastity was universally acknowledged, and whose extraordinary beauty
was the more admired, as she made use of no arts to
heighten or set it off.

Acte was the first person who made an impression on
his heart. He became excessively in love with her; [1] and
this passion seemed to be authorised by the silence of
his preceptors, who connived at it through a false policy,
or rather approved of his debaucheries; alleging that
it was better to allow of these criminal pleasures, than
that the chastity and modesty of the Roman ladies should
be violated by the impetuosity of this Emperor's lewd
inclinations. But their true motive was, to make use of
Acte by way of counterpoise to the power of Agrippina,
imagining that their own authority would be more considerable as the Empress's decreased. Thus Nero, meeting with no opposition, gave himself up to the gratification of his appetites without the least reserve.

Some of his friends were very sensible of the ill-treatment Octavia received from him, and had sufficient
honour and courage to tell him of it; but these remonstrances were in vain, and produced no good effects on a
prince that was not always in a humour to listen to them,
so they only served to increase rather than cure the evil;
for Nero, who consulted nothing but his passions,
answered brutally, that Octavia [2] ought to be content with
the simple ornaments of a wife; and he would probably
have divorced her then, if Burrus, his tutor, seeing how
far he carried matters, had not told him, with a good

[1] Sueton. vit. Ner. Tacit. Ann. 13.
[2] Sueton. vit. Ner. Tacit. Dio.

deal of liberty and resolution, that if he must needs put away Octavia, he ought at least to give her back her portion, meaning by that, that he was obliged to her for the Empire.

If the Emperor's love for Acte had caused no other affliction to Octavia than the loss of his heart, she would never have given herself any trouble about the matter, for it gave her no sort of jealousy or uneasiness. She saw him, with great indifference, carrying on his detestable amours; and thought herself sufficiently revenged by the contempt that this unworthy Emperor brought upon himself, in yielding to the seductive caresses of a prostitute. But Acte set no great value on his affections; for it was his fortune, not his love, that she aimed at, and the throne was what she aspired to. Full of these flattering hopes, she employed all her charms to win Nero, and found him so susceptible, that she soon perceived she had all the qualities she could wish for that were necessary to promote her success; corruption of heart and manners, aversion to virtue, a natural propensity to vice, hatred for Octavia; everything, in short, seemed to favour this coquette in her ambitious designs.

Besides, Nero was plunged in the most infamous pleasures, and surrounded with debauched and effeminate youths, whose sentiments were as low as their birth, and from whom he could learn nothing but what was vile and base in the highest degree. Burrus and Seneca chose rather to keep at a distance and neglect their duty, when they saw their labour was to no purpose, and that their instructions were thrown away upon the depraved nature of their pupil, who despised their lessons and precepts. On the contrary, Otho, that well-known debauchee, whom a resemblance of manners had recommended to the Emperor; Petronius, so clever in inventing pleasures, and chief manager of Nero's amusements; Crescens, a vile wretch that had been a slave; Vatinius, who, weary of struggling with poverty in a poor shoemaker's shop, where he had passed his younger days, had found out the secret of insinuating himself into the good graces of the Emperor, by the most shameful means, and in spite of the deformities of his body, which was crooked and disfigured; Tigellinus, who from the meanest extraction raised himself to the highest pitch of grandeur by all manner of wickedness; Anicetus, another freedman, who afterwards was the worthy instrument he made choice of when he put his mother to death; Pythagoras, to whom he caused himself to be solemnly married, to gratify his monstrous lewdness with detestable and newly-invented pleasures, being quite weary of such as were in the ordinary way; Sporus,[1] whom he had the folly to marry as a wife, after a ridiculous attempt to make him change his sex; Senecio, Serenus, and an infinite number of such like excrements of the Empire, were the worthy masters and patterns that Nero imitated and copied; so that, if he had not been naturally vicious, he could not but have become so by infection.

Among all these unworthy favourites and base flatterers, Senecio [2] was the person he chose for his confidant in his amour with Acte, because his inclinations were the most conformable to his own. This great familiarity was insupportable to Agrippina, who had often attempted to break through it, especially when she knew that Senecio favoured her son's intrigue with Acte, for

[1] Sueton. vit. Ner. 28.   [2] Tacit. Ann. 13.

she could not bear to have that courtesan put upon a level with her in point of authority; and Nero, who had not yet divested himself of all humanity, but pretended to keep some sort of restraint with his mother, quitted Senecio for a time, and made use of Serenus for his amour, who pretended to be in love with Acte himself, and publicly gave out that the presents Nero sent his mistress by him were his own. But these restraints did not long suit the inclinations of Nero, who was not of a temper to bear with such tedious and troublesome formalities: besides, it is no easy matter to conceal a violent passion so that it shall not break out some time or other. Thus Nero, being weary of dissembling, began to visit Acte with less reserve and circumspection, and soon after, without affecting secrecy at all, gave himself entirely up to Senecio, and despising the remonstrances and threats of his mother, resolved to marry Acte.

Two great obstacles stood in the way of this marriage; Octavia was to be divorced, and a woman who had been a slave was to be exalted to the throne of the Empire. The first would have been a flagrant injustice; and the second, a novelty that would have been thought monstrous. To put away Octavia could not but provoke the senate, and cause a revolt among the people, who perfectly adored the family of the Cæsars. To marry Acte would have been to despise all classes in the city, and infinitely to degrade the imperial majesty, by placing a slave on the throne. Nero's love, however, would soon have triumphed over all these difficulties, in spite of his preceptors' remonstrances, had it not been for his apprehension that the people's minds would be so alienated from him by this marriage as to incline them towards the young prince Britannicus, whom he thought already but too formidable. These considerations were what stopped his career. He had invented reasons (such as they were) for putting away Octavia, and gave himself but little trouble about getting them approved of by the senate; for he had absolute control over those timid and slavish persons of whom it was composed, who, sacrificing their duty and honour to the advancement of their fortune, conformed themselves entirely to Nero's will, or rather to all his crimes, not being ashamed of dishonouring their character by most servile and mercenary complaisance. Acte's obscure birth was not an insurmountable obstacle; for Nero had resolved to make it appear that she was of royal extraction; and for this purpose two persons [1] of rank, who had been consuls, had promised, by a shameful condescension, to swear that she had kings for her ancestors. This fabulous genealogy was to have put her, whose father had been a miserable slave, upon an equality with the noblest lady in Rome. And Nero, to authorise this pretended royalty of his mistress, adopted her into the family of Attalus king of Pergamus in Asia, who was possessed of immense riches, and, dying without children, left the Roman people his heirs; thus, everything was arranged for the celebration of this marriage, when, making the reflections which have been already mentioned, he bethought himself that, before he should venture to make such an experiment as might not be approved of by all the world, it behooved him to get rid of Britannicus, who was able to form a powerful party against him, as his pretensions to the throne were universally acknowledged. [2] This young

[1] Sueton. vit. Ner. Xiphilin.   [2] Tacit. Ann. 12.

prince, who was in the fifteenth year of his age, was by no means to be despised, both on account of his personal merit, as also of that affection which subjects always have for their lawful prince; besides that, Agrippina, who had fallen out with Nero, was continually threatening him with her intention of carrying Britannicus into the camp, of disclosing to all the world the iniquitous proceedings that had been carried on, her incestuous marriage, the unjust and violent death of Silanus, the murder of Claudius; and in short, declared that she would let all the earth know that Nero only governed the Empire on commission, and that it was high time to restore it to the son of Claudius, who was the true and lawful heir.

Nero did not relish these terrible threats, which made a deep impression on him; he could not help being prodigiously alarmed, and from that time forth looked upon Britannicus as his greatest enemy. He therefore determined to cut him off by poison, not daring to use any violent methods. Pollio, tribune of a prætorian cohort, (a man destitute of honour) was the infamous instrument this detestable prince made use of to take away the life of Britannicus, son of his Emperor, his benefactor, his colleague, his brother-in-law, and his brother by adoption. Locusta, a famous poisoner by trade, (who, as an historian says, was for a long time one of the principal springs of the government) was employed upon this occasion. She [1] was at that time in prison, under the guard of Pollio, for exercising her profession a little too freely at the expense of a great many people's lives; and her liberty was promised her, provided she did the business effectually. These terms were immediately accepted,

[1] Tacit. Ann. 12. Sueton.

and she prepared a poison for Britannicus, which was given him by his own preceptors, but it did not take effect, either because it was made up too mild, for fear that, if it operated too powerfully, there might be room for suspicion; or perhaps because the prince might have been speedily delivered of it by a natural evacuation. Nero, who did not understand such trifling work, threatened Pollio, and ordered him to put Locusta to death, being convinced that one or other of them had on purpose frustrated his intention, that they might not be liable to the odium of this horrid piece of iniquity, but, if it must be done, that all the blame might be thrown upon the Emperor. However, they promised to give Britannicus so subtle and violent a poison, that he should be carried off instantly. It was accordingly prepared in the Emperor's chamber, and in his presence: and, to remove all cause of mistrust from the young prince, it was given him at table, where nothing was ever served up, that had not first been tasted. They presented him a mess of soup that was boiling hot, and it was tasted before his face, because the poison was not yet put into it. The prince, just as they imagined, found it too hot, and desired that a little water might be poured in to cool it. This was immediately done; but the water contained so strong a dose of the poison, that, as soon as the prince tasted it he fell down dead, losing, in a moment, all the faculties of life and respiration.

Octavia, who was present at this tragical spectacle, and whom Nero, to conceal his crime, endeavoured to persuade that it was only one of those fits to which he said Britannicus was subject, was reduced to the cruel necessity of smothering her grief, that she might not seem to suspect Nero, and of affecting a calm and serene countenance, whilst her heart was labouring under the most bitter affliction. She had certainly the greatest reason to be grieved, for by his death the celebrated Claudian family was extinct. She had always reckoned upon her brother as the only person who might one day bring about a happy change in her condition. For, though the bad treatment she continually experienced excited the compassion of all the world, yet her friends, who for the most part were timid and without power, could only give her their good wishes, but none were willing or able to do her any essential service.

Britannicus's sudden death was also a mortal blow to Agrippina; for, as she had no hand in that murder, she was astonished when she saw him perish by such horrid perfidy. She mingled her tears with those of Octavia, when they were at liberty to indulge their grief without witnesses; the Empress embraced her with the greatest demonstrations of affection, and gave her the most evident tokens of sincere love and friendship; there was a similarity in their condition, that inspired Agrippina with such humane sentiments as she had till then been a stranger to. But this last abominable action of Nero's was not the only vexation she had to undergo; for the favour and influence Poppæa enjoyed gave her still more anxiety. Nero had begun to show less fondness for Acte; but he was no sooner delievered from the slavery of that intrigue, than he fell into a state of captivity more complete and more durable than the other, by becoming so excessively enamoured of Sabina Poppæa, that nothing would content him but marrying her; and because the authority of his mother was an insurmountable obstacle to the accomplishment of his desires, he resolved to shake off that intolerable yoke, by putting to death her who had given him life. Poppæa had taken a great deal of pains to bring him to this; and Nero, not being able to refuse her anything, but arming himself against all remorse, with the highest ingratitude and most barbarous fury determined to commit an execrable parricide, and dip his hands in the blood of that mother who had procured him the Empire. Thus Providence was pleased to permit that this ambitious Empress, who had perpetrated so many crimes to exalt an unnatural son to the throne, should meet with a just reward, and receive from that son the punishment she deserved.

Octavia was now the only victim left to be sacrificed to the brutal cruelty of Nero, and the restless jealousy of Poppæa. As it would have been very dangerous to attempt anything by way of violence against the life of a princess who was loved and admired by all the world, and whose conduct was irreproachable, so, on the other hand, it was no easy matter to do the business by poison, without its being perceived. The Emperor therefore resolved to be himself the executioner of his poor innocent wife and strangle her secretly; but, meeting with difficulties in all these methods, he determined at last to divorce her. This was the expedient which the infamous flatterers about the Emperor desired, to rid him of this incomparable princess,—those sycophants, who were more solicitous about their own interests than for the honour of their master, and had nothing so much at heart as the perpetuation of their power and authority by flattering his passions. Tigellinus was the chief of these. That insolent favourite had so insinuated himself into the good graces of the Emperor, that he was the companion of all his debauches, and generally arranged them. As the authority of the Emperor was in a manner vested in him, and he possessed the secret of maintaining himself in his friendship by the most infamous methods, he made no scruple of affronting all the persons of quality and distinction in Rome, who dreaded his power and malice. In his whole person was to be seen a certain brutal air that made him feared, even by those, who, a while ago, had never so much as heard of him; and joining insolence,[1] which generally accompanies good fortune, to the unpolished rudeness which is always the consequence of a bad education, he troubled himself about nothing but how to preserve the influence and riches that he had acquired by artifice and iniquity. As he had a mean soul, was mercenary and corrupted by long practice of the most infamous vices, and was capable of every crime, he found it an easy matter to promote his interests by all the wicked means he could think of.[2] It must not therefore be wondered at, if (being such as he has been described) he advised Nero to divorce the virtuous Octavia, and marry the shameless Poppæa. Reasons were sought for to authorise this divorce; and because the princess's virtue could never be called in question, they were forced to have recourse to her being childless, and made that a

[1] Tacit. Ann. 14.
[2] Sophonius Tigellinus, who was become extremely odious by his vices and wickedness, had the good fortune, during the reign of Galba, to preserve not only his life, but his power, notwithstanding the cries and importunity of the people, who earnestly desired his death. But the Emperor Otho, to ingratiate himself, granted their request. Tigellinus was then at Sinuessa, and when they brought him this dismal news, he committed a crime which in itself deserved the punishment that was decreed him; for this infamous and corrupt man had the courage to anticipate it by cutting his own throat with a razor.

pretence for entreating Nero to put her away, that he might have successors by another wife. Upon this the Empress was separated from her husband; and in lieu of the Empire, which was her portion, they gave her the inheritance of Plautus, and assigned her Burrus's house to live in, which was looked upon as a sad presage for her.

This was not sufficient for Poppæa. Octavia's presence alarmed her ambition, and she thought it was of the greatest importance to her to get rid of one so disagreeable to her; but it was necessary to lay some crime to her charge, for which she might deserve to be banished, and it was impossible to find any true one. Tigellinus, very fertile in mischievous expedients, found no difficulty in this, but cheerfully undertook to make her as guilty as she pleased. One of Octavia's domestics, being corrupted by that infamous courtier, became the accuser of his mistress. He deposed that the Empress had a gallant named Eucer, a slave and a native of Alexandria, a player on the flute by profession; and upon this malicious accusation, the most chaste and virtuous Octavia was to be proved a prostitute. Her women and the ladies that attended her were put to the torture; and in order to extort from them false evidence against her, the most frightful instruments of punishment, such as were most capable of shaking the firmest resolution, were displayed before their eyes to intimidate them. They imagined they had gained their point, when some of them, being extremely terrified at the dreadful sight, yielded to their importunity; but if the force and violence of the tortures, the threats of Tigellinus, the weakness of their sex, and the presence of Nero's infernal ministers, and Poppæa's

jealousy, prevailed upon some of those poor women to
waver in their duty, by deposing contrary to their con-
sciences (having no other method of procuring a cessation to their torments, but by wrongfully accusing their
innocent mistress), yet there were others who, in the
midst of their sufferings, gave evidence to the truth with
wonderful intrepidity, openly publishing the Empress's
innocence, and justly praising her wisdom, prudence and
modesty, their fidelity being proof against the tortures
that were made use of to corrupt it. Thus the horrid
trick was unmasked, to the unspeakable shame of
Octavia's enemies. The truth was victorious, and this
black accusation only served to lend a new lustre to that
virtue which it was designed to blast. Tigellinus,
Octavia's bitterest enemy, was put to the greatest confusion by one of these women, who had the boldness and
courage to affront him to his face; for, as he was interro-
gating her, and asking her, in his brutal manner, if it was
not true that her mistress had prostituted herself to Eucer
the musician, she answered,[1] with a generous sort of contempt, that the least clean part of Octavia's person was
infinitely purer than his scandalous mouth; a mortifying
reproach, which could not but have killed him with shame,
if so base a soul had been capable of it.

But, by the most monstrous iniquity and injustice, the
Empress's innocence, that had been proved beyond all
contradiction, and was universally acknowledged, was
forced to give way to infernal calumny and falsehood.
Octavia was banished to Campania, and guards set over
her, as if she had been a state prisoner, whose dangerous
practices were much to be feared. The people soon gave

[1] Tacit. Ann. 14.

evident tokens of their inclination and affection for the Empress, who was treated so unworthily; they even showed it in a manner neither timid nor silent, for they exclaimed openly against this unjust banishment. On every side nothing was to be heard but murmurings and complaints against Nero and indignation against Poppæa, who had occasioned this exile. The Emperor was soon informed of this, and was mightily alarmed at it; for nothing is more to be apprehended than the popular fury in its first heat, as there is no barrier capable of stemming such a torrent. This had such an effect upon him, that, pretending to be very sorry he had banished Octavia, he recalled her immediately.

As soon as she made her appearance in Rome, every heart was filled with joy and cheerfulness. The people demonstrated it in such a manner, as was not very respectful to the Emperor's mistress; for they threw down the statues that had been erected in her honour, and at the same time raised up those of the Empress that were pulled down, crowning them with flowers, carrying her images about the streets in triumph, and into the temples with the same veneration as those of the gods. They highly commended Nero for having taken his lawful spouse back again. One could see in every countenance that serenity which the exile of the Empress had banished; and nothing was spoken of but pleasures and rejoicings. In short, everybody gave such sincere demonstrations of their satisfaction, that it looked as if every individual had made his fortune by the return of the Empress.

This excess of public joy had very bad consequences for Octavia. The haughty Poppæa was more exasperated than ever because of the insults that she had received and the utter contempt that the people had shown for her upon this occasion by overthrowing her statues. She reflected that this fury of the people had intimidated Nero, and had in a manner compelled him to recall Octavia, and did not doubt but the Emperor, since he so much regarded the humours and caprice of the mob, would, some time or other, settle his affections again upon the Empress, and consequently that she herself would, sooner or later, fall a sacrifice to the good of the public; she therefore employed all her charms and cunning to prevail upon Nero to banish Octavia again. She threw herself at his feet, and shedding tears in abundance, told him, with a most insinuating air, that it was wonderful he should, in such a manner, permit his authority to be despised, and stoop so low as to condescend to the will and pleasure of a mob; that their having got the better of him upon this occasion, was a shameful triumph of the people over the prince; that it was the first instance of an Emperor's yielding to an insolent multitude, to whose caprices he prostituted his dignity, when he could tamely suffer a person, whom he honoured with his affection, to be grossly affronted; that this rising of the people was an indication of what he had reason to fear for his own person, if they were to be humoured in this manner; that Octavia's power was more to be apprehended than he imagined, and that she had given a specimen of it in this late mutiny of the people, who had insolently prescribed laws to him, in forcing him to recall a person he had thought fit to banish. In short, she knew how to manage him so well, that Nero, imagining both his honour and his safety required that Octavia should die, or rather, not being able to refuse this victim to the jealousy of Poppæa, by whom he was rather bewitched than enamoured of her, signed an order for her execution. It was agreed upon that it should not be carried out in Rome, for fear of exciting a sedition, but that Octavia should be sent away again, when it would be an easy matter to compass it.

The great difficulty was to fix some crime upon her with a tolerable appearance of probability, since she had been before accused of one not at all credible. The declaration of Octavia's women had put that affair in a clear light, and was a decisive proof of their mistress's innocence. But, if those proofs had not been so strong as they were, the high esteem she enjoyed and her blameless conduct would have sufficiently excused her. They therefore found it necessary to add to the crime of adultery that of attempting to disturb the state and to cause her to be accused by somebody who was to charge her on her own confession, and one who should hold such an office that there should be a probability of her making use of him to intrigue with in order to form a party and, to make that person entirely her friend, she was to purchase his interest at the expense of her honour. To invent such a horrible calumny and shamelessly adhere to it in the case of a princess, whose innocence and prudence were known to all the world, certainly required the basest and wickedest wretch that could be procured, and such a one Anicetus was thought to be. He was commander of the galleys at Misenum, and the same person who had been employed in the death of Agrippina.

They were not at all deceived in the man they had made choice of; it was not to be supposed that he would refuse to commit any crime, after having spilled the blood of Agrippina. He was sent for, and Nero told him that it was not enough that he had delivered him from his mother; he expected he would also free him from the plots and evil designs of his wife; that, in order to do this, it was not necessary he should put her to death himself, or have recourse to any other violent measures; it would be sufficient if he affirmed that he had committed adultery with her. The Emperor assured him that he could not possibly do him a greater piece of service, and promised that he should be extremely well rewarded; and (that it might not be in his power to refuse) he told him that, after having trusted him with a secret of such importance, he could not do otherwise than put him to death, if he made any scruples, so that it might not be possible for him to reveal it.

Anicetus, who had no reputation to be solicitous about, for he had forfeited it by a number of crimes, was easily persuaded to undertake this work of iniquity; and accordingly, being tempted by Nero's promises, and intimidated by his threats, he confessed that he had been guilty of adultery with the Empress, and affirmed it before the Emperor's friends, or rather before the accomplices in his crimes, who were all people capable of any mischief, and had been assembled on purpose. This action completed Anicetus's wickedness and Octavia's misfortunes, who was in one moment accused, judged, and condemned. Never was a case less examined into, for all the judges were of the same opinion; and the consequence of Anicetus's confession was that Octavia was immediately sentenced to be banished, as if she had been convicted by the fullest evidence in the world. Anicetus's crime was also taken into consideration; he was banished to Sardinia, but care was taken to let him want for nothing as long as he lived.

The equity of this sentence was very much called in question, or rather, nobody doubted the partiality of it, because the assembly was made up of people without honour, and entirely devoted to Nero and Poppæa. The Emperor published aloud the traitorous designs that Octavia had formed against him and the Empire; he declared that she had not been ashamed to corrupt Anicetus, the captain of the galleys, whom she had prevailed upon to act jointly with her in this conspiracy, at the expense of her honour, prostituting herself shamefully to him, in order to make sure of the fleet. But in vain do people endeavour to disguise falsehood, for it is generally discovered by the very mask that is designed to hide it; and the precautions that are most commonly taken to carry on a cheat happen to be the means of its being found out. For Nero (to make this story of Octavia's adultery more readily believed) reported that she had caused herself to miscarry, in order to conceal her guilt and shame from her husband and the world, without recollecting that the first time he had a mind to divorce her (not being able with all his malice to lay any crime to her charge), he had been forced to have recourse to her barrenness, which, he said, was such as rendered her incapable of giving him successors. This (to the great shame and confusion of Nero) proved the falsehood of his assertion about the miscarriage.

As to Anicetus's having owned his crime, which was mentioned as an undeniable proof of Octavia's guilt, it was evident that it ought to have had no weight, and that the confession of that infamous officer did not deserve any credit. The assertion of a man who had committed so many crimes ought never to have been believed; nor was it reasonable that Agrippina's executioner should be deemed an equitable accuser of Octavia. But how could it be expected that justice should take place in so partial an assembly, made up of mercenary courtiers and syco-phants who were entirely devoted to Nero?

In the meantime unfortunate virtue was sacrificed with-out pity to triumphant jealousy, and the false and imaginary crimes of Octavia were expiated by a punish-ment that was but too real. This unhappy Empress was banished to the island of Pandataria; and never did any banished person excite so great nor so just a compassion in the hearts of the Romans. People spoke of the exile of Agrippina and her sisters, and of that of Julia, daughter of Augustus, but it was remembered that the former had found many comforts in the place of their banishment to mitigate their grief, and that none of them had suffered without having but too well deserved it; that, after all, their punishment had been preceded by many a happy day they had passed at Court, and that the pleasures they had formerly experienced might in some sort counter-balance their misfortunes. But they saw nothing to com-fort Octavia, nor anything to lessen their sorrow and con-cern for her cruel treatment; since, without ever having in her whole life given the least reason to be complained of, she was unmercifully punished for imaginary faults, of which the bare accusation was worse to her than death.

She was conducted to the place of her exile, and on the road such rudeness and incivility were shown her, as her escorts should have been ashamed to exhibit even to the most vulgar and mean criminal. She was perpetually stunned with the noise of centurions and soldiers, who, adding the authority of the Emperor to their natural

insolence, treated her without the least pity or compassion, which sufficiently demonstrated the orders they
had received, not to spare her in the least.

But, though this behaviour of her guards (equally
cruel and insulting) was but a melancholy presage of her
last misfortune, and she could easily read the sentence of
her death in the conduct of her persecutors, yet she could
not prevail upon herself willingly to renounce that life
which was so loaded with bitterness and affliction. She
was but twenty years old,[1] and might reasonably have
flattered herself with the hopes of enjoying some fortunate moments, if she survived Nero, the author of all
her misery; and according to all appearance, his reign
would be but short, as that of tyrants generally is; for
that unworthy Emperor was doing everything in his
power to bring destruction upon himself, by an infamous
indulgence in all manners of monstrous pollutions and also
by the horrible cruelties he every day committed.

But Octavia never had the pleasure of seeing this
happy change in her fortune; for, no sooner was she
arrived at the place of her exile, than notice was given her
to prepare for death. This charming and virtuous Empress could not hear this dreadful sentence without
trembling. She pleaded that, being divorced from Nero,
she ought not any longer to be reckoned his wife; and
as she had renounced that position and all pretensions to
it in favour of Poppæa, they ought to spare her life,
since she did not intend to interfere with the good fortune
of her rival; that she would, from that time forth, look
upon herself as only sister to the Emperor, and conse-

[1] Ac puella vicesimo ætatis anno inter centuriones et milites præsagio
malorum iam a vita exempta, nondum tamen morte acquiescebat.
(Tacitus).

quently it would not be in her power, even if she were disposed, to be any obstacle to Poppæa's designs.

She invoked Germanicus (from whom both she and Nero were descended) and called upon Agrippina, who, though she had been the cause of all her misfortunes, had nevertheless treated her with less cruelty. But neither her tears nor her sighs could soften the hard hearts of those who were commanded to put her to death. They bound her and opened her veins; but the blood flowing but slowly, on account of the great terror she was in, they stifled her in a bath, and with her, the beauty, virtue and graces of the best Empress that ever was born of the family of the Cæsars.

Octavia's death put an end to Poppæa's jealousy, but not to her cruelty; for, not being content with having sacrificed this illustrious victim to her hatred, she must needs have her head brought to her. This object, so worthy of compassion, was to her a charming spectacle; she feasted her eyes upon it, and Rome had the inexpressible mortification of seeing, in the hands of an infamous prostitute, the head of the most worthy princess that ever honoured the Empire. The people were in the utmost affliction at the tragical end of this poor unhappy Empress. Her death was honoured with tears that were never shed with more sincerity, and which were certainly due to the merit of Octavia, who was deserving of a better destiny.

POPPÆA

SECOND WIFE OF NERO

HERE is nothing so bad that a person over fond of power is not capable of it. He will make no scruple to violate the most sacred laws, to break through the strictest bonds, or commit the most heinous crimes to gain his ends. The history of Poppæa will furnish us with sufficient proofs of this assertion; for, if she had not been ambitious, she would not have been guilty of so many prostitutions, she would not have persecuted the innocence of Octavia, or have prevailed upon Nero to murder his mother.

She was the daughter of Titus Ollius, who had formerly been quæstor,[1] and would have obtained the highest offices,[2] if he had not been involved in the misfortunes of Sejanus, whose friendship, after he was disgraced, was (to those who partook of it) as great a misfortune, as his hatred was in his prosperity to those who were so unhappy as to feel it effects. Her mother was that famous Poppæa, whose beauty and gallantries made so much noise in Claudius's reign.

Sabina Poppæa was so named after her grandmother. As for her father, though he had not much to boast of

[1] Sueton. vit. Ner.   [2] Tacit. Ann. 13.

in point of birth or capacity, yet he had always skill enough to insinuate himself into the good graces of the Emperors, who employed him sometimes at the head of the armies, where he performed such actions and [1] behaved so well as to entitle him to the honour of a triumph and the consulship, and at other times in the government of provinces, where he passed some part of his life in continual fears and alarms from the malice of those false accusers, who were so much encouraged and listened to by Tiberius. He dreaded them so much, that to prevent the consequences of the machinations of those mischievous creatures, he decided [2] to put an end to his life, which he did with great precipitation, as if he had a mind to disappoint Fortune, of whose caprices he was so much afraid.

Poppæa had received from nature every advantage except modesty. She was reckoned the most perfect beauty in the world. Her charms were of that sort which strikes at first sight, and forces the admiration of all beholders. Her countenance and features were beyond description; their effect was heightened by youth and improved by a sweet and delightful air, which became her wonderfully. She had a peculiar grace when speaking, and her voice had such a sweetness as was not to be resisted; her conversation was enchanting in its vivacity and sprightliness. In short, she was altogether charming, and she knew how to heighten and set off her charms to advantage with the most captivating and becoming ornaments of dress; so that, if she had possessed good qualities proportionate to her beauty, she would have been the most accomplished person in the universe.

[1] Tacit. Ann. 6.   [2] Dio. lib. 58.

But, whether the bad example of her mother had influenced her so far as to compel her, in a manner, to give herself up to vice, or whether her natural inclinations to debauchery and libertinism were so violent, that every consideration had to give way to them, or lastly, whether her ambition was the cause of all her irregularities, it is certain that she abandoned herself entirely to them, and made so shameful and vile a use of her charms, that, as an historian observes, she made no difference between her husbands and her gallants. Her duty and reputation were never put in the scale against her ambition; the desire she had to advance herself extinguished every sentiment of honour, and she never failed to sacrifice to her vanity all the advantages of her mind and person, whenever they could be instrumental to her preferment. As to her wit, she had as much of it as enabled her to act her part very well in company, and could give it such a turn as made her agreeable to people of all characters; she was, upon some occasions, as skilful a prude as she was a coquette upon others.

She passed her youth in her mother's house, which was a school of debauchery and prostitution; there it was that she received the first homage of those who came in crowds to make their offerings at the shrine of her beauty, against the powerful attractions of which it was next to impossible for any man to defend himself. At first indeed she received all her adorers with a good deal of indifference; she even affected not to display her charms to the utmost advantage, but rather to be shy and reserved,[1] avoiding to be seen much in public, and when she did go abroad (as Tacitus observes) she wore a veil that

[1] Xiphilin. in Ner.

covered half her face, whether it was that this became
her best, or that the beauty of what appeared might
excite a desire to see the rest; but this restraint and
affected modesty not being suitable either to her inclinations or her designs, she soon threw off the mask, and
showed herself in reality such as she was, receiving
indifferently the incense of flattery from whatever quarter it came, and her house was open to every one.

She had too many charms not to be surrounded with
admirers.   Rufus Crispinus was one of the most
assiduous.[1]   She was so well satisfied with his addresses
that she married him.   The issue of this marriage was
the young Crispinus, whom Nero afterwards put to
death, for reasons as unjust as they were ridiculous.[2]
This marriage, however, put no constraint upon Poppæa,
for Crispinus, who was excessively in love with her, and
knew that she had never been used to be thwarted in
anything, was so foolish and convenient a husband, as to
indulge her so far as to suffer as many as pleased to have
free access to her and to offer up the same tribute of
praise and homage that she had been used to from all
persons of mark and distinction in Rome.   A brilliant
assembly met every day at her house, and she was continually surrounded with crowds of flattering courtiers,
who came to adore her beauty; it was the general
rendezvous of play, amusements, and pleasures, and
it was among these zealous votaries of her charms that

---

[1] Sueton. vit. Ner.

[2] This young lad, playing one day with other children of his age,
diverted himself and his companions with imitating a king. This was
told Nero, who looking upon it as ominous, and considering that it
foretold the Empire to Crispinus, became so cruelly jealous, that once,
when they were amusing themselves with fishing, he ordered the poor
boy to be thrown into the sea.

she exercised that talent, in which she excelled, of entertaining her auditors with her bewitching conversation,
and answering, with incomparable grace and affability,
the delicate compliments that were paid her by all that
were present. But Crispinus soon perceived that his complaisance was carried a great deal too far, and was attended with serious consequences. He found by sad experience, that those marks of esteem, which look so like
friendship, are often the dangerous and ensnaring attacks
of a lover; and that those diversions, those parties of
pleasure which women are so fond of, and the familiari-
ties they admit in such places, are generally the forerunners of their ruin, and the destruction of their virtue.

Of all those that frequented Poppæa's house Otho
seemed to be the most remarkable. This young man was
descended from a very illustrious family and was extraordinarily handsome. Besides these advantages, he was
the Emperor's favourite and inseparable companion,
partner in all his follies and vices, privy to all his secrets,
and obtained whatever he pleased to ask, for it was
through him, and by his interest, that all favours were
conferred; so that those who were happy enough to make
Otho their friend might look upon their business as done.
Being therefore so powerful at Court, it was no wonder
that Poppæa was extremely civil to him, and that he
should easily insinuate himself into the good graces of a
woman who had such vast designs. He was continually [1]
praising her beauty, and never visited her without being
loaded with presents, nor went away without leaving behind him evident tokens of his prodigality, which, with
her, passed for generosity and greatness of soul; so that

[1] Tacit. Ann. 13.

by these great extravagances, accompanied by the most gallant and polite behaviour in the world, this cunning courtier so managed his affairs, that Poppæa soon became sensible of his merit, and thought herself obliged to recompense his liberality.

There is nothing that more speedily and effectually captivates the hearts of some women than presents. It is the rock that their strongest resolutions split upon, and that virtue must be proof against everything, that does not yield to the all-conquering gold. A lover who is rich and liberal is already in a very fair way of succeeding, and may be said to be within sight of his happiness; whereas others, with all their birth, wit, and merit, have many a weary step to take before they make any considerable progress; but there are few Danaes that are not to be won by the golden shower. Poppæa, having received so many presents and favours from Otho, imagined herself not at liberty to be so ungrateful as to make no return. The great interest and influence of the courtier flattered the ambition of this haughty woman, and put a thousand projects of grandeur into her head, which were vastly increased by the promises he made her, so that her mind was sufficiently filled with ideas of splendour and authority. She now thought of nothing but Otho; Crispinus became insupportable to her; she hated him mortally, proved unfaithful to him, and gave herself up entirely to Otho.

This favourite, when he first began to pay his addresses to Poppæa, had something more in his head than his own interests.[1] It is reported that Nero had not been insensible to this lady's charms, but some remains of respect

[1] Plutarch. Tacit. Histor. 1.

for his mother, who had already made a great noise about
his amour with Acte, obliged him to proceed with caution;
he therefore charged Otho, his chief confidant, to prepare her heart for him. But, as it is the most difficult
thing in the world not to act a double part in this sort of
commissions, which put the fidelity of the agent so much
to the test, the favourite became terribly smitten with the
charms of Crispinus's wife; and whether he imagined that
Nero was not very solicitous about this conquest, being
taken up with Acte, or that he was glad to secure Poppæa
to himself, or lastly, that he believed it necessary to his
fortune to get her into his power, that at a proper time
he might, through her means, promote his own advancement, and preserve his interest with Nero, by sacrificing
to him the charming Poppæa, he married her after Crispinus's death, which happened very opportunely.

As he was violently in love with her, he never ceased
to boast of her extraordinary beauty; and especially he
affected, before the Emperor, to dwell much upon the
regularity of her features, and the inexpressible gracefulness of all her actions, often declaring how happy he
was, in possessing [1] the finest woman in the universe.
His constant repetition of this excited Nero's curiosity;
and as he was not yet thoroughly acquainted with
Poppæa, he was very desirous to be himself a judge of her
merit, that he might see whether she was deserving of all
the praises that had been so lavishly bestowed upon her.
He saw her then, and finding that she was even more
beautiful than she had been represented, he was immediately rather bewitched than enamoured with her.

Poppæa, who carried her views much further than

[1] Tacit. Ann. 13. c. 46.

Otho imagined, like a skilful woman took advantage of
her husband's false measures. She at once observed the
impression that her beauty had made upon the Emperor,
and entertained no doubt that, if she could win his
affections, it would be the certain means of accomplishing
her vast designs. She resolved to spare no pains to complete this glorious conquest, or rather this unjust usurpation. In order to do this, she set all her charms to work;
tender and passionate looks, insinuating caresses, and
magnificent apparel; in short, everything that could
possibly ensnare his heart was put in practice, and with
great success. For, as she had a peculiar art in captivating as many as she had a mind to please, she found it no
difficult matter to draw into her net a prince, who was not
of an age nor humour to exercise the virtue of self-denial,
nor did he hesitate a moment whether he should gratify
his inclinations or not. He attributed to real love the
false tokens of affection which were given him by this
artful coquette, and became so violently enamoured, that
he could no longer live without her.

These assiduities alarmed Otho, whose passion had in
a manner changed its nature as soon as he was Poppæa's
husband, for he could not bear the thoughts of Nero's
sharing with him the possession of her; on the contrary,
he repented that he had so inadvertently procured himself a dangerous rival, who did not know what it was to
be contradicted in his pleasures. It is by no means safe
to hold disputes with one's master and Emperor, against
whom one cannot even make use of one's advantages; for
it leaves one no other choice than that of yielding, or
bearing patiently all the consequences. Whatever dis-
agreeableness there may be in doing one or the other,

Otho was obliged, whether he would or not, to submit to it; but not without such evident affliction, as lay very heavy at his heart, and soon showed itself in his countenance, which Poppæa took notice of.

It is certain that she had a real esteem and affection for Otho, but the splendour of the throne afforded her more flattering and charming ideas than any other consideration. Her ambition was the only master she served; it was not Nero that she desired, but she could not help adoring his fortune; so that the endeavours she made use of to triumph over his heart were not on account of any love she had for his person, but in order to promote her own advancement and to make him purchase her favours at the price of the Empire. But as she was not sure of meeting with this extraordinary success, she could not resolve to part with Otho entirely, that she might at least secure one of her admirers. To bring this about, she conducted herself with great cunning and policy, and affected to be very reserved, knowing that by such behaviour she could not fail of pleasing Otho, who was jealous, and at the same time, of irritating Nero's desires; for she was not ignorant that disgust and indifference are very often the effect of a too easy conquest, some favours being only valuable in proportion to the difficulty with which they are obtained; that love often ends in the possession of the object beloved, and that Nero, who was naturally very inconstant, might possibly soon be cured of his passion, if he could gratify it upon too easy terms.

She managed her design with great address; for, as she possessed, in an eminent degree, the talent of assuming every character that suited her convenience, she began to put on the prude, and affected mightily to blame her past conduct. At first, she industriously avoided being alone with Nero, or even holding any long conversations with him. A strict modesty, and a severe kind of circumspection in her manners, succeeded that mirth and cheerfulness she had been hitherto remarkable for. She now delivered long harangues upon prudence and discretion, which she resolved to practise in all her words and actions. In short, she showed upon every occasion so austere a regularity, that, on Nero going to pay her a visit one evening when Otho was absent, she denied herself somewhat rudely, saying, that she could not, without being guilty of a crime, rob Octavia of her husband's affections; [1] that she had all the reason in the world to be faithful to Otho, who had everything in him that was commendable, both in his person and inclinations; [2] that after all, she was married to Otho, and would never give her husband any reason to dissolve a marriage that he had made very valuable to her by a most agreeable life, such as Nero with all his sovereign power could not exceed.

Poppæa could not possibly have acted more for her purpose, and the snare was too well laid for Nero to escape. This false modesty and reservedness inflamed the Emperor's heart more than if she had been ever so liberal of her favours, but it nearly proved fatal to Otho; for Nero, having taken it into his head that Poppæa's behaviour was all owing to the orders she had received from her husband, was so enraged at it, that, in the first heat of his anger, he even threatened to put to death him who had kindled it. He entirely withdrew all the

[1] Plutarch in Galb. [2] Tacit. Ann. 13.

affection he formerly had for him, deprived him of his
confidence and intimacy, and would certainly have made
him feel the utmost effects of his displeasure, if it had
not [1] been moderated by Seneca. This philosopher, who
was always using his best endeavours to calm the impetuosity of his pupil's furious and ungovernable disposition
by mild and gentle counsels, was besides a good friend of
Otho's. He represented to the Emperor (who had not
yet thrown off all respect for his tutor), that a revenge
like this could not but make a great noise in the world,
and publish abroad the true reason of Otho's disgrace,
which was by no means fit to be known; that there were
other methods of getting rid of his rival, without having
recourse to those violent remedies, since he had nothing
to do but to send him from Rome on some pretence,
and then he might see Poppæa as much as he pleased,
without a rival. Nero, who perhaps had not quite
divested himself of all friendship for a man he had been
so intimate with and had opened himself to upon all
occasions without the least reserve, especially in his most
secret debaucheries, and to whom he had (in a manner)
given the key of his heart, approved this expedient of
his perceptor. He made Otho governor of Lusitania,
and by so doing procured for himself the satisfaction he
so ardently wished for, of seeing Poppæa without a rival.

It may be asserted that Otho was himself the author of
his misfortune; and that which he imagined would be a
means of preserving his fortune and interest had like to
have cost him his life. He found himself obliged to quit
Rome and Poppæa, and set out for Lusitania full of
sorrow and jealously, plainly perceiving that, under the

[1] Plutarch.

glorious title of governor, he was condemned to a rigorous banishment. So true it is, that there is no reckoning upon the friendship of great men, nor is there any solidity in their professions of kindness, especially when their favour has been obtained by crimes and iniquity.

In the meantime Otho so managed his affairs that what he thought was his disgrace proved extremely to his advantage. He behaved [1] in his government with so much moderation and wisdom, that all his past irregularities were forgotten. The bad impression which his dissoluteness and debaucheries had created in everybody's mind was quite obliterated, and his exactness,[2] integrity, and the regularity of his conduct made people conceive so high an opinion of him, and so effectually gained him the hearts of all the world, especially the army, that afterwards they all declared for him, and elevated him to the throne.

Nero, being now delivered from his rival, omitted nothing that could re-instate him in his former happiness, and regain the good graces of his mistress; he exhausted his whole stock of complaisance and courtesy, and even condescended to make the most humble submission, which was the shameful mark of his defeat and slavery.

Besides this, he loaded the haughty Poppæa with rich and magnificent presents, broke off all commerce with his once beloved Acte, of whom she was jealous, and, to carry his respect as far as it could go, promised to marry her. This was just what she aimed at; for being infinitely more in love with Nero's rank than his person, and her

[1] Sueton. vit. Othon. Plutar. in Othon.
[2] Tacit. Ann. 13. Histor. 1.

ambition being without limits, she was aiming at no less than mounting the throne; and there was nothing she was not capable of doing, to gain this important point. Her charms were not the only engines she set to work upon this occasion, nor was it without design that she entertained in her house soothsayers, and those sort of people who foretold events,[1] whom she consulted and employed in her most secret affairs. But there were two great obstacles in her way, that seemed to be an almost insuperable check to her soaring hopes, and these were the authority of Agrippina, and Nero's marriage with Octavia, obstacles which, it must be owned, were such as one would think could never be got over; but ambition is not easily repulsed. It is a passion that nothing puts a stop to, nothing discourages. There are no difficulties it is not ready to encounter. Its desires increase in proportion to its acquisitions, and its gratification is so far from satisfying, that it only serves to make it aspire after new honours and dignities. So far is it from bearing a superior, that it cannot endure an equal, for everything that comes in competition with it is exposed to its fury and persecution.

It is true that Poppæa did not dip her hands in the blood of those who opposed her, but she was not less guilty of their destruction, because in fact, she was the occasion of it.[2] After she had made herself absolute mistress of the Emperor's heart, she forgot nothing that could contribute to the ruin of such people as either by their offices, power, or interest, were in a position to obstruct her most ambitious schemes. Sometimes she irritated the Emperor against his mother, by inspiring

---

[1] Tacit. Histor. 1. c. 22.   [2] Dio. lib. 61.

him with mistrust and suspicions, by making him jealous
and afraid of her authority, which, she said, Agrippina
was endeavouring to make supreme and independent.
At other times she suggested that his mother had very
bad designs against him, and that, as she had given
him the Empire, she imagined she had a right to deprive
him of it if she thought proper. She did not scruple
to invent bitter things against Octavia, spreading false
reports about her, and artfully insinuating that she was
intriguing against Nero, and seducing the people. When
she had fair opportunities, she would throw in a provoking [1] sort of raillery, reproaching him, that instead of
being Emperor, he was more a subject than other people;
that his submission could not be called respect or filial
duty, but the dependence of a slave; that he was only
looked upon as Agrippina's pupil, who kept him in a
subjection like a child. "In short," said she (with one
of those enchanting irresistible looks, which she knew
so well how to put on, and at the same time letting fall
some tears) "what reason can you have for deferring
" any longer our marriage, if it be true that you are
" your own master? Or what objection can anybody
" have against it, that ought to be of sufficient weight
" to hinder you from accomplishing your desires? Do
" they find any fault with my person? Is my beauty
" surpassed by that of any other, and does it not deserve
" a suitable return of love and tenderness on your side?
" Can anybody pretend that my birth does not entitle
" me to the honour of being your wife, when it is remem-
" bered that the highest dignities of the republic have
" been held by my family? Have not my ancestors been

[1] Tacit. Ann. 14.

" honoured with the same glorious ornaments, wherein
" consists the lustre and grandeur of the noblest houses
" in Rome, namely, the rods of the consulship, and the
" laurels of the triumpher? Can I not reckon in my
" family many generals who have deserved the Empire,
" and whose extraordinary services have been judged
" worthy of great rewards? But is it not rather the case
" that Agrippina is apprehensive that my advancement
" may be a check to her pride and unlimited ambition;
" and that the attachment to your interests, to which our
" marriage would of course commit me, would naturally
" oblige me to disclose to you her pernicious designs, and
" so publish to the senate and the people all her crimes
" and her insatiable avarice? If your mother (continued
" this artful woman), who is so accustomed to rule you
" like an infant, cannot bear that I should live with
" you, restore me to my husband, give me back to Otho.
" I am ready to go to him, were it to the furthest corner
" of the world; and when I shall be at a distance from
" the inevitable dangers to which I see you exposed, it
" will be less grievous to me to hear the insults heaped
" upon my Emperor spoken of, than to be a sad spectator
" of them."

These keen and cunning remonstrances made a great
impression on the Emperor, the more so, because Poppæa
was assisted in her designs by those who had access to
him; who, seeing their authority weakened, or rather
quite eclipsed by that of Agrippina, were very glad to
make use of Poppæa's interest in opposition to hers, but
at the same time did not imagine that Nero would carry
his fury and resentment so far, as to put his mother to
death. But such is the deplorable weakness of those who

are possessed with the demon of irregular and unlawful amours, that they are blinded by their tyrannical passion, and it becomes impossible for them to refuse it anything. They are forced to subscribe rashly, and without examination, to everything it exacts, not even sparing those that are nearest to them, or having the least regard to the laws of nature.

The haughty Poppæa, after having brought the Empress Agrippina to destruction, resolved to do as much for Octavia, now the only person that hindered her marriage with Nero. As she had admirable talents for gallantry, there was nothing capable of exciting desire that she did not put in practice to inflame the Emperor, and she succeeded so well, that Nero perfectly adored her, so that, not having it in his power to deny her anything, he put away Octavia, banished her, and soon after married Poppæa, with whom he was rather bewitched then enamoured.

The people, who are easily reconciled to whatever the sovereign thinks proper to do, without giving themselves much trouble about the justice of the matter, are very often by that means imposed upon, and for want of consideration become approvers of those faults and vices which they would otherwise abhor. They therefore erected statues in honour of the new Empress, giving by this base piece of flattery a shameful and unjust approbation to the scandalous marriage of Nero, and consequently to the treatment poor Octavia had met with. Poppæa, finding herself at last exalted to the throne of the Empire, which she had so ardently wished for, thought of nothing but enjoying her new dignity; but her triumph did not last longer than Octavia's disgrace, for

the scene soon changed for both of them. The people,
who are generally very fickle and inconstant, had no
sooner reflected upon the unjust and injurious banishment of Octavia, and the cruel treatment this only remaining branch of Cæsar's family had received, than they
began to murmur, and loudly demanded that Claudius's
daughter should be recalled. All the town was in an
uproar, nothing was to be heard but complaints, which
soon reached the ears of Nero, who, fearing the caprice
of the multitude, pretended to repent that he had sent
her away, and immediately recalled her.

The news of the Empress's return was received with
universal approbation. The whole town went out to
meet her, and never had such great satisfaction been seen
in the countenances of the Romans, to the great vexation
of Poppæa, whose statues they threw down with great
marks of contempt, and at the same time carried Octavia's
about the streets in triumph. But these demonstrations
of love and affection, which the people with so much
warmth showed this unfortunate princess, only hastened
her destruction; for Poppæa, provoked to the highest
degree at being thus wounded in her most tender part,
and having her statues trampled under foot, was inconsolable. She thought herself affronted in the cruellest
manner, and drew conclusions from it that were not very
favourable to her designs, for she could not then doubt
but that the inclinations of the Romans were for Octavia;
accordingly, concluding that she could never be safe upon
the throne as long as Octavia lived, since Nero, solicited
by the supplications and complaints of the people, (whose
hatred she saw he was apprehensive of) might at last
open his eyes to the unjust manner in which he had

treated his lawful wife, who had given him the Empire, she resolved to lose no time, but to sacrifice Octavia as soon as possible to ensure her own peace and safety.

In order to persuade Nero to this, she thought it necessary to call in to her assistance the utmost efforts of her charms, and employ the most delicate strokes of her policy. She very dexterously identified the Emperor's interests with her own; she exaggerated the power of Octavia, her influence with the people, her evil designs; and to make Nero more susceptible of the impressions she intended to give him, she insinuated, that this importunity of the people in favour of Octavia amounted to no less than a downright revolt against his authority. Then (adding the most enchanting look she could possibly put on to the irresistible charms of her all-persuading voice) she threw herself at his feet with her face bathed in tears; and in this posture, which even gave her an additional beauty, she told him, " that however desirous she " was to render indissoluble the bands of a marriage, " which would make her his inseparable companion, and " consequently procure her the greatest honour she could " possibly aspire to, yet it was not her intention to make " him any such request. No," continued she, " that is " not the favour I have to ask; I come to put my life " under your protection. The seditious partisans of " Octavia, sheltering themselves under the specious " name of the people, undertake in the time of peace what " they dared not attempt during the war; for if you " consider the affair, you will find that, when they lately " took up arms, it was against you that they did so. " They seem to want nothing but a leader, which Octavia " will find without giving herself much trouble. In

" short,[1] since, by all appearance, my life is what they
" aim at, I would take the liberty to ask what I have
" done to forfeit it, what crime or mischief I have com-
" mitted; whom I have had the misfortune to injure or
" displease; is it because I may probably give lawful
" heirs to the Empire, that the people are so exasperated
" against me; or does Rome prefer to see upon the throne
" the infamous posterity of a miserable player on the
" flute?" (meaning Eucer) to whom (by a horrible
calumny) Nero gave out that Octavia had prostituted
herself.

" Your interests, however," added she with great art
and subtlety, " shall always be infinitely dearer to me
" than my own. If it be true that I have done harm to
" anybody, or if you are determined to have the people
" for your master, do not wait until you are compelled
" to recall Octavia; do it with a good grace and not
" under compulsion. Let it not be at the instigation or
" rather command of a brutal and insolent mob. The
" public welfare and yours ought in all reason to take
" the place of my own private advantage. Sacrifice me,
" then, to the good of the State, or rather to the un-
" reasonable hatred of the people. Let me die a martyr
" to the persecutions of Agrippina and the jealousy of
" Octavia, or if you please, say to the interests of the
" State; I am quite ready to submit to your good pleasure
" in all things. But, if you have not a mind that a con-
" fused multitude, a mutinous rabble should prescribe
" laws to you, if you can resolve to show that you are
" Emperor, and have yet some small kindness for Pop-
" pæa, put her life in safety by punishing those who

[1] Tacit. Ann. 14.

" threaten it. Nothing will be easier for you than to
" prevent the like seditions for the future; for, since
" Octavia is the only cause of them, you have only to
" deprive the people of all hope of seeing her again at
" Rome as Empress, and some other suitable husband
" may easily be procured for her."

Never was slander set out in more plausible colours,
nor imposture invented with more specious marks of
probability. Nero gave in to it at once; he listened very
attentively to this studied discourse of Poppæa, which
she pronounced with such artifice, that the Emperor did
not in the least doubt the truth of what she said. He
was alarmed at this pretended intrigue of Octavia, and
was afraid of that poor princess, weak and defenceless
as she was; for Poppæa knew so well how to support her
assertion, by making the danger appear certain and
imminent, that Nero, believing his life was at stake, if
Octavia was suffered any longer to enjoy hers, had her
cruelly put to death; for, after having dipped his hands
in his mother's blood, the greatest crimes cost him but
little trouble, nor did he scruple to become the murderer
of his innocent wife. Poppæa, finding her jealousy appeased, her power established, and her marriage secured,
would no longer deny herself the pleasure of being
revenged on those who had opposed her designs, and of
heaping favours upon such as had been her friends.

Doryphorus, secretary of petitions, forfeited his life
for the liberty he had taken of disapproving of the Emperor's passion for Poppæa; Gessius Florus,[1] for being
the husband of Cleopatra, Poppæa's intimate friend, was
made governor of Judæa, Nero being unable to refuse

---

[1] Joseph. Antiq. Jud. lib. 20.

her anything, nor could he prevail upon himself to run the risk of disobliging her whom he rather adored than loved.

He admired her beauty as much as she valued it herself, and never omitted an opportunity of extolling it, which he did by the most delicate and studied praises. He went so far as to compose [1] verses upon the delightful brilliancy of her hair, which he compared to amber.

It is certain that Poppæa was an accomplished beauty; but it must also be confessed, that never did anybody take more care to preserve their charms; for in order to keep and heighten those graces that had [2] procured her so many admirers, she spared neither cost nor pains. Besides prodigious sums, which she laid out in the composition of the most costly washes and pomatums for her complexion, she [3] caused to be maintained, with vast care and at great expense, five hundred she asses that had just had young, which were milked every day to make [4] a bath for her; for she had been informed that nothing was comparable to it for preserving the skin and keeping it from wrinkles, those cruel effects of age, and wherever she travelled,[5] she was attended by this ridiculous equipage.

Great variety of the finest apparel and most precious jewels wonderfully increased her natural beauty. She appeared every day in the most magnificent clothes; her furniture was sumptuous, and her equipage the most brilliant that could be imagined. The mules attached to her litter were adorned with the most costly harness, and were shod with solid gold instead of iron; the traces and

---

[1] Plin. Hist. nat. lib. 17. cap. 3.   [4] Plin. lib. 38. c. 11. Juvenal. Sat. 6.
[2] Plin. lib. 11. c. 41. lib. 28. cap. 12.
[3] Juvenal Sat. 6.   [5] Xiphilin in Ner.

reins were all wrought with gold thread [1] and wire, and
she never appeared in public without all these tokens of
her unbounded pride and vanity. Never was there seen
such prodigious luxury. As she had nothing so much at
heart as the desire of pleasing, she had that perpetually
in view in all her actions. She had recourse to her look-
ing-glass every moment, in order to study her looks and
gestures, and one day this haughty Empress, not thinking
herself so handsome as usual, and foreseeing with sor-
rowful heart the sad but inevitable decline of her charms,
which the fatal laws of time would not spare, wept
bitterly, and prayed the gods that she might die before
she grew old.

Though she applied her beauty to very bad purposes,
she affected to be very modest, and had an outside appearance that deceived people. It was without doubt
this external show of virtue that induced Josephus to
launch out into the praises of this Empress; or else we
must suppose that it was in consideration of the particular obligations that illustrious Jew was under to Poppæa,
who often honoured him with her protection upon occasions when he had the most powerful courtiers, and even
kings, to oppose. This appeared in the affair of Felix.

Felix was the brother of Pallas, remarkable for his
influence and power in Claudius's reign (whom he governed as he pleased), and for his immense riches, which
were the fruits of all the extortions he had been guilty of,
which at last hastened his death. Felix was sent as governor to Judæa, where, being supported by his brother's
interest at Court, he exercised his authority with that
haughtiness [2] and brutal pride which is natural to those,

[1] Plin. lib. 33. c. 11.   [2] Tacit. Ann. 12.

who, from a low condition, have been exalted to honours
and great employments. Among a number of arbitrary
things which he did, in order to create a high opinion of
his power, he caused some of the Jewish priests to be
apprehended, upon a very slight pretence, loaded with
chains, and sent to Rome to be tried. Baronius is of
opinion, that these were the people who had made a vow
not to eat or drink till they had killed St. Paul.[1]

King Agrippa, whose father was so powerful at Rome,
happening to be interested in this affair, made such strong
representations at Court, in conjunction with Felix, that
the prisoners were put into close confinement and treated
cruelly at Rome, without any one being at the trouble of
examining whether they were blamable or not. Josephus, who was their friend, knowing their innocence,
resolved to go and defend their cause. He embarked [2]
for that purpose, and upon his journey happened to meet
with Aliturius, a Jew and a comedian, mightily esteemed
by Nero (who was very fond of that sort of people, and
used to appear upon the stage among them) and also by
Poppæa. It was no difficult matter for Josephus, being
a person of great distinction and consideration among the
Jews, to make this man his friend, who was rejoiced at
having an opportunity of doing a service to a country-
man and a person of Josephus's merit. They travelled
together, and were no sooner arrived at Rome, than
Aliturius made what haste he could to recommend as
warmly as possible Josephus's cause to the Emperor and
Empress, to whom he likewise presented Josephus afterwards. This illustrious Jew told his story so gracefully,
and with so much good sense, that Nero and Poppæa

---

[1] Baron. ad An. Ner. 2. acta 32.   [2] Joseph. in vita sua.

were charmed with him; the latter especially was so
glad to oblige Josephus, that she undertook his business
herself, and interceded for the prisoners with the Emperor. So powerful a recommendation could not fail of
being victorious; the prisoners were immediately acquitted and set at liberty, in spite of all the intrigues of
the King of Judæa and Felix; and Josephus, besides
gaining his cause, received from Poppæa such magnificent
presents as were worthy of his merit and the high rank
of his benefactress.

Poppæa looked upon her exaltation to the throne as
the greatest happiness that could possibly befall her,
because she did not know the value of that which was
offered her by Heaven, the knowledge of the true religion that St. Paul would have instructed her in, and
persuaded her to embrace.

St. Paul,[1] the first time he resided at Rome, had made
some acquaintances at Nero's Court; it is even confidently
affirmed that he kept up a correspondence with Seneca,
though many authors are of opinion that those letters are
fictitious, being unworthy of St. Paul and Seneca,[2] and
the work of the same impostor; but it is generally agreed
that Seneca must have known St. Paul,[3] whose reputation
and doctrine, being very extraordinary, made a great
noise, and were much talked of. Be that as it may, it is
certain that St. Paul was well known to many of Nero's
officers, since he says himself that [4] his bonds were become famous at the Emperor's Court.[5]

[1] S. Chrysost. advers. Vituper. vitæ Monast.   [2] Godeus, Hist. Eccles.
[3] Baron, ad. Ann. Ner. 12. S. Chrysost. in Act. hom. 54.
[4] Ad Philip. 1. 13.
[5] It cannot be denied that St. Paul had acquaintances in Nero's
family. "I would have you to know," says he himself to the Philippians,

In all likelihood it was by means of the friends St. Paul had in the Emperor's palace that he found opportunities of speaking to Poppæa. He represented to her, with a generous freedom, the disorders of her past life; and finding her well enough disposed to hear him, he explained to her the mysteries of the Christian religion, and exhorted her to embrace its precepts and practice its rules. These remonstrances being made with that true apostolical zeal for which St. Paul was so remarkable, operated very powerfully upon the Empress, which Nero perceived. It was touching him in the most tender part, to inspire Poppæa with such sentiments as he could not approve of. He was informed that it was St. Paul who had given her the austere lessons, which had made her so discreet and modest; and in the first transports of his rage he had him apprehended, loaded with irons, and shut up in a close prison, after having abused him with all the opprobrious names he could think of, and treated him as a knave, corrupter and vagabond.[1]

St. Peter and St. Paul were confined together, and were afterwards companions in their martyrdom. They were

"that what has happened to me, far from doing harm, has much contributed to the advancement of the Gospel, for my bonds are much spoken of in the Emperor's palace, and among all the Romans." It is even certain that this apostle had converted to Christianity many officers of Cæsar's household; for towards the end of the same epistle, he says to the Philippians, "all the saints salute you, especially those of Cæsar's household." This has induced St. Jerome to assert, that St. Paul contrived to form a Church in the very palace of the Emperor, his persecutor. He goes further still, for he will have it that Seneca turned Christian, and corresponded with St. Paul; he even places him in the rank of saints, and ecclesiastical authors. It is true, that there are but few people who do not deny the veracity of those letters, but on the other hand it is generally taken for granted that St. Paul must have been personally acquainted with Seneca, his doctrine and imprisonment being so much talked of at Rome.

[1] This place is now called San Pietro in Carcere. It was formerly called Carcer Tullianus.

shut up in a frightful dungeon, but even there the guards were not able to resist the words of life that flowed from their mouths, so that, being fully convinced of the truth of that holy religion which the apostles taught, these gaolers were immediately baptised, and a few days after, being accused and convicted of being Christians,[1] they suffered, with wonderful intrepidity, a glorious martyrdom for the faith of Jesus Christ, which they embraced.

The narrow limits of St. Paul's prison bore no proportion to his zeal. This good[2] apostle, having made his guards his friends, found means by his emissaries to exhort the Empress Poppæa to yield to the force of truth, and profess that faith which he had preached to her, but his endeavours were without success; for as the steps she had taken towards virtue by his advice were only some weak efforts, her vicious habits soon reassumed their former strength, in spite of the salutary doctrine of the apostle, which Nero took care to put a stop to, and prevent its having the designed effect; for being told that even from the dungeon the apostle did not slacken his endeavours, nor cease to instruct the Empress, but that he was continually pressing her to conform herself to the precepts of a religion, the sanctity of which did by no means suit his inclinations, he had him beheaded without the town, and the same day St. Peter was crucified by his order.

Poppæa returned to her former abominations. Still intoxicated with her beauty and her power, she applied herself more and more to the preservation of the one by the charms of the other; and the Emperor, who loved her as much as ever, finding her in every respect the same as

[2] Martyrol. Rom. 2. Jull. [3] S. Chrysost. advers. vit. Monast.

she was before, set no bounds to his complaisance. But
what inflamed him yet more was the hope he had of her
bringing him an heir to the Empire, for, to his excessive
joy, the Empress was with child. He demonstrated his
satisfaction by all the ways he could think of, amongst
the rest numerous vows to the gods for a happy delivery
were not forgotten.

The senate, the people, and all the orders of the city
were too good courtiers to be backward in paying their
respects, and showing how they shared in the good fortune of the Emperor. Poppæa was brought to bed at
Antium of a girl, who was named Claudia, and was immediately honoured with the title of August, as well as
her mother. Nero, seeing his wishes accomplished, indulged himself in an excess of joy.[1] He caused the most
sumptuous and magnificent games to be celebrated according to the Athenian ceremonies. He dedicated a
temple to the goddess of Fecundity, in gratitude for the
fertility of Poppæa; and that nothing might be wanting
to do honour to the princess's birth, he caused games and
shows to be represented in a theatre beyond the Tiber,
where was assembled an innumerable multitude of
people, to hear the songs and hymns that were composed
on this occasion in honour of young Claudia; and the
Emperor himself must needs perform a part among the
musicians.

The obsequious senate went in a body to Antium in
great ceremony, to congratulate the Empress upon her
happy delivery; all the orders did the same, and each
strove to outdo the other in respect and courtesy.

But this joy was soon turned into mourning; Claudia

[1] Plin. Tacit. Sueton.

lived but a few months; and as Nero did not at the time of her birth know how to confine his satisfaction within reasonable bounds, so on the other hand his grief at her death was no less immoderate. This accident was matter of fresh trouble to the senate, who, being obliged to regulate their sentiments and conduct according to those of the Emperor, were now obliged to express as much affliction as they did joy before. They proposed to immortalize the young princess, build temples in honour of her, and appoint a priest to officiate daily. In short, they carried their flattery and submission to the utmost degree of impiety. Poppæa's affliction was much keener and far more just; for, if Nature had been silent upon this occasion, her interests required that she should sincerely lament the death of this child, because, by its birth, Nero's usual fickleness of temper seemed to be much changed for the better. Besides, her having a child had done much to win her the hearts of the Romans in general, which had been much alienated from her by the murder of Octavia. The Empress, however, proved with child again, which renewed her hopes, and in all probability would have crowned her desires as well as those of the Empire, if Nero had suffered her to die a natural death.

This prince had long since shut his ears against the wise remonstrances of good people, and had given himself up entirely to the pernicious flattery of mercenary courtiers, who laboured for their own advantage, and not for the honour or interest of the Emperor, who amused himself with such things as were quite below his dignity, and thought of nothing but his dancing, plays, and music, in all which he affected to excel the rest of mankind. But his greatest ambition was to drive a chariot; this piece of folly he carried so far, that he left Rome, and took a long journey into Greece, on purpose to show his skill and address, as we shall see presently.

Poppæa, not being able to endure that the Emperor should thus lower himself, and employ all his time in such low exercises, which exposed him to the laughter and ridicule of the world, endeavoured to reclaim him, by condemning those vile and mean occupations, which brought an indelible stain upon his glory and the imperial dignity. To this purpose she employed her prayers, caresses and tears, but all in vain. She next had recourse to reproaches and raillery, but this method, instead of producing a good effect, proved fatal to her. For the unnatural prince, not being able to bear some provoking expressions used by Poppœa in reference to his driving a chariot, gave her such a kick [1] on the belly that she died immediately.

When the Emperor had recovered from the transports of his fury, he was inconsolable. He caused all imaginable honours to be paid her body, which was embalmed after the manner of those of the ancient kings. It was carried with great pomp and magnificence to the mausoleum that was erected for the Julian family; and if Pliny is to be credited, more perfumes were consumed on her funeral pile, than Arabia produces in a year.[2] In short, as if the Emperor had a mind to make her amends for the life he had deprived her of, he made her a goddess, and caused divine honours to be paid her. Her funeral panegyric was pronounced with great form and cere-

[1] Tacit. Ann. 16. Sueton. vit. Ner. Xiphilin.
[2] Plin. Hist. Nat. lib. 12. c. 18.

mony, in which her transcendent beauty was not forgotten. Nero seemed more in love with her after death
than before, if possible; his passion was then as infamous, as it had been violent in her lifetime; and the laws
of modesty will not permit us to relate the manner in
which history [1] affirms that this libidinous prince treated
the person of his freedman Sporus, whose face had some
resemblance to that of Poppæa.

[1] Aurel. Victor. Epitom. Sueton. vit. Ner. Xiphilin.

MESSALINA

THIRD WIFE OF NERO

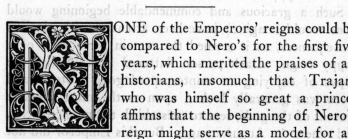ONE of the Emperors' reigns could be
compared to Nero's for the first five
years, which merited the praises of all
historians, insomuch that Trajan,
who was himself so great a prince,
affirms that the beginning of Nero's
reign might serve as a model for all
kings to imitate.[1] The manner in which he intended to
govern, and the rules he laid down to regulate his conduct were so approved of by the senate and all the people,
and gave them so high an idea of the happiness of his
reign, that they were ordered to be engraven on a tablet
of silver. Augustus was the pattern he was to copy;
and to show that he intended to be an exact imitator of
that excellent prince, he obliged himself [2] to perform
some action of generosity, clemency, or liberality every
day. Persons who were in affliction might depend upon
finding a sure refuge with him. He eased the people
by the suppression of new taxes, and by a diminution of
the old ones. He supported indigent virtue and nobility
(made contemptible through poverty), by delivering
from misery and wretchedness those senators of illustrious birth, who by the vicissitudes of fortune were be-

[1] Aurel. Victor. Epitom. in Ner.   [2] Sueton. vit. Ner. c. 12.

come extremely poor, and by his liberality enabled them
to maintain their dignity with honour and credit. In
short, he made such necessary and beneficent regulations,
that the senate, being charmed with so glorious a prospect, returned him public thanks in due form; but Nero,
with inimitable grace and modesty, said he had not yet
been so happy as to deserve them.

Such a gracious and commendable beginning would
(one would imagine) have been attended with glorious
consequences, as it seemed the certain forerunner of a
happy reign. Each person flattered himself with the
hopes of enjoying an uninterrupted good fortune, and
Nero was generally looked upon as the most valuable
present of the gods, sent to reëstablish the public felicity,
and renew the Augustan age. But this Emperor did not
long answer the great expectations that all the world had
conceived of him. His manners changed with his fortune, and he divested himself of his good qualities, in
proportion to the encouragement he gave to flatterers,
becoming wicked with them by contagion. He suffered
himself to be hurried on by a bad example, and at last
giving himself up to all manner of crimes, he clearly
proved that, from Ahenobarbus and Agrippina, nothing
could proceed but what was pernicious and detestable.

After he had shaken off the intolerable yoke of his
mother's authority and that of his preceptors, which
placed him under a grievous restraint, all those shameful
vices, which rendered him the scourge of Rome and the
republic, broke out like a torrent. Instead of Augustus,
who at first he declared should be his model, Caligula,
the worst of all the Emperors, was the person he said he
was resolved to imitate; he kept his word, for he sur-

passed him in all sorts of wickedness to that degree, that
his name, which before furnished an idea of a most accomplished prince, incurred afterwards such hatred and
public execration, that it became the expression and
image of a detestable tyrant; so that whoever was afterwards to be branded with that infamous character was
called a Nero.

His monstrous lewdness defiled every part of his body.
He invented such brutal pleasures as were never thought
of before, and there was neither [1] condition, relationship
nor sex, that could be secure from the infamous and
abominable flames of his incontinence. His horrible
cruelties filled Rome with blood and tears. He put [2]
his aunt Domitia to death, to possess himself of her
estate; though this lady was so extremely old, that, if he
had had but a little patience, it must have fallen to him in
due course. Rubellius Plautus, his near relation, was
afterwards sacrificed to his jealousy, though he had retired to Asia, that he might give no offence to Nero; but
this voluntary banishment did not protect him, for the
barbarous Emperor sent emissaries thither on purpose to
assassinate him, with orders to bring his head to Rome.
He indulged himself in the base and poor satisfaction
of examining it, and adding insult to cruelty, said, in a
jocose way, that he did not think Rubellius had so large
a nose. Pallas was also the object of his cruelty and
avarice; for Nero had him poisoned, in order to seize
the immense riches of this freedman, who had insolently
abused his good fortune, and accumulated prodigious
wealth by rapine and oppression, which he forfeited by

[1] S. Chrysost. advers. Vituper. vitæ Monast.
[2] Sueton. vit. Nero. Tacit.

an untimely end, a just punishment for having put so
many persons to death in order to glut himself with
their spoils.   After having made the citizens of Rome
sufficiently sensible of his inhumanity, he exercised his
fury against Rome itself, destroying its magnificent buildings, temples, and palaces,[1] by setting the town on fire,
which he contemplated with great pleasure from the top
of a tower, and saw preying with raging violence and
impetuosity upon the most sumptuous edifices in the
noblest streets in Rome, which he said gave him an agreeable notion of the burning of Troy.   Nothing could
better paint his character than this burning of Rome,[2]
on purpose to gratify his diabolical curiosity, and that
he might also be thereby furnished with an opportunity
of indulging the implacable hatred he bore the Christians, whom he accused of this horrible action, and so
threw the blame upon them, punishing those poor innocent people for a crime that nobody was capable of but
himself.

To attempt to give particular details of all the crimes
this infamous prince was guilty of, would be an endless
task.   It is sufficient for our purpose to say, that after
having shed the blood of Brittanicus, his mother, and
his wife Octavia, in order to marry Poppæa, whom he
also killed as has been related, he soon after resolved to
marry again, and at first had thoughts of Antonia, his
first wife's sister, and his own sister by adoption.   But
Antonia was not so charmed with the dazzling pomp
and magnificence of a throne (however captivating it
may seem to vulgar eyes), as to accept his proposal; for
she was very sensible that, notwithstanding its splendid

[1] Dio. Tacit. Sueton.   [2] Baronius.

outside, which makes it so ardently desired by ambitious people, it generally produces innumerable troubles and vexations, and that this exalted post, so much coveted, is surrounded with dangerous precipices. These judicious reflections induced her to refuse the offer of Nero, whose brutal temper she could not but be very well acquainted with.

It cannot be denied that Antonia's conduct upon this occasion was the height of prudence. The misfortunes of Octavia and Poppæa were terrible examples for her, and as she had a right way of judging in all things, she looked upon the treatment those two Empresses had met with to be no other than what she might herself expect; for which reason she steadily persisted in her determination never to marry a prince with whom she could not be an hour in safety. This refusal cost her her life,[1] for Nero, whose impetuous desires would admit of no contradiction, accused her of having designs against the Empire, and upon this accusation (which was supported by no sort of proof) put her to death.

His choice fell upon Messalina, grand-daughter of Statilius Taurus, who, in Augustus's time, had been honoured with a triumph and the consulship.

This lady was famous in Rome on account of her great riches and her wit; and though she had had already three husbands, from whom she was separated by death or divorce, she was yet very beautiful. These good qualities procured her abundance of admirers, and in spite of certain suspicions about her virtue, she managed to provide herself with a fourth husband.

This was Atticus Vestinus, Nero's companion in all

[1] Sueton. vit. Ner. Tacit. Ann.

his debaucheries, and sharer of all his secrets. This senator had the skill to insinuate himself so far into the Emperor's good graces, and to acquire such a degree of familiarity with him, that he frequently took the liberty to pique him by the most cutting railleries. Nero did not tolerate it without a good deal of impatience, but as he had trusted Vestinus with all his affairs, and had entirely opened his heart to him, he dare not reprimand him, for fear he should reveal the shameful secrets he had become acquainted with. Vestinus, however, when he married Messalina, was not ignorant that Nero had made very free with that lady. Their gallantry was so much talked of at Rome, that it is not at all probable that Vestinus should have been the only one that knew nothing of it, for she regarded her reputation so little in that affair, that she made no manner of secret of it, nor did she think proper to carry her scruples so far as to put her honour in competition with her fortune; accordingly she laid herself out to attract him as much as possible, being sensible that this amour could not but furnish her with the means of gratifying her vanity to the utmost. But, as she had but small hopes of succeeding in all her ambitious schemes, she prevailed upon herself to take up with Vestinus for her fourth husband, who paid very dear for the honour of marrying the Emperor's mistress, for Nero resented it so much, that he waited only for a fair opportunity to destroy him.

This he thought offered itself very opportunely in the poisoning conspiracy which was fatal to so many honest men. But as there was not the least shadow of proof that Vestinus had had any hand in that plot, nobody could be found willing to accuse him. Nero being at last quite

weary of seeing a man live whom he hated mortally
(especially since he was now at liberty by Poppæa's death
to marry Messalina), ordered his veins to be opened,
without seeking for any further pretence, and by that
means got rid of a person, who from being his greatest
favourite, was become extremely odious to him. Vestinus
was at table in his own house, entertaining a great number of his friends at supper, when the instruments of
Nero's cruelty came thither to put him to death. They
forced him into a warm bath, and opened his veins so
that he bled to death.

This tragical event did not cost Messalina many tears,
as she was sure that Nero would soon make her amends
for her loss. He did so in fact, for he married her, and
caused her to be honoured with the glorious title of
August. This new Empress at first found great charms
in the brilliant lustre of the throne, but soon after perceived it to be full of cares and anxieties. Nero's irregular conduct was an inexhaustible source of bitterness,
which Messalina was the more sensible of, as she was
forced to lament in secret, and without complaining, for
fear that her remonstrances, if she should venture to
make any, might prove as fatal to her as they had been
to Poppæa, whose place she filled; for Nero was no
longer capable of following wholesome advice, being entirely guided by his extravagant desires and caprices.

The Emperor, not being satisfied with the crimes he
had already committed, added fresh murders to those he
was already stained with, and under pretence of punishing such as had been engaged in Piso's conspiracy, filled
Rome with blood. Silanus Vetus, and all his family were
the objects of his rage; Annæus Mela, Seneca's brother,

and father of the poet Lucan perished under his accusation, as well as Petronius, the most agreeable debauchee of his time; Pætus Thrasea, the senator, famous for his great offices and dignities, in which he acquitted himself with honour; Barea Soranus, illustrious for his nobility and high station, as well as for his firm and immovable probity, precious remains of ancient Roman virtue; Corbulo, in whom was also to be seen a true image of old Rome, being the firmest support of the empire; Seneca, and a vast number of others of the first rank, augmented the number of victims that this tyrant sacrificed to his cruelty.

Messalina had many other reasons for the trouble and vexation she underwent from the conduct of Nero; his follies and extravagances continually prepared for her fresh matter for sorrow and discontent. His having passed his youth in singing, driving chariots, and music, might be excused; but even when he became Emperor, nothing would satisfy him but displaying his abilities in such low exercises as were not at all suitable to his dignity, and this upon such occasions as most required that he should put on a gravity conformable to his rank, for example, before Tiridates, who was come to Rome on purpose to receive from the hands of the Emperor the crown of Armenia. On this occasion, Nero, being unable to restrain himself for any considerable time, as soon as the ceremony of the coronation was over, took this king to the theatre, and in his presence, having clothed himself in green, must needs show his skill in driving a chariot, not being at all ashamed to degrade himself by those mean occupations. But however unworthy they were of an Emperor, there

was no lack of sycophants and flatterers, who extol even
the vices and greatest faults of princes, who mightily
commended his great address and activity; Nero, being
then persuaded that it was a pity to shut up such rare
talents inside Rome, resolved to give proof of them in
foreign countries, in order to obtain the crowns that
were given to the best performer in driving chariots,
acting, the best singer and the best player on the harp,
for this was his greatest ambition. He could not bear
that anyone should dispute these glorious titles with him,
and it would have been very dangerous to become his
rival. He accordingly left Rome, and stopped in all
the towns upon the road. He there publicly exhibited
himself to the people in all the squares and theatres,
and most ridiculously displayed to all the world that
great skill and address he so much prided himself upon,
supplicating the approbation of all the spectators; and,
after having gone through all Achaia, he returned to
Rome, loaded with one thousand eight hundred crowns,[1]
which he was more proud of than if he had gained as
many victories over the greatest enemies of the republic.

These unworthy occupations did not stop the course
of his cruelties and lewdness, for he never desisted from
them but in order to spill the blood of some citizen, or
dishonour some illustrious family. He filled up the
measure of his iniquity at last, and there was no way of
reckoning up his crimes but by the number of his actions.
This tyrannical government caused the provinces to re-

---

[1] The Romans honoured with a crown those who had distinguished
themselves in war, fighting in the capitol, public sports, any particular
science, or even combats in the amphitheatre. As these crowns were
given upon different occasions, they were made of different materials.
There were ten kinds of them.

volt, and decided them to shake off the intolerable yoke.
Vindex, governor of Celtic Gaul, was the first that declared against Nero. Galba, who commanded an army
in Spain, and Otho, governor of Lusitania, did the same,
and their example was followed by the people of Rome,
who were resolved to withdraw their allegiance from
a prince who had made himself odious to all the earth.
Galba was proclaimed Emperor by the legions, and this
election was confirmed by a decree of the senate, who
declared Nero an enemy of the republic, and condemned
him to death.[1] He was informed that there was a most
painful and ignominious end preparing for him; and
seeing himself hated by all the world, betrayed by his
subjects, and finding no compassion from anybody, not
even in the hearts of those who had been partakers with
him in his crimes, he killed himself, that he might not fall
into the hands of those who were in quest of him to
sacrifice him to the public hatred, and before he gave
the fatal stroke, he cried out, what a pity it was that so
skilful an artist should perish in such a miserable
manner.

Nero was at dinner when the news of the revolt of
the armies was brought him. He tore the letters to
pieces, overset the table, and broke two Corinthian vases
of immense value, which he called Homerics, because of

[1] Nero hearing that the senate had declared him an enemy to the
republic, and condemned him to be punished, according to the ancient
form [*more majorum*], asked what was meant by the ancient form. He
was told that the criminal was to be stripped quite naked, his head
placed between the two arms of a pitch-fork, and whipped till he expired; afterwards he was to be thrown down the Tarpeian rock, and
then dragged with a hook and thrown into the Tiber. This made him
tremble, and one of those that were with him having advised him to
forestall all these indignities to which his body would be exposed, by
courageously putting an end to his own life, Nero answered that he
should be extremely obliged to him if he would show him the way.

the verses of Homer which were engraven upon them. Then, enclosing in a golden box some poison which was prepared by Locusta, he went to the Servilian gardens, whence he despatched some of his most faithful freedmen to Ostia to secure a ship, with orders to have it always in readiness. He endeavoured to persuade the tribunes and captains of his guards to accompany him in his intended flight, but some made scruples and difficulties, and others absolutely refused.

He formed a great many designs, without being able to come to any resolution, hesitating whether he should take refuge among the Parthians, or throw himself upon the mercy of Galba by appearing before him as a suppliant. Sometimes he thought it would be best that he should show himself in public at the orators' tribunal in deep mourning, in order to excite the compassion of the people, of whom he intended to ask pardon for all his past faults; and if he should find it impossible to obtain forgiveness, to request that at least they would leave him the government of Egypt. In fact, a speech that he had composed for that purpose was afterwards found among his papers; but it is thought that his fear of being torn to pieces by the mob prevented his adopting that course. However it was, he resolved to defer his further deliberations till the next morning, and in the meantime went to bed, but awoke about midnight. Perceiving that his guards had quitted their posts, he got up immediately, and sent some of his friends for information, but not hearing from anybody, he went out into the streets, attended by a few persons, and knocked at several doors; but finding everywhere a profound silence, he returned to his chamber, where somebody had been in his absence and carried off his bedclothes, and the golden box that had the poison in it.

In this wretched condition he sent about for Spicillus or some other gladiator, to put him to death, for he could meet with nobody that would do him this last piece of service. " What then," said he, " have I neither friend nor enemy ? " and then ran as if he was determined to throw himself into the Tiber.

But changing his mind he looked about for some secret place to hide himself in, till he could consider a little what was best to be done. Upon this, one of his freed-men, named Phaon, offered him a little house he had four miles from Rome; so (bare-footed as he was, having nothing on but his shirt and an old ragged cloak that somebody had thrown over him, with which he covered his head) he held a handkerchief up to his face, and mounted a horse, accompanied only by four persons, of which number his beloved Sporus was one.

He had scarcely set out when he felt the earth trembling under him, and was horribly terrified with dreadful flashes of lightning. As he passed near the camp, he heard the soldiers cursing him with bitter imprecations, and wishing prosperity to Galba. He met some persons on the road, who said to each other, " These people are pursuing Nero." One asked him, " What news of Nero at Rome ? " and, his horse starting at the same time, his face was uncovered with the shock, and he was recognised by one of the guards, who saluted him. Coming to a narrow by-way, they were forced to quit their horses among bushes and briars, with which Nero's feet were much wounded, notwithstanding the clothes that they had wrapped about them, and with great difficulty got at

Bathing scene typical of the luxurious baths of Rome

last to a wall that was just over against the house. They had not however an opportunity of entering it secretly, so that Phaon advised him to conceal himself for a while in a cavern where gravel had been dug, but Nero said that he would not be buried alive; and being very thirsty, he was forced to take some water out of a ditch with his hand. He then sat down, and fell to pulling the thorns out of his cloak, which was all in tatters with them, and was afterwards obliged to creep upon all fours like a beast, through a narrow hole in the wall, which they had made on purpose. As soon as he had got into a little room, he threw himself upon a bed, where there was nothing but an old blanket and a wretched bolster; and as he was very hungry and dry, they brought him a piece of black bread, but he would not eat it, so was content with a draught of warm water.

All those that were present solicited him to anticipate, by a voluntary death, the evils and insults with which he was threatened; accordingly he caused a grave to be made before his face, and ordered that it should be covered with a piece of marble, if any could be procured. He also gave directions for water to be procured to wash his corpse, and wood to burn it. He wept at every word, with repeated lamentations that so skilful an artist should ever die. In the meantime, a courier arrived to give him notice that the senate had declared him an enemy to the State, and that he had been condemned to die after the ancient manner. He enquired what sort of punishment that was, and being told that the criminal was stripped naked, his neck fastened to a post with the arms of a pitch-fork, and in this posture, was whipped till he expired, he fell into a terrible horror;

and, in order to avoid so dreadful a death, resolved to be his own executioner. He therefore took two poniards into his hand, but, after feeling the points of them, put them up again, saying, that his last hour was not yet come. Sometimes he would entreat Sporus to bewail and lament his miserable fate, and then turning to all about him, would beg that some one of them would kill himself and show him an example, for otherwise he would never have the courage and resolution to do it. In the midst of this perplexity, he heard the horses' feet of those who were come to apprehend and conduct him to Rome. He then pronounced a Greek verse, the sense of which is, " a confused noise of horses strikes my ears," and repeating these words, he took the poniard again, and attempted to kill himself, but having neither strength nor heart to do it, he was assisted by Epaphroditus his master of petitions.

The moment he received the mortal stroke, the captain entered the room, and pretending to have come to his assistance, endeavoured to stop the bleeding. But Nero, looking at him, said, " It is too late: is this your fidelity? " Saying these words he expired, his eyes starting out of his head in a most frightful manner.

He had strictly charged those who were near him, that his head should not be given to anyone, but that his body should be burnt entire. Icelus, Galba's freedmen, granted his request, though he was but just come out of prison, into which Nero had thrown him, as soon as the revolt was known.[1]

The delights of a court and the charms of a throne had made too powerful an impression upon Messalina's

[1] Sueton.

mind, not to inspire her with a strong desire to enjoy them again. She even flattered herself with those golden hopes, especially when Otho (to whom she had not been indifferent) wrote her very tender letters, full of esteem and affection. And it is certain, that he had resolved to marry her, and waited for nothing but to carry out successfully the designs he had upon the Empire; but this hasty joy of Messalina did not last long, nor did Fortune perform for this princess what she had seemed to promise her. She frequently raises people only in order to precipitate them so much the lower, and accordingly abandoned Otho, when he had the greatest need of her; and, as if she had repented of having exalted him to the throne after the death of Galba, she immediately hurled him down again; or rather, Providence would not permit that Otho should long remain in quiet possession of the throne, which he had acquired by a horrible murder, as if it were to convince ambitious people, that nothing is less durable than a usurped power, and that the diadem rests upon a very precarious foundation, when placed upon a guilty head. In fact, after Galba had been assassinated by Otho's treason, the Empire became in a manner a prey to whoever took a fancy to it. Vitellius was proclaimed Emperor at Cologne, but Otho's party was the strongest, because he had the city of Rome on his side. He did not however make the most of his advantage, for, instead of waiting for several legions that were coming to join him from Illyria, he went to meet Vitellius, and offered him battle. He was not even present himself at the action, which was the cause of his ruin, for his army, not being encouraged by their chief, was entirely defeated. As soon as Otho heard of it, he killed himself through despair, that he might not survive his misfortune; but left an affectionate letter for Messalina, in which he bade her adieu for ever.

The same blow that put an end to Otho's life destroyed Messalina's hopes. This princess's ambition might be said to have been extinguished in Otho's blood; for, seeing all her projects brought to nothing by the death of him who, she imagined, would promote her again to the throne, she gave herself entirely up to the study of oratory, for which she possessed all the natural qualifications, and gave sufficient proofs of it by orations which she delivered in public. These were so full of learning and erudition, that the most famous orators of her age might have been proud of them; and in this occupation she passed the rest of her life.

HE Emperor Servius Sulpicius Galba
united in his person two of the most
illustrious families of Rome. He was
related [1] to the Empress Livia, who
took him particularly under her protection, and advanced him to the
highest employments, which he ob-
tained before he arrived at the age prescribed by the
laws. For a long time he was called Livius Ocella,
which name he took from Livia Ocellina, whom Galba
his father had for his second wife. This lady, though
very rich and handsome, condescended to make great advances to Galba the father, upon account of his nobility,
though he was of small stature, very ill made, and even
hump-backed, which defects of nature he took care to
conceal as much as possible by wearing a robe that was
very wide and long, and high-heeled shoes. Ocellina,
however, did not esteem him a whit the less for these
defects, though informed of them by Galba himself,
who made no secret of them to her; for being resolved
she should have no reason to reproach him with having
deceived her, he took her one day aside, and putting
off his robe, made her observe all the above-mentioned

[1] Sueton. vit. Galb. Plutarch. vit. Galb. Tacit. Hist. lib. 1. c. 13.

deformities. This sincerity, which is so little practised, so won over Ocellina, that she preferred him to the rest of her admirers, and married him; but having no children by him, she adopted Servius Galba, whom he had by his first wife, Mummia Achaica, who is the person of whom we are now speaking.

Galba had many lucky presages which promised him the Empire. Augustus [1] one day assured him of it. Tiberius [2] said openly, that Galba would reign in his old age; and a soothsayer foretold, that one of his family would be Emperor, but that it would not happen very soon, which made Galba say, that it would be so when a mule brought forth young. This prodigy came to pass, however; and, after that Galba reckoned upon it as a certainty.

With all these advantages, added to his immense riches and great hopes, Galba might have made his choice among the ladies, and many considerable offers were made him, but he found so much merit, wisdom and modesty in Lepida, that he infinitely preferred her to the others, and married her. He had no reason to repent it, for Lepida fully answered his expectations, repaying his esteem with the most tender affection. Her virtue and fidelity were always such as to give no room for censure or detraction. They lived together with mutual satisfaction and happiness, when Agrippina, whose mind was filled with ambitious projects, and who was looking about for somebody to assist her in the accomplishment of them, took it in her head to select Galba, as a proper person for her purpose, and hoped to prevail upon him to divorce his wife Lepida, in order to marry her.

[1] Sueton. vit. Galb.   [2] Tacit. Ann. 6.

Agrippina was then widow [1] of Domitius Ahenobarbus
her first husband. To her royal birth she added the
most captivating beauty, a lively wit, and an unbounded
ambition, which was founded upon the highest pretensions. She wanted nothing but a husband as ambitious as
herself, who might act in concert with her in promoting
her views and designs, and imagined Galba to be just
such a man, on account of his nobility, high office, and
vast influence at Court, but especially, the happy prog-
nostications of his future grandeur.

In order to succeed in this important undertaking,
from which she had formed such hopes and expectations,
she was of opinion, that it would be best to dispense with
those ordinary formalities and rules which the laws of
decency seem to require, and which do not admit of
ladies making the first advances. She therefore got over
all those scruples; and being afraid of losing her fortune
if matters were to go on in the ordinary course, she was
resolved she would have no reason to reproach herself
with having missed her aim, by adhering too strictly to
fashions and customs, and therefore made no difficulty
about taking the first steps in this affair, and that in the
most passionate manner.

Galba, who saw into her very heart, knew how to make
the proper distinction between real affection and policy;
and knowing the deep designs of this princess, he was
determined not to serve as a tool for her ambition; so,
in order to let her see that he was not to be imposed
upon by her deceitful behaviour, he affected to show as
much indifference as she had weakness. Besides, Galba
had no sort of inclination to part with Lepida, whose

[1] Sueton. vit. Galb.

virtue and prudence he was so well acquainted with, in order to marry Agrippina, whose husband he knew would be exposed to all her infidelities, and many other disagreeable trials, as were Passienus and Claudius.

Agrippina, however, was not discouraged. She employed the whole force of her beauty, which was very dangerous when armed with all the charms that a woman knows how to make use of, when she has a mind to please; and wherever Galba went, she was sure to be there, with all that art and nature could furnish, to captivate his heart.

He never had been exposed to such formidable enemies before; but they found him so strictly on his guard, owing to the high idea he had of Lepida's virtue, and the bad opinion he had conceived of Agrippina, that those powerful darts, which had been fatal to so many others, were launched in vain at him, and Agrippina found herself reduced to the melancholy condition of striving to no purpose.

Any person but Lepida would have been alarmed, and would certainly have been apprehensive that Galba would at last yield to those charms which were almost irresistible, and think himself obliged, like a man of gallantry and politeness, to make a suitable return, but she showed no signs of jealousy; on the contrary, she gave her rival full scope, without fearing that Agrippina's endeavours would work the least alteration in her husband's heart. Her mother was not quite so easy. This lady, who was extremely shrewd, and knew Agrippina to be capable of using every stratagem to seduce her son-in-law, was tormented with that jealousy of which Lepida had not been susceptible, and conceived such a hatred against Agrippina, that she could scarcely keep it within bounds. She managed however to smother it for some time, but being at length weary of swallowing this vexation in silence, she was resolved it should break out on the first opportunity; and soon after, chance furnished her with a very favourable one.

She happened to be at an assembly of ladies where Agrippina was one of the company. They were talking of indifferent subjects, but Lepida's mother [1] artfully turned the discourse upon Agrippina's fresh gallantry, and rallied her upon it, with a malicious kind of affectation. Any other person would have been put out of countenance; but she, who was mistress of great assurance, and was so proud as not to know what it was to yield to anybody, instead of cunningly evading the snare that was laid for her, defended herself with great heat and fury, and turned the conversation more and more upon that topic. The raillery became serious. Lepida's mother, excited by her jealousy and resentment, reproached Agrippina with her shameful attempt upon Galba, the scandalous advances that she made him, and the artifices she continually employed to gain her point. Agrippina, who was not easily put to silence, replied in the most provoking terms she could think of. The dispute grew exceedingly warm, a quarrel ensued, and at last open war. From words they came to invectives, then to the most abusive language they could invent, and at last to downright blows. Never was there a more diverting scene; the other ladies interposed, in order to separate the two heroines, and by their prudence hindered the combat from lasting long. Victory did not

[1] Sueton. vit. Galb.

declare itself on Agrippina's side, for she went away
very roughly handled by her antagonist, so that Lepida's
mother remained mistress of the field of battle.

If Agrippina could have prevailed upon herself to have
as much regard to decency as ambition, she would never
have behaved in such a manner to Galba as made her
the jest of the whole town; but she was not of a humour
to be governed by the dictates of reason. The distinguished rank of Galba, his important offices and high
expectations, gave her such flattering ideas, that she was
convinced she could not build her hopes upon a better
foundation than the fortune of that senator and a union
of herself with him by marriage. She had been so accustomed to make conquests in Rome, that she had very
few doubts as to the success of this; nor did it enter into
her imagination, that Galba would be able to resist the
power of her charms, to which so many others had
yielded without making any great resistance.

But Galba, who knew Agrippina perfectly well, and
who looked upon this behaviour of hers either as a sign
of shameful weakness, or an artifice due to her ambition,
despised all her attempts, and showed her, by his indifference, that he had no sort of inclination for her.

Agrippina perfectly perceived it; for Lepida being
dead, and also her two sons, Galba resolved never to
marry again; he therefore obstinately [1] refused all the
offers that were made him, and preferred the sweetness
and tranquillity of a single life, to the troubles, vexations,
and many disagreeable accidents that too often happen
in marriage. Happy would it have been for him, if he
could have been contented to deserve the throne, without

[1] Sueton. vit. Galb.

attempting to be Emperor; but he suffered himself to
be blinded by ambition, which proposes to itself nothing
less than crowns and sceptres, and generally casts down
those whom it has exalted. Thus Galba was hastening
to his destruction, and to put an end (upon a throne)
to a life already far advanced, which he might have
finished quietly and calmly in his private capacity. It
was [1] at Carthagena that he shook off the obedience that
he owed to Nero. The several prodigies that promised
him success, the flattering predictions that were made
him of his future grandeur, the pressing solicitations of
Vindex, who commanded in Gaul, and the jealousy of
Nero, who had sent orders to the intendants to put him
to death, prevailed on him to suffer himself to be proclaimed Emperor; he did not, however, at first accept the
title, choosing rather that of Lieutenant-General of the
Senate and People of Rome, to show, by this false
modesty, that he did not desire the sovereign authority,
but that it was only against that of Nero that he declared
himself.

Galba was far from being secure in his enterprise,
especially after the death of Vindex, who was defeated
by the troops of Virginius Rufus, governor of Upper
Germany, who being ignorant that Vindex and their
general, Rufus, were secret friends, attacked Vindex, who
expected no such thing, and who being defeated killed
himself from grief and despair; but Galba being informed of Nero's death at Clunia, and that the senate
had proclaimed him Emperor, took the road to Rome.

At Narbonne [2] he met the deputation from the senate,

[1] Plutarch vit. Galb.
[2] Zonar. Ann. i. Tacit. Histor. i. Plutarch vit. Galb. Dio. lib. 64.
Sueton. vit. Galb.

which he received very graciously, but refused Nero's
furniture, which they had brought to accommodate him
on his journey. This modesty gave them a good opinion
of him, but it was soon destroyed by the bloody executions which he caused to be carried out on the road, and
his entrance into Rome. To this great severity he added
a shameful avarice, which lost him the esteem of the
soldiers, who finding themselves disappointed of the
money that had been promised them in Galba's name,
began to murmur and declare that they were not satisfied
with an Emperor that was elected in Spain, independently
of the other legions, and that they insisted upon having
one who should be agreeable to all the armies.

This was, as it were, a signal for revolt; for Otho, who
had flattered himself [1] that Galba being very old would
have adopted him, finding those hopes frustrated by his
adopting Piso, was so provoked at this preference (which
he reckoned a great injustice, because he had been one
of the first that declared for Galba, and had brought over
to his interest the country of Lusitania, of which he was
governor) that he intrigued with the soldiers against
him, and they corrupting others, took part with Otho,
whom they saluted Emperor, and brutally assassinated
Galba, who, upon the report of their rebellion, had come
into camp to appease the tumult.

[1] Tacit. Histor. i.

POPPÆA

WIFE OF OTHO

THO had no other wife but Sabina Poppæa, who has been spoken of already. He was determined to marry Statilia Messalina, Nero's widow, but death prevented him, as we have observed. He reigned but three months and two days, from the 15th of January to the 17th of April.

GALERIA FUNDANA

WIFE OF VITELLIUS

NE has need of great moderation and command of one's passions, not to be very fond of sovereign power; for nothing is more difficult to be resisted than the charms of authority over others, though it is generally attended with circumstances that are disagreeable enough. The almost inevitable dangers which attend ambitious people, the dreadfulness of the fall with which they are threatened, the terrible examples of so many illustrious unhappy persons, who have met with tragical and violent deaths from that exalted position which they have attained after infinite labours, troubles, and (too often) heinous crimes—all these are not strong enough to remove from our eyes that fatal veil that conceals from us all the dangers and uglinesses of an elevated station, and shows us only the fair side of grandeur, by which we are lamentably imposed upon; so that multitudes of people choose rather to be unfortunate in high life (especially upon the throne) than happy in the enjoyment of a calm and quiet, but inferior rank. Agrippina was assured that her son's gaining the Empire would be her ruin, and that he would certainly put her to death; this princess, however, being devoured

by an unlimited ambition which never gave her a
moment's rest, consented that Nero should dip his hands
in her blood, if she might but have the unspeakable satisfaction of seeing him invested with the imperial robe.
She could bear the thoughts of his becoming her murderer, provided that murderer was Emperor.

Sextilia, Vitellius's mother, had very different sentiments. She never wished for her son's exaltation,[1] but
looked upon the flattering predictions of his future
grandeur as direful omens, that bespoke nothing but misfortunes. And when she saw him general of the army
and Emperor, she bewailed his wretched condition.
Galeria Fundana, his wife, had no more pride and ambition than her mother-in-law; she [2] did not suffer herself
to be dazzled with the false lustre of a throne; and whatever [3] a mistaken historian has been pleased to assert
upon this subject, this princess, in the imperial palace
and in the centre of the greatest pomp and magnificence,
was as humble as in her own private chamber before
her husband had any grandeur to boast of. Her heart
was unalterable and proof against all changes and accidents. It was always the same, and the various vicissitudes of Fortune, which she experienced in every shape,
sufficiently justify this character of her.

However flattering the predictions of the astrologers
had been, with respect to Vitellius's advancement, neither
his father nor his mother were pleased with them, because they foresaw the evils and misfortunes that it
would be attended with, and the tragical death he would
probably suffer, after a short reign. For this reason
they took all the measures they could think of to hinder

[1] Sueton. vit. Vitell.   [2] Tacit. Histor. lib. ii.   [3] Dio.

the accomplishment of them, by keeping him out of the way of office, but Fortune betrayed their designs, and we shall see that the very means they made use of to frustrate what the soothsayers foretold only served to fulfil it. They sent him, when a child, to Capreæ, whither Tiberius had retired to hide his abominations. In such an infamous school as this, and under such masters, what sort of lessons could it be expected he would learn? He had nobody to copy but those who served as instruments of the monstrous impurities of the Emperor, so that Vitellius could imbibe nothing but vicious and corrupt principles or an exact imitation of those detestable patterns he had continually before his eyes; and accordingly, it was by an abominable prostitution of himself, that he began that course of wickedness, in which he afterwards became so skilful a master.

His crimes were so many steps, by which he attained to dignities and high offices, because they made him agreeable, and even very dear, to Caligula, Claudius, and Nero, to whom nothing could more effectually recommend any person than great vices. In fact, he obtained the highest offices from those three Emperors. He was made commissioner of the public works, in which he did not acquit himself too honestly; for he was accused [1] of having sacrilegiously stolen the ornaments of the temples, and the gifts that were offered up to the gods, which, being of gold and silver, he applied to his own use, and substituted vessels of copper and brass in their stead. He behaved with a good deal of moderation, when pro-consul of Africa, and when he returned home, married Petronia, daughter of a person who had been

[1] Sueton. vit. Vitell.

consul, and by her had a son called Petronianus after his
mother, which son was born with only one eye, which disfigured him extremely; he was, however, heir to Petronia,
and she prevailed upon his father to give him his
freedom. She had a particular reason for taking this
precaution; for, knowing Vitellius's disposition to prodigality and debauchery, she was in hopes, by this ceremony, which made him independent of his father, to
secure her fortune to her son. But this expedient was to
no purpose; for Vitellius, having dissipated all his money
in expensive and most extravagant entertainments, and
not knowing how to procure more to carry on his excesses, had recourse to the barbarous expedient of murdering his son, to seize his riches. He accused him of
having a design to assassinate him; and, to make his
story gain credit, he gave out that Petronianus, being
touched with remorse for his intended crime, had swallowed the poison himself that he had prepared for his
father.

Vitellius and Petronia did not live together upon the
best terms in the world, so he divorced her, and as soon
as she was at liberty, she married Cornelius Dolabella,
a senator of an illustrious family. This hasty marriage
provoked Vitellius in the highest degree, and so exasperated him against Dolabella, that even Time, which over-
comes all things, could never get the better of it; for as
soon [1] as he became Emperor and had a full opportunity
of being revenged, he exercised his power against Dolabella, and cruelly put him to death.

Vitellius did not wait long after his divorce without
taking another wife, and married Galeria Fundana,

[1] Tacit. Histor. lib. ii.

whose father had been prætor. She was not remarkable
for beauty, but rather the contrary, and spoke thickly;
but she had a great share of prudence, moderation and wisdom, and a reputation without reproach.
These were rare qualities at a time when vice was in
fashion, and at a Court where rules and maxims, quite
opposed to virtue and chastity, were consistently followed. The issue of this marriage was Publius Vitellius,
who had also an impediment in his speech, like his
mother, so much so that he was almost dumb. Fundana
also had a daughter, who, after the misfortune of Vitellius, her father, furnished Vespasian with an occasion of
showing his generosity, by procuring a very advantageous
match for this girl.

Vitellius having, as we observed, made himself master
of all sorts of vices in Capreæ, gave himself entirely up
to debauchery.[1] The detestable examples that he had
seen in that infamous island, were the fatal seed which
future opportunities brought to maturity, and he found
but too many of them in the reigns of Gaius Caligula,
Claudius, and Nero, into whose good graces it was impossible to be admitted without being vicious. He worshipped no other god than his belly, and carried his
insatiable gluttony to such a pitch, that he consumed all
his substance in feasts and entertainments, by which
he impoverished himself so much, that when Galba gave
him the government of Lower Germany, he had not
money to defray the expenses of his journey, nor any
resources wherewith to procure them; so after trying
all manner of ways to no purpose, he was at last forced
to mortgage his house to some farmers of taxes, who

[1] Sueton. vit. Vitell. 2.

lent him some money upon it, and lodged his mother
and Fundana, his wife, in a very poor apartment.

This expedient, which could not but be grievous to
Fundana, did not however extricate Vitellius out of his
difficulties, for it was not sufficient for his present necessities; and if Sextilia, his mother, had not sold her jewels,
Vitellius would have been forced to stay at Rome, for
want of money to set out; he would, even yet, have
found it impossible to proceed, if he had not, during
the whole journey, subsisted by sharping and cheating.

This extreme indigence of Vitellius was very mortifying to Fundana, his wife; to be banished from her house
by utter poverty must have been very heart-breaking to a
lady who had always lived in great affluence; but those
excessive expenses naturally lead to ruin and destruction.
Luxury, intemperance, and the gratification of those unbounded appetites, cannot fail of bringing along with
them poverty and wretchedness.

Galba's making choice of Vitellius to command the
troops in Germany surprised all the world.[1] Everybody
knew that he was neither worthy nor capable of it. In
reality, he[2] had never done anything in his life, but eat
and drink, gamble, perfume himself, and plunge into
the most infamous pleasures. He had a base soul, given
to flattery and incapable of any sentiment of honour.
He was insolent, brutal, and even cruel, to those that
yielded; timid and supple to those that resisted. Those
who have a mind to justify Galba for singling him out
from the rest of mankind for the above-mentioned post,
say that in Vitellius he imagined he had found a man
from whom he had nothing to fear, as he would never

---

[1] Sueton. vit. Vitell.   [2] Eutrop. Sueton. Tacit. Ann. xiv. c. 49.

be at leisure to intrigue, on account of his gluttony, which required whole provinces to satisfy it.

Vitellius was received in his government with great demonstrations of joy. He affected a certain [1] air of popularity, which won him the hearts of all, especially those of the soldiers, who not being at all pleased with the severe and covetous temper of Galba, and always desirous of changes and novelties, saluted him Emperor, and gave him the surname of Germanicus. This election came [2] very opportunely, for it was made but a few days before the news of Galba's death arrived, and Vitellius immediately resolved to go and fight Otho, who, at Rome, had seized upon the throne.

Otho was at once informed of it; and whether he dreaded the event of the war, or through moderation, or perhaps cowardice, he endeavoured to stop Vitellius, by proposing terms of accommodation. He [3] wrote him several courteous letters, made him considerable offers, in particular to divide the Empire with him, and marry his daughter. Vitellius answered him very politely, but yet refused the conditions, so that, the negotiations being broken off, they began to lay ambushes for each other. Immediately each endeavoured to strengthen his army as much as possible by seducing the soldiers of his antagonist; afterwards the quarrel ran so high, that they wrote the most insulting letters to each other, filled with the most bitter affronts and invectives, reproaching each other with the greatest crimes, which, in fact, were so many truths, for it was difficult to say which was the

---

[1] Sueton. vit. Vitell. 7.
[2] Plutarch. vit. Othon. Sueton. vit. Oth. vit. Vitell.
[3] Suet. vit. Oth. Tacit. Histor. lib. 1. c. 74. Plut. vit. Oth.

more worthless man of the two; and at last they attempted to assassinate each other, but unsuccessfully.

If, during this quarrel between Otho and Vitellius, Fundana was full of fright and alarm for herself and her family, it was not without good reason. She was in Otho's power at Rome, and did not believe him generous enough to resist the strong inclination he had to be revenged on his enemy, in the person of his wife and children. Vitellius himself apprehended it more than once, for he wrote [1] to Titianus, who commanded in the city for his brother Otho, that if Fundana and his children were ill-treated, he would use him and his sons in the same manner by way of reprisals. But Otho behaved with the greatest politeness upon this occasion, for, instead of doing the least injury to that princess or her children, he took particular care of them; whether it was through generosity or fear, nobody knew; but this conduct, from whatever motive it proceeded, teaches us that one never ought to be revenged on one's enemy by showing resentment to his children or anybody belonging to him.

The issue of the war, however, was not favourable to Otho. His troops were defeated at the battle of Bedriacum; and finding that the legions and provinces (ever ready to join those who enjoy success), declared for Vitellius, he refused to survive his shame, but killed himself, and that with a resolution, that nobody expected from the effeminate life he had led. This united all parties in favour of Vitellius, who was then universally acknowledged. He was in Gaul, when he heard that his generals had gained the victory, and that Otho was dead;

[1] Tacit. Histor. i. c. 75.

and then it was that he began to show himself in his
proper colours. At first, indeed, he performed some few
acts of clemency and justice, but as this was not at all
natural to him, he could not long endure the restraint,
and consequently threw off the mask, showing himself as
he really was, without the least affectation or hypocrisy.
He set out for Rome, and all along the road left evident
marks of his gluttony and cruelty, the latter of which
cannot be better evinced than by those words, so worthy
of a tyrant, that he was heard to utter as he passed over
the field where the Battle of Bedriacum had been fought,
and which was covered with dead bodies, whose horrible
stench infected the air. He rejoiced at the sight of this
dismal spectacle, and cried out,[1] " How charming is the
smell of an enemy when dead, but a dead citizen has a
still more agreeable odour."

The news of Otho's death, and Vitellius's approach,
was soon carried to Rome,[2] by those who desired the
honour of being the first messengers of it, to Fundana
and Sextilia, the new Emperor's mother and wife.

Everybody strove who should show most complaisance
and respect to the two princesses; flattery performed its
part, according to custom, and soon declared on the side
that Fortune smiled upon; but all this zeal and these
honours made no impression upon Fundana, nor upon her
mother-in-law. They looked upon the elevation of
Vitellius as a snare that Fortune had laid for them, and
even as the greatest misfortune that could happen to
him, whose downfall they saw approaching in proportion
to the increase of his grandeur. The murder of Galba,
the untimely end of Otho and the other Emperors that

---

[1] Sueton. vit. Vitell. c. 10. [2] Tacit, Histor. ii.

had preceded them, were melancholy presages of what
Vitellius had to expect from the Senate, the people, and
the legions, who are always disposed to change sides and
take part with the strongest. Accordingly, when Vitellius
wrote to his mother, assuming the surname of Germanicus, Sextilia said openly [1] that that was not the name of
her son; that she had brought a Vitellius into the world,
and not a Germanicus. But Vitellius was not content
with taking that name, to which he was in no sort entitled,
not having one of that great prince's good qualities, but
he must needs confer that honour upon his son, too, and
heaped upon him all the honours and dignities belonging
to a Cæsar. He even caused all the army to go to meet
him, though he was yet but a young child, and almost
dumb. This [2] was not the only instance of his vanity; it
was still more conspicuous in his magnificent entry into
Rome, which was the most splendid that had ever been
seen, and the more ridiculous, because Vitellius, of all
men living, was the least worthy of it. He went to the
Capitol with a most splendid equipage, and there finding
his mother, saluted her with the title of August. But
what was most astonishing was, that he had the insolence
to deliver a pompous eulogy of his virtues to the Senate
and people, which was what they had never heard of
before, and with insupportable impudence laid a particular stress on his sobriety and temperance, even before
those who had been a hundred times witnesses of his
drunkenness and horrid debaucheries, and who at that
very time knew that all the high roads in Italy were
crowded with people whose business it was to furnish his

[1] Tacit. Histor. ii.
[2] Sueton. vit. Vitell. c. 11. Tacit. Hist. lib. ii. c. 89.

table with the most costly and delicious rarities that could
be procured from distant countries, to supply the exorbitant luxury of his entertainments. In fact, Josephus
does not scruple to affirm that, if he had reigned long, all
the revenues of the Empire would not have sufficed to
defray the expense of that single item.

An historian [1] has certainly given a wrong character of
him in endeavouring to make him pass for a miser, as
there are numerous instances of the contrary. He
thought that Nero had been neither lodged nor furnished
magnificently enough in his golden palace; and Dion [2]
gives us to understand that the Empress Fundana was
something of that opinion. He says that she entered
into the imperial palace with a ridiculous pride, and a
contemptible disdain, as thinking none of the rich furniture good enough for her, but, on the contrary, despising
everything she saw, notwithstanding what Tacitus tells
us of her humility and moderation. According to all
appearance, Dion must be mistaken, for it is not at all
probable that a woman just come out of a pitiful hired
chamber, where she had not the common necessaries of
life, should in so short a time forget her recent miserable
lot, and so suddenly conceive such proud and insolent
ideas as to imagine the most precious furniture in the
world, which had served so many Empresses, not good
enough for her. There is the more reason to suspect
Dion's veracity in this particular,[3] because it was remarkable that Fundana's behaviour was all of a piece,
and [4] that she was just the same upon the throne, as she
had been in her lowest station. She never affected a

[1] Aurel Vict. Epit.   [3] Xiphilin. in. Vitell.
[2] Dio. lib. lxv.   [4] Tacit. Hist. lib. ii. c. 64.

haughty carriage, never made use of her influence and
interest but to do good, and to confer favours, as we
read she did in behalf of Trachalus, who wrote Otho's
speeches, whose life she saved.

It would have been very well if Vitellius had imitated
her, but this prince, being hurried on by his bad conduct,
and the violent counsels of Triaria, his sister-in-law, a
most insolent, proud, and tyrannical woman, became a
monster of cruelty and all sorts of debauchery. He took
for his model the reign of Nero, and never was model
better copied. Gluttony and inhumanity were the two
main hinges upon which all his actions turned. Junius
Blæsus,[1] a Senator of great quality, and the most honest
man in Rome, fell under the weight of an artful and
unjust accusation, and Vitellius, not content with putting
him to death, desired to feast his eyes with the sight of
his execution. Two sons [2] of a man he had condemned,
who threw themselves at his feet to entreat his pardon
for their father, became his companions in punishment,
and were executed together with him whose life they
interceded for. Finally, he caused his mother to be
starved to death, under the pretence of a vain and idle
prediction that had been made him, that he should reign
long if he outlived her; as if those who murdered their
parents were, in a peculiar manner, to be blessed with
long life, whereas it is promised to none but such as
honour them. It is true there are people of opinion that
Sextilia killed herself, that she might not any longer have
the mortification of seeing the scandalous life her son led,
and that, foreseeing the misfortune with which he was
threatened, she asked poison of him, and he was cruel

[1] Tacit. Histor. iii. c. 39.   [2] Sueton. vit. Vitell.

enough to give it her. But, supposing it were so, he would not be less guilty of her death, since even among heathens [1] those were reckoned authors of a crime who did not hinder it when they could.

Never was gluttony carried to such a length as by Vitellius. He always made four, and sometimes five,[2] plentiful meals a day, to satisfy, if possible, his greedy appetite, which he was sometimes so little master of, that very often, during [3] the sacrifices, he could not forbear dragging the entrails of the victims out of the fire and devouring them half-raw in public. It was his custom to invite himself to dine with his friends, which was done at such excessive expense that the least of those entertainments cost immense sums. That which his brother Lucius Vitellius gave him seems incredible, for we read that [4] two thousand fishes were served up at table, and seven thousand birds, all of choicest quality, besides innumerable other things. But the profusion of this Emperor was never displayed more than at a famous entertainment he gave, where one single dish cost more than all his brother's feast, for he filled it with the livers of pheasants, the tongues of scars, peacocks' brains, the entrails of lampreys, and all sorts of fish and birds that were the most difficult to be procured. All these excesses and prodigalities, which were without bounds or judgment, show us what man is capable of when absolute power is added to depraved and vicious inclinations.

In the meantime, whilst Vitellius was giving himself no trouble about the cares and fatigues of government, but laying that burden upon his freedmen, thought of nothing

---

[1] Senec. Troas. Act. ii.
[2] Eutrop. in Vitell.
[3] Sueton. vit. Vitell.
[4] Eutrop. Sueton. vit. Vitell.

but how to satisfy his passions, and passed whole days
and nights at table, Vespasian, who was become very
illustrious by an infinite number of glorious actions, was
proclaimed Emperor, and acknowledged as such throughout all the East. Primus Antonius, one of his generals,
at the head of the Illyrian legions, entered Italy, and
gained two battles,[1] took and sacked Cremona, and in
these three actions destroyed above thirty thousand of
Vitellius's men, so that the whole Empire declared for
the conqueror, excepting the city of Rome, and even
that soon after abandoned Vitellius to his evil destiny.

This prince, being at last roused from his lethargy, saw
his danger, but not till it was too late, and did not begin
to think himself unfortunate till he was irretrievably lost.
Resolving, therefore, to quit his sovereign dignity, and
yield it up basely to his antagonist, he went out of the
palace in deep mourning,[2] accompanied by Fundana, his
children, and his domestics, his son being carried in a
litter, as it were in a funeral procession. In this condition, which inspired with pity even those who had no
reason to love him, he passed through the soldiers, and,
having assembled them as well as the people, he told
them, in very moving words, that he renounced the Empire for the sake of peace, and for the public weal; that
he had no other favour to ask of them, but to have

---

[1] In one of these battles in which Primus Antonius defeated the troops
of Vitellius, an accident happened that made both parties curse the civil
wars. One of Primus's soldiers having mortally wounded another belonging to Vitellius, and falling upon him to strip him, found him to
be his own father. They knew and tenderly embraced each other, which
showed the father's affection for the son, and the grief of the son for
having had the misfortune to be his father's murderer. The wounded
man died, and his son had only the melancholy consolation of burying
him who had given him life.

[2] Tacit. Histor. 3. 67.

compassion on his brother, his wife, and children. At the
same time surrendering his sword as a mark of his giving
up the sovereign authority, he offered it to the Consul,
Cæcilius Simplex, who refused it; he then retired into
the Temple of Concord.

It was a very melancholy sight to see the Empress
Fundana go out of the palace, leading her little daughter
by the hand, and shedding copious tears for her husband,
whose unhappy destiny had reduced him so low as to seek
for shelter in the compassion of the people. But all these
sighs and tears were in vain. Antonius's troops entered
Rome, and seized upon the palace. Vitellius, who had
also gone thither, and had just risen from one of his usual
entertainments, being frightened at the noise which the
soldiers made, withdrew secretly and retired to his wife's
house, where he had no sooner arrived than he took it
into his head to return to the palace, which he found
desolate, for all his people had left it. He then hid himself behind a bed in the porter's chamber, where he was
attacked by the dogs and cruelly bitten by them till the
blood ran down. He was soon [1] discovered, and rudely
dragged out of his lurking-place. The soldiers led him
about the town with his hands tied behind him, and to
complete his confusion they placed the point of a poniard
just under his chin, that he might be obliged, whether
he would or no, to hold up his head. They affronted
him in all the ways they could think of, threw dirt and
dung in his face, and called him gormandizer and in-
cendiary, and after they had tormented him and insulted
him by all manner of injuries, they put him to a slow and
painful death, and then threw his body into the Tiber.

[1] Tacit. Histor. ii. Sueton. vit. Vitell. Eutrop.

Lucius Vitellius, the Emperor's brother, and the young Vitellius, were also sacrificed to the public peace. Mucianus, chief favourite of Vespasian, thought proper to stifle all the seeds of discord in the blood of this young prince. Vespasian was not so rigorous in regard to Vitellius's daughter; he married her very honourably, which was the only consolation of Fundana, who passed the remainder of her life in grief and affliction.

DOMITILLA

WIFE OF VESPASIAN

LAVIA DOMITILLA is less known by her life, which was very obscure, than by the honours that were paid her after her death, and when Vespasian was settled upon the throne. She was daughter of Flavius Liberalis, intendant of the revenues, an employment [1] far above his hopes, for he was of so low an extraction that Domitilla, his daughter, was slave to Capella, a Roman knight, originally an African, till, after he had by long service [2] qualified himself for the above-mentioned post, his daughter was, upon his account, declared free and a citizen of Rome.

Vespasian was a prætor in Caligula's time, when he married Domitilla. She was not his first attachment, for Cænis, freedwoman of Antonia, Claudius's mother, was the object of his affections for a long time, and he loved her extremely, even when he married Domitilla.

Vespasian being descended from a mean family, would, without doubt, have remained in obscurity, only that evil Fortune has its revolutions as well as prosperity. But Narcissus, who at that time was very powerful at Court, having taken him under his protection, gave him prefer-

[1] Sueton. vit. Vesp.   [2] Aurel. Vict. Excerp. in Tit.

ment and advanced him by degrees to considerable offices,
which furnished him with opportunities of exercising
his rare and valuable talents. It was by his interest
that Vespasian was made lieutenant of a legion, at the
head of which, in Germany and in Britain, he performed
such glorious actions as gained him the highest reputation, and were afterwards recompensed by the priesthood,
a triumph, and the consulship. The duties of the latter
obliged him to repair to Rome, where he found his wife,
Domitilla, brought to bed of a son, whom he called Titus,
and who succeeded him in the Empire.

These great honours and distinctions began to arouse
Vespasian's ambition, which, together with certain
favourable predictions of his future grandeur, flattered
him very agreeably, and caused him to think that there
was nothing he might not aspire to. Some oracles had
promised him the Empire, and he thought his exploits
seemed to pave the way for him to that supreme dignity.
In reality, two powerful nations conquered, twenty
strong towns taken, a considerable island subdued, two
battles won, and all this in so short a time, were beginnings illustrious and glorious enough to stimulate the
hopes and expectations of a man naturally ambitious, and
who, being exceedingly influenced by superstition, was
much impressed by what had been foretold should shortly
happen to him. But all these hopes, this charming prospect of sovereignty, and these vast ideas, seemed to fall
to the ground when Narcissus, who was his patron and
only support, was ruined; and, to tell the truth, he and his
wife, Domitilla, were nearly undone by this accident, for
the Empress Agrippina, having conceived an implacable
hatred against Narcissus, involved in her resentment all

his friends and dependents; and after having destroyed her enemy, resolved to do the same by all those of his party. The absolute power she had acquired over the Emperor Claudius made everything easy to her, but as she was desirous to give a sort of colour to her persecutions, she suborned people to accuse of heinous crimes all such as she had a mind to ruin, that it might seem the punishment of transgression rather than of their attachment to Narcissus.

Vespasian, who by [1] having received innumerable favours and benefits from Narcissus, was become very zealous for his interests, plainly perceived that it was by no means safe for him to stay at Rome, where his life was every moment in danger, that Agrippina wanted only a plausible pretence to destroy him, and, according to all appearance, it would not be long before her fertile invention supplied her necessities. He therefore very wisely resolved to retire with his wife, Domitilla, into some remote country. This voluntary banishment saved him, as it procured him a safe shelter against Agrippina's persecutions, and furnished Domitilla with an opportunity of regaining her husband's affections, which Cænis had robbed her of, and both of them had the satisfaction of seeing their family increased by the birth of Domitian and a daughter, who was called Flavia Domitilla, after her mother, but who died soon after.

The storm being over, and Agrippina having satisfied her revenge, Vespasian, weary of a rambling and inglorious life, returned to Rome, which he looked upon as the proper theatre for him to display his talents in, and raise himself afterwards to the highest dignities; but

[1] Sueton. vit. Vespas.

From the painting by Georges Rochegrosse

The populace insulting and tormenting Vitellius in the streets of Rome before putting him to death

Fortune had a mind to try him once more, and make him sensible of her caprices. For, during Nero's journey to Achaia, Vespasian, who accompanied him, had the misfortune to displease the Emperor by falling asleep whilst he was singing. Nero was so offended at this want of courtesy that he forbade him his presence. Vespasian was far from being sure that this resentment would not be carried further, and, being well acquainted with the Emperor's violent temper, thought it best to withdraw as soon as he could. He retired again, and continued in exile till the danger was over, which, luckily for him, happened very soon, and Fortune, who would not lose sight of him, made him ample amends afterwards for all his vexations and disappointments.

The Jews,[1] who always looked upon their subjection to the Romans as an insupportable and shameful yoke, notwithstanding the protestations they had made of submitting to no king but Cæsar, being seduced by some vain predictions that seemed to promise them the Empire,[2] resolved to shake off an obedience that they only rendered with the utmost regret, and upon this foolish supposition they brutally assassinated their Governor. The news [3] of this rebellion put Nero into a strange fury,

---

[1] Sueton. vit. Vespas. Tacit. Histor. i. c. 10.

[2] There was among the Jews an old prophecy that the empire of the world was to fall into the hands of certain persons who were to come from the East. And Josephus, the historian, informs us that in Nero's time there was found among some old documents in the temple of Jerusalem, a prophecy which affirmed that about that time should spring up from among the Jews one that should command the whole earth. The Jews did not fail to explain this flattering prediction in favour of themselves, and not doubting but the time of their deliverance was near at hand, they revolted against the Romans. Josephus, like a skilful courtier, put a political construction upon the words, and attributed the meaning of them to Vespasian.

[3] Nicephor. Calist. Histor. lib. iii.

and he resolved to extirpate that nation, which neither threats, pardons, nor punishments could influence.

Nero, having need of a skilful general for this important expedition, immediately thought of Vespasian as a man of consummate judgment and experience, and nobody was more capable of answering the expectations that all mankind entertained of him. He therefore put himself at the head of the legions, marched into Judæa, and soon made himself master of all the province, except the town of Jerusalem. During these military operations Vespasian lost his wife. Her death did not make much noise, because there had been nothing very remarkable in her life, so that it was not till flattery was pleased to make her a divinity that Domitilla was much spoken of.

After the death of Nero, the Empire was divided into factions. Galba reigned but a little while, because Otho, who aspired to the sovereignty, had him massacred. However, he did not long enjoy that dignity which he had procured by so great a crime, for he was but a few months upon the throne.

Vitellius having made himself odious by his excesses and horrid debaucheries, Vespasian, who was then at the head of a very considerable army in the East, was proclaimed Emperor. At first he made some difficulty about accepting the sovereign power, which the legions had conferred upon him with so much ardour and zeal, but being at last overcome by the pressing solicitations of Mucianus, Governor of Syria, who promised to give him all the assistance in his power, he took the names of Cæsar and Augustus, and marched towards Rome to give battle to Vitellius, who had dishonoured the Empire by a scandalous, dissolute, and effeminate life.

When he was at Alexandria, some of the inhabitants brought him a blind and a lame man, who desired him to cure them, having, as they said, been assured by the god Serapis that Vespasian had the power of so doing, if he would condescend to touch with the end of his foot the leg of the cripple, and put some of his spittle upon the eyes of the other. The Emperor [1] had too much good sense to give credit to any such vision, and refused to comply with their request, that he might not expose himself to being laughed at, but at last, not being able any longer to resist the importunity of these poor wretches, and the solicitations of his friends about him, he was prevailed upon to do it, and it is confidently reported that they were both immediately healed. This event has been much spoken of, and people have argued different ways about it. As we are in no way concerned in the affair, the reader is at liberty to judge of it as he thinks proper, but those who conclude it to be downright flattery will certainly form the truest judgment of it.

Though Vespasian had a great deal of merit, it is certain that he owed, in a great measure, his advancement to the shameful and iniquitous lives of his immediate predecessors, Otho and Vitellius, especially the latter, who was altogether unworthy of the Empire, and to the two generals who declared for him, and served him with a fidelity, courage, and skill equal to that of the greatest warriors of ancient Rome. Licinius Mucianus [2] was one of them, of whom it is said that his vices at least balanced his virtues, if they did not exceed them, and that he was fitter to make an Emperor than to become one himself. The other was Primus Antonius, a Gaul, a native of

[1] Tacit. Histor. iv. Sueton. vit. Vesp.   [2] Tacit. Hist.

Tolosa, who in his childhood was surnamed Becco—that is to say, the bill of a cock. He had been convicted [1] of great crimes, for which he was expelled the senate, but Galba [2] reinstated him without enquiring into the reasons of his expulsion. After this mortifying disgrace, he went and offered his services to Nero, who did not set any great value upon him, but Antonius [3] managed matters so dexterously by his intrigues, that he procured the command of an army. He was exceedingly brave and enterprising, the very man for a bold action. He perfectly understood the art of war, and was intrepid in the greatest dangers; but, on the other hand, he was ill-natured and quarrelsome, loving broils and factions, dangerous in time of peace and idleness, ever ready to plunder and to shed blood. Such were the two generals who made Vespasian Emperor by the extraordinary services they rendered him.

As soon as he arrived in Rome he strove to improve the state of affairs in the city, for everything had undergone a great alteration owing to the troubles and disorders of past times. He rescued from obscurity and oblivion the name of Flavia Domitilla, his late wife, by granting her immortality. Temples were erected to her honour, altars built, and priests instituted, who were called Domitillans. In short, they made an idol of a woman, so that Vespasian's wife, who had scarce been known at Rome in her lifetime, was exalted to the sky by a posthumous honour, and by an impious apotheosis, increased the number of the divinities.

Cænis, the freedwoman, found her account in the advancement of Vespasian, for as he had always loved

---

[1] Sueton. vit. Vitell.   [2] Tacit. Ann. 14.   [3] Dion. lib. 65.

her, he took her into his palace, and always treated her with as much respect as if she had been his wife. It must be confessed, too, that she was worthy of it, for she had [1] a vast and extensive genius, capable of the greatest undertakings, and a penetration that nothing could escape. She first perceived and disclosed to her mistress, Antonia, the ambitious designs of Sejanus, of which that princess informed Tiberius. To all these qualities she added a profound policy, and the most discreet conduct, by which she always maintained herself in the good graces of Vespasian, studying his humour and conforming entirely to his inclinations, and as she was well acquainted with this prince's covetous temper, she was very industrious in finding out methods of satisfying the almost insatiable desire he had of amassing money. All the offices [2] in the Empire were for sale. The governments of provinces, and the command of the armies were given to those who bid highest. The priesthood, which was a sacred dignity, and the absolution of crimes were bought and sold. A scandalous and sacrilegious traffic was carried on even in such things as belonged to religion. In short, the unworthiest of mankind might aspire to the most honourable and important posts, provided he came with a purse well furnished, and addressed himself to Cænis. Taxes were imposed upon all manner of things, and everywhere the traces of this monstrous avarice were to be seen. Vespasian eagerly seized every opportunity of heaping up riches, and all profit was welcome from whatever quarter it came. His son, Titus, taking the liberty one day to represent to him the shamefulness of laying a tax upon urine, the Emperor, giving him a piece of money to

---

[1] Xiphilin.   [2] Dio. lib. 66.

smell, told him that it had no bad scent, thought it proceeded from what he so much condemned. About this
time Cænis died, to the great regret of Vespasian, who
did not long survive her. He sullied the latter part of
his reign by the death af Sabinus,[1] whom he put to death

[1] The history of Sabinus deserves to be particularly taken notice
of or rather the fidelity and conjugal affection of his wife. Sabinus
was a person of high rank, very rich, and had a good share of ambition.
His wife's name was Eponina, a lady of great virtue and beauty. During
the troubles in Gaul, which lasted all the time that Otho, Vitellius, and
Vespasian were disputing for the Empire, there was scarce a general
of an army, or governor of a province that did not imagine he had very
good pretensions to the throne; Sabinus was one of those, and suffering
himself to be hurried away by his ambition, consented that the army
should salute him Emperor. The support that he met with from his
countrymen, the inhabitants of Andematunnum (supposed to be the site
of the modern Langres) put this bold undertaking into his head: besides, he pretended to be descended from Julius Cæsar, who had had
an intrigue with his grandmother during his residence in Gaul. As,
in addition to being excessively vain, he was very rash, he turned his
arms against the Romans, which revolt had very bad consequences for
him. His troops were entirely defeated; and of all those who had
joined him, some fled and others killed themselves, that they might
not fall into the hands of the Roman generals, who gave no quarter
to these rebels, but punished them as their crime deserved. Sabinus
might have made his escape into the remote parts of Gaul, where he
would have been secure, if he could have prevailed upon himself to
abandon his wife, whom he loved extremely, and by whom he was
equally beloved. He flattered himself that in time he might be able
to obtain his pardon, and so resolved to conceal himself till the troubles
should be over. At his country house there were great subterraneous
caves that could not possibly be discovered, except one was let into
the secret. In fact, of all Sabinus's domestics, who were very numerous,
there were but two of his freedmen (in whom he had entire confidence)
who were acquainted with these caves: these he conferred with in
private, and acquainted them with his intention to hide himself in one
of these caves till he should have a proper opportunity of procuring
his pardon; but in the meantime (to hinder any search from being
made after him) he proposed to give out that he had poisoned himself.
Sabinus therefore assembled all his servants, and told them that after
the misfortune that had happened to him in the miscarriage of his
attempt, he was convinced that, if he should be so unhappy as to fall
into the hands of those who had put all the rest of his party to death,
there was no punishment his enemies would think cruel enough for him,
for which reason he was determined to destroy himself. He returned
them thanks for their services and fidelity, and dismissed them all,
except the two confidants. To these he gave proper instructions, and

for a crime which, on account of a nine years' repentance,
and the tears of a wife and two young children, deserved

then buried himself in the bowels of this dismal cavern, ordering his
house to be set on fire, which was soon consumed to ashes. This action
was attributed to Sabinus's despair, especially since the two freedmen
reported everywhere that their master, to escape the Emperor's pur-
suers, had taken poison and then burnt himself in his house, that they
might not have the pleasure of insulting his body. What confirmed
this story was Eponina's going into deep mourning and being inconsolable for the loss of her husband, for she really believed it to be true,
as Martialis, one of the freedmen, had protested to her that it was.
She cried and lamented excessively, as any affectionate wife would do,
who had been deprived of a husband she loved above all the world.
She was visited by all the persons of distinction in the neighbourhood,
who did not fail to comfort her in all the ways they could think of;
but Eponina, being determined not to outlive this unspeakable affliction,
took no nourishment for three days. The news of Sabinus's death was
soon spread abroad, and there was nobody that doubted it in the least.
Eponina's deep and unfeigned mourning, the house burnt, the servants
dismissed, everything contributed to confirm the story. In the meantime, Sabinus was kept well informed of everything that passed by the
trusty Martialis, and being afraid that his wife would really die of
grief, thought it high time to undeceive her; he therefore despatched
his faithful servant to let her know the true state of things, and to
entreat her at the same time not to make any alteration in her conduct,
lest it might reveal what was of such importance to him to keep secret.
So Eponina, carrying on the deceit, wept and lamented as much as ever
to all appearance, but her inconceivable impatience to see her dear
husband again would not admit of delay; she therefore paid him a visit
as soon as it was dark, and returned before day without being perceived by any body. This practice was continued for seven months,
but as it could not be carried on any longer without great trouble and
danger, she ventured (in order to spare herself the one and avoid the
other) to have him carried into the city to a house she hired for that
purpose, her own in the country being burnt. He was so well wrapped
up among some furniture, that it was impossible to find out the trick;
but after a while, reflecting that it might become known by some
accident, especially since she was visited by so many people, it was
thought wise to remove him again into his den. All this succeeded
as well as they could wish, and this lady had, by her discreet and
prudent conduct, the satisfaction of seeing her husband as often as
she pleased, in his gloomy retreat, during nine years, without the least
suspicion of any such thing. But what was most to be admired in this
affair was, that Eponina being with child, and very justly apprehending
that her pregnancy would soon be taken notice of by the ladies, who
saw her at the assembles or the temples, or especially in the bath, she
daubed herself with a certain ointment, which had the property of
making the flesh swell, and puffing up the skin; thus, by the size of her
legs, arms, and the rest of her body, she perfectly well disguised her big

to be pardoned. This was such an act of severity, or rather cruelty, as could not have been expected from an

belly, which was looked upon as the consequence of her disorder. She afterwards had the courage and resolution to suffer the pains of her delivery without complaining, and to be brought to bed, without the least assistance, of twins, which she nursed herself in the cavern, all the time that Sabinus remained there.

At last, however, Eponina's being so frequently absent created some suspicion, for people began to be persuaded that there must be some mystery in this behaviour. She was so narrowly watched that Sabinus's retreat was discovered. He was immediately arrested, loaded with chains, and conducted to Rome, with his wife and two children. As soon as they appeared before Vespasian Esponina threw herself at the feet of the Emperor, and presenting the twins, told him (with tears running down her cheeks) that long ago she had had a mind to implore his clemency in behalf of her husband, who had been misled by his imprudence, bad advice, the misfortunes of the civil wars, and the desire of being protected against the insupportable oppressions of tyrants; that he had indeed been prevailed upon to make himself the head of a party, for the above-mentioned reasons, rather than from any motives of ambition, or desire of reigning; that she had been frequently tempted to throw herself upon his mercy, and inform him that her guilty husband was still alive, but had waited on purpose till the children she then had the honour to present to him were of an age to join their tears and sighs to those of their afflicted mother, that the number of the suppliants might the more effectually disarm his indignation. "I brought them," said she, "into the world in a kind of sepulchre, and may say that they have never beheld the light till now. Be moved by our tears, our sighs, and our misfortunes, and look with compassion upon our misery."

So melting a discourse, and the melancholy sight of Esponina all this while upon her knees, with her two children, with uplifted hands and broken hearts, begging pardon for their poor father, touched to the very soul all that were present; and nobody doubted but the Emperor would grant the life of Sabinus at the ardent request of an afflicted woman, and the irresistible tears of the two innocents, who besought his pity in so tender a manner. So rare an example of conjugal love even required that Vespasian should give up Sabinus to the generous fidelity and affection of such a wife; but the Emperor was inexorable. He condemned Sabinus to death, in order, by this unseasonable and too rigorous severity, to intimidate others from revolting against their prince.

Eponina seeing her husband lost beyond all hopes, resolved to share with him his last punishment, as she had done all his former sufferings, and putting on a haughty and masculine countenance, told Vespasian with a surprising air of intrepidity, that he might be assured she did not look with horror upon death, since she had had the courage and resolution to pass nine years of her life with Sabinus, in the terrible darkness of a cave under ground, which might properly be called being

Emperor, who, in other respects was far from delighting
to shed blood.

buried alive; that she was, even in that lamentable situation, more
satisfied than he upon his throne. She then with great boldness reproached him with his cruelty. Thus, after having given an admirable
example of fidelity and conjugal love, she showed as remarkable a
one of her heroic courage and nobleness of mind.

MARCIA FURNILLA

WIFE OF TITUS

HE Emperor Titus was a prince endued
with great virtues, though when a
private person he had been very dissolute and debauched. He was educated at Claudius's Court, with Prince
Britannicus, where he pursued the
same studies, and under the same
masters. This was the origin of that great intimacy that
existed between them ever after, and nearly proved fatal
to Titus, for [1] he was almost poisoned with Britannicus
by tasting the soup that was prepared for that prince.

Titus, when at Court, had a presage of his future
grandeur, for one day Narcissus, secretary and favourite
of Claudius, sent for a physiognomist to know his
opinion with regard to the destiny of Britannicus, and he
assured him that Britannicus would never be Emperor,
but that the other, pointing to Titus, would.

Titus [2] was extraordinarily handsome, which perhaps
in some measure influenced the soothsayer in his favour.
In his countenance there was a majestic air, mingled with
sweetness, which had something in it so noble that anybody would sooner have taken him for a prince than an
inferior person. He was [3] extremely skilful at all exer-

[1] Sueton. vit. Tit. [2] Tacit. Histor. i. c. 2. [3] Eutrop. lib. 7.

cises, had a wonderful memory, a great facility in composing, both in prose and verse, and was so [1] dexterous at counterfeiting all sorts of writing that it was impossible to distinguish the true from the false; he used to say, that if he had had a mind, he could have been a very great rogue.

After he had served some time in Germany and Britain as military tribune, he took a fancy to study the law, and pleaded at the Bar; and when he returned to Rome he married Arricidia Tertulla, daughter of a knight, who had been præfect of the prætorian guards; but this lady dying soon after, he married Marcia Furnilla, who was descended from one of the most illustrious families in Rome. He was forced to separate from her in a little time, for Vespasian, his father, being taken up with the conquest of Judæa, employed Titus under him; and afterwards, when he quitted that country, to take possession of the Empire upon Vitellius's death, he left Titus in command of the army, in which position he acquitted himself with all the ability of the most experienced general, performing the duty both of captain and private soldier. He took the city of Jerusalem after a long siege, during which the Jews suffered all that a nation, who had drawn upon themselves the wrath of God, could suffer, and the obstinate resistance offered by that wretched people only served to heighten the glory of the conqueror.[2] The city

---

[1] Sueton. vit. Tit.

[2] During the siege, the Jews suffered all the calamities that can be imagined, especially so dreadful a famine, that a woman was constrained to kill her sucking child, and devour it after it was roasted. The noble and magnificent city was torn up from the very foundations, and Titus caused the plough to pass over it. Above eleven hundred thousand souls perished with hunger and all sorts of hardships during the siege, besides ninety thousand that fell into the hands of the

was taken by assault on the 8th of September, which day was also remarkable to Titus for the birth of a daughter, of whom Furnilla was delivered at Rome, who was named Julia; we shall see by the sequel that this young princess did not inherit the virtues of her father.

Titus, however, during his stay in Judæa, was not so taken up with his military occupations as not to find leisure for other matters: his attachment to the Princess Berenice, sister to King Agrippa, employed no small proportion of his time. Her charms made so deep an impression on him that in the excess of his passion he promised to marry her.

After the expedition to Judæa, Titus returned to Rome, covered with laurels. He was received with the greatest demonstrations of joy, and the Senate decreed him the honour of a triumph jointly with his father, amidst the applause and loud acclamations of the whole city, which gazed upon him with admiration. But soon after he greatly diminished the favourable idea that people had conceived of him, by his irregular behaviour. He gave himself up entirely to all sorts of vice, and frequently passed whole nights in debauch, with the most dissolute and abandoned of mankind, indulging himself in the most infamous pleasures, and to all these excesses added the greatest degree of cruelty, so that everybody was of opinion that he would make a second Nero.

He was much despised on account of his violent attachment to Berenice, for people could not endure that he should be so extremely fond of a stranger, as they were

Romans when the city was taken, part of whom were sold for slaves, and the rest sent to Rome, where they were condemned to hard labour, in the construction of a vast amphitheatre.

apprehensive that he designed to raise her to the throne;
and the death of Cæcina, a person of great distinction,
who had been consul, was attributed to his jealousy. It
is true that this action was excused in some measure by
the apparent necessity of anticipating the dangerous plans
of that ambitious senator, who was sowing the seeds of
rebellion among the soldiers; and it was given out that a
speech had been found upon him, most artfully composed
and calculated to stir up the army to a revolt, which he
was to have addressed to the legions. People of the
greatest penetration [1] considered that this was only a pretence made use of by Titus to cover a horrid assassination, and that it really was due to his jealousy, for he
imagined that Cæcina was not indifferent to Berenice, and
not being able to bear this rival, determined to get rid of
him, which he did in a most scandalous manner, quite
unworthy of a great prince; for, having one night invited
him to supper, he was not ashamed to violate the sacred
laws of hospitality so far as to have him massacred as he
was retiring from the banqueting hall, in order to go to
his house.

It may well be supposed that Titus was too much in
love with Berenice to have any great regard for his wife;
he therefore easily prevailed upon himself to divorce her,
which confirmed people in their belief that he was determined to place his mistress upon the throne. This was
such a monstrous innovation that it prejudiced all the
world against him; the Romans detested the very
thoughts of it, as much as they had abhorred the designs
of Mark Antony in favour of Cleopatra, to whom he had
promised the Empire.

[1] Excerpt. Aurel. Victor. in Tit.

Titus, however, soon gave people sufficient reason to alter their opinion with regard to his conduct, for, no sooner was he become Emperor by the death of his father than he showed himself the very reverse of what he had been before; it seemed as if he had changed his nature and inclinations together with his fortune. His glory and reputation (with an ardent desire to do everything in his power to please the Romans) were now become his prevailing passions, so much so that the day of his elevation to the throne put the finishing stroke to his love for Berenice, or rather he had virtue enough to deny himself, for this prince, who in contempt of the laws had been a slave to a foreigner, was now become a slave to those laws in opposition to that princess. He bade her therefore depart to her own country, and obliged her to go and hide in Judæa the powerful charms that had captivated him to such a degree. By making such a sacrifice (which no doubt went to his very heart) he was resolved[1] to give an unmistakable proof of the command he had over his passions. Their separation was very moving. Berenice reproached her lover very tenderly, in a manner capable of melting the hardest heart.

She reminded him of all the marks of affection she had given him, and the sincerity of it, which had induced her to quit her own country and travel over so many provinces with a lover that was now so ready to part with her; she reproached him with the promises he had so often repeated, not only to love her always, but even to marry her, which he now had it in his power to do. Titus, on his part, protested that nothing could be so grievous to him as those severe laws of the Empire, which laid him

[1] Sueton. vit. Tit.

under the cruel necessity of banishing from his presence
one who was so dear to him. Berenice, overwhelmed
with sorrow and despair, was forced to set out for the
East, to repent at leisure of her credulity in having accompanied Titus to Rome, in hopes of becoming his wife,
which had made her despise reputation and everything
that was dear to her. She gave all those of her sex an
instructive lesson, and taught them how little they ought
to depend upon the flattering promises which lovers are
so liberal of in the ardour of their passion, which they
generally violate as easily as they make them.

Titus's whole occupation, from that day forward, consisted in endeavouring to make the world happy. All the
virtues that were necessary to render a prince perfectly
accomplished showed themselves in his conduct and behaviour so conspicuously that he was called " the delight
of mankind," a title infinitely more glorious and desirable
than all those proud and pompous surnames with which
his infamous predecessors had been so undeservedly
honoured, who ought to have been called tyrants, rather
than fathers of their country.

Among the rest of his good qualities, Titus carried
generosity as far as it could go. It was his greatest
pleasure to grant favours, to make presents, and to do
good offices, and he was often heard to say that nobody
ought to quit the presence of a great prince but with a
contented heart. His hand was ever ready to bestow,
and he had so great and noble a soul, that one night,
recollecting that nobody had asked anything of him the
preceding day, he lamented it as if it were a great misfortune, and said, as he was sitting down to table, " Alas!
my dear friends, I have lost a day! " Sentiments truly

worthy of a great Emperor, and so well expressed in those few words that they have been taken notice of and transmitted to posterity by all the historians! He displayed his magnificence in the great and costly repairs that he caused to be carried out in Rome, and especially in the construction of that stupendous amphitheatre begun by his father, which he finished and brought to the utmost perfection, a work, the remains of which are still the wonder and admiration of all the world.[1]

If such a prince as this had lived to a great age, it would have been an inestimable blessing to the world, but unfortunately his life was short. He died in the third year of his reign, and people had good reason to believe that his brother, Domitian, who succeeded him in the Empire, was the contriver of his death.

---

[1] When this amphitheatre was entire, it was by far the noblest building in Rome. Martial speaks of it with great admiration in one of his epigrams.

> Omnis Cæsareo cedat labor amphitheatro.
> Unum præ cunctis fama loquatur opus.

In the middle of this amphitheatre was erected the great statue of Nero, called the colossus, on which account that place was known by the name of the Colosseum. Here it was that the Romans indulged themselves in the cruel pleasure of seeing men fight against wild beasts; and in this place Ignatius, Bishop of Antioch, was exposed to the lions. This amphitheatre is now half in ruins but the noble remains of it give us the highest idea of its Roman grandeur. There is a devout inscription on that side of it next to Constantine's triumphal arch, and another on the opposite side.

DOMITIA

WIFE OF DOMITIAN

————————

EAUTY and virtue do not always go together; on the contrary, it is an old observation that they seldom meet, for natural temperament generally triumphs over prudence and modesty, which too often prove but weak barriers against violent and depraved appetites. We have seen what an ill use Julia, Poppæa, and others of like character made of their charms, and we have now to relate in what manner Domitia employed hers.

She was daughter of Domitius Corbulo, one of the greatest men that ever Rome produced. His virtues, both civil and military, put him upon a level with the most famous generals and ablest politicians of ancient Rome. Honest and incorruptible, he had nothing at heart but the glory of acquitting himself well in all his actions. Prudent as he was in his undertakings, intrepid in dangers, and impenetrable in his designs, he was almost sure of success in all his projects, nor could that success be ever attributed to chance. Of the greatest presence of mind, so that he was ever furnished with almost infallible resources, even against accidents that could least of all be foreseen, by his consummate experience in the art of war he had the secret of making every event turn to his advantage. It was a common saying of his,[1] that a general should know how to beat the enemy with every kind of weapon and by indefatigable labour.

Besides all this, he was endued with so inviolable a fidelity, even in regard to his enemies and those of the Empire, that the very barbarians loved and esteemed him, though he was their greatest terror. In short, his uprightness,[2] vast abilities, numerous victories, and the triumphs with which he was honoured, rendered him so universally admired that everybody judged him worthy of the throne.

Domitia Longina, being thus of importance through her father, was yet more so by her beauty, for which no lady in Rome could be compared to her. She was then in the bloom of her youth, and possessed that irresistible charm that seldom fails to gain admirers. All the young men of quality and distinction eagerly sought her alliance, and Aelius Lamia, of the ancient and illustrious family of the Lamians, was proud of the honour of marrying her.

This senator (who by a fabulous sort of genealogy was made to descend from the gods themselves through Lamus, son of Neptune) possessed all the good qualities that it was possible for a man to have, and would have captivated any other heart but that of Domitia, but this lady was too much a coquette to confine her inclinations within the narrow limits of conjugal fidelity, for, by the loss of her father, whom Nero (that enemy to all virtue) sacrificed to his brutal fury, she was deprived of all those good examples and lessons which he had been very

---

[1] Domitius Corbulo dolabra, id est, operibus hostem vincendum esse dicebat. Frontin. Stratagem. lib. 4. c. 7.

[2] Tacit. An. 15. c. 27.

assiduous in giving her, and her ambition, added to her natural inclination to amours, turned the daughter of the wisest and greatest of men into the most abandoned and debauched courtesan in Rome.

Domitian, second son of the Emperor Vespasian, was the first who, by his particular attachment to her, gave room for suspicions that were not at all favourable to her reputation. People could not but have a very indifferent opinion of her virtue, since she received that prince's addresses with so much complaisance, and in such a manner as must needs be taken notice of by all the world, so that nobody imagined her capable of offering any great resistance to the ardent advances of Domitian, who was the only person that could advance her fortunes. Lamia, being more interested than others, did not fail to make these reflections; he could not help being much alarmed, nor were those alarms without foundation, for scarce was Domitian [1] upon the throne than, making use of the sovereign power he was thus invested with, he brutally forced Domitia from her husband and married her soon after,[2] honouring her with the title of August, without troubling himself with any of those formalities that Augustus thought himself bound to observe when he married Livia, for he did not do so till he had consulted the gods and their pontiffs, and made profuse apologies to Tiberius Nero, her husband.

As violent and sudden passions are seldom lasting, people were of opinion that Domitian's would easily be extinguished by the liberty he had of gratifying it, and that he would soon be weary of a woman over whose virtue he had made so cheap a conquest. Besides, there

[1] Dio. lib. 67.   [2] Suet. vit. Domit.

were powerful reasons of State, that seemed to plead hard for his putting away Domitia. The Emperor Titus,[1] his brother, had a mind to marry him to his daughter, Julia, a princess of admirable beauty, nothing inferior to that of Domitia, and their temperaments were pretty much alike in point of gallantry. But love is seldom directed by maxims of policy, and Domitian was too fascinated to prefer his fortune to his passion, especially as he had [2] already a daughter by Domitia. He was therefore deaf to all that could be said upon that point, and steadfastly refused the alliance that his brother offered him; so that it was with great indifference that he saw Titus give his daughter, Julia, to Sabinus, his cousin-german, though the Empire was her portion.

It was impossible for Domitian to give his mistress a greater mark of his esteem than his rejecting, for her sake, one of the most amiable ladies in Rome, and the highest fortune in the world. So great a sacrifice seemed to promise her no less than an unchangeable affection, but nothing is so uncertain as the caprices of love, for it often happens that it is near its end, when it appears most firm and durable.[3] Julia was no sooner married to Sabinus than Domitian became desperately in love with her; he was quite indifferent, when he might innocently have indulged an affection for her, and violently smitten, when he could not love her without crime, for such is the miserable depravity of human nature, that it hardly ever happens that men ardently desire anything except what is unlawful.

That which most contributed to inflame Domitian was

---

[1] Suet. vit. Domit. 22.   [2] Suet. vit. Domit. 3.
[3] Sueton. vit. Domit. 22.

that Julia, notwithstanding the contempt he had shown for her, was far from resenting it; on the contrary, she took care to let him see that she could forgive him, without doing any great violence to her feelings. She had the reputation of not being over cruel, and accordingly thought Domitian made her sufficient amends for the slight he had put upon her by his repentance, which she was determined to believe real and sincere, and therefore gave herself up to him without reserve. They shamefully abused the liberty of seeing each other as often as they pleased, which nearness of kindred furnished them with, and Julia made no scruple of prostituting herself to him who a little before had despised her, and her behaviour in this respect plainly showed that disorderly appetites and delicacy are incompatible.

Matters went on more scandalously after Titus's death, for there was an end of all constraint and decency when that Emperor was no more,[1] and our two lovers, having nothing now to fear, gave full scope to their infamous passion. There was one thing that seemed to interrupt their brutal felicity. Sabinus was the husband of Julia, and Domitian was become ridiculously jealous of him, as if he himself had the sole right to a possession, which Julia could not give him without being guilty in the highest degree; he therefore determined as soon as possible to get rid of this troublesome obstacle.

Domitia, meanwhile, soon perceived a great change in the Emperor, but far from complaining she, on the contrary, saw this alteration with great indifference, comforting herself with reflecting that at most he was only taking revenge for her numerous infidelities with regard to him;

[1] Suet. vit. Domit. 22.

and, as if she had resolved to copy him exactly, and regulate her conduct according to his, she abandoned herself publicly to libertinism, as soon as she found that he did so without reserve. She carried her impudence and prostitutions as far as they could go, and with an almost unparalleled insolence and audaciousness, gave herself [1] up entirely to the vilest and most contemptible of mankind. Paris, the comedian, with whom she was become furiously in love, was the person she was fondest of, and whom she encouraged without the least regard to shame or decency.

Nor did Domitian, for his part, give himself much trouble about his wife's conduct, for, being taken up with the intrigue with his niece, he was [2] satisfied with divorcing her, conformable to the advice which the senator Ursus gave him; as for Paris, he had him assassinated in the open street. This was all the revenge he took upon Domitia, but he would have done better if he had taken the advice that some people gave him, and had put an end to her evil ways and her life at the same time, by prudently and justly employing against her the punishment he inflicted upon the innocent Sabinus, whom he put to death upon ridiculous pretences, in order to enjoy his wife without a rival. But he had soon reason to repent of his proceedings in both these cases. Domitia lived to dishonour him more and more by her infamous behaviour, and the death of Sabinus (who had stood so much in his way), which he imagined would procure him the free possession of Julia, only served to occasion her destruction; for no sooner had Domitian cut off Sabinus, whom

---

[1] Sueton. vit. Domit. 3.   Aurel. Victor. in Domit.
[2] Sueton. vit. Domit. 3.   Xiphilin. in Domit.

he looked upon as the fatal obstacle to his happiness, than he abandoned himself entirely to his ungovernable passion for Julia, who, on her side, was not ashamed to behave with her uncle just as she might have done with her husband; in short, they lived together in such intimacy that Julia became with child.

Then it was that they were sensible of their folly in having inconsiderately put to death a man who would have been so necessary to their abominable commerce. They were ashamed that all the town should see the scandalous fruit of their incest, and that the whole Empire should know that an uncle had carried on such a shameful amour with his niece. So true it is, that even those who possess sovereign power, and consequently are above being called to account, are still desirous to conceal their vices. Domitian then, resolving to take such measures as should hide from the world the crime he had been guilty of with Julia, and which otherwise must soon be discovered, had recourse to another piece of iniquity, for [1] he persuaded her to swallow a potion that was to cause a miscarriage, and history informs us that it was not the first time she had had recourse to that wicked expedient. But it happened that this murderous draught operated so much more powerfully than they expected, that it occasioned the death of Julia. [2]

The death of Julia reinstated Domitia in the Emperor's good graces. His love for her having been rather lulled to sleep than extinguished, he recalled her, under pretence that the people entreated that favour of him, and ridiculously declared, [3] that she should again be ad-

---

[1] Dio. Lib. 67. [3] Sueton. vit. Domit. 13.
[2] Sueton. vit. Domit. 22. Dio. 16. Plin. Epist. 11.

mitted to his sacred bed. He did not reflect that the
same reasons for which he put her away existed still, and
were even stronger than ever. This inconsistency and
want of thought exposed him to satire and criticism.
People said he had committed a great fault, either in parting with her without sufficient provocation, or in recalling her without amendment, so that his behaviour became
the common topic of conversation, but the liberty people
took proved fatal to many of them. Subjects may
lament the faults of their prince in silence, which never
makes them culpable, but kings are not to be jested with.[1]
Helvidius was put to death for having composed some
verses, in which, in the characters of Paris and Oenone,
he made reflections upon the Emperor's having divorced
Domitia. Lamia also lost his life for expressing himself
somewhat too freely upon that subject, though he had
certainly a better right to do so than anybody, as his wife
had been forced from him by violence. In short, everyone that had dared to blame the conduct of that tyrant
experienced his cruelty, for these railleries were the more
insupportable in that he was conscious of their being true.
He could not but call to mind [2] the infamous debaucheries
of Domitia with all sorts of vile, low, and contemptible
wretches, as well as the horrid excesses she had been
guilty of with Paris, the comedian, whose public punishment sufficiently proved his crime, and as these tormenting reflections augmented his anger, in proportion as
they increased his shame, he breathed nothing but rage
and fury. One of Paris's pupils [3] was immediately executed, because there happened to be some resemblance

[1] Sueton. vit. Domit.   [3] Sueton. vit. Domit.
[2] Aurel. Victor. in. Domit.

between his master and him. Hermogenes, a native of
Tarsus, underwent the same fate for having made use of
some offensive expressions in a history he had written.
At last, not knowing whom to exercise his resentment
upon, he made everybody feel the effects of his vengeance
without respecting virtue, relationship, age, or innocence.
Glabrio, who had been consul, and who they say, was inclined to the Christian religion, and Flavius Clemens,[1]
his own cousin-german, were of the number of those who
were executed by this tyrant. Domitilla, wife to the
latter, was banished to the Island of Pandataria, and
Flavia, another of his own near relations, to the Isle of
Pontia, where she received the palm of martyrdom.

It might have been expected that Domitia would have
taken warning by the punishment inflicted upon Paris, the
comedian, and all the other bloody executions we have
mentioned; but, so far from altering her behaviour, she
rather grew worse, for her having hitherto escaped the
punishment she deserved encouraged her to go on in the
same way; she imagined that, as she had carried her
abominations to the highest pitch, without their having
been attended with any very bad consequences, she had
nothing further to apprehend; so, not content with giving
herself up entirely to all kinds of debauchery, she even
boasted of it, and publicly committed those crimes which
any other would, at least, have endeavoured to conceal.

It is amazing that this Empress, such as she has been
described, should have met with people who have highly
extolled and commended her; Josephus, however, that
celebrated historian, and in other respects so honest a
man, has not been ashamed to do this: he has represented

[1] Sueton. vit. Domit. 15.

her as a most virtuous princess, and has lavished upon
her a profusion of mercenary and self-interested praises,
in return for the many substantial favours she honoured
him with, and for having taken him under her immediate
protection.

Procopius has also followed the example of the above-
mentioned Jew, and painted her in the most beautiful
colours, as a princess endued with virtue and every good
quality.   By this extraordinary and undeserved commendation, we may see that there are none so bad as not to
be approved of by some people, if they have but power
and authority.

But Domitian, who knew his wife better than anybody,
could not prevail upon himself to think so well of her.
He was thoroughly informed of all her conduct, and was
well assured that there was nothing she was not capable
of after the life she had led; he therefore determined to
punish her, once for all, according to her deserts, and put
her to death.   The day intended for this execution was
to have been fatal to a great many others as well as her;
for the Emperor, having taken a dislike to a number of
his courtiers, had resolved to put an end to his jealousies
at the expense of their lives, and with this view he had
drawn up a list of such persons as were to be sacrificed
to his fury, and Domitia, his wife, was the first upon
the roll.   Petronius, Parthenius, grand chamberlain, Nor-
banus, and several others were also of the number of
those who were destined to destruction, and certainly they
would have had but a few hours to live, if they had not
been saved by a kind of miracle.

The Emperor kept about him a young child, whose
prattle he was very fond of, who entering one day into

Domitian's chamber, when he was asleep, found a paper at the bed's head, under the bolster, and carried it away with him for a plaything. Domitia, meeting with the child, began to divert herself with him. While caressing the boy she soon spied the paper, which she took from him and read. But what was her surprise when she saw her own name among those who had but a day to live. Being in possession of this important list, she lost no time in assembling all those who were equally concerned in it with herself, and in order to prevent the misfortune which threatened them, she informed them of the danger they were in, and proved it by producing the document.

The time was very short, the peril excessive, and consequently it was no season for hesitating what to do; they therefore immediately agreed that there was but one way to prevent the evil, and that was to be beforehand with Domitian, by dealing him the blow which he had prepared for them. This was accordingly done, and Domitian, who was massacred in his bed, left a useful lesson to all bloody tyrants, that a miserable and untimely end is often the just punishment which they bring upon themselves by their violence and cruelty.[1] History informs us of nothing further relating to Domitia, but, from what we have seen of her, we may venture to take it for granted, without doing much wrong to her memory, that she passed the remainder of her life after the same manner, and that, since the constant fear of punishment she

[1] It is confidently affirmed, by all the historians, that at the very moment when Domitian was being assassinated at Rome, it was known at Ephesus; for the famous magician, Apollonius of Tyana, who was then haranguing the people of Ephesus, stopped short, and began to cry out: " Strike the tyrant, strike him "; and he declared to all present that at that instant the Emperor was being killed at Rome.

was in during her husband's life was not strong enough
to influence her behaviour, she did not alter her conduct
for the better, under the reigns of Nerva and Trajan,
who were not guilty of cruelty, except to the Christians.

AUTHOR'S COMMENTARY
THE FIRST EMPRESSES
AND
NERVA

HE Roman Empire was never so flourishing as in the reign of Augustus, who, properly speaking, was the founder of it. This prince, by the good fortune of his arms, his moderation, and the wisdom of his government, knew how to make his authority respected, without rendering it odious, and though people, who have been always accustomed to independence, are apt to be exceedingly averse to the beginnings of slavery, yet the Romans, who had ever been so jealous of their liberty, were brought by degrees to bear this new yoke, because Augustus had the secret of making it easy, by stripping it of all that was disagreeable.

But it must be confessed that he was indebted to the Empress Livia for a great part of his glory. The most prudent and judicious of his actions were reckoned the fruit of her counsels and advice. It is thought that the magnanimity which he exhibited in pardoning Cinna and his accomplices for their conspiracy, contributed more to his grandeur and happiness than the most important of his victories, and everybody knows that it was a conversation he had with Livia that determined him to pardon those great men. Nothing fixed him so securely upon the throne as this well-timed piece of clemency to those who had a mind to deprive him of it, and this politic generosity was the effect of his consultation with the Empress, who had, generally speaking, a better way of judging than himself.

The other ladies (wives to those Emperors who succeeded Augustus, and were commonly called the twelve Cæsars) had neither the abilities, greatness of soul, prudence, nor policy of Livia. They were, on the contrary, remarkable for nothing that was to their advantage, but rather brought more dishonour upon the Empire than the worst of their husbands, who in reality were only instruments which the Empresses made use of to carry out their designs and gratify their passions. Cæsonia, who disordered the brain of her husband, Caligula, by the love-potion she gave him, made herself accountable for all his bad actions. Messalina and Agrippina, by their cruelty, ambition, covetousness, and debauchery, were the severest scourges that ever Rome and the provinces groaned under. And Julia, Poppæa, and Domitia made themselves scandalous throughout the whole Empire by their infamous lives. Such were the first Empresses.

Plotina, indeed, went a great way towards reinstating the Empire in its original splendour. She had Livia's good qualities, without her pride and haughtiness, but, of those Empresses that succeeded her, few had her virtues; and many of them trod in the steps of Messalina and Julia, as we shall see in the history of their lives.

Domitia and the rest of those who conspired against Domitian, offered the throne to several persons, who were afraid to accept it, because they looked upon those offers as so many snares that were laid for them; but Nerva, at last, being dazzled with the lustre of the sovereign authority, was prevailed on to comply with their request.

He was grandson of Cocceius Nerva, the famous lawyer, whom Augustus so much honoured with his esteem. He was a moderate and prudent man, of a peaceable disposition, a great lover of books, and of learned men. Martial has given us a fine picture of Nerva, and represents him to be a person endued with every good quality. Domitian was afraid of him, because certain soothsayers had predicted that he should be one day Emperor. This so alarmed the tyrant, that he was several times within a little of putting him to death, but an astrologer, who loved Nerva, and whose skill in fore-telling events Domitian had a great opinion of, assured the Emperor that Nerva would not live many days, and saved his life by this stratagem.

As soon as the news of Domitian's death was spread abroad, Nerva was declared Emperor. The Prætorian cohorts paid him their homage immediately, but at the very time when the new Emperor was very agreeably employed in this ceremony, there came a report that Domitian was not dead. Nerva was struck with such terror that he was not able to speak a word, but Par-thenius encouraged him by protesting solemnly that he knew the former report to be true, and that he had noth-ing to fear from that quarter.

The senate heard with great joy that Nerva was chosen, and confirmed the election, knowing the great merits of this prince, and having all the reason in the

world to hope for better times, and they soon found that
they were not mistaken in their judgment. The new Emperor immediately recalled all those whom his predecessor
had banished, and restored to them their estates, which
the cruelty of Domitian had deprived them of, issued
severe laws against informers, and punished with death
the slaves and freedmen who had accused their masters.
He expressly commanded that no statues of gold or silver
should be erected in his honour, and sold his plate, furniture, and a great part of his land to supply the necessities
of the State. Upon every occasion he gave evident tokens
of his beneficence and goodness, and made proper regulations to reform the abuses that had crept in by the negligence of former Emperors; but, being timid, and not
having resolution enough to alter certain customs which
yet ought by all means to have been abolished, and knowing that he was despised on account of his old age, he
looked out for a person of vigour and intellect whom he
might associate with himself in the government, and
selected Trajan to be his partner in the Empire.

It is not certain that Nerva had no wife, but it would
be very difficult to prove that he had, for the reasons
that some modern authors allege to show that, when
Trajan was adopted, Nerva's wife was alive, do not seem
to me to be convincing. Neither is it very probable that
he had children, for it is not to be supposed that he would
have gone out of his own family for heirs to the throne.
Be that as it may, he could not possibly have made a more
worthy choice, or thought of a man more capable of
raising the Empire to its former glory than Trajan, who
at that time was at the head of a powerful army in Germany. He gave him the title of Cæsar, with the sur-

name of Germanicus, and soon after honoured him with that of Emperor, making him his colleague in the sovereign authority, of which in a little time he left him entirely in possession by his death.

PLOTINA

WIFE OF TRAJAN

LPIUS TRAJANUS was a Spaniard, born in the town of Italica, of an ancient family, but not very illustrious. His father, indeed, distinguished himself in Vespasian's wars against the Jews, where his exploits made him known to the Emperor, and procured him his esteem, together with the consulship, and the honour of a triumph.

Trajan, at the time of his adoption, was in the prime of life, between the giddiness of youth and the slowness of old age; agreeable enough [1] in his person, of a large frame, but well proportioned, his neck muscular and head large, which were reckoned indications of prudence and fortitude, as well as of strength of body. His countenance [2] was always serene, without the least signs of melancholy, anger, or any other passion, that might have altered the sweetness and majesty that shone in every feature of his face. His grey hair seemed to command respect, but what most of all ingratiated him with the people were the excellent qualities, civil, military, and political, which were happily united in his person. He was so skilful in the art of war, which he had been bred up to from his youth, that it was a matter of doubt which

---

[1] Dio. lib. 68.   [2] Spon. recherches curieuses d'antiquité.

deserved to be most esteemed in him, the general who
gave his orders with so much judgment and discretion,
or the soldier who obeyed with so much fidelity and
valour. Sober, watchful, indefatigable, he taught his
troops, by his own example, how to endure hunger,
thirst, and all sorts of hardships, and forced them,
whether they would or not, to love him, by cheerfully
undergoing the same inconveniences with the meanest of
them. He was so little given to pride and ostentation
that he used to converse familiarly with the soldiers, and
yet had the secret of maintaining his authority in such a
manner that they never failed in point of respect, for
though he condescended to a familiarity with them upon
certain occasions, he took care not to make himself so
cheap as to be contemptible. Incapable of disguise and
artifice, he always spoke plain truth, mortally hating all
those subtle and ambiguous expressions that make a man
so impenetrable that one cannot approach him without
shyness and mistrust. His whole endeavours were how to
make himself loved, not feared.[1] He visited his friends
without ceremony, without guards or attendance, and invited himself familiarly to their houses, where, laying
entirely aside all state and grandeur, he put himself upon
an equality with the rest of the company. Men of learning were frequently the objects of his generosity and
magnificence, for though he had not applied much of his
time to study, yet he knew how to distinguish true merit,
which he greatly esteemed, and never suffered to go unrewarded. It would be very difficult to find a prince so
strict an observer of justice, for, if he ever seemed to
deviate from it in some measure, it was upon occasions

[1] Xiphilin. in Trajan. Aurel. Victor.

where he had to decide against his own interests. He kept in awe, especially in the beginning of his reign, the intendants and collectors of the taxes, who were accustomed to perform their office in so vexatious and oppressive a way, that the manner of doing it was more grievous than the taxes themselves. He did not fill his coffers with the blood and sweat of the people, but, on the contrary, demanded of the provinces no more than his needs absolutely required, for which reason he had always the satisfaction of finding that they gave with pleasure and cheerfulness. He treated the people kindly and affectionately, as if they had been his children, and the Senate with respect. As for slanderers and flatterers, those pests of mankind, he banished them from his Court. He gave his favourites but a very limited power, and even took care to choose none but persons of probity and honour, who could not but be acceptable to the people, when approved of by such a prince.

It would be endless to enter into details of all Trajan's good qualities; but, on the other hand, I should be guilty of a fault not to be pardoned in an historian were I to conceal his faults and vices. He was so much given to wine that he often passed whole nights in that kind of debauchery, and Hadrian, his successor, used to acknowledge that he owed his being adopted by the Emperor to his complaisance in bearing him company upon those occasions. He was never accused of having transgressed in point of chastity with women, but with too much justice a more shameful and brutal vice was imputed to him. He was by no means exempt from vanity, but gave evident tokens of it, even upon some occasions that were quite beneath a great prince, who was acknowledged to

have excellent sense, for he not only permitted [1] the
people to call him Lord (which Augustus would never
allow), but suffered them to offer sacrifices at his statues,
which was an impiety Tiberius absolutely forbade. He
also caused magnificent triumphal arches to be erected
in his honour, and his name to be engraven upon all the
buildings he either made or repaired.[2]

Such was Trajan, who was chosen by Nerva to succeed
him, in order to raise the Empire to its original glory and
splendour. He fully answered to what was expected from
him, but it must also be owned that the felicity of his
reign was in a great measure attributable to Plotina, his
wife. History is silent as to her family and her country.

It is thought,[3] however, that she was either sister or a
near relation to Pompeius Planta, Governor of Egypt,
who was much esteemed by Trajan; but it is certain that
most of the historians who mention Plotina speak of her
with great commendation. Trajan married her long before he was adopted by Nerva. She was not handsome;
there was even something in her countenance so grave
and serious as made her appear disagreeable, but her
manners were extremely pleasing, for her exaltation
made no change in her conduct, nor could anybody ever
reproach her with pride or haughtiness. She was so far
from coveting those pompous titles which the preceding
Empresses assumed so undeservedly, and with so much
ostentation, that she refused those which the Senate entreated her to accept, and nothing made her humility and
modesty appear to greater advantage than the comparison people made between her behaviour and the insolent

[1] Dio. lib. 55.
[2] Aurel. Vict. in Constanti.
[3] Tristan. Comment. Historiq.

vanity of other Empresses, who took upon them the proud
title of " mothers of their country," whereas, in reality,
they were its most cruel scourges, dishonouring by their
crimes that throne to which Plotina was an ornament.
There never was a more judicious princess, for her advice was always such as tended to the good of the public
and the honour of Trajan, as Julian, the Emperor,
acknowledged, who was a better judge of merit than of
the true religion. In short, Plotina contributed exceedingly to the glory of Trajan, and the splendour of his
reign.

Nobody could charge her with any of those flagrant
crimes and abominations of the Empresses who preceded
her, for she always seemed innocent and blameless, never
apparently deviating from the strictest rules of decency
and good manners.

It cannot, however, be taken for granted that in reality
she was deserving of the eulogies lavished upon her by
Pliny,[1] who calls her a woman exempt from all suspicion,
and beyond the reach of censure; but a panegyric is not
always a proof that the person praised is worthy of it,
especially when it happens that he who commends lies
under great obligations to the other. Some there are
who deny this rigid virtue that Pliny ascribes to Plotina,
and to say the truth, when one comes to examine closely
the great regard that this Empress had for Hadrian, it
looks as if there was at least as much policy in her virtue
as in Pliny's commendation. The true motives of
Plotina's extraordinary zeal for Hadrian's interests upon
all occasions may easily be perceived by the help of a little
reflection, and without much difficulty, or straining the

[1] Plin. Epist. lib. 9.

point, it will be found that the friendly protectress was neither more nor less than a kind of mistress. A great many credible authors are of this opinion, and have observed that Plotina made good use of her dissimulation to promote other views, and the better to gratfy her passions, especially her amour with Hadrian. It is true that this Empress knew so well how to take her measures, and put on a fair outside, that her failings were, for the most part, extremely well concealed, but all her care, attention, and prudery could not protect her against public report, for people did conclude, in spite of all her efforts to disguise it, that Hadrian was by no means indifferent to her.

Plotina was with Trajan at Cologne, when he received the news of his adoption in a letter Nerva himself wrote him. This adoption, which did credit to Nerva's judgment, was also an extraordinary honour to Trajan, because it was entirely owing to his merit, Nerva having preferred him [1] to all his own relations and friends, and associated him in the Empire, though a stranger and at a distance from Rome. This choice was approved of by all the orders of the city, the legions, and the provinces, and, indeed, it may be said that the whole Empire, being well acquainted with Trajan's merit, consented cheerfully to the election.

The new Emperor could not immediately leave Germany, where his presence was necessary, but was obliged to remain there till he had put matters upon a sound footing, which he was able to do in less than three months; he then set out, with Plotina, his wife, to take possession of his dignity at Rome, where he was much

[1] Dio. lib. 68.

wanted. They were received with the greatest demonstrations of joy, amidst the general acclamations of the
people, who showed all possible tokens of their affection
both for him and Plotina, and the latter appeared so
much the more worthy of it, as her humility upon this
occasion was more admired than her fortune. When they
returned from the Capitol whither they went immediately upon their arrival at Rome, and were ascending the
stairs of the palace, followed by a vast multitude of
people, who were paying their respects to them, the
Empress turned towards them, and being desirous to
show that the pomp and splendour of the throne had
made no alteration in her, she,[1] with the greatest
affability, protested that, if it should be her fortune to
quit it, she would do so with the same pleasure and satisfaction she then felt. These were such sentiments of
moderation as had not been found in persons of her rank,
and extremely ingratiated her with everybody.

The many good qualities of Trajan gave room to hope
that this reign would be mild and equitable, neither were
people deceived in him, for he fully answered their expectations. He set himself in the first place to make proper
regulations for the good of the city, and to reform abuses.
He restored to masters [2] the right they formerly had over
their freedmen, which Domitian had deprived them of.
There are some historians who attribute the idea to
Nerva, and will have it that Trajan only carried it out,
but Martial gives all the honour of it to Trajan.[3] He
also deprived these freedmen of the audacious liberty they
enjoyed of accusing their masters, that fatal permission,

[1] Dio. lib. 68. Xiphilin. in Trajan.   [3] Mart. Ep. 34.
[2] Dio lib. 68. Xiphilin. Aurel. Vict. Eutrop.

that had been attended with such tragical consequences! After having sufficiently provided for the security of the public, he entertained them with sports, feasts, and agreeable shows. The people had not, for a long time past, enjoyed those amusements with so much satisfaction, because they were now perfectly safe during their diversions, which was not the case in the preceding reigns. The cruelty of the former Emperors made the spectators quite incapable of any pleasure in these games and pastimes, being in continual dread and apprehension lest some mischief should befall them, for those who were obliged to be present at them, for fear of disobliging the Emperors, were all the while in constant expectation of death, since it frequently happened that a horrible massacre succeeded the shows, whereas, under Trajan, everyone was safe. Nobody had need to fear any other kind of death than a natural one, except they were guilty of some crime to deserve it, for neither the covetousness of the prince, nor jealousies, nor cruelty, nor the Empress's revenge, could give anyone reason to be uneasy. Slanderers were not listened to, except in order to stop their mouth, and punish their malice; riches did not render the possessors of them criminal, for the Emperor made his own happiness consist in that of his subjects. Thus nobly and commendably did Trajan employ his life, in which he was extremely encouraged by the example and advice of Plotina, who, in a great measure, inspired him with these godlike sentiments, and gave him more prudent and salutary counsel than he could have had from the wisest and most learned men.

But Trajan's extraordinary care and attention for the city began to diminish the vigilance that was necessary for the provinces, where the governors and intendants, depending on the Emperor's goodness and the confidence he placed in them, exercised their rapines and extortions with so much the more boldness, as nobody dared to complain of them, for the Emperor had such an aversion to slanderers that he was apt to run into the other extreme, so that it was difficult for the miserable and oppressed to get access to him; he did not consider, that in being deaf to calumniators, he also stopped his ears against fraud and injustice. It was, however, a happy circumstance for such unfortunate victims as had fallen a sacrifice to the greediness of those bloodsuckers that, though they were not able to lay their grievances before the Emperor, they were sure to meet with a kind reception from Plotina, who was ever ready to give them a gracious hearing. She always took care to keep herself thoroughly informed in these matters, and so became well acquainted with the cruelties and violent proceedings of these tyrants. She perceived that to be rich in any of the provinces was reason sufficient for a man being the object of their persecution, and that there was no way to escape the fury of these leeches but giving up all they had to their insatiable greediness. She could not hear of these evils, without being full of compassion for the poor oppressed countries, and indignation against the offenders, and therefore resolved to let Trajan know how far these dangerous abuses had gone. She then gave him details of all the infamous methods those iniquitous commissioners took to enrich themselves. She represented to him the irreparable injury which these miscreants did to his reputation, since his not punishing injustice was authorising it. In short, she argued with so much strength of reason and good sense, that Trajan owned himself to blame, and at once remedied these disorders by reprimanding severely the delinquents, and putting the government of the provinces upon such a footing, and under such wise regulations, as secured them for the future against the extortion of those harpies.

It was universally acknowledged that these wise measures were owing to the zeal and prudent advice of Plotina, and the Senate, with great justice, decreed her the glorious title of August, which had been often prostituted to the most infamous Empresses. Marciana, the Emperor's sister, being also endued with the same good qualities, received the same mark of their favour. However, their moderation was such that they both refused that honour, which others had so much coveted and usurped, imagining that Trajan's not accepting the title of Father of the Commonwealth, which he deserved, ought to be to them an example of humility worthy to be imitated; nor would they consent to accept them, till Trajan had been with great difficulty prevailed upon to accept the above-mentioned title, together with that of "the best of men," which clearly demonstrates the high opinion they had of the goodness of his heart and his affection for his people.

The excessive honours conferred upon Trajan were understood by him as laying him under fresh obligations to use his utmost endeavours for the good of the public; and, in reality, he gave himself up entirely to it. The most effectual method he could think of for that purpose was to appoint none to public offices but persons of merit and probity, in which he was so fortunate that it seemed as if he had collected the votes of the public before he filled up the vacancies, so that his Court was composed of none but such as were remarkable for honour and reputation.

Hadrian, his near relation, held the first rank, which he was entitled to, both on account of his birth and his merits. Licinius Sura, whom the Emperor made use of to signify his pleasure to the Senate and people, was the person he put most confidence in, and trusted with all his secrets. There was also Julius Severianus, a senator of high rank and such merit that Trajan thought him worthy of the Empire; Attianus, who together with the Emperor had been guardian to Hadrian; Pliny, famous for his erudition, his eloquence, and his politeness; Lucius Quietus, a Moorish prince, equal to the greatest generals in his intrepidity and his experiences in the art of war; Palma and Senecio, greatly esteemed by Trajan; Tacitus, so remarkable for his history and wise maxims; Celsus, and many other great men, who by their merit justified the choice of the Emperor, who honoured them with his friendship; Frontinus, illustrious for his military exploits, his knowledge of the laws, and the great capacity with which he had filled the most important posts; Saturninus, whose judgment was decisive in all performances of wit and learning; Martial, whose poetry was so much in fashion in the reign of Domitian, and who continued his epigrams, till, finding himself not so much favoured at Trajan's Court, as he had been at Domitian's, retired to Spain, his native country; Juvenal, so celebrated for his satires, for which he was banished from Rome, and so many others, that it would be tedious to the reader were we to give a list of them.

The ladies were equal ornaments to the court of

Trajan, nor was the Empress Plotina worse attended than he. They consisted chiefly of the Princess Marciana, the Emperor's sister, Matidia, daughter of that princess, also Sabina and Matidia, her daughters again. These were of the first class.

There were also Paulina, sister to Hadrian, Domitia, their mother; the daughter of Severianus, and Calpurnia, Pliny's wife, who was also well received at Court.

As the Emperor had no children by Plotina, the Princesses Sabina and Matidia, his nieces, were the more respected, for they were looked upon as the daughters of Trajan, and consequently all persons of quality and distinction paid their court to them. Marciana was a widow when she arrived at Rome with Trajan on his return from Cologne, and in all probability her daughter Matidia was so likewise, for history does not mention the names of their husbands. These princesses always showed a respectful deference for Plotina, and the Empress, on her part, never omitted any oportunity of giving them marks of her esteem and consideration. Never had there been seen so charming a unity as among these illustrious persons.

Sabina was the eldest of Matidia's daughters, and most beloved by Trajan; she was regarded as heiress to the throne. Hadrian was very assiduous in paying his respects to her, and though his heart was not so much concerned as his ambition, yet he always affected a great passion for her, being persuaded that, if he could be so fortunate as to marry her, it could not but extremely contribute to his advancement. In order to promote this he ran into such expenses as ruined him, without his gaining much ground in his amour; for, though he was handsome,[1] had a great deal of wit and learning, and was a man of gallantry, he had not the secret of making any great impression upon Sabina's affections, so that all his efforts and endeavours were in a manner lost upon her. He never would have been husband to this princess if Plotina had not employed all her interest with the Emperor to bring it about, for he was not much in favour of it, as he never sincerely loved Hadrian.

The Empress, however, was resolved to secure the Empire to Hadrian, and was therefore bent upon this marriage. Sabina brought her husband for dowry the hopes of succeeding Trajan, and Plotina thought it of the utmost importance to her that Hadrian should reign after her husband, as she would then be assured of having a share in the government. Thus the Empress, urged by her own interests, as well as her inclinations for Hadrian, left nothing undone that could possibly promote this match, and succeeded in her undertaking, in spite of the dislike the Emperor had for him, and the princess's indifference. For, as she was extremely politic, and might justly be called Ulysses disguised in women's apparel, as had been said of Livia, she induced Sura, the Emperor's most intimate confidant, to propose it to him, and afterwards taking proper opportunities of mentioning it to him herself, she managed it so that the Emperor gave his consent.

This grand alliance did not, however, contribute much to the fortune of Hadrian, for Trajan seemed to forget that Hadrian had the honour of being so nearly related to him, and neglected him entirely, at the same time promoting his favourites, whose interests people

[1] Spon. recherc. cur. d'antiq.

imagined he ought not to have had so much at heart, and who perhaps did not possess the merit of Hadrian. Plotina put the Emperor in mind of this, and the consulship, which Trajan gave him, was the fruit of her solicitation.

Those who were clear-sighted imagined they could easily perceive, in the zealous interest in Hadrian's affairs, which Plotina showed upon all occasions, something that went a good deal further than bare friendship; and his attachment to the Empress, and his extraordinary assiduity to be agreeable to her were looked upon as not so much the effects of esteem or gratitude as of love. Be that as it may, it must be confessed that if there was an amour between them, the Empress managed her conduct with so much circumspection, and knew so well how to contrive all her schemes, that she exposed herself very little to censure, for at most it could amount to no more than a suspicion. She certainly made very good use of her great cunning and address, for, though there was a vast deal of artifice in the excessive tenderness and affection she always showed her husband, yet, as she had the secret of making him believe she was sincere, he had the highest esteem for her, and thought much better of her than she deserved, according to the opinion of a great many people, who would needs have it that, in her private conversation, she did not behave with that strictness and regularity that she pretended to, and with which she imposed upon Trajan.

After the Emperor had given a new appearance to the city, by the good order he established in it, by the magnificent buildings he adorned it with, and by the reformation of many abuses that Domitian had either introduced or permitted, and which Nerva had not been able to correct, he turned his thoughts towards reinstating the Empire in its former lustre, and humbling its enemies, who were encouraged, by the negligence and misconduct of Domitian, to undertake anything. Decebalus, King of the Dacians, was one of those that had most affronted the Romans. This prince was as good a general as he was a politician,[1] skilful in seizing all advantages and abounding in resources and expedients; after having defeated the Roman legions in two battles, he had made Domitian pay very dearly for a peace, and exacted a tribute which he received regularly every year, a most shameful monument of the victory gained by those barbarians. Trajan, who could not endure to submit to this disgrace, which he looked on as an intolerable scandal to the Roman Empire, resolved to be revenged upon these people in his turn, and to wash out with their blood the shame of the victory they had obtained over the Romans, and the infamous conditions the latter had been forced to submit to in consequence of it. He therefore seized upon the first pretence that offered to declare war against them, and marched from Rome at the head of his legions, taking Hadrian with him.

The Emperor's approach astonished the barbarians, for Decebalus knew very well that it was not the Romans he had conquered, but Domitian,[2] a cowardly and effeminate prince, wallowing in luxury, an enemy to labour and fatigue, and incapable of any laudable ambition. He was now to learn that he would not find it so easy a task to defeat Trajan, who, he knew, was brave, experienced, and as good a soldier as he was a general. He therefore

[1] Dio. lib. 57.   [2] Dio. lib. 68.

did his utmost to avoid coming to a battle, but Trajan was too fond of glory to be contented with merely threatening his enemy. In fact, notwithstanding their ingenious contrivance of engraving upon a large mushroom, which was presented to the Emperor, near the enemy's camp,[1] some lines in Latin, in which the Dacians and neighbouring nations prayed the Emperor to return and not break the peace, Trajan, far from complying with their request, attacked them immediately. This was one of the bloodiest battles that had ever been fought, and may be said, in one sense, to have been fatal to the conquerors themselves, so many brave men did the Romans lose in this action, without mentioning the prodigious number of wounded, whose misfortune furnished the Emperor with an opportunity of demonstrating his excessive goodness, for, as they wanted linen to dress the wounded men, he tore his shirt in pieces for that purpose, and sacrificed his apparel to the miseries of the poor soldiers.

Trajan exerted all his skill and generalship upon this occasion. He carried on the war so vigorously that he penetrated even to the enemy's capital, through the midst of dangers, took the sister of Decebalus and the castle, whither she had retired, and constrained that king to implore the clemency of the conqueror, who, indeed, granted him a peace, but upon such terms as gave the Romans ample satisfaction for the ignominious one that had been extorted from them before. But what was most to be admired in Trajan was, that after he had prescribed the conditions of the peace, he should be so much master of himself, in the height of his success, as

[1] Xiphilin. in Trajan.

to preserve his humility and moderation to that degree that, though he was crowned with laurels, in the midst of victories, and the acclamations of the legions, he insisted that King Decebalus should send ambassadors to the Senate, to request them to confirm the treaty.

If it was a most agreeable sight to the Romans to see the Dacians, who had been so insolent and flushed with their victory, forced to acknowledge the authority of the Senate, and sue for pardon and peace after their misfortune; it was no less glorious for Trajan, when the ambassadors entered the Senate, with their hands joined like slaves, serving as heralds to bring tidings of the Emperor's victories, and in the humblest posture confessing their defeat. But Rome was soon after entertained with a much more agreeable show in the person of Trajan himself, who arrived covered with glory. The Senate decreed him the honour of a triumph and the title of Dacicus, which he had so well deserved. This ceremony was followed by many combats of gladiators, and all those other diversions that were usually provided for the people upon the like occasions.

Trajan had the satisfaction of finding in Rome the same order and regularity that his wisdom had established there, and which the prudence of Plotina had maintained in his absence with such ease and facility as proved her capable of everything that was great and noble. The Empire had not, for a long time, enjoyed the happiness of so mild and happy an administration. The provinces no longer feared the attacks of their enemies, nor the extortions of usurers. Trajan's valour and consummate experience left them nothing to apprehend from the one, and his justice put a stop to the extortions of the other; every single person enjoyed what he had, peaceably and quietly. The city no longer beheld the blood of her most illustrious citizens running down the streets. People were not alarmed, either by the cruelty, avarice, or ambition of Plotina, for, as she was solicitous about nothing but the public good, her whole thoughts were employed in contriving the welfare and prosperity of every individual person. None had reason to complain of her authority, so that it might well be said that if Trajan was the terror of the barbarians, Plotina was the delight of the Romans. She was not distinguished from the other ladies of the city, either by the magnificence of her apparel, the haughtiness of her carriage, or the number of her servants, but by her generosity, her unbounded inclination to do good, the sweetness of her manners and behaviour, her anxiety for the glory of Rome, the goodness of her heart, and the extraordinary pleasure she took in conferring favours. These amiable qualities could not but procure her the love and affection of all the world.

The strict union and friendship that always subsisted between the Empress and Marciana, her sister-in-law, was also the effect of Plotina's wisdom and prudence and the value she set upon that princess's merit. There was no emulation, envy, or jealousy on either side to create a coolness or diminish their mutual affection, no striving against each other, except as to which should be most courteous, for there was such a conformity of inclinations and sentiments between these two ladies, as made them always of the same opinion, and this agreement was the occasion of the perfect tranquillity and happiness that the city and the Court enjoyed, for they

were not laid under the disagreeable necessity of refusing Marciana the respect that was due to her, for fear
of incurring Plotina's displeasure, nor, on the other
hand, were they apprehensive that Marciana would
grudge the Empress what was due to her rank.

Plotina's behaviour was the same in regard to Matidia
and the two princesses, her daughters. She showed so
much complaisance for them, and espoused their interests
with so much zeal and cordiality, that they were not sensible of any superiority of hers over them, so it must be
acknowledged that Plotina's exaltation [1] only served to
furnish her with opportunities of showing her humility.
Their living together in so much harmony gave Trajan
infinite pleasure; he saw, with great satisfaction, this
good understanding among the ladies of his Court so
nearly allied to him, his wife, whose worth and merit
he so much admired, his sister and nieces, who were
also as dear to him as possible. Thus, having no domestic affairs that gave him any uneasiness, he was the more
at leisure to attend to the good of the public. He frequently denied himself his innocent recreations, rather
than that justice should not be administered, and used
often to stop [2] in Livia's Porch, in the market place or
Forum of Augustus, and other places, to listen, with
great patience and attention, to the people's complaints,
and caused everybody to be paid their due with such
justice and equity, as was no less commendable than it
was rarely met with.

In the meantime, whilst Trajan, depending on the
treaty of peace which he had concluded with the barbarians, was taken up with regulating and embellishing

[1] Plin. lib. 16.   [2] Dio. lib. 68.

the city, Decebalus was secretly stirring up the adjacent princes to a revolt. In order to persuade them to it, he endeavoured to convince them that his interest was theirs; that they ought to look upon the Romans as their common enemy; that they might be assured that, when once Dacia was conquered, their countries would also fall a prey to the ambition of the victors; that if they had any regard for their liberty, they should prevent this misfortune by joining their forces against the Emperor.

This cunning and deceitful prince, at the same time that he was corrupting his neighbours, took care to fortify his towns, to store up arms, provisions, and ammunition, to raise troops, to encourage and receive all deserters from the Roman army, and by all these preparations threatened a speedy irruption into the Empire. These operations plainly showed his design, and Trajan was soon informed of it. He communicated this to the Senate, and after they had declared Decebalus an enemy to the Empire, and resolved to punish him for his perfidiousness, the Emperor marched to give him battle.

It was during this expedition that Trajan caused to be made over the Danube the famous bridge that was reckoned one of the most surprising pieces of work that was ever undertaken, being apprehensive that the river might be frozen, and his army, by that means, deprived of all succour. He then penetrated into the enemy's country, and reduced Decebalus to such a miserable condition that the barbarian, perceiving he could not avoid being taken, and fearing that he would be forced to grace the Roman triumph, killed himself in despair. The Emperor had his head cut off, and sent it to Rome. He conquered all the country of Dacia, and made it a province, planting a colony in it, and giving his own name to several of its towns. He distributed among his troops the riches that King Decebalus imagined he had safely hidden, as he had deposited them in ditches which he had dug in the channel of a river, and turned the watercourse another way for that purpose. Thus Trajan put an end to a war that for a long time past had given the Romans prodigious trouble and uneasiness. Trajan performed wonders in this expedition, and his example encouraged the soldiers to such a degree that a Roman knight, who was wounded, being told that there were no hopes of his recovery, instead of being dejected or losing courage, resolved to signalise the last moments of his life by an action that gloriously evinced his resolution and intrepidity; returning to the battle,[1] he fought with more fury than ever, as he had nothing to be solicitous about, and killed a great many of the enemy, till at last he dropped down dead with loss of blood.

The Emperor having put everything upon a satisfactory footing in Dacia, returned to Rome, where he was received with the greatest and sincerest demonstrations of joy. A triumph was immediately decreed him, magnificent trophies were erected in his honour, and there is still to be seen a most superb monument of his glory, called Trajan's Column, erected in the square which is also called Trajan's Square, and which the Emperor Constantius most admired of all the curiosities in Rome. It is, to this day, reckoned the noblest piece of antiquity in the world, and the greatest example of the ancient Roman magnificence. On it there are represented all

[1] Dio. lib. 68.

the victories, battles, and exploits of Trajan. It was
begun on his return from the Dacian War, and was not
finished till seven years after. Plotina caused to be put
on the top of it the urn which contained his ashes, in
place of which Pope Sixtus V. set up the statue of St.
Peter.

The conquest of Dacia carried the reputation of
Trajan to the most distant nations, and rendered his
name an object of respect even to those barbarians whose
names were scarce known or heard of, and whose ambassadors came in crowds to pay their respects, or rather
adoration, to the Emperor. The Indians came from the
furthest corners of the earth to implore his protection,
and these strangers, who were admirers of his virtue,
were also witnesses of his magnificence, which he displayed in those famous combats of gladiators and wild
beasts, games, sports, races, and all manner of shows,
which lasted many months.

But these diversions did not so occupy Trajan as to
make him give himself up to an effeminate idleness. He
showed himself as great in time of peace as in war, by
taking indefatigable pains to lighten the afflictions the
city laboured under, and by giving the most generous and
convincing proofs of his affection for the citizens, who,
at that time, were severely chastised by the hand of
Providence, for they suffered extremely from the plague,
fire, famine, earthquakes, and an extraordinary inundation of the Tiber. He embellished the city with a number of buildings, especially the famous Circus, whose
structure and magnificence proclaimed aloud the Emperor's greatness of mind. Besides this, he took care
to have the laws strictly observed. Three of the vestal

virgins who had broken their religious vows experienced
his justice in a terrible manner, for, how rigorous soever
the penalties were in consequence of their crimes (especially a breach of chastity), Æmilia, Martia, and Licinia
did not fear to incur them. They carried on intrigues
with three Roman knights, who were as rash and as
little scrupulous as themselves. Lucius Veturius was the
first beginner of this dangerous intimacy, and he conducted it with so much circumspection that nobody knew
of it. The vestals, under shelter of their respected dress
and the sanctity of their profession, were contriving
secret pleasures, and sacrilegiously trampling under foot
those solemn vows of which, in public, they pretended to
be the zealous observers. Their vigilance to preserve
unextinguished the sacred fire of the goddess Vesta
served for a blind to conceal their own criminal flame.
The gallants, on their side, were equally concerned to
keep the secret, and consequently took care not to take
any steps that could lead to discovery, for the same
punishment being reserved for their crime, it was incumbent upon them to use the same precautions. It may
well be imagined that this intrigue cost the lovers a great
deal of anxiety and solicitude, for it was no easy matter
to deceive the public and the Great Vestal, who kept a
strict watch upon the behaviour of the rest. They would,
notwithstanding, have been too cunning for both, had it
not been for an unlucky accident that revealed the mystery. Veturius had, among his domestics, a servant who
was his confidant in this affair, for people who are engaged in business of that kind must needs trust somebody. This man, having some slight reason to be displeased with his master, thought he could not be more

effectually revenged than by accusing him and his companions of this sacrilegious intercourse with the three vestals. Such offences as these were never pardoned in Rome. Trajan immediately took cognisance of it, and there was no want of proofs against the unfortunate criminals, upon which they were condemned to suffer the punishment which the law inflicted in the like cases.

This severity, though very rigorous, was not to be compared to the cruelty which this otherwise good Emperor exercised towards the innocent Christians, against whom he issued very bloody decrees, which were put in execution with great barbarity. Pliny, who was then governor of Bithynia, wrote to the Emperor, that, after having made the most diligent enquiry he could, he did not find that the Christians were guilty of any fault; that their principles were wise and prudent, and their actions free from everything that was bad. Upon this remonstrance Trajan, knowing Pliny to be a person of the greatest candour and veracity, made another decree, whereby it was forbidden to persecute them merely upon account of their religion, but at the same time ordered, that if they were informed against and convicted, they should be punished. In this the Emperor, who was so great a lover of justice, contradicted himself, for in forbidding that they should not be molested only for being Christians, he declared them innocent, but in commanding that they should be chastised when convicted, he judged them guilty.

About this time died Licinius Sura, the most sincere friend that Trajan had, and to whom he was in a great measure indebted for the Empire. He was extremely afflicted at this loss, and honoured him with a most sump-

tuous funeral, and a magnificent statue, which he caused
to be erected to the memory of this valuable favourite,
a noble monument of his sorrow and gratitude. It cannot be denied that in Sura the Emperor had a faithful,
honest, and zealous friend, whom he knew to be worthy
of his esteem and the trust he reposed in him, in spite
of the endeavours of certain malicious persons, who,
being jealous of the favour he enjoyed, did all that was
in their power to make him suspected, by insinuating
that he had a design upon the Emperor's life. Trajan,
who was incapable of entertaining so outrageous an
opinion of the best subject he had, showed by his behaviour that he did not suppose him guilty of so black
a crime, and, by so doing, quite discouraged those calumniators;[1] he did not, however, punish them, because
they sheltered themselves under a specious show of zeal
for his welfare and interests. Having one day invited
himself to his favourite's house, he sent away his guards
and officers, and remained with him alone; afterwards he
asked for Sura's physician (whom he consulted) and his
barber, whom he ordered to shave him and clip his eye-
brows; he then went into the bath, and afterwards sat
down to table, without showing the least mistrust at
what had been told him, and the next morning, at his
levee, he said pleasantly to his courtiers, that if Sura
had had any evil designs against him, he had missed the
finest opportunity in the world.

Sura being dead, all the men of mark and distinction at
Court strove who should succeed him in the Emperor's
good graces. Hadrian, by his wit, knowledge, birth (and
especially by the honour he had of being nearly allied to

[1] Dio. lib. 68.

the Emperor), seemed to have the best claims, but all his merit would have been insufficient, if Plotina had not come in very opportunely with her assistance. She spoke very warmly in his behalf, furthered his interests with so much dexterity, and knew so well how to turn the Emperor's heart towards him, that Trajan, who was always complaisant to the Empress, invested Hadrian with the consulship, appointed him governor of Syria, made him his confidant, though he could not prevail upon himself to trust him as he had done Sura, and preferred him to the distinguished post of leader of the army that was to serve against the Parthians, not in the least suspecting (as may well be imagined) that he was conferring all these benefits upon his wife's lover, whilst he only thought he was heaping favours upon his niece's husband.

I shall not enter into details of all that Trajan did in this war, which his ambition induced him to undertake, for that would lay me under the necessity of composing a history on purpose.[1] Plotina went with him into the East, together with the princess Matidia, and exhibited, in those remote countries, the same moderation and humility that she had done at Rome. The Emperor, however, was not always successful in his enterprises. The siege of Atra put a stop to his conquests, for he was obliged to abandon that undertaking, after losing a great number of his men, especially in the last assault, where he fought in person, and gave ample evidence of his intrepidity; for, being piqued at the obstinate resistance of the enemy, he put off his imperial ornaments

[1] Dio. lib. 68.

to perform the duties of a common soldier, and took less care of himself than became his dignity.

This siege was the last of his exploits, for as soon as it was raised, he found himself indisposed, and it was thought that his illness was the effect of Hadrian's treason, but some imagined it to be a dropsical and paralytic disorder. Notwithstanding this illness, he resolved to return to Rome, being earnestly entreated by the Senate to come and receive the fruits of his victories. He left the command of the army with Hadrian, whom he had made governor of Syria, and set out for Rome, accompanied by the Empress and the princess Matidia, but upon their arrival at Selinus, a town in Cilicia,[1] the Emperor found himself much worse, because of the heat of the dog-days, and was not able to proceed. His disorder increased every day, and at last he was seized with a flux, which carried him off.

Plotina, who during Trajan's illness had leisure to provide against his death, took her measures accordingly, and contrived everything to the advantage of Hadrian, who was then at Antioch, and as she was afraid that his absence might be prejudicial to him, she omitted nothing that could possibly promote his interests. We have already observed that Trajan never really loved Hadrian, and far from naming him to succeed to the throne, had made up his mind to make no choice at all of a successor; whether it was in imitation of Alexander, whom he had taken for a model, or that he did not think Hadrian worthy of it, he left the Senate and the legions at liberty to act as they should judge proper in that affair.

[1] Afterwards called Trajanopolis.

Plotina considered how important it was to Hadrian to have it thought that Trajan had adopted and appointed him his successor, for she well knew that the respect the Senate and the troops had for Trajan would almost secure the Empire to whomsoever he should have pitched upon, but that, on the other hand, Hadrian was not loved and esteemed so much as to give him reason to flatter himself that he should be preferred to so many great men who were worthy of it. She took care not to press Trajan to name Hadrian for his successor, for fear his choice should have fallen upon some other person, or that her mentioning any such thing to him should have a contrary effect, and make him show his dislike to Hadrian. As soon, however, as the Emperor was dead, Plotina, who kept it very secret, sent in all haste for one of her courtiers, in whom she could place entire confidence, and having put him into Trajan's bed, caused a great number of senators and officers of distinction to come into the chamber, in whose hearing the pretended sick Emperor declared, with a faint and dying voice,[1] that he chose Hadrian for his successor.

Plotina immediately caused letters to be written to the Senate, to acquaint them with this, and as they could not be signed by Trajan, who was dead, she signed them herself, pretending that the Emperor was not able to do it, because of his extreme weakness; at the same time she despatched a courier to Antioch, to inform Hadrian of the Emperor's death.

This good Emperor was universally regretted by the whole Empire, and Rome never shed tears that were more sincere. Those of Plotina were certainly more

[1] Spartian. in Hadrian.

politic than otherwise; she found reasons for consolation in the kindness and esteem that Hadrian had for her. In the meantime she made, in public, all possible demonstrations of sorrow for her unspeakable loss, and after having caused the Emperor's body to be burnt at Selinus, and enclosed his ashes in a golden urn, she set out for Rome. Hadrian, who came with all speed from Antioch, carried the urn himself on board the ship, and then returned thither, not forgetting to offer the Empress the utmost acknowledgment of his gratitude.

Plotina and Matidia carried to Rome the precious re-remains of Trajan, with which they were entrusted. The urn was received by all the orders of the city with the greatest respect, and placed upon the superb column that Trajan himself had erected in the square, which is distinguished by his name. The Empress Plotina had the same power and authority that she had enjoyed during the reign of Trajan. Hadrian, who was beholden to her for the Empire, had that respect for her which he was obliged by all the ties of gratitude to have for his benefactress. But nothing could more testify his attachment to her, than the excessive grief he felt at her death. He appeared in deep mourning for nine days, erected a temple in her honour, composed a beautiful poem in praise of her, had her immortalised, and dedicated a magnificent mausoleum to her memory in the town of Nemausus,[1] the noble ruins of which are yet to be seen.

[1] Nîmes.

SABINA

WIFE OF HADRIAN

EAL happiness is not always to be met with in a high rank or exalted station, for frequently it happens that great vexations are attendant upon great fortunes, and kings upon their thrones are surrounded with cares, jealousies, and bitter anxiety. Sabina was not at all the more fortunate for being raised to the empire, but on the contrary fell a sacrifice to her grandeur. Hadrian became Emperor by her means, but that did not hinder him from being his wife's tyrant and persecutor: she found herself no better than a miserable slave in the most elevated dignity in the universe.

Sabina was daughter of Matidia, niece to Trajan, and grand-daughter to Marciana, that prince's sister, whose names were not so much as known (such was the obscurity of their husbands' fortunes) till Trajan obtained the throne. Marciana and Matidia, her daughter, were widows when Nerva adopted Trajan, which certainly is the reason that history makes no mention of their husbands' names, who, in all probability, were not very con-

siderable in the empire. But Trajan being invested
with the sovereign power, his glory could not of course
but reflect upon all his family, and from that time Marciana, his sister, Matidia, his niece, and the young princesses, Sabina, and Matidia, his niece's daughter, were
always treated with the fitting respect due to their rank.
The Senate, who were sure never to omit any opportunity
of flattering and paying their court to the Emperor, gave
them the most pompous titles, and among the rest that
of August was not forgotten; and as Trajan was exceedingly fond of his sister, and had also a great affection
for his nieces, the Court, the city, and the provinces
had the same regard for them that they had for the
Empress herself.

Sabina was the eldest of Matidia's daughters, and because Trajan had no children, she was looked upon as
his daughter; so that whoever she married was thought
to bid fairest for the empire, which was no small addition to her merit, and served mightily to heighten her
good qualities. Besides these great prospects and expectations Sabina had this additional advantage, that few
could compare with her for beauty or virtue. In her
countenance [1] might be read that modesty and prudence
for which she was so much distinguished; and she never
encouraged any pleasures or diversions that were the
least in the world inconsistent with the strictest decency.
She had a sort of gravity in her looks that was the true
picture of her mind, and which afterwards furnished
Hadrian with a pretence to dislike her, and give out that
he could not endure her gloomy and melancholy temper,
as he called it; [2] but the complaints of some husbands are

[1] Tristan Comm. Hist.   [2] Spartian. Hadrian.

much to be suspected, and one ought to be very cautious how they give credit to any man when he is speaking ill of a wife he hates.

Of all those who paid their addresses to Sabina, and who aspired to the honour of marrying her, Hadrian was, without dispute, the most remarkable; for besides the advantage he had of being related to Trajan, and of having had him for his guardian, he possessed many excellent qualities, which were the more conspicuous, as he had the secret of concealing perfectly well all those vices that might have eclipsed them. He was tall, very handsome, had a comely figure, and hair that curled naturally, and a thick beard, which he took care not to have shaved,[1] because it hid some defect in his chin. He had so strong and robust a constitution that he generally travelled on foot and very seldom had any sort of covering upon his head even in the depth of winter, a most extensive genius, and so good an understanding that he was capable of penetrating the most abstruse sciences, and, in fact, there never was an Emperor that was master of so much knowledge as he. His memory was prodigious; he was thoroughly acquainted with all the roads he had ever travelled, and all the rivers he had met with in his journeys, and could call every soldier in his army by his name. He had so extraordinary a wit and vivacity, and so happy a facility at composing, either in verse or prose, that in the first he could speak extempore, and that as correctly as if he had had leisure to prepare his discourse. But this prince had also great faults: he was a great dissembler, cruel, cunning, debauched, vain, envious, and very jealous of other people's

[1] Spon. recher. curieu. d'Ant. Spartian.

good fortune; he had an unbounded ambition,[1] and not
content with being superior to other men in rank and
power, he also pretended to be infinitely above the rest
of the world in wit, learning and abilities, not being
able to endure those who were thought to excel him,
whom he persecuted as much as possible, as it happened
to Apollodorus,[2] and would have happened to Favorinus,
if that sophist had not been wise enough to give him
the honour of the victory in a dispute they had about a
word. The philosopher had it in his power to have
proved and maintained his assertion beyond all doubt,

[1] Dio. lib. 69.

[2] Apollodorus, a native of Damascus, was the great architect whom
Trajan employed in the construction of the famous bridge that he made
over the Danube, and several other magnificent buildings. Hadrian was
present one day at a conversation that Trajan had with Apollodorus
about an edifice he intended to erect; and as Hadrian prided himself
upon his skill in every art, he must needs give his opinion upon this
occasion, which was opposed to that of the architect. Apollodorus
finding himself contradicted in a science which he, very justly, imagined
he knew more of than Hadrian, answered him, with an air of contempt,
"Go and divert yourself with your painting, for the matter we are now
treating of is far enough beyond your reach." Hadrian, who did then
pass a good deal of his time in that amusement, was so stung with this
piece of raillery that he could never forgive it, for as soon as he was
Emperor he wanted only a pretence to be revenged upon him. In fact,
he banished him from Rome, but a little while after he carried his
resentment still further, and Apollodorus furnished him with an opportunity to do so; for Hadrian having built a temple in honour of Venus,
he sent the model to Apollodorus, as if it were to know his opinion of it,
but in reality to let him see that he could do without him, and that fine
buildings might be executed without his help. Apollodorus, having
examined it, found several faults, and not being as cautious of offending
the Emperor as in prudence he ought to have been, observed that the
statue of Venus which was placed in the temple, and which was represented in a sitting posture, was too high in proportion to the building;
for, added he, joking, when the goddess has a mind to rise and go out
of the temple, she will not be able, except she stoops. Hadrian, who
thought he had done the finest thing in the world, was extremely mortified when he himself perceived the error he had been guilty of, and
for which there was no remedy but pulling down the roof of the temple,
which was not elevated enough: he was, however, so exasperated at
Apollodorus, that on a frivolous pretence he put him to death.

and being asked by his friends why he gave up the point so easily, answered: " Do you imagine me such a fool as not to acknowledge a person, who has thirty legions at his command, to be the most knowing man in the world?" So dangerous was it to contend with Hadrian in any branch of learning.

Hadrian, with all his good qualities and skill in concealing his vices, was never able to secure the esteem of Trajan; whether it was that that Emperor had a natural aversion to him, or whether he perceived a great many faults in him in spite of his art, or lastly, whether those courtiers, who were in favour, took pains to prejudice the Emperor against him. It is certain that Severianus, who was married to Paulina, and in whom Trajan put entire confidence, was the first that gave the Emperor information that Hadrian had dissipated his fortune; and that prince (generous and munificent as he was) could not endure those unnecessary expenses, which foolish prodigality incurs from want of judgment, and sharply reprimanded Hadrian for it. Be it as it may, Trajan never approved of the match between Sabina and Hadrian, whatever pains the latter took to bring it about. Nothing is more manifest than that Hadrian did not care for his wife Sabina, and that all his pretended esteem and affection for that princess was only the effect of his policy; so that it was Plotina who received the sincere tokens of his love, whilst he could afford Sabina nothing but cold and forced civility, even before Trajan's death. Sabina possessed no qualities that were agreeable to her husband, except her high rank and her portion—that is to say, the empire; these flattered his ambition, but never captivated his heart.

Hadrian was, however, too cunning not to disguise his real sentiments, and to conceal his dislike with the contrary appearance, but this artifice would never have deceived Trajan, if the official endeavours of Sura (in whom the Emperor placed all his confidence), added to the warm persuasions of Plotina, had not, in a manner, forced his inclinations, and broken through all obstacles to promote this marriage, to which Trajan did not consent but with the utmost regret. This sufficiently appeared [1] from the slender regard the Emperor had for Hadrian, though it might be said that he was become his son-in-law by his marriage with Sabina, and consequently that he never intended him for his successor. His being raised to the throne then was entirely the work of the Empress, which she accomplished by the stratagem we have already taken notice of, and in which she was assisted by Attianus, who had been Hadrian's guardian, and the senator Similis, who was then in great esteem at Rome. This person did Hadrian great service upon that occasion, for which he was but very ill rewarded.

Hadrian was at Antioch when the news was brought him of the Emperor's death. He caused himself to be proclaimed Emperor immediately, without waiting for the determination of the Senate, under pretence that the State could no longer remain without a head; and this was the reason he alleged in his letter to the Senate, when he desired they would confirm the election. He solemnly protested, with horrible imprecations, that he would never put any senator to death, let his crime be what it would, which promise he was so far from performing that he broke it frequently; for, as he was very

[1] Dio. lib. 69.

inconstant in his friendships, he persecuted all those whom he had loved, and to whom he was under the greatest obligations. This odd and unaccountable conduct soon after induced Similis, an officer of great honour and merit, to retire into the country, where, far from tumults, business and courts, he passed seven years in calm and quiet solitude, and reckoned that his whole life till then went for nothing, of which he had a mind to inform all the world by ordering this epitaph to be written upon his tomb:

> Hic jacet Similis,
> Cujus ætas multorum annorum fuit,
> Ipse septem dumtaxat annos vixit.

" Here lies Similis, who was in the world many years, but only lived seven."

He died in the 76th year of his age.

As soon as the new Emperor had settled and regulated matters in the East, he set out for Rome, where he did not question but his presence was necessary. He was received with great demonstrations of joy. The Senate decreed him the triumph that had been prepared for Trajan, and gave him the title of Father of his country. Sabina was also declared August; and the Senate, being desirous to show some particular mark of their esteem for the Empress, as niece to Trajan, honoured her with a new title, and called her a second Ceres. The Emperor celebrated his entry into Rome [1] by games and sports, and a very magnificent show which he exhibited on his birthday; he distributed a great deal of money among the people and soldiers, and endeavoured by his bounty, and all possible means, to acquire the goodwill

[1] Faber, c. 8.

and esteem of everybody; but at the same time he behaved so ill towards the Empress his wife that it was
plain he had never loved her. In fact, as his sole reason
for marrying her was to obtain the throne, which he
had long sighed after, as soon as he was in possession of
it and Sabina had nothing more to give him, he made
her little better than his vassal. This is too frequently
the consequence of those marriages which are founded
upon motives of interest or policy; for as nothing is
sought after but riches or grandeur, the parties are
quite indifferent to each other, so that nothing remains
but grief and remorse for having so dearly bought those
chains that they are neither able to break nor support.
Sabina cruelly experienced the truth of this, for Hadrian,
who during Trajan's life had appeared so fond of her,
was no sooner seated on his throne than, weary of dissembling, and far from setting any value on her, either
on account of her person, or for her having procured
him the empire, he, on the contrary, showed her the
utmost contempt, and treated her in so insulting and
brutal a manner that she was infinitely more a slave
than an Empress. Such unjust and blamable conduct as
this could not certainly be justified; [1] but Hadrian endeavoured to excuse himself by alleging something odd
and disagreeable in the Empress's temper, [2] and gave
out that her humour was insupportable, the ordinary
pretence of bad husbands. But Sabina was not silent in
regard to Hadrian's behaviour, when she found herself
so cruelly dealt with; she was too sensible of this usage
to bear it without complaining. One day, having been
worse treated than ordinarily, she reproached him with

[1] Aurel. Victor.   [2] Spartian.

his ingratitude and ill-nature, which, she said, was unbecoming in a prince.

Nor did she think herself obliged to keep it secret; on the contrary, she was in hopes that its being known could not but cover him with confusion, which might have a better effect than all her remonstrances and expostulations. So she made no scruple to lament openly her hard lot in being thus tied to a man of so intractable a disposition and so evil a mind.[1] But Sabina gained nothing by publishing her misfortunes, but, far from it, she ruined her position more than ever, for Hadrian, who by his supreme dignity was out of everybody's reach, and little valued what people thought or said of his conduct, made no alteration for the better in his manner of acting, but rather otherwise; for he proceeded to such a pitch of brutality as to put her upon the footing of a maid-servant and talked of divorcing her, but certain reasons of policy hindered him from going that length. He kept, however, no sort of restraint with her, but showed her the utmost contempt, and that in so shameful a manner as has branded his name with eternal infamy, for, not content with settling his affections elsewhere, and dishonouring, by his inordinate appetites, the most illustrious families, even those of his intimate friends, [2] he became desperately in love with a young man named Antinous, a Bithynian, whom he abused by a horrible brutality, and carried his scandalous and detestable weakness for that infamous object of his passion to an excess that is almost incredible. This, it may be imagined, could not but provoke Sabina in the highest degree; [3] she looked upon Hadrian as a monster she ought to avoid more than a

[1] Aurel. Vict. in Hadrian.   [2] Spartian.   [3] Tristan. Comm. Hist.

wild beast, and her aversion to him became so great that she did all that was possible to prevent herself having a son by him, for fear that an heir sprung from him might inherit his vices and be the ruin of mankind, and she was not ashamed to boast of this.

The whole empire was a witness to this division between the Emperor and Sabina, who, notwithstanding her hatred of Hadrian, accompanied him on all his journeys during his whole reign. His curiosity [1] induced him to visit all the provinces of the empire, notwithstanding the bad weather and the inclemency of the worst climates, with which the poet Florus reproached him in some humourous verses, in which he tells him that, if being Emperor would oblige him to travel through Britain and suffer the excessive cold of Scythia, he would not accept it upon those conditions. Hadrian, who was always very ready at repartee, answered him in such a manner that the poet did not come off best in it, for he composed some extempore verses in the same metre as those of Florus, in which he says that he would not for the world be Florus, who was always haunting taverns and scandalous places, and that it was more honourable for an Emperor to travel than it would be to act as Florus did, and to be over-run with vermin. It is to be observed that among the Romans a man would be extremely ashamed to have been found in a tavern. We have not thought it amiss to insert here the poet's verses and the Emperor's answer.

> Ego nolo Cæsar esse,
> Ambulare per Britannos,
> Scythicas pati pruinas.

[1] Spartian.

The Emperor answered by these verses:—

Ego nolo Florus esse,
Ambulare per tabernas,
Latitare per popinas,
Culices pati rotundos.

The subject's good or bad fortune depends in a great measure upon the very looks of the prince: when he condescends to smile upon anyone, that person will be sure to meet with respect from everybody; and on the contrary, the unfortunate man upon whom he frowns is shunned and avoided by all the world, as if he carried infection about him; the inclinations of mankind will ever be of a piece with those of the sovereign.

Sabina, whilst Trajan was alive, saw all the grandees of Rome at her feet, and particularly Hadrian, who paid his court to her with the greatest respect and assiduity; but, no sooner was he invested with absolute power, and had begun to show his hatred of the Empress, than she was not only abandoned by those who had in a manner adored her before, but even treated most insultingly, by such as were permitted, if not ordered, so to do. From that time they lost all sort of respect for her, nor was there anybody who had not impudence and assurance enough to affront her, by everything they could invent that could cause her trouble and vexation. Among those who carried this liberty to the greatest lengths, Suetonius, secretary to Hadrian, and Septicius Clarus, distinguished themselves in so brutal a manner that the Emperor (desirous as he was to have her mortified and ill-treated upon every occasion), could not hear of it with patience; he deprived them of his confidence and friendship, dismissed Suetonius from his employment, and gave it to

Heliodorus, whom he then loved as much as he hated
him afterwards.   It is true that Hadrian could not endure Sabina : [1] he used her barbarously, and even obliged
a great many of his courtiers to do the same; but it was
the highest disrespect to him for anybody to insult the
Empress without his permission.   I know that some
have attributed the disgrace that befel Suetonius to his
having expressed too much compassion for that unfortunate princess, but I see no authority for that conjecture.

Hadrian was in Britain when Suetonius, his secretary,
forfeited his good graces; and there it was that he was
informed of Plotina's death.   By the immoderate grief
which he showed upon that occasion, it was evident that
the passion he entertained for her was rather love than
anything else.   Sabina's condition was not, however, the
more tolerable upon that account, nor did he think himself obliged to give her a greater share of his esteem for
having lost Plotina : she was still the object of his hatred
and persecutions, and Antinous that of his affection;
but the untimely end of that infamous wretch, which
happened not long after, was a fresh subject of grief
for the Emperor.   It is credibly reported that while
Hadrian was walking one day upon the banks of the
Nile with his favourite, the latter fell into the river, and
was drowned, except we rather choose to believe what
an historian [2] has asserted, that the Emperor offered
him up in an execrable sacrifice that he made to prolong
his own life, which (as the magic which he had long
practised informed him) would be the case, provided he
could meet with a man who should voluntarily consent to

[1] Spartian.   [2] Dio. lib. 69.

be put to death for that purpose, but which nobody could be prevailed upon to do but Antinous. Be that as it may, Hadrian, on the death of that abominable favourite, committed incredible follies and extravagances. He wept like a child, and to mitigate his sorrow, or else to show his gratitude to Antinous, he erected temples and set up statues in honour of him, and placed among the gods the disgrace of mankind.

Hadrian's perpetual journeys did not a little contribute to dissipate his affliction, but his custom of going bare-headed (let the cold be never so intense) and his other fatigues, so damaged his constitution, that he contracted dangerous disorders. He was pretty far advanced in years, which, added to the slight hopes he had of being cured and the contempt he began to perceive that people had for him on account of his age, made him think it high time to look about for a successor. At first he determined upon Severianus, his brother-in-law; but afterwards changing his mind, he was more inclined to Fuscus Salinator, his grand-son, than to Nepos his intimate friend. Gentianus, and many others in their turn, were also in his thoughts, but they all became odious to him, as if his intention to give them the Empire had rendered them guilty of having designed to rob him of it. At last, contrary to everybody's opinion, he [1] pitched upon Lucius Aurelius Verus, whom he adopted, and declared him Cæsar, though he knew by his magic art (as it is pretended) that he would not survive him, and consequently could never be Emperor. In fact, Verus died on his return from Pannonia, and the very day upon

[1] Spartian. Dio. Xiphilin.

which he was to have delivered a panegyric, that he had composed in honour of his benefactor.

This threw Hadrian into new perplexities about the choice of a successor; but after deliberating a while he fixed upon Titus Antoninus, whom he adopted upon condition that he should adopt Marcus Aurelius, and Lucius Verus, son of him who had died lately. Hadrian had been always extremely fond of Lucius Verus's father (too much for both their reputations), for malicious people attributed his resolving to make him his successor to very shameful motives.

Hadrian having thus settled the succession did great honour to his judgment, and was much approved of by all the world, but he mightily tarnished what good qualities he had by his cruelty, especially in the last year of his life. Severianus, his brother-in-law, and Fuscus, were the first that were sacrificed to his rage, under pretence of their having aspired to the throne. Càtilius Severus, Intendant of Rome, was disgraced, being also accused of having designed to usurp the Empire, so that he lost the dignity he possessed by endeavouring to exalt himself to the sovereignty. But the most illustrious of these victims, as well as the most unfortunate, was the Empress Sabina, whom this cruel Emperor put to death, just when she had conceived expectations of a better fate from her husband's illness. Hadrian, after having persecuted her unmercifully, was resolved she should not have the satisfaction of outliving him, and of thereby being compensated for all her sufferings; he treated her with such extraordinary rigour and severity that he constrained her to put an end to her own life, or, rather, he poisoned her, as it was generally believed. Thus perished this poor unhappy princess by the barbarity of him whom she had raised to the empire. After her death he was pleased to procure her immortality, and find her a place among the divinities, as if this impiety could make her happy in another world whom he had rendered so completely miserable in this. The senators did not scruple to grant those impious and ridiculous honours to her whom many of them had deprived of that which was justly due to her upon earth.

Hadrian's death took place soon after that of Sabina. His indisposition increased daily, and instead of deriving any benefit from the physicians, he complained that they had killed him. He caused himself to be carried to Baiæ, in the Campagna of Rome, to try what the change of air would do for him; but, far from observing the diet the doctors had prescribed him, he ate everything that aggravated his complaint, and thereby hastened his end. He saw its approach with great anxiety as to his future state, and composed some verses upon that subject which have made his last moments remarkable. He died at Baiæ, in the arms of Titus Antoninus, whom he had sent for, and his body was burnt in Cicero's house at Puteoli.

FAUSTINA THE MOTHER

WIFE OF ANTONINUS PIUS

HE name of Faustina is as remarkable in history as that of Messalina, and for much the same reason. In the Empresses who were known by these two names, the same inclinations, vices, and debaucheries were predominant; for it does not appear that the wife of Marcus Aurelius Antoninus had any right to reproach the wife of Claudius, nor can it be said that Faustina (the mother) was at all more virtuous than Messalina, whom Nero married after he had killed Poppæa.

Annia Galeria Faustina was daughter of Annius Verus, and sister of Lucius Aurelius Verus, whom the Emperor Hadrian declared Cæsar, and who died soon after he had received that honour. She was of a very ancient family, and her ancestors, who came originally from Faventia, had filled the most important posts in Rome with great honour and reputation; but neither her noble extraction, nor the favour her brother was in with Hadrian (who certainly loved him more than was consistent with decency), contributed so much to her advancement as her beauty. The medals of her that still exist represent her as a most amiable person. She had a peculiar sweetness

in her countenance, a gay and lively disposition, a very
insinuating manner, an amorous temperament, and was
extremely fond of pleasures and diversions, which unhappy tendency was the occasion of all those horrible
irregularities to which she abandoned herself.

Her mother's name was Rupilia Faustina, daughter
of Rupilius Bonus, who had been consul, but came of an
obscure family. Some affirm [1] that he never was really
consul, but that he was only honoured with the consular
insignia, for his name is not in the list of consuls. It
is very probable that she was indebted to her beauty for
her distinguished marriage with Annius Verus, [2] who
on his father's side was descended from Numa Pompilius,
second King of Rome, and on the other from a King of
the Salentines. Be that as it may, Faustina, of whom we
are now treating, was the offspring of this marriage.

If Verus and his wife took much pains to give their
daughter good ideas of virtue, it must be confessed that
they laboured upon a very ungrateful soil, and that her
shameless and most scandalous behaviour is to be attributed entirely to the depravity of her nature, in which
she resembled her brother Lucius Aurelius Verus, whose
licentious and debauched life caused his wife Fadilla so
much trouble and vexation, and which she might have
spared herself, as it was far from having any good effect
upon him.

Faustina, besides her illustrious extraction and her
extraordinary beauty, was the most agreeable person in
the world; she was of a cheerful and lively disposition,
full of wit and vivacity, but there was something in all
her conduct that was not at all [3] consistent with the

[1] Casaubon. not. in Capitol.   [2] Eutrop.   [3] Capitolin.

modesty of her sex, especially at parties of pleasure. On such occasions she did not pride herself upon an over-strict observance of the rules of decency, which were always very irksome to her, but, on the contrary, made no scruple of giving full vent to her natural temper, being quite unguarded both as to her words and actions, in which she discovered the strongest inclination to libertinism. Her friends were willing to hope that her indiscreet behaviour proceeded rather from her giddy un-thinking youth than from a natural bent that way, and that when she was married she would grow more sedate and reserved, but it was not in the power of anything to make an alteration in her for the better, her bad habits becoming every day more ungovernable, so that in a little time she threw off all kinds of restraint.

Faustina's temper and genius induced her parents to marry her betimes, and certainly they could not have found a husband more worthy of her than Titus Anto-ninus, who possessed the highest qualifications. He was originally from Nîmes in Languedoc. His family re-mained for some time in obscurity, but Titus Aurelius, having been made twice consul, owing to his extraordi-nary merit, after passing through all grades of office, it became very illustrious. His son Aurelius Fulvius, who was also honoured with the consulship, was remarkable for his honesty and integrity. This person had, by his wife, Arria Fadilla, Titus Aurelius Antoninus, known since his exaltation to the empire by the name of An-toninus, and who was one of the greatest princes that ever sat upon the throne. He had received from nature and education all the advantages and virtues that were

to be wished for in a great monarch. He was [1] tall and
well proportioned, had a most amiable countenance, and
such sweetness and majesty in his face, as gained him
the esteem and affection of everybody. It was even observed that he greatly resembled Numa Pompilius, whose
virtues and good qualities were revived in him. He was
liberal [2] without prodigality, magnificent without ostentation, polite without affectation, easy and agreeable in
his manner, cheerful in his conversation, exempt from
ambition in his private life, and from pride and haughtiness, when holding the most honourable offices. He was
exceedingly esteemed for his probity, learning, and eloquence, and loved for his moderation, goodness, and
sweetness of temper. All these virtues made his reign
glorious, and acquired him the surname of Pius, which
does more honour to his memory than all those pompous
titles, which were so liberally bestowed upon the other
Emperors, and which were due rather to vanity and
flattery than to truth and real merit.

These rare and excellent qualities soon distinguished
Antoninus, and procured him the highest offices; those of
quæstor and prætor he filled with great honour and magnificence, and acquitted himself with so much wisdom and
capacity in everything he undertook, that he was thought
worthy of the consulship, which accordingly was bestowed upon him. His colleague in that exalted dignity
was Catillius Severus, a very ambitious man, whom
Hadrian would have made Emperor, if he had not discovered that he too earnestly wished for it.

It was during his exercise of this important office that
he married Faustina, and this match was the source of

[1] Capitolin. Spon.   [2] Eutrop. Aurel. Vict.

all his misfortunes, as it attached him to a person whose character was directly contrary to his own. For she, who was in the flower of her age, delighted in nothing but pleasure and amusement; whereas Antoninus, having reached years of maturity, was grave and thoughtful, which was not at all agreeable to a young person of great vivacity, who could relish nothing but mirth and laughter.

It is very difficult for a wife of this sort to behave with that care and circumspection which virtue and decency require; for conjugal fidelity is seldom strictly observed when it has to contend with an impetuosity of constitution, especially when opportunities and temptations are sought after instead of being avoided; and it is much to be feared that a woman who is so excessively fond of amusements will not always insist upon their being perfectly innocent. Faustina, who was born with strong and violent passions, looked upon the gravity and reserve required of married persons as an intolerable constraint. All Antoninus's merits were not strong enough to defend her against the attacks of those crowds of admirers who surrounded her, and who, by their poisonous maxims and seductive flattery, encouraged her in those vicious propensities to which she was naturally but too much inclined.

For some time after her marriage she lived in her ordinary manner, but soon after, she began to indulge her disposition for gallantry, and so by degrees shook off the very appearance of modesty and virtue, till she was irretrievably plunged into vice, and her debaucheries became the common topic of raillery and ridicule.

It is certain that Antoninus was informed of his wife's

behaviour, which was publicly talked of, for she was
so little solicitous about her reputation that she did not
endeavour to conceal her crimes. But even if the Emperor had had so little penetration as not to discover it,
it cannot be supposed that his friends should be so little
zealous for his interests as not to let him know that his
wife was the laughing-stock of all Rome. However, he
did not proceed to violent measures, for, though he was
thoroughly instructed in Faustina's shameful conduct,
and was extremely disturbed about it, he chose to dissemble his vexation and remain quite silent about the
affair.

Debauchery is always inexcusable, but was the more
so in Faustina, upon whom it was, on many accounts,
incumbent to have been more than ordinarily careful of
her conduct. Her husband was very faithful to her,
and was worthy of all her affection; and besides, her
marriage with Antoninus was no reason for her exempting herself entirely from the authority of her parents,
whose esteem she ought by all means to have preserved.
She had also children to whom she should have shown
a good example, and whose education was of the utmost
importance, but her appetites got the better of her
reason, so that she followed her own inclinations rather
than the good advice that was given her, and dreaded
neither the resentment of her husband (who she knew
was incapable of revenge), nor the indignation of her
parents, whose remonstrances she despised. So, instead
of giving her children good instruction, she encouraged
them to tread in her steps, and we shall see in the sequel
that Faustina, the only daughter she had left, being

influenced by so scandalous and pernicious an example,
became a monster of impurity.

Whether Galerius Antonius and his brother (sons of
Faustina) died before or after their father came to the
throne is what the learned differ about, for history does
not decide; but we are informed that the eldest of the
daughters, whose name is not mentioned, and who was
married to Lamia Silanus, died before Antoninus went
into Asia, whither the Emperor sent him as pro-consul.
Faustina accompanied him thither. She would have
been heartily glad to have dispensed with that journey,
which deprived her of all the pleasures of Rome, where
her beauty and the delight she took in being admired
procured her so many adorers; but as there was no help
for it she was forced to submit. She went then with her
husband to the East, where he had some presages of his
future grandeur, and had daily opportunities of demonstrating such a sweetness of temper and such moderation
as nothing could disturb, for it was proof against all
provocations, of which he gave a signal instance on his
first entrance into his province.

This illustrious pro-consul, on his arrival at Smyrna,
took up his lodging for that night in the house of the
sophist, Polemo,[1] because it happened to be at that time
empty, the owner being absent; but the very night that
Antoninus arrived there Polemo came home. He was a

[1] Care must be taken not to confound this Polemo with other philosophers of that name. The person of whom we are speaking was a
native of Laodicea. He was a man of great distinction in Smyrna,
and had formerly been sent on a deputation by the inhabitants to the
Emperor Hadrian, who received him very honourably at Rome, and
showed him considerable marks of his esteem, which had rendered this
philosopher so proud and insolent that he thought himself above all the
world.

man very full of conceit, and so insupportably vain and
haughty that he imagined himself equal to the gods.
The great influence he had with the Emperor, who was
fond of that sort of people, flattered his pride so much,
and made him so insolent, that he kept no restraint with
anybody, as sufficiently appeared upon this occasion.
This sophist, finding his house [1] occupied by the pro-
consul, fell into such a rage that he made the street echo
again, and after having railed at Antoninus in the most
brutal manner, he sent him word to go out of his house
instantly and procure himself a lodging elsewhere, without considering that common prudence, as well as good
manners, required that the pro-consul (whom it was very
dangerous to provoke) ought to be treated with more
politeness : that it was in the highest degree unbecoming
and indecent to oblige the wife of a pro-consul of Asia
(extremely fatigued with a long journey) to rise out of
bed at so unreasonable an hour and wander about in the
dark to look for a lodging, and that he ought at least to
have waited till the next morning.

A less mild governor than Antoninus would have punished the incivility of Polemo, and so brutal an affront
would have induced any other in his place to have kept
possession of the house he had selected for his quarters,
in spite of its impolite owner, which he might have done
by the assertion of his authority; but Antoninus, who was
all goodness and complaisance, would not stay a moment
in the house against the master's will, but gave it up to
Polemo, though at midnight, and it was almost morning
before he could find another lodging. This incident became known at Court, where Antoninus's mildness was

[1] Philostrat. vit. Polem.

not less admired than Polemo's insolence was disapproved. Hadrian, who had a great regard for Polemo, was angry and vexed at his impoliteness, and, for fear that Antoninus should resent it, he condescended to make up the matter between them, and took pains to reinstate the philosopher in the pro-consul's good graces.

Antoninus was as much beloved in Asia as he had been at Rome, and for the same reasons. He behaved with so much justice [1] and probity, and governed that province with such prudence and goodness that he eclipsed the virtues of his grandfather, who had ruled it so wisely, and was so much extolled. The Emperor heard with great joy how exceedingly Antoninus was esteemed in the East, and putting all confidence imaginable in the soundness of his judgment and advice, he recalled him to Rome, to receive the benefit of his counsel and assistance. Faustina was in raptures at this. She quitted Asia with great pleasure, in order to return to Rome, where she could recommence her intrigues; in fact, she there renewed her gallantries, and the more her husband was valued for his good qualities, the more she gave loose to her vicious inclinations. Antoninus smothered in his breast the disagreeable reflections which this irregularity of his wife occasioned, and, by carrying his complaisance too far, pardoned those crimes that he ought to have punished. Whether he was incapable of the least severity, or whether he imagined it would rather increase than cure the evil, or that he hoped to conceal his dishonour by pretending to be ignorant of it, he permitted his goodness and the sweetness [2] of his temper always to intercede for Faustina, who, for her part, made a very bad use of his

[1] Capitolin.   [2] Capitolin. in Tit. Anton.

indulgence, and did not fail to furnish the public with ample matter for raillery and censure.

As nothing encourages vice so much as impunity and bad example, so Faustina could never have gone calmly on in such a course of life if she had found it attended with any bad consequences. Antoninus could not prevail upon himself to use severity against his wife, though she dishonoured him; Annius Verus, who was grown old and decrepit, was not in a condition to make himself much respected by his daughter; and as for Lucius Aurelius Verus, her brother, instead of giving her good advice, he showed her the worst example in the world, for, as if their being born of the same mother had given them both the same inclinations, he gave himself up as entirely to debauchery as his sister. Never was man such a slave to infamous pleasures; for, not content with ordinary ones, he invented new kinds of vice, and outdid the most depraved princes in effeminacy. Among other odious monuments of his unbounded incontinence, history mentions [1] a particular sort of bed, strewn with roses and lilies, the scene of his abominations with his infamous concubines.

Fadilla, his wife, was extremely sensible of the affronts her husband put upon her, and far from being of as pacific a temper as Antoninus, her brother-in-law, she lost all patience, and railed at Verus in all the provoking language she could think of, and reproached him with his scandalous way of life and his contempt of her, who did not think herself at all inferior to any of those objects of his affection he was so fond of. In short, she worried him so much that once he told her in a great passion that he took a wife merely to maintain the honour and

[1] Spartian. in Æl. Ver.

dignity of marriage, not for any satisfaction that was to be expected in a married state; so that she ought not to be surprised if he looked for pleasure elsewhere. Thus Faustina and Verus, by their vices and infamous conduct, were a scandal to all Rome, while Fadilla and Antoninus, by their wise and prudent conduct, were the glory and ornament of it.

Verus's debaucheries, however, did not spoil his fortune; for Hadrian, finding himself declining every day in health, resolved to name him his successor, and adopted him. The Emperor made him prætor, Governor of Pannonia, and consul, and had so great a regard for him that a letter from this new Cæsar had more influence over him than the most earnest solicitations of any of his courtiers.

It is affirmed (notwithstanding) that Hadrian (who knew Verus to be entirely unfitted to govern the empire) never intended that he should be invested with sovereign authority, but that this adoption was the infamous price of that brutal complaisance which he showed the Emperor, who knew that Verus would never sit upon the throne, which made him say that he had adopted a god, and not a son. The result verified his prediction; for Verus died soon after, without leaving any other mark of his dignity than a pompous funeral.

Although Hadrian did not design that Verus should succeed him, yet he could not make up his mind whom to leave the empire to, till he considered the virtues and good qualities of Antoninus, and then he determined in his favour; and perceiving that his illness increased, he convoked the Senate, and declared that he adopted Titus Antoninus, and, having made his will, he appointed him his heir and successor to the throne; he added that it was [1] at the persuasion of Polemo that he was prevailed upon to make that choice, that the merit of this action might make Antoninus forgive the insult he had received from the philosopher at Smyrna. Hadrian died soon after.

Nothing could have been more agreeable to the whole world than this choice, for never had the empire a more worthy master. The first thing the new Emperor did was to express his gratitude to his benefactor by procuring him immortality. He thought he could do no less than place Hadrian among the gods, who had provided him so exalted a station upon earth. He did not, however, find it so easy a matter as he had imagined, for the late Emperor, having put to death several of the most illustrious senators, had rendered his memory odious; and far from granting him divine honours, on the contrary, they were much inclined to break all his ordinances, and destroy everything that might do him honour with posterity.

Antoninus was much afflicted at this disposition of the Senate, and endeavoured by all the arguments he was master of to give them a more favourable opinion of Hadrian; but his reasons had no great weight. He represented to them that if they revoked and annulled what Hadrian had done, it would follow that he himself could not be their Emperor, at the same time that they were expressing so much joy at his being so; " for," said he, " if you suppress the dispositions of the deceased, if you will not execute his last will, do you not thereby refuse to accept me, to whom he bequeathed the throne?"

[1] Philostrat. vit. Sophist.

Then, on his shedding some tears, the senators were so moved that they altered their resolution, and he obtained his request; so that he who had been the tyrant of the State became a divinity.

Antoninus signalised the beginning of his reign by pardoning all those who had been condemned to death by Hadrian; for he said that it should not be in the power of anybody to reproach him with having dishonoured his accession to the throne by such odious executions. These generous sentiments saved the lives of a great many persons, who were so many heralds to proclaim his clemency. In fact, those who had been banished were recalled, prisoners were set at liberty, sentences of death were revoked, and the Senate honoured those marks of his goodness by decreeing him the title of merciful, and the glorious name of father of the State, which no Emperor had better deserved. The same decree granted Faustina the title of August; for the Senate did not think they could well refuse the Empress the same honour they had conferred upon other princesses, however unworthy they had been of it.

Faustina's exaltation to the throne, the pompous title that had been given her, and the supreme rank with which she was honoured, required that she should live in a different manner from hitherto. She could not, without the utmost degree of shame and scandal, indulge herself in those liberties that had so much dishonoured her, and which certainly did not become an Empress, upon whose conduct the eyes of all the world were fixed; but all these considerations could not extinguish in her that invincible desire of pleasure which had obtained such an absolute empire over her heart, and obstinately resisted every reflection that tended towards a restraint of her passions.

After the new Emperor had acquitted himself of the duty he owed to the memory of his predecessor and bene-factor, he displayed his magnificence and generosity to the people, among whom he distributed large sums of money; he paid the troops the legacies that Hadrian had bequeathed them, and made them considerable presents in addition. The towns of Italy and the provinces also partook of his liberality; but Faustina [1] could not help looking upon this excessive generosity of Antoninus as downright prodigality, and reproached him with it in very sharp terms.

She told him, with an air of discontent, that he ought to be satisfied with dissipating in gifts and presents the public treasure, without wasting his private fortune in needless and superfluous expenses. Nobody expected to find this wonderful economy in Faustina, who ought her-self to have been a little more sparing of her favours; for, at the same time that she was so thrifty in point of money, she did not scruple to be exceedingly prodigal of her honour. Antoninus would, notwithstanding, have willingly excused her covetousness, if he could have pre-vailed upon her to be more chaste and virtuous; he re-proved her for this low and self-interested way of think-ing, and answered that, since he was become Emperor, he had nothing he could call his own, not even his private patrimony, which was become that of the public; which remarkable words sufficiently prove the goodness of his heart and the love he had for his subjects, whom he looked upon as his own children, and, in fact, took all

[1] Capitolin. in Anton.

possible measures to make them happy. He exterminated the quadruplators, that dangerous class of people,[1]
he did away with all those offices and posts that were of
no manner of use to the public, as he looked upon it as
unjust that the people should be burdened with those
who contributed nothing to their benefit. He strictly
charged all the governors of provinces not to be guilty
of extortion, put none into posts of importance but persons of known probity and honour, and never undertook
any war but when there was an absolute necessity for
it, being much more desirous to maintain peace in the
empire than to enlarge its bounds, and more solicitous
about the public tranquillity than his own glory. He
had continually in his mouth that remarkable sentence
of Scipio the African, that it was better to save the life
of one citizen than to destroy a thousand enemies. Never
did prince make so moderate a use of his power. He
was easy of access, and gave everybody a hearing, not
only with patience, but with the greatest condescension
and affability. No person whatever was forbidden to
approach him; he listened attentively to the poor and
unfortunate, without pride or haughtiness, for nobody
had occasion to bribe any of his courtiers to procure an
audience: the doors of his palace were open to everyone,
and never had favourites fewer opportunities of squeez-
ing money out of the people than during the reign of
Antoninus.

But of all his good qualities none were more conspic-

[1] The quadruplators were so called from being entitled to the fourth
part of the substance of those who were convicted of crimes upon
their accusation. They did an infinite deal of mischief in Rome; for
in order to enrich themselves, they made it their business to blacken
the characters of those who had money.

uous than his mildness and sweetness of temper. He
never was known to revenge an injury, so that those
who had the most grievously offended him had nothing
to fear from his resentment. He gave Polemo, who
had treated him so brutally at Smyrna, an instance of his
extraordinary moderation. The professor, being informed that Antoninus was on the throne, went to Rome
to congratulate him upon his accession. His arrival
put everybody in mind of the insolence with which he
had refused his house to Antoninus, when he went there
to exercise his pro-consulship; and people expected that,
if it was possible for him ever to show any tokens of his
displeasure, it would be to a man who had so grossly
affronted him; but Antoninus, who was perfect master of
himself, and looked upon revenge as a poor low passion,
received Polemo with great marks of esteem and consideration; he even embraced him tenderly, lodged him
in a handsome and convenient apartment in his own
palace, and, in a joking manner, gave orders that it
should be such a one that he should run no risk of being
turned out of it. By this agreeable and ingenious raillery
Antoninus was minded to let the philosopher see that
he had not forgotten his incivility, though he had forgiven it; and showed that, if he did not express any signs
of his displeasure, it was not to be attributed to stupidity,
or his being insensible to insults, but to his heroic virtue
and nobleness of soul. This rare example of meekness,
at the same time that it secured him the affection of the
Senate and people, served as a lesson to all those about
him; for he would never have mentioned this affair at all
had it not been to instruct others how they should behave
in the like cases; he brought it in very opportunely upon

another occasion, when an actor, who had been driven out of the theatre by Polemo, came to complain to him. The Emperor asked what time of the day it was when this happened; the other answered, "At noon." "I," said the Emperor, "was turned out at midnight, and never complained at all."

Antoninus had reigned three years, with all the wisdom and goodness that has been described, which made him a blessing to all the world, for which he was justly called the "delight of mankind," when his wife, Faustina, died in the thirty-seventh year of her age. Her debaucheries, which had caused the Emperor so much vexation, would, one would think, have furnished him with reasons for consolation. He, nevertheless, regretted this Empress, in spite of her infamous behaviour.

He caused all the honours that had been granted to the preceding Empresses to be conferred upon her, and placed her among the gods, where the Senate had already introduced the Agrippinas and Messalinas. Rupilia Faustina, her mother, was yet alive, and received the compliments of condolence usual upon those occasions. She had the satisfaction of seeing the Emperor, her son-in-law, doing particular honour to the memory of Faustina; for Antoninus, not content with causing her to be immortalised, and dedicating the most sumptuous games in honour of her, built a temple, which he filled with the statues of this new divinity, and being resolved to grant her extraordinary privileges, he ordered that her image should be solemnly carried in procession to the shows that were exhibited in the Circus.

After the Emperor had paid the last tribute to the memory of his wife, by all the honours that could be thought of, he employed himself entirely in State affairs. He repaired old buildings, and erected new ones. He relieved the provinces, that had been afflicted with the plague, famine, and earthquakes, especially Cyzicus, whose famous temple (the grandest and most magnificent building in the world) had lately been thrown down.[1] He also rebuilt, at his own expense, the houses that had been burnt down at Carthage, Narbonne, and Antioch; so that it may be said that there was no province where some monuments of his liberality, compassion, or magnificence were not to be seen.

Never was prince so great a lover of peace, and at the same time so formidable. The most distant people thought themselves happy in being under his protection and owning him for their sovereign lord, so much were they captivated with his uprightness and the mildness of his government. His power extended to the remotest corners of the earth. His name was revered and respected by all the Kings in alliance with the Roman Empire, even strangers and barbarians; so that he maintained peace and tranquillity in the world more by his reputation alone, than his predecessors had done by force of arms.

One of the greatest benefits he could possibly have conferred upon mankind was to instil virtuous notions into the mind of Marcus Aurelius, whom he had adopted,

[1] Cyzicus was one of the most remarkable towns in Greece, both for size and beauty. It was situated on an island in the Propontis, and had a communication with the Continent by two bridges. It was famous for its marble fortresses and towers; but most of all for the temple, which was an astonishing piece of work, far surpassing anything that was to be seen in Asia for its size and magnificence. The pillars were fifty cubits high, and each made out of an entire stone. The island is still celebrated for its marbles.

and who was to succeed him, jointly with Lucius Verus, pursuant to Hadrian's will. He therefore took care to choose for him such tutors as had the greatest reputation, and sent to Chalcis for the celebrated Apollonius, whose pride and arrogance furnished Antoninus with an opportunity of showing his extreme goodness. That philosopher, being arrived at Rome, took up his lodging in a private house, instead of going directly to the palace. The Emperor being told that he was come, sent for him in order to commit the education of his adopted son to his care, but Apollonius, full of his surly philosophy, and looking sternly at the Emperor's messenger, told him that it was not the duty of the master to go and wait upon the scholar, but the pupil's to go and pay his respects to his master. Antoninus was not at all offended at this impertinent and ridiculous vanity, but laughed at it, saying he was surprised that this great philosopher should not have found out that it was not quite so far from his lodging to the palace as from Chalcis to Rome.

It may be taken for granted that such a prince as Antoninus (since he took so much care of his adopted son's education) did not neglect that of his daughter Faustina, but he did not find in her the same good disposition as in the other, for Marcus Aurelius copied Antoninus, whereas Faustina unhappily trod in the steps of her mother.

We shall see by the sequel that she carried her lasciviousness and shamelessness as far as it could possibly go. Antoninus had not the mortification of seeing it, for he died in the twenty-third year of his reign, after having governed the empire with so much wisdom, justice, moderation, and glory that it might more fitly be said of him

than of Trajan or Augustus that he should either never
have been born, or should never have died. Towards the
latter end of his life he issued that famous decree that
St. Augustine has so much commended, by which husbands were forbidden to accuse their wives of adultery
when they were themselves guilty of the same crime;
and which subjected the men, when they offended in that
way, to the same penalties that were incurred by women
of that character. Never was Emperor so much regretted by his subjects, who had all of them so high an
idea of his honour and integrity that the most remote
and barbarous princes thought themselves happy when
they could prevail upon him to be the arbitrator of their
differences, in which cases his opinion and judgment was
always regarded as final.

FAUSTINA THE YOUNGER

WIFE OF MARCUS AURELIUS

EN'S love and study of philosophy is not always what procures them the esteem and affection of their wives; on the contrary, it has often been the case that too much gravity and studiousness in a husband has been the occasion of his spouse's infidelity, and who knows whether the younger Faustina would have carried her irregularities to so great a length if her husband had been less a philosopher? She was the daughter of Titus Antoninus, as we have before mentioned, and in her father she had the most perfect model of virtue, but her headstrong passions and the violence of her temperament hurried her away, in spite of the best instruction and example. It is generally vain and fruitless to attempt to counteract Nature, so Faustina, who was born with vitiated and depraved inclinations, imitated the vices of her mother, as if it had been decreed that all of that name were to be utterly shameless. If the face can be reckoned a true image of the soul, no great prudence or discretion was to be expected from this princess, for her physiognomy seemed to foretell her natural humour and disposition. She had a small head, a somewhat prominent face, [1] a long neck, small but very

[1] Spon. recher. curi. d'antiquité.

lively eyes, and a giddy, thoughtless look. She was incapable of reflection or modesty, and never allowed the rules of decency to enter into rivalry with her own humour and inclinations, so that few women have carried their debauchery and shamelessness to such an excess. It is certain that the fact of Marcus Aurelius not giving himself much trouble about her conduct, and the too great complaisance he always exhibited towards her, contributed not a little to her scandalous behaviour, for an unrestrained indulgence has generally that unhappy effect. A husband who resolves to shut his eyes against all his wife's failings betrays himself, for it is not at all safe or prudent to give too much liberty to some women, who make no other use of it but to dishonour themselves and all who belong to them.

When the Emperor Hadrian adopted Antoninus, he ordered that he should give Faustina his daughter to Verus; but, as soon as Hadrian was dead, Antoninus, thinking [1] there was too great a disproportion between his daughter's age and that of Verus, acted quite contrary to Hadrian's intention, and decided to marry her to Marcus Aurelius, though he was already betrothed to Ceionia, daughter of Lucius Ceionius Commodus.

Marcus Aurelius belonged to one of the best families in Rome, being descended from Numa Pompilius, whose wisdom and goodness he imitated. His first name was Annius Verus, but as soon as he was adopted he took the name of Marcus Aurelius. His ancestors had always held considerable rank in the Senate, but his personal virtues rendered him infinitely more illustrious than his birth, or his connections by marriage, who included all

[1] Capitolin. in Marc. Aurel.

persons of quality and distinction at Rome. In him were to be seen all manner of good qualities, without any faults. From his childhood he was inclined to be grave, moderate, and liberal, and preserved, even in the exercise of the sovereign power and all the splendour that attends it, his simplicity of manner. He passed the greater part of his youth in the study of the Stoic philosophy, and continually conversed with people of that profession: he even affected their sedate and serious air, and imitated them in the minutest things, not disdaining to wear (after their example) the long cloak, in which he was not ashamed to appear in public, for which reason he was always styled "the philosopher." He greatly injured his health by too close application to study, and the many disorders which he complained of all his life were to be attributed to it.

As soon as Hadrian was dead, Antoninus adopted Marcus Aurelius, and at the same time resolved to marry him to his daughter, though she had been intended for Verus. Faustina, the mother, proposed this to Marcus Aurelius; and, as he was not a man to do things rashly, but, on the contrary, weighed and considered all his actions, he desired time to think of it. Antoninus, however, gave him the title of Cæsar, initiated him into the College of Salian Priests, appointed him consul for the next year, and, in short, heaped upon him all those honours that were usually bestowed upon such as were intended to succeed to the throne. All this made no impression upon Marcus Aurelius, who had so imbibed the maxims of the Stoics that he was quite insensible to honours that were sufficient to gratify the most unlimited ambition; and, making his whole pleasure consist in his philosophy, he gave himself up entirely to it.

The time being expired that he had asked before he could determine about the marriage, he accepted with gratitude the honour of being the Emperor's son-in-law, and married the Princess Faustina. The nuptials were celebrated with all possible magnificence, and the Emperor displayed upon this occasion his great generosity and bounty. But what in due time completed their happiness was the birth of the Princess Lucilla, whom Faustina was delivered of, and as this more endeared him to the Emperor, he had new dignities conferred upon him. He was created tribune, with the power of pro-consul, which last office, far from making him arrogant, rendered him if possible more meek and humble; and he behaved with as much duty and respect to Antoninus as if he had been his own son. There never was so beautiful a union between a father and son-in-law, who made it their whole study and occupation to give each other reciprocal tokens of their esteem and affection.

There were not wanting, according to custom, many envious people, that could not bear this happy agreement, as they imagined that Marcus Aurelius's favour and influence with the Emperor eclipsed theirs.

There are always in Courts corrupt and mischievous flatterers, who think to advance their own fortune by insinuating themselves into the good graces of the Prince at the expense of other people's reputations, pretending to be more zealous than ordinary for his interests; and it is next to impossible for the best of kings to be always upon their guard against the venom of this dangerous class of people. Valerius Omulus was one of this char-

acter. This artful and wicked courtier, who had the
Emperor's ear, never failed to take advantage of the frequent opportunities he had of endeavouring to create
mistrust and jealousy in Antoninus with regard to Marcus Aurelius; and whenever it was in his power to put a
malicious construction upon any actions of him or his
family he was sure to do it.

Cunning and imposture were the more dangerous in
him, as he had a great deal of cleverness, and knew how
to give weight to mere trifles; he also possessed the
secret of employing raillery with great success, in order
to gain his point; but under pretence of mirth and joking,
his way was to give mortal stabs to those whom he had
a mind to injure. Omulus adopted this method to give
the Emperor a bad impression of his son-in-law. Domitia
Calvilla, Marcus Aurelius's mother (a lady who prided
herself upon her wisdom and piety towards the gods)
went regularly every day to pay her devotions before
an image of Apollo, that was in her garden. She was
performing this duty one day, when the Emperor and
Omulus saw her at the feet of this statue in a very humble
posture. Omulus, perceiving the Emperor looking very
attentively at Domitia, would fain have put a bad construction upon this attitude of hers, which he ought
rather to have commended. He insinuated to Antoninus
that his death was what she was begging from the god
with so much earnestness; then, turning towards the
Emperor, with a malicious smile, " It is not difficult,"
said he, " to guess at the petition Domitia is offering up
to Apollo; it can be nothing but your death that she is
requesting, in order to procure the empire for her son."

Antoninus, whose prudence and natural goodness

would not suffer him readily to entertain an ill opinion of anybody, did not fall into the snare that was laid for him, nor did he in the least alter his conduct towards Calvilla or Marcus Aurelius; so that the perfidious courtier had no other satisfaction than that of having discharged a malicious arrow with no other results than revealing his odious character. This is very often the only fruit that such base flatterers and parasites reap from their diabolical attempts to do ill offices to innocent people.

Titus Antoninus being dead, the Senate (agreeing with him as to the merit of Marcus Aurelius) declared him sole Emperor; but he, being a religious observer of his word, would not fail in the promise he had made to Hadrian to take Lucius Verus as his colleague in the empire; he accordingly did so, and, though he had but a very indifferent opinion of this prince, he thought himself obliged to declare him his colleague, gave him the title of Cæsar and August, and from that time promoted the match between him and his daughter Lucilla.

It was then that the empire had, for the first time, two Emperors, who governed in concert with equal authority, for till that time the sovereign authority had been always lodged in one single person. Marcus Aurelius was very well pleased to divide both the honour and the fatigue of rule with Verus, that he might be more at leisure to indulge his favourite passion, the study of philosophy. In fact, he cultivated it upon the throne with the same assiduity as when he was a private person, nor did he think it at all inconsistent with his dignity to frequent the Academies, and to take Lucius Verus, as his colleague in the empire; he accordingly did so, and lis-

tened with great attention to the lessons of such philosophers as were of high reputation, whence he returned
filled with the maxims of the most austere virtue and
wisdom.

This was not at all suitable to Faustina's taste, whose
coquettish and lively disposition could but ill relish such
serious conduct,—she, who could not live but in the midst
of pleasures and diversions. Accordingly, whilst Marcus
Aurelius was amusing himself in his study with his philosophical pursuits, she (unmindful of her birth and
dignity) was giving full scope to her vicious inclinations;
and the Emperor, too much taken up with his meditations, troubled himself but very little about his wife's behaviour, who knew so well how to make the most of this
supine indolence, that she was resolved to deny herself
nothing. The Emperor Verus was not less complaisant
to his passions and desires than Faustina, and in all his
actions showed the vast difference there was between
him and his father-in-law; but the misfortunes which, at
'that time, afflicted Rome and the empire, roused him at
last from his diversions and pleasures. The Tiber overflowed the city, destroyed the finest buildings, and
swamped all the country. In addition there was a dreadful famine and plague; and, as if all the judgments of
Heaven were united to punish the Romans, the Parthians, after having driven out of Syria Atidius Corne-
lianus the Governor, openly declared war, which they
had been meditating for many years past.

The Emperors applied themselves with vigour to repair the loss and damage occasioned by the inundation,
the scarcity, and the pestilence; and after having sent
experienced generals and troops against those barbarians,

and the inhabitants of Britain, who had also revolted, it was agreed that Verus in person should take a journey into Syria, to chastise the Parthians for their rebellion, and that Marcus Aurelius should remain at Rome, where his presence was necessary. The Senate authorised all these resolutions.

Marcus Aurelius accompanied his colleague as far as Capua, and then returned to Rome, but being soon after informed that Verus was taken ill at Canusium, he ordered the Senate to offer vows for his recovery, went himself to pay him a visit, and did not quit him till he was well enough to proceed on his journey to Syria. About this time Faustina was brought to bed of the Princess Fadilla, whom Caracalla afterwards put to death, and of whom we shall have occasion to speak hereafter. She had afterwards another daughter, called Justina, who died young, according to some historians, but others say she lived long enough to imitate her mother. As for Faustina the Younger, she exactly copied Messalina in her shameful and most infamous behaviour, so that it would be difficult for one who has the least regard for decency and good manners to mention such things without horror. I know, however, that the rules of history oblige him who writes it to report the vices as well as the virtues of those whose lives he undertakes to give an account of. For my part, I wish I were able to report with more circumspection, and in terms more consistent with modesty, these horrible and shocking crimes; but yet, if too thick a veil be thrown over the meaning of an author, it is entirely hidden. After all, when one has read the history of Messalina, Julia, and Agrippina, there will be no great room for being surprised at any

thing that can be met with in that of Faustina, who trod
in their steps; for, while Marcus Aurelius was shut up
in his study, contriving the best means to humble the
enemies of the empire, or indulging his philosophical
tastes, the Empress his wife was abandoning herself entirely to the gratification of her appetites by the most
scandalous behaviour. The confidence she had in the
Emperor's goodness encouraged her to dishonour him
by the most horrible libertinism. She was not content
with procuring gallants of quality and distinction, and
bestowing upon them those favours which her too studious husband neglected, but gave herself up to all
comers, so that her prostitutions became quite public;
and having by degrees brought matters to such a pass
that she blushed for nothing, and being not in the least
afraid of her husband, who seemed insensible of her
conduct, she gratified without restraint her infamous inclinations.

Orfitus, Utilius, Moderatus, and Tertullus were
some of her lovers, who lived with her in a disgraceful
intimacy.

The public, which observes every step that is taken by
persons of high rank, was thoroughly acquainted with
Faustina's debauches. The eyes of all the world were
upon her; and scandal, which spares neither nobility nor
dignity, grandeur nor authority, was not more indulgent
to the Empress than to other people. Marcus Aurelius
could not but be informed of these excesses of his wife,
for it would have been impossible for the gallantries of
Faustina (who set so small a value upon her reputation)
to escape his knowledge. At least, he must have known
of her intrigue with Tertullus, as he surprised them

together one day at dinner; and so great a familiarity must needs have given him to understand that they had had meetings more secret and more criminal. He had even the mortification to see that his wife's imprudence furnished matter of ridicule to the theatre; for one day, when the Emperor was there,[1] the actors had the rashness and assurance to introduce this subject upon the stage, and acquaint him with his wife's prostitutions to his face, which would have been a very dangerous attempt under a less mild Emperor than Marcus Aurelius, and in all likelihood the comedy would have had a tragical end; for an actor, who represented a stupid husband, enquiring of his slave what was the name of his wife's gallant, the slave named him three times, and said it was Tullus; but the husband, who pretended not to have heard him, repeating the same question, he answered it was Tertullus.[2]

Marcus Aurelius certainly stood in need of all his philosophy, and all he could do was to endure his shame and vexation in secret; so, affecting to know nothing of his wife's gallantries (though she took so little pains to conceal them), he was put to a severe trial.

In the meantime, whether the rigid maxims of the Stoic philosophy or the rules of policy absolutely required that he should pretend ignorance upon this occasion, he certainly continued to give his wife such tokens of his love and affection as she was little worthy of, and having a mind to justify his insensibility on so tender a point, he undertook to impose on posterity by making believe that he had the best opinion in the world of his wife, and pro-

[1] Jul. Capitolin. in Marc. Anton.
[2] i.e., Ter-tullus, "thrice Tullus."

testing in his moral reflections [1] that he looked upon his having a wife of so good a character to be a particular favour of the gods. But unluckily this was a useless precaution, for the reputation of the Empress Faustina was incapable of defence.

Verus did not behave with more discretion in Syria than Faustina did at Rome, and we shall see presently that his conduct did not give his colleague less trouble and vexation. However, the Roman generals under him [2] managed so successfully that they beat the enemy. Verus did not fail to claim all the merit of it, and when the war was at an end he appointed Avidius Cassius Governor of Syria, whose bad and suspicious behaviour soon gave Verus reason to mistrust him, and he wrote to Marcus Aurelius to let him know that in Cassius they had a very dangerous enemy to fear.

Whether it was that the Emperor's philosophical maxims made him think himself independent of Fortune, and that the decrees of Providence were inevitable, or that he imagined this information was only the ill-grounded suspicions of a person who thinks of nothing but his pleasures, he answered his colleague that, if the gods had so ordered it that Cassius was to be Emperor, it was not in the power of man to reverse their decrees, and that it was better to submit with patience than attempt a resistance that would be in vain. In this way of reasoning there might be a good deal of philosophy, but very little truth or policy; and accordingly we shall soon see that when Cassius openly revolted, Marcus Aurelius did not look upon it in that light, and that his

---

[1] Marc. Aurel. Antonin. op. de. seip.   [2] Capitolin. in Ver.

submission to the gods was not so blind and passive as it appeared.

In the meantime Verus adorned his brows with the laurels that others had won, and received at Rome the honour of a triumph which was the reward of a victory he had had no hand in, notwithstanding all his boasting. He there continued his horrible debaucheries, with which he had corrupted all the towns in Syria; nothing like it had ever been seen, and when we come to read in the following chapter of the actions of that prince, it will appear that no injustice was done him when he was compared to Caligula, Nero, and Domitian, the worst of emperors. His incontinence respected nobody, for he lived in a criminal intimacy with Faustina, his mother-in-law, and was not ashamed to defile the bed of Marcus Aurelius, his father-in-law and benefactor, by a shameful incest and odious ingratitude. This disgraceful intercourse between Verus and Faustina cannot indeed be doubted, when we consider that he was invested with sovereign authority, and that he was incapable of setting any bounds to his infamous passions, while Faustina had neither shame nor modesty, so that they both burnt with the same flame. It is said that Verus, far from making a mystery of this intrigue, was very proud of it, and even could not forbear boasting of it to his wife.

Lucilla was strangely surprised to find that her mother was her rival; for though she well knew that Faustina lived a strange life, she did not imagine that she could possibly carry her irregularities so far as to have an amour with her son-in-law. She was so exasperated that she could not control her anger and jealousy; and, forgetting the respect she owed her mother, she reproached her bitterly with her scandalous behaviour with Verus. There are some crimes of such a nature that those who are guilty of them cannot bear to be thought so, be they never so shameless; and a woman must be a monster if she does not show some little signs of bashfulness when she is reproached with her crimes; thus Faustina, long as she had been accustomed to vice, had not the assurance to endure her daughter's just indignation, but on the contrary was covered with shame and confusion; she further conceived such an implacable hatred to Verus that his death was afterwards attributed to this piece of indiscretion, and reckoned the effects of Faustina's revenge.

If Marcus Aurelius was really acquainted with all these things, it must be acknowledged that they afforded him as good an opportunity as he could have desired to exercise his philosophy, and that his being able to endure it could have been owing to nothing less than his being a downright Stoic. He maintained his character, however, always appeared insensible of his misfortune, and seemed not to perceive what all Rome saw plainly enough. This over-strained complaisance (not to say stupidity) only served to encourage the Empress in her vicious habits, and embolden her to commit those abominations in which she indulged herself at Gaieta in the kingdom of Naples, so called from Gaieta Æneas's nurse who died there.[1] Marcus Aurelius went thither upon some occasion, and Faustina accompanied him. There it was [2] that she abandoned herself to such prostitutions

---

[1] Tu quoque litoribus nostris, Aeneia nutrix.
Aeternam moriens famam, Caieta, dedisti.—VIRGIL, AENEID, vii. 1, 2.

[2] Capitolin. in Marc. Aurel. Victor.

as would scarce be believed, were it not so well attested
by the most credible authors as to leave no room for
doubt.

It was no longer to senators and knights only that she
was so liberal of her favours (that would have been an
insupportable restraint) : it was now men of the vilest
condition, the most abject and contemptible, that were
the objects of her depraved inclinations; for, as she was
no longer curbed by any rules of shame or decency, she
kept no sort of restraint, but put up, as it were, her
honour to auction. She did not blush to be seen publicly
in the amphitheatres and on the quays, where she caused
numbers of sailors and gladiators to pass quite naked in
review before her, and singled out such as she liked best.

She thus obliged the whole empire to be witness of her
shameless debaucheries,[1] for neither the obscenity of
this spectacle, nor any reflection, nor motives of shame or
decency were strong enough to stop the fury of her
unparalled impudence, or set bounds to her lasciviousness. Never had vice been seen that could be compared
to this. It was during these debauches, and during this
miscellaneous intercourse, that Faustina became with
child, and nothing but corrupt fruit could be expected
from a pregnancy that was the consequence of such
scandalous proceedings. The Empress's dream did not
a little contribute to strengthen the general suspicion,
and seemed to foretell the devilish nature of the child
that was to be born. She dreamed that she was delivered
of two serpents, one of which was more venomous than
the other; and this fatal presage was but too well verified, to the great misfortune of the empire. Faustina

[1] Capitolin. in Marc. Anton. Aurel. Victor.

was delivered of twins, one of which was Commodus, the scourge of mankind; the other was Antonius, who in all probability would not have deserved a better character if he had lived. Commodus's depraved nature, the mischievousness of his heart, his corrupt inclinations, and his exceeding great love of shows and gladiators, made people believe (and with good reason), that Marcus Aurelius was not his father, but rather one of those gladiators that had partaken of the Empress's favours. I know that there are authors who, to palliate the crimes of Faustina, or to save the honour of the Emperor (about which, as about her own, she was so little solicitous), have invented a fabulous account of this pregnancy of Faustina. They say that Faustina, having seen a handsome gladiator, became mightily smitten with him. This passion threw her into a state of melancholy which alarmed Marcus Aurelius. So good a husband could not possibly neglect to procure his wife the medicine that was proper to cure her; he asked her then the cause of her illness, and was informed that it was occasioned by her love for this gladiator. This sort of distemper a little disconcerted the philosophical phlegm of the Emperor, and because the remedy which he saw she was desirous of concerned his honour a little too much, he consulted the Chaldæans as to what was to be done, told them the nature of her indisposition, and requested them to employ their art on this occasion. These wise people were of opinion that the gladiator, who had caused the Empress's disorder, should have his throat cut, and that the Empress should drink his blood. Marcus Aurelius was obliged to consent to this prescription, and also to contribute his part to the cure; for part of the ceremony was that he should go to bed with the Empress after she had drunk the bloody potion. Everything was done accordingly, and with great success; but because the imagination of Faustina had been warmed by her idea of the gladiator, she conceived Commodus, who in consequence had always the inclinations of a gladiator. It is true that the historian who relates this says it was only a report that did not gain much credit; nor is it indeed very likely that Faustina should be so scrupulous as to languish for love of a gladiator.

It is wonderful that Marcus Aurelius, who was so great an admirer of virtue, and who was well acquainted with his wife's prostitutions, should have been able to dissemble so long, and that he should not have reflected that, by neglecting to punish such horrible disorders, he made himself an accomplice in them, and was liable for his share of the disgrace. Besides, he could not doubt but all Rome was well acquainted with his wife's scandalous behaviour, for among his courtiers there were some who had his honour and interests so much at heart as to take the liberty of reproaching him with his impolitic silence. They represented to him the infamy with which Faustina dishonoured his family, and the insults she inflicted upon her husband and her Emperor; then they declared that such abominations demanded that she should be made an example of, since to pretend ignorance in this case was to authorise her proceedings; that so unseasonable a clemency was a shameful weakness, that Faustina had justly forfeited a life she had sullied with innumerable adulteries, prostitutions and debaucheries; and, in short, that if he could not prevail upon himself to put Antoninus's daughter to death, he ought at least to divorce her, since she had not been ashamed to dishonour their marriage by the most scandalous and most punishable transgression.

Marcus Aurelius heard all this with indifference, and answered coldly that, if he must needs part with Faustina, he could not avoid restoring her portion; meaning that, having received the empire from the liberality of Antoninus, who at the same time gave him his daughter, he could not, consistently with justice and gratitude, put her away without giving her the empire which she had procured him. This answer silenced his advisers, for none after that would give themselves any trouble about it; so, Faustina, being persuaded that the Emperor's great respect for Antoninus would always protect her against the treatment she deserved, went on in the same way, and continued to live as she had hitherto done: so true is it that, where there is no fear of punishment, there is nothing to restrain vice.

The Emperor Verus also continued the same course of debaucheries; but the rebellion of the Marcomanni interrupted his infamous pleasures, for the revolt of those barbarians was of such importance as to alarm Rome, and Marcus Aurelius, in spite of his philosophy, was extremely perplexed. He omitted none of those pagan superstitions that were practised in those days in order to render the gods propitious; but as it was to impotent divinities that he addressed his vows, he was obliged to prepare for his defence, and to look for that succour from force and the courage of his legions, which his sacrilegious offerings could not obtain from his gods. The Marcomanni in the meantime horribly ravaged the provinces, and at the same time the plague raged in

Rome, and daily swept away vast numbers of people. Marcus Aurelius did all that was possible to put a stop to the terrible effects of this dreadful calamity, and, after having given the necessary orders to relieve them, he set out with his colleague at the head of his army for Aquileia. The approach of the Emperors, who had made great preparations for this war, intimidated the barbarians, and detached from their alliance some of the neighbouring princes whom the rebels had won over to their interests, and at the same time the Quadi, having lost their King, declared that they would have no other but such as the Emperors were pleased to give them. Verus, who was deprived of his pleasures by this journey, and had only quitted Rome with a great deal of regret, longed to return thither. He represented to Marcus Aurelius that, the war being at an end, there were no more enemies to fight; and that such a dangerous sickness had attacked the army as would soon utterly destroy it if they were not soon put into quarters. Marcus Aurelius, who weighed and considered things in a very different maner, was very cautious how he yielded to his colleague's reasons and pretences, and told him that it was very probable this pretended submission of the barbarians was only an artifice to get the army disbanded, in order to make sure of their work as soon as that was done. Verus, who could not avoid showing deference to the opinion of his father-in-law, was forced to give up the point; but as soon as they had passed the Alps, Verus, who had no liking for the fatigues of war, and the further he got from Rome, the more he wished to return thither, used so many arguments with Marcus Aurelius that at last he prevailed upon him to suspend operations, and go and consult with the Senate about the most suitable measures to be pursued.

It was in the beginning of winter that they set out again for Rome, and with the same equipment, but between the towns of Concordia and Altinum, Verus was seized with an apoplectic fit, which carried him off.

Marcus Aurelius continued his journey to Rome, where he caused a superb funeral to be prepared for his colleague. He procured him the honour of immortality, and gave the most debauched man that ever existed a rank among the gods. This done, he resolved to reduce the barbarians, and marched against them with a formidable army. That of the rebels was no less so, being much more numerous; for besides the Marcomanni, there were large bodies of Germans, Quadi, and Vandals. To those were joined the Sarmatians, and the Iazygans— people accustomed to the fatigues of war, used to all sorts of hardships, and as irreconcilable enemies to the Romans as the Marcomanni themselves, against whom Marcus Aurelius had assembled all his forces, which indeed were much diminished by the plague. The Emperor's skilful management, however, supplied this defect; so that he was victorious over the barbarians. This astonished but did not discourage them, for, urged on by their despair, they exerted their whole strength, and resolved to make a last effort. And certainly it may be affirmed that never was the Roman empire in so great peril.

The Roman army that was in the territories of the Quadi, being unfortunately encamped in a very disadvantageous situation, the barbarians besieged it.[1] The

---

[1] Dio. lib. 71.

Romans were shut in by mountains, ditches and defiles, and could not possibly extricate themselves without yielding at discretion to the enemy, who reckoned upon destroying them without striking a blow. Among the Romans there were a great number of soldiers wounded, and many that were infected with the plague, which spread more and more, and made terrible havoc. Their misery was still more increased by the excessive heat, from which, and the want of water, both men and horses suffered extremely, so that it looked as if all the evils that could be imagined were united to ruin the army. The barbarians, who suffered from none of these inconveniences, and who were well informed of the miserable condition of the Romans, felt sure of a complete victory, and that without losing a man; since they imagined that the Romans could not but be undone by being so hemmed in, and took it for granted that their distressed condition would compel them to surrender.

Marcus Aurelius was never in so much perplexity, and did not fail to implore the protection of all the tutelary gods of Rome; but these prayers were without success. As this was the greatest danger the troops had ever been in, the Emperor was extremely embarrassed, but in the midst of his perplexity a captain of the Prætorian Cohorts reminded him that in the army there was one legion entirely composed of Christians, who did not worship the Roman divinities, and that he saw no reason why, in this case of extreme necessity, application should not be made to them to invoke the God of the Christians, and supplicate from him that help which they stood so much in need of, for that no means ought to be neglected. Marcus Aurelius immediately sent for the officers of that legion, and entreated them to beseech the God whom they served to deliver them from their extreme peril. They did so, and were heard: for the Almighty, willing to manifest His power in favour of those who called upon His name, afforded them the assistance they so earnestly prayed for. Scarce had they finished their devotions, when the sky, which till then had been very clear and serene, suddenly became dark, and soon after, the Romans had the unspeakable satisfaction of feeling an abundant shower of rain fall upon their camp, which cooled the air and supplied them plentifully with water for the soldiers and the cattle, which were ready to expire with thirst and at the same time there fell upon the barbarians such violent hail, accompanied with dreadful thunder and lightning, that they were struck with a panic and fled, abandoning their camp and baggage to the Romans, who pursued them and slaughtered most of their army. Marcus Aurelius acknowledged that this miraculous delivery was owing to the prayers of the Christians, honoured that legion with the glorious surname of Thundering, and showed a great esteem for the Christians ever after.

I know that the enemies of the Christian religion, in order to weaken as much as they can the truth of this event, or attribute it to any other cause than the above mentioned, give out that the escape of the Romans was owing to the enchantments of the magician Arnulphus; and some flatterers, to pay their court to the Emperor, spread it abroad that the gods had shown them that peculiar favour out of regard to Marcus Aurelius's piety. We leave it to the reader to examine the authors and historians that write of this fact, where he will meet with arguments enough to refute these idle dreams.

This important victory greatly increased Marcus Aurelius's glory and reputation, and made him a terror to the barbarians. The legions proclaimed him Imperator with loud acclamations, a title they were accustomed to give their generals after a notable victory, which in this sense had a different meaning from what the word usually imports; but he would not accept the honour, though he had deserved it so well, till after the Senate had confirmed it to him by a solemn decree, which also bestowed upon him the title of Germanicus. They could not indeed do too much for an Emperor for whom no reward was too great, especially considering how they had prostituted the most honourable and high-sounding titles to the basest and most unworthy tyrants. But if, on the one hand, they justly heaped honours upon Marcus Aurelius, on the other it must be owned that Faustina, to whom the Senate was also very liberal in that respect, was not in the least worthy of them. For whilst the Emperor honoured the throne by his virtues, the care he took to defend the empire, and the many victories that were due to his skill, Faustina gave herself up without reserve to her brutal pleasures, and became the shame and disgrace of the empire by her infamous prostitutions. The Senate, however, bestowed upon her all the honours they could think of, and decreed her the proud title of " mother of the armies." They likewise struck a medal with this inscription (Divæ Faustinæ August. Castror. consecratio), when at the same time she deserved the utmost contempt instead of honours. The barbarians were in such consternation at

their loss that Marcus Aurelius would in all likelihood
have entirely subdued them, and would have reduced
their country to a Roman province, if the news of the
revolt of Cassius, who had caused himself to be proclaimed Emperor in Syria, had not obliged him to march
against that rebel, who, for a long time past, had
ardently desired to mount the throne, and who had his
spies at Rome. The Emperor then perceived that
Verus's suspicions were not groundless, and that in
Cassius he had indeed a dangerous rival. This revolt
made it necessary for him to make peace with the Germans upon as reasonable terms as could be had, so, deferring to another opportunity the more effectual
humbling of those people, he determined in the first place
to fight Cassius.

Avidius Cassius was descended from the famous family
of that name, which was very distinguished during the
republican period of Rome, and was extremely jealous
of its liberties. He inherited that hatred which his
ancestors had shown upon all occasions against such as
assumed excessive power. Cassius was an odd mixture of
virtues and vices very opposite to each other. He was
sometimes severe and cruel, and at other times humane,
mild and polite. Sometimes he affected great piety and
devotion towards the gods, and soon after showed a
thorough contempt even for what was most sacred in
religion. On certain days he wallowed in wine, and
carried his debauchery to the greatest excess, and then
again he would live in the other extreme; so that this
mixture of good and bad qualities caused him to be
compared to Catiline, and he was rather pleased than
otherwise when people gave him that name. He was so

strict an observer of military discipline that it might rather be called cruelty than strictness, for he punished the smallest crimes most rigorously. Marcus Aurelius, who looked upon him as a man capable of doing good service and of keeping the troops to their duty, gave him very important posts, in which he had always acquitted himself well, and to reward him for his good behaviour, made him Governor of all Syria, where, after he had made all his preparations, he thought proper to rebel against his Emperor and benefactor.

It is reported that he was excited thereto by Faustina, because this Empress, in whom the love of pleasure had not extinguished that of power, imagining that Marcus Aurelius, being frequently sick, had not long to live, and being desirous of finding some able protector who might be a friend to her and her children in case of accidents, and even secure the throne to herself, thought nothing could more effectually do this than a suitable alliance; and she was persuaded that in the whole empire she could not have selected anybody more capable of anwering her purpose than Cassius, whose exploits had procured him the highest reputation. With this view it is said she wrote to him to seize the empire as soon as he should hear of the Emperor's death, and promised to marry him. But it is not at all probable that Faustina ever had any such design, for besides that, in reality, she never showed any tokens of ambition (as her capital vice lay another way), her letters to Marcus Aurelius, wherein she exhorts him never to pardon Cassius or his accomplices, sufficiently clear her of that crime. It is more likely that Cassius, suffering himself to be hurried on by his foolish hopes, and being at the head of a considerable army, beloved by his troops, much respected in Syria, and prompted by his ambition and the sycophants that surrounded him, gave out that Marcus Aurelius was dead. Whether he really believed it was so, or that by this false report he desired to induce the army to choose themselves a master, it is certain that he flattered himself with being able to seize the empire.

The news of this revolt caused Marcus Aurelius considerable annoyance. Cassius's great reputation, the high esteem he enjoyed among the troops as well as in the provinces, and the affection the army had for him, rendered him very formidable. The Emperor at first kept it very secret, but perceiving that his men were already forming themselves into parties, he resolved to conceal it no longer, and having assembled the legions, told them that it was not so much his design to break out into complaints and show his resentment against his enemies as to express his grief at being engaged in a civil war, and at finding himself betrayed by a man who had been always faithful to him hitherto, and whom he had never offended.

" What friendship," said he,[1] " can for the future be safe from treason, or what virtue secure? If this revolt were only against me I should despise it, and scarcely think it worth my while to trouble myself about it, but it is more against you than me that he turns his arms; he attacks the State and we cannot defend it without shedding the blood of the citizens. As for me, my dear companions, though I am exposed to dangers in foreign countries, remote from Rome and my family, loaded with years and infirmities, I shall neither spare

[1] Dio. Lib. 71.

pain nor care to make Cassius return to his allegiance; it remains with you to do your part. The victory depends upon your behaviour. Let us consider that our principal enemies, being Cilicians, Jews, Syrians and Egyptians, are an effeminate sort of people, over whom we have been accustomed to triumph. Fear not their numbers, your valour is worth much more than their multitudes. Cassius has more reputation than merit; but if he were a greater general than he is, what could the boldest lion do at the head of a herd of deer? Is it the exploits he performed against the Parthians that they boast so much of? Is it not to your courage that he owes them? Are we not more obliged to other generals for them than to him? I am persuaded that his revolt is the effect of his foolish credulity, and that the report of my death, which was spread all over Syria, has induced him to enter upon this rash enterprise, and consequently, my being now alive and in good health should make him desist from his ill-judged undertaking; but suppose he should not have already given up all hopes of success, it cannot be doubted but our approach will disconcert him, for he is well acquainted with your valour, and cannot but respect my dignity. If I have anything to be apprehensive of, it is that he will probably fall a victim to his despair, and destroy himself rather than support the shame of his defeat, or that some other will kill him to punish his audacity. I desire neither the one nor the other. I should look upon it as a very great misfortune, as I should be thereby deprived of the sweetest fruits of the victory—I mean the pleasure of pardoning an enemy, and showing my affection for a man who has betrayed me. In short, it would rob me of an opportunity of proving that there yet exists in some men the precious remains of that ancient generosity for which our ancestors were so remarkable."

In the meantime the Senate declared Cassius a public enemy, and confiscated his estate for the benefit of the Emperor; but Marcus Aurelius, who had no sentiments but what were noble and disinterested, having refused it, it was deposited in the public treasury. As to the revolt, it was almost as soon extinguished as begun. Cassius was killed by a centurion, who was jealous to deliver the Emperor from an enemy who was by no means to be despised, and whose violent and untimely death served as an instructive lesson to rebels, to teach them what is generally the consequence of ambition and power unjustly usurped.

Faustina was all this time employed at Rome in taking care of her daughter the Princess Fadilla, who was ill. Marcus Aurelius informed her of Cassius's rebellion, and desired her to meet him, that they might consult together what measures were proper to be taken. Whether she had nothing to say to Cassius's crime, or whether her intention was to cover her perfidiousness by an artificial appearance of indignation against the author of this conspiracy, she answered the Emperor that she would come to him as soon as possible, but that, in the meantime, she entreated him not to pardon one of the rebels, since the punishment of those miscreants was the greatest mark of kindness he could show their children. "You cannot but know," said she, "that it is very false policy to pardon such guilty people; for if they do not meet with the chastisement they have deserved, they naturally become bolder. I remember that Faustina, my mother, represented to your father, Antoninus, when this very Cassius had attempted his life, that he ought to have a greater regard for his own children than anybody else, and that an Emperor who neglected the safety of his wife and children was destitute of true affection. Our son Commodus," continued she, in her second letter, " is yet very young, and Pompeianus, our son-in-law, is grown old, and they have no support but you. If you suffer Cassius to live, you expose them to his fury and resentment. Take care how you forgive those who have dared to commit so heinous a crime."

Marcus Aurelius, whose heart overflowed with goodness and sweetness of temper, could not prevail upon himself to agree with this opinion; for, no sooner had he heard of the death of Cassius, than he showed public marks of grief and affection. His moderation even went so far as to make him intercede with the Senate on behalf of the rebels. " I acknowledge your kindness," says he, in the answer to his wife's letter, " in taking so much care of me and my children. I have read several times the letter you wrote me at Formiae, in which you advise me to punish Cassius's accomplices, but I cannot bring myself to follow your counsel, which is so opposite to my nature. I am, on the contrary, determined to spare the life of his wife, children, and son-in-law; and I will entreat the Senate so to moderate the rigour of the law in their favour that they may neither be condemned to too cruel an exile nor otherwise suffer too severe a punishment. Nothing is so worthy of an Emperor as clemency. It is that virtue that has placed Julius Cæsar among the gods, and has immortalised the memory of Augustus, as well as that of your father, Antoninus, who was honoured with the glorious title of gracious and merciful. If, in this war, my orders had been obeyed, Cassius would yet be alive. The gods will grant me their protection in recompense for my moderation. I intend Pompeianus, our son-in-law, to be consul next year."

Nothing more sublime than this can be met with in a heathen. His excessive goodness appeared yet more in the letter he wrote to the Senate entreating them not to shed the blood of any person of quality, and to recall those who were banished or proscribed. " How unfortunate I am," said he, " that it is not in my power to recall from the grave those who have lost their lives by this rebellion, for I can never approve of an Emperor revenging his own private injuries. Pardon, therefore. I beseech you, Cassius's wife, children, and son-in-law. But why do I intercede for persons who have been guilty of no fault ? Let them live, and that without fear or apprehension ; for I would have them feel that they live in the world during the reign of Marcus Aurelius. Let them quietly enjoy the inheritance of their forefathers, and full liberty of action and going where they think proper, that, wherever they are, they may be living instances of your clemency and mine."

Such were the sentiments of Marcus Aurelius, transmitted to us by his letters, which have been preserved, and which will ever be a monument of the nobleness of soul and generosity of that excellent prince. He gave real and convincing tokens of it to the unfortunate family of Cassius, for he caused their father's property to be restored to his children, and took under his protection Druantianus, his son-in-law, and Alexandria, his daughter, whose grief and affliction for the deplorable end of her father he lessened and mitigated by heaping upon her all manner of benefits.

The Senate could not do otherwise than extol the clemency of the Emperor; Rome echoed again with the hearty acclamations and unfeigned praises that were so unanimously bestowed upon this best of princes, and Marcus Aurelius, after having regulated and put everything on the best footing in the city, set out for Asia, in order to stifle by his presence all the seeds of war, and entirely reduce to their obedience those towns and provinces that had followed the party of Cassius. Faustina accompanied her husband on this journey; but the fatal period of her debaucheries, together with that of her life, was come. She died in a village at the foot of Mount Taurus [1] which Marcus Aurelius made into a Roman colony, and called it Faustinopolis, after his wife. Some say she was carried off by a sudden death, others that she died of the gout, and there are not wanting those who affirm that she destroyed herself to avoid the shame she must have undergone by her confederacy with Cassius being discovered. Be it as it may, Marcus Aurelius was inconsolable at the death of his wife, and upon this occasion his philosophy abandoned him; for, giving himself up entirely to his affliction, he wept as bitterly as if he had lost the most virtuous wife in the world. He himself pronounced her funeral oration, caused all sorts of honours to be paid her, and requested the Senate to make her a divinity. The Senate, long since accustomed to be very prodigal of honours, and to fill heaven with such goddesses, granted immortality to Faustina, and placed among the divinities her who by her infamous life had

[1] Dio. lib. 71. Capitol. in Marc. Antonin.

been the disgrace of human nature. He further ordered, by a flattering decree that savoured much of impiety, that statues of silver should be erected in the temple of Venus to the honour of Faustina and Marcus Aurelius; that an altar should be raised there, where all the girls of Rome, at their marriage, should be obliged to offer sacrifice, together with their husbands; that a golden statue of Faustina should be erected in the amphitheatre, in the very spot where she had been accustomed to sit at the public shows, and that every time the Emperor took his place there, the principal ladies of Rome should range themselves round the statue of Faustina to do her honour. Marcus Aurelius, for his part, indulged his grief by all the marks that he could possibly give of his love and esteem for his wife. He instituted games which he called Faustinian, and built a most magnificent temple to Faustina, which afterwards was dedicated to Heliogabalus, as if it was its fate to be always consecrated to the most infamous divinities.

When the Emperor had settled everything in the East to his satisfaction, he began his journey towards Rome. He entered the city in triumph, having his son Commodus at his side, whom he created his colleague in the consulship. He entertained the people with the most curious and sumptuous shows, and provided with admirable judgment and foresight against the necessities of the State, causing the laws to be put in force throughout the whole empire. Such transcendent virtues made this prince dear to all the world, and brought into vogue that famous sentence of Plato, that those empires cannot but be happy that are governed by philosophers.

The throne being rendered vacant by the death of

Faustina, the Princess Fabia, sister to Verus, had hopes
of filling her place. With this view she put in practice
all those arts and means that a woman knows how to
make use of, when she has a mind to please. The most
severe philosophy is not always proof against the darts of
love. The most insensible Stoic may be rendered
tractable by the charms of a beautiful woman, and a
tender, insinuating look frequently alters in a moment the
firmest resolutions. Fabia took all the necessary steps [1]
to make Marcus Aurelius comprehend her meaning, and
armed her looks and glances with such fire as she
imagined could not fail to inflame the Emperor's heart,
but certain domestic reasons outweighed this lady's pretensions. Marcus Aurelius could not make up his mind
to give his children a step-mother, nor make a suitable
return to her who wished to become so, and who doubt-
less sighed more ardently for the throne than his affections. The Emperor, therefore, having taken for a
concubine the daughter of one of his intendants, applied
himself indefatigably to put everything in a good condition. He was thus gloriously employed when he was informed that the barbarians were meditating a new revolt. He resolved to spare them no more, but to humble
them so effectually that they should never again be able
to create fresh troubles. After having declared war
against them with the usual ceremonies, [2] he left Rome

[1] Capitolin. in Marc. Anton.
[2] There was at Rome, in the Temple of Mars, a pillar, upon which
was placed a lance, which was preserved there with great solemnity
and superstition. When the Emperor was to declare war against any
nation, he went with great ceremony into this temple, and, after having
offered sacrifices for the prosperity of his arms, turned the point of this
fatal lance towards the people or nation against whom the war was to
be carried on, and by this ceremony war was declared.

accompanied by his son Commodus,[1] whose tender years
he intended to train to virtue, and with great rapidity
marched against the enemy, over whom he soon after
gained a victory, which the barbarians disputed with him
from morning till night, only, as it were, to enhance his
glory, and manifest his consummate valour and experience. This advantage must have been followed by the
entire destruction of these united nations, if death had
not stopped him short in the midst of his glorious career,
for a few days after this battle he was taken ill. He knew
immediately that he was come to the last period of his
life, and therefore assembled his friends in his chamber,
presented his son to them, entreated them to be a father
to him, to instruct him, and to give him their advice.
He delivered so moving a speech that they all wept, and,
after having given Commodus the wisest and best advice,
he died. Nothing could equal the affliction of all classes
in the city, of the armies, the provinces and the whole
empire. He was universally acknowledged to have been
the best prince that ever reigned.

His death gave room for an infinite number of suspicions. Some attributed Marcus Aurelius's sickness to
the fatigues of the war. Dion assures us that he knows
for certain that the physicians, who were employed by
Commodus, hastened his death, at the instigation of that
unnatural and wicked prince, who longed to have the
reins of the government in his own hands. Others
affirm that when the Emperor perceived his son to be of
a depraved and corrupt nature, his life began to be a
burden to him, so that he put an end to it by abstaining
from nourishment. It is beyond dispute that Marcus

[1] Dio. lib. 71.

Aurelius's greatest trouble and vexation proceeded from Commodus's bad disposition. The latter had already given evident signs of horrible cruelty and all sorts of vices, notwithstanding all the pains his father took to inspire him with noble sentiments,[1] by committing the care of his education to none but such preceptors as were most remarkable for virtue and abilities, but the malignity of his inclinations was more powerful than all the Emperor's endeavours. Whatever occasioned the death of Marcus Aurelius, the whole empire was in the greatest affliction imaginable. The excessive honour that was paid to his memory, the unfeigned tears that were shed at Rome, and the deep mourning that every family put on, were glorious proofs of the high esteem people had for his rare and valuable qualities.

[1] Dio. lib. 71.

LUCILLA

IRTUE and merit are not hereditary: from a mild and good father often are born children who are wicked and depraved; and the more the good qualities of the parent are remarkable, so much the more does the degeneracy of the son appear in an odious light. Vice is so ingrained in the constitution of some people that nothing can correct or alter it, so that one often sees the best education, example and instruction, thrown away when cast upon an ungrateful soil. Marcus Aurelius, as we have seen, was a most accomplished prince; in him was to be admired a collection of all the virtues, civil, military, and political; but unfortunately his children had nothing of the kind to boast of. His son Commodus was one of the most vicious princes that ever lived—a heap of tyranny, cruelty, and everything that was diabolical. In Lucilla, eldest daughter of Marcus Aurelius, ambition and lasciviousness were predominant qualities: his other children dishonoured their high birth and dignity by the most infamous actions; and it was observed that even those who died in their childhood had discovered a strong propensity to vice. So true it is,[1] that

[1] Lamprid. in Commod.

children bring into the world with them the good or bad
seeds which brighten or tarnish their lives, and which are
brought to maturity as occasions and opportunities occur.

Lucilla was born at Rome, in the first year of the
marriage of Marcus Aurelius with Faustina. Her birth,[1]
which filled the town with joy, also furnished the Emperor Antoninus with an opportunity of distributing
his bounty to the people, and of honouring his son-in-law
with the most important dignities. He gave him the
tribunate and pro-consular power, and raised him so high
that he left him nothing to wish for but the empire, which
he also inherited at the death of the above-mentioned
Emperor.

Although Lucius Verus, as well as Marcus Aurelius,
was the adopted son of Antoninus, yet the latter did not
show him the same tokens of his esteem and affection as
the other, for he never set any great value upon him.
But Marcus Aurelius was no sooner Emperor than he
not only created him Cæsar, with the title of August,
but also made him his partner in the sovereign authority,
and in order to lay him under a yet more sensible obligation, he betrothed him to his daughter Lucilla, though
they were not married till two years later, in the East.

Verus was a handsome man, tall in stature,[2] and his
countenance commanded respect. His hair was long and
very fair, and he took so much care of it that he used to
rub gold dust into it to brighten its colour.[3] He had an
impediment in his speech, and was very viciously inclined,

---

[1] Tillem. sur. M. Aurèle.
[2] Capitolin. in Ver.
[3] Dicitur sane tantam habuisse curam flaventium capillorum, ut capiti
auri ramenta respergeret, quo magis coma illuminata flavesceret.
(Capitolinus).

much given to gaming, intriguing, and so excessively to wine, that we shall presently see to what a pitch he carried all these irregularities, especially the latter, in which he indulged himself to that degree that he was generally drunk, and his face was covered with pimples.[1]

He was at first very grateful to the Emperor Marcus Aurelius for the extraordinary favours he had received from him, and showed it upon all occasions by the great deference and respect with which he treated him, as if he had been his superior, or father, rather than his colleague and equal. And because Marcus Aurelius's greatest delight consisted in the study of philosophy, Verus, although he had but very little taste or genius for the sciences, by a politic sort of complaisance, also pretended to be a philosopher. But it is the most difficult thing in the world to sustain, for any considerable time, a borrowed character; for, some time or other, the mask will drop off, and show people in their proper colours. Verus was soon weary of counterfeiting, and because Marcus Aurelius's grave and austere manners laid him under an irksome and disagreeable restraint, he longed for a fitting opportunity of quitting Rome, that he might be at liberty to do as he pleased.

The revolt of several barbarous nations happened very opportunely. The Parthians, whom Trajan had subdued, shook off the yoke of obedience, and stirred up all the people of the East. The Chatti, a wild sort of people that dwelt in the district of the modern Hesse-Cassel, dispersed themselves all over Germany, and Britain threatened an insurrection. Aufidius Victorinus was selected in order to humble the former, and Agricola the

[1] Spon. recherch. cur. d'Antiq.

latter; but it was thought necessary that Verus should go in person against the Parthians, who were the most formidable, and that Marcus Aurelius should stay at Rome, to take care of domestic affairs, and the education of his family.

Lucilla was then in the bloom of youth, being about fourteen years of age, and Marcus Aurelius took great pains to cultivate her mind, in order to make her worthy of the high rank to which she was destined. She was beautiful, and Verus owed her his affection and esteem, both on account of her personal merit and out of gratitude for the obligations he was under to her father. But the disproportion of their age did not at all contribute to the union of their hearts, Lucilla being, as has been observed, extremely young, and Verus thirty-two years old; and accordingly, it will be seen that he never entertained any great passion for her, any more than she did for him.

Marcus Aurelius, being well acquainted with Verus's vicious inclinations, was very glad when he set out for Syria, and was in hopes that if he was once at a distance from the pleasures of Rome, he would not be so much exposed to temptations, and might contract habits of sobriety and temperance by the fatigues of the war and travelling; while Verus, on the contrary, flattered himself that, being at liberty, and having nobody to stand in awe of, he might the more easily gratify his voluptuous passions. He kept himself, however, within bounds at first, but as soon as he came into the country called Apulia, he gave himself up entirely to hunting and gaming; he went thence to Athens, in a vessel magnificently adorned and loaded with musicians, who made the neighbouring shores echo with soft and effeminate airs; and on his arrival at Antioch, he left the care of the war to his generals, who were officers of experience, and plunged into all sorts of luxury and debauchery, taking no more trouble about the army than if he had come thither only for diversion. By this conduct, so injudicious and so little conformable to his rank, he became the jest and scorn of the Syrians, who despised a prince that made his shameful debaucheries the whole business of his life; but, when they found that he proceeded so far as to make attempts upon the chastity of their wives and daughters, he became the object of their aversion.

Marcus Aurelius heard all this with so much grief that it was one of the things that most exercised his philosophy. In the meantime, in spite of Verus's indolence, the Roman arms were successful. Vologeses, King of the Parthians, was driven out of Armenia. Cassius took Ctesiphon, and destroyed the famous palace of the kings, which passed for a wonderful building; he also besieged Edessa in Mesopotamia; Babylon, Seleucia, and many other strong towns were taken, and all those provinces, which composed the kingdom of the Parthians, were entirely brought under the Roman yoke.

Verus was as much elevated with these successes as if they had been owing to his own military efforts. He ridiculously caused himself to be named Parthicus and Armenicus, and arrogated to himself, with equal pride and injustice, titles that showed the importance of those victories, the glory of which he usurped, though the merit belonged to others. He gave monarchs to such nations as were used to kingly governments, distributed the provinces among the senators of his retinue, and made Avidius Cassius governor of Syria, which was by far the most important post.

This great dignity only served to excite his ambition, and made him long for something higher still. He concealed it, indeed, under a specious show of his great love of liberty, and exclaimed against Emperors at the very time when he was hatching the perfidious design of seizing the sovereign authority. When Verus sent him orders, he received them with contempt, and executed them with negligence; he never ceased to blame the present government, and to sow everywhere the seeds of sedition. Sometimes he spoke of Verus's debaucheries with insolent rashness, and at other times vented his mischievous raillery and scoffing against Marcus Aurelius, whom he called an old good-for-nothing philosopher. Verus, who thought he saw something in the conduct of Cassius that was very suspicious, was convinced of it when he heard of the liberties he took. He was further informed that Cassius was collecting money by all the means he could think of, which he imagined proceeded from some deep design. He gave Marcus Aurelius notice of all this, and informed him that Cassius, who aimed at nothing less than absolute power, was so much the more to be feared, as he had the secret of insinuating himself into the affections of the legions.

Marcus Aurelius, whose philosophical soul soared far above the ideas of other people, answered his colleague that he had received his letter, in which he perceived uneasiness and ill-grounded suspicions rather than greatness of mind. "If the gods," said he,[1] "have determined to raise Cassius to the throne, all attempts to break

[1] Vulcatius Gallicanus.

through their decree will be labour in vain, for, according
to the maxim of your grandfather, no prince ever put
his successor to death; but if, on the contrary, Cassius
is not authorised by Heaven, he will bring his own
destruction upon his head. After all, we must not treat
as a criminal a person whom nobody accuses, and to
whom no fault is imputed but that of being loved by the
soldiers. If we should use a man ill who has always
shown a great deal of merit, people would not fail to say
that he had rather fallen a victim to our mistrusts and
jealousies than that he was chastised for any crime he
was guilty of. As for my children (continued he), I
should see them perish with great indifference if they
deserved less to be beloved than Cassius, and if his life
be of more importance to the empire than the offspring
of Marcus Aurelius."

These are great sentiments, but it must be confessed
they are not altogether as consistent with sound judgment
and policy as one could wish. Cassius had in his youth
shown evident marks of excessive ambition, so that he
was not so little dangerous as to be contemptible. Verus,
however, thought he had done all that was incumbent
on him to do in acquainting his father-in-law with what
was going on; so without giving himself any further
trouble, he followed his infamous pleasures as usual.
His palace was turned into an abominable seraglio, filled
with women of the worst characters, with whom he passed
his time in the most dissolute manner; and not satisfied
with that, he also kept a number of young boys, whom he
brutally abused. He passed the winters at Laodicea,[1]
and the summer at Antioch, leaving everywhere shameful

---

[1] Capitolin. in Ver.

marks of his scandalous debaucheries; and his time was taken up entirely by day as well as by night in gaming, dancing, and gluttony, with the most abandoned wretches, whom he made the confidants of all his secrets, and trusted with the most important affairs.

Verus's unworthy conduct was the greatest affliction imaginable to Marcus Aurelius, and he concluded that the most likely way to put a stop to or, at least, to restrain it in some measure, was to send the Princess Lucilla into the East that she might marry him; he communicated his design to the Senate, and, after consulting them, declared that he would himself accompany his daughter into Syria. Lucilla was in the prime of life, being about seventeen years of age. She was well enough acquainted with Verus's character, and consequently did not leave her father's palace to be conducted into so remote a country without great regret. Nor can it be wondered at that she was very loth to become the wife of so dissolute and debauched a prince. But Marcus Aurelius was of opinion that this marriage would fix his affections, and that the princess's presence could not but be a curb to his violent and irregular passions. He therefore set out from Rome and arrived at Brundusium, but finding that his enemies had industriously reported that under pretence of going with the princess into Syria, his real design was to deprive his colleague of the honour of having terminated the war, he resolved to show the innocence and uprightness of his intentions by returning to Rome, leaving his daughter to proceed on her journey under the care of his sister Cornificia, and Pompeianus, uncle to Verus. Upon this occasion he gave a remarkable instance of his humility and dislike to show and splendour, for, being told that the provinces had notice of his journey and were making great preparations to receive him and his daughter with the magnificence that was due to them, he caused letters to be written to the governors and proconsuls, that they should not permit the people to meet the princess, or show her any sort of honour, for he was well aware that these extraordinary expenses had to be defrayed by the provinces, though the pro-consuls would not fail to claim all the merit and receive the reward of them.

In the meantime the news of the Emperor and his daughter being on the road soon spread over Syria. This made Verus extremely uneasy, for he was not at all pleased that his father-in-law should be a witness to his behaviour, and still less did he desire a wife to be a perpetual obstacle to the gratification of his depraved appetites, but, above all he dreaded that Marcus Aurelius would be thoroughly informed of his supine indolence and indifference to affairs. So he determined to parry the blow by going as far as Ephesus to meet him, under pretence of saving him the trouble of so long and so fatiguing a journey, and there it was that he received the Princess Lucilla, and heard with great joy that Marcus Aurelius had returned to Brundusium. He there married the princess, and conducted her with him into Syria, where she led a very uncomfortable life, for Verus, continuing his debaucheries and despising the young Empress, gave himself up more and more to his shameful and infamous pleasures. Marcus Aurelius was informed of it, and finding that even his daughter's presence was incapable of making any alteration in Verus's conduct, he recalled him on pretence that, the war being finished, it was but just that he should return to reap the fruit of his labours, and receive the honour of a triumph which the Senate had decreed him.

Verus would gladly have been exempt from this honour, for glory was not his predominant passion. A prince that is plunged in debaucheries is very little solicitous about his reputation; but he could not possibly refuse what his father-in-law requested of him, nor show a contempt for the reward with which the Senate had thought proper to recompense his victories (to which, for all that, he knew he had not at all contributed). He accordingly set out for Rome, and carried his princess with him. Lucilla was as much rejoiced at leaving Syria as her husband was sorry; for as he never looked upon her in any other light than as a spy upon his actions, he had never shown any regard or affection for her. She was in hopes that Verus would be ashamed to take such liberties and indulge himself in such infamous pleasures so much at Rome as he had done in the East. But bad habits are not so easily got over. Verus was the same in all places, or rather worse, if possible, after his return from Syria, for it was his constant practice to drink all night, and towards morning to run about the streets in disguise, committing all those follies that had made Nero the execration of Rome, except his cruelty. He caused an apartment [1] to be fitted up in his palace, which was called the Emperor's tavern, where he used to assemble his companions in debauchery, and which was the scene of his abominations. He never left the table but in order to gratify his more shameful appetites, which he did without respecting the sacred laws of Nature, not

---

[1] Capitolin. in Ver.

even being ashamed of living with his sister Fabia, and Faustina his mother-in-law, in a horrible and incestuous intercourse.

Lucilla had long been acquainted with his infamous intimacy with Fabia; his excessive complaisance for her, and the absolute power that she had over her brother, sufficiently evinced their criminal intercourse. Lucilla was jealous of it, and continued so till her husband's death. Marcus Aurelius perceived then that by changing climates one does not change one's nature, for in recalling Verus from Syria he but furnished him with fresh objects of debauchery, and so was a melancholy witness to those scandalous irregularities, which before he had only heard of at a distance. Verus now became a heavy burden to the good Emperor, for the infamous life he led, added to his bad treatment of the Princess Lucilla, grieved him beyond measure; and the more so since he kept it to himself, and made no complaints.

To this vexation was added that of the revolt of the Marcomanni, who being determined to shake off the Roman yoke, declared war against the empire. Marcus Aurelius was much alarmed, and assembled the Senate to consult what measures were proper to be taken at this juncture, and after all the necessary preparations had been made it was resolved that the two Emperors should conduct the army in person. This design was the effect of Marcus Aurelius's judicious prudence, for on the one hand he was apprehensive that, if Verus should remain at Rome, he would do a great deal of mischief by his debaucheries, and on the other hand he was afraid that, if he was sent singly against the barbarians, he would precipitate the empire into some dreadful misfortune, or would abandon the army to pursue his pleasures. They set out, then, together, but with very different sentiments, for Verus was very unwilling to quit Rome, on account of his abominable pleasures; wherefore, they had no sooner passed the Alps than he prevailed upon his father-in-law to return, for the reasons we have already mentioned. As they were upon the road near Altinum, Verus was suddenly attacked with an apoplectic fit. He was immediately taken out of his chariot and bled. They carried him to Altinum, where he lived three days, but in a state of insensibility, and died, little regretted, except by his partners in iniquity.

No innocence can be proof against slander. There were people malicious enough to cast the blame of Verus's death upon Marcus Aurelius, whom they accused of having poisoned his colleague at an entertainment, and of having caused him to be bled at Altinum, when it was bad for his disorder, with a design to hasten his death. Others will needs have it that Faustina committed the crime by giving him poisoned oysters to eat, in revenge for his having indiscreetly communicated their amour to Lucilla; and lastly, there are not wanting those who impute it to Lucilla herself, and allege that she was moved thereto by her jealousy, on account of his intrigue with Fabia, whom she hated and considered to be the most dangerous of her rivals, being a person who had no sort of regard for her reputation, and who scrupled at nothing that could advance her influence and authority.

It was probable, that Lucilla was easily consoled for the loss of her husband, whose contempt for her, together with his scandalous debaucheries, caused her considerable vexation. Reasons of State and paternal authority had

induced her to consent to the match, not any mutual inclination or affection between them; besides, the princess
was so young, and Verus had lived so little at Rome, that
they had scarcely an opportunity of knowing each other,
much less of contracting any intimacy. But the princess
did not long enjoy her liberty; no sooner was Verus
dead than her father proposed another match for her,
which was by no means agreeable to Lucilla; not that she
had any sort of dislike to marriage in general (for a
father that provides a husband for his daughter is always
very favourably listened to), but it was Marcus
Aurelius's choice of the person that she could not prevail upon herself to approve of. It was not consistent
with the Emperor's way of thinking to proceed in those
matters according to the rules and maxims of policy:
he did not require that his son-in-law should have either
nobility or riches, but thought it sufficient if he had
virtue and moderation, and imagined he had met with
one of this character in Pompeianus. He was originally
of Antioch, a senator whose reputation recommended him
more than his birth, a man of profound wisdom and
gravity of disposition. This last merit Lucilla could
willingly have dispensed with, nor was she at all backward in giving her father evident proofs of her aversion
to this match. The Empress Faustina was [1] also much
against it, and offered many reasons to support her
opinion. She did not think him in any sort her equal in
point of birth and fortune, but that was not the motive
of the princess's reluctance; she did not see in Pompeianus that youth and vivacity that were so agreeable
to her; she could have tolerated a considerable abate-

[1] Capitolin. in Marc. Anton.

ment of his excessive wisdom and virtue, provided he
had been younger and of a more gallant disposition.
The fact of Verus's having been too great a lover of
pleasure was no reason why she should desire a husband
who was too old to have any relish for it, and such a one
she took Pompeianus to be, who, being in the decline of
life, always wore a composed and serious countenance
suitable to the austerity of his profession. The resistance
of the Empress was not, however, strong enough to
make the Emperor alter his resolution: he insisted absolutely upon this match, and Lucilla was obliged to undergo
all the uneasiness and vexation that is naturally the consequence of a forced obedience. Pompeianus became the
Princess Lucilla's husband. He had a son whom he
named after himself, and, as Dion informs us, a daughter
called Lucilla.

This illustrious alliance procured him the respect of all
Rome, which before had the highest opinion of his
merits; and though he could not boast of that high
dignity that Verus possessed, yet he was very much
esteemed, and the honour that was due to him as son-in-
law to the Emperor was paid him by everybody. The
princess his wife lost nothing of the privileges and precedence that she had always enjoyed as Empress. She still
maintained in the amphitheatre and all public assemblies
the rank that she held in Verus's time, for that prince's
death [1] did not deprive her of any of those advantages.
She was still distinguished by all those pompous ornaments that accompanied her dignity, and it would have
been well if she had also observed the decency that became it; but though she was very tenacious of her own

[1] Herodian. lib. 1.

rights and prerogatives, she forgot that there was a duty
due from her to her husband. As she had only married
Pompeianus in compliance with her father's will, she did
not think it incumbent on her to be faithful to a husband
to whom she had never given her heart, so she dishonoured her marriage by shameful prostitutions. Unhappy fate of ill-matched nuptials! Where an absolute
authority, which cannot unite hearts and affections,
obliges a very young woman to accept a man advanced in
years, she is sure to take vengeance upon the husband,
whom she betrays, for the forced submission she is compelled to yield by a tyrannical parent, who insists upon
being obeyed.

Lucilla, being of a sprightly disposition, and then
about twenty-four years of age, could not reconcile herself to the grave and serious behaviour of Pompeianus,
and therefore endeavoured to find elsewhere that life and
vivacity that was so suitable to her own humour.[1] Quadratus (of a very noble family in Rome) was the person in
whom she met with all she desired. He was a charming
youth, full of fire, spirit and gallantry, and very rich,
which not a little contributed to the gratification of his
amorous inclinations. Quadratus soon perceived that he
was not indifferent to Lucilla, with whom he became
passionately in love, and by the assiduous court he paid
the princess, gave occasion for such discourse and censure as was not at all favourable to her; but soon after,
the intrigue was carried on with so little air of mystery
that it was no secret at all. This crime was an introduction to more scandalous proceedings; for, finding in
Commodus, her brother, a heart as corrupt as her own,

[1] Herodian. lib. 1.

she made no scruple about [1] living with him in shocking
and unnatural intimacy. By these incestuous favours she
preserved that pre-eminence of rank which her brother
allowed her after the death of Marcus Aurelius, and it
was at the expense of her honour that she purchased
those vain distinctions which she regarded with so much
pride and affection. But as of all honours none are so
precarious as those which are procured by guilt, so Lucilla
soon had the mortification of being forced to yield to
another the rank she had held with so much pomp and
ceremony.

Crispina, Commodus's wife, not being able to endure
that Lucilla should claim a right to that precedence
which she claimed to be due to herself, resolved to
assume, upon all occasions, the rank which belonged to
her as Empress. This divided the Court into parties, but
Commodus had no sooner declared his opinion than it
was followed and agreed to by everyone according to
custom; so the homage that was used to be paid to
Lucilla was now given to Crispina, and Lucilla herself
was obliged in decency to pay her court to her sister-in-
law, notwithstanding her pride. It is a very difficult
task for those haughty spirits who have been accustomed
to see all the world acknowledge their superiority to be
forced to give up their heart's desire and follow those
with respect and submission whom they used to precede.
It is not without great regret and vexation that they are
compelled to bend beneath the insupportable yoke of
dependence; for people never submit with a good grace
when they do so by compulsion. Lucilla could not,
without the utmost rage and jealousy, bear to see Crispina

[1] Dio. in Com. lib. 72.

fill up the place which was hers before, and assume that superiority over her which she herself had made the reigning Empress feel before her elevation. She looked upon herself as quite eclipsed by Crispina, considered that she was despised when her sister-in-law was respected, and that the claims of Commodus's wife were an attack upon those of Verus's widow. This occasioned an implacable hatred and jealousy between the two princesses; and Lucilla, who was not a person to keep it shut up in her breast, resolved that the Emperor, who permitted this distinction so much to her prejudice, should be the object of her indignation. She therefore determined to dethrone him and place some other in his stead, who, by sharing the empire with her, might reinstate her in her former glory and splendour. She was the more exasperated against her brother because, in order to gain his support in her interests, she had not scrupled to prostitute herself to him by a shameful and detestable incest, which was known to all the world. At first she thought of many things which opposed this dangerous resolution, but her passion soon removed all the obstacles that her reason suggested, so after having hardened her conscience, she thought of nothing but how to execute her intention, and find out a proper person to be her accomplice in the crime. Pompeianus, her husband, did not seem fit to conduct such an affair, nor dared she run the risk of trusting him with a secret of that nature; besides, he had a friendship for Commodus, and was not, in her opinion, capable of entering into so black a plot. Quadratus was therefore the man she selected to be the instrument of her revenge, and the executor of her scheme.

Lucilla took a favourable opportunity to communicate

the matter to him and prepare his mind for it. There are certain moments when complaisant lovers can refuse nothing to the objects of their passion, and a skilful, cunning woman knows how to make the most of them. The princess, knowing how much she was adored by her gallant, communicated her affliction to him, and at the same time put on the most melancholy aspect to make him the more sensible of her grief. She complained bitterly of the affront she had received from Crispina,[1] who, by robbing her of the honours that nobody had ever disputed with her before, degraded her from the rank that was her right as daughter of one Emperor and widow of another; and because everything that a fine woman and a mistress asserts, when she is in affliction, proceeds from her mouth with such an insinuating and irresistible air as goes to the bottom of the heart, Lucilla found no great difficulty in prevailing upon Quadratus to agree to whatever she had a mind to. They therefore resolved to murder Commodus, who had preferred his wife's interests to those of his sister. But as the undertaking was dangerous, Quadratus thought it expedient and safest to obtain the assistance of others. The secret, then, was communicated to Quintianus, a bold, enterprising young man, and many other persons of distinction. Quintianus undertook to deal the mortal blow, and Quadratus, who was rich, was to be very liberal of his money and scatter it plentifully among the people, who they supposed would be so taken up with gathering it as not to think of revenging a murder that procured them so great an advantage.[2]

Quintianus, though courageous enough, was not suffi-

[1] Herodian. lib. i. c. 19.   [2] Herodian. lib. i.

ciently discreet, for, as the Emperor was to go through a dark passage on his way to the amphitheatre, in which the assassin stood ready to perform his bloody work, Quintianus contented himself with only showing him the poniard and saying in a meanacing tone, "See here what the Senate sends thee!"[1] This imprudence[2] and blustering threat only served to reveal the conspiracy, and to bring upon Quintianus the punishment he justly deserved for his treason and stupidity. The Emperor's guards fell upon him immediately, and dispatched him in a moment.

Lucilla was all this time in apprehension about the success of this perilous attempt, and was ready to die with fear when she was told that the Emperor had escaped unhurt. Commodus caused the affair to be thoroughly sifted, which resulted in a number of executions. Quadratus was one of the first that was sacrificed to the Emperor's fury, because he was found to be most guilty, and Lucilla was condemned to a rigorous banishment in the island of Capreæ, a punishment in no sort proportionate to the enormity of her crimes; nor did she come off so cheaply, for Commodus, who was resolved to give full scope to his revenge, ordered her to be put to death, and to say the truth she had merited no less. This haughty and lascivious princess thus brought her destruction upon her own head, and, in order to gratify her unlimited pride and procure herself those vain and empty honours she was so fond of, came to a tragical and untimely end.

[1] Hunc tibi pugionem Senatus mittit.
[2] Lamprid. in Com. Herodian. lib. 1. Dio. lib. 72.

CRISPINA
WIFE OF COMMODUS

AND

MARCIA
CONCUBINE OF COMMODUS

T is very difficult to correct the defects and imperfections that are innate in our constitutions, and become part of our very being; nor does it often happen that the most careful education and most powerful examples of virtue operate so strongly as to alter our nature. That which is born with us may be modified, but seldom conquered; for generally it happens that whatever seeds Nature has sown in our minds, such will be the fruit they produce.

Nobody could have taken more pains to instruct a son and instil into him noble and virtuous sentiments than did Marcus Aurelius. His whole conversation tended to inspire Commodus with mildness, humanity, and all those good qualities which he himself possessed in so eminent a degree. In addition, he gave him the most skilful masters, whom he chose from all who were remarkable for learning, probity, and good morals in the whole empire. All these precautions, cares, and precepts were however in vain; for the depraved nature of Commodus was such that no instruction could work upon it, nor was it in the power of anything to reform his vicious inclinations. The malignity of his heart showed itself from his very cradle, and he was but twelve years old when he gave an instance of such barbarity as one would not imagine so tender an age to be capable of. Being at Centumcellae (now called Civita Vecchia), and having a mind to take a bath, he caused the person who had the care of the bath to be thrown into a furnace, because the water was rather too warm. He was prodigiously passionate, impetuous and violent; all which appeared in every feature of his face. He had fiery eyes [1] and a wild and furious look, casting here and there such horrible glances as seemed to threaten with sudden destruction those to whom they were directed. He was not ill made in his person; his shape was well proportioned, he had a manly countenance, a good complexion, fair curly hair; but notwithstanding all this, he had the manner of a wicked, corrupt man: his conversation was filthy and obscene, without restraint or coherence, like that of a drunken man: his manners were low, base, contemptible, altogether unworthy of a man of his birth and rank; he employed his time in nothing but jumping, whistling, and acting more like a buffoon than an Emperor; profaning his palace with horrible debaucheries, and turning his apartment into a scene of prostitution and infamy, where, with his execrable companions of the same stamp, he plunged himself into the most shameful excesses of drunkenness and impurity, too prodigal to care what expense he incurred, and too corrupt to have

[1] Lamprid. in Comm. Spon, recherches. curieuses d'Antiq. Herodian.

the least regard to decency. This was the melancholy prelude to the abominable life of Commodus, son of the wisest and best of all the Roman Emperors.

The sort of people he was surrounded with continually encouraged him in his vicious practices, nor could he endure any about him but such as flattered his passions. Marcus Aurelius, having once a mind to banish from the palace certain officers who had employments in the young prince's household, and who, instead of instilling into him notions of virtue and honour, gave him very pernicious lessons, Commodus was so afflicted at it that he fell sick, and the Emperor carried his complaisance and indulgence so far as to recall those unworthy and perfidious wretches, who did not fail to perfect the work they had begun.

Marcus Aurelius was thoroughly informed of all these irregularities, and therefore resolved to carry the prince with him into Scythia, where the rebellious Marcomanni had recommenced hostilities; and in order to curb the impetuosity of his passions, he thought it best to marry him betimes, sooner, indeed, than he would have done if the movements of the barbarians had not laid him under the necessity of settling the matter as soon as he could, that he might be at leisure to make preparations for the war, or if the prince had been more discreet; so the marriage was celebrated with considerable precipitation. The Emperor, knowing that his presence was absolutely necessary in Scythia, did not take much time to hesitate about the choice of the lady, but immediately selected Crispina. She was one of the handsomest women in Rome,[1] daughter of the senator Bruttius Præsens, whose

[1] Trist. Com. Hist.

merits had been several times rewarded with the consulship; but she did not possess her father's good qualities. She was of an amorous disposition, and so susceptible to love that, whatever gravity and reserve the high rank she was now raised to required of her, her temperament got the better of her reason; she dishonoured her dignity by the most scandalous libertinism, which was the cause of her ruin, and of the untimely death with which Commodus afterwards punished her infamous behaviour. It is very likely that when the Emperor married her to Commodus she was innocent, or at least had been circumspect enough to conceal her gallantries. But we shall see that her becoming a wife, far from fixing her inclinations, only served to furnish her with opportunities of gratifying her unfortunate appetites.

After the celebration of these nuptials, the Emperor and his son set out for Scythia. Some historians say that the new Empress accompanied them; be it as it may, Marcus Aurelius, who had resolved to extirpate those barbarous people, was seized in the midst of his victories with a disorder that soon laid him in his grave; and it was with a great deal of reason generally believed that his perfidious son was the author of it, and that the physicians, who had the care of him, purchased the favour of Commodus at the expense of his father's life.

In the meantime, the Princess Lucilla enjoyed at Rome all those honours that had always been paid to the Empresses, and although her second husband [1] was a person of inferior dignity to Verus her first, the Emperor her father deprived her of none of those rights and prerogatives which were due to the Emperors' wives, and

[1] Herodian. lib. 1. c. 20.

she took care to assume, with great pride and haughtiness, the most pompous distinctions. Crispina looked upon the pretensions of Lucilla as an attack upon her own privileges; she imagined that the precedence belonged rather to the reigning Empress than to the widow of an Emperor, and especially since she was married again to a private senator; so, as she was no less vain than her sister-in-law, she everywhere took her place, and insisted upon it as her indisputable right. Lucilla was so enraged at this that she was resolved to have Commodus, her brother, assassinated, and to raise in his stead some other person to the throne, who, being under obligation to her for it, would re-establish her in all the splendour of that rank she had hitherto enjoyed, and which was now taken from her. We have already seen what was the issue of this conspiracy; it merely served to furnish Commodus with a fair pretence of exercising his cruelty, for the assassin, who had undertaken to give Commodus the fatal blow, only threatened him and showed him a dagger, telling him that it was a present the Senate made him. The Emperor ordered him to be seized, and he suffered that death which he so well deserved.

Commodus could never forget the words of Quintianus, who intended to have murdered him. They made so deep an impression in his mind,[1] that he ever after looked upon the Senate as a body of men composed of his greatest enemies, whom he ought to get rid of by all means. This was the beginning of that implacable hatred he conceived against them, and which caused the shedding of blood and tears in abundance in Rome. He put to death the most illustrious of the senators, especially all

[1] Herodian. lib. 1. c. 22.

those who had been friends of Marcus Aurelius. Pater-
nus, colonel of his guards, whom he accused of having
a design against his life; the brothers Condianus, who had
served with great distinction in all his father's wars,
were some of the first sacrificed to his rage. Salvius
Julianus, who commanded one of his armies, also fell a
victim to his jealousy.

If he was dreaded on account of his cruelty, he was
not less detested for his incontinency, which he carried to
such a pitch as to debauch all his sisters, and to have
criminal commerce with his other nearest relations.[1] It
was his custom to expose his concubines in his presence
to the brutal lust of all who desired them, and one of
his mistresses whom he loved most he called his wife,
though she least of all deserved his affection, on account
of her numerous amours and intrigues.

There was no sort of abomination that he did not
indulge himself in to that degree that nothing had ever
been seen like it.

Crispina was a witness of all these horrible proceedings, but she would have been in the wrong to complain,
since the life she herself led was not much better. This
Empress, being hurried on by her strong passions and
the impetuosity of her temperament was not intimidated
by the bloody executions her husband ordered every
day, but being encouraged by his example, greedily
sought after opportunities of gratifying her inordinate
appetites, and lived in a most infamous and scandalous
manner. She was, by her prostitutions, thoroughly
avenged for his contempt of her, and whilst he was dis-

[1] Lamprid. in Com.

honouring the empire by his excesses and debaucheries, she was disgracing both him and the throne by her shameful and impudent conduct. But as these reprisals are often attended with bad consequences, so a woman ought not to expect to go on unpunished with such a husband as Commodus. Crispina soon found the truth of this by sad experience, for happening to be once surprised with one of her gallants, Commodus was so sensible of the dishonour and affront, that he banished her to the island of Capreæ.

The Empress Lucilla had also been exiled to the same place, so that the two princesses, who had been so hotly engaged in disputes about rank and precedence, met there. Some say that common misfortune united them in a strict friendship. It is, however, certain, that they were both put to death in that island, for Commodus, who had always in his mind Quintianus's attempt upon his life, and knew that his sister was the cause of it, never could forgive those two unfortunate princesses the crimes they had been guilty of.[1]

This execution was followed by a great many others. Rufus and Capito (persons who had been consuls), Vitrasia Faustina, his own near relation, Crassus, proconsul of Asia, and a large number of great men, illustrious by their nobility and merit, lost their lives by order of this tyrant; and if Sextus, son of Maximus, so remarkable for the vivacity of his wit and learning, escaped his fury, it was owing to an artifice he made use of to deceive those who were to have sacrificed him to the Emperor's barbarity.[2]

[1] Dio. lib. 72.
[2] Sextus, who was in Syria, being informed that his father had been put to death, and not doubting he would be served the same way, had

Perennis, chief favourite of Commodus, persuaded him to these cruelties, for, having acquired an absolute power over the Emperor, he could influence him as he pleased; so, whoever he had a grudge against, he had nothing to do but to invent some lie to make Commodus jealous of him. By this method he easily got rid of all those who he thought might be in any way prejudicial to his interests. This infamous wretch directed all the affairs of the empire as he thought proper, and applied to his own use the forfeited estates of all those whom he had caused to perish by his diabolical slanders, thus heaping up immense riches with a design to distribute them among the soldiers as soon as a fair opportunity should offer recourse to a stratagem to avoid falling into the hands of the instruments of Commodus's cruelty, who filled all Syria with their murders. He drank a great quantity of blood, and then, mounting on horseback, spurred the animal on purpose to make him rear; then, contriving to fall gently, he pretended that the horse had thrown him, and caused himself to be carried into the house by his servants, where he made as if he were almost dead, vomiting the blood he had swallowed as if it had been occasioned by his fall. The report of this accident was soon spread abroad, and came to the ears of the Emperor's agents, who were even told that he was dead. They had no room to doubt it when Sextus carried the trick so far as to cause a man to be put into a coffin and to be burnt, with all the usual ceremonies, as if it were his body. In the meantime he began to grow very weary of being shut up in his house, so ventured out of his prison, wandering from one town to another in disguise, and altering his voice for fear of being discovered. He was known, however, notwithstanding all these precautions, and orders were given from Court to arrest him. Several persons were executed merely for happening to be like him, and their heads sent to Rome. Others, who were accused of having protected this condemned person, had their estates confiscated, and many of them were put to death, though they had never known or seen him, so that nobody was certain whether the real Sextus was dead or alive. After the death of Commodus, there started up a person who called himself Sextus, the son of Maximus, who demanded his father's dignities and inheritance. He was interrogated, and answered every question correctly, even about family affairs, which it was next to impossible for a stranger to be acquainted with. Pertinax, who knew that the true Sextus understood Greek very well, which he had learnt in Syria, spoke to him in that language, but the impostor, not being able to comprehend what the Emperor said, was banished from Rome in disgrace.

of raising himself to the throne. He caused the most important military employments to be given to his son, and attributed to his valour and capacity whatever exploits were performed, or victories obtained, by the courage and experience of the generals, and at last carried his impudence and boldness to such a pitch as to dismiss from their employments the bravest officers belonging to the army in Britain, that he might fill up their posts with such people as he could depend upon.

All these things (together with the information the Emperor received from several parts, to the effect that Perennis aspired to the throne) at last roused Commodus from his lethargy, but what put the finishing stroke to the ruin of this insolent minister was the arrival of fifteen hundred soldiers from the Roman army in Britain, who said they came to defend the Emperor against the treasonable designs of his false favourite, who was secretly endeavouring to raise his son to the throne. Cleander, for whom the Emperor had a very great regard, was the author of this report; he knew so well how to irritate Commodus against Perennis that the iniquitous favourite was immediately massacred by order of the Emperor, who was no sooner delivered from his most shameful dependence upon Perennis, than he became equally the slave of Cleander.

This man, who had been the sport of Fortune, was a native of Phrygia, and was taken to Rome amongst other vile and common slaves. After various adventures [1] he found out the secret of insinuating himself into the Emperor's family, where he managed so well by his arts and intrigues, that he became chief of those whose office

[1] Dio. lib. 72. Herodian. lib. 1.

it was to sleep in the Emperor's chamber, then colonel of the Prætorian Guards, and at last so powerful and so high in favour with Commodus, that he married him to Damostratia, one of his concubines, and vested him with absolute authority.

It happened to Cleander just as it frequently happens to those whom Fortune raises from a state of obscurity. He became insolent, proud, ungrateful, and made no other use of his excessive power than to pave himself a way to a greater. Master as he was of all the fortunes of the Romans, he made and unmade consuls at his pleasure, having created no less than five-and-twenty in one year, which had never been done till then, and which no Emperor ever ventured to do since. (Severus, who afterwards sat upon the throne, was one of these consuls). He sold all employments, civil and military, and raised to the rank of senators the most abject of mankind, provided they had but money enough to purchase it; and in order to stop the mouths of those whose zeal for the Emperor's service might have induced them to find fault with him, he caused Burrus,[1] the Emperor's brother-in-law, to be put to death, accusing him of aspiring to the throne, at the very time when he himself was taking all the measures he could think of to procure that supreme dignity.

Thus did Commodus betray himself by his indolence, and by suffering his favourites to exercise unlimited power; whilst he himself, entirely taken up with his irregular passions, thought of nothing but how to gratify them. He passed whole days in fighting and killing wild beasts in the amphitheatre; and as if this butchery made

[1] Lamprid.

"Chatter of Birds"

From the painting by Georges Rochegrosse

It was a custom among Romans of wealth and distinction to keep beautiful children to amuse them with their antics and prattle. In this colorful picture we have an intimate insight into the sensuous luxury of ancient Rome

him as celebrated as the greatest military exploits would
have done, he caused himself to be named the Roman
Hercules, carried a club and wore a lion's skin. He
converted his palace into an infamous seraglio, where he
maintained three hundred women and as many boys, who
were the miserable victims of his monstrous lasciviousness. He was so foolish as to give his name to the city of
Rome, calling it the colony of Commodus, and Marcia
was accused of having persuaded him to this ridiculous
piece of extravagance, for, of all his concubines, none had
so much power over him as she.

Marcia was extremely beautiful, very witty and cunning, capable of the greatest cabinet intrigues. She had
the secret of insinuating herself into the good graces of
Commodus, by her complaisance and all those artful
caresses that women of her character are well acquainted
with, and practise with great success where they have a
mind to please; so that if she was not declared Empress,
she may be said to have had at least the same honours
and authority as if she had been. She had [1] a great
esteem for the Christians, though she could not prevail
upon herself to imitate the sanctity of their lives, but
espoused their interests upon all occasions, and procured
them [2] many favours; whence it resulted that the Church
enjoyed peace and tranquillity during Commodus's reign,
though at the same time nothing was to be seen at Rome
and in the provinces but slaughter and blood, the terrible
effects of his cruelty. This favourite mistress had such
influence over the Emperor that he could refuse her
nothing.

He was not ashamed to carry his complaisance so far

[1] Herodian. lib. 72. Xiphil. in Com.   [2] Baron. ad. an. 182.

as to change his name, and cause himself to be called Amazonian, to do honour to the picture of Marcia, where she was represented in an Amazonian dress, which this artful woman affected to wear, as most becoming to her. But the greatest instance of this Emperor's weakness, and of his being bewitched with the charms of Marcia, was his going publicly to the amphitheatre in the habit of an Amazon, in order to show his mistress how much [1] he was delighted when she obliged him so far as to appear in that graceful equipment. This base and unworthy behaviour furnished ample matter for laughter and ridicule to the Romans, when they beheld their Emperor in the circus, dressed like a woman, and degrading his dignity by such a scandalous and shameful metamorphosis : but what will not inordinate passions bring people to !

Thus Commodus abandoned the affairs of the empire, and troubled himself with nothing but his fooleries, whilst Cleander, insolently abusing the blind confidence which the Emperor placed in him, was labouring to establish his own authority, by using all the means he could think of to make himself popular, without reflecting that the method he took was only hastening his own ruin. In fact, when the city was afflicted by the plague to such a degree that two thousand people perished daily, and at the same time by a dreadful famine, Cleander heaped up vast stores of corn, intending to distribute it among the people, and so purchase their favour and protection by this politic and self-interested bounty; but Papirius, superintendent of corn supplies, having seen through Cleander's intention, made him the dupe of his

[1] Lamprid.

own artifices; for his having collected such stores of
corn made it so dear, that the effects of the famine began
to be worse than the plague. Papirius, who hated
Cleander, seeing the people ready to mutiny, accused the
favourite of being the occasion of this scarcity, and of
having ambitious designs. The people were the more
exasperated against him because, just at that time, a
woman, followed by a great number of children, made
great lamentation, and cried out bitterly against Cleander.
These seditious exclamations so animated the people
against him, and so convinced them of his being the
author of all their sufferings, that in a tumultuous manner
they went directly to Commodus, who was without the
city pursuing his diversions, and demanded that he should
surrender Cleander to them. Cleander having heard of
this, sent immediately a detachment of the Guards
against the mutineers, and killed a great many of them.
Those who could escape ran into the city, carrying the
alarm and confusion along with them; the people took
up arms, and Rome became the theatre of the most
terrible Civil War.

Commodus, in the meantime, being plunged in his
sensual and infamous pleasures, knew nothing of this
sedition, nor did anybody care to inform him of it, for
fear of incurring the indignation of Cleander, who made
the Emperor do just what he pleased; but the Princess
Fadilla, whose birth and rank put her above any fears
of that nature, went to her brother, and throwing herself
at his feet all in tears, represented to him the melancholy
condition of Rome, and the imminent danger he himself
was exposed to from the fury of the people, who were
become ripe for any mischief, owing to the insolence and

tyranny of Cleander; at the same time she revealed to
him the perfidious and ambitious designs of that haughty
courtier, who aimed at nothing less than the throne.
This information was too interesting not to make a great
impression upon Commodus; but what decided him to
sacrifice Cleander to the clamours of the people was the
complaints of his dear Marcia, who, pretending great
fear and apprehension for the Emperor's life,[1] represented the danger as much greater than it really was, and
said everything that could possibly exasperate him
against Cleander; and as nothing is more fitted to persuade than the insinuations of a darling mistress, Commodus condemned to death the unfortunate favourite,
whose fall also involved that of many others, for it then
became criminal to have had any friendship or intimacy
with him.

Cleander's ambitious views greatly increased the mistrust of the Senate the Emperor had entertained ever
since the conspiracy of Lucilla; for, imagining that he
ought not for the future to put confidence in anybody, he
involved in his suspicions and resentment people of the
highest rank and quality, and nothing but their destruction could satisfy him. Papirius, who had contributed
to the ruin of Cleander; Julianus, Governor of Rome,
whom the Emperor used to call father; Julius Alexander,
a brave and experienced general; Mamertinus and Sura,
and a large number of great men were the victims of his
fury.

These bloody executions did not in the last interrupt
his follies and debaucheries. He was every day in the
amphitheatre amongst the gladiators, showing his skill in

---

[1] Dio. lib. 72.

killing wild beasts, and boasting of his famous exploits. Sometimes he appeared in a very odd and curious dress, with a lion's skin thrown over his purple robe spotted with gold, holding a club in his hand, in imitation of Hercules, whose name he had taken; and at other times he would dress himself in women's clothes, in the sight of all the people, and drink to them, that he might have the pleasure of hearing them cry out, "Long live the Emperor." He would then go down into that part of the amphitheatre where the combats took place, and fight with the gladiators, slaughtering, without mercy, those who contended with him, though those poor unfortunate creatures were forced to spare him out of respect, not daring to exert themselves. The Senate authorised by their base acclamations this shameful and cruel behaviour; for when it happened that he killed a bear or lion, or any other animal, they would join their flattering applause to that of the people, and servilely cry out, " Thou overcomest the world.[1] Thou art the conqueror, O brave Amazonian!"

In short, after having disgraced the empire by innumerable crimes, which it would be tedious to particularise, he took it in his head to substitute himself in the place of the consuls whom he resolved to put to death,[2] and to appear upon the theatre as consul and servant of the gladiators; for, among a vast number of ridiculous titles that he assumed, that which he took most pleasure in was that of first champion among the followers of the gladiators, who with his own hand had killed about twelve hundred men. The first day of January, which among the Romans was one of the most solemn in the

[1] Dio. lib. 72. Xiphilin. in Com.   [2] Herodian. lib. 1.

whole year, was the time he made choice of to entertain
the public with this fantastic scene, and communicated
his design some time before to his beloved Marcia.

Marcia, who foresaw the consequences of this monstrous project, opposed it as much as possible, and represented to him the infinite shame and scandal that it would
bring upon him and the Roman people; that his own
reputation and interest absolutely required that he should
not be so infatuated with gladiators, especially since he
never went among them without endangering his life,
and putting himself in the power of wretches who were
destitute of all sentiments of honour or principle. She
endeavoured to corroborate her arguments by a thousand
caresses, embracing his knees, and shedding a torrent of
tears, but nothing was capable of making him alter his
resolution.

Lætus and Eclectus, captains of his guard, also took
the liberty to expostulate with him upon that subject,
but with no better success; in vain did they represent to
him the disgrace that this monstrous novelty would bring
upon the empire. Commodus, who was not to be influenced by reason or sense, commanded them to arrange
and prepare everything for the ceremony; and looking
upon those zealous officers as rash and presumptuous
censurers of his conduct, turned away from them abruptly
with indignation in his countenance. In fact, he was
so provoked that they should have the impudence and
assurance to make these remonstrances that he determined to put them to death the next day, and entering
his closet, drew up a list of those who were to be executed, which he concealed at the head of his bed. Lætus
and Eclectus were not the only condemned persons, for

Marcia, who had endeavoured to divert him from his purpose, was also of the number; and the most illustrious among the senators were destined to the same fate, the tyrant intending to enrich his gladiators with their spoils. But matters happened quite contrary to his expectations, for Commodus fell himself a victim to his own cruelty. His design was discovered, and he was put to death by the hands of those very people whose blood was to have been spilled the next morning.

It was a custom among the Romans of quality and distinction to keep beautiful children to amuse them with their agreeable prattle. They went about almost naked, having scarcely anything on them but diamonds and jewels. The Emperor had one of these boys, whom he was so fond of as to let him frequently sleep with him, and called him Philo-Commodus, or the favourite of Commodus. This little boy was so indulged as to be at liberty to do whatever he pleased, so that the officers and guards never hindered him from going in and out of the Emperor's chamber as often as he had a mind. This child was accidentally the occasion of Commodus's infernal designs being discovered, for, as he came out of the Emperor's room with the fatal paper in his hand, Marcia was apprehensive that it might be of consequence, and took it from him. Her curiosity prompted her to read it, and it may be easily conceived that she was extremely surprised and terrified at discovering the Emperor's barbarous intention. "And is it thus," said she, "thou inhuman monster, that thou intendest to recompense the love and attachment I have always had for thee? Have I for so many years past suffered thy insolence and brutal temper to be rewarded at last with a cruel and unjust death? But no, it shall never be said that a barbarous and bloody tyrant could thus treat a woman who has not deserved such usage at his hands."

It was idle to waste time in reflection, for every moment was precious, and Marcia did not throw them away in useless meditations. She immediately sent for Eclectus, with whom history tells us she had an intimacy that was not very consistent with virtue, and showing him the paper, "See here," said she, "the handsome treatment that is preparing for us to-morrow." Eclectus, as soon as he was informed of the Emperor's intentions and of the danger he was in, trembling with fear, sent the paper, well sealed up, by a person he could trust, to Lætus. Lætus, not less surprised and alarmed than the other two, went directly to them to consult what was to be done. It was soon determined in this secret council that Commodus should be poisoned, and that without loss of time. This seemed the more practicable plan, as Marcia had been used to give him what he drank. The plot succeeded. Commodus, returning much heated and thirsty from the bath, called for something to drink, and Marcia presented him a cup of excellent wine, but of so dangerous a composition, that as soon as he had taken it he felt a great heaviness in his head (Dion will have it that they poisoned the meat that was served up to him at supper). Marcia and Eclectus caused everybody to withdraw from the Emperor's room, on pretence of keeping him quiet that he might sleep; but when the conspirators saw that he vomited with great violence, they were terribly afraid,[1] lest he should get rid of the poison by that means, and the whole affair be discovered. They

[1] Dio. lib. 72.

were the more apprehensive of this, as the Emperor seemed to suspect something by certain threats that he uttered. They therefore thought it the surest way to induce Narcissus, a famous wrestler, remarkable for his great strength, to smother him in his bed, and promised him great rewards. He undertook the business, and strangled the Emperor, after which they conveyed the body out of the chamber and covered it with a carpet.

Marcia and her accomplices were in dreadful apprehension of what was to happen as soon as it should be known that the Emperor was dead. They thought it absolutely necessary that some senator of merit should be proclaimed Emperor, who would be agreeable to all the orders of the city, and able to protect them against the fury of the soldiers, who they knew would be enraged in the highest degree at the death of a prince who allowed them great liberties. Pertinax was thought a proper person to fill the throne. They, therefore, declared him Emperor without further delay, and gave out that Commodus had died of apoplexy. We shall presently mention the circumstances of Pertinax's election, so at present shall only add that the new Emperor harangued the soldiers, and did not forget to speak very honourably of Lætus, who had given him the empire.

The consul Falco could not hear Lætus praised without expressing great indignation, and as he was not a man to dissemble his real sentiments, neither from complaisance nor policy, he declared openly to Pertinax that no good was to be expected from him, since he was capable of tarnishing the beginning of his reign by shamefully commending a man who had dipped his hands in the blood of his Emperor, and showing marks of his esteem for Marcia and Eclectus, who had been the instruments of Commodus's cruelty.　Pertinax answered with great moderation.　He told Falco that a young man as he was did not consider what it was to be under a necessity of obeying; that Marcia and Lætus had acted by compulsion, and that as to their having put the Emperor to death for his tyranny, it sufficiently showed that they did not approve of it.

Pertinax was too sensible of the obligations he was under to Marcia not to take her part; in fact, she received from the new Emperor great tokens of his gratitude during the three months that he reigned, but she did not escape punishment.

Julianus revenged the death of Commodus; for this Emperor, to whose elevation Lætus had much contributed, imagining that he, together with Marcia, afterwards favoured the party of Severus, put them both to death, and caused Narcissus, who had strangled Commodus, to be exposed to the wild beasts.

TITIANA

WIFE OF PERTINAX

T looked as if Pertinax had only escaped the tyranny of Commodus to fall a sacrifice to Fortune, and that he had only made his life famous by the most glorious exploits to lose it miserably upon the throne. Happy is the private individual, and wretched the Sovereign! He soon found, by experience, that the most exalted stations are often dreadful precipices. He was born at a village in Liguria, the son of Helvius Successus, a seller of firewood, who, having made a little money by his occupation, was resolved to bring up his son to learning, and educate him as well as his moderate circumstances would admit of.[1] It was not long before Pertinax gave tokens of a superior genius, and of being destined for greater things; for he learned and practised so well the art of war upon every occasion on which he was employed that he was looked upon as a person of consummate experience, capable of filling the highest posts. In fact, it was he who, by his extraordinary prudence and resolution, appeased the legions that had revolted in Britain;[2] and it may be affirmed that he saved the island for Marcus Aurelius, who knew so well the importance of this service and the merit of

[1] Capitolin. in Pertin.　　　　[2] Dio. lib. 73.

497

Pertinax that he several times extolled him in full Senate:
glorious commendation, when given by a prince as much
an enemy to flattery and dissimulation as Marcus Aurelius was.   But it was not only by empty praises that this
magnificent and generous Emperor rewarded the glorious
actions of Pertinax; he was promoted to the most honourable posts, and afterwards raised to the consulship—
that sublime dignity that drew upon him the jealousy
of a large number of envious people, who could not bear
he should become their equal,[1] little foreseeing that one
day they were to have him for their master.

There was something in his countenance extremely
agreeable; he had a large forehead, fair hair, gracefully
and naturally curled,[2] a very majestic air, and was tall.
He spoke well, and behaved upon all occasions with great
affability and sweetness of temper.   His principal failing
was love of money, which he still exhibited even when
he was Emperor.   He was fond of pleasures, and we
shall see that they were not always consistent with
decency.   He was not lacking in learning, for, before
he had any military employment, he exercised that of a
grammarian at Rome with great success, having succeeded in that science the famous Apollinaris, who had
been his master.

Pertinax, having by his merit surmounted the disadvantage of the meanness of his birth, and having, by his
great and eminent services, gained the Emperor's esteem,
looked out for an alliance that might bring him influence
and honour.   He selected Flavia Titiana, a lady of great
talent and vivacity, more inclined to consult her inclinations than her duty.   She was the daughter of Flavius

[1] Dio. lib. 71.   [2] Spon. Recher. curi. d'Antiq.

Sulpicianus, who on account of his riches was reckoned one of the principal senators. She was easily prevailed upon to listen to Pertinax's addresses, for, as she was of an amourous disposition, she did not hold out long against the solicitations of a handsome person, especially one who made a great figure in Rome, and might reckon upon the highest preferment. This marriage, then, was soon concluded; but neither of the parties piqued themselves upon over-strictness in conjugal fidelity. Pertinax, in a little time, provided himself with mistresses, whom he liked better than his wife; and Titiana, by an odd sort of taste, grew so in love with a certain player upon the harp as to abandon herself without reserve to that passion; nor, indeed, did she take much pains to conceal it, for all Rome soon became acquainted with the scandalous intrigue.

It might reasonably be supposed that Pertinax would have been greatly provoked at such an infamous intrigue which so much dishonoured him, and that he would have been induced to punish his wife for so shameful and notorious a breach of chastity. However, he gave himself very little trouble about it; whether it was that, being as much to be blamed as she, he thought he had no right to reproach or punish her for a crime he was equally guilty of himself, or that he despaired of ever curing an evil that had taken too deep root; or lastly, that, being entirely taken up with Cornificia (with whom he was rather bewitched than enamoured),[1] he had no leisure to take notice of what went on at home. Be it as it may, he left Titiana at full liberty to act as she thought

---

[1] Jul. Capitolin. in Pertin.

proper, and she made so bad a use of her opportunity
that all the city were witnesses to her shamelessness.

They passed a good part of their life after this manner. As for Titiana, her behaviour was such as entirely
lost her the esteem of all modest people; but it was not
so with Pertinax, for he did not find that it hurt his prospects in the least. He was made pro-consul of Africa,
in which post he acquitted himself so well that Commodus, much as he hated virtue, respected his, and rewarded
him with the government of Rome, in the exercise of
which office Pertinax showed so much moderation and
capacity that he was extremely popular with everybody,
the more so because Fuscianus, his predecessor, had been
rigorous and severe. This wise conduct gained Pertinax
universal esteem, and contributed not a little to his being
made Emperor; for after Commodus had been killed, the
authors of that assassination, fearing (and with great
reason) that it would be attended with dreadful consequences to them, imagined that the soldiers would be
the more easily induced to overlook that affair if some
person of great merit and excellent qualities were chosen
to succeed him. Pertinax was thought worthy to be
immediately selected for that purpose, and proclaimed
Emperor; for, Commodus having been despatched in the
night, and the fatal morning approaching when the conspirators were to be sacrificed to his fury, Lætus, Eclectus, and some others of their party went and knocked
at Pertinax's door. The porter had no sooner perceived
Lætus with the soldiers than, seized with fear, he ran
to his master's chamber to tell him that the captain of
the Emperor's guards wanted to speak with him in all

haste. As soon as he had said this Lætus and Eclectus entered the room.

Pertinax, to whom the untimely and tragical end of so many illustrious senators was a sufficient warning of what he had to expect, made no question that they came to put him to death by the tyrant's orders: however, he remained very calm: for, as it was no more than what he had daily expected from Commodus, who had not spared even his father's most intimate friends, he showed the greatest intrepidity, and without rising from his bed, or changing countenance, told them that, having had the honour of being very intimate with Marcus Aurelius, he was much surprised that he had been suffered to live so long; that for many years past he had expected every night to be his last. " What do you wait for, then (continued he)? [1] execute the orders of Commodus, and by giving me a speedy death, put an end to the alarms and apprehensions in which I have passed so much of my time." " Your fear wrongs your merit," answered Lætus; " it is not your life we are come for, but our safety and the prosperity of the State. The tyrant is no more: we have made him suffer that death which he had prepared for us. We are come, then, to offer you the empire, because we know nobody so worthy of it, and are sure that the whole world will approve of our choice."

Pertinax, imagining that they were laying a snare for him to work his ruin, interrupted Lætus, and without giving him time to proceed: " Cease," said he, " to make a jest of a poor unfortunate old man, and by your flattering offers to induce me to do or say something that is to

[1] Herodian, lib. 2. c. 4.

cost me my life." " Well," replied Lætus, " since you
will not believe me, look at this paper, and see if it be not
the handwriting of Commodus, with which you are well
acquainted; read the sentence of death which was to have
been executed against us to-morrow morning, and you
will be sensible of the danger we have escaped." Pertinax,
seeing an air of truth and sincerity in their manner of
proceeding, and as they had been always his good friends,
began to take courage; and at length, suffering himself
to be persuaded by them, told them he was ready to do
whatever they should think proper.

After Lætus and Eclectus were sure of Pertinax, they
thought it absolutely necessary to sound the feelings of
the legions. Lætus, who was captain of the guards, did
not doubt that he could easily bring them over to his
opinion, as his rank gave him great authority in the army.
In the meantime they caused the news of Commodus's
death and Pertinax's election to be spread abroad, that
it might be generally supposed to have been carried out
with the approbation of the army.

Pertinax, however, notwithstanding all the proofs that
had been given him of Commodus's death, could not feel
at ease, nor prevent himself being cruelly agitated with
different passions, sometimes fear, sometimes hope; for,
when he reflected upon what Lætus and Eclectus had told
him, he was at a loss what to think of the matter. In
this uncertainty he sent one of his domestics, in whom he
had entire confidence, to find out the truth; but his
apprehensions were quite removed when the messenger,
on his return, affirmed that he had seen the dead body of
Commodus in the arms of those who were carrying him
out of the palace.

In the meantime Lætus acquainted the soldiers with
the death of Commodus, telling them that he had been
carried off by an apoplectic fit, and proposed Pertinax as
his successor, whose courage and virtue, he said, they
were well acquainted with. The people expressed great
joy at their deliverance from the tyranny of Commodus,
and uttered loud acclamations in honour of the new
Emperor; the soldiers also, being rather hurried on by
the general torrent than in pursuance of their own inclination, acknowledged Pertinax for Emperor, and took
the oath of fidelity. Pertinax, amidst all the honours
that were paid him, imagined he foresaw great difficulties in his way. He could not bring himself to believe
that a man so obscurely born could be firmly settled on
the throne which had just been filled by a prince of so
noble an extraction, or that so many illustrious senators
would easily acquiesce in the command of a person so
infinitely beneath them. Agitated by these serious reflections, he could not help feeling very anxious and
solicitous, and when he came to the Senate he would not
assume, nor suffer the people to give him, any of the
honours that were due to the dignity they had conferred
upon him. He was, however, received in the Senate
with the highest tokens of satisfaction and respect, and
saluted with the titles of Emperor and August. Pertinax thanked the senators for their good will, but refused
the empire on account of his age, which, he said, would
not permit him to act with that vigour and circumspection
so absolutely necessary for an Emperor, and which was
not to be expected from a person so far advanced in life.
He added that the Senate contained many members who
were infinitly more capable of governing, and at the same

time taking Glabrio by the hand, who was descended
from one of the most noble families in Rome, and was
then in his second consulship, he would have made him
sit down in the seat appointed for the Emperors. " Very
well," said Glabrio, " since you think me more worthy of
empire, I yield up my pretensions to you, and I join my
request to that of the Senate that you will accept it."
At that instant the senators all rose up, and approaching
him, insisted upon his taking the place which his modesty
and humility had made him refuse. As soon as he was
seated, he made a speech full of wise reflections and
noble maxims, entreated the Senate to partake with him
the care of the State, and, after having offered the
accustomed sacrifices, retired to the palace of the Emperors.

The same day that Pertinax was declared Emperor,
the title of August was voted to Titiana, his wife, and
the Senate, by a solemn decree, conferred that of Cæsar
upon young Pertinax, the Emperor's son, but the new
Emperor would not suffer his wife to accept the above
title; [1] whether it was that he did not yet think himself
secure enough in his authority and so was not willing
that she should accept honours she might soon be forced
to give up, or that, reflecting on the meanness of his
birth, he thought it inconsistent with the modesty which
became him, or else, being persuaded that everybody was
acquainted with Titiana's behaviour, he was ashamed
that she should be honoured with a title she so ill deserved. [2] But the Senate, being resolved to acquit itself
of everything that decency and politeness required, entreated the Emperor not so suffer Titiana to refuse an

[1] Jul. Capitolin. in Pertin.   [2] Jornandes.

honour which they had with great pleasure decreed her, and which all the Empresses had accepted. Pertinax, however, with an obstinacy that agreed very well with his name, replied that it was sufficient that he himself had, at their request, accepted the sovereignty, which he confessed he was unworthy of, and that he would never consent that his son should be called Cæsar till he deserved it. And further, to show that he was not proud of his new dignity, he refused to allow his children to be brought up in the palace, nor did they ever appear with that magnificent distinction of rank and apparel which had been always bestowed upon the children of Emperors.

The excellent qualities of Pertinax, and his prudent conduct, had given everybody a high idea of his fitness to rule, nor were they mistaken. He began his reign by establishing the most useful regulations. He banished from the city those pests of all society, the informers, who were such enemies to the public peace and tranquillity; he suppressed the burdensome taxes which obstructed trade and commerce; he gave those lands that had been long neglected and reckoned barren to anybody who would cultivate them, and exempted them from all duties for ten years; he paid all the arrears of pensions and what was due to the officers and troops, and corrected the abuses and disorders that had crept into military discipline. His manners were in no way altered by the change of his condition, for his friends found in him the same freedom and familiarity. He conversed with them without ceremony or laying them under any disagreeable constraint; invited them to dine with him in an affable manner, and gave them the same liberty as if they were at their own houses, Titiana never sitting down with him at table when he had other company.

We do not well know how this princess conducted herself after her husband's elevation to the throne, history being almost silent in regard to this; but it is very probable that his short reign did not furnish her with many opportunities of showing whether it would have had any influence upon her behaviour or not, for the wise changes and regulations this Emperor made not being agreeable to the soldiers, especially the Prætorians, who were accustomed to extraordinary license under Commodus, they repented that they had chosen an old man, whose strictness was by no means suitable to their way of living, and resolved to have an Emperor who would not be so severe. Lætus fomented their discontent, for this officer, under pretext of having raised Pertinax to the empire, thought he had a right to aspire to everything. He accused the Emperor of ingratitude as often as he was refused anything, though his requests were such as could not be granted without injustice. Pretending to pity the soldiers, who, he said, had to do with an Emperor who was an enemy to their pleasure, he so animated them against him that two hundred of the most seditious went to the palace in order to put him to death.[1]

---

[1] Falco, a senator of very illustrious family, who was then consul, and who probably aspired to the empire, had also done his utmost to stir up the Prætorians to a revolt, and had very lately encouraged a slave of his to demand, in a most insolent manner, that Pertinax should give up the imperial palace to him, which he pretended belonged to him, being, as he said, son of Fabia, the Emperor Verus's sister. His impudence was, indeed, punished, the slave having been publicly

The Empress Titiana no sooner perceived this mutinous troop than she ran in great fright to give the Emperor notice of the danger he was in. It certainly would
have been no difficult matter for the Emperor to have
driven away, or even to have killed the greater part of
this audacious mob, for he had about him a sufficient
guard, both of horse and foot, besides a great number
of other people, who might have shut the gates of the
palace; or if he had pleased he had it in his power to
have retired to a place of safety till the sedition was
appeased; but considering it beneath his dignity to flee
at the appearance of danger, and flattering himself that
his presence would soon stop the fury of the soldiers,
and make them return to their allegiance, he advanced
to meet the Prætorians with an air of resolution, and
spoke to them thus, in a firm and intrepid tone of voice: [1]
—" Is it an action that will add much to your glory, O my
companions! to murder your Emperor? Thanks to the
gods, I have lived long enough; nor has my behaviour
been such that I should be afraid to die. No; it is but
what I have expected for a long time past. But shall it
ever be said that those whose duty it was to guard and
protect their Emperor have been so perfidious as to
assassinate him? Would it not be an eternal and indelible dishonour that future ages would reproach you
with? And, after all, in what have I offended you?
If you regret Commodus, did you not know that he was
to die, as sure as he came into the world? And supposing it to be true that his death was not a natural

whipped; but that chastisement was in no way adequate to his crime,
so that Pertinax's having afterwards sent the slave back to his master
may be said to have been a very ill-judged piece of clemency.
[1] Herodian. lib. 2.

one, can you accuse or even suspect me of having conspired against him? You have been witnesses of my conduct, and I am not conscious that I have given any one of you reason to complain of it, since I have never refused you anything you have required of me with the least appearance of justice."

The Emperor's presence, his grave and majestic countenance, and this moving discourse, put a stop to their fury for a time; they seemed disconcerted, and showed signs of repentance, not being able to look him in the face. They had sheathed their swords, beginning to feel ashamed of their abominable enterprise, when one of the soldiers, more insolent and brutal than the rest, ran him through the body with his sword, and encouraged the others to do the same. Eclectus, seeing the Emperor wounded, drew his sword, killed two or three of the mutineers, and defended his Emperor, till being mortally wounded himself he fell down dead, showing a rare example of loyalty and faithfulness. Pertinax, seeing them determined to kill him, covered his head with his robe, prayed the gods to revenge his death, and never attempted to make any defence. The infamous villains, not contenting themselves with shedding his blood, were so inhuman as to cut off his head, and to carry it into their camp upon the end of a lance.

Such was the tragical end of Pertinax. He died extremely regretted by the Senate and the people, who expected from his love of justice the reformation of those abuses that Commodus had introduced. This unfortunate prince had several presages of his death; for, three days before it happened, while he was in the bath, he saw the figure of a man threatening him with a sword;

the day before he was killed the stars were observed to shine in the day as if it were night; and in the victim that was sacrificed no heart was to be found, which the heathens reckoned to foretell some grievous misfortune. He left a son and a daughter by his wife Titiana, who hoped to preserve her rank and the honours that had been paid her, when she saw that Sulpicianus, her father, had a prospect of the empire by the soldiers putting it up to auction to the highest bidder; but Julianus's intrigues got the better of him, so that Titiana had the mortification of passing the remainder of her life as a private individual.

MANLIA SCANTILLA

T is very dangerous to follow the dictates of ambition, which generally occasions the downfall of those it has a mind to exalt. Scantilla, hurried away by her vanity, persuaded her husband to aspire to the throne, and to scatter his treasures with a liberal hand, to procure the sovereign authority; but this advice proved fatal to him, for, by so doing, he purchased a miserable and untimely death.

Thus we frequently die martyrs to our pride. But, if we are disposed to carry our reflections further still, we may attribute Julianus's ruin to another cause; for, if it be true that he was concerned in the murder of Pertinax, it may reasonably be concluded that Providence would not permit him long to enjoy a dignity which he had procured by so black a crime.

Marcus Didius Severus Julianus was a native of Mediolanum (Milan),[1] and grandson, through his mother, of the celebrated Salvius Julianus, the lawyer, who did so much honour to Hadrian's reign. He was brought up under the Princess Domitia Lucilla, mother of the Emperor Marcus Aurelius, who procured him the highest offices. He married Manlia Scantilla, by whom

[1] Spartian. in Julian.

he had Didia Clara, whom he married to Cornelius Repentinus.

History does not inform us either of the family or character of Scantilla; but it is easy to conjecture that she had more vanity than prudence, since it was at her instigation that Julianus bought the empire at the very time when all the senators of rank and merit were trembling at the horrid assassination of Pertinax, whose misfortunes served them as a warning of what was to be expected from the fury and brutality of the soldiers.

When the Prætorians had glutted themselves with the Emperor's blood, they retired into their camp, and posted sentinels to hinder the people from approaching. Their not meeting with any punishment from this execrable action increased their insolence, for, seeing that nobody attempted to revenge the death of Pertinax, and that no senator presented himself to succeed him, they had the effrontery to set up to auction the chief dignity of the world.[1] In fact, they caused a soldier, remarkable for a loud voice, to mount the wall of the camp, and proclaim that the empire was to be sold, and that they would take upon them to give it to the highest bidder.

Sulpicianus, father-in-law of Pertinax, was then in the camp, having been sent thither by the late Emperor, in order to appease the soldiers, who he had heard had mutinied, but as soon as he was informed of his death, he entreated the Prætorians to choose him in his stead, and offered them great sums of money to do so; but whilst they were bargaining about the price, Julianus was told of the soldiers' resolution to sell it. He was at the table with some of his friends, and this news flattered ex-

[1] Herodian. lib. 2.

tremely his own and his wife's ambition. Her heart
immediately leaped at the throne, and the brilliancy
of the enchanting object dazzled her. For, not reflecting
upon the danger of this high station, though she had
so recent an example of it before her eyes, she persuaded
her husband to quit the table, and immediately to make
an offer to the soldiers. She represented to him that,
as the empire was to be sold, nobody was better able
to purchase it than he, who had more money than any
other senator, and that it would be the height of imprudence to lose so favourable an opportunity. Didia
Clara joined her entreaties to those of her mother, that
her father might not fail to procure himself an honour
in which she was to have so large a share, and of which
she was, no doubt, in hopes of being one day the heiress.
In short, the parasites that were at supper with Julianus
importuned him to go, without losing a moment, and
tempt the Prætorians with such an offer as could not
be resisted; and all together solicited him so strongly
that he rose from table, went directly to the camp, and
shouted out to the soldiers that if they would choose
him Emperor he would give what price they pleased. The
guards told him what Sulpicianus had offered, and declared they would not sell it so cheap. Julianus represented to them that, in listening to Sulpicianus they did
not consider what prejudice they did themselves, for
that the strict alliance there was between him and Pertinax ought to be the strongest reason in the world for
rejecting him, since they might be sure that he would not
fail to revenge the death of his son-in-law. After having
said all that was calculated to render his antagonist suspected, he made them an advantageous offer. The

soldiers communicated this to Sulpicianus to try if he would give more, and this scandalous traffic lasted a considerable time, for Sulpicianus within the camp, and Julianus without, endeavoured to outbid each other.[1]

At last Julianus made so tempting an offer (also promising to pay ready money) that they immediately made him mount the walls into the camp by a ladder, for they would not open the gates. After they had agreed upon the terms, he was declared Emperor, and they gave him the surname of Commodus. In the evening they conducted him to the Senate, amidst (not the acclamations) but the imprecations of all the people, who reproached him with the infamous bargain he had made for the empire, which he had not been ashamed to purchase in so scandalous a manner.

Julianus, leaving the soldiers at the door, went into the Senate to take his place, and after he had seated himself in the Emperor's chair, he made the following infamous speech, as it has been transmitted to us by one who was present.[2] " Perceiving, O venerable fathers, that the throne is vacant, I must tell you that I think nobody more worthy to fill it than myself. I shall not take up much of your time by praising myself, or putting you in mind of my virtues, for I believe none of you are ignorant of them. I am persuaded you all know me very well, so without giving you further trouble, I beg to inform you that the army has thought proper to choose me Emperor, and I am come hither that you may confirm their choice." The Senate bore with this arrogance. That timid body of men, having lost all

[1] Xiphilin. in Did. Jul. Dio. lib. 73. Herodian lib. 2.
[2] Dio. lib. 73.

sentiments of freedom, and being incapable of any generous resolution, declared him Emperor, elected his family into the number of patricians, and by the same decree honoured Manlia Scantilla his wife, and Didia Clara his daughter, with the sublime title of August.

Whilst all this took place in the camp and in the Senate, the two ladies, who were become princesses without knowing it themselves, were in the utmost impatience about Julianus's negotiations; but they were not long kept in suspense, for the emissaries soon let them know that the Prætorians had elected Julianus, that the Senate had not only ratified their choice, but had conferred upon them the title of August, and that the new Emperor, who was coming, desired they would meet him.[1]   It is easy to conceive the joy they felt upon this occasion, for people do not often mount the throne with indifference; but it was not long before very disagreeable reflections succeeded those first transports; for, through all these flattering honours and titles, the princesses could perceive that Julianus's elevation was but a melancholy forerunner of some dreadful calamity, and therefore it was not without a kind of regret that they proceeded towards the palace, which they entered with secret horror, for fear of some impending misfortune counterbalancing their present satisfaction, and not without good reason; for the first object that presented itself to their view was the body of the murdered Emperor stretched upon the ground.   This tragical sight made no impression upon Julianus, but on the contrary, furnished him with matter for mirth and ridicule; for, not dreaming of this affair being attended with any bad consequences

[1] Spart. vit. Did. Jul.

from the senators, whose approbation he had extorted, after having basely purchased the consent of the soldiers, he brutally insulted the dead body of Pertinax, of whose death he was not innocent; and, after making himself very merry about the frugal supper that had been prepared for him he ordered the most costly and delicate provisions the city could supply to be procured for him, supped most luxuriously, played at dice, and ordered the comedians to come and dance before him.[1] The yet smoking blood of his predecessor (still lying dead in the palace) was not capable of moderating his excessive and ill-timed rejoicing; nor did the probability of his meeting with the like fate (which had made Scantilla tremble) give him any sort of concern.

The day after, the senators went with all formality to the palace to pay their respects to the Emperor, and accompany him to the Senate; they were obliged to pretend great joy at his elevation, though they were extremely afflicted. They carried, however, their flattery so far that they decreed him the title of Father of the State, and ordered a statue of silver to be made in honour of him. Julianus thanked the Senate for having confirmed the choice of the army, and for the titles they had conferred upon his wife and daughter, but was so modest, or rather so politic, as to refuse some other honours they were inclined to give him. From the Senate he went to the Capitol, still attended by the senators, who were very liberal of their false tokens of esteem; but the people, not so skilful at dissembling, no sooner saw him than they poured out a torrent of insolent and affronting language, called him parricide, and reproached him with

[1] Dio. lib. 73.

having usurped the throne. This taunting reception disconcerted him, but he dissembled his resentment, and, in order to appease the people who he found were enraged against him, he promised them a great sum of money. This offer only served to exasperate them the more; thousands of voices were heard in a moment crying out that they would have none of his money, and that he was a base villain who made it his whole business to corrupt the Romans by cunning and bribery. Then Julianus, being no longer master of his passion, commanded the guards to fall on them, who accordingly killed a great many of those who were nearest. This violence made them lose all patience; they never ceased to pour out horrible imprecations against him and the soldiers that chose him for money, and even flung stones at him. They afterwards wept aloud for Pertinax and bitterly lamented his death. They called to their assistance the armies that were in Syria, and Niger who commanded them, whom they entreated to come speedily and avenge the detestable scandal brought upon the empire by a base and infamous usurper.

Julianus was too sensible of the consequences of these threats not to be alarmed. From that time he affected great civility towards the senators and people of distinction, and promised them all they could desire, but nobody paid any heed to these promises, because they were out of all proportion, and such as did not become an Emperor.[1] He made his son-in-law Governor of Rome, and settled upon Didia Clara, his daughter, an income proportionate to her rank and her new dignity of August. In short, he omitted nothing that was necessary to

[1] Dio. lib. 73.

strengthen and establish his authority, which was odious
to everybody who had not had a hand in his election, and,
in a little time, even to the soldiers who were the authors
of it, because he could not pay them what he had promised. This made people inclined to believe that his power
would be of no long duration; at least, there were few
who did not wish it. There even happened a kind of
prodigy which confirmed this opinion, and filled people's
minds with superstition, for, as Julianus was offering sacrifice to the god Janus, whose statue was erected before
the Senate House, three bright stars were observed near
the sun. The soldiers looked earnestly at them, and said
that so unusual a phenomenon must needs portend some
great misfortune to Julianus. In fact, three generals
soon after revolted, which made him totter on his throne:
Septimius Severus, Clodius Albinus and Pescennius Niger.
The first commanded in Pannonia, the other in Britain,
and the last in Syria. They had great authority in their
respective provinces, and were at the head of the three
most considerable armies in the empire. As they have
a great share in this part of the history, it will not be out
of place to give some account of them.

Decimus Clodius Albinus was from Adrumetum in
Africa. He belonged to a family that had furnished the
State with many great men, so that whatever some
authors have said to the contrary, it is certain that
Albinus was of very illustrious birth. His father,
Ceionius Postumius,[1] gave him the name of Albinus,
because he was extremely white when he was born. He
was tall, had curly hair, a high forehead, so weak a
voice that it resembled that of a eunuch, and a wide

[1] Capitolin. vit. Clod. Albi.

mouth. He was [1] so great an eater that incredible stories are told upon that subject. He served with considerable reputation under Marcus Aurelius and Commodus, the latter of whom gave him the privilege of assuming the title of Cæsar as often as he thought fit, which, notwithstanding, he never made use of. Such modesty was very agreeable to the Senate, to whom he said their ancient authority ought to be restored. In Gaul he gained several victories, which procured him the government of Britain. He perfectly understood the art of war; he was grave, and a strict observer of military discipline, but his good qualities were eclipsed by great vices; for, besides that he was a bad master and a worse husband, unjust towards his domestics and of an insupportable temper towards his wife, his behaviour was very inconsiderable towards the rest of the world; severe to an excess, the least fault [2] with him was unpardonable; he was very neat in his dress, but slovenly at his table, which was very plentiful, but not very elegant. Sometimes he drank no wine at all, and at other times would indulge in it to excess.

He frequently abandoned himself to more shameful vices, but it is mentioned amongst his virtues that he never indulged in anything that was unnatural; on the contrary, he was always an utter enemy to such practices. With all these faults and so few good qualities, we read that he was beloved by the senators and people of rank more than any other prince, to which the cruelties of Severus contributed not a little.

Pescennius Niger was descended from an equestrian family, of no great distinction, and yet not mean. He

[1] Spon. Recher, cur. d'Antiq.   [2] Capitolin. vit. Albin.

After the painting by W. Kotarbinski

A Roman Bacchanal

was well-built, had an engaging countenance and a ruddy
complexion, his voice was so powerful that when he
spoke in the camp he could be heard a thousand paces
off; he wore his hair in natural curls, and it was so black
that he was called Niger from it. He drank a good deal,
but ate little. He had been several times consul, and
had filled many important posts, civil and military, to the
general satisfaction, having always behaved with prudence and moderation. He had given, upon all occasions, undoubted proofs of his zeal and devotion to the
public welfare. He was very rigorous in matters of
military discipline, keeping the soldiers strictly to their
duty, by remonstrances as well as his own example, and
making them carefully avoid luxury and everything that
was likely to diminish their courage; for when he was
encamped near the Nile, on the soldiers desiring he would
allow them wine, he answered that he was surprised at
their request, considering how near they were to the
river. He is accused of having been a great dissembler,
ambitious, fickle, and a slave to his pleasures, which cost
him the empire. It was said of him [1] that he was a
good soldier, an excellent officer, an admirable general,
an illustrious consul, a man who distinguished himself in
peace and war, but an unfortunate Emperor; and when
his virtues are compared with his vices, it will be found [2]
that the former were not such as to entitle him to great
commendation, nor were the latter so glaring as to justify
his being called a bad man.

Septimius Severus was a native of Leptis in Africa.
His name agreed very well with his disposition, for he
was cruel, vindictive, and furious. He was reckoned the

[1] Spart. vit. Pescen. Nig.　　　[2] Dio. lib. 74.

most covetous of all the Emperors, for in his actions and
projects he never had anything in view but his own
advantage. Never was a man a greater master of dissimulation, so that his heart[1] and his tongue never
agreed, as he was cunning and deceitful. He expressed
the greatest friendship for such as he was most desirous
to deceive, concealing his deep designs under a fair
appearance of frankness and sincerity, being neither
afraid nor ashamed to make use of the most execrable
oaths and imprecations that people might give credit to
what he said, in order to deceive them the more easily.
He was very skilful in the art of war, for which he had
the greatest genius of any of the Roman Emperors, and
especially he was an extremely capable commander.[2]
As he was vigilant and indefatigable, and possessed, in
short, all the requisite qualities that are necessary to
make a perfect general, so it may be said that he was
more indebted to his own extraordinary talents for his
preferment than to Fortune. He was an enemy not only
to idleness, but to rest, for when he had but a few
moments to live he asked if there was not something to
do. He had a very vigorous and robust constitution,[3]
till he was violently attacked by the gout. His countenance was majestic, his hair was fair and curly, he wore
his beard long, and had a most melodious voice. He
was not expensive either in his dress or table. In his
youth he had been guilty of very bad actions, notwithstanding which, by the favour of his uncle, Septimius
Severus, he was made a senator. Marcus Aurelius gave
him the quæstorship, and afterwards named him pro-

---

[1] Herodian. lib. 2. Vict. Epit. 1, Dio. lib. 76.
[2] Dio. lib. 75.　　　　　　　　[3] Dio lib. 76.

consul of Africa, where he gave a very brutal instance of his severity. An eminent citizen of Leptis, meeting him one day in the street, went to salute him, thinking that as there had formerly been great intimacy between them he might venture to take that liberty; but Severus ordered that he should be immediately beaten with a stick, saying at the same time,[1] " My friend, take care another time how you treat a Roman magistrate with too much familiarity." Commodus promoted him still higher, at the request of Lætus, his favourite; for, after having given him several posts, in all of which he behaved with great rigour, he made him commander-in-chief of all the armies in Illyria.

Such were the three generals who revolted against Julianus, and disputed for the empire. Rome and all the provinces were divided into factions, parties, and cabals; the horrors of the famous triumvirate, which cost Rome so much blood, were renewed. Of these three competitors Niger seemed the most powerful, for, besides that his command was the most considerable (as it extended not only all over Syria, but reached also through Phœnicia, and all the countries bordering upon the Euphrates), he possessed the affections of the Romans, who looked upon him as a man extremely zealous for the State, and the only person that could make them amends for the loss of Pertinax, whose virtues they said he possessed. He was extremely beloved by the troops, and much esteemed in Syria, where he had governed with the greatest lenity and mildness.

Severus was neither so well beloved nor so powerful, but he was more active, more laborious, and more crafty

[1] Spart. vit. Sev.

than Niger; very skilful at making the most of conjunctures and events, and nobody was so capable of conducting an affair of importance. As for Albinus, the only thing in which he had an advantage over the other two was his age;[1] so he was reckoned more capable of making another person Emperor than of being a good Emperor himself.

Niger was informed of what took place at Rome; he was told that the people only waited for him to choose him Emperor, that they hated Julianus, and that even the soldiers who had raised him to the throne could not endure him. In short, they advised him not to delay a moment his coming to Rome, where everyone was for him. Niger, who was not inclined to take so important a step without mature consideration, assembled the officers of his army and the principal people of Syria, to whom he communicated the letters he had received from Rome. They all solicited him to take advantage of the favourable disposition of the people towards him, and promised to risk their lives for his service. Niger was very glad to find them so zealous for his interests, but, that they might never afterwards accuse him of having undertaken this affair of his own accord, " I protest to you," said he, " that it is not ambition that prompts me to deprive Julianus of the empire, but I cannot refuse the Roman people the assistance they ask from me against a tyrant that oppresses them.[2] The empire stands in need of someone to manage it; I am invited to Rome for that purpose, but I will do nothing without your approbation, for, since you are willing to share with me the dangers and difficulties of this undertaking, it is but reasonable

[1] Capitolin. in Albin.   [2] Herod. lib. 2.

that I should be guided by your counsels." Nothing was then to be heard but acclamations and shouts of joy; the army and the people strove who should first proclaim him Emperor; he was invested with the purple robe, and all the other imperial ornaments, conducted in state into the temples of Antioch, and afterwards to his house, which they had taken care to adorn with all the insignia of sovereignty. Fame soon carried the news of his election to the most distant provinces, and ambassadors arrived from all the neighbouring Kings and Satraps to congratulate him upon his elevation to the empire, and to offer him their assistance. He received them with all possible tokens of gratitude and generosity, thanked them for their courtesy, but answered that he hoped there would be no occasion to take up arms or shed blood to establish his empire. In fact, imagining that he had nothing to fear, instead of going directly to Rome to get his election confirmed by the Senate, he amused himself with one diversion or other at Antioch, and endeavoured to gain the hearts of the Syrians by entertaining them with games, shows, and races, which were extremely agreeable to those people, who are very fond of things of that nature.

Severus, in the meantime, being well informed of all these matters, and seeing the empire within the grasp of anybody who would seize it, assumed in Pannonia the title of Emperor, but proceeded with more caution. He exaggerated to the officers of his army and the soldiers the miserable condition to which the empire was reduced by the unworthiness of him whom the Prætorians had chosen for money, and by that means had rendered venal the first dignity in the world. He represented to them

the inhuman massacre of the Emperor Pertinax, whose
merit they were well acquainted with, having so often
experienced his goodness when they served under him.
He then encouraged them to revenge that horrible murder, and concealing his design with this specious pretence,
he managed them so cleverly that they proclaimed him
Emperor with great demonstrations of joy, and gave him
the surname of Pertinax, which was much respected in
Illyria. He did not stop there, for he distributed a
large sum of money among the troops, and made magnificent promises to the officers of his army, and the
governors of provinces, without the least intention of
fulfilling them. By his cunning and intrigues he won
over the armies in Gaul; [1] and after he had secured all
those from whom he thought he had anything to fear, he
determined to set out directly for Rome. But he was
not one of those who look no further than the present;
he reflected that, after having conquered Julianus,[2] he
would have Niger and Albinus to deal with. The first,
indeed, did not appear very formidable, because of his
indolence and want of activity; and he despised the second, as being, in his opinion, a greater lover of pleasure
than glory, and not capable of carrying out any noble
enterprise; [3] but he was much afraid of having them
both on his hands at once, which it was his business by all
means to hinder. In order to effect this he made use
of a stratagem, which succeeded admirably. He entered
into a sham treaty with one of his competitors, to prevent their coming to a real agreement. He thought it
would be a vain attempt to make any proposals to Niger,
who was so elevated with the invitations he had received

[1] Spart. in Sever.   [2] Dio. lib. 72.   [3] Herod. lib. 2.

from Rome that he could never be brought to compound for anything less than the empire; but he concluded that Albinus would probably lend a favourable ear to his offers, because he knew him to be naturally credulous. Besides, Severus imagined it was more to his interest to treat with Albinus, who, being nearer to him than Niger, might be in a condition, with the troops he commanded in Britain, to dispute the throne with him. It was, therefore, to him that he addressed himself, sending him a trusty officer with a very courteous letter. He communicated to him his design of delivering Rome from the tyranny under which it groaned under Julianus; made him an offer of dividing the sovereign authority with him, and even solicited and exhorted him to take upon himself the government of the empire, " which," said he, " stands in so great need of a chief nobly descended, and in every way qualified to restore it to its ancient splendour, such as is not to be met with but in you." And, in order the more effectually to deceive him and remove all grounds of mistrust, he wrote a letter to the Senate full of commendations of Albinus, who, he said was worthy of the throne; and immediately caused money to be coined with his image, which he assiduously circulated, and erected statues in honour of him as to an Emperor.

Albinus was the more easily drawn into this snare, as he did not love fatigue or trouble, though his valour was never called in question. He flattered himself with the hopes of enjoying supreme power without running any risk to acquire it. He accordingly accepted the offer of Severus, and remained very quiet in Britain, waiting for the issue of this important affair.

Severus, having nothing more to fear from that quarter, endeavoured to convince his troops that they were all perfectly safe with regard to Niger. "Can you," said he, "apprehend any danger from the army in Syria, which is composed of voluptuous and effeminate Orientals, who have never been accustomed to the hardships of war? You see that Niger, instead of hastening to Rome, is plunging himself into all the luxuries of Antioch, and gives his legions no other occupation than that of seeing sports and shows. Know," said he, with a confident and haughty air, "that, at the first report of my election, the Syrian legions will be glad to join me. My name is not unknown to them, and they will not be desirous of contending with my troops, who, they are well assured, surpass them in number, as well as in courage and experience. Come, let us, without further loss of time, set out for Rome, and we shall soon see that all obstacles will fall before us. We will revenge the deplorable death of that venerable old man, of Pertinax, who was so worthy to command, and of whose virtues you can never be unmindful." This speech so encouraged the soldiers that they were eager to march, and wished for nothing so much as the word of command. Severus, like a crafty and experienced man, took advantage of this ardour, and immediately directed his course towards Rome, without quitting his arms or loitering upon the road, except just to give them time to breathe. He gained a wonderful hold upon their affections during this long march, by living with them in a familiar manner, without ceremony or distinction. He constantly wore his armour, fared just as his soldiers did, and in short, put himself more upon the footing of a companion than a general.

The news of Severus's approach soon reached Rome. Julianus, who did not in the least suspect him, was strangely surprised when he heard of his revolt. He went immediately to the Senate, and obliged them to declare Severus an enemy to the State. They also pronounced the same sentence against the soldiers of his army, if they did not quit him and return to their allegiance in a certain number of days. In consequence of this, Aquillius, who had caused the death of so many senators under Commodus, was sent to assassinate Severus; and Valerius Catulinus was appointed to take the command of the forces in his stead, as if it had been so easy a matter for a senator to displace a general at the head of such a numerous body of troops, who adored him. In the meantime, Julianus made great presents to the Prætorians, besides paying them all that he had formerly promised, in order to bespeak their favour. He caused some regiments of horse to enter the city,[1] and sent for the marines from the port of Misenum. Nothing was then to be seen in Rome but bustle and confusion, arms, encampments, and disturbance, as if it had been an enemy's country. The soldiers,[2] horses, and elephants were regularly trained and exercised to prepare them for battle, which threw the citizens into great consternation; in the midst of which, however, nobody could forbear laughing to see Julianus very busy fortifying the palace with gates and iron bars, remembering that Pertinax would not have been killed if the Prætorians had found him so well prepared—foolish precautions, which sufficiently showed the timidity of that prince, and only served to expose him to the ridicule of all the world. It

[1] Herodian. lib. 2.   [2] Dio. lib. 73.

was then that he caused Marcia and Lætus to be put to death; divine justice had decreed that the murderers of Commodus should sooner or later meet with their deserts, for assassins have nothing better to expect.

In the meantime Severus, having taken all the towns in Italy, throughout which the terror of so formidable an army had caused a general panic, hurried towards Rome, where he had already found means, by one stratagem or another, to introduce a great many of his soldiers. This quite disconcerted Julianus, who could perceive that everybody was ready to forsake him and join the conqueror. The Prætorians, who had given him the empire, were no longer able to defend him, even if they had been willing; for, having been long accustomed to pleasure and idleness, they were so destitute of skill and courage as to be scarcely capable of military duties, and besides, they had no real affection for Julianus. In this perplexity he assembled the Senate, and requested that they would depute some of their body, together with the priests and vestal virgins,[1] to approach Severus, and entreat him not to disturb the peace of the city, and destroy the liberties of the State, as if a few religious ceremonies could stop soldiers, who are seldom much troubled with qualms of that nature. For this reason the Senate represented to him how useless it would be to have recourse to such fruitless expedients, and Quintillus, who had been consul, took the liberty of telling him that a prince who had not courage to fight his enemies was not worthy of the empire, and this bold reproach was supported by several other senators. Julianus was so provoked that he immediately ordered the soldiers to

[1] Spart. vit. Julian.

compel the Senate to obey, or else to fall upon and
massacre them; but as he found his authority extremely
weakened, he thought it best to abandon his foolish and
mad intention, and going in person to the Senate he
caused them to issue a decree, by which he associated
Severus with himself in the empire, and sent Crispinus
to him with the decree, having at the same time given
him secret orders to destroy him. Severus, not being
easily imposed upon, suspected the truth, refused the
proposal, sent Julianus word that he would rather have
him for an enemy than a colleague, and, by the advice of
his officers, sent after Crispinus, and had him arrested
and put to death, which was acknowledged to be the just
punishment of his base undertaking. Thus this unworthy Emperor, not knowing which way to turn, had
recourse to strange, extravagant, and unusual religious
ceremonies, ridiculously hoping by those means to change
the hearts of the Romans, and make their arms drop out
of the hands of his enemies. He also took it into his head
to make use of certain magical enchantments, by way of
learning what was to happen to him, but gained nothing
by his impious curiosity; for the near approach of Severus,
to whom all the towns had readily submitted, soon taught
him that a great deal more than his iniquitous sacrifices
was necessary to disarm those victorious legions, and that
if magical practices can hurt anybody, it is only those
who employ them. In this extremity he had a mind to
give up the empire to Pompeianus, son-in-law of Marcus
Aurelius, who was then at Terracina;[1] but that wise

---

[1] Pompeianus had a house at Terracina, whither he always retired
when any change happened at Court, or when he found it necessary to
screen himself against whatever attempts the Emperors might make to
destroy him. Pertinax offered him the empire, but he excused himself

senator, who looked upon this offer as a gift which it was
not in Julianus's power to make him a present of, returned him thanks very politely, but pleaded his usual
infirmities and excused himself. At last Julianus, being
quite at a loss what to do, and forsaken by all the world
(even the Prætorians who had elected him, upon
Severus's promising them that they should be forgiven,
provided they offered no opposition and delivered up the
murderers of Pertinax), retired, with Repentinus, his
son-in-law, into the palace, and there began to lament
and bewail his miserable condition.

In the meantime Messalla, who was consul, having
assembled the Senate in the Temple of Minerva, laid
before them the state of affairs. The death of Julianus
was the first matter discussed. Severus was declared
Emperor, and it was also resolved that Pertinax should
have divine honours. Two deputations, very different
from each other, were despatched. The most distinguished senators were sent to Severus to carry him the
imperial ornaments and invite him to Rome, to take
possession of the throne, which the Senate prayed him
to accept. At the same time others were despatched to
kill Julianus. They found him in the palace in a pitiable
condition, and endeavouring in vain to implore the

on account of his great age, and a disorder of the eyes, which, however, was reported to be only a pretended one; for, towards the end of
Commodus's reign, finding that that tyrant had put to death the most
illustrious of the senators, he was violently seized with the pain in his
eyes, and never appeared in the Senate; but as soon as Pertinax (whom
he knew to be a wise and good prince) was on the throne, he attended
the Senate as formerly, and had no further ailment. Again, when
Pertinax was massacred his pain returned, and he retired to Terracina,
where he was when Julianus sent for him to offer him the empire, but
his eyes would not permit him to accept it. This, nevertheless, would
not in all probability have been any hindrance to him if another
Pertinax had been elected.

clemency of Severus, to whom he offered to yield up the empire, desiring only that he might be allowed to live. The tribunes, without minding his expostulations, executed their orders and despatched him, the unhappy prince crying out all the while, "What harm have I done; have I put anybody to death?" Thus the unfortunate Julianus purchased, at the expense of his life, the pleasure of reigning two months.

The death of this poor Emperor occasioned, as may well be supposed, the most bitter affliction to Scantilla, his wife, and to Didia Clara, their daughter. We have seen that at their first entrance into the palace they had a sort of presentiment of what was to happen, and that they had the mortification of seeing it verified by the tragical end of this prince, which was entirely owing to their ambition and imprudent advice. They begged Severus to give them leave to bury him in the tomb of his ancestors. The new Emperor did not refuse them this request. He spared their lives, but deprived them of the sublime title of August, and took away from Didia Clara the patrimony that her father had settled upon her. Thus these two princesses, after enjoying for a very short time the shadow of empire, fell into their original obscurity. It seemed as if the highest rank in the universe had been lent them for two months, only that Fortune might have an opportunity of making them feel more sensibly the weight of their disgrace.

JULIA

WIFE OF SEVERUS

AND

PLAUTILLA

WIFE OF CARACALLA

ULIA, wife of Severus, was one of the Empresses who made most noise in the world. Her high position, gallantries, love of knowledge, and esteem for learned men, her troubles, and even her death, have made her name famous in history. Fortune raised her from a comparatively humble position to the first dignity of the world, and afterwards plunged her into the deepest afflictions; so that the different events of which her history is composed, the sorrows, anxieties and vexations that she suffered, the secret annoyances that agitated her heart under the appearance of grandeur and amidst all the pomp and splendour that surrounded her, have made even a heathen confess that there is no rank so elevated, no prosperity so complete, as to afford perfect happiness upon earth.

Julia Domna Pia was born at Emesa, a town in Phœnicia, daughter of Julia Soemias, and of Bassianus, priest of the sun, which the Phœnicians adored under the name

of Elagabalus. She had a sister called Julia Mæsa, who by her marriage with Julius Avitus, a native of Apamea, had two daughters, Soemias and Mamea; the eldest was mother of Avitus Bassianus, known afterwards by the name of Heliogabalus; and of Mamea, who was the youngest, was born Varius Alexianus, who was afterwards called Alexander Severus. Julia's family was not very illustrious, but the high rank to which this Syrian arrived made amends for any deficiency in point of descent. We shall see that these four women had no small share in the affairs of the empire, during the reigns of Severus, Caracalla, Macrinus, Heliogabalus and Alexander.

Julia was very beautiful, and by nature had the strongest inclination to make a bad use of her charms. Everybody who saw her was captivated by her, many found her far from cruel, and her licentious life sufficiently proves that beauty and discretion are not often to be met with in the same person. She had a most agreeable humour and ample wit, but was artful,[1] malicious, and full of dissimulation, as the Syrians generally are. She had a very fertile imagination, a wonderful facility in seeing through the most difficult affairs, and so true a judgment that, among a variety of sentiments and opinions, she seldom failed to choose the best; for which reason the Emperor Severus, who was well acquainted with his wife's unerring instinct, consulted her upon all important occasions, and was frequently guided by her counsels. Her judgment was very sound, she spoke with grace, and wrote elegantly; she was capable of managing the most intricate intrigues of the cabinet, so that it is

[1] Spart. in Carac.

generally believed that Caracalla had no minister or
Secretary of State who could better acquit himself in the
duties of his office than Julia his mother did, as long as
she managed affairs. She cultivated those rare talents
she had received from nature by a close application to
learning, philosophy, geometry, and all the sciences; she
also spent a large proportion of her time [1] in the useless
study of judicial astrology, and loved to be in the company of sophists and other learned men, whose conversation she much admired. Happy would it have been for
her if she had never desired any that was more dangerous; and if, whilst training her mind with philosophical
ideas and notions, she had also equipped her heart with
wise and useful maxims. But those grave and serious
occupations did not so entirely employ her thoughts as
to prevent her finding time to gratify inclinations that
were not so commendable. As, like the rest of her nation,
she was prodigiously fond of sports, shows, and all those
diversions that flatter the senses, she never appeared more
beautiful than upon those occasions, when she was sure
to make conquests. She was always then in high spirits,
full of life and vivacity, which could not fail to procure
her a crowd of lovers, who certainly did not amuse her
with philosophical topics alone. She was soon as skilled
in affairs of gallantry as in more serious matters, and,
suffering herself to be hurried on by her desires, she indulged herself in liberties that dishonoured her. This
charming Syrian was also as greedy of honours as of
pleasure, and her heart (softened as it was with luxury)
was fully as susceptible of ambition as of any other passion, which was fostered and fortified by the hopes [2] of

[1] Dio; Philostrat. vit. Apollon.　　[2] Spartian. in Sever.

that high and brilliant fortune which her horoscope had promised her.

Julia was in the height of her beauty when she left Phœnicia to display her charms at Rome. Whether it was that she had any particular business that obliged her to undertake that journey, or that, being elated with flattering hopes from her noble extraction, she did not think Emesa a town important enough to afford her opportunities of pushing her fortune, she repaired to the capital of the world, which she looked upon as the proper stage for her to appear on, in order to advance herself, which she thought could the more easily be brought about there because of the frequent changes and revolutions that happened in that city. She depended entirely on her beauty, and her own skill in managing it to the best advantage, together with the favourable predictions she had of her future grandeur; nor was she mistaken in her conjectures, for, soon after, she married Severus, whose birth and family we have already taken notice of, as also of the offices with which Marcus Aurelius had honoured him. He was tribune of the people when he married Marcia, of whose family and country we do not find that any certain account can be given; nor have we any proofs of either her virtue or of her husband's affection for her, except this, that, after he was become Emperor, he erected statues in honour of her memory long after her death. Severus had two daughters by her, both of whom (according to a modern author) were called Septimia, after their father. We shall see what was their destiny. Marcia died soon after Severus's return from Gaul, and it was not long before he had thoughts of a second marriage. He had, for a considerable time past, had certain presages [1] of the sovereign authority. These pleasing auguries flattered his ambition very agreeably, and, as he was not a man to neglect anything that could contribute to his advancement, he looked out for a wife who might enter into his pretensions and assist his projects. In order to find one fitted for his purpose he secretly consulted the astrologers about the persons who were proposed to him, and particularly whether they were destined to high advancement, for he had great faith in those fooleries and superstitions. He was told there was a Syrian woman concerning whom the most skilful augurs had foretold that whoever married her would one day be Emperor.

These lofty hopes and expectations Severus reckoned as the greatest merit in Julia, for, though her beauty was sufficient to captivate any heart, yet Severus laid much greater stress upon the extraordinary degree of power and authority he was to acquire by her means. The conformity there seemed to be between what was foretold of him and the predictions concerning Julia made him believe that they were marked out for each other, so that Severus's thoughts were from that time devoted to bringing about this marriage, for which purpose he set his friends to work, and they met with all the success they could desire. Severus had a very considerable reputation at Court, having received from the Emperor great marks of his esteem, for, though he had many faults, yet he was too cunning not to conceal them. So Julia, looking upon him as a man who could not fail of preferment, accepted his proposals. Their nuptials were celebrated in the Temple of Venus [2] near the palace, and the Em-

[1] Dio. lib. 77. Spart. in Sever. Xiphilin.   [2] Dio. lib. 74.

press Faustina, who must needs honour the ceremony with her presence, was so obliging as to cause an apartment to be prepared for them in the palace.

Amidst all his matrimonial pleasures Severus was not unmindful of his interests. He was persuaded that an idle, voluptuous life would conduct him neither to glory nor promotion, and that nothing less than an extraordinary reputation was capable of raising a man to offices of importance, so he was determined to lay hold of every opportunity of showing his talents. Marcus Aurelius, who set a great value upon him, made him Governor of Gaul, and he behaved there with so much moderation that he gained a wonderful hold upon the hearts and affections of the people. Julia, who accompanied her husband on his journey,[1] was brought to bed of a son at Lugdunum (Lyons), whom they called Bassianus, after his grandfather by the mother's side, and who was afterwards surnamed Caracalla. About two years after she bore another son at Rome, who was called Geta.

It is not necessary to mention here the troubles in which Rome was involved after the murder of Commodus, since we have already treated of those matters, as also of Severus's pretence for conducting to Rome the army that he commanded, and which had declared him Emperor. As soon as they were informed of his approach, the Senate (who out of complaisance to Julianus had declared him an enemy to the State, which had greatly offended him), being apprehensive that he would revenge the affront, were very desirous to make peace with him, and endeavoured by all the means they could think of to gain his goodwill. A hundred of the senators went to

---

[1] Aurel. Vict. Epit. Eutrop.

the camp to pay him their respects, and congratulate him upon his arrival in the name of the whole body. Severus declared that he was only come to revenge the murder of Pertinax, and as this was the honourable motive of his errand with which he concealed his ambition, he punished very rigorously all those who were concerned in that prince's death. He ordered the Prætorians to present themselves before him, not with their arms, but adorned with laurel branches, in the same manner as when they assisted at the shows or any public ceremony. He made them believe they were to take the oath of fidelity, and flattered them with fine promises. The Prætorians, not suspecting anything, made their appearance accordingly, unarmed and covered with laurel, as upon a day of rejoicing. But they were no sooner come into the presence of the Emperor, who was seated upon a throne, than, on a signal that had been agreed upon, they were surrounded by the soldiers of the army, who, turning towards them the points of their spears and javelins, put it out of their power to make the least defence. Then Severus, looking on them with an air of indignation, thus addressed them. "If I intended to chastise you in proportion to your crimes, I should be at a loss to find out a punishment rigorous enough. You have not been ashamed to dip your hands in the blood of that venerable old man and worthy Emperor, whom it was your duty to have defended at the expense of your lives; and the empire of the world, which our ancestors looked upon as the greatest reward of virtue and nobility, you have most scandalously put up to auction, as a thing of small value. But what further enhances your guilt is that, instead of maintaining Julianus in the supreme dignity which you were pleased to sell him, you have most perfidiously betrayed him. However (base and unworthy wretches as you are), it is not my intention to make you expiate by your death that of Pertinax, whom you brutally assassinated, but, on the other hand, I will not trust myself with soldiers who make nothing of perjury, and the most heinous crimes, whose swords are yet besmeared with the blood of their Emperor whom they have murdered. You shall be indebted to me for your lives, undeserving as you are to breathe the common air; but that you may everywhere carry about you the marks of that justice which I owe to the memory of Pertinax, I command my faithful soldiers to strip you instantly of every military ornament, which shall not any longer be dishonoured by you, and at the same time I charge you at your peril to be gone far from hence, and to suffer, in some distant place, the eternal shame of your infamous actions; and if any of you be ever found within a hundred thousand paces of Rome, I swear that you shall be put to death without mercy." This order was executed on the spot. These miserable assassins were immediately divested of all their military insignia, and banished in the most ignominious manner. Severus was received in Rome with great demonstrations of joy. His entry was as magnificent as the most superb triumph. The Romans, to show their satisfaction, wore white robes, and crowned themselves with flowers; the senators in their robes of ceremony saluted the Emperor at the gate of the city, and assured him of the sincerity of their vows for his prosperous reign. That day everything wore the look of joy and gladness, and nothing was to be seen in the streets but flowers, crowns of laurel, and fires, in which were consumed great quantities of perfumes in honour of the Emperor's arrival. Nothing was to be heard but shouts and acclamations. The people strove with one another who should shew the greatest marks of esteem and respect, and everybody was so desirous to see the Emperor that prodigious numbers climbed upon walls and other eminences to get a sight of him and hear him speak, as if Fortune had presented them with something quite new, and till then unheard of.

Severus went the next day to the Senate, and made a courteous speech, but a very artful one. He protested that he would never have consented to his election but in order to revenge the death of Pertinax, and to restore the ancient families to their former glory and splendour. That he would never put any senator to death except he were first condemned by the Senate; that he would not encourage or listen to informers; that in his manner of governing he would take Marcus Aurelius for a model, and that he would not only take the name of Pertinax, but also his character. These fair-sounding words were generally approved; but several of the old senators, who had been long acquainted with Severus, whispered that it would not be prudent to reckon too much upon the promises of an artful man, who had never kept his word any further than was consistent with his own interest. In the meantime, the Senate decreed to Severus all the honours that had been bestowed on preceding Emperors; nor was Julia forgotten. The Senate conferred upon her the title of August, together with that of Mother of the State and also of the Armies, and several others that flattery thought proper to invent. Then were the happy predictions accomplished. She saw herself exalted to that rank which her birth had given her hopes of, nor was she at all inclined to lose or waive any of her privileges, for elevation and prosperity did not fail to produce in her the ordinary effects,—pride and insolence. Intoxicated with her high fortune, she remembered no more by what steps she had climbed up to it. She treated with haughtiness, and even contempt, the greatest persons in the empire, and looked upon herself as infinitely superior to those who a little before were greatly above her.

Severus greatly endeared himself to the Romans, by procuring immortality to Pertinax, whose memory everybody had the greatest respect for, also by the sports and rejoicings that followed his entry into Rome. The marriage of the two princesses his daughters furnished him with another opportunity of diverting the people with games and shows. One of them he gave to Aetius, whom he made consul, and the other to the consul Probus, upon whom he would have conferred the government of the city, but he was politic enough to refuse it, for, the better to make his court to the Emperor, he alleged that he regarded the honour of being his son-in-law as infinitely above what that office could procure him. These nuptials were celebrated with all the pomp imaginable, for Severus omitted nothing that could possibly contribute to their magnificence, knowing how acceptable those sumptuous shows were to the people.

He heaped favours upon his two sons-in-law, made several very useful regulations, and having settled matters in Rome, set out for the East to fight Niger, who was so taken up with the luxuries of Antioch that he never dreamed of war. Severus's expedition was attended with all the success he could desire.[1] A bloody battle was fought in Cilicia, where Niger's troops were defeated, and he himself was forced to flee with precipitation; but that did not save him, for he was wounded near Cyzicus, by some of Severus's people, and was found half dead in a bog. In this condition he was brought before the conqueror, who immediately ordered his head to be struck off and sent to Rome.

The Emperor made a very cruel use of his victory, for he put to death most of the senators who had taken the part of Niger, and banished the rest. He punished rigorously those towns that had afforded him any assistance, or shown him any affection. Byzantium (now Constantinople) felt the fury of the soldiers and the resentment of Severus; and Emesa would have experienced the terrible effects of his indignation if the Empress Julia had not stood in the gap, and solicited pardon for her country. He caused Niger's wife and children to be put to death, and by this extreme severity made himself very odious; for which reason there was hardly anybody that did not desire Albinus for Emperor, because of his sweet disposition. It is even credibly reported that, during Severus's stay in the East, many of the most illustrious senators wrote to Albinus and entreated him to come to Rome.[2] Severus being informed of this, conceived a mortal hatred against Albinus, and endeavoured to get rid of him by all manner of base and treacherous means; but these only turning to his own confusion, he declared war against him without further ceremony, being persuaded thereto by Julia. This princess, perceiving that Albinus was much more beloved

---

[1] Herodian. Spartian.   [2] Capitolin. in Albin.

than Severus, and that the number of his well-wishers would prodigiously increase if he had time to make friends and the necessary preparations, induced her husband to break with him and march against him. She met with no great difficulty in making the Emperor (over whom she had acquired an absolute power) do whatever she had a mind to. At the first sign of the war nothing was to be seen in the empire but troubles, cabals, and factions. Foreign princes, distant towns, and even the senators espoused the interests, some of Albinus and others of Severus; so that the people, being fatigued with these disputes, which exhausted both their blood and treasure, declared openly that they were quite weary of them. Besides this, there happened a sort of prodigy that filled people's minds with fear and superstition; [1] a kind of fire appeared in the air, so bright and flaming, that they were afraid the city was going to be reduced to ashes. But soon after, they were agreeably relieved from this apprehension, when they perceived a small shower like dew falling, which seemed white like silver. In fact, some having taken it in their heads to wash pieces of brass with this water, it gave them the colour of silver; but this whiteness disappeared in a little time, and the pieces remained brass as before.

The issue of this war was not favourable to Albinus; he was beaten near Lugdunum, and his defeat secured the empire to Severus. Never was a conqueror more brutally cruel; he cut off Albinus's head and sent it to Rome; he put to death the wife and children of his enemy, and fell with unparalleled cruelty upon all his adherents, and after having shed their blood confiscated

[1] Dio. lib. 75.

their estates. His revenge extended afterwards to Rome, where he caused the strictest search to be made after all those of Albinus's party, and under pretence of punishing them, he seized upon their possessions, and filled his coffers with their riches. Nothing took place in the city but accusations, executions, and funerals. The noblest of the senators—men who had been consuls and Roman knights—forfeited, for supposed crimes, not only their lives, but also their fortunes, which Severus immediately took possession of, for his covetousness was equal to his cruelty. Never had there been an Emperor so greedy of money. The vast treasures that he heaped up only served to whet his appetite, and make him still desire more. He exacted with the utmost severity the usual taxes, and invented new ones, for fear, said he, of some unforeseen accident, thus making his insatiable covetousness pass for wise precaution: so that his thirst after money was as fatal to Rome as the most cruel war.

It is astonishing that a prince of such a temper and so inflexible in his resentment should be so insensible to his wife's gallantries, who indulged without reserve those appetites that highly dishonoured both the Emperor and herself; for Severus could not be ignorant that the Empress did not scruple to abandon herself to her shameful pleasures, which were known to all. Severus, however so cruel to all the rest of the world, carried his complaisance for her to such a degree that he appeared ignorant of those prostitutions which he ought to have chastised. She was so artful that, by her insinuating and well-timed caresses, she could calm him in the midst of his fury, and manage him as she thought proper. In fact, she was so confident of the power she had over him that,

if some historians are to be credited, she was not afraid
of entering into a conspiracy against him, being well
assured that she would be able to extricate herself from
the consequences in case it should be discovered, as indeed
it happened; for, in spite of certain knowledge he had
that his wife was privy to the plot, he showed her the
greatest marks of kindness and affection, and treated her
as if she had been the best wife in the world. This appeared upon the following occasion. Severus, being one
day so very desirous to know who was to succeed him
that it made a strong impression on his mind, dreamed
that a person called Antoninus would reign after him;
and so, taking it for granted that this was an infallible
prediction, he brought his son Bassianus, who was his
favourite, into the camp, and gave him [1] the name of
Marcus Aurelius Antoninus, in the presence of all the
legions.

Julia, who loved Geta, the younger of her two sons,
much more than Bassianus, the elder, represented to him
that by having given Bassianus only the surname of
Antoninus, which was a presage of the empire, he seemed
to exclude his second son from that dignity. Severus,
finding that the Empress was desirous that Geta should
have the same chance as his brother, was unable to
refuse her that satisfaction, and though the dream only
called upon one Antoninus to be Emperor, Julia's will
prevailed over that of the gods, so great was the Emperor's complaisance for her. He did not carry it so
far in regard to his sister. She had quitted Leptis, the
place of her birth, and came to Rome, bringing with her
a son that she had. The Court showed her all possible

[1] Spart. in Sev. in Get.

honour and respect, for her being so nearly related to the Emperor procured her the homage of all people of quality and distinction; but all this was to be attributed to courtesy and politeness, not to her merit, for her coarse and rustic air, together with her not being able to express herself in Latin except in a ridiculous manner, instead of bespeaking the favour of the people, had a contrary effect, and furnished sufficient matter for raillery and laughter. Severus, who saw nothing agreeable in his sister, was ashamed of her, and annoyed at her arrival, for which reason he made them some presents and sent them both back again to Leptis.

About the same time Mæsa, sister to the Empress, also arrived at Rome, and brought thither her two daughters, Soemias and Mamea. They met with a kinder reception and more courteous treatment than the Emperor's sister, and, to tell the truth, they were of quite different characters.[1] Mæsa was a lady of infinite merit, prudent and virtuous beyond the reach of calumny—of a genius capable of penetrating the most intricate sciences. Never was there a woman who better understood the practice or constitution, as one may say, of the Court. She was as skilful at concealing her own sentiments as at penetrating those of others, and knew how to make all events turn to her advantage. It was evident that the elevation of Heliogabalus, and afterwards of Alexander, her grandsons, to the throne, was due to her policy and courage. She acquired in Severus's Court such experience in politics as stood her in good stead afterwards. She lived in the strictest intimacy and friendship with Julia, very cunningly shutting her eyes against the notori-

[1] Herodian. Lamprid. Spartianus.

ous irregularities of her sister, while she carefully avoided making herself disagreeable by reproaches and remonstrances, which never fail to give offence. She always showed the greatest deference and respect to Severus, for which reason he was very fond of her, and so complaisant that she could do almost what she pleased with him, and as she was extremely clever at foreseeing events long before they happened, she employed her great influence and favour with the Emperor to amass great sums of money, which she knew would one day do her good service.

Mæsa was a widow when she quitted Syria for Rome; she brought up her daughters in the maxims of the Court, and took care to instil into their minds the principles of her own policy. Her endeavours were not thrown away, for we shall see in the sequel that they knew how to make the most of their mother's lessons. These princesses did not always remain at Rome; they accompanied the Empress in all Severus's journeys, who was frequently at war with barbarous nations, being desirous to signalise himself by exploits less odious than those he had performed against his fellow-citizens. His arms were generally successful, but the town of Atra in Arabia put a stop to his progress, for, after he had made inconceivable efforts to take it, he was to his disgrace obliged to raise the siege. He there had the mortification of seeing a considerable part of his army perish and his laurels withered by a turn of fortune which grieved him beyond measure.

This put him into so ill a humour that Crispus, tribune of his guards, fell a victim to his rage upon this occasion, and forfeited his life for having repeated some verses that seemed to reproach the Emperor with the blood of so many soldiers and brave officers whom he had sacrificed to his caprice and ambition, especially by his obstinacy in attempting to take Atra.

We shall not trouble ourselves to follow Severus in all his voyages and travels to the East and into Britain, but will rather examine and give an account of what took place in his own family, about which he seemed so indifferent himself. While he, being hurried away by his ambition, was taken up in pursuing his Eastern conquests, his wife Julia was dishonouring him by her prostitutions, and his children by her debaucheries; being at last informed of this, he resolved to make their education the principal object of his care. Caracalla was then but fourteen years of age, and his brother some years younger. The Emperor took them, and their mother with them, into the East, to wean them if possible from the pleasures of Rome, and to get them out of the way of being corrupted by those insidious and dangerous flatterers who never fail to make a fatal impression upon young and tender minds. But, by the bloody executions which he carried out daily, he rather gave them lessons and examples of cruelty, which operated but too strongly upon Caracalla, who was by nature inclined to that as well as all other vices. The viciousness of his temper did not, however, appear while he was a child; on the contrary, he seemed to be very affable, good-natured, and inclined to good actions, which perhaps might have been due to his having been educated by Proculus, who professed the Christian religion, and was greatly esteemed by Severus. But flattery, pleasures, and bad examples soon got the better of Proculus's endeavours, and, not-

withstanding all the care and trouble he took to inspire
him with noble inclinations, he had no other sentiments
than such as were depraved and vitiated. Geta's education, on the contrary, was more powerful than nature,[1]
for in his childhood he exhibited something very rude
and indocile in his manner, and was much inclined to
sensuality and covetousness, but all his failings vanished
as he grew riper. He became humane, polite, and accomplished, free, and easy of access,[2] entertained his friends
cheerfully and agreeably, the nobles with affability, and
men of learning with great marks of esteem. Upon all
occasions he gave proofs of his mild and gentle disposition, and when he was but ten years old he interceded
with his father, as much as he possibly could, on behalf
of those who had taken part with Niger and Albinus,
being always inclined to commiserate the unfortunate.
From the difference of temper in these two brothers proceeded that antipathy they always had to each other;
one affected to blame what the other approved, and those
whom Geta loved the other was sure to hate. The
flatterers that were about them made it their business to
nourish and promote this disagreement by their poisonous
reports; for, on pretense of being devoted to the interests
of these princes, they never ceased to animate them
against each other.

Geta was the Empress's favourite, for, besides that he
was the handsomer of the two, she found him much more
dutiful and complaisant. She dreaded the furious and
violent temper of Caracalla, and clearly saw that Geta
was infinitely more beloved by the Romans than his
brother. She, however, did all that lay in her power

[1] Tertullian ad. Scapulam c. 4. [2] Herodian. lib. 4.

to make them live on good terms; the Emperor also took a great deal of pains with the eldest to reform him, and, as marriage has been always reckoned the best restraint against the impetuosities of youth, he formed the design of marrying him to Plautilla, daughter of Plautianus, his favourite, who was one of the mainstays of the government, during all the time that he continued in favour, and was a conspicuous example of the instability of fortune after his disgrace.

Plautianus was a native of Africa, of very obscure birth. His youth had been sullied by many crimes [1] for which he was banished his country, and he afterwards insinuated himself into the good graces of Severus by another crime, for which he deserved to have been rigorously punished. [2] He acquired such great favour and influence with this Emperor, and became so powerful that the lives and fortunes of the Romans were at his disposal. Severus made him a senator, and at the same time gave him other offices that till then had been incompatible with the former dignity. He heaped riches upon him, and gave him all the opportunities he could desire of acquiring more. This encouraged him to commit horrible cruelties and acts of injustice. Fortune did in his case what she generally does in the case of those whom she raises from nothing to great honour; she made him insolent, and being quite intoxicated with his grandeur and authority, he looked upon himself as vastly superior to the rest of mankind. When he passed through the streets the great number of domestics that preceded him obliged all those they met either to turn

[1] Herodian. lib. 3.
[2] Ut vero alii affirmant, flore magis ætatis per stuprum conciliatus.

aside or to cast their eyes downward, that they might not presume to look at him, as being unworthy of so great an honour. Never was there seen such excessive pride, for everybody prostrated themselves before this idol of the Court. Nothing was to be seen but statues of the most sumptuous materials erected in honour of him, and nobody swore but by his Fortune; public prayers were composed for his preservation and prosperity, though the people would have rejoiced if he had been annihilated, for they were never fond of excessive power, and Plauti- anus's was the more detested because to him were at- tributed all the cruelties of Severus, who was never weary of shedding the blood of the most illustrious citizens. Thus this minister was at last as much hated as the Emperor, and more feared than he.

Though Severus was very jealous of his authority, yet he could tolerate that this insolent and overgrown favourite should assume so extraordinary a degree of power, and was so infatuated with him that he was desirous to have him for his successor; [1] so it became a common saying that the sky would fall sooner than that Severus could ever be unkind to Plautianus. Julia, for her part, could not bear that Plautianus should enjoy this monstrous and excessive power, for, accustomed as she was to treat people of the highest rank and distinction in the empire with haughtiness, it was intolerable to her to yield to one so infinitely beneath her, and to see a man who had risen from nothing dispose of everything accord- ing to his absolute will and pleasure. She did not fail to put in practice all her art to undermine him, if possible, but in vain. Plautianus—who did not love the Empress,

---

[1] Dio. lib. 76

because he knew she hated him—parried her strokes and turned them against herself, for, as he knew his own strength, he undertook to accuse Julia of all her intrigues, and had the boldness to assure the Emperor that he could prove his assertion. Severus very carefully suffered his favourite to attack the Empress's honour by these accusations, and was a quiet spectator of his insolence, without endeavouring to silence him. It is not unlikely that he was very glad of Julia being thus mortified, and secretly rejoiced at her suffering from Plautianus the reproaches she so justly deserved, and which he had not courage to address to her himself. Be that as it may, Julia had the vexation to see that the Emperor sacrificed her to Plautianus's revenge, and found by experience that nothing was to be got by contending with a favourite who was so firmly rooted in the Emperor's affections. From that time she ceased to give herself any trouble about State affairs, and devoted herself solely to the study of philosophy, so that, instead of those flattering courtiers with whom she used to be surrounded, she admitted none but sophists and learned men, and passed her time in disputing with them, more for amusement and to dissipate her vexation than to display her knowledge, though few had a greater share of it. Among the philosophers who had free access to her, none was more remarkable than Philostratus. He was a professor of rhetoric, and had published a famous book entitled "The Lives of the Sophists," which he dedicated to the Emperor Severus. Julia honoured him with her particular esteem, made him her secretary, and engaged him to write the life of Apollonius, for the Empress, having read the history of that celebrated magician which Damis, a great friend of the impostor, had composed, and not thinking it done as correctly as it should be, entreated Philostratus to undertake it.

Plautianus's triumph over Julia could not but add greatly to his pride and insolence, for, meeting with no obstacles in his way, and having undoubted proof of the absolute power he had acquired over the Emperor, he carried his views further still, and imagined there was nothing he might not attempt. Then it was that he threw off entirely the mask, and appeared in his proper colours. He gave himself up to the most infamous vices, even such as were contrary to nature; and at the same time that he indulged himself in all sorts of abominations he took it into his head to be excessively jealous of his wife, and could not endure that she should take the most innocent liberties. In his own family he was severe and tyrannical, prohibiting every diversion or amusement, and carried his ill-nature to his wife so far as not to permit her to pay the visits that courtesy required, nor so much as to speak to the Emperor or Empress.

About that time a comet happened to appear which caused great speculation, as the most trifling thing did among the superstitious heathens. People would needs have this to be a prodigy that foretold some great event, but few imagined that the ruin of Plautianus was threatened; for the Emperor himself acknowledged that he did not believe it was possible he could ever be prevailed upon to hurt him. Plautianus was not ignorant of this: he knew his own power, and made a very bad use of it; for being intoxicated with his ambition, he thought of nothing but how to raise himself still higher, and humble everybody else. The more favours the Emperor granted him, the more he asked, but he worked only for himself, and did not think it necessary to make friends. One seldom meets with generosity in upstarts of this kind, their extraction and their sentiments being generally of a piece, while everything in them shows the baseness of their origin. Plautianus, amidst all his grandeur, could not help reflecting very often upon the obscurity of his own birth, not by way of becoming more humble and modest, but in order to obliterate it by some splendid alliance. There was no lack of illustrious families in Rome, but none of them were great enough for his vanity, nor seemed fitted to carry into execution his exalted schemes. None less than members of the Imperial family were sufficient for his purpose; for, feeding his imagination upon the most flattering and pleasing hopes, he did not doubt but his fortune would be so firmly established, if a great match of that sort could be brought about, that he would not only have nothing to apprehend in regard to his present grandeur and power, but would have opportunities of carrying out even loftier designs.

This ambitious scheme being thus decided upon, he only waited for a proper time to propose it to the Emperor, intending, as soon as he could conveniently do so, to recommend his daughter Plautilla to be married to Caracalla the Emperor's son. Severus himself furnished him with an opportunity; for, having resolved to procure a wife for his son, as we have observed, he communicated his desire to his favourite Plautianus, who did not fail to make use of all his power and interest to persuade the Emperor to approve of the above-mentioned match. The Emperor, who was unable to refuse him anything he asked, consented immediately, and informed Caracalla of this resolution.

Plautilla was very handsome,[1] but not agreeable in temper and manners; for, as pride and great fortune are generally inseparable, she had acquired a certain haughty air that was not at all pleasing, especially to Caracalla, who hated Plautianus, and everything belonging to him, because of his excessive power and insolent behaviour. It does not appear that Julia was consulted in this affair, but in all probability it would not have been conformable to her inclinations, for it is not reasonable to suppose that she could ever have approved of a match between her son and the daughter of her mortal enemy, who had nothing but her fortune to recommend her; while at the same time, he had all the illustrious families of the empire to choose from, and might have selected some lady to whom Plautilla could not be compared for beauty and merit.[2] Caracalla received his father's commands with a pretended obedience and respect, but with a very grave and discontented countenance, which notwithstanding did not make Severus alter his mind; thus Caracalla became Plautianus's son-in-law by marrying his daughter.[3]

These nuptials were celebrated at a happy conjuncture, for the Emperor was just returned from the East, covered with laurels which he had gathered there in his successful wars against the Parthians, and bringing with him a prodigious number of captives. His triumph and the marriage of his son were a double motive for the magnificent presents that he made the Prætorians and the people. To these liberalities he added all the usual diversions, such as sports, races, and shows. The re-

[1] Tristan. Comment, Histor.   [2] Dio. lib. 76.   [3] Herod. lib. 3. c. 35.

joicings lasted many days, and Plautianus contributed largely to their splendour and magnificence. He entertained the people with several wild beast shows, and regaled the senators with a most noble banquet; but it was not observed without the greatest indignation, that in order to give his daughter a magnificent retinue and a melodious band of musicians, he caused a great many to be made eunuchs on purpose, which was a cruelty unheard of in Rome;[1] he further chose for that purpose the children of very considerable families, and even selected some married men—a novelty that was no less a mark of his insolence than of his brutal disposition.

The new princess brought by way of dowry immense sums of money to her husband. It is asserted that there was enough of it to have married fifty Queens; it was all carried into the palace, and the people passing through the streets saw those monstrous heaps of gold and silver, which they looked upon as spoils taken from them, and the fruits of Plautianus's rapine and plunder.

As for Caracalla, he did not show, amidst all these rejoicings, a satisfied and contented countenance, for, as he had been compelled to marry Plautilla quite contrary to his inclinations, he plainly discovered that his heart had not been at all consulted in the affair, and that his compliance with his father's will was extremely distasteful to him, for which reason he lived, even at first, upon a very indifferent footing with her, but this soon after degenerated into a downright aversion, by reason of her proud and haughty behaviour, as well as her peevish and restless temper. For, after she became wife to the presumptive heir to the empire, she grew daily more imperi-

[1] Dio. lib. 76.

ous, and claimed to govern Caracalla as his father was governed by hers. Whatever he said or did incurred her censure, for she took upon her to control all his actions and conduct, and blamed them in terms so provoking as vexed him beyond measure, for he was not naturally of a very patient disposition. These disputes,[1] reproaches, and complaints increased more and more the weight of his matrimonial chains, and consequently, his hatred of his wife. She became the most disagreeable object in his sight, and her presence so insupportable that he ordered a separate apartment for himself. In short, matters came to such a pass that, in the course of the violent and furious quarrels they had together, he often threatened that, as soon as the Emperor died, both she and her father should perish together.

This alarmed Plautilla; for, as she had had time and opportunity to study her husband, and became well acquainted with his disposition, she knew him to be a man capable of keeping his word, which furnished her with matter for very serious and melancholy reflections. The miserable condition of several of the earlier Empresses extremely agitated her mind, and filled her with frightful apprehensions. In this perplexity she went to pour out her grief and tears in the bosom of her father, to whom she communicated all her terrors and afflictions.

Thus those favourites of Fortune, who, to disguise the lowness of their extraction, purchase great alliances, only procure for their daughters intolerable slavery, and sacrifice their peace and happiness to their own restless ambition; for the man who sighs more after the dowry than the lady, has, generally speaking, nothing but con-

[1] Herodian. lib. 3.

tempt for his wife, as soon as he has got possession of her riches.

Caracalla's threats and treatment of Plautilla exasperated Plautianus exceedingly, but at the same time greatly alarmed him; for he considered that in all probability the young prince would soon have it in his power to execute his intentions. He saw the danger he was in, and could think of no way to prevent it but by seizing the throne. The undertaking was difficult and hazardous, but he found it absolutely necessary, and thought it worth his while to make a bold and desperate attempt, when a throne was to be acquired and at the same time his life and treasures secured. In the meantime a thousand obstacles presented themselves to his imagination, and made him hesitate what to do on this important occasion. His enterprise was no less than that of hurling Severus from the throne, assassinating the Emperor and his children, and seizing the supreme power. To do this he must first make himself master of the palace, cut the throats of all the guards or corrupt them, have a sufficient body of troops at his command, and be well assured that the army would all this time remain quiet spectators of the whole scene. He had to form a party whose fidelity he could depend upon, and associate with him in this design people who were capable of supporting him. In a word, he had to overthrow the whole State, which in the present condition of things was no easy matter to do. In this anxiety of mind, and amidst these bitter reflections, he was so agitated between hopes and fears that he was observed to be pale and trembling, and it was easy enough to read in his countenance the vexation of his heart;[1] so that Plautianus was a prey to terrible alarms and the most cruel perplexities.

Just at the time when Plautianus was meditating this great stroke, Mount Vesuvius vomited an extraordinary quantity of fire, and with so much noise and roaring that it was distinctly heard at Capua. This, according to the ideas of those superstitious times, was looked upon as the forerunner of some great change, and Plautianus's ruin soon after verified this conjecture.

Geta, the Emperor's brother, being very ill, and finding himself near his end, sent for his brother, and talked to him with the freedom of a man who, having nothing more to fear, speaks his mind without artifice or disguise. He represented to him the great danger of giving Plautianus so excessive a power, which he might make use of against his benefactor; disclosed to him all the pernicious designs and projects of that ambitious man; told him that, in raising his favourite to such a height, he was acting quite contrary to his own interests and those of his family; that, by the excessive honours which he had heaped upon him, he only spurred him on the more to gratify, if possible, his insatiable desire of power and riches; and, in short, convinced the Emperor that, in his conduct toward that haughty minister, he had shown an unpardonable stupidity and want of discretion. Severus, who in the main was a person of good sense, found his brother's reasoning to be so much the more solid and judicious as he had himself made some serious reflections upon the too extensive authority he had suffered Plautianus to assume by degrees. He was displeased at the great number of statues which he had

[1] Dio. lib. 62.

observed to be erected at Rome and in the provinces in honour of his favourite,[1] some of which were placed among those of the Emperor's family and nearest relations, as if he had been their equal. From that time he resolved to humble him, and show him less regard than he had hitherto done. This coldness of the Emperor had a speedy effect upon the proud and surly minister. He became somewhat more tractable, but was not at all discouraged, not doubting but he should soon find the way back to his master's affections. He looked upon this alteration in the Emperor's behaviour as due to some ill turn done him by Caracalla, who, he knew, had frequently made his grandeur, riches and authority, the subject of conversation with his father, and took every opportunity of setting the Emperor against him. Plautianus, on the other hand, strictly observed the conduct of his son-in-law, and kept a sort of register of all he did, which he reported to the Emperor, and did not fail to put the worst construction upon everything, without considering that, by endeavouring to hurt the prince, he only hastened his own destruction; for Caracalla, who was informed of all this, hated him so much the more, and laboured the more zealously to compass his ruin.

Plautianus made no question but his death was the aim of Caracalla, and the object of all his intrigues. The prince's hatred of him was too obvious to leave any room for uncertainty, and this caused him the greatest apprehension; for, whatever friendship the Emperor had hitherto shown him, he could not flatter himself with the hopes of its continuing, especially since he now no longer received those tokens of it which the Emperor had been

[1] Spartian. in. Sever.

always so lavish of with regard to him. On the contrary, he could not but look upon this change in the Emperor's behaviour as the beginning of his disgrace, and the fore-runner of his misfortunes. The affliction of his daughter, together with her husband's threats, with which she had just acquainted him, greatly augmented his fears; every-thing, in short, gave him warning of his danger, and showed him plainly that he was on the brink of destruc-tion. Full of these melancholy thoughts, he considered what measures to take, and how he should avoid his im-pending ruin; but the means he had recourse to had an effect quite opposite to what he intended, and proved fatal to him, for, having determined to massacre the Emperor and the prince, he went to work the wrong way, and so fell a victim to his ill-concerted scheme. In order to perpetrate this horrid crime, he addressed himself to Saturninus, a centurion in the Prætorian Guards, who upon every occasion had shown a particular devotion to his interests. He sent for him one evening into his chamber, and, having caused everybody to retire, "It is now time," said he,[1] "that you should give me the strongest proof of that zeal and friendship you have always professed for me, and that you should receive such a substantial token of my gratitude as shall be pro-portionate to the important service I expect from your affection. It is in your power to raise me to the throne, or, rather, you have an opportunity of sharing the sov-ereign power with me. In labouring to advance my fortune you promote your own. It is a question of de-priving Severus of the throne, and of getting rid of Cara-calla, who is ready to ascend it. Do not let this proposal

[1] Herodian. lib. 3.

terrify you; the enterprise, no doubt, appears difficult, but when it is maturely considered it will be found to be not only practicable, but easy. You know that nobody is permitted to enter the Emperor's chamber but the officer of the guard, and it happens very opportunely that you are in waiting. There is no difficulty in the matter, for you have nothing to do but to make use of your privilege; you have free access to the Emperor's room, and also to that of Caracalla; you may plunge your dagger into them both without meeting with the least obstacle. I need not tell you that there is not a moment to be lost, for we can never have a better opportunity. Go directly to the palace, as if you had some affair of importance to communicate to the Emperor from me, and despatch both him and his son. This generous action will exalt you to the post I now hold, for, if you share with me the danger of this undertaking, it is but reasonable that you should divide the spoils with me. But I must at the same time inform you that of necessity you must decide upon one or other of these two things: you must either prepare to take away the Emperor's life or to lose your own; for, in short, my interest absolutely requires that I should not leave you in a condition to abuse the confidence I place in you, by revealing the important secret I have now confided to you."

This discourse filled Saturninus with horror; but as he was extremely cunning, he did not appear to hesitate a moment between his duty to Severus and the magnificent rewards that Plautianus offered him. He was convinced that, if he showed any scruples, Plautianus would think nothing of putting him to death, even by accusing him of the very crime which he refused to commit; he accordingly pretended to enter very readily into this project, begged Plautianus to give him instructions in writing, and, in order to convince him that he looked upon the affair as settled, he prostrated himself before him, and saluted him as Emperor. This afforded Plautianus infinite delight; he was rejoiced at having found a man so well fitted for his purpose, and gave him the writing he desired, without reflecting that, in case his enterprise should not succeed, he was leaving in Saturninus's hands a decisive and incontestable proof of his crime; but he was so blinded with his ambition that he did not consider the fatal consequences his imprudence might be attended with. He, therefore, immediately dismissed Saturninus, and charged him, as soon as he had massacred the Emperor and his son, to inform him without delay, that he might lose no time in seizing the palace before the Emperor's death should be known.

Matters being thus arranged, Saturninus hastened to the palace with the order Plautianus had given him, but fully determined to make a very different use of it from what the minister intended. He sent the Emperor word that he had a secret of the greatest consequence to impart to him, and being immediately admitted into his chamber, " I am sent by Plautianus," said he, with tears in his eyes, " to kill you; but, contrary to his intentions, I come to save your life. Your favourite, having most ungratefully resolved to possess himself of your throne, has commanded me to put you and your son to death. It is probable that you would not easily be brought to believe him capable of so much perfidy, if I did not bring ample evidence to prove my assertion. By this written order you will see whether I speak truth. I pretended to accept this commission very willingly, for fear some less faithful officer should undertake it without scruple or difficulty."

The great regard that Severus always had for Plautianus pleaded very strongly in his behalf against Saturninus's accusation. He was inclined to believe that this pretended conspiracy was the effect of Caracalla's malice, who, he imagined, had a mind to ruin the favourite. He felt so convinced of this that he immediately sent for his son, and reproached him with the base artifice he had made use of to destroy one who was so useful to him, and whom he honoured with his affection. It was useless for the prince to protest he was innocent, for the Emperor pronounced him guilty. Saturninus, seeing that the Emperor obstinately refused to be convinced, notwithstanding the proofs he had given him that it was really as he had affirmed, began to be terribly alarmed, not doubting but the storm would fall upon his own head, if he should be so unfortunate as not to convict the criminal. He then addressed the Emperor thus: "What clearer demonstration can you desire of Plautianus's treason than his own handwriting, together with his seal? But if that be not sufficient, give me leave to send one of my soldiers to Plautianus to inform him that his orders have been executed, and you will see him come immediately to take possession of the palace and throne, which must put the matter beyond all doubt or question."

It happened just as Saturninus had said. Plautianus was no sooner informed by the soldier that the business was done than, abandoning himself to the flattering hopes of reigning, he fancied he was already on the throne. He put on his armour with all possible speed under his robe, and made what haste he could to the palace, which he entered without meeting with the least resistance. As soon as Saturninus saw him, he paid him the respect due to the Emperor, and taking him by the hand, conducted him into the chamber, where, he told him, the bodies of the two princes were weltering in their blood. The first object that presented itself to his view was the Emperor and Caracalla, both alive and well. Nothing more was necessary to show him that he was betrayed. Severus [1] reproached him with his ingratitude and the enormity of his crime in attempting the life of the benefactor who had heaped riches and honours upon him, and given him so many marks of his confidence and affection. Plautianus was at first greatly confused, but soon recovering himself he put on a bold and impudent countenance, and told the Emperor that if anybody had accused him of so black a treason it was a false and scandalous aspersion, maliciously invented to ruin him. He then went on to complain of this horrid plot, as he called it, with such an air of innocence, ingenuousness, and resolution that Severus began to be moved, and did not know what to think, but unluckily for Plautianus it was by some accident discovered that he had on his armour. Caracalla, pointing this out to the Emperor, said to his father-in-law, " What, you come to the palace at an unseasonable hour without being sent for, you wear a breastplate under your robe, and all this without any design? Do people arm themselves with so much precaution to go to supper? " And at that instant, without giving him time to answer, he took his sword from him, gave him a blow on the face, and would have killed him on the spot if the Emperor had not hindered him. The unfortunate minister was,

[1] Herodian. lib. 3.

however, soon put out of pain, for the Emperor ordered him to be killed directly in his presence.[1]

All this while the Princess Plautilla was with the Empress Julia in her apartment, not dreaming of her father's misfortune, but an officer went and informed her of it, and in the most brutal manner. Entering the chamber unceremoniously, " See here," said he, " a part of your father," at the same time throwing at her a handful of Plautianus's beard that he had plucked off his face. These words pierced her heart, for with her father she lost her only support, and was left exposed to the barbarous persecutions of a tyrannical husband, Plautianus being the only person who could check the furious and violent temper of Caracalla. She shed floods of tears, and her affliction was the more bitter as nobody took any pains to mitigate it, for the Empress, instead of endeavouring to comfort her and sympathise with her in her sorrow, gave full vent to her joy. She could not forbear expressing her satisfaction at the death of Plautianus, in spite of the reasons she had to conceal it, in accordance with all the rules of decency and good manners; but she had suffered too much from the insolence of that haughty favourite to dissemble the pleasure which the news of his death afforded her. Plautilla had but too much reason to dread the consequences of this tragical affair, for the prince, being no longer withheld by the fear of his father-in-law, appeared in his natural colours, and showed his brutal disposition with so little restraint that he became the terror of all the city.

His wife Plautilla was the first to experience the terrible effects of his vengeance, for, as he had only

[1] Herodian. lib. 3. Dio. lib. 76.

married her in pursuance of his father's commands, he was resolved to make her suffer for the constraint that had been put upon him. Sometimes he would reproach her [1] with her father's misfortune, and heap the most insulting language upon her, and at other times would assiduously look out for opportunities of mortifying and vexing her; at last he became so cruel that it was not his fault that she did not perish miserably.

Whether Severus had still some remains of compassion for the family of Plautianus whom he had so much loved, or that for decency's sake he would not quite desert Plautilla, and abandon her to her husband's ill humour and resentment, he contented himself with banishing her to the island of Lipari, together with a son she had, where these illustrious exiles lingered out a wretched life in continual apprehension of a violent and untimely end. They were not only refused the means to enable them to live in any way suitable to their rank, but were denied even common necessaries.

The death of Plautianus delivered the two princes, Caracalla and Geta, from a disagreeable spy upon their actions, but it furnished them with an unhappy opportunity of abandoning themselves to all manner of excess and debauchery; for they were now no longer in awe of that minister, who used to reprimand them without ceremony. In vain did Severus employ remonstrances and threats, for the poisonous insinuations of flatterers were greedily listened to, whilst the irksome advice of their father was held in the utmost contempt; so that these two brothers, so different in their tempers, so inveterate against each other, so divided in their opinions, and born

[1] Herodian. lib. 3.

with inclinations so opposite, agreed perfectly in everything that was bad, and joined in the same crimes.

The Emperor being no longer governed by Plautianus, undertook to reform several abuses, for which purpose he made use of Papinianus, cousin of the Empress, and a famous advocate. He gave him very important posts, which this worthy man filled with great credit; so that upon this occasion merit was justly rewarded,—a thing which rarely occurs. Severus, at the instigation of Papinianus, made a number of salutary and judicious laws; but at the same time it must be confessed that those ordinances, so admirable in intention, became inhuman by the severity with which they were put into force; for the Emperor, being hurried away by his natural sternness, caused them to be carried out with inexorable cruelty. He prosecuted and punished robbers without the least mercy, not considering that his own insatiable avarice made him infinitely more guilty than those he put to death with so little compassion. He issued terrible edicts against adulterers (of whom, Dion says, there were a great many thousands convicted after a strict investigation), and at the same time neglected to restrain his sons, who filled Rome with their debaucheries. Those of the Empress Julia were even more scandalous; and, if the historians have not given us a special list of her crimes, they have at least said enough to convince us that she led an abominable life, and that it was not necessary to enter into details of them. Severus, however, who was so severe against women in general, treated his own wife with an indulgence that dishonoured him. He was jealous to avenge other men in that respect, but permitted his own wife to be as unfaithful to him as she pleased, which encouraged her to continue in her immorality. Thus the Emperor, who knew so well how to rule the State,[1] was quite ignorant how to manage his own family. He was so careful in reforming the conduct of others that he neglected the behaviour of his own wife and children. He could not, for all that, plead that he was unacquainted with these things, for he was but too frequently a witness of them, especially of the implacable hatred of his sons for each other; their quarrels caused him much trouble and vexation, but he had not the secret of preventing them, nor of influencing their behaviour. He attempted this, by taking them away from Rome, where the sycophants, with whom they were surrounded, were perpetually corrupting and setting them at variance. With this view he took them with him to Britain, whither he was obliged to go to quell the barbarians, who terribly ravaged that province. The Empress Julia and her sister Mæsa accompanied the Emperor on this journey. He was very successful in this war, and destroyed above fifty thousand of the barbarians. He penetrated into the heart of Caledonia, and obliged the enemy to come to terms; or rather, he granted them peace upon such conditions as he thought fit.

Julia received, in Caledonia, all the honours due to her rank, as far as the rude and uncivilised inhabitants were capable of paying them; but not finding in the women of the country the politeness of the Roman ladies, she often used to rally them with a great deal of wit and vivacity, and sometimes in a very provoking manner; but the august dignity of Julia, and the respect they owed the wife of the Emperor of the world, shut their mouths, and

[1] Spartian. in Sever.

secured the Empress, at first, against repartees that would not have been very agreeable; afterwards, however, when they came to be better acquainted with her, they gave their tongues more liberty, and did not always leave Julia the satisfaction of triumphing. One of the better sort of these women had so little regard for the Empress as to reproach her with her prostitutions with as much good sense as resolution, and Julia, who had attacked her in an offensive manner, was given to understand that, even in Caledonia, people were not ignorant of her debaucheries. Dion tells the story as follows:[1] Argentocox, a person of consideration in Caledonia, had a wife who was full of wit and vivacity, and never at a loss for a repartee. She went one day to pay her respects to the Empress, and Julia, having turned the conversation upon the customs and manners of the women, rallied the lady upon their gallantries, and the little fidelity shown to their husbands. The Empress was not so innocent in that respect as to be beyond the reach of recrimination, and it is not at all politic to touch upon certain subjects that may be turned against one's self with so much advantage. It is true that the women of Caledonia were not, at that time, remarkable for chastity, but Julia, without being a Caledonian woman, had the same inclinations as they had, and gratified them in a more shameful manner.

The Empress, having pushed her raillery a little too far and accused the Caledonian ladies of being quite unmindful of the rules of decency in their amours, and of carrying on their intrigues publicly, the other replied with great firmness, " It is true that we women do not manage

[1] Dion. lib. 76.

our love affairs quite so cunningly as the Roman ladies, but it must be owned that our not taking much pains to conceal our gallantries from our husbands is rather a mark of our sincerity than otherwise, as we do not endeavour to impose upon them; and besides, the merit of our lovers is some sort of excuse for our misconduct. You Roman ladies," continued she, " behave with more artifice, policy, and slyness, but at the same time act with more shame, dishonour, and infamy; nor are your proceedings less scandalous for being secret, for you often prefer the vilest and most abject wretches to your illustrious husbands, and, under an appearance of modesty, you commit, unknown to your husbands, whom you dishonour and impose upon, the most abominable prostitutions." This answer quite abashed the Empress, and cured her of bantering. It is probable that the laugh was all on the side of the Caledonians (as the Romans called the people of modern Scotland), and the Empress was thus taught that she was in the wrong to reproach the Caledonian ladies with a crime for which she herself was much more to be blamed. But this was not the only mortification she met with; for the behaviour of her two sons in Britain caused her more acute vexation, especially the attempt that Caracalla made upon his father's life, which was a specimen of what he was capable of, and showed her what she had to apprehend for herself.

This wicked and unnatural prince, looking upon the Emperor as the only person that could put constraint upon him, was determined to shake off the yoke of dependence, to which he had not, for a long time past, submitted but with great impatience. He resolved to

kill his father, whose life was far too long to suit his
ardent desire of reigning, and he was within a very little
of successfully carrying out his design; for Severus being
one day on horseback, at the head of his legions, and in
the presence of the barbarian troops, Caracalla drew his
sword, and was going to run his father through behind
his back, if he had not been frightened at a great and
sudden shout, raised by those who were also on horseback behind him. The Emperor, turning about at the
noise, saw the naked sword in his son's hand, and at once
guessed for what reason he had drawn it. The consternation which he saw depicted in the countenances of those
who had cried out, plainly showed him the intentions of
his perfidious son, which were also manifestly apparent
in his looks. It is easy to guess at Severus's grief and
indignation; he had, notwithstanding, presence of mind
enough to conceal it in a great measure, and was so
politic as to pretend that he did not think his son capable
of so horrible an action; but at night, when he had retired to his chamber, and dismissed all his attendants,
except Papinianus and Castor, the latter of whom was
the most faithful officer he had, he sent for Caracalla,
called for his sword, and placing him in the midst of
them, looked at his son with an air of sorrow rather than
anger, represented to him the horror of the action he had
been about to commit, of which the barbarians, as well
as the Romans, were to have been witnesses. "If you
have a mind to take away my life," he continued, "do
so now. Here I am, loaded with years and infirmities,
and not in a condition to defend myself. But if you are
at present loth to wash your hands in the blood of your

father, order Papinianus to assassinate me; he will execute your orders, for you will then be Emperor." [1]

This remonstrance was the only punishment that Severus inflicted upon his son, but we are informed that it caused him so much vexation that his life became a burden to him. He had even a mind to put an end to himself by eating more [2] than his stomach was able to digest. He succeeded with the help of Caracalla, who finished by treason what he had not been able to do openly. It is reported that, finding himself very ill, he caused to be read in his presence, and in that of his children, the fine discourse that Micipsa delivered to his, to persaude them to live together like good friends, and which is to be found in Sallust. He then caused the urn, into which his ashes were to be put, to be brought to him, which he took in his hands and addressed these words to it: " Thou wilt soon enclose him who once thought the whole world too little for him." Then making a public and sincere acknowledgment of the frailty of this life and all its grandeur, " I have been," said he, " all that a mortal can be, and what [3] satisfaction does it afford me now? "

He died at Eboracum; and, in spite of his sordid avarice and extreme cruelty, he was so well beloved that it was said of him, as it was said of Augustus, that he ought either never to have been born or never to have died.

Julia had his body burnt with the usual ceremonies, put his ashes into a costly urn, and set out for Rome, accompanied by the Princess Mæsa and her two sons: but neither the death of their father, nor the constant

---

[1] Dio. lib. 76.   [2] Herodian. lib. 3.   [3] Spartian. in Sever.

sight of the urn which contained his remains, nor the
deep mourning of the Empress their mother, could induce them to lay aside, even for a while, the envenomed
hatred and animosity they bore each other.   They did
nothing during the whole of the journey but dispute,
quarrel, and bitterly reproach one another.   Caracalla
could not bear that his brother should claim any authority
or receive any of the honours due to the Emperor.   Geta
alleged, with great heat and violence, that he had a right
to an equal degree of power with his elder brother, because it was always Severus's intention that it should be
so, and he had declared it to be his resolution, for which
reason he had ordered that the statue of Victory should
be placed alternately in their chambers.[1]   The Empress,
who clearly foresaw the terrible consequences that these
perpetual quarrels would be followed by, made use of
all the persuasive remonstrances and entreaties she could
think of to appease the two brothers.   She also assembled
all those who were most distinguished by their rank and
wisdom to settle the prerogatives and privileges of the
two princes, and used all possible means to pacify them.
She omitted nothing, in short, to make them friends, and
was in hopes she had succeeded when she had brought
them to an apparent reconciliation, and they had given
each other mutual tokens of affection.   But we shall
soon see that there was no sincerity in all this, for their
hatred was only smothered, not extinguished.

Caracalla was no sooner arrived at Rome than he

[1] The Emperors had always in their chamber the statue of Victory,
which was one of the divinities for which they had the greatest respect.
Nobody had this privilege but the person who was invested with the
sovereign authority.   Wherever the Emperor went this statue was
carried along with him, and it was always placed in his chamber, or in
his tent.

stained his entry with the blood of a great number of persons.[1] The physicians, who refused to put his father to death, were the first that were executed, and died martyrs to their fidelity. Castor, chamberlain to the late Emperor, Evodus, to whom this young tyrant owed his education, and many others, perished by his order. He dismissed Papinianus from his post, which he so highly honoured by his upright behaviour, and considered all those as his mortal enemies who had endeavoured to make peace between him and his brother.

Plautilla was all this while overwhelmed with grief and affliction in the Island of Lipari, where she suffered all sorts of inconveniences; thus, by the severity of her banishment, she sufficiently expiated the part she had had in her father's insolent behaviour. Besides this, she had the mortification of losing her son, who was her only comfort, and by whose means she hoped one day to see all her misfortunes brought to an end; but Caracalla was resolved not so soon to forget the uneasy moments she had cost him and the forced submission that had been extorted from him when he was compelled to marry a woman he hated, and who was the daughter of his greatest enemy. The mere thought of the annoyances heaped upon him by Plautianus and his daughter roused his fury, and he looked upon the banishment of his wife as but a slight chastisement, not at all proportionate to the affronts he had received from her; his rage and indignation demanded that she should be more rigorously punished, nor was he long before he gave himself that cruel satisfaction. He sent the instruments of his vengeance to Lipari,[2] who, with the utmost brutality, put

[1] Dio. 77. Herod. lib. 4. Spartianus.   [2] Dio. lib. 76 & 77.

this unfortunate princess to death, who seemed to have been exalted by her immense treasures only in order to become the sport of Fortune. Thus miserably perished Plautilla, who might have been infinitely happier in private life than she could possibly have been upon the throne. Plautius, her brother, who had been her companion in banishment, was also put to death with her. Caracalla extended his hatred not only to Plautianus but to all those that belonged to him, and avenged in the person of the children the crime of the father.

Thus Caracalla signalised the beginning of his reign in a manner which could not but alienate from him the heart and affection of everyone, and inclined them towards Geta, his brother, who was better natured and of a more humane disposition; and, although each of these princes had his guards, his apartments in the palace, and his separate Court, yet Geta's friends were more numerous than his brother's, for, of those who seemed to be attached to the elder, the majority were influenced only by considerations of interest or policy, very few by inclination; this exceedingly increased Caracalla's jealousy and hatred of his brother, which he soon showed, for he was not a man to dissemble in that respect. From that time they kept upon their guard against each other's attempts; Caracalla laid snares for Geta, and was under continual apprehension of falling into those which he imagined his brother had contrived against him. They neither ate nor conversed together, but lived, in short, like declared enemies.

This inveterate hatred that existed between the two brothers made Julia very uneasy, and was a great grief to all Severus's friends, who were apprehensive that the

insuperable aversion they had for each other could not
but be productive of some great misfortune, and were of
opinion that there was no better way to prevent it than
that they should divide the empire between them. They
consented to this, and after a great deal of wrangling, it
was agreed that Geta should have Asia and Egypt, and
that Caracalla should have all the rest. Nothing remained but to put this project in execution; but the Empress interposed with tears, for, finding herself by this
division under the cruel necessity of parting with one of
her sons, she used all her endeavours to hinder the separation. In this she consulted her maternal affection more
than her prudence; she did not consider that, in persuading the princes to stay at Rome and govern the
empire together, she exposed them to the very misfortunes she ought, of all things, to have avoided. Her love
for her children got the better of her discretion upon
this occasion, for the thoughts of losing one of them
affected her so, that she was no longer able to endure
her affliction; she shed copious tears, and then, casting a
most tender look upon the two princes: " You have at
last," said she, " my dear children, hit upon the secret
of dividing the earth between you; but what method will
you find of dividing your mother? For how do you
imagine I can ever prevail upon myself to consent that
I should be deprived of one of you? Rather than it
should come to that, cut me in halves,[1] and take each of
you a part of me. Let it be said all over the world that,
after having divided the earth and the seas, you have
divided your mother also." These words were interrupted with sobs and sighs; and Julia pronounced them

[1] Herodian. lib. 4.

in so moving a voice that the two princes were at a loss how to proceed. The Empress, perceiving that her tears began to have the desired effect, approached her sons, embraced them both with all the marks of affection that Nature can inspire, and besought them in a most tender and irresistible manner, to think no more of a separation that could not fail to cost her her life.

The tears and supplications of Julia persuaded her sons to abandon their design of reigning separately, but they were not strong enough to create an affection between two persons, whose hatred to each other had taken such deep root. They continued to show their mutual animosity upon every occasion, being always at variance in their views and inclinations, and never of the same opinion in the election of magistrates and the administration of justice, to the great loss and prejudice of those concerned. At the public games, the combats of gladiators, and at all times, the people were witnesses of this scandalous breach; each of the brothers kept up, protected, and favoured a faction, and openly declared against the other; they brought matters to that pass at last that they could not endure one another, either together or at a distance; they laid snares for each other perpetually, were not ashamed to try and bribe their cooks and domestics to poison their respective masters; and, as each was in continual dread of his brother, they had no other occupation than that of discovering or laying snares for one another. At length Caracalla, being quite weary of this work, resolved to put his brother to death, whatever it cost him; and in order to do it without risk or danger, he had recourse to the most horrible treachery that the blackest malice could invent;

for, as he knew his mother desired, above all things, that they should be reconciled, he pretended he had resolved to live for the future upon good terms with his brother; he made the most solemn protestations of this to the Empress, and told her that she should have the satisfaction of seeing her two sons united for ever, as far as depended upon him. He entreated her, for that purpose, to bring Geta into his chamber,[1] where she should have all the proofs that it was in his power to give of his sincere friendship for him.

As people are naturally ready to believe what they earnestly wish for, Julia, being deceived by the perfidious protestations of her eldest son, was persuaded that at last Nature had begun to operate in his heart, and that he was now fully determined to behave in a different manner from before. Believing this, she therefore sent for Geta, and entreated him to come to her apartment, where his brother was minded to give him convincing tokens of a sincere reconciliation. Geta, who knew his brother well, gave no credit to this; but as it was the Empress that requested it, he thought he might venture to go to her house. Certainly the most cautious person could not have suspected such a malicious artifice; but alas! Julia's apartment, which ought to have been inviolable, became the scene of Geta's destruction, for this unfortunate prince had no sooner entered the room than the soldiers that Caracalla had concealed revealed themselves immediately with their swords drawn, and looked about for him that was to be sacrificed to their master's vengeance. At the sight of these assassins, the young prince (being in no doubt as to their design) thought he

[1] Dio. lib. 67.

could not do better in this extremity than shelter himself as well as he could in the Empress's bosom. He threw himself into her arms, and embracing her with all his strength: "I am undone, my mother," said he; "my dear mother, save me." The Empress clung to her son, and endeavoured to protect him, even at the cost of her own life, but neither so moving a sight nor the respect due to the Empress were able to check the fury of these murderers; they ran him through the body several times, though in the Empress's arms, so that it might be said that his blood returned to the bosom from whence it came. Julia was covered with it, and was wounded in one of her hands, either by the soldiers or by Caracalla himself, who had the barbarous cruelty to come into the chamber, and be not only a spectator of this horrid tragedy, but also a sharer in it.

It is easy to imagine Julia's grief; but what is almost incredible is that Caracalla's brutality went so far as to forbid his mother to enjoy the poor comfort her tears could afford her. Both she and the ladies who were with her were obliged to stifle their grief, for fear that Caracalla should serve them in the same way. The Empress was even reduced to such an excess of misery as to be forced, notwithstanding the bitterness of her sorrow, to seem rejoiced at the death of her son, because there were spies placed about her by Caracalla to take note of everything she said, and of her every look.[1] The infamous Caracalla went directly to the camp, his hands yet reeking with the blood of his brother, to put himself, as he said, under the protection of the soldiers, where he gave them a long account of the dan-

[1] Dio. lib. 77.

gerous conspiracy his brother had formed against him. The next day he went to the Senate, where he endeavoured to justify himself and palliate his crime by declaring that what he had done was in his own defence, as his brother intended to have begun with him, if he had not anticipated him. He carried his dissimulation further still, for he entreated the senators to grant his brother immortality; and imagining that this pretended respect for his brother's memory might impose upon the public, he caused him to be placed among the gods, not grudging him a place in Heaven, provided he was no longer troubled [1] with him upon the earth.

Whilst Caracalla was seeking excuses for this horrid assassination, Julia, now enjoying a little freedom, gave free vent to her tears, which had been restrained by the dread of his furious temper. She deplored the misfortune of her son, whom she had lost in so dreadful a manner, and who had met with his death in the very arms of her who had given him life. Her sister, her nieces, and the other ladies also greatly lamented the death of Geta, and sympathised with her in her grief, but their compassion nearly proved fatal to them; for Caracalla, happening to go into his mother's chamber just at the time when they were bewailing the death of the poor prince, was within a very little of having them massacred instantly, and of mingling their blood with their tears, which he looked upon as his accusers. If Lucilla, daughter of Marcus Aurelius (a princess whose age, birth, and rank had procured her the greatest respect from all the Emperors that had reigned since her father), escaped

[1] Spart. in Get.

his rage for the moment, it was only in order to expiate soon after, by her death, the crime she had been guilty of in pitying Geta. For Caracalla, finding there was no danger of anybody revenging the death of his brother, fell like a fury upon all those that had served and loved him. Afterwards, his relation, Pompeianus, grandson of Marcus Aurelius, and a great number of illustrious persons who had laboured to preserve peace and union between the two brothers, were put to death for having zealously endeavoured to unite them. Helvius Pertinax, son of the Emperor of that name, who was the darling of the Romans, forfeited his life for having made this fratricide of Caracalla's the subject of his wit. Papinianus, the pride of the empire and the greatest upholder of the laws,[1] was executed for refusing to justify this murder, for the tyrant insisted on this excellent man making a speech in the Senate to prove that Caracalla was in the right when he killed his brother, as if it was as easy to excuse that horrid action as it was for him to commit it. Foolish man, that he did not consider that Papinianus's extraordinary merit would only make this abominable affair more talked of, and that the efforts he himself made to justify it convinced people more and more of its enormity!

All these bloody executions threw Julia into terrible fright and alarm, for nothing could possibly give her greater reason to fear for her own life than the dismal end of Geta, who had died by the hand of his unnatural brother. In the meantime, whether Caracalla had a mind to appease his mother's grief and merit her pardon, or whether he thought her useful to him, he gave her

[1] Spartian. in Caracal.

great authority, and behaved to her with great respect.
He ordered that all the honours due to her rank and
dignity should be paid her, which was a great consolation
to the Empress in the midst of all her misfortunes. He
trusted her with the management of several important
duties, especially that of answering the petitions and
memorials that were presented to the Emperor; he
granted the privilege of Roman citizens to the town of
Emesa, where Julia was born; he gave the rhetorical
chair of Athens to Philiscus the Sophist at her request,
in opposition to the solicitations of the greatest persons
in his Court, who interested themselves for other rhetori-
cians; in short, he showed great consideration for her.
All these favours and marks of kindness were not, however, capable of entirely consoling her, for she was overwhelmed with the sad remembrance of her son Geta,
whom she had always loved much more than his brother.

I am not ignorant that some authors have accused
Julia of having purchased these honours from Caracalla
at the expense of her own, that she lived with him in an
incestuous intimacy, and that she even married him. It
is reported that, as Julia was yet beautiful (more so than
many younger ladies who were reckoned handsome),
when she was one day with the Emperor in an exceedingly magnificent and becoming dress, he was so smitten
with her charms that, looking very amorously on his
mother, he sighed, and said, " Indeed I should be very
glad, if it were permitted me." Julia, who had only
called all her charms to her assistance with a view to
inflame her son, being rejoiced at her conquest, answered,
that it was his own fault if he denied himself anything
he had a mind for. "Are you not," said she, "absolute

lord and master? [1]   Is it not you who give laws to all the
world without being accountable to anybody for your
actions?   Have you not a right to do what you please,
without being exposed to censure like other people?"
Julia's reply soon removed all obstacles; he married his
father's widow, and added this unnatural crime to all
the rest.   This is what Spartianus tells us, but the gen-
erality of authors deny this marriage.   Be that as it
may, all historians agree in this, that Caracalla, having
no colleague to be apprehensive of nor rival to fear,
gave free scope to the cruelty of his nature, which he
exercised upon people of all ages and conditions.   Nothing was to be seen in Rome but tragical and bloody executions.   His barbarity caused him to accuse innocent
men of horrid crimes, and his desire for money made him
oblige them to buy their freedom dearly.   He ruined the
senators by the extravagant expenses that he compelled
them to meet.   He recklessly squandered the funds that
Severus, his father, left him, upon his flatterers and the
soldiers, to ingratiate himself with them and secure their
commendation; he was, in short, guilty of all the crimes
that might have been expected from a prince who had
sullied the beginning of his reign with execrable murders.

Julia had too much good sense not to foresee the bad
consequences of this management; she represented to
him that these vain and excessive expenses could not fail
to ruin him; that it might, indeed, be consistent with
good policy to ingratiate himself with the solders, but
that there was no necessity for enriching them; that,
since he had exhausted all the means of getting money
that could possibly be thought of, by such exorbitant

[1] Spartian. in Caracal.

taxes and oppressions that all the provinces were ready to mutiny, she did not see what further methods he could have recourse to.

The Emperor looked upon these wise remonstrances as the timid ideas of a woman who was apt to carry her apprehensions too far; for, in order to convince his mother that, notwithstanding his extravagance, as she called it, he had resources that she knew nothing of, he shewed her his sword, pronouncing at the same time these words, which paint in lively colours the character of a true tyrant: "Let not my expenses cause you any anxiety, for, as long as this remains, we shall not want money." This was the fatal method he put in practice at the expense of many a life; but this sword, dreadful as it was to multitudes of people, could not furnish him with money as often as he had occasion for it. He was soon so reduced [1] as to be forced to coin false money, pieces of lead plated over with silver, or of copper gilt.

This prince's foolish prodigality was not the only vice the Empress endeavoured to cure him of; there was no sort of excess she was not necessitated to remonstrate against, for never had a man such depraved inclinations; so that it may be said all his actions were crimes. He continually took part in the combats in the circus, degrading his dignity with the low amusements of driving chariots, killing wild beasts, and fighting with gladiators —unworthy occupations, that procured him the nickname of Tarantus, who was a little, ill-made, crooked, contemptible gladiator. He caused all those governors of provinces who had been intimate with his brother Geta to be put to death. Even the Vestal Virgins were not

[1] Dio. lib. 77.

exempt from his persecutions; he caused several of them to be buried alive because he found them too virtuous, and as many as had the resolution to despise his solicitations and threats, died martyrs to their chastity, and underwent the punishment which by the laws they were liable to for the contrary.[1] He filled with blood and tears all the provinces he visited, and cruelly massacred the inhabitants of Alexandria, by way of revenge for their having spoken some disrespectful words of him,[2] and feasted his eyes with the cruel pleasure of seeing the execution. He deceived the King of Parthia by a most treacherous and perfidious action; for, pretending to enter into a close alliance with him, he sent him a magnificent embassy and sumptuous presents, accompanied by a letter desiring his daughter in marriage.

Though the Parthian thought of nothing less than the Emperor's using any artifice or deceit, but took it for granted that he was sincere, he yet excused himself, upon account, as he said, of the great difference there was between the two nations in point of customs, manners and language, while thanking Caracalla for the honour he proposed to him.

The Emperor redoubled his entreaties, pretended he could not live without the Parthian princess, sent other ambassadors to Artabanes, her father, and more costly

---

[1] Herodian. lib. 4.

[2] The inhabitants of Alexandria were accustomed to allow themselves great liberties, and to be very free with the characters of princes; some of them had acted thus in regard to Julia, nor had the Emperor escaped their licentious tongues. He was informed of it, and was so provoked that he adopted a cruel method of being revenged; for going thither afterwards, he caused all the youth of the town to be assembled in a large square, on pretence of having a mind to form them into a phalanx, in imitation of Alexander the Great, and then put them all to the sword.

presents, and promised him eternal friendship, confirming it with horrid oaths and imprecations. The barbarian King, being deceived by these artful promises, yielded to the Emperor's importunate solicitations, and convoked the princes and great lords of his Court to go with him to meet the Emperor, while the subtle and crafty Caracalla entered the Parthian dominions as far as Ctesiphon, the metropolis. He was received in all the towns through which he passed with the greatest acclamations. The inhabitants, to do him the more honour, burnt vast quantities of rich perfumes upon altars adorned with flowers, according to the fashion of the country, and Caracalla returned his thanks and acknowledgments for these extraordinary marks of their respect and esteem, making to all appearance the sincerest protestations of friendship and gratitude.

Artabanes, attended by all his Court, received the Emperor in a vast plain near the capital with concerts of instrumental music and singing, with which an infinite number of people, who accompanied their King, made the air echo. This interview of the two monarchs took place with mutual assurances of esteem, friendship, and fidelity. Refreshments were provided in abundance for the Roman and Parthian armies; the latter, having great curiosity to see the Emperor, quitted their ranks and pressed as close upon one another as if Caracalla had been made in a different form from other men. The Emperor, seeing a favourable opportunity to execute the perfidious design that he meditated, gave the signal that had been agreed upon, and that instant the Romans fell, sword in hand, upon the Parthians, who dreamed of no such thing, but thought they were only come to a wedding, and had no other arms than their musical instruments. The slaughter was terrible. Artabanes had the good fortune to escape on horseback, though with great difficulty, and after Caracalla had given his soldiers [1] all that the Parthians had been forced to abandon, that they might be the better able to save themselves by flight, he returned into Mesopotamia, sacking, pillaging, and burning everything that came in his way, and leaving behind him dismal tokens of his march.

Caracalla was as proud of this odious and perfidious action as if he had gained the most important victory in the world. He insolently informed the Senate by letter that he had conquered the Parthians and subdued the East. The poor-spirited and timid Senate, who knew the truth of the matter, were not ashamed to applaud him. They gave him the surname of Parthicus, decreed him a triumph and the same honours that the greatest hero was ever entitled to, which this base Emperor received as no more than what was due to him. He called these rapines and plunderings his military occupations, and it was for fear they should be interrupted that he left the administration of affairs to his mother. She was then at Antioch, and had with her her sister Mæsa, to whom Caracalla had given the title of August, and who lived in great state and splendour. The Empress's two nieces, Soemias and Mamea, also continued with their mother during their widowhood. Mamea was married again to Julianus, a person much inferior to Marcianus, her first husband, but Caracalla let her enjoy the same rank and the same honours she had in Marcianus's lifetime, and

[1] Herodian. lib. 4.

which were continued to her as long as Julianus lived, but his death happened soon after.

All these princesses were extremely concerned at Caracalla's foolish and impious proceedings, whereby he exposed himself to the ridicule as well as the hatred of all the world. He ran about from town to town and was never to be seen but in the circuses and amphitheatres, among the gladiators and that sort of low, contemptible company.

The Empress and Mæsa her sister saw him, with great grief, give himself up entirely to those unworthy occupations that made him so much despised, and lamented bitterly on account of his cruelties, for which he was so odious. They were justly apprehensive that it could not be long before the fate of those tyrants whom he imitated would overtake him, and the event soon after justified their fears.[1] Julia, who received all the letters that were written to the Emperor, and which came by way of Antioch, having one day opened a packet that came from Rome, found among the rest one from Flavius Maternianus, governor of the city, to Caracalla, informing him that a soothsayer, who came from Africa, had affirmed that Macrinus would soon reign, and giving him warning to be upon his guard. This news alarmed the Empress, who gave her son speedy notice of it, but all her diligence was in vain, for the report of this prediction having spread over Africa, other letters arrived with several particulars and circumstances connected with this prediction. The Emperor was very busy driving a chariot when these letters were delivered to him, and being resolved not to inter-

[1] Dio. lib. 78.

rupt his noble exercises, gave them to Macrinus to read,
with orders to report the contents. Macrinus immediately read the information that was given to the Emperor about what the astrologer had foretold, and did
not doubt but it would be at the expense of his life
that they would endeavour to make the soothsayer a liar,
if he did not prevent it without loss of time. He thought
it much better to verify the prediction by killing the
Emperor, against whom he had also a particular grudge
on account of some provoking language he had lately
used towards him. Thus, being prompted by his resentment, his ambition, and especially the great danger he
was in, he corrupted two tribunes of the guards, and
Martialis, another of the officers, who were all exasperated at the Emperor's treatment of them, and encouraging them to be revenged of the affronts they had
received, prevailed upon them to be the Emperor's exe-
cutioners.

Caracalla had a great many presages of the misfortune
that threatened him; his father's ghost appeared to him
with a naked sword in his hand, and said to him, in a
most frightful voice: "As thou didst kill thy brother so
I will kill thee," and the spirit of Commodus, that he
had invoked with horrible enchantments, foretold him a
tragical death, by saying to him: "Begone to the punishment that is prepared for thee." But this Emperor had
no need of any other presage of his miserable end than
his own tormenting fears and reflections. In the meantime he persisted in his abominations and debaucheries,
without troubling himself with futurity. An Egyptian,
named Serapion, having had the boldness to tell him he
would die soon, and that Macrinus would succeed him,

Caracalla put him to death, instead of amending his ways in consequence of this important warning.

Macrinus, finding that the Emperor had information from all parts that his fatal hour drew near, and that it was in everybody's mouth that he himself was to be the author of his death, resolved to defer no longer the accomplishment of his design, and Caracalla furnished him with an opportunity for it. The Emperor, being told that the Parthians, extremely resenting his cruel usage of them, had raised a formidable army to be revenged, thought it high time to make preparations against them, but before he left Mesopotamia he resolved to go to Carrhæ, to visit the Temple of Luna, and offer sacrifices. He left Edessa, attended only by a few domestics and the officers of his guard, amongst whom were the conspirators; and as they had a right by virtue of their office to be near his person, they had an opportunity of assassinating the Emperor without meeting with any obstacle. In fact, as they were upon the road, Caracalla having occasion to alight from his horse, went a little aside by himself. Martialis, who waited only for the favourable moment, ran to the Emperor as if he had been called, and just as the Emperor turned himself about,[1] gave him a stab with his poniard which laid him dead upon the spot.

The murderer had presence of mind enough to join the rest of the company as if nothing had happened, but was so imprudent as to hold the bloody dagger still in his hand, which was a sufficient proof of his crime; for if he had thrown it away nobody would have known who had done it; but a Scythian of the guards, seeing him with the poniard, shot him through the body with

[1] Dio. lib. 78. Spartian. Herodian. Lib. 4.

an arrow. The news of the Emperor's death was soon
published in the army; the soldiers, who had been always
very fond of him, because of the liberty he allowed them,
ran to Carrhæ to see his body, and Macrinus, who was
the author of this tragedy, went thither also, affecting
to be much afflicted, but in reality very joyful; and, the
better to avert from himself all suspicion, he pretended
to weep bitterly. This artificial grief concealed his
treason for some time, and the more because, with much
seeming respect and piety, he caused the body to be
burnt with great magnificence, put the ashes into a costly
urn, and sent them to Julia.

The Empress was already informed of her son's
tragical death, and at the same time, that Macrinus was
the author of it. Never was there seen so much affliction,
for Julia, giving herself up entirely to her grief, filled
Antioch with her cries and lamentations, dashing her
head against the wall, and giving herself such blows upon
the stomach that the cancer she had in one of her breasts
was exceedingly inflamed; she tore her clothes, and refused to take any nourishment, on purpose to starve herself. Afterwards, to indulge her rage, she poured forth
all the insulting language and invectives against Macrinus
that her despair could dictate, in hopes that her son's
murderer would also be provoked to become hers.

People were surprised to see Julia shed such floods of
tears upon this occasion, and thought her son's crimes
would furnish her with reasons sufficient for consolation,
especially since it had been all along observed that she
never had any great or real affection for him. The
politicians and those who pretended to be so thoroughly
acquainted with the Empress were of opinion that she did

not so much bewail the loss of her son as that of the
authority she had till then exercised with so much pomp
and splendour, and which was now to vanish into nothing; and certainly her future conduct justified these suspicions. For Macrinus, who had made himself Emperor by his intrigues, not thinking it proper at first to
make any changes, that he might not be supposed to
have had any hand in Caracalla's death, wrote Julia a
letter full of expressions of esteem and respect, entreated
her to make no alterations in her household, domestics,
guards, or officers, and let her enjoy all the prerogatives
and honours that she had been entitled to in the reigns of
Severus and Caracalla.

These flattering and courteous offers wonderfully
mitigated the Empress's affliction and sweetened her sor-
rows. She no longer endeavoured to shorten her days.
She was so sensible of Macrinus's courtesy and politeness that she would gladly have recalled all that which,
in her first transports of grief and indignation, she had
said against him. But unluckily, all her shocking and
insulting expressions had been taken notice of, and carefully collected by those parasites who made it their
business to report them to the Emperor, and so aggravated them in the telling that he was mightily exasperated. He was told that this princess, being accustomed
to rule, would never endure to see herself reduced to the
condition of a private person; and that, after having held
the reins of government under her husband and her son,
she would not fail to carry on intrigues, and endeavour by
underhand measures to establish her power.

Macrinus knew Julia to be a woman of skill and
courage enough to form such designs. The acquaintance

she had in Antioch, and the cabals she was capable of entering into against an Emperor who was not very firmly settled on his throne, made her no contemptible foe. In short, he forgot all the civil and polite letters he had written to her, and commanded her to quit Antioch. This order was the death blow of her hopes, and put an end to all her schemes; but, as she was determined not to yield to her misfortune till she had tried everything that might prevent it, she resolved to go to Rome, where she flattered herself that it would not be impossible for her to form a party that might espouse her cause and enter into her views. This resolution was abandoned as soon as entertained. She considered that the memory of Caracalla was too odious to give her any hopes of success. It was not very probable that the Romans would be so zealous in the cause of the mother of a tyrant, who had treated them with so much inhumanity, as to take up arms in her behalf; thus, seeing no remedy for her misfortune, and besides, being grievously tormented with her cancer, she killed herslf by a voluntary abstinence from food.

Thus perished the celebrated Julia, who had undergone such a variety of fortunes. For if, as a heathen observes,[1] she was raised up to the highest pitch of grandeur, so, on the other hand, it was accompanied by so many misfortunes, cares and anxieties, that she may be reckoned one of the most unhappy princesses that ever existed.

[1] Dio. lib. 78.

AUTHOR'S COMMENTARY

THE CAPRICES OF FORTUNE

HERE never was a man yet who could find out the secret of entailing prosperity upon his family. The same age, generally speaking, sees its own work fall to nothing: frequently the son or grandson of opulent parents falls into misery and poverty, and passes from honour to obscurity with as rapid a course as the great-grandfather leaped from rags to riches. Fortune makes a jest of human hopes and projects, and takes pleasure in frustrating all our plans. Even those things we most admire are built upon such precarious and slight foundations that they are not to be reckoned upon at all; for the very props upon which they depend are often the occasion of their fall.

Plautianus raised himself to that prodigious height of grandeur that, if he had had the least degree of moderation, there was nothing left for him to desire; but that virtue is seldom to be met with in such persons as blind Fortune has drawn from the dirt, and exalted to a state of honour infinitely beyond their merit and expectation. That insolent favourite, who made such bad use of his influence and riches, was in hopes they would protect him from the changes and vicissitudes of Fortune; and this was the motive that induced him so earnestly to desire that his daughter should be married to Caracalla, in order firmly to establish himself by a great and glorious alliance; but that was just what ruined him. Caracalla, indeed, never loved Plautianus, but by being his son-in-law he became his mortal enemy. The uneasy constraint, or rather the bitter vexation, in which he lived from the time that his father compelled him to marry Plautilla inspired him with the strongest desire to be revenged, which he was so little able to conceal that he could not hinder himself from openly declaring to his wife that as soon as Severus should die the cruellest effects of his indignation should fall upon both her and her father.

These threats could not but terribly alarm Plautianus, knowing, as he did, Caracalla's violent temper; for he could easily judge what he was to expect from a furious young prince who was extremely provoked with him. This made such an impression upon his mind, and caused him so much concern, that he could find no remedy for it but that of anticipating him by taking away his life and usurping the throne. At first this undertaking seemed so difficult and hazardous that he abandoned all thoughts of it, but afterwards he considered that, whatever danger it was attended with, it was necessary; and therefore he set about it in good earnest. While he continued in these tormenting agitations, floating between hope and fear, he was pale and trembling. Thus we see that, even when Fortune seems to smile most, we are secretly tormented by care, sorrow, and perplexity.

NONIA CELSA

WIFE OF MACRINUS

OTHING recommends a woman so much as beauty, but virtue is the most precious ornament of it; and happy are those whose whole behaviour is influenced by prudence and discretion. A certain poet is of opinion that the number of those is but small; but, whatever that satirist has been pleased to assert, beauty and modesty are not incompatible; and, without going any further for examples than such as the history of the Empresses has furnished us with, we have observed that Calpurnia, Agrippina, wife of Germanicus, Octavia, Sabina, and many others, joined the most consummate prudence and virtue to the charms of their persons, and were not at all the less chaste for being handsome. It cannot be denied that multitudes of women have made a very bad use of their beauty. A great many instances of this have been already given in the course of this history, and the Empress Celsa is going to afford a fresh proof of it.

She was the daughter of Diadumenus, whose family is not much known, but who was probably related to two great men of that name, remarkable for their skill in the law, and for their good qualities. The Empress

of whom we are now to treat did not inherit their virtue;
she was of a very amorous temperament, and a great
lover of pleasures. She willingly permitted a crowd of
admirers to entertain her with their passion, and listened to them with that sort of complaisance which is a
sure sign of the progress such flattering discourses make
in the heart of the person to whom they are addressed;
so that what at first was only an agreeable amusement,
in a little time became a commerce of gallantry that
exposed her very much to the censures of the public, for
which the irregularity of her conduct gave but too much
reason; for she proceeded from one degree of libertinism
to another, till at last she had not the least shadow of
modesty left; so true it is that when a woman has once
broken the ice, and transgressed the rules of decency,
there is nothing so bad but that she is capable of it.

Of all Celsa's lovers, Macrinus had perhaps the least
reason to hope for success. He was a Moor by birth, of
a very obscure family, and possessed none of those good
qualities that could make amends for the meanness of his
extraction, and other imperfections; on the contrary, he
was disagreeable in his person, for his head was bald,
his nose turned up; he was of a coarse and clumsy build,
of very poor natural parts, ill-natured and cruel, and
there was something in his countenance that was coarse,
and not at all pleasing. Notwithstanding all these disadvantages, Celsa did not disdain to give him a favourable hearing, and even the strongest proof of his not being indifferent to her. Celsa was one of those women
who stand in need of a husband for a screen, and to patch
up their broken reputations. She could not hope to find
one among those to whom she had been very liberal of

her favours; successful gallants are generally least of all desirous to be husbands; it was reserved for Macrinus to marry the mistress of all his rivals.

Celsa's marriage to Macrinus did not put a stop to her dissolute behaviour; on the contrary, it only served to furnish her with more opportunities of indulging her passions. Macrinus, as we have observed, was not amiable enough to defend his wife's heart against the importunate attacks of innumerable polite and genteel lovers who paid their court to her with great assiduity, and the vicious habits she had contracted were too strong to be influenced by the rules and punctilios of decency. She therefore denied herself none of those pleasures which are prohibited by marriage, but gave herself up entirely to the bent of her inclinations without the least reserve or restraint, so that her gallantries and debaucheries became the subject of everybody's discourse. Verses were composed and very assiduously circulated, for fear anyone should remain ignorant of her prostitutions; but Celsa, who was past all blushing, carried it off with an amazing impudence, and was the one person who was the least put out of countenance upon that score; for, having hardened herself against all that could be said to her disadvantage, and fearing neither the tongues nor pens of critics, she added to the number of her lovers [1] by making the first advances herself.

Favours that were so cheap one might imagine were not valuable enough to procure her gallants much above the ordinary stamp; she, however, made an illustrious conquest, and that was the Emperor Severus, who was so captivated as to become one of them. Riches and

[1] Capitolin. in Macrin.

honours entered with this prince into the habitation of
Macrinus, so that her other lovers vanished. Severus
was never weary of heaping benefits upon Celsa's husband. This upstart, who till then had been forced to
get a livelihood by mean occupations, was all on a sudden
raised to the highest offices; and in a few days gained
more by his wife's talents than he had been able to do
in his whole life by his industry. The public, who are
not easily imposed upon, took it in this sense, and did
not fail to attribute the favours the Emperor bestowed
upon Macrinus [1] to those which he received from Celsa.
It has been always observed that none are so likely to
make great and rapid fortunes as those whose wives are
beautiful and complaisant enough to oblige princes.
Macrinus, who had been a notary, and had even been
forced to appear in the amphitheatre among the gladiators, was, by the influence and interest of Celsa, put
upon a level with the greatest persons in the empire;
and his wife's having found the secret of subduing the
Emperor's heart was more advantageous to her husband
than if he had defeated all the enemies of the State.
Thus monarchs who are slaves to their passions frequently confer upon the base and unworthy instruments
of their vices those honours and preferments that ought
only to be the rewards of true merit and of worthy
actions.

Just about the time that Macrinus was coming into
favour at Court, Celsa was brought to bed with a son,
whom she named Diadumenus, because he came into the
world with a sort of string bound round his forehead,
something in the shape of a diadem. Those who were

[1] Tristan. Comment. Histor. Capitolin.

sent for to draw his horoscope did not fail to make the most flattering predictions upon this happy circumstance. They promised Celsa that her husband would be Emperor, that the child ought to be looked upon as the son of a person who was one day to be invested with the sovereign authority, adding that he himself would, in due time, be exalted to that supreme dignity.

The death of Severus made no alteration in Macrinus's fortune; for Caracalla, who was entirely governed by his odd humours and caprices, added new favours to those which his father had so profusely lavished upon Celsa's husband, and honoured him with one of the highest and most important posts in the empire, for which unworthy choice, as we have observed, he paid very dear; for Macrinus was not ashamed to become the assassin of his benefactor. He committed that crime [1] with so much precaution that at first nobody suspected him; and when Audentius, who, as well as Macrinus, was præfect of the Prætorian Guards, had refused the empire on account of his great age, the army, upon a report that the Parthians were approaching, elected Macrinus with a great deal of precipitation, thinking him the fittest person to stop the barbarians, who, they believed, were ready to fall upon them. In fact, Artabanes, highly exasperated at the perfidious behaviour of Caracalla, put himself at the head of a very powerful army, and set out in all haste to attack the Romans, who, on their side, prepared to defend themselves. Two or three battles were fought, in which vast numbers were destroyed on both sides. The Parthians claimed the honour of the victory, and celebrated it with great rejoicings. They lost, how-

[1] Herodian. Spartian.

ever, as many men as the Romans, who ridiculed the barbarians for priding themselves upon their imaginary victory. Macrinus, in the meantime, who was neither general nor soldier, and was very impatient to get his election confirmed by the Senate, did not disdain to treat with Artabanes. He sent him ambassadors, who asked him if he had well considered against whom he had fitted out such an army?—that if he only desired to be revenged on Caracalla, he might rest contented, since that base and unworthy Emperor had already met with his just deserts for that horrid treachery, in which nobody was concerned but himself. That Macrinus, who was elected Emperor, had nothing so much at heart as to be upon good terms with the Parthians, and to observe religiously the treaty of peace that Caracalla had violated; that he offered to restore to him all the spoils that the Romans had taken from the Parthians, and also the prisoners; and, to give him a proof of the desire he had to repair, as much as in him lay, the affront that Caracalla had put upon him, he would make him a present of a great sum of money. Artabanes, who had no personal pique against anybody but Caracalla, accepted these proposals and retired.

Macrinus was no sooner elected than the troops felt aggrieved on account of their not having upon the throne one of Antoninus's family, and their discontent was shown by a deep silence throughout the whole army. Macrinus's friends, being apprehensive that they would choose some person related to Antoninus (for there were several of them among the officers), advised Macrinus to give his son Diadumenus the name of Antoninus, in order to ingratiate him with the legions; and Macrinus, knowing how dear that name was to the army, gave it to his son, and made him his colleague in the empire.

The news of Caracalla's death having been brought to Rome, the citizens, by their countenances, expressed their satisfaction at being delivered from the cruel oppressions of that tyrant. Macrinus's election was not indeed what they desired, for they could not perceive in this new Emperor either birth or merit; but, after Caracalla, they did not think it possible they could fall into worse hands. This was what the senators repeated many a time, with transports of joy, when Macrinus informed them that the legions had made choice of him to supply the place of Caracalla. The Senate (now quite stripped of their liberties) approved this election, decreed to Macrinus all the honours and titles that were now inseparable from the sovereign authority, and confirmed to Diadumenus the surname of Antoninus.

If in Macrinus Rome had an Emperor without merit, in Celsa they had an Empress without modesty—her prostitutions were known to everybody. It was, however, to her that all the orders of the city went in the most respectful manner to pay their homage.

The Senate, more flattering again than the people, exhausted their whole stock of adulation, declared her August, and honoured with the most pompous titles a woman whom her scandalous debaucheries had covered with infamy.

Macrinus lost no time in acquainting his wife with his exaltation to the throne, and the honour the legions had conferred upon their son, in giving him the name of Antoninus. It appears from the letter he wrote her upon this occasion that the Romans had a greater veneration for the above-mentioned name than for that of their gods, and that their infatuation for it even amounted to impiety, for which reason Macrinus protests to Celsa that he held himself less obliged to them for the empire than for the surname of Antoninus, which they had given his son. His words are as follows:—" I have just now received a most valuable present; you will, no doubt, imagine I am going to speak of the empire that the legions have honoured me with, but it is far beyond it, for the throne has frequently been bestowed upon very unworthy men. Know, then, that you are become mother to Antoninus, and they have given me an Antoninus for a son: what a piece of good fortune for you and for me! what glory to our family! what a presage of happiness to my empire! May the gods grant, and especially the celestial Juno, whom you revere so religiously, that I be found worthy of being father to Antoninus, and that in our son his virtues as well as his name may revive."

It was not only Diadumenus who borrowed a name, for Macrinus changed his own for that of Severus. Happy would it have been for him if, when he mounted the throne, he had abandoned his vices altogether with his name, but it is not so easy a matter for a man to leave off bad habits; greater efforts are necessary for that than Macrinus was capable of. It is true that, in order to ingratiate himself with the Romans, he made very good regulations, and among others, inflicted heavy penalties upon adulterers, certainly not considering how many people his wife would render liable to them. He punished false accusers with death, which severity stifled, as it were, the infectious breath of those serpents who cost so many people their lives. He made a great many other useful ordinances, but he caused them to be executed with such rigour as more than counterbalanced the usefulness of them, and alienated from him the people's affections; these laws were rather looked upon as the effect of his cruelty and ill-nature, than of any desire he had to prevent vice and promote virtue.

Diadumenus, at an age that ought to be distinguished by nothing but mildness and sweetness of temper, gave marked signs of the opposite qualities; for Macrinus, after having put to death the chiefs of a conspiracy that was formed against him in Asia, was inclined to pardon those that were least guilty, but his son blamed his clemency, and complained of it to his mother. She was then at Rome indulging her vicious appetites, whilst her husband and her son were making the East tremble with their violence. She there received her son's letter, in which he gave a specimen of what he was capable of. "It appears," says he, "that the Emperor is unmindful of your interest and his own, since he can so easily prevail upon himself to forgive. You ought to make use of the power you have over him to persuade him to punish Arabianus, Tuscus, and Gellius, whom he has pardoned; for by putting them to death he will effectually hinder them from doing us any further harm." Diadumenus did not stop there; he wrote to his father to the same effect, and omitted nothing he could think of to rouse him to revenge. These letters became public, and they gave everybody a very bad impression of a prince who could give such early signs of inhumanity. Macrinus, however, did not stand in need of his son's exhortations to cruelty; he daily gave but too evident proofs of it, by treating the soldiers with extreme rigour, and suffering them to want even common necessities, while he was wallowing in luxury and pleasures at Antioch. He was dreaded on account of his severity, and hated for his effeminacy.

People could not endure the brutal haughtiness which he affected, and which was so far from causing the obscurity of his birth to be forgotten that it only served to put everybody in mind of it. But what most disposed the legions to revolt was their discovery that he was the murderer of Caracalla, whose name and memory were very dear to them. It was then that they heartily repented having raised to the empire that infamous assassin, and determined to place Antoninus Heliogabalus, who was nearly related, and perhaps was son to Caracalla, upon the throne.

This young prince was extraordinarily handsome. He was then at Emesa with Mæsa, his grandmother, who, after the death of her sister, the Empress Julia, had been ordered to quit Antioch, where she lived in such magnificence as aroused the jealousy of Macrinus. She retired then to Emesa, the place of her birth, with her daughters, Soemias and Mamea, and thither she conveyed the immense riches which she had amassed during the reigns of Severus, her brother-in-law, and Caracalla, her nephew. Her two daughters were widows, and had each of them a son. That of Soemias was named Avitus Bassianus, and was afterwards known by the name of Heliogabalus; Mamea's son was called Alexianus, who, some time after, took the name of Alexander. Mæsa educated them very carefully, and dedicated them to the Sun, which the inhabitants of Emesa adored by the name of Elagabalus. She even made them priests of that divinity, to which the neighbouring nations, kings, and satraps rendered superstitious worship, and sent magnificent presents. Bassianus, who was older than his cousin Alexianus, exercised the office of the priesthood. He appeared in a purple habit, spotted with gold, wearing a sort of diadem, or tiara, adorned with jewels, whose lustre set off the majesty of his countenance, which was the admiration of everybody, especially the Roman soldiers who were encamped near Emesa, and who often went into the temple to be present at the sacrifices of Heliogabalus, whom they saw perform the office of pontiff with extraordinary pomp, and in a most graceful manner. But what made this young prince so dear to the troops was the report that Mæsa [1] gave out that he was the son of Caracalla, which perhaps was true enough. Her emissaries industriously spread this rumour, and said that Caracalla, having fallen desperately in love with his cousin Soemias when she was at Court, had had a son by her, and that this was Heliogabalus, whom Macrinus had deprived of the empire, which was his right. Mæsa, on her side, very cunningly persuaded the soldiers to believe whatever she pleased, by making them great presents, and promising them very considerable rewards if they would defend the son of Caracalla against the snares and designs of Macrinus. Eutychianus and Gannys, Mæsa's freedmen, made the most of this favourable disposition of the legions, who listened very attentively to all these words. They told them that they ought to prefer the son of Caracalla, who had loved them so entirely, to Macrinus, the man of yesterday, the murderer of their Emperor, equally incapable and unworthy of governing the empire. That,

---

[1] Capitolin. in Macrin. Lamprid. in Diadumen.

after all, their own interests required that they should place Heliogabalus upon the throne, because that would lay Mæsa under a great obligation to them, who would not fail to distribute her riches among them.

The soldiers (a class of men for the most part extremely fond of changes), and who were already much averse to Macrinus, on account of the harsh manner in which he treated them, lent a favourable ear to these proposals, and even promised to do whatever should be required of them. Mæsa, perceiving that the troops were favourably inclined towards her, and that she could pretty safely depend on their endeavours and assistance, in consideration of the recompense she had led them to hope for, like a skilful woman seized the happy opportunity that presented itself to place her grandson upon the throne. She left Emesa in the night with all her family, and brought Heliogabalus into the camp, clothed in a magnificent robe that Caracalla had sometimes appeared in, which was artfully contrived on purpose to put the legions in mind of him. Eutychianus whispered it about that Mæsa was inclined to distribute a large sum of money among the troops; he gained over the principal officers, while those whom he could not prevail upon to declare for him, since they felt uncertain about the issue, he persuaded to stand neutral. As soon as day appeared, they presented Heliogabalus to the soldiers, who proclaimed him Emperor, and put on him the imperial purple robe, giving him the name of Marcus Aurelius Antoninus. After this ceremony came Mæsa's present. She caused gold and silver to be thrown among them in great abundance, nor could she possibly have done so more opportunely, for the soldiers immediately reported that they had found a son of Caracalla, and that Mæsa was distributing money lavishly among the troops; this made the soldiers flock together from all parts, in order to get their share of the booty, and these were so many additions to the new Emperor's party.

Macrinus was informed at Antioch of what was taking place in Phœnicia, but did not think a faction conducted by a woman was much to be feared; so, without stirring from Antioch, he contented himself with sending Julianus, præfect of the Prætorian Guards, with some troops to disperse the rebels; but this detachment, instead of fighting, joined them. For those who were in the camp, having made Heliogabalus mount the walls, told the new comers that he was the son of Caracalla, and reproached them with their unpardonable ingratitude, in taking up arms against the son of an Emperor, from whom they had received so many benefits, and at the same time showed them bags full of money that Mæsa had given them. The sight of these was more persuasive than all that the others could allege; Macrinus's soldiers, to obtain the like reward, fell upon their officers, killed them, and then, being admitted into the camp, acknowledged Heliogabalus for Emperor and took the oath of fidelity to him. Mæsa knowing full well that they had not betrayed Macrinus for nothing, recompensed their perfidy, and sent Julianus's head to Antioch, whence Macrinus had already started (for he had heard what condition matters were in) in order to fight his antagonist; but afterwards he changed his design and returned to Antioch, whence he wrote to the governors of the provinces, and to the Senate, letters full of contempt for Heliogabalus, who, he said, was a silly blockhead, and whom he declared an enemy to the State. He then thought it expedient to be liberal to his soldiers, whom he did his utmost to exasperate against those who had taken part with the rebels; he gave his son the title of August, and thinking he had taken all the precautions that were necessary, remained very quiet at Antioch.

In the meantime Mæsa was resolved to pursue her aim, and having caused the army to quit their camp, conducted it towards Antioch in order to besiege Macrinus, or else oblige him to come to a decisive battle. Macrinus then began to think the affair was no laughing matter. He marched out of Antioch to fight the enemy. The two armies met between Phœnicia and Syria.

That of Macrinus had a great advantage over the other, for besides the superiority of numbers, he had good generals; whereas Heliogabalus had nobody fit to command his army, for Gannys, who acted as general, had never served, and had done nothing all his life but amuse himself. Upon this occasion, however, the old observation, that good luck is better than skill, was verified; for Gannys at first gave his adversary sufficient trouble, Heliogabalus's troops fighting desperately, knowing that if they did not conquer they could expect no mercy on account of their rebellion. But some time after, not being able to resist the efforts of the Prætorians; they were put to flight.

Mæsa and Soemias seeing affairs change to their disadvantage, alighted from their chariot, and throwing themselves into the midst of those who fled, reproached them, with tears in their eyes, with their shameful behaviour to a prince they had just sworn to be faithful to. These remonstrances, accompanied by every argument they could think of that was capable of moving the soldiers, had such an effect, that they returned to the battle. At that instant, Heliogabalus put himself at the head of his troops sword in hand, and shewed such resolution and courage, as would not have been expected from one of his age. The fight began again with more fury than ever, but with different result, for Heliogabalus's soldiers having beaten the first rank of their enemies, those that were worsted put their whole army into confusion. The Emperor seeing this, gave up all for lost, and a panic seizing him, he fled with some of his most faithful officers. The Prætorians continued the fight with great obstinacy, and maintained the honour of their corps; but Heliogabalus calling out to them, asked for whom it was that they fought and exposed their lives thus, since Macrinus had deserted them, whereupon they all declared for him, upon his promising that he would allow them to retain their rank according to their request.

Macrinus, who had taken off his imperial robe that he might not be known, got away as fast as he could, intending to go to Rome with all possible expedition, to consult and assemble his friends, but he was taken at Chalcedon, where he stopped to repose a little, and the soldiers cut off his head. Some of them were inclined to spare Diadumenus, and would have done so, had it not been for the letter he wrote to his mother about the conspiracy of Gellius; this proved fatal to him. Thus perished Macrinus, after a reign of fourteen months; its short duration shows that nothing is so precarious as power procured by unlawful actions. History makes no further mention of Nonia Celsa.

ANNIA FAUSTINA
JULIA CORNELIA PAULA
JULIA AQUILIA SEVERA
WIVES OF THE EMPEROR HELIOGABALUS

JULIA VARIA SOEMIAS
HIS MOTHER

JULIA VARIA MÆSA
HIS GRANDMOTHER

FTER Macrinus was put to flight, his army having declared for Heliogabalus, Mæsa conducted her grandson to Antioch, where the honours due to the Emperor were paid him, and he received the oath of the legions. Mæsa, who was full of schemes and projects, thought it fitting that the new Emperor should write to the Senate to entreat them to confirm his election, but his letter was not well calculated to bespeak their favour; for, whereas the preceding Emperors had never assumed any title till after they had been decreed them by the Senate, he insolently took, by his own authority, those of Emperor, Cæsar, August, Happy, son of Antoninus, and several other pompous surnames. The obsequious Senate confirmed, however, what the soldiers had done, and, the more to please the new Emperor, they honoured in an extraordinary manner the memory of Caracalla, whose son he pretended to be. By the same decree the title of August was conferred upon Mæsa and Soemias, together with all the honours that had ever been given to the mothers of the Emperors.

The senators, for all this, regretted Macrinus extremely, and not without reason; for he could not possibly have had a more unworthy successor. To say the truth, Heliogabalus was very handsome, well made, and had a very agreeable countenance; but never did a fair outside conceal a more polluted soul. In him was to be found an unhappy collection of all sorts of vices. He possessed the malice and cruelty of all the tyrants that had ever reigned; gave himself up entirely to the most abominable lewdness; carried luxury, prodigality, and insolence to the highest pitch. Being informed that the Senate had ratified his election, and that he had nothing more to fear, he signalised the beginning of his reign by a horrible piece of barbarity and ingratitude, namely, the execution of Gannys, to whom he owed his education and the throne. This freedman had been preferred at Court by the interest of Mæsa, who had always had a great esteem for him, because she had always found him faithful, and very zealous for the welfare of her family. In fact, Gannys, who had been tutor to Heliogabalus, acquitted himself of that duty to the general satisfaction; Heliogabalus himself was a witness of his behaviour at the last battle, which ended decisively in his favour, and was so convinced of the important service he did him upon that occasion that, in one of those fits of good humour to which he was now and then subject, he was inclined to choose Gannys for a stepfather, by making him marry his mother, Soemias, and to declare him Cæsar. These favours would have been no more than Gannys deserved, and would have done honour to the new Emperor's gratitude and acknowledgment. Soemias's reputation, indeed, was none of the best, for she led a very dissolute life; but Gannys was not so fastidious as to refuse to be the Emperor's father-in-law.

In the meantime, instead of honouring him, Heliogabalus put him to death. This cruel and ungrateful Emperor, not being able to endure that Gannys should be a spectator of his conduct, and especially since he took the liberty to advise him, ordered him to be executed, and was not even ashamed to dip his hands in the blood of that faithful servant by giving him the first blow himself.

This bloody affair was succeeded by a great many more equally unjust. Nestor, whom Macrinus had made colonel of the Prætorian Guards, and Agrippinus, who commanded in Syria, were put to death because they had fought for their Emperor; Pica and Rianus, who governed Arabia under Macrinus, lost their lives for not betraying their master; and Heliogabalus punished in them a fidelity he ought to have rewarded. But he was not content with persecuting virtue, he gave credit to vice, and honoured the greatest crimes. He debased the highest dignities in the empire by making them venal, or bestowing them on miserable eunuchs and infamous people who had been slaves, who were only known by their abominable lives, so that in heaping the greatest preferments on those unworthy wretches he left no recompense for true merit. He would not condescend to wear

a Roman habit, as all his predecessors had done,[1] but
chose his dress after the manner of the Phœnicians and
Medians, which indeed was very graceful and magnifi-
cient, but at the same time savoured of the luxury and
effeminacy of those nations. At last he quite forgot all
the decorum that decency required, and which was suitable to his rank; and abandoning himself entirely to the
most brutal debaucheries, passed the winter at Nicomedia
in those shameful occupations. Mæsa, his grandmother
(than whom nobody understood the world better), did
not see all this without being sensibly concerned: it
grieved her to the heart that her grandson should be
remarkable for all sorts of bad qualities, and she was
apprehensive that the Romans could never be brought
to endure an Emperor who had nothing of the Roman
about him, not so much as the fashion of his clothes. She
gave him many wise admonitions upon that subject, but
the flatterers he encouraged destroyed the force of her
arguments. Heliogabalus, continually surrounded by
those sycophants, and corrupted by their maxims, looked
upon the advice of his grandmother as the mere whims
of an old-fashioned woman, who would needs have him
wear the Roman dress for no other reason than because
all the former Emperors had done so. On the other
hand, Soemias, by her pernicious counsels, effaced the
little impression that Mæsa's good sense had made upon
her son; and, by a base approbation of his behaviour,
encouraged him in the gratification of all his vicious passions. Thus this prince, being hurried away by his irregular appetites, seduced by his young courtiers, and supported by the bad example of his mother, gave himself

---

[1] Herodian. lib. 5. Lamprid.

up to the most shameful course of life that can be imagined, and even went beyond Caligula, Nero, or Domitian, whom he professed to imitate.

It is no new thing for flatterers to extol the weaknesses and vices of princes, and to applaud those actions that most deserve to be blamed; but it is not common to see a mother encourage her son in everything that is infamous. This, however, Soemias did, and this was the more blamable as she well knew that all the misfortunes Caracalla drew upon himself were owing to his cruelty and his debaucheries; she had therefore great reason to apprehend the same fate for her son. It is true that a young man seldom learns any good from a mother who is herself a libertine, and Soemias was too regardless of her own reputation to be very solicitous about that of Heliogabalus. Mæsa, indeed, who looked further into things, and weighed consequences, gave him better counsel; for instance, that he should go to Rome, where she said his presence was necessary; and, in fact, Macrinus's chief mistake had been his not going thither immediately after his election, but continuing at Antioch. The Emperor was at last convinced of what importance it was to him to gain over the Senate, and as soon as the winter was over set out for Rome.

His arrival there only served to make people regret Macrinus, for he renewed at Rome all the excesses that he had practised at Nicomedia. He went to the Senate, and obliged the senators to invite Soemias, his mother, and Mæsa, his grandmother, to take their places among them. This was a monstrous innovation, and a scandalous degradation of the senatorial dignity. The proudest of the Empresses, and even those who had carried their authority the greatest lengths, never dreamed of assuming any such privilege; and we have observed in the life of Agrippina that the Senate broke up one day when she attempted to do the like. But the senators had now no longer the probity and resolution of their forefathers; the Emperor's will and pleasure was become the only law. Heliogabalus caused that to be permitted to Soemias and Mæsa which Agrippina could never obtain, and which Livia never had the assurance to ask for. Thus the Senate entreated them to assist at their meetings, they took their places next to the consuls, voted, signed, and, in short, performed all the functions of senators.

Heliogabalus did not stop there. Not content with having made his mother a member of the Senate, he must needs put her at the head of another Senate, where she performed the office of president. He created a Senate of ladies, and appropriated to that purpose a palace that was situated upon the Quirinal; and in this grave tribunal were decided all weighty matters connected with the sex,[1] particularly styles and fashions, order of precedence, and what best became each form and complexion. It was there deliberated which ladies had a right to be carried in a chair, which in a litter, who should be permitted to go on horseback, and who were to have the privilege of wearing gold or jewels. They very solemnly issued decrees about dress and other affairs of that nature as being of the greatest importance to the welfare of the public, and they assembled as frequently, and with as much regularity, as if the weightiest affairs of the empire were transacted among them.

[1] Lamprid. in Heliogab.

If Soemias shone at the head of this ridiculous Senate, Mæsa was equally conspicuous in military matters. She appeared in an amazon habit at the camp, reviewed the Prætorian cohorts, and had the management of everything relating to the army. Thus did Heliogabalus, by his foolish and unprecedented infatuation, overturn all order and decency. One of the most extravagant things he introduced was the worship of his favourite god Elagabalus [1] with strange and unheard of ceremonies. This god he caused to be brought from Emesa to Rome, built him a temple, which was one of the most magnificent in the city,[2] and had everything that was most sacred and revered carried out of the other temples into it, especially the celebrated statue of Pallas, which Æneas brought from Troy. Thus he caused the Romans the mortification of seeing a new and strange god preferred to Jupiter; and, by an unaccountable whim, he took it in his head to marry his god Elagabalus to Urania, that famous divinity that was so much respected in Africa. He caused it to be brought from Carthage, and celebrated the wedding at Rome and in the provinces with great pomp, saying that there was never a fitter match than that Elagabalus should marry Urania; that is, that the sun should marry the moon. But the tragical part of this new sort of worship was that the Emperor, to do honour to his god, in a brutal and abominable manner, sacrificed children, whom he chose

---

[1] Elagabalus was a surname given to the sun, which was adored by the people of Emesa. This divinity was nothing but a great stone, round at the bottom, and ending in the shape of a cone. It was black, and had some curious characters engraven upon it. The Phœnicians pretended that it fell from Heaven, and had the greatest veneration for it.

[2] Herodian. lib. 5.

out of the most illustrious families; and whilst these hellish sacrifices were going on, he celebrated the praises of his god in hymns, which he sung in the Syrian language, and made Soemias and Mæsa do the same.

We shall not take upon ourselves to enter into the details of Heliogabalus's life, which was one continued succession of all sorts of crimes; for it would only be a mark of disrespect to the reader, and of our small regard for decency, were we to enumerate the horrible acts of lewdness and lasciviousness that this detestable prince committed; we prefer to draw a veil over those shameful pollutions. After he had provided his god with a wife, he thought proper to choose one for himself; and, as he deprived the Carthaginians of their Urania in order to marry her to his Elagabalus, so he took it into his head to rob Pomponius of his wife Faustina. Annia Faustina was one of the most accomplished ladies in Rome, remarkable not only for her nobility, but the incomparable beauty of her person. She was great granddaughter to the Emperor Marcus Aurelius, whose name and memory were held in the highest veneration among the Romans. She was then in the prime of her youth; and, at an age wherein there is but little discretion to be expected, she shewed [1] such prudence and virtue as had not been met with in her predecessors of that name.

When it happens that nobility, beauty and virtue are united in a young person, there can be no lack of admirers. The charming Faustina had abundance of them, but Pomponius Bassus was the happy man who, for his extraordinary merit, was preferred to all those who aspired to the honour of possessing the princess. Honour

---

[1] Dio. lib. 79. Tristan. Comment. Hist.

and goodness were hereditary in his family, which had been also rendered illustrious by the most important employments, he having been Governor of Rome, and afterwards consul. It might safely be affirmed that there was not in Rome a more honourable man that Faustina's husband. They lived together in that happy calmness and tranquillity which in marriage is generally the consequence of reciprocal love, until Heliogabalus, being smitten with the charms of Faustina, looked upon her as a lady worthy of his esteem and affection. At first he contented himself with showing her all those tokens of his passion that are so natural to an assiduous lover; but whatever pains he took to make himself understood, Faustina, defended by her own virtue and her husband's merit, gave him no hopes of success; so that the Emperor, in the midst of all his pomp and splendour, made no impression upon the princess's heart.

The obstacles that violent love may meet with do not always prove a remedy; on the contrary, they very often serve only to heighten it. Heliogabalus, perceiving that Faustina's virtue gave him but little room to hope for those favours that he had so easily obtained from other ladies less cruel, resolved to put her husband to death, in hopes that Faustina, who would not listen to him as a lover, might without difficulty be prevailed on to receive him as a husband, especially as he was invested with the sovereign authority. Thus was Pomponius already condemned, and nothing was wanting but to lay some crime to his charge that might furnish a fair pretence to put him to death; but, as that senator's conduct had always been without reproach, it was absolutely necessary to invent some calumny, the ordinary resource of tyrants. Heliogabalus complained that Pomponius took upon him to censure all his actions, that whatever passed in the palace was criticised by him; that Pomponius and his friend Messala had set up a sort of tribunal, where they were so audacious as to sit in judgment upon the conduct of Emperors, who ought not to be accountable for their behaviour; and, upon these false and imaginary crimes, the Emperor accused Pomponius and Messala to the Senate.

There was nobody present that did not know that Faustina's beauty was all Pomponius's crime. Heliogabalus's attachment to that charming lady and the absurdity of his complaint sufficiently declared the motives of his accusation; and the sequel justified these suspicions. Messala was no more blameworthy than Pomponius. That senator had been twice consul, and was so influential that he had caused the Emperor Julianus to be declared an enemy to the State, and Severus to be elected Emperor. He was a man of great firmness and resolution, never influenced in the Senate by complaisance or flattery; and as he had nothing in view but the public interest, he was either useless or a hindrance to the Emperor's projects. Heliogabalus, therefore, during his residence at Nicomedia, sent for him thither, pretending that he stood in need of his assistance, but in reality to get him out of Rome, where he was apprehensive that he would oppose him; for there was nobody in the Senate more dreaded by the Emperor and his sycophants than Messala, who was always intrepid and immovable.

The rank that these illustrious men held in the Senate, the high esteem they enjoyed at Rome, and their virtue and reputation, deserved at least that the matter should

be enquired into, and that judgment should not be too
hastily given in a matter of so much importance; but
Heliogabalus was too much in love to wait the issue of
these tedious proceedings; so, forgetting that he himself
was the accuser of Pomponius and Messala, he would
needs be their judge also; and as they were too odious to
him to make it a matter of doubt whether they should be
punished or acquitted, he resolved to make sure of his
work. He therefore ordered them to be executed, and
by that flagrant piece of injustice delivered himself, in
Pomponius, from one who stood between him and the
object of his passion; and, in Messala, from a magistrate
who had revived the ancient liberty of Rome.

The tears that Faustina shed did honour to the merit
of Pomponius; but Heliogabalus found the means to dry
them. As it was not his intention to suffer her to remain
long in mourning, he redoubled his solicitations, and
pressed his point so eagerly and with so much importunity
that he prevailed upon Faustina to venture upon a
second marriage. In fact, she became wife to the Emperor, and was immediately honoured by the Senate with
the title of August. It might be imagined that Faustina,
being now amply recompensed for the loss of Pomponius,
had reason to promise herself a great deal of happiness.
By marrying the Emperor she had ascended the throne of
her ancestors, and the violent love he had shown for her
seemed to afford her reasonable grounds to hope for its
continuance; but pleasures that are procured by crimes
are of no long duration. The Emperor soon found those
insipid which he had not scrupled to purchase with a
horrid murder. He was no sooner married than he was
disgusted with Faustina, and showed that nothing is a

more effectual cure for love than possession. He conceived for Cornelia as irresistible a passion as he had done before for Faustina.

Cornelia Paula belonged to one of the best families in Rome. It is generally imagined that she had been married before, and was a mother of children at least, Heliogabalus's pretext for marrying her seems to authorise this supposition. This prince, whose love was as soon cooled as warmed, no sooner saw Cornelia than he was persuaded it was impossible he should ever love anybody else; he paid his addresses to her very earnestly, and to cut short the matter, spoke of marriage. The misfortune of Faustina, whom he had abandoned notwithstanding all her merit, did not plead very much in his favour. A man who is fickle, always ready to change, is not very likely to secure a lady's affections, and Cornelia did not fail to reproach the Emperor with his having cast off, without any reason, the most amiable person in Rome. Be that as it may, the Emperor was provided with a plausible excuse, and Faustina's barrenness furnished him with it. He even informed the public of the motives of that divorce, and endeavoured to make it appear a convincing proof of his wisdom and prudence that he should look out for a wife capable of giving him heirs and perpetuating the empire in his family, of which he said Faustina gave him no hopes; whereas, in Cornelia, he had all the reason in the world to expect the accomplishment of his desires, as she had already been a mother. These arguments, together with the dazzling prospect of the throne, induced Cornelia to supply the place of Faustina, and run the risk of meeting with the same fate. The nuptials were celebrated with incredible magnificence.　Never had there been seen at Rome so pompous a ceremony.　The Emperor went to enormous expense upon this occasion.　All classes in the city partook of his bounty, and he heaped favours upon the senators, the knights, and the senators' wives.　He gave the soldiers and the people several splendid entertainments, followed by all manner of shows and games; among the rest (what had never been seen before at Rome) a bloody battle between tigers and elephants.

The Senate went in a body to pay their respects, or rather homage, to the new Empress, and at the same time presented her with the title of August, which included all the honour that could be bestowed upon the wives of the Emperors; for they did not think they could possibly show too much zeal for a princess to whom Heliogabalus had given such extraordinary tokens of his esteem and affection as to exhaust his treasures in honour of her. Nothing could be a greater instance of this prince's want of judgment and reflection than his not considering the bad consequences of precipitate marriages.　It looked as if he had put himself to this excessive expense for no other reason than to make his inconstancy the more remarkable and to put a greater affront upon Cornelia; for, a few days after his marriage, he divorced her, and deprived her of the title of August.

So sudden an alteration struck the city with astonishment.　People had, but a week before, been witnesses of the extraordinary pains the Emperor had taken to obtain her good graces, and were quite at a loss to guess what could occasion so quick and unexpected a change. Cornelia was very handsome, and her person extremely agreeable; her birth [1] was worthy of her fortune, and her behaviour had been always consistent with decency; but, notwithstanding all this, she became in so short a time a heavy burden to this whimsical and ridiculous Emperor. Heliogabalus was sensible of his unjust conduct in this affair, and was not a little embarrassed to invent a plausible excuse for it.

Cornelia had done nothing to deserve such insulting treatment; and the public, who will criticise even the actions of monarchs, were very curious to know what sort of pretence the Emperor would find out to lend colour to his inconstancy; but Heliogabalus was cunning enough to give reasons that nobody could contradict. He said, that he could not bring his delicacy to be reconciled to certain bodily imperfections [2] from which Cornelia suffered, being well convinced that her modesty would not permit her to disprove his assertion.

The marriage was no sooner dissolved than this fickle prince ran after new pleasures. He looked out for a third wife, whom at last he found among the Vestal Virgins, not being at all ashamed to add this abominable and sacrilegious action to all the rest of his crimes. The vestals were young girls who consecrated their virginity to the Mother of the Gods by the most solemn vows, the breach of which was punished with death. They were held in great veneration at Rome. Their institution was sacred, their authority much respected, and their persons inviolable. There was, at that time, a vestal named Julia Aquilia Severa, daughter of the senator Aquilius Sabinus, who had been twice consul in Caracalla's reign. She was one of the handsomest ladies in

[1] Herodian. lib. 5.　　　　[2] Dio. lib. 79.

Rome, and the vestal's dress, instead of diminishing, heightened her beauty. The Emperor was so captivated with her charms that he fell in love with her at first sight; and, not being a man to deny himself anything he had a mind for, he paid frequent visits to the charming vestal. This alarmed the rest of that society; they were too well acquainted with the Emperor's impious character not to suspect his intentions, and therefore watched him very narrowly.

Severa was not so cruel. She prevailed upon herself to bear, with great patience, the Emperor's assiduities; for nothing so much flatters the vanity of a woman as to see a man at her feet to whom all others are inferior. She therefore received his visits very willingly, and listened attentively to his proposals of marriage. It is probable that she was not at all sorry to be compelled, by absolute power, to dispense with those vows which in all likelihood she had made without consulting her inclinations, and at an age when she was not competent to judge of the difficulty she might find in keeping them; for the vestals were admitted too young to consider the burden of the yoke they imposed upon themselves, so that instances were not wanting of their dishonouring the sanctity of those engagements by their gallantries, their oaths not being strong enough to get the better of their constitutions and the impetuosity of youth. Be it as it may, Heliogabalus, in contempt of what was most sacred among the Romans, carried off the vestal, married her, and proclaimed her August.

The Senate looked upon this odious and detestable match as the forerunner of some terrible calamity to the empire. The laws had been always strictly put in force

when a vestal had deserved punishment for breach of
chastity, nor had the accomplices in the crime ever
escaped the penalty; but, upon this occasion, the authority
of the Senate was superseded, and they were reduced to
the sad necessity of deploring a misfortune for which
there was no remedy. Heliogabalus easily perceived the
deep sorrow that this marriage caused to all classes in
the city, as not only the strictest laws, but the most
ancient and religious custom of the Romans had been
thereby trampled under foot. The people exclaimed
against it as an unheard of crime, capable of drawing
down upon them the indignation of all the gods. A deep
silence reigned among them, and such melancholy was
seen on the countenances of the citizens that all the city
seemed in deep mourning.

Though Heliogabalus did not usually give himself
much trouble about justifying his actions, he yet thought
it incumbent on him to excuse the step he had taken;
but he did it in a manner that was more offensive than
the action itself, that was, by jesting about a crime for
which,[1] as an historian says, he deserved the worst of
deaths. He wrote to the Senate that, of all the failings
a man was subject to there was none that more entitled
him to pardon than those which were the effects of his
frailty; that it was very difficult to resist the violence of
love; that Severa's beauty did not give him time to reflect;
that his passion had surprised his reason, but that, in
short, the mischief being done, there was no help for it;
that, after all, he did not see any reason they had to cry
out so much against what he had done, for if all was
considered it would be found that it would be no very

[1] Herodian. lib. 5.

strange thing for a priest of the sun to marry a vestal. That, on the contrary, they ought to rejoice to see two sacred persons united by the solemn bonds of marriage, because from the union of a pontiff with a vestal nothing could be produced but a race that must be celestial rather than mortal.

Severa found it no difficult matter to exchange her plain and simple dress for the imperial ornaments, and it must be confessed that her consent to this marriage could be attributed to nothing but unbounded ambition, for besides the breach of her vow, which she scandalously violated, the inconstancy of Heliogabalus, who thought nothing of marrying and unmarrying himself as often as he pleased, ought to have made her reject his solicitations. He exalted his mistresses to the throne only to have the pleasure of hurling them down again, without giving them time to taste the sweets of sovereignty.

Faustina and Cornelia, reduced to their former condition of life, lamented their foolish credulity, and it was not to be expected that Severa would be able to fix the wavering heart of a prince who was incapable of a perfect and constant affection. Accordingly, it was not long before her fall administered some consolation to the disgraced Empresses. Heliogabalus soon becoming tired of his favourite vestal, divorced her, and at the same time took the opportunity to ruin her father Sabinus. It would not have been consistent with the rest of his conduct if he had remained for any time without some new amour, for with him the conclusion of one passion was the beginning of another. He substituted another Empress in the place of Severa, and as speedily got rid of her for a fifth, and her again for a sixth. And so great a

jest did he make of his marriages, and such was the
mutability of his temper, that he took Severa back, and
re-established her in all the glory and splendour he had
just stripped her of. If Severa had the satisfaction to be
reinstated she had also, on the other hand, innumerable
annoyances to submit to from the odd caprices, fickleness, and debaucheries of Heliogabalus, for never did any
of the Emperors carry excesses to such a pitch. Not content with abandoning himself entirely to all sorts of
pollutions, he generally passed the night in those infamous
places that were appropriated to lewdness, where he
brutally substituted himself in the place of the most remarkable courtesans, counterfeited their voices and
gestures, and, prostituting himself to the bestiality of
those whom the fury of their debaucheries had brought
thither—such as buffoons and slaves—filled Rome with
his abominations, so that it was said of him that he was
a man for every woman, and a woman for every man.

His monstrous lasciviousness was only interrupted by
acts of cruelty or folly, for his very diversions were fatal
to somebody. Sometimes he took it into his head to cause
so great a quantity of flowers to be thrown from a gallery
upon the senators, who went to pay their court to him,
that a great many were smothered. He passed whole
days in driving chariots, and it was generally in the
presence of the Princesses Mæsa and Soemias that he
chose to show his skill in that low exercise, which exposed
him to the ridicule of the people. At last, after innumerable follies and extravagances, he went so far as to be
formally married to a miserable slave named Hierocles,
who, in a short time, became one of the richest and most
powerful men in the empire. He was delighted to be

called the mistress, the wife, the queen of Hierocles, and,
that he might look the more like a woman, he had himself close shaved, took a distaff, and employed his time
in spinning and other feminine occupations, to the great
dishonour of the sex he intended to imitate. Thus do
men commit the most unaccountable actions when they
cease to be directed by reason and discretion.

Mæsa was in the utmost confusion at this shameful
behaviour, and could not without the greatest concern be
a witness of the scandal Heliogabalus brought upon the
imperial dignity, which could not fail to end in some
dreadful misfortune. She made use of all her art and
address to correct her grandson's evil courses and persuade him to reflect a little upon the consequences of
such irregularities, but it was all to no purpose. Heliogabalus was entirely guided by his mother, who encouraged him in his debaucheries, and by her own licentiousness set him an abominable example, for this vicious
princess, forgetting the reserve and modesty of her sex
and the regard which was due to her rank, abandoned
herself to the most scandalous debaucheries and prostitutions.[1] Thus, far from opposing the depraved inclinations of her son, or endeavouring to reclaim him,
she was quite satisfied with his course of life, and even
commended him for it.

Heliogabalus's odious government became an insupportable yoke to the Romans, the weight of which he
every day increased by his cruelties and ridiculous behaviour, which was equally detestable and contemptible.
But what made the people lose all patience was his mad
design to declare the infamous Hierocles, who but the

[1] Lamprid. in Heliogab.

other day was a wretched slave, Cæsar, and his successor
to the throne. Mæsa did all [1] in her power to dissuade
him from this resolution, which could not fail to bring
eternal shame upon the empire. She represented to him
the injury he would thereby do himself and his family,
and, in order to intimidate him, she told him that so
unworthy a choice could not fail to cause a sedition, and
make the Senate, the officers of the army and the people
revolt, but Heliogabalus, looking upon these remonstrances as so many impertinent reprimands, lost the
respect he had till then shown to his grandmother, and
answered with violent threats. Mæsa's arguments had,
however, made such an impression upon his mind that
he was afraid of executing his project; so true it is that
wholesome advice has generally a good effect, even upon
those who are determined not to follow it.

Mæsa, perceiving how difficult, or rather impossible, it
was to work upon the obstinate temper of her grandson,
so as to effect any considerable alteration in him, was
convinced that a revolution could not be far off; for
Hierocles had obtained such an ascendency over the
Emperor that he was trusted with all his secrets, invested
with his authority, and was the channel through which all
favours at Court were to pass. This roused the jealousy
of all the nobles, who could not bear that this upstart
should have absolute control of the empire and dispose
of their lives and fortunes. Mæsa foresaw the consequences, and had no doubt that a change would soon
take place; she was even apprehensive of being involved
in the misfortunes that threatened the Emperor, so that
from that time she thought of taking care of herself and

---

[1] Dio. lib. 79.

abandoning her grandson to his evil destiny. The brilliant appearance she had made at Court with the Empress Julia, her sister, and the power she had enjoyed during the reigns of Severus and Caracalla, gave her such a taste for grandeur that she could not endure the idea of returning to the obscure private life she had been forced to be content with in Macrinus's time, and which she had reason to look forward to, if the prince who should succeed Heliogabalus should happen not to be favourably disposed towards her. She therefore did her utmost to arrange matters so that the empire might devolve upon somebody she could reckon upon, who would preserve to her her rank and authority, which she was most solicitous about.

She could think of nobody more proper for her purpose than young Alexianus, her grandson, cousin-german to Heliogabalus, and son of Mamea; and she thought she might the more easily procure him the empire as he was next heir, Heliogabalus having no child. If the Emperor could be induced to adopt him, she imagined there would be no difficulty in the matter; but, as Heliogabalus was of a very obstinate temper, she knew she would need all her skill and address to carry her point without exasperating him. Mæsa had, however, so studied him, and was so well acquainted with his temper, that she succeeded; for as she knew his weak side, she watched the favourable moment, and finding him disposed to listen to her, she gave him to understand that it could be nobody's interest so much as hers to give him such advice as would prove most to his advantage, and prevent those evils she was apprehensive of. " It is certain," said she, " that the empire alone would require all your attentions, but the office of priest of the sun must necessarily take up part of your time. Two such important offices are too much for one person. Your zeal for Elagabalus is, without doubt, very commendable, but your care and concern for the welfare of the empire cannot be less than your respect for that adorable divinity. I agree with you that all this is fatiguing and laborious, but nothing hinders you from laying part of the burden upon some other person, which would leave you more at leisure to attend to the service of your god. Choose somebody you can depend upon, but take care how you trust a stranger; it would be putting too great confidence in him, for of all things you must beware of selecting one who would be likely to arrogate all the authority to himself, and by degrees employ the power you have put into his hands against you. Look out for someone in your own family upon whom you may safely rely.

" There is Prince Alexianus, your cousin, than whom I think nobody better qualified in every respect, and from whom you have nothing to fear; for, besides that he is too young to cause you any jealousy, he has the honour to be related to you, and consequently cannot but have your interests at heart."

The Emperor, in whom some respect for his grandmother still lingered, especially when she did not attempt to lay him under any restraint, approved the proposal, and even looked upon it as a striking token of her love and affection for him. He carried Alexianus to the Senate, where he declared that he adopted the young prince for his son. He gave him the name of Alexander, made him Cæsar and consul, and protested that it was his god Elagabalus that had inspired him with this thought.

The Senate authorised his choice, and the people heard
it with great joy.

After Heliogabalus had adopted Alexander he thought
he had a right to require what he pleased of him, and
because he had associated him in the empire he was
resolved he should imitate him in his follies. Mamea,
the young prince's mother, on the contrary, laboured in
secret to instil good ideas into his mind, and to keep him
aloof from all the pleasures, or rather madnesses, of the
Emperor. She was a woman of modest and regular life,
and employed all her time in giving her son a good education. She took no part in her sister's debaucheries,
so that her reputation was as illustrious as that of
Soemias was infamous. She acquired great experience
in State affairs with Mæsa, her mother, who during the
reigns of Severus and Caracalla had a great share in the
government. These two Emperors greatly esteemed
Mamea for her wisdom and other qualities, and Caracalla
allowed her to retain the rank and honours she became
entitled to when married to Macrinus, although strictly
speaking she had forfeited them by her second marriage
with Claudius Julianus, who was of inferior rank. But
nothing did her so much honour as the care she took to
inspire her son with sentiments of moderation and
humanity, and to make him hate all those diversions that
were inconsistent with purity and decency, by giving him
privately such good lessons and advice as served for an
antidote against the infectious example and conversation of Heliogabalus, who seemed determined to make
him a partner in his vices, as he had done in his dignity.
She had, further, the precaution to cause masters and
preceptors to visit him secretly, who taught him the

sciences, and such exercises as were becoming his rank
and quality, and formed his tender mind to virtue, in
spite of all the Emperor's attempts to make him in love
with those low, shameful, and contemptible occupations
in which he himself employed his time, and for which
Alexander showed a great aversion.

As nothing more binds and cements friendship than a
conformity of sentiments and inclinations, so nothing is
more apt to disunite than a difference in temper and
humours. Heliogabalus and Alexander were born with
quite opposite characters, so that it would have been very
unusual if there had been a perfect union between them.
Accordingly, the Emperor, not finding in his colleague
that taste for the shameful pleasures, gross amusements,
and frequent cruelties that he himself was so fond of,
began to hate him, and repented that he had adopted him.
The people's affection for the young prince much increased his jealousy and dislike, so that he was determined
to destroy his partner. He commanded Alexander's
officers and domestics either to massacre or poison him,
but found them so faithful to their master that neither
his threats nor promises could influence them. Besides,
Mamea was so vigilant and so continually upon her
guard against the Emperor's plots and designs that she
would never suffer her son to eat or drink anything that
came from Heliogabalus or those belonging to him, being
very careful to have all his provisions dressed by her
own servants, on whom she could safely depend; and,
that Alexander might have it in his power to ingratiate
himself with the troops, she furnished him with money to
distribute among them. This liberality gained him, indeed, the affection of the soldiers, but it irritated Helio-

gabalus more and more against him, for he knew that by these means Alexander was endeavouring to corrupt the legions; he therefore hesitated no longer about putting him to death, but resolved to do it at all costs, and that Mamea should be served the same way for being, as he suspected, the person in reality responsible; but, not content with taking away his life, he was minded to degrade him, and strip him of the name which he had given him at his adoption, together with the title of Cæsar. In fact, he sent people to erase his name and title from all inscriptions where they had been inserted.

This attempt ended in quite a different manner from what Heliogabalus intended, for, as soon as the above orders began to be put into execution, the soldiers mutinied, and flocked to the palace to defend Alexander, who they no longer doubted would fall a sacrifice to the Emperor's resentment; and, being informed that Heliogabalus had withdrawn to another palace, they ran thither to assassinate him, and would have done so had not Antiochitus, præfect of the Prætorian cohorts, put a stop to their fury, by reminding them of the oath they had taken to Heliogabalus, and which they were going to violate by murdering him. They were even forced to carry Alexander into the camp to convince the soldiers of his being alive. Thus this wicked Emperor, by attempting to destroy his cousin, did him the greatest possible service, contrary to his intentions.

This evident token, however, of the soldiers' affection for Alexander provoked Heliogabalus beyond all measure. He looked upon this sedition as the most violent attack upon his authority, and upon his cousin as his most formidable enemy. The more he perceived the soldiers loved him, the more did his hatred increase. He was so little able to conceal his aversion for the young prince that he could not help showing it upon every occasion, particularly the first day of the year, at which time Alexander, as consul, had to attend the Emperor to the Senate, and then to the Capitol, to perform the usual ceremonies. Heliogabalus had a mind to go thither alone, and not to allow his cousin to bear him company. Mæsa and Soemias represented to him that so glaring an exhibition of hatred would entirely alienate from him the love of the people; that by such impolitic conduct he would be acting against his own interests instead of hurting the prince. That so scandalous a mistake (the whole blame of which would certainly fall upon him) would furnish the soldiers with a pretence to revolt, which he ought by all means to prevent, as they seemed only too ripe for it already. That in so delicate a conjuncture he ought to be very careful how he omitted or changed anything in the ancient customs.

These remonstrances so intimidated the Emperor that, after having for a long time resisted the entreaties of the two princesses, he determined about noon to go to the Senate with Alexander and Mæsa, who took her place there as usual; however, he obstinately persisted in his resolution not to go to the Capitol, so as to deprive Alexander of the honour of performing the accustomed sacrifices upon that occasion (at which the consuls were to appear in all their pomp and splendour), and ordered them to be performed by the governor of the city, as if the consuls had been absent. His having been prevailed upon to take Alexander with him to the Senate did such great violence to his inclinations that he determined he should perish, whatever ill consequences it might be attended with.

His jealousy inspired him with these violent ideas, and fortified him at first against whatever might happen, but his timidity soon weakened his resolution, and made him apprehensive of the consequences. He could not doubt but the Senate and the armies, who had the greatest affection for Alexander, would not leave his death unpunished; but, on the other hand, he flattered himself that if the deed were once done, Alexander's most zealous friends, having nothing further to hope from him, would not give themselves much trouble about avenging his death. In this state of irresolution, he thought he could not do better than sound the people, and learn what their sentiments would be if they imagined that Alexander was dead. For this purpose he kept the prince within the palace, and gave out that he was dying. This news, being spread in a moment all over the city, caused general consternation amongst the people. Nothing was to be heard but murmurings and threats. The soldiers flocked together, refused to mount guard as usual at the palace, and, shutting themselves up in their camp, resolved to go directly to the Emperor and oblige him to deliver up Alexander to them.

This terrified the Emperor, and fearing that he had carried the matter too far, he conducted Alexander into the camp, accompanied by Soemias and Mamea. As soon as the prince appeared, the soldiers shouted for joy, and, by the ardent vows they offered for his prosperity, sufficiently shewed how much they had it at heart, at the same time remaining quite silent as to the Emperor. This was fresh matter of discontent for Heliogabalus,

and the fact of the soldiers preferring Alexander's welfare so much before his exasperated him to that degree
that the next morning he assembled the Senate, and condemned to death those who had appeared most zealous
in behalf of the prince.

This ill-timed severity was his ruin; the whole camp
mutinied, and though the Emperor had proscribed only
those whom he considered most guilty, the others could
not see their comrades sacrificed to his fury without apprehending the like treatment. They unanimously cried
out that it was high time to destroy the tyrant and raise
Alexander to the throne. Nothing is more dangerous
than the first transports of a popular insurrection: it is a
torrent that carries all before it. The Emperor, seeing
his life in danger, was inclined to have recourse to flight,
but being in the midst of the camp, whence it was no
easy matter to extricate himself, he implored the assistance of those about him. The præfect of the guards,
Hierocles, and some others who had accompanied him,
made some efforts to defend him against Alexander's
soldiers, and the skirmish in a little time became a battle.
Soemias and Mamea, perceiving that the fortune of their
respective parties depended on the issue of this fight,
separated. Each put herself at the head of her own
friends, and performed the part of general, encouraging
her soldiers with promises of reward, and endeavouring
to corrupt those of her adversary, so that these two sisters
were seen labouring to the utmost of their power to
procure each other's destruction.

During the combat Heliogabalus hid himself in a place
where were thrown all the excrements and filth of the
camp, and whither Soemias, his mother, followed him,

when she found that her party was beaten; but Alexander's soldiers, looking diligently for him, found him at last, and massacred him in the arms of Soemias, who held him fast as it were to protect him, and afterwards killed her, in like manner, with their poniards. The Senate were in raptures of joy at the news of his death, and the first decree they made was that no woman should ever be permitted to sit in the Senate. Such was the end of the infamous Heliogabalus, and his abominable life deserved no better one. It was foretold him that he should perish miserably by a violent and untimely death, and, in order to disappoint any that should attack him, he carried about him silken cords to hang himself with, a silver poniard to stab himself, and poison in a gold box, that he might choose what kind of death he liked best. He also caused a high tower to be built, in which he might take shelter in case of necessity; this he paved with silver and enriched with diamonds and precious stones, that, if he should prefer to cast himself from top to bottom to any of the other methods of death, it might be said that his end was magnificent.

History makes no further mention of the Empresses Faustina, Cornelia, and Severa.

THE DAUGHTER OF VARIUS MARCIANUS
MEMMIA
SALLUSTIA BARBIA ORBIANA
WIVES OF ALEXANDER SEVERUS

MAMEA
MOTHER OF THAT EMPEROR

FTER Heliogabalus had been killed in the camp of the Prætorians, the soldiers proclaimed young Alexander August, and attended him to the palace. More universal joy was never seen at Rome, where each individual seemed to promise himself all possible happiness from the prince's election. At the same time as the Senate declared him Emperor, they gave him the titles of August and Father of the State. They were also inclined to honour him with the surname of Antoninus, and the title of Great, which had been given to Alexander of Macedon, but the young prince refused it with a modesty that made him more worthy of it. It is certain that, if Alexander had reason to be well pleased at the zeal and affection that all classes in the city showed in his behalf, it must be also confessed that never prince of his age gave better proofs of being worthy of it. As to his person, he was very tall, well made, and had a most

agreeable countenanace, in which was something so manly
and warlike that it bespoke the love and respect of all
who approached him. His eyes were so lively and brilliant that people could not bear he should look steadfastly at them. His mental endowments were in no way
inferior to his bodily perfections, for in him all the virtues
were united in an eminent degree. He was mild, affable,
modest, humble, an enemy to vice and vicious people, as
careful to make others do justice as he was to do it
himself. To these noble inclinations Nature had added
an apt and docile disposition, which made him entirely
submissive to the advice of those who were entrusted with
his education, and who, not finding any bad habits in
this young prince to struggle against, had nothing to do
but to cultivate and bring to maturity the good seed which
had been sown in so fruitful a soil.

Alexander was but thirteen years old when he came to
the throne. The Senate decreed to Mamea, his mother,
the title of August, that of Mother of the State, and all
those honours which they had so lavishly bestowed upon
the wives and mothers of the Emperors. But it must be
acknowledged that, though many of those princesses
were unworthy of the pompous and magnificent honours
that had been decreed them, they were no more than
what Mamea deserved. She was exceedingly strict and
prudent in her behaviour, having never in her whole life
taken any step that could afford the least excuse for calling her virtue in question.[1]

Mamea thoroughly deserved the honours the Senate
had decreed her, were it only on account of the good
education she had given her son, and the care she took to

---

[1] Euseb. Hist. 6. 15, Nicephor. Call. Hist. 5. c. 17.

place no persons about him but such as were of known virtue and integrity. People of corrupt lives found no admittance into the palace, and especially those debauched instruments of Heliogabalus's shameful pleasures and cruelties were strictly prohibited. She banished all flatterers—that poisonous race of vermin with which Courts are often infected, and whose pernicious counsels are capable of seducing even the best disposed people. She did not stop there; for, being convinced that nothing is more pernicious, nor a greater promotion of vice, than idleness, she was careful to keep him well employed in such occupations as should not afford him leisure to run into those amusements that might have been prejudicial to him; for which reason she chose to be generally present when he was administering justice, or regulating the affairs of the empire.

It is certain that Mamea could not possibly have taken wiser precautions; but, on the other hand, it must be owned that the young prince's good disposition made her work very easy and agreeable. What a surprising progress will education make in a person so well inclined as Alexander! He was very attentive to the good advice of his mother and his preceptors, and followed it strictly. He showed the greatest zeal for the public good, and made excellent regulations for the government of the empire. One of the first things he did was to abolish the odd and fantastical worship of the god Elagabalus, and send back to Emesa the stone for which Heliogabalus had so ridiculous a veneration. He soon gave the city quite another appearance, by reforming the abuses that his predecessors had either introduced or connived at. He restored to the Senate their ancient splendour and dignity, by placing in it such persons as, by their merit and birth, were worthy of that honour, and by turning out those infamous people with whom Heliogabalus had filled it. In his reign no other qualifications were necessary as a recommendation to office than honour and probity; for Alexander (deaf to all considerations of friendship and kindred in the distribution of important posts) regarded nothing but merit and virtue.

Mæsa had the satisfaction of seeing these happy beginnings of her grandson's reign; and it must be acknowledged that she had greatly contributed to his noble sentiments and inclinations by her good advice. She died soon after at a very advanced age.[1] Alexander procured her immortality, and all those superstitious honours that were usually given to the mothers and wives of Emperors. He was not unmindful of the obligations he was under to this princess, who had prevailed upon Heliogabalus to adopt him.

The death of Mæsa brought fresh anxieties upon Mamea, for as the former of these ladies had been a very active and vigilant guard of all the young Emperor's actions and behaviour, so it now became more immediately incumbent upon her to supply that loss. To cultivate his mind with the attention that was necessary, and at the same time to take care of all the affairs of the empire, were no trifling occupations; her endeavours were, however, attended with such success that, in spite of those who rail at the government of women, it may be affirmed that the city and provinces were never ruled with more wisdom and prudence. As she was persuaded that nothing was so dangerous and apt to seduce a young

[1] Herodian. lib. 6.

man as being invested with absolute power, she selected (with the assistance of the Senate) sixteen persons, the most remarkable for gravity,[1] experience, and purity of manners, whose business it was to protect him against those vices and failings to which the impetuosity of youth is liable, and the pernicious influence of flatterers. Ulpian, a famous lawyer, who was without dispute the principal person of that select body of men, was particularly zealous in the business he undertook, and became so great a favorite with the Emperor that Mamea began to be jealous of him, for she could not bear that her son should have so great an esteem for anybody but herself.   At last, however, perceiving that Ulpian gave the Emperor no advice but what was salutary and discreet, she herself laboured for the advancement of that great man, and defended him against some mutinous soldiers, who, not being able to endure the authority that he assumed over them, would have killed him.   She also made him præfect of the Prætorian Guards, which dignity afterwards cost him his life.   The authority of these governors was, however, subordinate to hers, for Mamea did not suffer her son to be guided by them, except in so far as they conformed to her directions; and the Emperor paid so blind and implicit an obedience to his mother that he followed her advice even when he could not approve of it, for which he has been much blamed. People have reproached him [2] with being such a slave to his mother's opinion as to have been often thereby prevailed upon to act in a manner quite contrary to his reputation and interests.

The vigilance of these grave senators, who were as so

[1] Lamprid. in Alex. Herodian. lib. 6.   [2] Herodian.

many Arguses to watch the Emperor's conduct, did not appear to Mamea to be a sufficient guard against the temptations and violent outbursts of youth; she therefore thought it necessary, in order to prevent his running into criminal pleasures, to procure him such as were lawful. She determined to marry him, though he was but about fifteen years of age, and was of opinion that her own interest required that she should take this step, for as she gratified her ambition by enjoying the sovereign authority without control, so she took it for granted that any daughter-in-law of her choosing would lie under such obligations to her as to be very well satisfied with whatever share of power she was pleased to allow her, and selected a relation of her first husband for that purpose.

Varius Marcianus, a near relation of Alexander's father, had a daughter no less remarkable for the beauties of her mind than for those of her person; and though she could not boast of a very illustrious extraction, she was always reckoned upon a level with the most noble persons in the empire, on account of the many important victories of her father in Illyria, as well as the honour she had of being allied to the Imperial family. Mamea, flattering herself that it would be in her power to govern her as she did her son, proposed the match to Alexander, who, never having been accustomed to contradict his mother, made no objection. The Senate, with great pleasure and satisfaction, decreed her the title of August, and all the other marks of their respect that had been conferred upon the Empresses her predecessors, which Mamea was very well satisfied with, as it did honour to her choice. We shall, however, find in the sequel that these titles, particularly that of August, occasioned a misunderstanding between the two princesses that was attended with fatal consequences.

These nuptials having been celebrated, Mamea resolved to look out for a proper husband for the Princess Theoclea, her daughter, and determined in favour of the son of Maximinus, who, from a shepherd, became a soldier, and chief of a legion which Alexander had given him command of, after having made him a senator, not knowing that in this officer he was heaping favours upon his murderer. Maximinus, the father, was, without dispute, a good soldier and brave officer, but of rough, unpolished manners, that savoured of the rudeness and barbarity of his nation and the lowness of his birth. It is reported that his son Maximus was more civilised, but at the same time more proud and insolent. It was, however, to him that Mamea resolved to give her daughter; but as the Emperor, her son, was not then at Rome, she communicated her design to him by letter. Alexander did not like it; for, as he was very fond of his sister, he was apprehensive that the princess, who had been brought up at Court and well educated, would never be reconciled to the sour and morose tempers of the Maximins; but, as he had the greatest desire to oblige his mother, he contented himself with representing to her that he could not indeed but acknowledge that Maximinus was a good officer, and that he had a great regard for his merit; but that there was something so disagreeable in his manners and person that neither the air of the Court nor his long service in the army had been able to correct it. That the princess, his sister, having been used to Greek customs and polite society, would find it extremely difficult to endure a father-in-law of such a character. That, though the son was of a disposition somewhat more tolerable, yet he did not think it reasonable that a princess possessing her accomplishments should be matched with a person who, in his opinion, was not equal to her in any respect, particularly with regard to his temper. That, since she was inclined to marry her daughter, he thought she could not find a more suitable husband than Messala, who was a Roman of illustrious birth, adorned with all the good qualities that could be desired, and who, in all probability, would one day make a considerable figure in his military capacity. He added, nevertheless, that he did not venture to oppose her inclinations; but, on the contrary, left her at full liberty to act as she thought proper. It is very likely that Mamea approved of her son's arguments, since she made no further mention of this marriage.

Though Alexander loved his wife extremely, he did not give himself up so entirely to the pleasures of marriage as to neglect the welfare of the State, which was always the principal object of his care. He abolished some of the taxes and lessened others, and never allowed his private interest to interfere with that of the public. As for the arts and sciences, he rescued them from the contemptible situation his predecessor had left them in, by honouring with his protection and liberality those great men whose genius and learning he admired. He founded schools [1] in which he settled all sorts of professors, and gave pensions to a certain number of scholars who were of rank, but in poor circumstances.

He erected many sumptuous buildings and repaired others, adorning the city with a great number of statues.

[1] Lamprid.

But what ingratiated him most of all with the people was his esteem for those who behaved well, and the care he took to punish such as deserved chastisement, especially those who were corrupt or partial in the administration of justice, in which case he never pardoned even his best friends. His palace was open to all those who were distinguished for virtue and goodness, but such as were of a contrary character he could not endure. He carried this so far that, according to the historians, he would not permit people of indifferent reputation to pay their respects to his wife nor his mother, as if there had been something infectious about them. He was a strict observer of justice, but, at the same time, his severity was always tempered with mildness and clemency; for, during his whole reign, he never ordered any person to be put to death, leaving capital crimes to the decision of the Senate. No flatterers could gain admittance to him, as he considered them to be his most dangerous enemies. As he was sincere in his words and actions, he detested cunning and artifice; but, above all, he hated those who, holding high offices, made a traffic of their influence and interest, for, in those times, as well as the present, there were persons at Court who received money and presents for services which they promised to do, but never did. Very ready to give words, they would undertake to obtain, from the Emperor or his ministers, favours and offices, which they forgot as soon as the petitioner was out of sight. Vetronius Turinus excelled in this trade. He had insinuated himself [1] in such a manner into the good graces of the Emperor that he became his chief favourite, though he had very little to recommend him.

[1] Lamprid. in Alex.

To tell the truth, Alexander put such confidence in this
man, who had no one good quality, as did but small
honour to his character, for the public, who did not find
in Turinus that merit that might have been expected
from the high degree of favour he was in, thought Alexander either not so judicious as he ought to be, or too
complaisant. Turinus, in the meantime, lost no opportunity of making the most of his interest, and did not
scruple to receive money from all those who had favours
to ask, and addressed themselves to him. He encouraged
the people as much as possible to apply to him, and
boasted that he could do what he pleased with the Emperor, promising them success with so much assurance
that whoever was so happy as to gain his friendship had
no doubt of obtaining all he could wish for. It was,
however, but very seldom that he gave himself any
trouble about those whose money and presents he had
received; but if they happened to succeed, by whatever
means it was, he took the merit of it to himself.

Alexander had some suspicion of this traffic, and was
extremely provoked at it; but being determined to find
out the truth, he ordered a person who requested a favour
of him to apply to Turinus, and then to come and let him
know what passed. Turinus did not fail, as usual, to
promise to recommend his case to the Emperor; and soon
after, having met the petitioner, he assured him that his
business was going on satisfactorily, and he did not doubt
but he would succeed upon a second application; but gave
him to understand that he did not employ his interest
gratis. The other bound himself before witnesses to pay
him a great sum of money.

The Emperor was acquainted with the whole transaction; he granted the favour required, for which Turinus received payment, though he had done nothing to entitle him to it. Alexander, having got all the information he wanted, ordered Turinus to be apprehended, and that all who had anything to allege against him should be heard. The consequence of this was that he was convicted of innumerable acts of this kind. He was condemned to be tied to a gallows, under which was kindled hay and green wood, which suffocated him. The crime he had committed was called "selling smoke," so that his punishment was conformable to his guilt.

Alexander, however, drew a useful lesson from this iniquitous proceeding of Turinus; it taught him not to trust anybody with his secrets for the future, except Ulpian, whose fidelity he knew he could depend upon, nor to permit any other person to solicit favours. By this commendable behaviour, together with his affability and modesty, he acquired the love and esteem of all the world. He would never permit anybody to call him Lord; and his humility was such that he used to visit his friends familiarly, and, inviting himself to their houses, would sit down among them without ceremony or distinction, acting less like an Emperor than a private person. At his table was served nothing but what was common, and all those who were remarkable for honesty and goodness were admitted to it with as much freedom as if he had been their equal.

If this excellent prince could not be reproached with pride or extravagances, neither was he ever accused of any excess in his apparel, which was always plain, without jewels or embroidery; he seldom went to the expense of silk garments, his virtue being his chief ornament.

This frugality served as a model to his courtiers and all persons of distinction, who were ashamed to fare more delicately than the Emperor himself. The ladies had the same example to follow in the Empress, by Alexander's direction; for an ambassador from the East having presented her with two pearls of an extraordinary size and weight,[1] the Emperor would not permit her to wear them, saying he would never consent that his wife should introduce the pernicious custom of wearing rich jewels; so he ordered them to be sold by auction.

The Empress could have wished that Alexander had been less rigid than he was upon this occasion. It was not without considerable regret that she saw the pearls that were intended to adorn her person likely to pass into other hands; but she was spared that mortification, for nobody offered to bid for them.[2] Whether it was that the price was excessive, or that people were afraid to encourage an extravagance that the Emperor took so much pains to discountenance, the pearls were brought back to the Empress, though she had not the satisfaction of making use of them; for Alexander sent them to adorn the statue of Venus.

The Emperor's zeal to suppress luxury was the more worthy of praise, as it did not proceed from sordid avarice, a vice unworthy of a great prince, but from the most consummate prudence; for, by careful retrenchment, he was always in a position to defray necessary expenses, and then it was that he displayed his magnificence and generosity. In fact, he blamed covetousness as much as prodigality, and did not, as history informs us, spare his mother in that respect; for, perceiving that she had re-

[1] Lamprid. vit. Alex.   [2] Lamprid.

course to scandalous and sometimes unlawful methods to heap up money, he told her one day, in a respectful manner,[1] that so great economy did not become a princess of her rank, who ought, on the contrary, to be liberal and beneficent; that he could not conceive what use she intended to make of the treasure she was scraping up with so much pains and trouble, and by such ways and means as did not appear to all the world to be strictly consistent with innocence.

Mamea, who never wanted presence of mind, was not at a loss for a specious and plausible pretence for her avarice. She represented to her son that, money being the sinews of the State, and the very life of affairs, particular regard must be paid to it. That she did not lock up her money in her coffers for her own private advantage, but to employ it to good purposes when need arose. That if the soldiers, who are continually given to change, should revolt against him, there was no speedier or more effectual method to bring them back to their duty than a reasonable distribution of money. That a well-timed bounty among the legions would maintain them in their fidelity; for that the troops would never fail to support that side where most money was to be got; and, in short, that it was in order to prevent or extinguish rebellions that she heaped up those riches for which he reproached her.

These reasons appeared sound, but did not satisfy Alexander, who was not desirous of gaining the goodwill and affection of the soldiers upon such conditions. He looked upon this extraordinary precaution of his mother as unworthy of the glory of his reign, and was of opinion

[1] Herodian. lib. 6.

that, the more the legions were interested, the more they were to be suspected.

If Mamea's covetousness caused Alexander a great deal of vexation, her ambition was not less a cause of anxiety to him.

She had received from the Senate all the honours that flattery could invent, and even more than had ever been conferred upon the wives or mothers of any of the preceding Emperors. They had decreed her, not only the title of August, but also that of Mother of the Armies,[1] of the Senate, and of the State. Thus, it might reasonably have been imagined that this would have been sufficient to gratify her vanity; it was all, however, too little to cure her of the ridiculous jealousy she had conceived at her daughter-in-law's enjoying the title of August, which she thought was due only to herself. She ought to have considered that an empty title was all she had to boast of, for Mamea engrossed all power and authority to such a degree that she did and ordered everything according to her own will and pleasure. This unbounded ambition caused her to treat the young Empress in a most inhuman manner, for, without having the least regard either for her rank or for the love her husband had for her, or in short, for common decency and good manners, she suffered herself to be so hurried away by her passion as to use this unfortunate princess extremely ill, and persecute her cruelly.[2]

Alexander had never been in so disagreeable a situation; this misunderstanding between his mother and his wife gave him a great deal of trouble; for, if he had taken part with Mamea he must have sacrificed a most amiable

---

[1] Spon. Miscel.   [2] Herodian. lib. 6.

wife, who loved him above all things; and, on the other hand, he could not think of contradicting his mother, to whom he owed his fortune. The Empress was well aware of the vexation these disputes must needs cause her husband, and was prudent enough not to require that he should declare for her; but that she might not be exposed to Mamea's envy and ill-nature, she quitted the palace, and retired to her father's house, imagining that by this voluntary banishment she would cease to give her mother-in-law any further cause for jealousy. This precaution was very discreet, but it did not satisfy Mamea, for wherever the young Empress was, she was still August, and the Emperor's mother could not endure that any person but herself should enjoy that title. She did not therefore suffer the Empress to be quiet in her retreat but, on the contrary, found means to persecute her even there; and not content with that, she could not help showing marks of her indignation to Marcianus, the Empress's father, having been informed that he was much displeased at her injustice and cruelty towards his daughter.

Marcianus was not courtier enough to have learnt the art of dissimulation; he could not be an indifferent spectator of the ill-usage his daughter met with; so, thinking it useless to complain to Alexander of Mamea, who kept him in the utmost subjection, and perhaps urged on by his ambition as well as resentment, he formed a conspiracy against his son-in-law.[1]

The rank he held in the empire facilitated this bold undertaking, for, besides the honour he had acquired by his victories, he was promoted by the Emperor, his son-

[1] Lamprid. Herodian.

in-law, to the highest offices, and was become very important from his near alliance with Alexander. Thus, depending on the great authority he had in the army, he took refuge in the Prætorian camp, as if to avoid the persecutions of Mamea; he there exaggerated the unlimited ambition of that princess, who in the name of her son, exercised a tyrannical power, and whose envy and jealousy had reached such a pitch that she could not endure that the Empress should take the title of August, which the Senate had decreed her, which all the orders of the empire had given her, and which was due to the Emperor's wife. After having done all that was possible to irritate the soldiers against Mamea, he put himself under their protection; but this scheme did not succeed according to his intention, for the troops were too fond of Mamea to consent to anything contrary to her interests. Marcianus, by this step, only discovered his design, and drew upon himself more and more the indignation of Mamea, to which he soon fell a victim. Instead of prevailing upon the soldiers to espouse his cause and revolt in his favour, as he was in hopes would be the case, he expiated his rashness by his death. The Empress shared her father's misfortunes, of which she had been the innocent cause, and was banished into Africa, whither she carried only the empty shadow of that grandeur and useless title that had occasioned her disgrace. Alexander, dearly as he loved her, had not the resolution to exert his authority in behalf of this unfortunate princess. He saw her condemned to an unjust and rigorous banishment without being able to afford her any other relief than his sorrow and affliction.

History does not inform us whether the Empress died

in exile, but we are told that Alexander married a second wife, who, in all appearance, was chosen by Mamea, and was probably one who did not insist upon the title of August. This lady's name was Memmia, daughter of the consul Sulpicius, and grand-daughter of Catulus. The Senate did not fail to decree her the title of August,[1] as may be seen by her medals, but it may be taken for granted that she did not accept it, for fear of bringing upon herself the misfortunes of the preceding Empress. She was not, however, exempt from pride and haughtiness, for it went much against her inclinations that the Emperor should go to the public baths, and mix familiarly with people of low degree, divesting himself of all his pomp and grandeur, as if this humility, so charming and commendable in a prince, was any real diminution of his glory. But Alexander was far above this poor way of thinking, and when his mother and his wife reproached him with his too great condescension (as they called it), he answered that by seeming to abase himself he was in reality exalted, and his authority the more firmly established. In fact, his sweetness of temper and affability so won him the affection of the soldiers that there was nothing they would not do to serve him, while at liberty to act according to their own inclinations and uninfluenced by traitors. This was sufficiently proved in his wars with Artaxerxes, King of Persia, who became formidable to Rome by his victories.

This new conqueror was a Persian by birth, a man of no family, but possessed of all those talents that were necessary to make a great man. After he had made himself general of the army, he attacked the Parthians, de-

[1] Lamprid.

feated them, and having killed their King Artabanes,
overthrew their monarchy, and re-established the government that Alexander of Macedon had abolished. These
successes so raised his hopes and expectations that he
flattered himself he would recover whatever had belonged
to the Kings of Persia, and reconquer all the dominions
the Romans had in Asia. As arrogance naturally follows
good fortune, this monarch, who was so proud of his
victories as to take upon him the title of King of Kings,
and to look down upon other potentates as his slaves,
wrote to all the neighbouring princes that they should
either furnish him with the usual auxiliary troops or prepare for destruction. These threats terrified the weakest
and most timid of the princes, but there were some who
only yielded after a vigorous resistance; and Alsawad,[1]
one of these Oriental kings, would perhaps have been
able himself to have rendered abortive all the vast designs of this brutal conqueror if he had not been betrayed
by the very person he thought he had least reason to be
apprehensive of. It was his own daughter who was guilty
of this horrible perfidiousness. This princess, dazzled
with Artaxerxes's triumphs and the extent of his power,
was not ashamed to deliver up her father and her country
to their bitterest enemy.

Artaxerxes had besieged Alsawad in a fortress, before
which he had the mortification of wasting a great deal of
time and losing a considerable part of his army without
making any progress. He was not, however, discouraged, for the resistance he met with, far from making him
raise the siege, made him the more determined to take
the fort at all costs. But, as he was not less cunning

---

[1] Eutych, annales.

than brave, he had recourse to craft where his good
fortune failed. He knew that Alsawad had a daughter
who was marriageable, and not doubting but the princess
would with great pleasure listen to a proposal from him,
he found means to inform her that, if she would let him
know the weakest part of the fortress, he would marry
her, and raise her to the throne of Persia. This flattering
offer had the desired effect.

Nothing is more calculated to tempt and seduce a
young girl who is nobly born than a splendid marriage.
The crown of Persia did not appear to the princess to
deserve to be neglected. She gave Artaxerxes a favourable answer by a note shot from an arrow, and, after the
terms and conditions had been adjusted by the help of
these flying ambassadors, the princess who was as desirous to take the Persian as he was to take the fort,
discovered to him a place through which he might make
himself master of the castle without danger or trouble.

Artaxerxes immediately made the best use of the intelligence he had got, and meeting with but little resistance,
took the place. The princess received, indeed, the reward of her treason, but it was not long before she also
underwent the punishment she deserved. The barbarian,
soon after he had married her, asked her one day very
cunningly how her father used to treat her. The
princess, who did not suspect the snare that was laid
for her, answered that he had always loved her beyond
anything in the world, and had never given her the least
cause for displeasure. " Thou art then unworthy to
live," replied the Persian in a fury, " for, if thou hast
been unnatural enough to betray thy father who loved
thee, and from whom, as thou hast confessed, thou didst

never receive any cause of displeasure, what fidelity can *I* expect from thee? No," continued he, casting on her a look of indignation and contempt, " I will not expose myself to thy treachery, and that which thou hast been guilty of deserves the most rigorous chastisement." That instant he commanded the princess to be tied by her hair to a wild horse, which, at full speed, dragged her till she was torn in pieces. Thus was Alsawad revenged upon his undutiful and perfidious daughter, by means of the Persian monarch, his greatest enemy; so true it is that there is no reckoning upon the fidelity of a person who has not been shown proof against temptation.

Artaxerxes having taken the fort in the manner related, conquered all the country bordering upon Mesopotamia, and carried his arms as far as Cappadocia. These rapid victories alarmed Rome. Alexander, by the advice of his council, wrote to the barbarian prince that the Romans were not people who could be easily overcome, which the Orientals had found to their cost under Augustus, Trajan, and many other Emperors; therefore he was not acting over wisely in exposing himself to the same misfortunes. This letter, however, had a quite different effect from what was expected; for the Persian, instead of being intimidated by these threats, pursued his conquests on purpose to let the Romans see he was not afraid of them.

The Emperor being informed of this, prepared for war, and everything being ready, he set out from Rome, accompanied by the Senate and an infinite number of people, who testified by their tears the affliction they felt at the departure of a prince, who, by his mildness, beneficence, and many other rare and valuable qualities, had so well deserved their esteem.

As soon as the army had arrived at Antioch the Emperor sent a second embassy to Artaxerxes, but to as little purpose as the former. Alexander being then convinced that it was in vain to parley any longer, marched directly towards this haughty enemy, and gained a glorious victory. The news had no sooner reached Rome than the whole city was in the greatest joy imaginable, and it is impossible to describe their satisfaction at his arrival there. He was received in triumph, and all classes of the city went out to meet him with as much zeal and eagerness as if each individual person was to meet his father after a long absence. Rome, they said, was now safe, since she possessed within her walls so inestimable a jewel as Alexander.

The Emperor was extremely sensible of the sincere tokens of affection shown him by the Romans, and distributed large sums of money among the troops and the people. To his extraordinary bounty and generosity he added all sorts of sports, games, and shows; but the revolt of the Gauls soon interrupted these diversions.

Alexander was mightily provoked that these barbarians who, under the weakest and least warlike Emperors had not dared to stir, should have the assurance to shake off the yoke of obedience in his reign, who had just subdued the Persians, who were looked upon as infinitely more formidable. He resolved, therefore, to make an example of them, and for that purpose set out again from Rome with Mamea at the head of a powerful army, leaving the people in great grief. It is said that a Druid met him on the road, and told him his expedition would not be attended with success, for that his soldiers would betray him. It is also reported that an astrologer foretold that he would be killed. These unfortunate predictions did not hinder the Emperor from marching, with the utmost diligence, to Moguntiacum (Maintz). Amongst his legions there was one composed of Pannonians, and commanded by Maximinus, who has been already spoken of. This officer was under the greatest obligations to the Emperor, who had brought him up, and had given him innumerable marks of his esteem; all this kindness, however, made no impression upon the ungrateful wretch, who had formed a design to put the Emperor to death, and took every opportunity of rendering him odious to the soldiers, often insinuating that it was a shame for troops accustomed to conquer to obey a prince who was entirely governed by a woman, and who had not resolution to fight the enemies of the empire; that instead of going directly against the barbarians, Mamea had prevailed on him to return into the East with her son, and was not ashamed to leave the army without a chief, fleeing in a manner before the enemy.

These seditious discourses had but too great an effect upon the minds of the soldiers, who are generally fond of change, and who, besides, were not over content with Mamea, from whom they never received the least largess or present, though she was immensely rich. They imagined that a new Emperor would be more generous, and that by massacring Alexander they would be entitled to great rewards from whomsoever they should choose in his stead. Thus animated by the perfidious arguments of Maximinus, and by the hopes of a considerable recompense, they resolved to get rid of Mamea and her son.

The treacherous Maximinus took advantage of the disposition of the soldiers, and seeing them determined to act conformably to his wishes, detached a band of these Pannonians to Maintz, where the Emperor was. The unexpected arrival of these tumultuous troops without being sent for immediately caused a great consternation. The Emperor's guards, either intimidated or corrupted, fled, and left their Emperor exposed to the fury of this mutinous cohort. Mamea came out to persuade the rebels to return to their duty, but she had no sooner appeared than the soldiers brutally murdered her, and cut to pieces as many as attempted to defend her.

Alexander, who was in his tent, being informed of this uproar, gave himself up for lost. He had indeed observed military discipline very strictly, but yet was the farthest in the world from cruelty. He was nevertheless always apprehensive that, sooner or later, he should experience the bad consequences of his mother's avarice. In fact, as soon as he perceived the assassins enter his tent, their swords smeared with his mother's blood, he cried out that Mamea's covetousness had undone him. He promised to distribute among them all the money he had, but nothing could prevail, for they despatched him in a moment; and never was a prince more undeserving of such a fate.

It is not known what became of the Empress Memmia. A modern historian [1] asserts that she had a son by Alexander who died young, but this does not seem sufficiently proved; nor is there any mention made of another wife of Alexander, to whom the medals give the name of Sallustia Barbia Orbiana. There is, however,

---

[1] Occo. Imperatorum Romanorum numismata.

no doubt but Alexander had three wives. Tristan confounds Memmia with the daughter of Marcianus, as if she were the same person; but Lampridius distinguishes them too clearly to give room for any such conjecture.

PAULINA

WIFE OF MAXIMINUS

ORESTILIA

WIFE OF GORDIANUS, THE ELDER

CRISPILLA

WIFE OF PUPIENUS

TRANQUILLINA

WIFE OF GORDIANUS III

E differ in opinion from Camerarius, who, in his notes upon the chronology of Nicephorus, asserts that Calpurnia, of the celebrated family of the Pisos, was wife of Maximinus, and that she was a lady of exquisite beauty and virtue. He was led into that mistake by misunderstanding a passage in Trebellius; for it is plain that the above-mentioned historian [1] affirms that Calpurnia was wife of Titus Quartinus, who revolted against Maximinus, as we shall see by the sequel.

The name of Maximinus's wife was for a long time unknown, but it is now the general opinion of learned men that this Empress was called Paulina. This princess

[1] Trebel. Trig. Tyranni.

665

possessed beauty and virtue, was of a very beneficent disposition, and inclined to mildness and clemency. She was a great enemy to injustice, and has been much commended for her endeavours to moderate the violence and impetuosity of her husband's temper. Maximinus [1] was born in a small village in Thrace. His father was a Goth, and his mother a Scythian; so that the two wildest and most barbarous nations of the earth were united in his person. He had been a shepherd in his youth. He was of a gigantic size, and incredible things are told of his strength, which was the beginning of his fortune; for, during the rejoicings at Court in honour of the birth of Prince Geta, he gave proofs of such prodigious strength before the Emperor Severus that he imagined such a man would be capable of doing good service in the army, and gave him a company in the guards, whence he rose by degrees to the highest office. As to his temper, manners and extraction, all were barbarous. He was brutal, cruel, covetous, and perfidious, and had all the vices of tyrants.

He served under Severus and Caracalla with great fidelity, but quitted the service when Macrinus seized the empire. He remained unemployed till Heliogabalus dethroned Macrinus, and then offered his service to the new Emperor, but did not meet with such encouragement as he hoped for, nor any of those marks of esteem that Caracalla and Severus had shown him. On the contrary, he conceived a very bad opinion of him from the behaviour of that vicious and depraved Emperor, who, on account of that extraordinary vigour and strength of Maximinus, so much talked of, asked him several very

[1] Ammian. Marcel.

impertinent questions. He accordingly seldom appeared at Court during his reign, but when Alexander came to the throne, he got himself introduced to him.

Alexander, being well acquainted with his merit, gave Maximinus a very favourable reception, presented him to the Senate, of which he made him a member, gave him the command of a legion, and afterwards of an army, thus exalting a man who was to be the author of his ruin. These excessive honours increased his ambition, pride, and insolence to a great degree; he had such a confidence in his strength that he imagined himself invincible, and able to undertake what he pleased. But what especially contributed to his pride and haughtiness was the great regard and esteem the Emperor and his mother Mamea had for him; the latter carried this so far as to have thoughts of marrying her daughter Theoclea to his son Maximus, and this would actually have taken place if, as we have observed, Alexander had not, with a good deal of difficulty, dissuaded his mother from her design. This was probably the cause of that secret spleen and resentment that Maximinus ever afterwards conceived against Alexander.

Young Maximus was, without dispute, one of the handsomest men in the world. Everything about him was amiable; [1] for which reason all the ladies in Rome, of that class that is not very scrupulous, were desirous to have him for a lover. He was magnificent in his apparel, and neglected nothing that could possibly set off his person. He was a great lover of gaiety and pleasures, was no enemy to gallantry, and in a word had every quality that could recommend him to the fair sex, and many

[1] Capitolin. in Maxim.

there were that sighed for him. It may be taken for
granted that the ladies did not admire him the less for
his being invested with the sovereign authority, for his
father had associated him with himself in the empire,
that the Senate and Roman people might be forced to
own (as he said) that there never was so beautiful a
prince upon the throne. Julia Fadilla was of the number
of his admirers, and as she was the most illustrious of
them, she bade fairest to be mistress of the young Emperor's heart.

She was grand-daughter of Antoninus,[1] and, together
with the nobility of her birth, Nature had given her that
dazzling beauty that all the princesses of her family were
endowed with. Maximinus, the father, who was willing
to conceal the obscurity of his own family by a grand
alliance, looked upon Fadilla as a person capable of doing
honour to his son; and whether the prince's inclinations
were conformable to those of his father and the lady, or
whether he was desirous to be nearly related to Antoninus, whose name and memory were so much esteemed
at Rome, Fadilla was selected to be his partner on the
throne. They were solemnly betrothed at Rome, and
the prince made the lady the usual presents upon that
occasion, which history tells us were magnificent, con-
sisting chiefly of necklaces, bracelets, and sumptuous
robes. The troubles that ensued soon after obliged him,
however, to quit his mistress, and put off his wedding
till his return. But he never had that satisfaction, being
involved in the misfortunes his father brought upon himself by his cruelty and avarice, which filled the empire
with blood and executions. He put all those to death

[1] Capitolin.

who had been the domestics, friends or councillors of Alexander, as well as those who were particularly acquainted with the lowness and obscurity of his family, and most ungratefully destroyed people who had been of great service to him at the beginning of his career.

He could not endure persons of high quality,[1] because their nobility seemed to reproach him with his own contemptible origin. People of good character were odious to him, because the comparison between their virtues and his vices made him appear in a worse light than he would otherwise have done. As for those who were rich, they were the objects of his most bitter persecutions, because their death enriched him with their spoils; so that, during the reign of this tyrant, nothing was so dangerous as the reputation of being virtuous or wealthy.

Paulina was secretly in the greatest affliction [2] at these cruelties, for, as she was born with quite a different disposition, she bewailed those evils to which she could afford no other remedy than her compassion. She did not doubt but her husband's conduct would bring upon him some terrible misfortune, and that the people and nobles of the empire, being driven to despair by so many vexations, would do their utmost to shake off a yoke that was become intolerable. She, therefore, did all that lay in her power to make him alter his behaviour, and to inspire him with more humane sentiments. Her entreaties and remonstrances sometimes put a stop to his fury, but soon after the tyrant would return to his own natural temper; his barbarity always got the better of her arguments, so that he stained all the provinces with

[1] Aurel. Victor. Epit. Capitolin. in Maxim.
[2] Ammian. Marcel. lib. 14.

the blood of the most illustrious persons, whom he sacrificed to his rage. After having robbed individuals, he pillaged the cities, and seized all their treasures and revenues, not sparing even the temples, which he plundered and stripped of their ornaments.

These excesses stirred up many powerful people to revolt, and provoked the Osrhoenians, who were the soldiers who had been most faithful to Alexander, and who extremely regretted his death. They were a troop who had been commanded by Titus Quartinus, who had been deprived of that employment by Maximinus, because Alexander had had an extraordinary regard for him. The disgrace of their general irritating them more and more against Maximinus, they accordingly proclaimed Quartinus Emperor, clothed him with the imperial robes, and paid him royal honours. Nobody was [1] more capable of maintaining this dignity, for he was nobly descended, and had acquired a very great reputation. But, whether it was that he could not reconcile himself to such a breach of his duty, or that he was doubtful of the success of it, he refused the empire, till, being compelled by the troops who had served under him in Syria, he resolved to try his fortune. What most of all prevailed upon him was the treacherous persuasion of his ancient friend Macedo, who was the principal author of the conspiracy, and who was hatching the blackest treason that could enter into the heart of man. For one day, when the unfortunate Quartinus was sleeping with great tranquillity in his tent, the infamous Macedo assassinated him, and had the brutality to cut off his head and carry it to Maximinus, in the hope of being rewarded for an action

[1] Herodian. lib. 7. Trebel. Pollio. 30. Tyr.

that deserved the most rigorous punishment. He did
not, however, receive for his baseness the recompense he
expected. The Emperor was, indeed, very well pleased
with the affair, as he was glad to get rid of a formidable
enemy, but, whatever benefit people receive from the
treason, the traitor is sure to be detested; Macedo was
put to death by order of Maximinus, who was informed
that he himself was the author of the conspiracy, and
the person who had prevailed on Quartinus to undertake
it. It is said that Calpurnia, Quartinus's wife, acquainted
the Emperor with this, and that her husband had engaged in the plot contrary to her advice. History gives
her an extraordinary character. She was of the celebrated family of the Pisos, remarkable in Rome for its
antiquity and the many eminent men with which it had
furnished the republic. Her illustrious birth was not, however, so great an honour to her as her virtues, especially
the regard she paid to the memory of her husband, to
which she dedicated the remainder of her life, and passed
the rest of her days in widowhood with so much modesty
and reserve that the regularity of her conduct was looked
upon [1] as a rare example of prudence and discretion, and
statues were erected to her honour.

This estimable lady had a silver basin of one hundred
pounds weight, upon which were engraven the famous
exploits of her ancestors.

The miscarriage of the several conspiracies that were
formed against Maximinus made him naturally more
proud and cruel. He allowed full scope to the ferocity
of his nature, so that rivers of blood ran all over the
provinces. He so encouraged informers and slanderers

[1] Trebel. Pollio. 30. Tyran.

that nothing was heard of but complaints and accusations. The high roads were filled with unfortunate wretches, who were dragged into Germany, where the Emperor then was, and who had been falsely accused of crimes, for which they were sure to suffer death if they had any possessions, for their property was always confiscated by the Emperor. No excuses or pleas of justification were listened to; they were condemned without proof, and punished without reason. Never did Rome groan under a more cruel scourge. Maximinus, incapable of remorse or compassion, thought only of gratifying his insatiable avarice, without fearing the dreadful consequences of his tyrannical behaviour, having taken it into his head that there was nobody so bold as not to tremble at the force of his arm. He did not reflect that lions, tigers, and elephants are subdued in spite of their great strength, as a buffoon told him one day in the amphitheatre. This would infallibly have cost him his life if the Emperor had understood Latin well enough to have comprehended the meaning of it, for he was not a man to permit anybody to give him advice. The words of the buffoon were these:

> Et qui ab uno non potest occidi
> A multis occiditur.
> Elephas grandis est, et occiditur;
> Leo fortis est, et occiditur;
> Tigris fortis est, et occiditur;
> Cave multos, si singulos non times.

The Empress Paulina sadly experienced the brutality of his nature, for as she seized every opportunity to inspire him, if possible, with some sentiments of humanity, she represented to him the danger to which he exposed himself; but he was so provoked at her importu-

nate warnings that he resolved to get her out of the
way, and accordingly poisoned her. This princess was
of so beneficent a disposition [1] that she was extremely regretted. The Senate did not fail to grant her the honour
of immortality, for though she had but little influence
over her barbarous husband, she had contrived to avert
a great deal of bloodshed.

The death of Paulina made Fadilla very impatient for
the return of the young prince, to whom she was betrothed. She was greatly vexed to see her hopes re-
tarded by the absence of him who was to raise her to
the empire, but her uneasiness would have been much
greater if she had known that his absence was voluntary,
and that it proceeded from his indifference. For, whatever argument the Emperor made use of to persuade
his son to go to Rome, where he said his presence was
necessary to keep the people in awe, he would not quit [2]
his father, so that his passion for the princess was not
so violent as he pretended to her. But though he could
not prevail upon himself to leave Germany from motives
of love, he ought to have done it at least for the sake
of his interest, and he had soon reason to be convinced
that the Emperor was in the right when he pressed him
so much to go to Rome, where he might have hindered
what happened there soon after, which cost him his life
and the empire. The revolt began in Africa, which
province was worn out by the oppressions of the commissioner whom Maximinus had sent thither, and who
exercised his authority as those of his profession are
wont to do—that is to say, with the utmost severity.
The people determined, therefore, to shake off this

[1] Zonar. Trist. Com. Hist.   [2] Capitolin. in Maxim.

tyrannical yoke, which was no longer supportable, and choose themselves another master.

Gordianus, pro-consul of Africa, seemed a fit person to fill the throne. He was a venerable old man, grown grey in the service and in the exercise of the highest offices, in which he had acquitted himself with honour. He was son of Metius Marullus, of the celebrated family of the Gracchi, and of Ulpia Gordiana, descended from Trajan; but if [1] he was illustrious by his birth, he was not less so on account of his great actions. He had been twice consul, and that dignity was, in a manner, hereditary in his family; he had afterwards held the government of Africa, where he distinguished himself by his conduct, his magnificence, and the noble use he made of his riches. He married Fabia Orestilia, daughter of Annius Verus, who, in all probability, died before Gordianus came to the throne. She was niece of Antoninus, and consequently related to Fadilla. They had a daughter and a son; Metia, the former, was married to Junius Balbus (who had been consul), and Marcus Antoninus Gordianus, the son, declared August along with his father, under whom he served as lieutenant-general in Africa. Gordianus, the father, was then very old, being nearly eighty years of age, but yet was reckoned a man fit for service and capable of disputing the empire with Maximinus. The people, then, who conducted this affair, went to Gordianus in the night, surrounded his bed, and with their drawn swords in their hands, told him they came to force the empire upon him.

Gordianus was alarmed at this proposal, and thought they were laying a snare for him. He pleaded his age,

[2] Capitolin. in Gordianos tres.

and reminded them of the fidelity they owed the Emperor, the danger to which they exposed themselves, and said everything he could think of to make them desist from their design, but his remonstrances only served to increase their obstinacy; they assured him that, whatever danger the undertaking might be attended with, they were ready to share it with him, and, seeing that he still refused to accept the empire, they told him that he must either consent or prepare for death. This alternative determined him to comply with their request; he preferred to run the risk of a remote evil, than meet with certain and immediate destruction. He suffered himself, therefore, to be invested with the purple robe, and after having associated his son with him in the government, he set out for Carthage with all the pomp and splendour of an Emperor upon his march. The Senate confirmed what was done in Africa, for, as the members were either relations or friends of Gordianus, and mortally hated Maximinus, who exercised his cruelties as much at Rome as in the provinces, they declared the Gordiani August, and Maximinus the enemy of the State.

Maximinus was informed of all this in Germany, and the news disconcerted him so much that he tore his robes, threw himself upon the ground, and drew his sword, as if it had been in his power to kill all the senators. He also made an attempt to kill his son, because he imagined that if he had followed his advice and had gone to Rome, his presence would have intimidated the senators. As soon as his anger began to cool, and he recovered the use of his reason, he assembled his troops, and took the road to Rome, fully resolved to exterminate the Senate, who had set a price upon his head in the decree that was issued

against him, and of which he had found the means to procure a copy.   He had every reason to expect good success, when he heard that the two Gordiani were put to
death; for Capelianus, who commanded the troops in
Mauretania, and who was attached to the interests of
Maximinus, being told of the election of Gordianus,
whom he hated, marched to attack him. Gordianus, the
son, went out of Carthage to meet him. The young
prince, having but little experience, was entirely defeated,
and lost his life. The old man was so stricken with grief
at the loss of his son and colleague, and with the apprehension of falling into the hands of his enemy, that he
strangled himself with his girdle.

The death of these two Emperors threw Rome into the
utmost consternation. The Senate, after the step they
had taken, thought they could not draw back; they deliberated about choosing some other person proper to
oppose Maximinus, and at last selected Balbinus and
Pupienus, two senators who were remarkable for their
merit and experience, as well in military as civil affairs.

Pupienus had married Quintia Crispilla, a lady of
great resolution.[1]   History does not mention her family
and her husband's reign was so short that she was scarce
known; but one of her actions, represented on a medal,
gives us a great idea of her courage. It does not appear
that she ever received the title of August any more than
her husband; so it is probable that the election of these
two Emperors was so precipitate that the Senate had not
time to confer upon them the honours that had always
been given to those who were invested with the sovereign
authority.

[1] Menestrier.

The excellent qualities of Balbinus and Pupienus justified the choice of the Senate, but did not please the people, who insisted upon their electing one of Gordianus's family, and threatened to massacre those whom the Senate had proclaimed, if that satisfaction was refused them. Though the senators saw their authority attacked by this sedition, they were so unwilling to fill the city with trouble and confusion that they carried young Gordianus, about twelve years of age, into the Capitol, declared him Cæsar, put on him the imperial robes, and, by bestowing upon this third member of the family the title of August, contented the people. Some historians inform us that he was son to Gordianus the second, but the opinion of those who assert that he was son of Metia Faustina, daughter of the old Gordianus, and of Junius Balbus, has been more generally received.

After this election the new Emperors prepared for war. Balbinus remained at Rome to take care of domestic affairs, and Pupienus went to Ravenna to meet Maximinus, who had already entered Italy, and who, having heard what had taken place at Rome, flattered himself with no less than the pleasure of sacrificing the whole Senate to his resentment; but his cruelty drew on him his destruction, for, coming before Aquileia, which had shut its gates against him, and not being able to gain admittance, either by threats, promises, or artifices, he resolved to storm the town, and to put all the soldiers and inhabitants to the sword.

This bloody design exasperated the garrison beyond measure, and made them resolve to defend themselves to the last extremity. The townspeople imitated their zeal, and showed a courage and resolution nothing inferior to that of the soldiers; and even the women were ready to hazard their lives to save the place. Maximinus, then, met with such resistance as made him mad with rage. He renewed the attack several times, but was always beaten back with great loss. It was upon this occasion that the women of Aquileia gave an instance of their courage that has been so much talked of and commended; for, the cords belonging to the machines being worn out, they all cut off their hair to supply the defect. There is great reason to believe that the Empress Crispilla, wife of Pupienus, who probably accompanied her husband thither, set an example to the rest in this affair. The Senate, to perpetuate the generosity of these heroines, built a temple, which they dedicated to Venus, and caused a medal to be struck in honour of Quintia Crispilla, who is there represented as a woman with her hair cut close off.

Maximinus, not being able to take the town, vented his fury upon the officers and soldiers of his army, whom he loaded with reproaches that were as impolitic as they were unjust, and which did not fail to provoke them in the highest degree. Seeing themselves, therefore, so ill rewarded for all their pains, they resolved to get rid of the discomforts of this tedious and troublesome siege, and at the same time secure themselves against the ill-treatment of Maximinus, who was hated and forsaken by all the world. They entered his tent when he was asleep, and massacred both him and his son.

Pupienus was so pleased to see himself delivered from this formidable enemy that he immediately despatched a courier to Balbinus with a letter, accompanied with the

From the painting by V. Checa

Race of Roman Chariots

usual ceremonies.[1] Never was news received with so
much pleasure, which was testified by all sorts of rejoicings, and by the hecatomb which the Emperor Balbinus
offered in gratitude to the gods. Pupienus arrived soon
afterwards at Rome, and was welcomed by the acclamations of the Senate and people, especially the former,
who, by honouring the Emperor Pupienus, intended to
vindicate and applaud their having elected him; and some
of them, in the transports of their joy, happened to draw
a comparison between Emperors chosen by the Senate,
and such as had been appointed by the stupid and ignorant soldiers (as they called them). This proved fatal
to the two princes; for the Prætorians, not being able to
endure Emperors who were elected contrary to their
inclinations, brutally assassinated them in the palace.

This tragical affair filled Rome with mourning.
Everybody was in the greatest affliction, except Fadilla,
who looked upon these two princes as persons who had
caused the destruction of the Maximins. But a new
admirer soon banished from her heart the image of
young Maximus. Toxotius was a senator of a noble
family,[2] remarkable in Rome for his accomplishments
and many good qualities, especially for the works that
he had composed in verse, and which were well received
by the public. Fadilla found in him merit enough to
make her forget that of young Maximus. Toxotius, as
well as herself, was descended from Antoninus, and,
though he had not an empire to offer her, he held a
very considerable rank in Rome. This marriage was

---

[1] When the messengers carried good news, the parcel that contained the letters, as well as the heads of their spears, was adorned with
laurel; but when bad, with black feathers.
[2] Capitolin. in Maxim. junior.

accordingly celebrated, and Fadilla had the satisfaction of adorning herself with the superb ornaments and magnificent robes that Maximus had presented her with when he was betrothed to her.

The massacre of the two Emperors would have been attended with bad consequences if the Prætorians who murdered them had not given out, to appease the people, that they did it with no other view than to secure the empire to young Gordianus, whom they at the same time presented to them, having conducted him from the camp.[1] At the sight of the prince, the misfortune of his colleagues was forgotten, and he was declared sole Emperor; and the Senate, whose authority had been used to yield to that of the troops, were forced to confirm the election. Gordianus took possession of his new dignity under unfortunate presages; for that very day there was so total an eclipse of the sun that people were obliged to light torches in order to go about their business and distinguish each other. This was reckoned a sure prognostic of the shortness of his reign, and the event verified these conjectures, to the great regret of all classes in the city, who loved this prince excessively; and certainly he deserved their affection. He was extraordinarily handsome, of a sweet and amiable countenance, and most agreeable humour: he wanted nothing, in short, but a few more years. His mother had, by I know not what false policy or blind indulgence, brought him up with eunuchs and freedmen, who had infused into him their corrupt sentiments, and at whose instigation he had done some very bad things. But Gordianus soon met with better advice and example in Misitheus, whose

[1] Herodian. lib. 8. Capitolin.

daughter he married. This person was in high esteem
at Rome for the gravity of his manners and prudent conduct, so that he had very justly acquired the reputation
of a great man. He had a daughter called Turia Sabina
Tranquillina, who had inherited her father's good qualities. In her were united the greatest beauty and strictest
virtue,[1] which recommended her to the Emperor's good
graces. He married her at Rome,[2] and the people, who
were extremely fond of Gordianus, celebrated his nuptials with all the rejoicings and magnificence that could
be thought of. Gordianus might have made a more distinguished alliance, but not a more profitable one; for
Misitheus was possessed of such eminent talents for important affairs that things soon put on another appearance; he corrected many abuses that had crept in since
the death of Alexander Severus, and made so good a
use of the authority that his offices bestowed upon him
that the Senate decreed him the glorious title of Guardian of the State.

Tranquillina, on her part, by the regularity of her
behaviour and excellent endowments, proved herself
worthy of the high rank to which Gordianus had exalted
her. Her life was innocent, and exempt from all suspicion of vice, free from pride and haughtiness, and she
made no other use of her power than to embrace, and
even seek after, opportunities of doing good. The ladies
of Rome had such affection for her that they erected a
statue to her honour, with an inscription that showed
how much she was valued and beloved. The Senate
made her August, and the provinces strove with each
other which should excel in the glorious monuments they

---

[1] Eutrop.   [2] Tristan. Comment. histor.

erected to show the perfect esteem they had for this illustrious Empress.

She had scarcely begun to taste the first sweets of her happy condition when the revolt of the Persians interrupted her felicity by depriving her of the company of her husband. This filled her with terrors and anxieties; for Sapor, King of Persia, made dreadful havoc wherever he went, so that the Empress felt he was no enemy to be despised. Artaxerxes, his father, when he left him the kingdom, had also bequeathed him his bloody and tyrannical disposition. He was of gigantic stature, of a furious and implacable temper, and one of the least torments that he inflicted upon those he had a mind to punish was to flay them alive. Gordianus, being informed of Sapor's acts of hostility, opened the Temple of Janus, declared war against the Persian with the usual ceremonies, and after having made the necessary preparations, marched against the barbarians, under the conduct of his father-in-law. His expedition was attended with success, for he soon retook the fortresses that Sapor had made himself master of, and put the tyrant to flight, pursuing him into his own territories. But the death of Misitheus was the conclusion of his prosperity. Whether the fatigues of the war had impaired the health of this incomparable man, or whether it was that his time was come, he found himself taken very ill of a flux. This unlucky accident greatly alarmed the Emperor. He sent for the most skilful physicians, who ordered such remedies as they thought proper, and which probably would have been effectual if a perfidious wretch had not found means to baffle them. Among the officers of the army there was an Arabian named Philip, who, besides

that he did not love Misitheus, eagerly desired his post
of præfect of the Prætorians. He was a man of very
obscure family, but had not the less ambition on that
account, and was capable of the greatest crimes to compass his ends. Misitheus's sickness offered him a fair
opportunity of advancing his fortune, and as he was not
in the least mistrusted, they were not upon their guard
against his attempts, so that Misitheus fell a victim to
them; for Philip having found means to convey poison
into the medicines, the general died. Gordianus was left
in a deplorable situation; as he knew nothing of Philip's
being the cause of his father-in-law's death, and having
no officer so capable of filling the vacancy as he, he gave
this treacherous Arabian the place, who, abusing the
Emperor's goodness and the confidence he put in him,
made use of his authority to bring about the ruin of his
benefactor. In fact, as ambition seldom knows any
bounds, he had no sooner attained to what he was so
greedy of but he wanted to be Emperor, and laboured
to destroy the person who had exalted him. Sometimes
he uttered seditious speeches against Gordianus, whom
he treated as a child, incapable of governing the empire
and conducting the armies; at other times he maliciously
contrived subjects and occasions for a revolt, by letting
the soldiers want provisions, and then throwing the
blame upon the Emperor. In short, he practised so many
stratagems that he got Gordianus to make him his partner in the empire. His pride was not yet satisfied, for
not content with sharing the throne with Gordianus,
he thought it beneath him to have the Emperor for his
colleague, and, with horrible ingratitude, massacred him
on the borders of Persia. Thus perished miserably this

young prince, whose virtues had made him so dear to
the Romans. The soldiers, whom Philip was not able to
corrupt, regretted their Emperor extremely, and erected
a magnificent tomb in honour of him, which showed
his merit, and the detestable character of his murderer.
Of all those who were concerned in this assassination not
one of them died a natural death. It is even credibly reported that they either killed themselves or were killed
with the same swords they made use of when they put
their Emperor to death.

MARCIA OTACILIA SEVERA

WIFE OF PHILIP

ITHERTO all the Empresses had been heathens, but in Otacilia we find a Christian princess. She is one of those of whom least mention is made in history; nor is it certainly known whether she was an Arabian, as well as her husband, or a Roman lady, as seems probable by her name. Her medals give her a serious countenance, a modest air, and a tolerable share of beauty. She had the good fortune to be instructed in the Christian religion,[1] but had not so much imbibed its maxims as to be exempt from ambition, or to be hindered from taking part in the crimes and unjust projects of her husband.

Octacilia married Julius Philippus, an Arabian, a man of very obscure family. His father was chief of a band of robbers, but he,[2] thinking his father's trade a very dangerous one, imagined he could do better for himself by turning soldier. He was handsome in person, had a masculine and warlike air,[3] but was rude and unpolished to the last degree, and, though he disliked his father's profession, he had all the inclinations and vices of it. He was audacious, insolent, and perfidious, having no sense

[1] Chron. Alex. Euseb. Hist. lib. 6.   [3] Tristan. Comment.
[2] Aurel. Victor.

of favours received nor gratitude towards his benefactors. He was ambitious beyond measure, and so forgetfull of the meanness of his birth that the higher he was raised the less he was satisfied. Dignities, that might be imagined sufficient to content the proudest of mortals, only served to make him desirous of more. He was, besides, very unsteady and fickle, and lacked thoughtfulness, though capable of reasoning with great soundness. His behaviour was so odd, even after he became Emperor, that he would frequently set up a loud laugh upon occasions where seriousness and gravity were most required, which showed the levity of his mind. He performed his duty so well when a common soldier that he was thought deserving of the highest military posts. It is, however, certain that he had more reputation than merit, for he often wanted resolution and courage where it was necessary, and, in fact, lost the empire by that means. It is generally taken for granted that he was a Christian (however unworthy he was of that glorious name),[1] nor can we question it, after all the proofs that the most learned historians, ancient as well as modern, furnish us with, and we shall see that he signalised the beginning of his reign by an instance of great Christian humility.

It is not well known what sort of life Otacilia led before her husband came to the throne, but in all probability she conducted herself prudently and without reproach. She had a daughter, whose name we are not acquainted with, who was married to Severianus, an officer not much known at that time, but afterwards gen-

[1] Euseb. Hist. lib. 6. Oros. lib. 7. Nicephor. lib. 5. Tillemont.

eral of the army in Macedonia, an office he was by no means fit for.

Philip had already attained to power and authority when Maximinus and the Gordiani disputed the empire; and it was during these troubles that his wife Otacilia was brought to bed of a son, who was called after his father. Otacilia took the greatest care of his education; she instructed him in her own religion, and inspired him with sentiments conformable to it,[1] to which may be attributed that modesty and reserve which he was always remarkable for, notwithstanding the impetuosity to which youth is subject, except we prefer to attribute it to the natural gloominess of his temper. However this may be, he was during his whole life of such a melancholy disposition that he was never known to laugh upon any occasion whatsoever.

If Otacilia infused into her son the maxims of Christianity, she did not follow them very strictly herself; for she was ever ready to second the ambitious views of her husband, and had her share in all the crimes upon which he built up his fortune, even the murder by which he obtained the throne.

As soon as Philip had obtained considerable and important employments, he conceived strong hopes of something higher; for the obscurity of his birth did not serve as a counterpoise to his pride. It was certainly carrying his expectations very high,[2] but nothing hindered him from hoping, however wild and extravagant his pretensions were. People as low and obscure as he had been Emperors, and the throne was actually filled by a young prince whose only support was the wisdom and experience

---

[1] Oros. lib. 7. Baron. ad an. 249.   [2] Capitolin. in Gord. 3.

of his father-in-law—a poor support, considering how the Prætorians took upon themselves to dispose of the empire, according to their own whims and fancies.

Philip's professing a religion that prohibits all crimes and injustice did not hinder him from pursuing such measures as he thought would promote his temporal interests. His ardent desire of sovereign power got so much the better of his conscience that he was hardened against all scruples and remorse; and, as he only consulted his ambition, he was resolved to open himself a door to the empire by treason and murder.

He therefore put Gordianus to death on the confines of Persia, and there was no sort of artifice that he did not make use of to conceal this horrid act. He wrote to the Senate that, the Emperor having died of sickness, the legions had chosen him. He spoke of Gordianus with the greatest respect, ranked him among the gods, and procured him a place in Heaven to make him amends for what he had deprived him of on earth. The Senate, who had neither authority nor courage enough to contradict the army, confirmed the election, declared him August, and decreed the same title to Otacilia. His first care was to make peace with the Persians, and he was so much in haste to get to Rome that he even consented to terms that were far from being honourable; so, having put an end to the war, he set out directly with the Empress.

Whatever precautions they had taken to keep the people in ignorance of the crime they were guilty of, they were, nevertheless, suspected. They arrived at Antioch towards the end of Lent, and as there were a great number of Christians in that town, they were desirous of

giving a proof of their religion, by going to church and
joining in the service that was performed on Easter-eve.
Babylas, the Bishop of Antioch (remarkable for his
courage and sanctity, and a most zealous upholder of the
discipline of the Church) being informed of what had
taken place in Persia, and hearing that the Emperor and
Empress were just at the door, went out to meet them;
and, far from being overawed by the presence of the
master of the world, stopped the Emperor, and hindered
him from advancing,[1] representing to him, with modest
but noble liberty of speech, that it was not proper he
should enter into the holy place with hands that were
besmeared with the blood of his Emperor and benefactor; that, after having committed so heinous a crime,
he could not take part in those sacred rites till he had expiated his guilt by performing a suitable penance. Nor
was the Empress exempted from the penalty, for neither
her sex, dignity, nor the lustre which surrounds the
supreme authority were thought by this holy prelate
sufficient reason for escaping the rigour of the Church.

Otacilia had virtue enough to sacrifice her grandeur
to her duty upon this occasion. She submitted, and
showed an edifying example of humility by undergoing,
along with the other penitent women, whatever the
Bishop of Antioch required of her. The Emperor also,
doing the same, received absolution.

This action made a great noise; it edified and rejoiced
all those who had the interest of religion at heart.
Origen, who lived at that time, wrote the Empress a
letter full of pious instructions becoming an apostle,[2]

[1] Chrysost. adv. gent. Nicephor. Cal. lib. 5. c. 25.
[2] Euseb. lib. 6. Vincen. Lirin. lib. 1.

and Saint Hippolytus, who was then one of the greatest bishops in the Church, addressed to her an exhortation worthy of his zeal.

After the Empress had given, at Antioch, so convincing a proof of her Christianity, she accompanied her husband to Rome, where, shortly after their arrival, the thousandth year of its foundation was celebrated with great rejoicings. Philip entertained the people with several kinds of wild beast fights, and upon this occasion made use of all those that had been destined for Gordianus's triumph. The Emperor did not, however, go to the Capitol to sacrifice as usual, which was attributed to his religion; but if he was a Christian, he was but a very imperfect one. He assisted at all the shows in the amphitheatre, and that with so much good humour that his son by no means approved of it; for Philip bursting out into fits of laughter one day [1] in the midst of the diversions, the young prince, thinking this very indecent in an Emperor, turned away his head and frowned, to show his dislike at it.

Otacilia did not scruple to indulge herself in many things that without doubt she would never have done if she had been more zealous for the religion she professed. Flattery, however, was not wanting to celebrate her praises, as well as those of many of her predecessors who were at least as unworthy of them. We find there were medals struck in honour of her with very pompous inscriptions and encomiums.

These rejoicings ended in an unfortunate accident, for Pompey's theatre took fire, and that superb edifice was reduced to ashes. This afflicted the Emperor extremely,

[1] Aurel. Vict.

but the account which he received soon after of the revolt of several of the provinces was a more painful and interesting subject of vexation.

In the first year of his reign he gave his son the title of August; and, the better to establish himself on the throne, he gave his brother Priscus the command of the troops in Syria, and made Severianus, his son-in-law, general of the armies in Mœsia and Macedonia. These offices were above the merit and capacity of the two officers. Priscus made so bad a use of his power that the Syrians rebelled, and chose for Emperor Iotapianus, who gave out that he was nearly related to Alexander; and Severianus behaved so ill in his command that the troops in Mœsia revolted, and invested with the purple Marinus, a person of very obscure birth and small experience. These two rebellions alarmed the Emperor, but he had about him some very skilful generals, who encouraged him by affirming that Marinus was incapable of conducting so important an enterprise, and consequently that this revolt would come to nothing. In fact, it happened just so; for Marinus was massacred by the same persons who had raised him up, and received the punishment due to usurpers.

But, as Philip knew that Severianus had not experience or skill sufficient to keep the troops and the province which he had been entrusted with in obedience, he resolved to send Decius thither to chastise the authors of the revolt, that this example of severity might intimidate such as were inclined to sedition.

Decius refused this post at first, but was forced to yield to the positive command of Philip, who little imagined that he was advancing a person destined by

Providence to be the avenger of Gordianus's death. Decius set out, then, much against his inclinations, and, before he arrived at the army, the motives of his journey were known. The rebels, being well acquainted with his character, and knowing him to be inexorable, thought they had no better method of obtaining his favour than by declaring for him, and expiating their guilt by making him Emperor, who came to punish them with death. Decius, whether through fear or pretending great humility, refused the purple; but seeing that they threatened to kill him if he made any further resistance, suffered himself to be proclaimed Emperor.

Philip was thunderstruck when he had an account of this election. He knew full well the valour and capacity of this new usurper, and was very sensible that the revolt which he was conducting was infinitely more dangerous than that which he was sent to put down. Decius, indeed, excused himself on account of his having been compelled to accept the imperial dignity, and promised to give it up as soon as he should arrive at Rome, but Philip looked upon this as mere artifice, and thought it was only a snare that his enemy was laying for him, to lull him asleep and surprise him, and marched directly to give him battle. The quarrel was soon decided. Philip was killed at Verona by the very soldiers who had encouraged his revolt against Gordianus; so that he who drew the sword to commit a horrid murder, perished in like manner by the sword.

The Empress Otacilia was at Rome, waiting with the utmost impatience the issue of this war. The reputation of Decius was sufficient reason for her dreading the consequences of it, nor were her apprehensions without

foundation.   She was in the greatest affliction when she
heard that Philip was dead, which she looked upon as the
melancholy forerunner of her son's destruction, so that
her grief on account of the evils she dreaded was as
great as for those which she actually suffered.   In fact,
she had all the reason in the world to fear that Decius
would sacrifice young Philip to the fortune of his own
children, and assure the empire to them at the expense
of her son's life.   Being, therefore, terrified with these
reflections and the approach of Decius, she took refuge in
the camp of the Prætorians, and put her son under their
protection.   But the camp was no place of safety for
her, for the soldiers, hearing that Decius had defeated
Philip and was proclaimed Emperor, massacred the
young prince in the arms of his mother, in order to entitle themselves to the favour of their new master.
Otacilia was spared,[1] because her life was of no consequence, for she was in no condition to intrigue.

If this Empress was really a Christian, the overthrow
of all her fortunes furnished her with a fair opportunity
of practising that resignation which Christianity teaches.
History does not inform us what became of her, but if
she lived a little longer she must have seen Decius forced
to abandon to another usurper the throne that he had
deprived her husband of, and from which Philip had
precipitated Gordianus.   And the destruction of all these
princes must have taught her that riches and honours
seldom continue long in families that have acquired them
by wicked actions.

[1] Vaillant.

HERENNIA ETRUSCILLA

WIFE OF DECIUS

OR a long time it was not known that Etruscilla was wife to Decius; some historians would needs have it that he was married to Orbiana, but it is generally taken for granted that Orbiana was the wife of Hostilianus, his son, and that Etruscilla was his. No mention is made of her family or country. Her medals give her but little beauty to boast of; they represent her with small eyes, a disagreeable countenance [1] and a mean air. She had a great many children before she came to the throne. Together with the title of August, all the honours that were usually given to the Empresses were conferred upon her; but she did not enjoy them long, for she owed them to the revolt of her husband, and the glory of bad actions is but of short duration.

Decius was born in a village in Pannonia, and served with great reputation under Maximinus and other Emperors. He was a man capable of doing good service, as well in peace as in war, and had a great many good qualities. But he eclipsed the merit of them by that furious barbarity with which he signalised the beginning

[1] Vaillant.

of his reign; for never did Emperor spill the blood of Christians with so much brutality.

He had scarcely taken possession of the empire than he had to defend it against an irruption of the Scythians, who spread terror through all the neighbouring provinces. The Emperor sent his son Decius into Thrace to put a stop to the rapid march of the barbarians, but though this prince wanted neither resolution nor skill, he saw the town of Philippopolis taken before his face, where a very large number of people were put to the sword. This misfortune obliged the Emperor to go and command the army in person, and in fact, his presence soon changed the situation of affairs.[1] He defeated the Scythians and the other barbarian nations who had joined them, took away from them all they had conquered, and obliged them to abandon all the country they had taken possession of. This success made him hope for still greater, and resolving to take advantage of the consternation his enemies were in, he was determined utterly to extirpate them.

Trebonianus Gallus, Governor of Mœsia, put this design into his head at the very time when he was hatching a scheme for taking possession of the throne. As he had known it filled by persons who had as little right to it as himself, he thought he might expect the same good fortune. Decius, without knowing it, was labouring to promote the designs of this ambitious man; for, being deceived by the false marks of zeal and affection shown him by Gallus, he was contriving with him the means of destroying the Scythians, not dreaming that this perfidious wretch was at that instant carrying on a secret

[1] Ammian. Marcel. lib. 31.

correspondence with the barbarians to ruin the Roman army. The Emperor fell a victim to this treason, for, the enemy advancing to fight him, he charged them so briskly that he killed a great number of them. But Gallus had given the barbarians notice to draw up their troops near a morass not far off, and then told the Emperor that he could never have a better opportunity of destroying them—that he had nothing to do but to pursue the Scythians towards the morass, and it would not be possible for them to escape. The Emperor, forgetting his usual prudence upon this occasion, took his advice, and intending to drive the enemy into the bog became so entangled in it himself that he was either smothered in the mud,[1] or else was so exposed to the arrows of the enemy, who were concealed, that they killed him. Thus perished this Emperor, whose memory will be ever detested on account of his cruelty to the Christians; and with him fell all the honours and fortunes of Etruscilla.

[1] Victor. Epit. Zosim. Lactant. de Mortib. Persec.

HOSTILIA SEVERA

WIFE OF GALLUS

ETRUSCILLA

WIFE OF VOLUSIANUS

ORBIANA

WIFE OF HOSTILIANU

HERE is so much obscurity in the history of those Emperors who reigned from Philip to Valerianus that scarcely anything certain can be advanced concerning them. What one author asserts is contradicted by another, and there is scarcely any fact in which they agree. We have seen by what perfidy Gallus came to the throne. History gives him for a wife Hostilia Severa, and yet says nothing of her. If it be of her that the chronicles of Alexander speak, when they mention the fury of an Empress who cut her husband's throat, we cannot entertain a very advantageous opinion of her. This, however, does not tally with the account we have of Gallus's death in another manner; for we find that this prince was massacred, together with Volusianus, his son, at Terni, whither he had gone to fight Æmilianus.

Volusianus, according to the opinion of a great many, married Herennia Etruscilla, daughter of the Empress of that name, and of Decius. They affirm that Gallus made this match, and at the same time adopted Hostilianus, his daughter-in-law's brother, that he might not be reckoned capable of so black an action as that of having caused Decius and his army to perish. But this artifice did not exempt him from the odium of that horrid crime, nor from the punishment that was due to it. Æmilianus revenged Decius by taking up arms against Gallus, which revolt also met with its deserts, for the soldiers rebelled and assassinated Æmilianus.

We have already observed that Hostilianus's wife was Barbia Orbiana. There are medals that represent that Emperor on one side, and on the other Orbiana, who seems to have been rather handsome than otherwise; this is sufficient to justify the assertion of those who deny that she was wife to Decius, as some will have it. It is true that many imagine there were two Empresses of that name, one of whom was wife to Decius, and the other of Hostilianus, who, they say, was only son-in-law to Decius; but there are so many difficulties in this, and so little probability, that I do not see how we can admit it without being much confused. Hostilianus died of the plague at Rome, after Decius's death.

MARINIANA

WIFE OF VALERIANUS

SALONINA

WIFE OF GALLIENUS

PIPARA

CONCUBINE OF GALLIENUS

ZENOBIA

WIFE OF ODENATUS

VICTORIA

WIFE OF THE TYRANT VICTORINUS

HE ladies are far from being incapable of heroism: there are many instances of women combining with virtue and sweetness of temper a masculine courage, great intrepidity, and other warlike qualities, which sufficiently proves that great talents are common to both sexes. There are numerous authors who have made it their business to celebrate the praises of such heroines as have acquired immortal honour by their great actions; but it may be affirmed that Zenobia and Victoria hold the first rank among such as were most distinguished and most remarkable. We shall find them an honour to the age in which they lived, by the rare and uncommon abilities which enabled them to govern and defend the empire, to the shame of all those Emperors who dishonoured their dignity by their voluptuous and effeminate lives; whilst these princesses, by the most glorious military exploits and consummate prudence, have deserved an everlasting esteem and reputation.

Æmilianus having been massacred, the soldiers proclaimed Valerianus Emperor, who commanded the army of Gallus. This general had acquitted himself with great honour in several important military posts, which, besides his being of noble birth, seemed to pave the way for him to the throne, of which everybody thought him worthy. He possessed all the qualifications necessary to form a great man. He was courteous and polite in his manners, had an honest, upright heart and vast experience in the art of war. He was mild, judicious, grave, an enemy to vice; and, in person, he was tall and well made, with a majestic air and a robust and excellent constitution. For all these reasons his election was so universally approved of that it looked as if the votes of all classes in the city and the army had been collected for that purpose.

Valerianus had two wives. The name of the first, who was mother to Gallienus, is not known; the second was called Mariniana, by whom he had young Valerianus. Many people have thought that she was daughter to Carvilius Marinus, who in the reign of Philip commanded the army in Pannonia. Her medals give her a grave and serious air, and it is conjectured that Valerianus made choice of her for that reason, hoping that her behaviour would be conformable to her physiognomy.

Valerianus took great care of his children's education, but his expectations were not altogether fulfilled, so true it is that nature and constitution often get the better of instruction and example. Gallienus possessed, indeed, all the good qualities that a prince ought to have. He was extraordinarily handsome, affable, generous, liberal, fond of doing good offices, never refusing what was requested of him without showing visible concern in his countenance, which consoled those whom it was not in his power to gratify. He had a considerable share of agreeable wit, and composed well both in prose and verse; he understood perfectly the art of war, and, upon occasion, could perform the duty of a soldier as well as that of a general. But, on the other hand, he had great vices that sullied and eclipsed all his virtues. He was so revengeful that he carried his resentment to the utmost degree of cruelty, and so jealous that he could not bear anybody who had more reputation than himself. His carelessness and indolence were such that he gave himself up entirely to his pleasures, and neglected affairs of the greatest importance. He suffered, with brutal stupidity, the greatest indignity and disgrace that had ever befallen the Roman empire; he basely abandoned his father to the insults of the barbarians, and gave himself no trouble about releasing him from the cruel captivity he endured among them. As for Gallienus, he revived the luxury of the most effeminate Emperors. He was always served in vessels of gold, enriched with diamonds. His robes and shoes were covered with precious stones, and his affectation extended even to his hair, which was powdered with gold dust. He was so voluptuous and extravagant that he despised all ordinary pleasures, being delighted with nothing but what was difficult to be obtained, and he would eat no fruit but such as was out of its natural season. He did not limit his pleasures to these whims and fancies, but plunged into all those shameful debaucheries that are most apt to debilitate both body and mind; thus he was quite unmindful of the condition of the empire, though it required his utmost care and vigilance.

His brother, young Valerianus, had all the necessary good qualities without any considerable faults. In person he was perfectly well proportioned, had an agreeable countenance, and something so civil and affable in his behaviour that he won the hearts of all who approached him.

He was learned beyond what could be expected at his age, and knew how to temper the vivacity of his wit with good sense. Such were the sons of Valerianus. This great man, having a mind to take from them all opportunities of debauchery, married them; and many are of opinion that the princes espoused two sisters,[1] natives of Clazomenae, a town in Ionia, that Valerianus's wife was named Cornelia Supera, and Gallienus's Salonina; but nothing can be asserted positively either about their names or family.

Salonina, whom the Greek medals call Chrysogona, was [2] extremely handsome; and, what was infinitely more valuable than beauty, possessed prudence and virtue, which wonderfully set off her charms. She had read a great deal, and much esteemed learned men, whom she honoured with her protection, particularly the philosopher Plotinus, who often received marks of her generosity. The Senate, after the election of Valerianus, hav-

[1] Tristan. Comment. Histor.   [2] Vaillant.

ing declared Gallienus Cæsar, conferred upon Salonina all the honours and titles that had usually been given to the Empresses, and it may be affirmed that in so doing they honoured virtue and merit. She had many children by Gallienus. Cornelius Saloninus,[1] Gallienus, Julia, and Gallia are the best known.

The great qualities of Valerianus caused extraordinary rejoicings at Rome when he was chosen Emperor. The Senate confirmed the election unanimously, and declared the Empress Mariniana August. Her exaltation only served to make her modesty and humility more conspicuous. It was a great satisfaction to the Emperor to see in his wife and daughter-in-law the virtues of which he gave them so illustrious an example; but the scandalous life of his son Gallienus caused him, on the other hand, as much displeasure as it did Salonina, to whom he showed the greatest coolness and indifference, whilst other women were possessed of his real esteem and affection.[2] Valerianus, whose austerity would not permit him to wink at these shameful proceedings, often reprimanded his son for his irregular life, but these wise remonstrances produced no good effect; on the contrary, they made Gallienus hate his father, and rejoice that he was in captivity. This misfortune happened to him in the sixth year of his reign, which was so fatal to Rome, for never was there known a time when the Romans had so many enemies upon their hands at once. There was scarcely one of the provinces that did not revolt. No less than thirty tyrants laid claim to the empire, and most insolently abused the authority they had usurped.

Valerianus was very successful in the beginning of

[1] Tristan. [2] Trebel. Pol.

these wars, but that with Persia was fatal to him. Sapor, the Persian King, who had given Gordianus a great deal of trouble, having conquered Armenia, carried his arms into Syria, took Antioch, the capital of the East, and then made terrible havoc in Cappadocia, which he ravaged, and took immense riches away with him. Valerianus, much afflicted at these losses, went into the East and endeavoured to repair them, but a much worse disaster happened to him in that country, for having imprudently and without precaution exposed himself to an interview with Sapor (who a little before had gained some advantage over the Romans) the enemy seized and carried him prisoner into Persia. Some affirm that he was taken after the loss of a battle. Be that as it may, Sapor used his victory, or his treachery, with great insolence. He led Valerianus, clothed in the imperial purple robe, in triumph, exposed him to the ridicule of the barbarous nations, and pushing his brutality to the highest degree of excess, exacted from the Emperor such mean and shameful offices as would not have been put upon the vilest slave, even so far as to make use of him by way of a footstool, when he wanted to mount his horse, or step into his chariot—a strange vicissitude of fortune, which teaches us that there is no permanent felicity in this world, and that everything is liable to change.

Mariniana met with the same fate as her husband, and fell into the hands of the Persians. Sapor [1] respected neither her sex nor her dignity. He treated her with the utmost brutality, so that a Roman Empress was forced to submit to such mortifications as would scarcely have been inflicted upon the meanest of women. There are

[1] Vaillant.

but few people who have philosophy enough to endure such heavy strokes of fortune as these. Mariniana, besides her own ill-usage, had always before her eyes that of Valerianus. The Persians made their chains daily more insupportable by adding to their miserable condition the most outrageous affronts. The poor unfortunate Empress, not being able to bear it any longer, died, and had the vexation of leaving the most illustrious person on earth in the power of his bitter enemies, who made a jest of his calamities.

The news of Valerianus's and Mariniana's captivity threw the empire into the deepest affliction, but if there was anybody who seemed insensible of it it was Gallienus. This unnatural son heard it with stupid indifference, and when he was condoled with upon that occasion, he answered very coldly that he knew his father was mortal, and was consequently liable to the same mischances as other men, and that he had at least this consolation that if his father was unhappy, he had always performed his duty, and fought valiantly. He showed no signs of grief, but went to Rome, and instead of taking proper measures for the Emperor's deliverance, he minded nothing but his infamous pleasures and debaucheries, passing the nights in brothels and the days in the baths.

Salonina was the more sensible of her husband's contempt as her beauty and conduct were such as entitled her to his utmost regard and affection. But his transitory amours were not what gave her most uneasiness; a very formidable rival became the object of her jealousy. It was Pipa, or Pipara, daughter of Attalus, King of the Marcomans, a princess whose charms were much talked of, and the report of which kindled in Gallienus's breast

so violent a passion that he imagined the happiness of
his life depended upon possessing so amiable a person.
He had, however, but small reason to flatter himself
with hopes of success in this affair, where his authority
was not sufficient to command it. The princess was not
his subject, and therefore not in his power. The Roman
law did not admit of his marrying a stranger, and there
was no law that the people had a greater respect for.
This law had cost Titus and Berenice many a sigh and
many a tear; nor did the son of Vespasian think proper
to infringe it, however ardent his love for that charming
Jewess.

All this was well known to Gallienus, but being to the
full as amorous, and less scrupulous than Titus, he
sought for expedients that might furnish him with the
means of gratifying his passion without openly violating
the laws; and the melancholy situation of the empire
seemed to him a happy conjuncture. The irruptions of
the barbarians into almost all the provinces alarmed all
the world, for the Roman empire seemed upon the very
brink of its ruin. Gallienus, taking advantage of this general consternation, but having much less at heart the
interest of the State than his own private amour, assembled the Senate, and represented to them the prodigious
number of enemies that seemed to be united for its utter
destruction; that it was impossible for one Emperor to
resist so many usurpers, for which reason he had thought
proper to make an alliance with some foreign prince, by
whose assistance he might be supplied with such an army
of auxiliary troops as should enable him to sustain all
these wars. That Attalus, King of the Marcomans,
seemed to him the fittest for this purpose, and best able

to defend the Romans; and that, in order to make Attalus the more zealous in behalf of the Romans, he imagined the best thing he could do would be that he should marry that prince's daughter.

Gallienus only made the proposal out of courtesy, and to show some little regard for decency, for he knew very well that nobody durst contradict him. There was not remaining in the Senate the least shadow of liberty or uprightness; the Emperor governed its opinions, and reversed its decrees when they were not conformable to his will and pleasure. This step then being taken, Gallienus sent an embassy to Attalus to demand the hand of his daughter. Formerly there was no prince upon earth who would not have looked upon such an alliance as the greatest honour, and have purchased it at any price, but matters were not now upon that footing; the Romans were now no longer feared and respected as they had been even by the greatest monarchs, who paid them homage, either voluntarily or by force. The barbarous nations were now convinced by experience that the Romans were not invincible, for they had seen upon the throne Emperors more worthy of their contempt than fear; hence it came to pass that foreigners no longer regarded either the Roman arms or the decrees of the Senate.

Attalus lent a favourable ear to this proposal, and seemed highly sensible of the honour that was designed him; but being more crafty than the Roman, and knowing how much Gallienus was smitten with his daughter, he was resolved to make him purchase her. He accordingly raised such difficulties as could not be got over without Gallienus's yielding to him part of Pannonia; and it was upon these conditions that the hand of the Princess Pipara was obtained, and she was conducted to Rome. The beauty of this charming stranger augmented Gallienus's esteem for her; he had not only the affection of a husband, but the complaisance of a lover,[1] and indulged his weakness so far as always to carry about him a lock of her hair.[2]

It was well for Salonina that she had acquired sufficient command over her temper to bear, with less uneasiness than might have been expected, this new amour; she contented herself with the outward civility that her husband was pleased to bestow upon her, and learnt philosophy enough to wink at his gallantries. The love she had for the sciences served to amuse her, and divert her thoughts from such reflections as would otherwise have been very troublesome. She had gained a great reputation among the learned, which, together with the respect shown her by all classes in the city, made her amends for the loss of her husband's heart, of which Pipara had robbed her. Her wisdom, prudence, and sweetness of temper procured her the love of all the Romans. Her behaviour was such as could not but win everybody's affections, for not the least pride or haughtiness was to be seen in her whole deportment. Her goodness frequently induced her to sacrifice her interests, and her indulgence was such as always inclined her to forgive any who had injured her. This was seen upon an occasion when she even seemed to carry her clemency a little too far.

There happened to arrive at Rome a jeweller, who, among some diamonds of great price, had a great many

[1] Excerpt. Aurel. Victor.   [2] Trebel. Pol. de Saloni.

false stones.. Some were of glass, but they were such admirable imitations that there was scarcely anybody skilful enough to find out the difference. This person went to Court, and presented his jewels to the Empress, who was struck with their beauty and lustre; she chose out those she liked best, and paid the price. The false being the most brilliant and best set, she selected them. She showed her purchase to the ladies and courtiers, who greatly admired them, but upon a closer examination the cheat was discovered. The Empress being very vexed and ashamed at having been imposed upon, gave orders to arrest the merchant; but, not being desirous to carry her revenge very far, she contented herself with putting him in a terrible fright.

The jeweller was congratulating himself on his good success, when he was seized [1] and conducted to prison. They gave him to understand that he was condemned to be torn to pieces by lions in the amphitheatre. The appointed day being come, the people flocked thither in great multitudes to satisfy their curiosity; the criminal was brought out, and every moment they expected to see half a dozen famished lions let loose upon him. The eyes of the people were fixed upon the den, where they were told the beasts that were to devour the jeweller were shut up. The signal being given, the door of the cave opened, and the jeweller almost fell dead with fear. At last, out flew a cock directly in the face of the malefactor, who was placed close by the den, which made him cry out and tremble prodigiously. The spectators, who expected a more bloody scene, could not forbear laughing heartily at the merchant's terror. A herald immediately proclaimed

[1] Trebel. Pollio. Gallien.

with a loud voice, that the trick had been revenged by another; and this was all the punishment that was inflicted upon the offender.

It would have been lucky for the inhabitants of Mœsia if Gallienus had been as merciful, but he punished that province with the utmost rigour for having encouraged the revolt of Ingenuus, whose death, however, did not deter many others from rebelling. Gallienus's effeminacy and the little care he took of the government exposed the sovereign authority to such a degree that it fell a prey to anybody who could lay hold of it, so that every day a new tyrant appeared. One of the most formidable was Cassianus Postumus, Governor of Gaul. He was a man of obscure birth, but had the reputation of being an extraordinary general and politician, possessed of excellent talents, as well for ruling a kingdom as for defending it valiantly, equally experienced in war and in peace. Gallienus thought him a man of so much merit that he trusted him with the education of his son Saloninus and the command of the army in Gaul. He even imagined he had discovered in this officer inviolable fidelity. But ambition corrupted him; he no longer looked upon Gallienus as his superior, but assumed the imperial purple at Cologne,[1] murdered Saloninus, and carried on his rebellion during seven years.[2]

In the meantime Valerianus was the sport of a barbarous Court, who insulted his misfortunes with the utmost brutality; but what most afflicted him was the undutifulness of his son, and his insensibility to the miserable captivity he groaned under. In fact, Gallienus plunged into a voluptuous course of life, and thought of

[1] Trebel. Pol. Trig. Tyr.   [2] Trebel. de Postum.

After the painting by R. Coghe

Sale of Slaves in a Roman Camp

nothing but how to please Pipara and gain her affections, indulging himself in the most shameful debaucheries; he seemed to forget entirely that his father and most of the provinces were in the enemies' hands, which stupidity emboldened the barbarians and tyrants to undertake what enterprise they pleased.

Sapor especially had carried his conquests very far into the empire; but Odenatus, King of the Palmyreans, checked his career. He was a prince of great courage, and inured to fatigue by the continual exercise of hunting, which he had been accustomed to from his childhood in the mountains of Palmyra (a city in the deserts of Syria, upon the confines of Arabia), where he endured heat, cold, and all the inclemencies of the weather with admirable patience. His ancestors had been always friends to the Romans, and he himself was no enemy to them, but was obliged to act cautiously with Sapor, whose power and ambition were become formidable to all the East; accordingly, when Valerianus was taken prisoner, Odenatus sent ambassadors to the Persian, loaded with magnificent presents; they also carried a submissive letter, congratulating him upon his victories, but at the same time entreating him to push his conquests no further for fear of irritating all the neighbouring princes. Sapor, whose prosperity had made him haughty and insolent beyond measure, looking upon Odenatus rather as his slave than an independent king, despised his embassy, and expressed great displeasure at the liberty this prince had taken in writing to him. He commanded the presents to be thrown into the river, and tore the letter in pieces in presence of the ambassadors, whom he charged to tell their master that he would soon let him know that it was not for a vassal to treat with his lord by ambassadors, and that he should dearly repent his temerity if he did not expiate his fault by coming to him immediately with his hands tied behind his back.

Odenatus was extremely sensible of this affront, and was determined to humble the intolerable pride of Sapor. His wife Zenobia strengthened him in his resolution, and encouraged him in his design. She was a most illustrious princess, originally of Syria, and a Jewess, if the ecclesiastical historians are to be credited. She was descended from Cleopatra, Queen of Egypt,[1] so famous for her beauty, and the misfortunes of Marc Antony, her lover. Zenobia had inherited her charms, but not her failings! She was considered the finest woman in the East, and had withal a certain masculine air that seemed to show her courage and intrepidity; she was of a brown complexion, and had large black eyes, whence proceeded such fire and vivacity as were irresistible. Over all her person were diffused charms that made her infinitely amiable, and the qualities of her mind were no less praiseworthy than her bodily perfections. She had great talents, and a courage incapable of yielding under difficulties. No undertaking could be too great for her abilities, natural and acquired, for she had cultivated and greatly improved her mind by study. She spoke perfectly well the Greek and Egyptian languages, and was mistress of the history of the East, of which she had made an abridgment. The philosopher Longinus was her preceptor, and instructed her in all manner of sciences. She was also desirous to become acquainted

[1] Athanas. Epist. ad Solitar.

with the Christian religion, but had a bad master in Paul of Samosata, who taught her his errors. She was naturally generous and magnanimous, which made her a lover of honour and glory. As she was careful and economical, she never incurred any unnecessary expenses; she was reserved in speech and behaviour, and so strict an observer of order and discipline that she was both feared for her severity and loved for her clemency, tempering one with the other, and seldom preferring the necessity of punishing to the pleasure of showing mercy.

Never was heroine so indefatigable in military affairs; she would frequently (notwithstanding the delicacy of her sex) march several leagues on foot with the troops. But none of her good qualities were more remarkable than her chastity. She was not only exempt from all suspicion of taking liberties that were not consistent with virtue, but we read that she would never allow any intercourse with her husband after she perceived herself to be with child. This princess, being informed of the insulting reception her husband's ambassadors had met with from Sapor, and seeing the insolent and provoking threats with which his letter was filled, persuaded him not only to break off all further negotiations with the Persians, but to enter into a strict alliance with the Romans, in order to be revenged upon him. Balista at that time commanded the Roman legions in the East. He was a very skilful officer, full of resources and expedients for conducting and provisioning the army. Odenatus let him know his intentions, and his proposals were received with great joy. He was put at the head of the army, and it was upon this occasion that he performed all those great actions mentioned in history. He defeated the troops of Sapor, and obliged him to repass the Euphrates with shameful precipitation. He afterwards carried his arms into Mesopotamia, and conquered all the East.

Sapor, astonished at this change of fortune, was glad to retire into his own dominions, and fled before Odenatus; but the latter, pursuing him vigorously into Persia, shut him up in Ctesiphon, the capital, where he kept him in continual alarm. Zenobia, accompanying her husband in all these military expeditions, shared with him both the fatigue and the glory of them.

These fortunate exploits re-established the prestige of the empire. Rome celebrated them with the greatest rejoicings, and looked upon Odenatus as its chief support. Then it was that the greatest lords of Persia were seen entering the city loaded with chains, and gracing the triumph of this prince, who was received with all possible marks of esteem and respect; and Gallienus, to honour the merit of the conqueror, made him general of all the East; for there were no dignities or posts commensurate with his deserts. Odenatus avenged the empire of the insults and mortifications that Sapor had inflicted upon it, and the Emperor found in him a general who was able to sustain his fortunes. He had so much the more reason to promote him, because, although sovereign master of the Roman troops, covered with laurels, and dreaded by the enemy, he added to the importance of his services the glory of a constant and unshaken fidelity, at a time when most of the Roman generals had shaken off the yoke of obedience, turned tyrants, and changed into so many empires the provinces they had been entrusted with. In fact, Macrianus had assumed the purple in

Egypt, Valens in Greece, Piso in Thessaly, Aureolus in Illyria, and were become bitter enemies to their benefactors. Even Balista had the baseness to abandon the service of the Emperor and join Macrianus, whose revolt he would have made very dangerous if Odenatus had not punished him as he deserved. Those provinces which did not fall a sacrifice to the usurpers were exposed to the incursions of the barbarians; the Scythians overran Asia, and the Goths made perpetual irruptions into Macedonia and Achaia. So many enemies having sprung up at once aroused Gallienus out of his lethargy; but what resolution could a prince take who was softened with pleasures, and enervated with all sorts of debaucheries? Young Valerianus represented to him the danger of the empire, and persuaded him to associate Odenatus with him as partner on the throne, in order to induce him, in his own interest, to defend the provinces that were to be his. Gallienus did not hesitate about it, but made Odenatus his colleague. He declared him Cæsar and Emperor, and gave him all the insignia of sovereignty, causing money to be coined with his image and inscription.

Zenobia ascended the throne together with her husband. She was declared August, and her sons received the title of Cæsar. It must be acknowledged that no Empress was more deserving of this high rank; for, of all those who had been exalted to the empire, either by their birth or their fortune, few were exempt from some great vice or other, and the most that could be said even of the best of them was, that they had some virtues mingled with their faults; but none were like Zenobia, endowed with all those talents and good qualities that were capable of doing honour to either sex. Odenatus, by new services that he rendered the empire, proved himself worthy of the honour that was done him. He made more conquests, and established peace throughout all the East.

Odenatus's victories excited the emulation of Gallienus. Those who had his reputation at heart made him at last sensible of the injury he did himself by leading a voluptuous life, whilst his colleague was acquiring honour and glory, and convinced him that he ought to sacrifice his pleasures to duty, and take up arms in defence of the empire; that all these revolts were owing to his indolence, and might have been prevented if he could have prevailed upon himself to chastise the rebels in person. Gallienus was subject to sudden resolutions that drew him out of his ordinary habits. It was thus not impossible for his intimates, by managing him skilfully, to inspire him with vigorous resolutions. These remonstrances had so good an effect that he resolved to tear himself from the arms of Pipara and all his pleasures. He put himself, therefore, at the head of his army, and marched to fight Postumus, who had established himself as a usurper. He showed in this expedition more courage than was to be expected from a prince who was abandoned to luxury, and an enemy to fatigue. He reduced the tyrant to such extremities that, finding himself not able to resist the Emperor, he made Victorinus [1] partner in his dignity, or rather his revolt. Victorinus was a man very skilful in the art of war. Nature had given him all the talents that were necessary to form a hero, and history assures us that he possessed all the good qualities of the

[1] Trebel. de Victorin.

most illustrious Emperors. But he was given to one vice
that tarnished all his virtues—he was so amorously inclined that he lost the affections of his officers by endeavouring to debauch their wives.

He was a son of the famous Victoria, or Victorina, a
princess of great courage and ambition, very little inferior
to Zenobia in point of merit. She was especially so
clever at managing the soldiers that she could do what
she pleased with them; and it was at her persuasion that
Postumus chose her son Victorinus for his colleague.
She was, in short, the most formidable of Gallienus's
enemies, for she had an enterprising genius; whatever
she undertook she executed with resolution, and generally
with success, so that she was looked upon as the most
dangerous enemy to the empire. She assumed the titles
of August and Mother of the Armies, and maintained her
dignity with great honour and reputation as long as she
lived. Thus was Victoria as much celebrated for her
great and heroic qualities in the West as Zenobia was in
the East; and it may be said that the empire was governed
by these two women.

After Odenatus had shut up the Persians within their
own borders, and recovered all that had been taken from
the Romans, he made very good regulations for preserving peace and tranquillity in the East. Zenobia
received in those countries all the honour that was due
to her, and it was given her with pleasure, because everybody was convinced that she was worthy of it. It might
reasonably be imagined that she had nothing to wish for
but the continuance of her good fortune; but what condition is so happy as not to be embittered with some
vexation or other? Zenobia, upon the throne, was

tormented with anxieties and jealousies that interrupted her felicity, and this princess, after having so gloriously contributed to the elevation of Odenatus's family, became its most cruel scourge.

Odenatus had, by his first wife, a son named Herodes, whom he loved exceedingly, though he was not very deserving of it. This young prince was of a mild and humane disposition, but, like all Orientals, a lover of pleasures and diversions, and fitter for gallantry than war. He carried his luxury to the highest pitch, and his father was so complaisant as to indulge him in it by supplying him with funds for his pleasures, for he made him a present of all the magnificent furniture,[1] precious jewels, and immense riches that he had taken from Sapor, and even gave him all that prince's concubines.

Zenobia had three sons, Timolaus, Herennianus, and Vaballath, from whom she expected great things. She educated them in the principles and after the manner of the Romans, had them taught Latin, and put them under the tuition of the famous philosopher Longinus, who instructed them in the sciences. In short, she omitted nothing that was necessary to qualify them for the throne, for which she intended them, hoping to prevail upon Odenatus to adopt them; but Herodes was a powerful obstacle to her projects. This young prince had been declared King of Palmyra jointly with his father, and when Gallienus and the Senate decreed the empire to Odenatus they made his eldest son his colleague. As Odenatus was extremely fond of Herodes, Zenobia could not help being jealous, and from this sprung that invincible aversion she always had for Herodes, and the ill

[1] Trebel. Pol. de Herod.

offices she never failed to do him on every occasion,
which were such as became the malice of a cruel step-
mother. Odenatus, however, knowing how much
Herodes was hated by Zenobia, only felt the greater
affection for him.

That sort of jealousy that proceeds from ambition is
the most dangerous kind. Zenobia, not being able to
bear the thought of her son-in-law mounting the throne,
which she imagined had been obtained more by her
courage and advice than by her husband's merit, resolved
to procure for her own sons the sovereign authority, and
not to stop at any crime to gain her point. A son-in-law
runs no small risk when a jealous step-mother is looking
out for means to put him to death, and the husband
frequently pays dearly for the favours he has conferred
upon any children he may have had by a former marriage.

There was in the Court of Odenatus a prince called
Mæonius, nearly related to the Emperor. They happened to quarrel as they were hunting together, for
Mæonius had several times had the presumption to kill
any game that came near Odenatus, and thereby deprived him of that satisfaction. Odenatus, being provoked at this want of respect, insulted him. Mæonius
was so irritated at this that he threatened Odenatus, who,
not being able to endure such audacious behaviour, was
going to kill Mæonius, and would probably have done
so if Herodes had not thrown himself at his father's feet
and interceded so strenuously for his cousin that Odenatus could not resist him. The quarrel being thus made
up Mæonius was as much in favour as before, but he
bore malice at heart, and was determined at one time or
other to be revenged upon Odenatus. We read that

Zenobia did all she could to heighten this discontent,[1] and never ceased to exasperate them against each other, till she had prevailed upon Mæonius to revenge the affront he pretended to have received. He communicated his design to Odenatus's nephew, and holding out the most flattering hopes, gave him to understand that if they could get rid of Odenatus they would have nothing to do but to possess themselves of his fortune and riches. Young Odenatus, being thus deluded, entered into the conspiracy, and they waited with great impatience for a favourable opportunity of putting their design into execution.

At the very time when this plot was going on, Odenatus was acquiring great honour. He had marched against the Persians, and was in a fair way of completing their ruin. He besieged Ctesiphon and took it, notwithstanding the obstinate resistance he met with. He afterwards vanquished the Goths, those barbarians who had overrun Asia, and who were no sooner informed of Odenatus's approach than they fled with precipitation; but Odenatus overtook them in time to deal great slaughter, and his presence terrified both the barbarians and the tyrants. All these advantages convinced the Romans that they could never value too much a prince who was capable of doing them such essential service, and they did not doubt the affairs of the empire would soon be put on a better footing than ever under the conduct of this great man. But the gods, says an historian,[2] being irritated against the State, had resolved to give them the greatest mark of their displeasure by depriving them of their chief support.

[1] Trebel. Pol. de Mæon. Zonar. Ann.   [2] Trebel. Pol. de Oden.

Odenatus having thus gloriously finished this campaign, halted at Ephesus, and made a considerable stay in that city, to keep the enemy in awe. He had his son Herodes with him, and when he was one night at supper a troop of the conspirators rushed into the room and brutally massacred both father and son. Mæonius and young Odenatus were the authors of this treason, and by that means gratified the ambition of Zenobia.

The death of Odenatus was reckoned the greatest misfortune that could possibly have befallen the empire. Gallienus, knowing how difficult it would be to repair such a loss, was extremely afflicted at it. The condition of affairs, and particularly of Odenatus's family, was quite changed. Zenobia caused her sons, Herennianus and Timolaus, to assume the purple robes and the other imperial ornaments, and presented them to the army with great pomp and magnificence. She seized the empire in their names, and took the title of Queen of the East, which she preferred to that of Empress. It gave her great pleasure to hear of Victoria's grandeur in those countries, where she made and unmade Emperors at pleasure, and, of her own authority, took the titles of August and Mother of the Armies. She interested herself extremely in everything that concerned Victoria, and wished for nothing so much as to be able to join her forces to those of this Amazon, that they might together conquer the whole world,[1] a project worthy of Zenobia's courage and ambition.

The Emperor Gallienus, being informed of Zenobia's behaviour, no longer regarded her as an ally zealous for the good of the Roman empire, but as one who was build-

[1] Trebel. Pol.

ing her own fortune on the ruins of the State. Zenobia, to tell the truth, seemed to have some such design, and did not show Gallienus all that respect that Odenatus did upon all occasions, never failing to communicate to him all his designs and undertakings. She demanded of the Romans neither succour nor advice, but governed the East with absolute and independent authority. Gallienus took such measures as he thought would put a stop to her proceedings and humble her pride; he sent Heraclianus into the East to command the troops, and gave him secret orders to attack Zenobia as soon as he should have a fair opportunity. But as he knew her to be a woman not likely to lay down her arms and divest herself of the sovereign power, which she had tasted the sweets of, his pretence was that he desired to subdue the Persians entirely, and flattered himself that, the true reason of his sending Heraclianus being thus concealed, she would not be alarmed at his arrival; but it was no easy matter to impose upon Zenobia. She looked upon Heraclianus as a man she ought to suspect, and therefore took care to prevent him making a party in the East by marching directly to meet him. She accordingly gave him battle, and defeated his army. She showed by this action that war under her conduct was not less formidable than in the hands of Odenatus, and that there are heroines capable of the greatest undertakings. She proved the truth of this assertion in the East, whilst Victoria sufficiently demonstrated it in Gaul. The latter governed in the name of her son, Victorinus, who had caused himself to be declared Emperor. We have observed that he might be compared to the greatest princes for his excellent qualities. He had [1] the courage of Trajan, the clemency and mildness of Antoninus, the gravity of Nerva, and the authority of Severus, but all these virtues were eclipsed by his incontinence. It is true that after he came to the throne he denied himself for some time, but nature got the better of his resolutions, and returned with greater violence than ever. He kept no bounds, but without reserve or decency gave full scope to his inclinations, and imagining that his authority placed him above all fear or censure, he did not scruple to indulge himself by corrupting his officers' wives.

A commissary of the provision supply, named Atticianus, who had been thus insulted, was more delicate in that point than others whom the Emperor had dishonoured, and who patiently submitted to their disgrace. Victorinus had debauched his wife, which he resented in the highest degree. He was neither indifferent nor politic enough to put up with such an injury; he bore it continually in mind, and could not rest without being revenged. Victorinus had offended so many in that way without their ever daring to complain that he did not apprehend he had anything to fear from a person much below a great number of others, who were timorous enough to wink at these gallantries; but no enemy is to be despised. Whilst Victorinus was at Cologne, thinking of nothing but his pleasures, and leaving all affairs to the conduct of his mother, Atticianus was hatching a conspiracy against him, which he carried on with so much secrecy and cunning that Victorinus received a mortal wound, which afforded him but just time to declare his son, Victorinus, August, and name him his successor.

[1] Trebel. Pol. de Victorin.

Victoria, who had persuaded him to this, confirmed it, and proclaimed her grandson Emperor. This prince was so young that he was incapable of governing, but this was so much the better for Victoria, who desired only the shadow of an Emperor, in whose name she might exercise an absolute authority.

The honour she had procured for her grandson was, however, fatal to him; for those who had massacred his father, not thinking their lives in safety under an Emperor so much interested to revenge his death, resolved to free themselves from the punishment they deserved by another crime. They therefore plunged into the breast of the young Emperor the very poniards that were yet reeking with his father's blood. This created more work for Victoria. She had been so accustomed to unlimited power that she exhausted all her resources to maintain it. Her chief object was to cause some general to be elected who should not be in a condition to govern by himself, for she apprehended nothing so much as having a master. Marius, she thought, would answer her purpose, and proposed it to the legions. She so well employed her talent of persuading that she got him proclaimed Emperor.

Marius had been an armourer. He was remarkable for his extraordinary strength, of which he had given surprising examples. He had passed through all military grades till he reached that of general, and when Victoria invested him with the purple it was understood between them that, however willing she might be to let him enjoy the honours of the government, she reserved the solid part of it for herself. Marius was no sooner elected than he assembled the soldiers, and spoke to them thus: " I

am sensible, my comrades, that I am liable to be reproached with the meanness of my first occupation. I
shall not deny that I have handled iron, for you are all
witnesses to it; but let people say what they will, I hope
to handle it yet for the good of the empire; for it will be
more honourable for me to do so at the expense of the
enemy than to plunge myself into pleasures and effeminacy like Gallienus, who has tarnished the splendour of
his birth by his infamous debaucheries. Let people
affirm that I was formerly an armourer, provided the
barbarians do but learn by experience that I still know
how to handle arms."

This modest discourse did more honour to Marius than
his dignity, as it seemed an undoubted proof of his
humility and moderation. There are but few upstarts
who have the courage to confess the obscurity of their
birth; they are more apt to obliterate the least traces of
their former lowness, and hope, by their riches and high
offices, to impose upon the world. The new Emperor,
with all his affected simplicity, was not, it seems, proof
against this sort of seductive pride, for a soldier, who had
learned his trade under him in his shop, coming to congratulate him on his exaltation, was received with great
contempt, which provoked him to that degree that, not
being master of his passion, he killed him on the spot,
saying, " This very sword you made yourself."

The death of Marius furnished new material for
intrigues at Court. Victoria, who trembled to think of
an election that might not be to her mind, dispensed her
money very plentifully among the officers and soldiers.
By this politic liberality she had so gained the affection
of the legions as to be almost sure of them upon any

occasion. She applied to them on behalf of Tetricus, a Roman senator,[1] who commanded in one part of Gaul, and who was her relation. She succeeded, and as soon as he was chosen she despatched a courier to give him notice of it, and exhorted him not to refuse a dignity that the army had thought proper to confer upon him. It is not often that such offers are rejected, for an empire is no present to be despised. Tetricus put on the imperial robe at Bordeaux, and showed that he was deserving of the honour that was done him.[2] He gave his son Tetricus the title of Cæsar, and soon after had an opportunity of signalising his courage and experience in Spain.

While he was engaged in that war, Victoria had the government of Gaul, and the entire conduct of all affairs; for Tetricus, who was as cunning as she, thought proper to humour her at first; but when he thought himself pretty well confirmed in his authority he resolved not to submit any longer to the yoke of an imperious woman, who, he knew, only made a tool of him, in order to concentrate all power in herself and gratify her ambition. Victoria, thus made the dupe of her own policy, was stung to the quick at this ingratitude, and would infallibly have made him dearly repent it if death had not prevented her. It is credibly reported that Tetricus, fearing the effects of her artifices and resentment, adopted means to put an end to her career. Thus perished the celebrated Victoria, who had filled Gaul, and, indeed, all the empire with her reputation.

At the time when this princess and Zenobia were gaining the admiration of all the world for their heroism, Salonina was as much esteemed at Rome for virtues that

[1] Trebel. de Tetric. Sen.   [2] Eutrop.

were less tumultuous, such prudence, mildness, and sweetness of temper as nothing could alter or disturb. The affronts that she received from Gallienus were not capable of diminishing her affection for his person, nor her attachment to his interests, of which she gave him an instance that nearly proved fatal to her.

The news of the Scythians making terrible havoc in Illyria having reached Rome, Gallienus tore himself from his debaucheries, and put himself at the head of his army to fight them. Salonina, who feared for her husband, whose soft and effeminate conduct she knew caused the troops to murmur, insisted upon accompanying him on his expedition. Some days after the army had reached Illyria, and the Emperor had left but a slender guard in the camp, having marched against the enemy with all his forces, the barbarians, knowing the Emperor's design, and that the camp was left in a manner defenceless, resolved to carry off the Empress, which they preferred to a victory. They therefore detached for this purpose a troop of resolute soldiers fitted for a bold undertaking, who marched so silently and with so much precaution that they came in sight of the camp without being perceived. Salonina nearly fell into their hands, in which case she would have undergone the same fate as Mariniana; for the enemy was but a very small distance from the camp when a soldier, who had gone out by chance, saw them and gave the alarm, and snatching up his sword and shield, met the barbarians and killed a great number of them. By his astonishing courage and resolution, he gave his comrades time to come to his assistance.

It is no difficult matter to imagine the terror of the

Empress, who knew upon what errand they came, and that the barbarians were persuaded they could not possibly gain a greater advantage over Gallienus than to rob him of his wife. Pipara would, no doubt, have been much obliged to them, nor is it probable that Gallienus would have broken his heart for the loss. Be that as it may, Salonina got off with the fright, and returned to Rome with her husband after he had dealt terrible slaughter among the Scythians, which was more owing to his good fortune than his merit.

The Emperor no sooner arrived at Rome than Aureolus, who had been so often rebellious, revolted again; and upon Gallienus's approach, retired to Milan, where he was besieged. The generals of the army imputed all these insurrections to Gallienus's effeminate life. Marcianus and Ceronius especially thought themselves highly dishonoured by being obliged to obey a prince who was so little worthy to command. Their ambition caused them to speak disrespectfully of Gallienus, to give the army a worse impression of him than they had already, and in order to get themselves chosen in his stead; but as they were secretly jealous of each other, they resolved to get Claudius proclaimed Emperor, who was a very deserving general, and much esteemed by the Senate and the legions. The better to succeed in this scheme, they gave Gallienus a false alarm, and had him informed that Aureolus had quitted Milan, and was in sight of the camp with a strong detachment.

Upon this Gallienus hastened to put his troops in order of battle, but the conspirators, watching a favourable moment, fell upon him and killed him, as well as young Saloninus and Salonina, who was deserving of a better fate. Such was the death of this Empress, who had done great honour to her station by her great wisdom and zeal for the public welfare.

It was soon known that the new Emperor was worthy of the high rank to which he was raised; his valour became very formidable to the barbarians and tyrants, and his other qualities of the greatest utility to the empire. He demonstrated his courage and experience in every battle he fought, and gave sufficient tokens of his wisdom and prudence by the excellent laws and regulations he established, proving himself equally meritorious in war and in peace.

While he was employed in subduing the Goths, Zenobia displayed her extraordinary resolution and intrepidity in the East, where she was making daily conquests and extending her dominions. She defeated the Egyptians, and destroyed a great number of their troops. Claudius, being informed of all these enterprises, sent Probus, who was one of his most skilful generals, into Egypt. The Palmyreans were at first put to flight, but Zenobia sending them a reinforcement, the troops of Probus were surprised and defeated, and the whole country was again in her power. Claudius, having the Goths upon his hands, seemed to take no notice of the affronts he received from the Queen of the East, and not being at liberty to give her battle, he thought it his best plan to amuse her with a treaty of peace till he could have a fair opportunity of being revenged. Then, having nothing to fear from Egypt, he turned all his forces against the Goths, over whom he gained that celebrated victory which cost three hundred and twenty thousand of the barbarians their lives. He also destroyed two

thousand of their ships. Those who escaped being put to
the sword by the Romans were cut off by famine and
pestilence. But this last scourge did not prey only upon
the Goths, for the Romans were greatly afflicted by it,
and the Emperor himself died of it at Sirmium. Quintillus, his brother, was elected in his stead, but not being
found capable of performing the duties of that high
post the soldiers killed him, and chose Aurelian in his
place. His character will be given in the following
chapter, so we shall say no more of him at present than
what relates to Zenobia's history. This princess had
conquered all Egypt, Syria, and the greater part of Asia
Minor. The alliance that she had made with Claudius,
and which was of his seeking, exceedingly flattered her
vanity, for she imagined the Romans were afraid, and
had not courage to attack her. She was so confident of
this that she did not now think it worth while to renew
the alliance with Aurelian that she had concluded with
his predecessor. Aurelian, provoked at being thus despised by a woman, resolved to humble her; but knowing
that Zenobia was not an enemy to be slighted, he assembled the greatest part of his troops and marched
into Syria.

Zenobia, hearing of all these preparations, made ready
to give the Emperor a fitting reception; and, being told of
his approach, marched out of Antioch at the head of her
army, having under her Saba, a very experienced general.
She met the Romans near the river Orontes, and there
the battle was fought. Aurelian, though full of valour
and courage, had recourse to a stratagem which succeeded. Zenobia's army was composed of Palmyreans
and other Orientals, who were in armour from head to

foot, which was so cumbersome that they were scarce able to move. The Emperor having observed it, pretended to flee before her to entice those Asiastics to a pursuit. They fell into the snare, for, taking it for granted that the Romans were afraid to engage, they followed them so close that in a little time they were out of breath. Aurelian, like an experienced officer, took advantage of their weariness, and causing his troops to face about, attacked them with such vigour that vast numbers of them were slain.

Zenobia was at the head of her army doing everything that could be expected from the ablest general, and encouraging her soldiers by her speeches, gestures, and example; but her harangues had not upon this occasion their usual effect. Her troops were put to flight, and she had the mortification of abandoning the field of battle to the conqueror, and of retiring to Emesa. She had scarcely reached that place, and collected the scattered remains of her army, than she was compelled to risk a second engagement; for Aurelian, resolving to make the most of the ardour of his soldiers and the consternation of the enemy, followed and overtook them near Daphne. Fortune was no more favourable to her now than before, for her army was defeated; and when she perceived that, whatever efforts she made, it was impossible to rally her men, she shut herself up in Palmyra, where she imagined she was safe. The town was defended by a numerous garrison, and the Queen had supplied it with all sorts of ammunition and provisions,[1] so that it was reckoned impregnable. The Emperor was convinced that the siege of this place would be tedious, difficult, and bloody; but,

[1] Vopisc. in Aurel.

on the other hand, he knew that the capture of it would put an end to the war, and that it would be very glorious for him to subdue Zenobia, whose reputation had filled all the empire, whereas all the advantages he had hitherto gained would be to no purpose, if he gave that princess time to repair her loss. This determined him to sit down before it. He found the undertaking as dangerous and difficult as he had foreseen, and if the Romans performed prodigies of valour to make themselves masters of the town, the besieged were not at all inferior to them in defending it. Aurelian called all his experience and intrepidity to his assistance, and exposed himself so much that he was wounded with an arrow. Zenobia, who feared more than death the shame of adorning the triumph of the conqueror, showed the courage, or rather fury, of an enemy driven to despair.

The length of the siege, the uncertainty of the issue, and the obstinacy of the besieged, made Aurelian repent more than once that he had undertaken it. He saw with great vexation that his conquests were likely to be interrupted and all his laurels withered before Palmyra, and that by a woman, who gave him more trouble than he had ever met with from an enemy before. He knew that at Rome he was ridiculed and made a jest of for being thus baffled by a woman; but he was not ashamed to give her the praise she deserved by declaring that she was not cast in the same mould as the rest of her sex, but on the contrary was by far the most formidable enemy the empire had. He wrote to his intimate friend Marcipor to justify himself. " I am informed," said he, " that with you people make their remarks upon my being at war with a woman, as if this Queen was less to be dreaded than the most consummate hero. I could heartily wish that those who are so given to raillery could see the astonishing quantity of provisions and all things necessary to the defence of a place that she has laid up in Palmyra. What arrows, arms, stores, and machines for throwing fire upon the assailants; what palisades to hinder them from approaching the walls! To give you a just idea of Zenobia, I shall only say that this princess does not defend herself like a woman, but like an experienced general, who, fearing to incur the penalties of misbehaviour, puts in practice all his skill and abilities to prevent his being conquered. And this I can assure you, that, in order to get the better of Zenobia, we have need that the gods (ever propitious to the Roman arms) should be favourable, and not fail us upon this important occasion."

Nothing does so much honour to Zenobia as this forced commendation given her by Aurelian, who without dispute was a great warrior, and a very good judge of true merit. It appears by this that Zenobia was as much dreaded by Aurelian as he was by his enemies. It was not his fault if this war was not terminated by treaty. He offered terms to Zenobia, promising her and all belonging to her security, and to leave the Palmyreans in quiet possession of all they enjoyed. But Zenobia was not a woman to put herself willingly in the power of the conqueror; far from coming to terms with Aurelian she sent him a haughty answer, capable of intimidating an Emperor who was less brave than he. In her letter she says: " I am surprised that you should propose to me to surrender. So great a hero as you ought to know that it must be by deeds of valour, and not by letters, that enemies are compelled to yield. You are the first that ever paid me such a compliment, and might have been better acquainted with me than to talk in that style. I would have you call to mind that I am descended from Cleopatra, and have no less firmness and resolution than she. Death seems to me, as it did to her, a lesser evil than slavery; nor should I think the greatest dignity in the world worth purchasing at the expense of my liberty. Do not imagine that you are speedily to be master of Palmyra, for the powerful assistance that the Persians are sending us is just at hand; the Saracens and Armenians will also help us, and how do you propose to deal with so many enemies—you who have found by experience that a band of Syrian robbers has been able to beat your whole army? Our allies will presently join us; we shall then bring down that pride of yours, which induces you to command us with so much haughtiness to surrender at discretion."

Aurelian was stung to the quick by this epistle, and was more than ever determined to take the town, cost what it would. He surrounded it with his army to prevent its being succoured, and a troop of Persians, which made an attempt to throw themselves into the place, was entirely defeated. The Palmyreans were thunderstruck at this accident, for notwithstanding what they had declared, their provisions began to fail. Then it was that Zenobia, despairing of help, and seeing neither the Armenians nor Saracens coming to her aid, for Aurelian had gained them over by presents, had but small expectation of being able to preserve the town. She foresaw, on the other hand, all the miseries that would be the consequence of its being taken by assault;

but on the other, she could not bear the thoughts of falling into the hands of the conqueror after the boastful letter she had written. Her pride presented to her all the horrors of slavery, and the shame of being compelled to follow the triumphal chariot of Aurelian. She chose, therefore, to run all risks rather than implore the clemency of an Emperor she had provoked by her obstinacy and the haughtiness of her letter. She knew she could prevail upon the Palmyreans to defend themselves to the last extremity, and had some small ray of hope that she might yet save the place if it were possible to procure any assistance. She resolved, then, to go out of the town secretly, and beg the King of Persia to furnish her with the auxiliaries he had promised, and then to put herself at the head of the troops and attack the Romans. Having taken this resolution, and used all the necessary precautions that everything should in the meantime be carried on according to her directions, she got out of the town privately, and with few attendants. Aurelian, however, had notice of her escape, and knowing of what importance it would be to secure her, sent after her some light horse, who went so fast that they overtook her upon the banks of the Euphrates, just as she was going to cross the river. She was treated with the utmost respect, and brought back to Aurelian.

The Emperor was in transports of joy when he saw Zenobia in his power. He understood better than anybody the value of this piece of good fortune, which made him master of all the East, and put an end to a war that gave him infinite trouble and anxiety. But the more this event gave satisfaction to Aurelian, the more insupportable was Zenobia's affliction. It would not be easy to describe the wretched condition to which this princess was reduced, who after having given law to the empire, saw herself a prisoner, and destined to the mortifying fate of serving as a trophy to those enemies she had often conquered. Her disgrace did not, for all that, quite sink her spirits; for in her countenance still reigned that air of grandeur and noble haughtiness so natural to those who are born to command. Neither the pretence nor reproaches of Aurelian were capable of shaking her courage and resolution; and when the Emperor asked her how she could ever think of acting as an enemy towards the Romans, to whom she owed her fortune, she boldly answered, that indeed, as far as he was concerned, she had always had the greatest esteem and respect for him, because she knew him to be worthy of the empire; but that she had never looked upon Gallienus and all those tyrants, who had taken the title of Emperor, as other than persons who disgraced their dignity by their shameful and scandalous behaviour.

Zenobia's capture was soon followed by the taking of Palmyra. The greatest part of the inhabitants resolved to hold out to the last, but the others opposed a design that could not be attended with any good consequences, and must needs end in the destruction of the town; they accordingly demanded quarter of Aurelian, and opened their gates. The Emperor carried away immense wealth from Palmyra, and after placing a strong garrison in it, went to Emesa, where he decided the fate of the captives. Those who had shown themselves most zealous for Zenobia, and had espoused her interests with too much warmth, were punished with death. Among their number was Longinus, who was accused of being the

author of Zenobia's letter to Aurelian. The soldiers
were very importunate that the princess should lose her
life; but the Emperor, though not very gallant, could
not prevail upon himself to treat with so much severity a
queen who had defended the Roman provinces against
the barbarians with great valour and intrepidity.
Aurelian also pardoned the youngest of her sons, named
Vaballath, who it is thought lived long after his mother's
misfortune; but it is uncertain whether he put to death
Herennianus and Timolaus, who had been declared
Cæsars before Odenatus died, or whether these princes
were already dead.

By Zenobia's capture and the reduction of Palmyra,
Aurelian added greatly to the reputation he had before
acquired. His name became the terror of the kings and
people of the East. They all sent ambassadors and
presents to him, to obtain his good graces; and it was
observed that Hormisdas, King of Persia, and son of
Sapor, who had so brutally treated Valerianus, was one
of the first to do honour to Aurelian, by sending him a
chariot covered with plates of gold, and enriched with
jewels, together with a purple mantle of so extraordinary
a lustre that the Romans had never seen anything comparable to it.

After the Emperor had restored tranquillity to the East
he set out for Italy, but was soon obliged to return.
Some factious Palmyreans persuaded the inhabitants to
revolt, massacred the garrison and the governor, proclaimed Emperor a relation of Zenobia, and caused him
to put on the imperial robe. This news put the Emperor
out of all patience. He returned into Syria in such
haste that he arrived at Antioch before the Palmyreans

knew that he was informed of their rebellion. But his approach struck them with such fear and consternation that they yielded without attempting to defend themselves. Aurelian treated them with the utmost severity, put all the inhabitants to the sword without distinction of age or sex, and entirely demolished the town. This rigorous proceeding did not, however, prevent a new tyrant from starting up. Firmus, a native of Seleucia, but who lived in Egypt, where he was of considerable importance, and who was nearly related to Zenobia, undertook to head the remains of that party, and got himself proclaimed Emperor. His revolt was at first attended with success, for he made himself master of Alexandria and all Egypt, but in the end he met with the same fate that generally overtakes rebels; he was taken, and expiated his audacious attempt by a horrible death.

The destruction of this rebel again reduced Egypt to obedience, and served to give Tetricus warning of what he was to expect. That senator had been for some time past weary of the authority he had usurped, and had thought of making his peace with Aurelian. But it was not so easy for him to make his soldiers return to their duty; these men are always inclined to sedition, and, as he had been beholden to them for his elevation, they thought they had a right to exact what they pleased from him. A prey to those fears and apprehensions that are inseparable from an unlawful and tyrannical power, he preferred a private, but peaceable condition, to a tottering and precarious command. He went, therefore, and threw himself at the feet of Aurelian, to be dealt with as the Emperor pleased. The Emperor laid hold of this opportunity to attack the army of Tetricus; he came

up with it near Châlons upon the Marne, and cut them
to pieces, for they fought without a chief, and, consequently, without discipline. By this victory Aurelian became master of Gaul, Spain, and Britain, which acknowledged Tetricus, and, after having put matters upon a
satisfactory footing, he went to Rome to reap the fruits
of his labours, and was received with the greatest applause and demonstrations of joy.

For a long time past the Romans had not seen so
superb a triumph. The captives of several nations followed the triumphal chariot with their hands tied behind
them, which sufficiently evinced the glory of the conqueror, but the principal ornament of this magnificent
scene, and which most of all attracted the eyes of the
spectators, was the Queen of the East, so loaded with
chains of gold, diamonds, pearls, and other precious
jewels that she was scarcely able to carry them, but was
forced, every now and then, to rest and take breath.
Tetricus and his son, and some Egyptians of the highest
rank, were captured at the defeat of Firmus, and the
chief lords of Palmyra did also great honour to this
splendid ceremony. It is true that some thought it
indecent that the Emperor should cause a woman and a
Roman senator, who had been consul, to grace the procession along with the Goths, Vandals, and other barbarians, but with regard to this Aurelian fully justified
himself to the Senate.

Such was the fate of the celebrated Zenobia. Aurelian
omitted nothing that could contribute to the mitigation
of her misfortune and the alleviation of her condition.
He treated her with great respect, and made her a present
of a fine estate near Tivoli, just by Hadrian's palace.

Many are of opinion that her son Vaballath retired into Armenia, where Aurelian gave him a principality; it is, however, certain that she left a son at Rome of that name. Baronius seems to think that she became a Christian, and that Zenobius, bishop of Florence, who lived in great friendship with St. Ambrose, was descended from her family, but other credible historians contradict this.

The Emperor did everything to repair the affront he had put upon Tetricus, by treating him ever after with great kindness, sometimes calling him his colleague, and even giving him the title of Emperor.

SEVERINA

URELIAN, of whom we have already spoken, was of very obscure birth, but his meanness was obliterated by his superior talents, his extraordinary merit, and by such great actions that nobody thought too much was done for him when he was made Emperor. He had excellent natural qualities, a robust and vigorous constitution, great courage, and a majestic deportment. He was vigilant, prudent, grave, a strict observer of military discipline; his great failing was cruelty, which made him inflict the severest punishments for the smallest faults. He put a great number of senators to death upon slight suspicions or accusations, without proof; and, under pretence of correcting abuses, he made a very bad use of the sovereign authority with which he was invested; for which reason it was said of him that he ought to have remained always a general, but never to have been Emperor—that he was a good physician, but drew too much blood.

He married Ulpia Severina, who, as some modern historians believe, and upon good grounds, was daughter of Ulpius Crinitus, who claimed to be descended from Trajan and whose virtues he had inherited. This alliance was advantageous to Aurelian; for as he was born without fortune, he found ample means in the generosity of his father-in-law, who adopted him, and shared his riches with him.

Severina was not handsome, but had a great soul, and noble inclinations. She accompanied her husband on all his expeditions, even when she was Empress, and did not a little contribute towards procuring him the affection of his troops, by a well-timed liberality, and her engaging behaviour to the meanest soldier. It is from inscriptions and medals that we have drawn the greatest part of what we have reported with regard to her; for the historians do not so much as tell us her name.

As soon as Aurelian was proclaimed Emperor, he set himself about regulating public affairs, which were in great disorder and confusion. He carried his arms into the East with so much success that all the strongholds, and even provinces, submitted of their own accord, for fear of incurring his displeasure and feeling the effects of his anger. Only the city of Tyana attempted to make any resistance; but that was done with so much courage and obstinacy as would in all probability have put a stop to his conquests, had it not been for the treachery of one of the inhabitants who opened the gates to him.[1]

[1] Aurelian was so provoked at the obstinacy of the citizens that he swore he would not leave a dog alive. This oath made the soldiers believe that the Emperor intended to destroy the inhabitants and give up the town to be plundered. This expectation made them perform prodigies of valour, which notwithstanding would have been to little purpose had it not been for a townsman, named Heraclammon, who showed the Romans a weak part in the fortifications, through which they might enter the place. As soon as it was taken, the soldiers prepared to destroy and plunder it entirely, and when the Emperor opposed it, they put him in mind of his oath. "Very well," replied Aurelian, "I swore that I would not leave a dog alive in Tyana, so I consent that you shall massacre all the dogs." The perfidious Heraclammon was, how-

It was a strange sight for the legions to see the Empress in the midst of camps and armies, sharing the fatigues of the war with the Emperor, preferring the noise and tumult of arms to the luxuries and pleasures of Rome, and doing honour to her sex by military exploits. This, together with her bounty, procured her the regard and affection of the legions; they could not but esteem a princess who distributed her riches among them, instead of wasting it, as other Empresses had done, in show and grandeur. These largesses were of great service in keeping quiet the mutinous and seditious dispositions of the soldiers, which had always been a most difficult matter. The Senate, to show their gratitude to the Empress, and express their sense of her merit, caused a medal to be struck in honour of her, with an inscription, which attributes to her the glory of having won the hearts of the soldiers, and of maintaining peace and harmony among the legions.

This was not the only mark of esteem the Romans bestowed upon her; for, when Aurèlian went to Rome to receive the reward of his good services, she shared with the Emperor all the honours that were decreed him; and there had never been seen at Rome a more magnificent triumph,[1] which was celebrated amidst the sincerest acclamations of the people and all classes in the city. To this was added all the games and shows that had ever been exhibited upon the like occasions, besides a naval engagement that was carried out with the greatest magnificence. Thus Aurelian, by entertaining

ever, put to death as the reward of his treason; for the Emperor said that a man who could betray his country could never be faithful to anyone.

[1] Vopisc. in Aurel.

the citizens with these amusements, caused the past sufferings and calamities to be forgotten.

After this, the Emperor thought it right to give a token of his piety as well as his grandeur, by erecting a very sumptuous temple, and dedicating it to the sun, a divinity which he revered with great superstition, and to which he attributed all the success of his arms. Severina also took part in this ceremony, and in concert with her husband paid her homage to the god in the new temple. It was upon this occasion that the solemn sacrifice which was offered to the sun (represented to us by the medals) was performed; so that Severina's piety ingratiated her as much with the citizens as her military accomplishments did with the troops.

A woman of this character certainly deserved the love and affection of her husband, and accordingly the Emperor thought he could never too highly esteem a princess who followed his fortunes with so much courage and alacrity, sharing with him all his dangers and troubles, and contributing so much to his glory and safety by being liberal to the soldiers, and that with such grace that they were more charmed with her manner of giving than with the gift itself. Severina, however, with all her merit, could never persuade the Emperor to be polite and complaisant, or to abate anything of a certain rusticity which he always affected; and she had the mortification of being refused a favour she earnestly requested of him.

Though purple was, at the time of the republic, the colour most in fashion among all the ladies of quality, it was afterwards reserved for the Emperors only, and became a badge of the sovereign authority, so that edicts were issued to prohibit private persons from making use

of it.   The ladies were, indeed, permitted to wear silk,
but it was at that time so scarce and dear that very few
could venture to carry their luxury so far.

Severina, by accompanying her husband in all his
wars, had acquired a martial air which she was very
proud of, and fancied that a purple mantle of pure silk
would add to her natural liveliness and vivacity, so that
she longed exceedingly to purchase one.

This piece of finery could not be reckoned an immoderate expense for the first lady in the world, who,
one would imagine, was not so strictly bound by general
rules; nor could Aurelian, without the utmost austerity,
refuse that little satisfaction to a princess for whom he
ought to have had more indulgence for many reasons;
for, if anything could have induced him to deviate from
his usual principles, it might reasonably have been presumed that he would do so upon this occasion.   But
Aurelian was too rigid to be influenced by motives of
courtesy and good manners.   The Empress employed all
her solicitation to no purpose, for Aurelian still persisted
in his obstinacy.   He represented to Severina that, by
being clad in silk, she would lower the value of gold; for,
though silk was very rare and curious, it ought not to be
put in competition with the most precious of all metals.

Severina, who knew the Emperor was not a man to be
easily dissuaded from his resolutions, was forced to
acquiesce, and was the less surprised at this refusal, as
it was not the first mortification of the kind she had met
with; for upon his coming to the throne, he allowed his
wife and daughter no other furniture than what he had
given them when he was a private officer.[1]

[1] Vopisc. in Aurel.

This humour of the Emperor was not attributable to that kind of sordid avarice that causes some people to grudge every little expense. It is true that he was no friend to luxury and show, but yet he could not be accused of covetousness, as was plainly proved by the use he made of his riches. The fault that might justly be imputed to him was that he did not know when to set bounds to his unreasonable severity, which made him a tyrant to the Senate as well as a persecutor of his own family, which he overwhelmed with affliction by putting his sister's son to death; and those who have been most zealous in their commendation of Aurelian, and have compared him to Cæsar and Alexander (whose military talents he indeed possessed) have not been able to excuse his inhumanity. By his excessive rigour he alienated from him the hearts of the Romans, who hated his government. This occasioned the conspiracy against him, by which he lost his life near Byzantium, when he was going to war with the Persians.

Severina was witness of her husband's misfortunes, and did not long survive them. She had by Aurelian one daughter, who was the mother of that Aurelian who, in the time of Constantine the Great, was one of the most illustrious ornaments of the Senate; and this is all that historians relate concerning Severina.

THE WIFE OF TACITUS
JULIA PROCLA
WIFE OF PROBUS
MAGNIA URBICA
WIFE OF CARUS

HE legions, notwithstanding Aurelian's severity, regretted his death extremely, and refused to choose a successor for fear of selecting one of his murderers. The army sent the Senate a letter full of his praises and imprecations against those who had put him to death, and desiring that they would make choice of one of their body who should be worthy to fill his place. The Senate was too well acquainted with the changeable and fickle temper of the soldiers, and knew too well the aversion they always had to such Emperors as had been created by them to expose any senator to the caprice of the troops. They had not forgotten the tragical deaths of Balbinus and Pupienus, who were brutally massacred only because they had received the sovereign authority from the Senate; and the miserable end of those two princes gave them to understand what any Emperor had to expect who was not chosen by the army. These prudent reflections determined the Senate to request that

the legions would elect whomsoever they should judge most deserving of the throne.

These mutual differences between the Senate and the army took up six months, and yet during this sort of interregnum the provinces all remained quiet and submissive to the authority of the Senate. But at last couriers arrived with the news that the Germans had passed the Rhine, and that the Syrians, no longer in awe of Aurelian, were beginning to revolt. The consul, Gordianus, accordingly assembled the Senate, and represented to them that the election of an Emperor could no longer be deferred. Tacitus, whose age and quality gave him a right to speak first, rising up to give his opinion, all the Senate with one consent voted him the empire, saying that he who was at the head of the Senate ought also to be at the head of the armies.

Tacitus, who was a very wise and judicious person, excused himself by alleging that a magistrate who had passed his whole life at Court and in the Senate, and who was upon the brink of the grave, was not capable of undergoing the fatigues of war, and that the legions would never be brought to obey a senator who was become an Emperor at once, without having passed through the military grades; this modesty only made him appear more worthy of it, and as to his great age, they mentioned Trajan, Hadrian, and Antoninus, who had come to the throne when they were very old. They told him that it was not his business to fight, but to command, and that strength of body was not so necessary a qualification in an Emperor as a sound judgment, according to the maxim of Severus, who used to say that it is the head that commands and not the body, and that it was

ridiculous to give the title of Father of the State to
boys, who stand in need of their tutors' lessons; that a
ripe age produced wise and well concerted designs,
whereas all the irregularities of Nero, Commodus and
Heliogabalus were less to be attributed to their vices
than to their youth.

The importunity of the Senate and the soundness of
their arguments prevailed upon Tacitus at last to accept
the empire, but he protested that he would do nothing of
himself. The Senate could not certainly have made a
more worthy choice, for in Tacitus were revived the
moderation and integrity of those wise senators who were
so remarkable in ancient Rome. If he was descended
from Tacitus the historian, as is generally believed, he
was of distinguished family, but, be that as it may, his
merit sufficiently recommended him. As for his wife, no
mention is made either of her name, family, or country.
She found in Tacitus the same aversion to luxury that
Severina met with in Aurelian, for her rank of Empress
was the only thing that distinguished her from the other
ladies. The Emperor, her husband, would never permit
that she should wear richer clothes than she had before
his election, for he was looked upon as the author of the
prohibition which his predecessor had made against
wearing gold or silver. It is not to be doubted but that
the Senate decreed the new Empress all the honours that
they had been so prodigal of to others, and that they
gave the most pompous titles to the wife of an Emperor
who was of their own creating. They wrote to the
governors of provinces, and to all the nations and kings
in alliance with the Romans, that the Senate had reassumed their ancient rights, that they would always,

for the future, elect the Emperors, and that they had now made choice of one of their own members to fill the throne; that, from that time forth, it should be by authority of the Senate that war or peace should be declared, and, in a word, that the State, being reinstated in its privileges and prerogatives, intended to have the principal share in the government. The senators congratulated each other upon the recovery of their liberty, and they made an experiment that seemed to assure them that neither the interest nor the will of the Emperor would any longer put a restraint upon their votes; for when Tacitus requested the consulship for his brother the Senate refused it. But this great joy was but of short duration, for Tacitus,[1] after having given the greatest proofs of his mildness, equity and justice, died of a fever, according to some, while, according to others, he was killed by some seditious soldiers.

Florianus, his brother, made himself Emperor as if he had had a right to succeed Tacitus; but he had to deal with a very powerful competitor in Probus, who was chosen by the majority of the soldiers, and whose merit greatly alarmed him. He knew that Probus was extremely beloved and esteemed by the Senate, the legions, and the people, and consequently that it would be very difficult to maintain himself in a dignity which a more worthy person than himself was in possession of; so the rash step he had taken was followed by another still more so, for he put himself to death by causing his veins to be opened.

Never did the troops make a choice that was so universally applauded, for the virtues of Probus eclipsed

[1] Eutrop. Aurel, Vict.

all those of his predecessors; so many good qualities had never been united in the same person. The sovereign authority only added to their lustre, by making them appear in a more favourable light.

For a long time it was not known that Probus ever had a wife, but Strada affirms that he did marry one Julia Procla,[1] whose family and country, as well as her good and bad qualities, were not mentioned. It is hard to say upon what grounds he builds his assertion that there ever was an Empress of that name. We find, nevertheless, that Probus left children behind him, who settled near Verona; but it nowhere appears that his wife's name was Julia Procla; he certainly had a sister called Claudia.

The reign of Probus was one continued series of victories. When he had punished the authors of Aurelian's death, he marched against the rebellious Gauls, and destroyed above seven hundred thousand of those barbarians. He subdued the Illyrians and the Getans, both which nations he compelled to submit to the Roman yoke. The East was afterwards the theatre of his triumphs, where he took an infinite number of strongholds, and defeated the Persians, who had so often rebelled. He would have utterly extirpated them, when he was massacred by some soldiers at Sirmium.

Marcus Aurelius Carus was elected in his stead. He was of Narbonne in Languedoc, and possessed the same virtues for which Aurelian, Tacitus, and Probus had been so much esteemed.

Magnia Urbica, his wife, is known only by her medals, for history is silent as to her family, or where she was

[1] Tristan. Comment. Historiq.

born. It is indeed acknowledged that there was an Empress called Magnia Urbica, for there are medals which give her the title of August, and on which she is represented with her two children standing before her. The difficulty is to know which Emperor she was wife of, because authors do not agree in that point; but, all circumstances considered, it seems plain that she was the wife of Carus and that the two children represented in the medals were Carinus and Numerianus, her sons. Numerianus had all his father's good qualities, but Carinus gave himself up to all manner of vices, so that the former was the delight of the army and the people, whilst the other, by his monstrous debaucheries, became the object of their aversion. All met with tragic deaths. Carus was killed by lightning upon the banks of the Tigris near Ctesiphon. Numerianus was assassinated in his litter by Aper, his father-in-law, who intended to seize the empire, and Carinus, after having several times defeated Diocletian, whom the army had chosen Emperor, was killed by an officer whose wife he had debauched.

PRISCA

WIFE OF DIOCLETIAN

VALERIA

WIFE OF GALERIUS

EUTROPIA

WIFE OF HERCULES

THE WIFE OF MAXIMINUS

ORTUNE respects neither rank nor grandeur, and the most exalted throne is no security against changes and revolutions. The Empresses Prisca and Valeria are proofs of this assertion. We shall see these two princesses, wives of the masters of the world, become wanderers and fugitives, reduced to all the misfortunes of a cruel destiny, and at last ending their lives by a violent death—a melancholy example of the instability and precariousness of everything in this world!

Nothing positive can be said about the family or country of the Empress Prisca. The historians do not even agree about her name. Some call her Alexandra, others Serena, and others again Eleuthera. It is not impossible that she might have had all those names, but it is certain that she was also called Prisca, and she is generally known by that name.

The ecclesiastical annalist speaks of her by the name of Serena, and makes her a Christian. He also asserts that she died a quiet and natural death, and that the Empress Valeria, her daughter, did the same, soon after she had married Galerius Maximinus. This he infers from there being no further mention made of her by ancient authors. We cannot hold the same opinion as Baronius, nor the Acts of Saint Susanna, upon which he grounds his authority, because it does not appear that they are more to be credited than Lactantius, who affirms the contrary, and who not only lived at that time, but held a post in Constantine's Court.

Tristan, in his Historical Commentaries, believes that Diocletian's wife, whom he calls Serena, was daughter of Serenus, who held then one of the most important posts at Rome. Be that as it may, Prisca was a woman of such extraordinary good qualities that it is reasonable to suppose she had some knowledge of the Christian religion, and at least practised it secretly. The prudence of her conduct, her humility upon the throne, and the great patience with which she bore the different persecutions she met with, seem to be proofs of her having been well acquainted with those divine laws.

Diocletian, who acquitted himself with honour in all his military duties, had by Prisca, his wife, a daughter called Valeria, whose beauty, though very great, did not do her so much honour as her virtue and the regularity of her life. She was educated by the Empress with all possible care and exactness, and instructed in the Christian religion. She followed very strictly the excellent example her mother gave her, and showed that the good lessons that had been taught her were not thrown away, but on the contrary produced excellent fruit.

After the death of Numerianus, the Roman army that had been led into Persia by the Emperor Carus chose Diocletian, who passed for one of the greatest generals of his time, and was thought the most capable of governing and defending the empire. He was born in Dalmatia, of a very obscure family. He was reckoned a great but very wicked Prince,[1] and in fact had many vices mixed with extraordinary talents. He was of commanding stature, had a grave and majestic air, but a rude and disagreeable countenance, was close and reserved, and a great master of dissimulation, always forming important designs, and never executing them till after he had well weighed and considered the consequences. He was generally victorious in war, and could never be accused of having failed by his own fault. He was so fertile in expedients that in the most desperate crcumstances, and such as seemed to be past all remedy, some resource or other was sure to present itself to his superior genius. He was nobly jealous of the glory of the empire, and so encouraged arts and learning that he deserved the pompous title that was given him of Restorer of the Golden Age. Before he was Emperor he used to say that nothing was more difficult than to reign well, and he afterwards justified this maxim by his conduct; for though he had resolved to imitate Marcus Antoninus he fell far short of his model, and exhibited scarcely any of the virtues of that great Emperor. He was, indeed, so far master of his passions that he knew how to curb and restrain them, but this victory was owing to his policy,

[1] Eutrop. Dioclet.

not to his virtue. He endeavoured to impose upon the
public, and succeeded, for he was thought exempt from
vice because he had the art of concealing it. He set no
bounds to his pride, for he caused the same honours to
be paid him that were given to the gods. His vanity
was so conspicuous in the luxury and splendour of his
apparel that even his shoes were covered with jewels.
He was also so avaricious that, in order to heap up
money, he did not scruple to commit the most flagrant
acts of injustice,[1] but was cunning enough to throw the
shame and odium of them upon his agents and instruments, who had acted by his order.

As soon as Diocletian was proclaimed Emperor, the
Senate, according to custom, conferred upon Prisca the
title of August, which honour rather increased her
humility than otherwise, and showed that there are some
few persons in the world of such exalted souls as not to
be influenced or corrupted by grandeur and high stations.
It is not known whether Prisca accompanied her husband
when he went to Rome to have his election confirmed;
but it is generally believed that she was in the East when
Diocletian associated in the empire his old friend Maximinus, who took the surname of Hercules, who, indeed,
had served with credit under the preceding Emperors,
but was of obscure extraction; this would have been no
dishonour to him if he had not at the same time plunged
into all the vices of the worst of tyrants. Hercules was
brutal in the highest degree, and so passionate that, in his
fury, there was nothing too bad for him to be capable of.
Never were the taxes collected with so much rigour and
violence as in his reign. He was covetous, unjust, with-

[1] Lactan. de mortib. persecut.

out honour or conscience, suborning false witnesses
against those whose riches he was resolved to be possessed
of, and beyond measure debauched, so that all lawful
pleasures were insipid to him. He did not scruple to
carry off by force any young girls whom he took a fancy
to, even in sight of their parents, whom he also compelled
to be witnesses of their dishonour, so, as an historian has
observed,[1] if his valour and military capacity rendered
his progress terrible to his enemies, his incontinence
made it not less so to women of virtue in those places
through which he passed. His person was as deformed
as his mind; he was of great size, but his coarse and
savage features and countenance, together with his black
thick beard, caused him to be looked upon with horror;
so it was not to be wondered at, that with his forbidding
aspect he was not able to gain the affections of his wife
Eutropia; on the contrary, it would have been more
surprising if that charming Syrian had not listened to
the solicitations of a passionate and handsome lover,
whose merit could not but place the imperfections of
Hercules in a more disadvantageous light.

Galeria Valeria Eutropia was not exempt from those
vices to which her nation was subject. Some authors say
she was nearly related to Eutropius, father of the Emperor Constantius.[2] She possessed great beauty, a
cheerful temper, and an amorous temperament, and was
very fond of pleasures and diversions. She was married
very young to a Syrian, whose name and family are not
mentioned; the fruit of this marriage was Theodora,
whom we shall see upon the throne. Her husband died
soon after the birth of her daughter.

[1] Lactan. de mortib. persecut. c. 8.   [2] Julian. Cæsar. 1. Victor. Epit.

Eutropia's beauty suffered nothing from her deep mourning, on the contrary it seemed to be rather heightened, for it is not probable that her countenance was of a piece with her dress. Nobody is more disposed to receive comfort than a young and amiable widow, whose vivacity and liveliness is naturally no friend to seriousness and grief, and who is surrounded by a crowd of admirers, vying with each other who shall be the first to make amends for her loss. A lover full of life and sprightliness soon obliterates the remembrance of a dead husband, for people are soon weary of fighting in vain after a shadow, and wasting their tears upon an object that can only amuse their imagination. Eutropia paid such respect to the memory of her husband as fashion and the rules of decency required, but did not think herself obliged to carry on the farce further than she was obliged; she therefore looked out for a new conquest, and was so fortunate as to make a very illustrious one. Hercules, notwithstanding his rough and unpolished disposition, was far from being insensible to the power of beauty. He was captivated by her charms, and soon found means to let her know it.

Hercules, as we have observed, had a most disagreeable appearance, and was more calculated to inspire fear than love; his mind was as uncultivated as his person, so that he was quite incapable of carrying on his amours gallantly, but his fortune spoke for him, and the lustre of the imperial purple made at least as deep an impression upon the heart of Eutropia as the greatest accomplishments could have done. Sovereign authority is a sort of veil that effectually eclipses the imperfections of whoever is invested with it. A lover who wears a crown is always

well received, and the eyes of his mistress, being fixed
upon that splendid mark of his dignity, have not time to
wander about to spy out the faults and deformities of his
person; for this reason, although Eutropia had an infinite
number of adorers, between whom and Hercules there
was no sort of comparison as to real merit, yet he had
the preference, as being most capable of gratifying her
ambition.

Reasons of State might possibly have weighed so far
with the Emperor as to induce him to marry Eutropia,
especially if it be true that she was related to Eutropius,
and consequently to Constantius, his son. The Emperors
made a point of marrying into their own families, for we
shall find that when Constantius was associated in the
imperial dignity, he was obliged to divorce his wife
Helena to marry the daughter-in-law of Hercules; thus
Diocletian, having formed the design of placing Constantius upon the throne, who was every day rendering
important services to the State, it is very probable that
he persuaded Hercules to marry Eutropia in order to
unite them beforehand to the Emperors by this alliance.
However it was, this was the first time that two Empresses were seen reigning at the same time.

It is true that Faustina, wife of Marcus Aurelius, and
Lucilla, wife of Lucius Verus, enjoyed at once the same
dignity, as did afterwards Julia, wife of Severus, and
Plautilla, wife of Caracalla, but we have observed that
this last was not looked upon by Caracalla as his wife,
because Severus his father compelled him to marry her;
she lived at Court only as daughter of Plautianus, and
not as wife of the prince, nor had she any sort of influence
or interest. As to Faustina and Lucilla, the mother

always maintained a superiority over the daughter; Lucilla could not be jealous of the honours conferred upon her mother, nor could Faustina envy her daughter the respect that was paid her, since it was of her own procuring. But when Faustina died, and Commodus had married Crispina, the case was altered. As she was then Empress, she claimed singly all the honours that were used to be given to the Emperors' wives, and which, she said, nobody could claim but the reigning Empress; she refused to share them with her sister-in-law, who thought she had a right to them as widow of an Emperor, and we have drawn attention to the confusions and quarrels that were occasioned at Court in consequence of the perpetual jealousies between these two princesses.

Prisca was not at all uneasy upon this account; she saw with great indifference Hercules's wife seated with her upon the throne, whereas Eutropia regarded the matter very differently. Prisca being guided by virtue and good sense, and perhaps by the pure maxims of the Christian religion, was an ornament to her rank and her station, and led such a life as was exempt from all suspicions and censures; Eutropia, on the contrary, indulged in such indecencies as were not at all to the advantage of her reputation. When she first came to the throne she indeed acted very cautiously, but the characteristics of her nation, added to her own natural temperament, soon prevailed, and she gave herself up to pleasures; and, however the fury and resentment of Hercules was to be dreaded, that did not hinder her from being extremely fond of a Syrian, who, being polite and agreeable, found the secret of insinuating himself into her good graces. A woman has a great deal more complaisance for a man of her own country than another, and such a one will always have a great advantage over a stranger. We cannot help leaning towards such a person, for there is implanted in everybody's heart a certain national partiality, that inclines us, whether we will or not, to give him the preference. Eutropia had this feeling for the handsome Syrian, nor had she virtue or resolution enough to withstand the solicitations of a lover who had everything she desired to recommend him.

Eutropia had been married some years to Hercules without having a child, which afflicted him very much,[1] for he was extremely desirous to have heirs. The Empress knew this, and it did not a little contribute to persuade her to an intrigue, which answered her expectations, for she became pregnant. This gave the Emperor all the satisfaction in the world, but, if anything were wanting to make it complete, it was the fear of having a daughter; his desires were, however, accomplished by Eutropia's being delivered of a son, whom he called Maxentius. The credulous Emperor received this present with transports of joy, and caused this shameful production of his wife's libertinism to be educated with all possible care and expense.

Some authors, who are more favourable to the Empress,[2] say that Hercules passionately longed for a son to perpetuate his family, and seeing his wife with child, waited the event with great impatience, and that Eutropia, being brought to bed of a girl, cunningly substituted a boy in her place, in order to ingratiate herself with her husband. It must be acknowledged, for the honour of the Empress, that there are historians who

[1] Vita Constantin. Auctor. Anony.   [2] Eutrop.

will have it that Maxentius was really the son of Hercules.   Be it as it may, the Emperor, who was more
interested than anybody in the birth of this child, looked
upon him as his son, and accordingly raised him afterwards to the throne.

When he himself was adopted by Diocletian as his
colleague, that Emperor did not less consult his own
interest than the friendship he had for Hercules.   He
saw the provinces exposed to the incursions of barbarians and the usurpation of tyrants, and, as it is
impossible for one Emperor to oppose so many enemies
at once, he was very glad to be eased of part of the
burden of choosing a partner.   Hercules had proved
himself capable of answering his expectations, for, having been sent against Ælianus and Amandus, who had
put themselves at the head of a band of robbers in Gaul,
he dispersed in a very short time that dangerous faction,
but at the same time demonstrated his cruelty by in-
humanly ordering the entire Theban legion to be massacred.   It was composed of Christians, and commanded
by Maurice, an experienced general, who knew how to
give Cæsar his right, but was not a man to prefer Cæsar
to God, or to make his fortune at the expense of his
religion.   Hercules being about to offer a sacrifice to his
gods to render them propitious to his designs, Maurice,
as well as the officers and soldiers of his troop, not being
able to prevail upon themselves to join in this idolatry,
stood aside, that they might not be partakers in those
abominations.   The Emperor, hurried on by his superstition to revenge his despised deities, thought he could
not take a better method to appease them than by putting
Maurice to death; and in order to intimidate the soldiers

by punishing a great many, decimated them. Those upon
whom the lot fell showed so much joy in imitating their
leader, and suffered the punishment to which they were
condemned with such surprising intrepidity, that the
tyrant, provoked at seeing himself overcome by these
martyrs, put the whole legion to the sword.

This act of violence was, as it were, the signal of the
persecution that was then kindled against the Church,
which was one of the most terrible that had ever been
known, for the oracle of Apollo having been consulted,
answered that the just persons of the earth hindered it
from speaking. It was not doubted that by this was
meant the Christians, so it was resolved that they should
be extirpated. Diocletian, who was most superstitiously
jealous of the honour of his gods, began with his own
family, and the first act of the persecution was committed in his palace.

The Empress Prisca, having the greatest veneration
for the Christian religion, had taken care to inspire the
Princess Valeria, her daughter, with the same sentiments,
and if they did not profess it publicly they were at least
Christians at heart. It is difficult to imagine that Diocletian was quite ignorant of the leaning these two
princesses had to Christianity. Their neglect of the
Roman deities and their compassion for the persecuted
Christians might have made him suspect that they paid
their adoration elsewhere; nor can it be supposed that
they could keep so strict a guard upon their whole
behaviour as not to reveal the favourable opinion they
entertained of a religion that the Emperor abhorred.
His affection for his wife and daughter had made him
often hesitate what to do, and had frequently induced

him to delay the execution of what the heathen priests had assured him it was his duty to do, rather than give offence to persons he so tenderly loved. But as soon as the oracle had roused his superstition by appearing unfavourable to the Christians, he formed the design of abolishing Christianity entirely, and of causing his gods to be universally worshipped, especially Jupiter and Hercules; and in order the better to pay his court to them, he imagined that he ought to compliment them in the first place with the lives of the chief persons in the empire.

Diocletian's conduct in this affair seems to have been extremely imprudent, and not of a piece with his behaviour in other respects, for he seldom did anything of consequence without having well weighed and considered it. It cannot but be acknowledged that he was very fond of his only daughter, as well as of his wife, who was so deserving of his esteem and affection; but by commanding them to assist at the sacrifice he exposed himself to the cruel necessity of either permitting his gods to be despised by the refusal of these princesses to offer incense to those fabulous divinities, or else of being compelled to expiate the contempt at the expense of those lives which were so valuable to him.

This disagreeable alternative did not, however, change his resolution, for the unbounded respect he had for his gods prevailed; he was of opinion that nothing ought to enter into rivalry with them, and thought his family should be the first to show an example of their submission to his orders, and of their zeal for the tutelary gods of the State.

This might have been a happy conjuncture for the

princesses, who were thereby furnished with a fair opportunity of ennobling their names and doing honour to
their faith, by refusing to pay to false deities that worship and adoration which they knew belonged only to the
true God. But whether they were terrified at the threats
of the Emperor, whose fury was never so dreadful as
when he was to revenge any slight upon his gods, or
whether it was that the princesses were not sufficiently
instructed in the principles of their religion, which commands us to confess its Divine Author, even in the
midst of tortures, before the potentates and tyrants of
the earth, and not to fear those who can only kill the
body—whatever was the reason, they had not resolution
enough to overcome the powerful temptation, but were
so weak as to conform to the command of Diocletian,
and offer, externally, the sacrifice which their hearts condemned them for. They preferred to their salvation
a life that they seemed to have preserved only to pass
in grief and bitterness, for, by avoiding the present evil,
they drew upon themselves a worse and more lasting one.
The bad example of the two princesses had indeed but
too many imitators, but there were a great number of
good Christians, upon whom it made no bad impression,
and who cheerfully sealed their faith with their blood.
Even the Emperor's palace served as a stage for the
triumph of some of his officers, who bore with a serene
countenance and intrepidity which was not to be shaken
either by threats or promises, the utmost efforts of his
rage. Sebastianus especially, a captain of the Prætorian
Guards, who was distinguished by his extraordinary
merit, made a noble confession of his faith in presence
of the whole Court, and confounded his persecutors by

suffering martyrdom, not only with courage and patience, but with joy and pleasure.

The Emperors did not, however, reap from this cruelty the advantage they expected, nor were they able to procure peace and tranquillity to the empire by appeasing the gods with torrents of blood, as they flattered themselves. The Christians were exposed to all the miseries and torments that the malice of men or devils could invent, but that did not hinder new revolts from creating new wars in all the provinces, so that the sovereign authority was never in so much danger of being totally overthrown. Carausius rebelled in Britain, where he made himself an absolute tyrant. The Persians, conducted by Narses their king, made irruptions all over the East. Egypt had chosen a new master in the person of Achilles, who had caused himself to be proclaimed Emperor at Alexandria, and even Italy groaned under the unlimited and independent power that Julianus had assumed; so that it looked as if all these enemies had arisen by common consent against the empire in order to divide it amongst them.

Diocletian and Hercules, finding so much upon their hands, resolved to take other colleagues who should be as much interested in defending the empire as themselves. They therefore gave the dignity of Cæsar to Galerius and Constantius, generals who were quite capable of humbling the rebels, and protecting the provinces they should be entrusted with. The former was the son of a peasant of Illyria. Romula, his mother, had an implacable hatred of the Christians, which she took care to instil into her son, the poisonous leaven of which fermented only too readily in his heart. He had in his youth been brought up as a shepherd, but afterwards took up the profession of arms, in which he became very skilful and had great success. However, neither the air of the army nor his long residence at Court were able to rub off the rust he had contracted, so that, in the most exalted stations, he still retained his former lack of polish. To tell the truth, he was a good officer, but (that excepted) he had not one commendable quality. There was something dark and gloomy in his countenance that sufficiently showed the sourness of his mind; and his loud, harsh voice, wild look, and continual frown inspired everybody with aversion to his person. He had the vices of the worst of the Emperors, and indulged them with the utmost brutality. As he was cruel and inflexible, he could never be prevailed upon to temper justice with mercy, a virtue so necessary to princes. His vanity surpassed that of the Emperors who were most accused of it; for, notwithstanding his base extraction, he carried his pride so far that, not content with being above other men in point of rank, he also claimed a superiority with respect to his family and origin, giving out that he was the son of Mars, who, he said, in the form of a dragon, had had connection with his mother, being very willing to dishonour her by so monstrous a union, rather than not be thought of illustrious descent. Besides all this, he was so covetous that, in order to gratify his insatiable avarice, he made all the provinces groan under the intolerable burden of his extortions.

Flavius Constantius was son of Eutropius, one of the greatest lords of Dardania, and of Claudia, daughter of Crispus, brother of the Emperor Claudius the Goth,[1] and

[1] So called from his victory over the Goths.

he honoured his nobility by the greatest virtues, especially sweetness of temper, affability, and the most engaging behaviour. He never filled his coffers with the riches of the provinces; for it was a maxim of his that it was much better the gold should circulate among the people than be treasured up by the prince. He had acquired so great a reputation in the army that Carus judged him worthy of the empire. Before the title of Cæsar was conferred on him, he married Helena, but he was forced to divorce her, conformably to the will of Hercules and Diocletian, who obliged him to marry Theodora, daughter of Eutropia.

About this time Maximianus Galerius married the Princess Valeria; and it is very probable that when Diocletian gave her to him he did not much consult the inclinations of his daughter, for it is certain that Galerius had none of the qualifications that were necessary to make him acceptable to so accomplished a lady. In his first wife's time he had led a most dissolute life, nor were matters much better after his marriage with Valeria, for he had a favourite mistress whom he preferred infinitely to her. It is true that the princess did not take this affront much to heart, for her virtue and good disposition made her unsusceptible to jealousy. She not only submitted to his ill treatment without complaining, but even showed him marks of esteem and affection of which he was by no means worthy; for, finding that she had no children, she adopted Candidianus, her husband's natural son.

By the creation of these new Cæsars there were four Empresses upon the throne. To all appearance Prisca, who was the oldest of them, preserved a kind of supe-

riority over the rest. The other Emperors owed their
fortunes to Diocletian, and gratitude required that their
Empresses should yield the precedence to the wife of
their benefactor. They were not, however, much exposed to the jealousy and disputes that are generally
occasioned by equality of rank and condition, for the
Emperors having divided the provinces that each might
protect his own part against the barbarians and tyrants,
the Empresses accompanied their husbands, and each in
her own territory enjoyed all the honours that are com-
bined with the supreme authority.

Galerius marched against the Persians, who had already conquered Mesopotamia. His first campaign was
not successful, for he was defeated by the barbarians.
Diocletian heard this news with great vexation; he was
so out of humour with his son-in-law, and gave him so
cold a reception [1] that he allowed Galerius to follow his
litter on foot for half an hour, though he was clothed
in the imperial purple, the lustre of which only served
to augment his confusion. This misfortune did not,
however, discourage Galerius, for he raised another
powerful army, and attacked the Persians again. The
Empress Valeria accompanied him in this expedition,
and shared with him the fatigue and the honour of it;
she even greatly facilitated the victory he obtained over
the enemy, for, as Diocletian [2] was very fond of his
daughter, she employed all her influence with him to
procure everything that was necessary to enable Galerius
to carry on the war with success, and so won the hearts
of the soldiers by her liberality that they were all ready
to lay down their lives to re-establish the reputation of

[1] Ammian. Marcel. lib. 14, Eutrop.   [2] Tristan. Comment. Histor.

the Roman arms. By these means Galerius defeated the Persians in Armenia, and Narses, their King, was put to flight, abandoning to the conquerer his Queen, sisters, children, and treasure, together with his camp and equipage. The Romans retook all that they had lost the year before, and if Galerius had been at liberty to have pushed his good fortune as he at first intended he would have absolutely destroyed the Persian empire. But Diocletian's jealousy was a piece of good fortune for the barbarians. He saw with envy the laurels with which Galerius was covered, and recalled him, pretending that it was high time for him to take some repose after his labours, and enjoy the honour of the triumph that was preparing for him.

Constantius in the meantime met with the like vicissitudes of fortune in Gaul. He was first surprised and beaten by the enemy, but afterwards defeated them near Langres.[1] Hercules subdued the Africans; and Diocletian having humbled the tyrant Achilles, made himself master of all Egypt; so that the four Emperors had the honour of re-establishing the fortunes of the State. The Senate decreed them a triumph, and Diocletian, accompanied by Hercules, went to Rome to reap the fruits of his victories. The Empress Eutropia undertook the journey with her husband, though she was pregnant. She had never been at Rome, and passionately longed to see the capital of the world. She was there brought to bed of a daughter, who was named Fausta; this was a new subject of joy to the city, and added very much to the splendour and magnificence of the triumph. It was celebrated with extraordinary pomp, and all classes

[1] The ancient *Civitas Lingonum*.

strove to out-do each other by the most flattering language upon this occasion. The Empress Valeria had the satisfaction of sharing all these honours with her husband, for the Senate, who were very assiduous in obtaining the good graces of Diocletian, for whom the other Cæsars had the greatest deference and respect, did not think they could pay their court to him more effectually than by conferring upon his only daughter the honours that had been granted to preceding Empresses, especially since she was so deserving of them. Besides the proud title of Mother of the Armies, with which none but the most illustrious of the Empresses had been dignified, they decreed her a crown of laurel, a glorious and special privilege that had never before been bestowed upon any woman, in consideration of her having had so large a share in and so much contributed to her husband's military exploits. They did not stop there, for, in order to immortalise her name and memory, they gave the name of Valeria to that part of Pannonia which is between the Drave and the Danube.[1] Thus liberal of her favours was Fortune to the princess, giving her no hint of the bitter afflictions that were soon to overtake her.

Diocletian, after the example of other Emperors, entertained the people with shows and diversions, but in so mean a way that, instead of gaining their esteem and affection, it afforded ample matter for raillery and ridicule, whereupon he was so affronted that he left Rome and went to Ravenna in such bad weather that he contracted a disorder, which emaciated his body and so enfeebled his mind that he was out of his senses for a considerable time. This accident made his colleagues

[1] Ammian. lib. 19.

lose a great deal of the respect they had hitherto shown him, and Galerius, his son-in-law, was the first who gave signs of this. For a long time past the submission that he had been forced to render to Diocletian had gone much against the grain with him. His late victory had so puffed him up that he imagined himself the only person capable of governing, and looked upon Diocletian and Hercules as old and worn out. He flattered himself that it would not be impossible for him to persuade them to abdicate, and then thought he could easily manage Constantius. He omitted nothing that he supposed necessary to carry out this project, but did not, at first, find them so ready to gratify him as he could have wished. People are not so eager to condemn themselves to a private life after having tasted the sweets of power and sovereignty; nor is it so easy for those who have been used to command to submit to a voluntary obedience. The two Emperors struggled a long time against all the efforts of Galerius, but were at last so intimidated by his threatening letters that, to avoid a civil war, they were forced to divest themselves of their dignity.

Diocletian did this with a great deal of solemnity. He assembled at Nicomedia all the officers of his army and the great men of his Court, and told them with tears in his eyes that his infirmities would not permit him to support the fatigues of war any longer, wherefore he was determined to give up his share of the government to his colleagues, who had all the talents that were required for so important a trust, and were in the prime of life. He added that Hercules had formed the same design. After a very moving speech he quitted the purple, as-

sumed the garb of a private person, and retired to
Salona, a town in Dalmatia. Hercules went through the
same ceremony at Milan, and, no doubt, with the same
regret; after which he went to Rome in his private
capacity. Diocletian desired that Constantine (son of
Constantius) and Maxentius, who passed for the son of
Hercules, should be created Cæsars, but Galerius, who
intended to make himself sole Emperor, opposed it.
He was, nevertheless, obliged to accept those two princes
for his colleagues, for Constantius when he was dying at
York, named Constantine his successor, and Maxentius
took upon himself that dignity of his own authority,
causing himself to be proclaimed Emperor.

By the abdication of Diocletian and Hercules the Empresses Prisca and Eutropia found themselves deprived
of their dignity. It is more than probable that they did
not quit it with a very good grace, for ladies do not
generally submit to a degradation without some sighs.
Be that as it may, it appears that it was not long before
Hercules repented of the step he had taken, for being
soon weary of a private life he reassumed the insignia
of sovereign authority, and again increased the number
of Cæsars. He would fain have prevailed upon Diocletian to imitate him, and sent a nobleman of his Court
to urge him to do so, but Diocletian very prudently
rejected the proposal. He declared to the envoy that he
infinitely preferred the tranquillity of his retreat to the
hurry and bustle of a Court, and in his letter he says:—
" I wish that you were at Salona to see my garden, and
the herbs that I have planted with my own hands; you
would not then endeavour to entice me away from my

agreeable retirement, to embroil myself afresh in affairs of State."

Of all the rivals and competitors of Galerius, Maxentius seemed to him the most formidable. This prince was full of ambitious designs, capable of forming vast projects, and, believing himself the son of Hercules, thought he had a right to aspire to the empire. As he did not receive his authority from anybody, but had seized it himself, Galerius treated him as a usurper, and sent Severus with an army against him, who, having attacked Maxentius, was put to flight and forced to take shelter at Ravenna. Hercules ordered him to be executed, though he had promised to save his life.

This piece of treachery furnished Galerius with a pretence to declare war against Hercules, and in order to be the better able to carry it on with success he took Licinius as a colleague. Hercules, being alarmed at the number of his enemies, endeavoured to procure the assistance of Constantine, and to that end gave him his daughter Fausta in marriage, but notwithstanding this close alliance, he soon formed very black designs against the life of his son-in-law. But he was the dupe of his own artifices, for Constantine, having discovered the mischief that was hatching against him, drove Hercules to such a pitch of despair that he killed himself. Galerius did not long survive him, but terminated by a shameful death a life which his cruelty and incontinence had made detestable. He was smitten with a horrible disease [1] in the most sensitive parts of his body, being devoured alive by worms, and such a stench proceeded from him as was offensive even to those who were without the palace.

[1] Lactan. de mortib. persecut.

The inexpressible noxiousness of this dreadful distemper did not hinder the Empress Valeria from attending her husband with all the care and affection that could have been expected from a woman who had met with the best treatment in the world, and giving such proofs of her dutifulness as he was in no sort deserving of. But the terrible and uncommon plague that he was afflicted with having obstinately resisted all the means that could be thought of for his recovery, he knew that he had nothing to expect but a miserable death. Then it was that he began to make dismal reflections upon his cruelty to the Christians, and issued an edict to put a stop to the persecutions he had set on foot against those poor innocent people, whose blood cried aloud for vengeance. At last, after having recommended his wife and Candidianus, his natural son, to the care of Licinius, he died without being regretted.

As soon as Maximinus was informed of his death he set out for the East to take possession of those provinces that had fallen to the lot of his uncle. But Licinius would not admit his claims; and this dispute obliging them to have recourse to arms, they determined to decide it by a battle. Means were, however, found to adjust the difference, and then they mutually swore to live in friendship with each other. As the territories of Galerius had been the subject of their quarrel, Valeria, who was resolved to live quietly and free from disturbance, yielded to Maximinus everything that he had a right to as belonging to her husband; but Maximinus with great courtesy declined it, and insisted upon her enjoying the riches that Galerius had left her. He gave the most generous tokens of a sincere friendship and esteem, and

even eagerly embraced every opportunity of contributing
to her pleasure and satisfaction.

There being now no rancour or animosity between
Licinius and Maximinus they both retired to their respective provinces; but before they separated they each
of them offered Valeria a revenue suitable to her rank.
She hesitated for a long time about what was best for
her to do. She knew that Diocletian, her father, was
drawing near his end, and that after his death neither
Salona nor Nicomedia could be a place of safety for
her; she therefore thought it best to pass the remainder
of her days either with Licinius or Maximinus, who, being beholden to her late husband for their fortunes, could
not in honour and gratitude but have a particular regard
for his widow, so all the difficulty lay in the choice she
should make. On the one hand she recollected that
her husband had very warmly recommended her to Licinius, which looked as if he had thereby declared his intention; but, on the other hand, she was not ignorant
that Licinius had a very bad character, and was even
afraid that, as she was not married, he might make her
some disagreeable proposals that should be directly contrary to the resolution she had taken of passing the rest
of her life in widowhood. These reasons determined
her to put herself under the protection of Maximinus,
who, being nephew to Galerius, would be most likely to
treat with kindness and affection a person who had been
the wife of his uncle and benefactor.

The Empress Prisca was so excessively fond of her
daughter that she could not bear the thought of separat-
ing from her. Besides, she hoped to be more at liberty
to practise the Christian religion with Maximinus than

elsewhere; for, though she knew him to be no friend to Christianity in general, yet she could not suppose that she or her daughter were to be subject to the rigour of whatever edicts he might issue against it. Diocletian did not think proper to oppose the princesses' design, for he had for a long time past been so used to solitude that he gave himself very little trouble about what was going on; his garden at Salona was all he cared for, and indeed, the disorders he was subject to would not permit him to employ himself in anything else. So he willingly consented to the departure of his wife and daughter. They were accompanied by Candidianus, natural son of Galerius, and Prince Severianus, son of the Emperor Flavius Valerius Severus.

These two princesses, by their virtue, beauty and merit, were the greatest ornaments of the Court. Prisca especially was highly esteemed for the prudence of her conduct; she never meddled with any State affairs, but passed her time in the performance of the duties of the religion she secretly practised. Valeria was yet in the height of her beauty, which was in a great measure owing to her having had no children; her modesty set off her charms, and the mourning habit, which she never quitted, added to her charms instead of having a contrary effect.

Maximinus at first behaved with the greatest politeness and civility to the two princesses. He showed Prisca all the deference and respect that was due to her age and quality, and treated Valeria as a kind and dutiful son would a good mother. The princesses thought themselves so happy that it was not in the power of anything to add to their felicity, congratulated each other upon their good fortune in having preferred Maximinus to

Licinius, and were far from regretting their former condition. As they were entirely their own mistresses, and at liberty to do whatever they pleased, they imagined that nothing could interrupt their tranquillity. The extreme complaisance of the Emperor and his eagerness to procure them all possible satisfaction made them forget all that had been disagreeable in their past life; but they little knew that this calm was so soon to be succeeded by a storm, and this state of peace and serenity by a cruel persecution.

The Empress Valeria was herself the innocent occasion of it; her beauty kindled in the heart of Maximinus a flame that was not to be resisted, so that in fact he was rather her slave than her protector; and as he had not been accustomed to curb his passions, he gave himself up to the violence of his love, without considering whether it was lawful or not. Neither the respect he owed to the memory of his uncle, nor the strict virtue of Valeria (which did not permit him to flatter himself with the least hopes of success) were strong enough to restrain him. He had unlimited power, which seldom permits those who are invested with it to act according to reason or religion: some people are apt to think everything lawful that is possible.

It is certain that Valeria could not have made a more dangerous conquest, for in Maximinus were united all the vices that can be imagined; he had an extreme aversion to the Christian religion, and an inexhaustible fund of brutality that made him dreadful to all the world; as he passed most of his time in drinking to excess, and consequently was never master of his reason, it cannot be wondered at that he fell into all other sorts of irregularities and debaucheries; particularly, his incontinence was carried to such a pitch that there was no security against it. As he was not a man to put in practice the virtue of self-denial, he thought of nothing but how to gratify those desires which were more and more excited by the beauty of Valeria; and not having the patience to wait till the expiration of her mourning, he was resolved to let her know it without further loss of time. He began with the usual complaisance, and studying what could be most agreeable to her; but Valeria, taking all this for an effect of his politeness, and far from imagining that it was anything more than bare civility, behaved in such a manner as gave the Emperor plainly to understand that she did not see into his designs; it was therefore necessary for him to come to a clear explanation. He did not, however, choose to do this himself, for the first steps in love are generally the most troublesome, and there are few men, however great their wit and assurance, who are not embarrassed upon such an occasion, especially when the declaration is to be made to a person whom it is unlawful for them to address in such language. Maximinus, who felt this sort of uneasiness, and was well acquainted with Valeria's austerity and reserve, gave this commission to one of his favourites, charging him to acquaint the princess with the impression her charms had made on him; and, that he might be more favourably heard, Maximinus gave him orders to declare that he had no other intention than to raise her to the throne, by marrying her after first divorcing his wife.

Valeria was thunderstruck at this proposal, and immediately reflected upon all the miseries that this fatal passion would involve her in. All the evils that the

most cruel and the most libidinous of mankind could
bring upon her crowded into her imagination. She felt
little gratitude to her beauty that had laid such a snare
for her, and plunged her into such deep distress. Her
inclination, as well as her religion, forbade her to think
of it without horror.

The emissary did not fail to exaggerate the violence
and sincerity of the Emperor's love, and the great advantage she would reap by this match. She acknowledged
herself infinitely obliged to the Emperor for the honour
he did her,[1] but added that, in her present condition, it
did not become her to listen to any proposals of that
nature; that the ashes of Galerius were scarce cold, and
that the mourning which she wore reminded her every
moment of her husband's death. Besides this, the laws
of decency would not permit her to accept the Emperor's
offer, for she could look upon him in no other light than
as the son of Galerius, since he had been adopted by him.
That it would be unpardonable in her to do the wife of
Maximinus so great an injury as to deprive her of her
husband's affection; and, in short, that it would be the
height of injustice, if he should divorce his wife who was
so worthy of his esteem, and by no means deserved such
treatment. She added that it would be very unseemly
for a person of her rank to marry a second husband, and
tarnish her widowhood by a fresh engagement.

The favourite did not fail to oppose all these arguments, but in vain; for the princess protested that she
had made a solemn resolution against ever marrying
again, and thereby cut short all hopes of her being prevailed upon to alter her mind, whatever brilliant and

[1] Lactan. de mortib. persec.

flattering promises might be made her. This answer, so little favourable to Maximinus's hopes, provoked him beyond measure, and changed his love into hatred. He resolved that Valeria should fear him at least, since she could not be brought to love him; and as it is usual for tyrants to pass from one extreme to another, he became her most cruel persecutor. At first he was determined to make her feel all the weight of his resentment, but some small remains of regard for Diocletian induced him to delay for a little time the gratification of his vengeance, which, nevertheless, only fell the heavier upon her afterwards. He turned her brutally out of her palace, seized all her effects, deprived her of her domestics, and inflicted upon her all the mortifications he could possibly invent.

The Empress Prisca, being involved in the same persecution, shared with her daughter in all these afflictions, and met with the same treatment. The princesses submitted to this inhuman usage with great courage and resolution, as far as they themselves were concerned; but what grieved them most was the affronts that were put upon many ladies of their retinue, whom they honoured with their friendship and esteem. Maximinus endeavoured to blacken their reputations, after having in vain attempted to corrupt them. This monster of impurity, against whose attacks no woman was safe, having found in these ladies a chastity that was proof against all his solicitations, thought he could not be more effectually revenged than by accusing them of the very crime he would have persuaded them to commit, knowing that a woman of virtue is more sensible of the loss of her honour than of her life.

An infamous Jew was thought a fitting tool to carry on this piece of work. He was a notorious villain, who had been convicted of the greatest crimes; but Maximinus promised him his pardon upon condition that he would accuse these ladies before Eratineus, Governor of Nicaea, where the Court then was. The Emperor, who knew that this magistrate was fit for his purpose, had made him judge of the case. Eratineus was of a cruel, arbitrary disposition, severe against those whom he had a mind to destroy, however innocent they might be, and indulgent to such offenders as he intended to screen from punishment, however guilty they were. He had a corrupt and mercenary soul, and was anxious about nothing so much as how to make his fortune without troubling himself about the means.

This villainous Jew, who rejoiced at having so fair an opportunity of exempting himself from the chastisement he had deserved upon such easy terms, greedily embraced the offer, and accused the ladies of the most horrible prostitutions. With these illustrious criminals there were two senators' wives who were nearly related to the Empress Prisca, and another whose daughter was one of the Vestal Virgins, and for whom Valeria had a particular regard. These ladies were all extremely handsome, and their beauty was adorned with such virtue as had enabled them to withstand all the advances of Maximinus, which was in reality the crime they were guilty of.

The accusation of this Jew, though supported by no proofs, was a sufficient reason for the condemnation of the ladies. So unjust a sentence made everybody tremble, for in such a case none could be secure. The people clamoured exceedingly against it, and a thousand voices were heard in the crowd, extolling the virtue and merit of the pretended criminals. This did not, however, save them, for as it was pre-determined that they should die martyrs to their chastity, the senators' wives and mother of the Vestal Virgin were accordingly executed without the city, and the iniquitous judge was not ashamed to feast his eyes upon this tragic spectacle.

But to his great confusion, as well as the Emperor's, it was not long before the wickedness of this action was discovered, for the Jew, having committed some new crime for which he was condemned to death, confessed the whole affair.

Maximinus's cruelty did not stop there. He condemned the two princesses to a strict banishment, and committed them to the charge of the most pitiless and hardhearted wretches who could be procured, who had orders to treat them with the utmost inhumanity. They were sent into the deserts of Syria, where they were reduced to the greatest misery. It was a melancholy sight to see two of the most illustrious persons in the universe, who had been always used to be treated with the greatest respect and distinction, dragged from town to town like the vilest offenders, and the objects of compassion of those who had had reason to envy their former splendour.

In all the places they passed through great multitudes flocked about them, some to gaze and gratify their curiosity, and others to be witnesses of the strange vicissitudes of Fortune, who frequently hurls people down from the highest pinnacle of grandeur to the lowest depth of wretchedness.

Valeria, however, found means to inform her father of all their afflictions, and Diocletian felt upon this occasion all that a father and a husband can suffer on account of the misfortunes inflicted upon a wife and a daughter. He sent a person of quality belonging to his Court to Maximinus to demand the Empresses; but he, looking upon Diocletian as a poor hermit who need not be regarded, despised the message.

Diocletian, having divested himself of all authority, and not being in a condition to command, had no other method of procuring redress than that of negotiating. He therefore deputed one of his near relations, who held considerable rank in the army, to obtain if possible what he had requested of Maximinus. The ambassador represented to him that both Galerius, his uncle, and he himself had been made Emperor by Diocletian's means, and though the latter, exhibiting extraordinary modesty, had resigned the empire, he had been always treated with the respect that was due to him. He added that nothing could be more reasonable than for a father and husband to demand his daughter and wife. But all these arguments and remonstrances were to no purpose, for they only served to increase Maximinus's cruelty. Instead of giving the Empresses their liberty, he increased the rigour of their exile. This deprived Diocletian of all patience; his solitude had not so infinitely broken his spirit as to render him insensible of this insulting treatment; on the contrary, it made so deep an impression on him that he felt tired of his life, and a new vexation that befel him made him resolve to destroy himself.

Licinius and Constantine, in order to cement the peace and friendship that existed between them, entered into a

close alliance.   Constantine married his sister Constantia
to Licinius, and the nuptials were celebrated at Milan.
Diocletian was invited to be present at the ceremony, but
as he had upon his abdication renounced all pleasures
and diversions, and particularly at this time, when he
was overwhelmed with grief on account of the misfortunes of his family, he returned thanks to the two
Cæsars [1] for the honour they did him, but desired, for
the above-mentioned reasons and on account of his age
and infirmities, to be excused.

This refusal was taken very ill by Constantine and
Licinius, and looked upon as an insult, in consequence
of which they wrote him such threatening letters and so
terrified the old Emperor that he killed himself. Maximinus did not long survive him, for, having quarrelled
with Licinius and declared war against him, the two
armies met near Adrianople. Maximinus addressed
himself [2] to his gods, and promised to extirpate the
Christians entirely if they would grant him the victory;
but Licinius, as is credibly reported, dreamt that if he
invoked the God of the Christians he would infallibly
conquer. However that may have been, Maximinus was
defeated, and obliged to flee with such precipitation that
he travelled sixty leagues in twenty-four hours, till he got
into Cappadocia, where, knowing that he was pursued,
he poisoned himself.

It was hoped that the death of Maximinus would put
an end to the sufferings of Prisca and Valeria, and, in
fact, Licininus had nothing to apprehend from two
Empresses who enjoyed no more than the shadow of
their former dignity, for, as there were no traces re-

[1] Eutrop.   [2] Lactan. de mortib. persecu.

maining of their past grandeur, they could not be objects of jealousy to the reigning Empresses. Besides, they were neither ambitious enough to intrigue, nor powerful enough to carry into execution any project that might be formed for their advantage. They thought of nothing but how to pass in tranquillity the remainder of a life that Maximinus had embittered with sorrow and affliction. Fortune seemed to give them some rays of hope that they might some day or other see better days, for, as soon as Maximinus was dead, Candidianus, Galerius's natural and adopted son, went to pay his respects to Licinius at Nicomedia, and was received with great courtesy, and great honour and respect was paid to him by order of the Emperor. Valeria, who had the interests of Candidianus much at heart, heard with great joy of the kind reception that Licinius had given him, and thence conceived good hopes of seeing her fortune reestablished. Full of these flattering ideas she resolved to go secretly to Nicomedia, that she might be a witness of the figure Candidianus made at Court. She therefore disguised herself, went thither, and had the satisfaction of seeing him receive all the respect and honour that was due to his birth. Severianus, being encouraged by this to try his fortune, went also to Nicomedia, and was treated in such a manner as gave him reason to hope. In fact, Licinius, looking upon Severianus as the son of his ancient colleague, showed him such distinguishing marks of his esteem as procured him great respect from all the nobles of the Court; but the same reasons for which they paid him all these honours were the cause of his ruin. Those who envied him his good fortune insinuated to the Emperor that he ought to be upon his guard against a prince who thought he had a right to the throne. They told him that his name alone was sufficient to make him dreaded, for that the son of an Emperor would be apt to believe he had good claims to a throne that had been in a manner hereditary in his family—that Severianus had a good share of ambition, and wanted nothing but a suitable opportunity of making himself head of a party.

Licinius listened to these artful insinuations, and began to look upon Severianus as a dangerous person. His jealousy was attended with cruel consequences, for, fearing he might one day have a troublesome competitor in this prince, he was determined to make himself easy in that respect, and resolved that Severianus should expiate with his life whatever designs of that kind he might have entertained. The unfortunate prince fell a victim to this inhuman precaution, and Candidianus was also involved with him in the same misfortune, when he had least reason to expect any such thing, for they were both put to death together. Valeria and Prisca, her mother, were proscribed, but being disguised, made their escape, and wandered about from province to province for fifteen months.

Their escape made Licinus the more eager to apprehend them. For a long time past he had been exasperated against Valeria, who had refused to yield up to him her right to Galerius's effects. Besides, as she was the daughter and widow of two Emperors, he looked upon her as one who, if not in a condition to form a party, was at least capable of encouraging some other person. The Emperor, after weighing and considering these things, thought he had reason sufficient to take away the lives of these fugitive princesses. He had them pursued by people, who took their measures so well that they were overtaken at Thessalonica, where he caused them to be tried as prisoners of State. It was certainly a difficult matter to convict them of any crime, but those are always guilty who have the misfortune to fall under the displeasure of the prince; accordingly, the corrupt judges knew their duty too well not to condemn them to death. They were conducted, therefore, to the place of execution, accompanied by a great multitude, who were drawn together by the novelty of the spectacle, and who beheld, with great astonishment, the heads of two Empresses cut off by the hands of the common hangman. The bodies were thrown into the sea. This was the tragical end [1] of Prisca and Valeria, who may be said to have died martyrs to their illustrious birth and their extraordinary virtue.

The Empress Eutropia had a happier destiny. After the death of Maximinus Hercules, her husband, she went to live with Fausta, her daughter, at Constantine's Court. As she was past the age of pleasure, she thought of nothing but how to pass the remainder of her life in peace and quietness, far from the noise and hurry of State affairs. She lived to see that happy change in the empire, occasioned by Constantine, her son-in-law, embracing Christianity, which Hercules and Diocletian had endeavoured to extirpate. This religion daily gained ground from that time, got the better of idolatry, and was professed at Court and in all the provinces. The Cross became the greatest ornament of the Roman ensigns and the crowns of the Emperors. Constantine was so assiduous in prop-

[1] Lactan. lib. 51.

agating the faith that not only the imperial family, but
the greatest part of the Court embraced Christianity;
Eutropia was one of the first to profess a religion that had
maintained itself in opposition to all the power of Emperors, who had exhausted all their malice and authority
to abolish it, though the Christians in their defence made
use of no other weapons than their patience and their
prayers.

After Eutropia had been instructed in the precepts of
the Gospel, she practised them with so much zeal and
strictness that all the indiscretions of her past life were
forgotten. She was as solicitous to promote Christianity
as Hercules her husband had been to destroy it. She
not only conformed to its laws, but used her utmost
endeavours to abolish all the impious rites of the Pagans,
and even some superstitions that had been introduced
among the Christians, to the scandal of their holy
religion, which more than anything evinced the soundness
of her belief. This was shown in her care to suppress
the annual ceremonies that were performed under the
famous Oak of Mamre, so remarkable in the Scriptures
for having been the residence of the patriarch Abraham,
and the place where the angels announced the ruin of
Sodom.

This was always celebrated in summer, and a vast
concourse of Jews, Christians, and even heathens used to
assemble there upon that occasion: the first,[1] to honour
the memory of Abraham, the second to solemnise the
apparition of their Messiah, who they imagined spoke
to the patriarch in the form of an angel; and the Pagans,
because they considered those angels to have been, in

[1] Sozomen.

reality, their own gods, whom they honoured by erecting altars there, upon which they placed idols, and offered sacrifices and libations; so that each of them, for one reason or other, had the greatest respect and veneration for that place, and this occasioned an odd mixture of Pagan ceremonies, Jewish superstitions, and Christian devotions. There was a great fair held every year in that place, which drew an infinite number of people from Phœnicia, Palestine, and Arabia.

Eutropia, taking a journey into Palestine, passed through the Valley of Mamre just when they were performing these ceremonies, and saw the impious sacrifices that the heathens offered to their idols, and the superstitions practised by the Christians, who imagined they were performing their duty in a very commendable way. She was extremely offended when she observed that God and the devil were worshipped in the same place; and that this valley, which had been sanctified by the solemn promises which the Almighty had made to Abraham, that from him should spring One in whom all the nations of the earth were to be blessed, should become a theatre of impiety and profanity. She resolved to do all in her power to remedy this evil, and wrote to her son-in-law upon this subject, informing him of what she had seen done by the Pagans, Jews, and even Christians, who all dishonoured that venerable place, some by their idolatrous libations, and others by their indiscreet practice of a mistaken devotion.

Constantine, who eagerly embraced every opportunity of signalising his zeal for the Christian religion, ordered all the idols to be burnt, the altars to be overthrown, and everything that savoured of Paganism and superstition to be destroyed. He caused a church to be built on the very spot, and laid under severe penalties those who in the future should dare to profane that venerable place.

History makes no further mention of Eutropia, but apparently she continued the rest of her life in the strictest practice of the religion she had once professed.

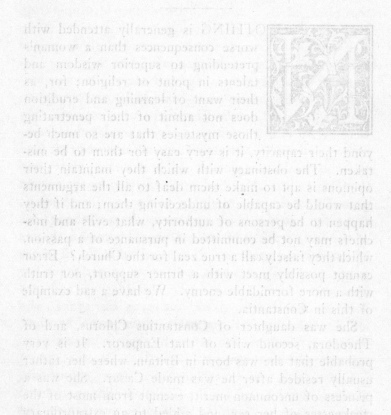

CONSTANTIA

WIFE OF LICINIUS

OTHING is generally attended with worse consequences than a woman's pretending to superior wisdom and talents in point of religion; for, as their want of learning and erudition does not admit of their penetrating those mysteries that are so much beyond their capacity, it is very easy for them to be mistaken. The obstinacy with which they maintain their opinions is apt to make them deaf to all the arguments that would be capable of undeceiving them; and if they happen to be persons of authority, what evils and mischiefs may not be committed in pursuance of a passion, which they falsely call a true zeal for the Church? Error cannot possibly meet with a firmer support, nor truth with a more formidable enemy. We have a sad example of this in Constantia.

She was daughter of Constantius Chlorus, and of Theodora, second wife of that Emperor. It is very probable that she was born in Britain, where her father usually resided after he was made Cæsar. She was a princess of uncommon merit, exempt from most of the weaknesses of her sex, and added to an extraordinary beauty the greatest perfections of mind. She had a masculine courage, a large share of discretion and prudence, and solid virtue. She was distinguished by the force of her genius, a penetrating judgment in the most intricate affairs, a surprising eloquence, a firmness and a resolution that was not easily shaken, and was above all so skilful at healing breaches and making up differences between people at variance that she seldom failed in her attempts that way. She was, however, obstinately attached to her own ideas, and could rarely be persuaded to abandon her first opinion, which was generally something extraordinary, and contrary to that of other people; she was very fond of being singular, even in religious matters, which occasioned great inconveniences and disadvantages to the Church.

Constantia was very young when the Emperor, her father, died at York. It is generally believed that she continued with Constantine, her brother, who was proclaimed Emperor with the universal approbation of the troops, and that she remained at Court with Theodora, her mother, and the Empress Eutropia, her grandmother.

The Prætorians at Rome, being extremely provoked when they heard of Constantine's election, would not accept an Emperor who had been chosen by the army in Britain without their consent, and of whose bounty they had not been partakers; they accordingly proclaimed Maxentius Emperor, the real or supposed son of Hercules, who had already resigned the imperial dignity. Licinius was chosen some time after, and increased the number of the Cæsars.

It would have been much to be wondered at if peace had long been preserved among four princes who had an equal share in the sovereign authority, for moderation is a virtue unknown to ambitious minds. Hercules, who had divested himself of supreme power, would gladly have reassumed it; and, the better to gain his point, he made a close alliance with Constantine, whose daughter he married; but it was not long before he conspired against his son-in-law, which cost him his life; for, finding that the conspiracy was discovered, he fled to Marseilles, where he was assassinated.

Constantine soon found another enemy in Maxentius, and, when he marched against him, had a sure presage of the victory he obtained, by the miraculous cross that appeared to him, with the results that are well known to everybody. This made him resolve to embrace Christianity, and Constantia followed her brother's example. She renounced idolatry, and became very zealous for the religion of Jesus Christ, whose maxims she followed with extraordinary fervour and devotion, which added a fresh lustre to all her other amiable qualities.

Constantine having defeated Maxentius, entered Rome in triumph, and then set the affairs of the empire in order, together with Licinius, his colleague; and, in order to cement a solid peace and friendship between them, he gave him in marriage his sister Constantia, who was then in the height of her youth and beauty.

The nuptials were celebrated at Milan with extraordinary pomp and magnificence. Constantine, who dearly loved the princess his sister, and had the highest opinion of her discretion and virtue, omitted nothing that could contribute to the splendour of this ceremony. To do it the greater honour, he invited Diocletian, but that prince desired to be excused, which refusal annoyed Constantine extremely.

Licinius was not worthy of so great an alliance. His birth was obscure, and though he pretended to be descended from the Emperor Philip, it is certain that he had no great nobility to boast of. It is true that he had a military appearance, and, in fact, was a good officer, and a great enemy to flatterers; but at the same time he was vicious beyond measure, and there was something haughty and severe in his deportment that sufficiently denoted that cruelty which appeared in all his actions. He was of a sour disposition, unjust, a great dissembler, covetous, and quite incapable of any sort of politeness. He was a declared enemy to men of learning, who, he said, were the pests of the State, and being very ignorant himself he avoided as much as possible and persecuted studious people, especially orators and lawyers, who, he said, ought to be exterminated, for that they were the ruin and destruction of empires. He was inveterate in his hatred of the Christians, and persecuted them with a fury that was equally inhuman and ungrateful. Besides, he indulged himself in the most shameful of all vices, and his incontinence spared neither age, sex, nor rank. Such was the husband that Constantine, for reasons of State, gave to his sister.

After the nuptial ceremony the two Emperors separated. One of the conditions of this marriage was that Licinius should do nothing against Christianity, for Constantine, who had embraced it, insisted upon his colleague's suffering the Christians to practice their religion in peace and quietness. Accordingly Licinius, though superstitiously attached to the worship of idols, pretended to have some regard for them. The fact of the Empress being of that profession, and the fear of dis-

obliging Constantine, who interested himself very much
in their favour, was what restrained him. Their blood
was, however, very often shed, which Licinius saw with
pleasure, and though he was artful enough to throw all
the blame upon the governors of provinces, it was easy
enough to perceive, by his forbearing to punish such as
committed those cruelties, that they were far from giving
him any offence.

The Empress was well acquainted with his implacable
hatred of the Christians, and made use of all the power
and influence she had over him to conquer in some
measure his aversion to them. She secretly informed
her brother of everything that was being done against
them in Licinius's Court, and the Church was beholden
to her for the tranquillity it enjoyed at that time. It
would, indeed, have been no easy matter for Licinius to
refuse anything that was requested of him by an Empress whose extraordinary merit and amiable qualities
rendered her so worthy of his esteem and affection. But
it was not by her solicitations only that Constantia was
serviceable to the Christians. They felt upon a thousand
occasions the effect of her goodness, and the liberal presents which she distributed among all of them who stood
in need of her assistance.

The success that Constantine had met with in his wars,
and which he with gratitude attributed to the protection
of the God of the Christians, and the public profession
that he and his family and all the nobles of the Court
made of that religion, prevailed also upon Licinius to
pretend a belief in those divine laws; but as soon as he
was at a distance from Constantine he forgot all the
promises that he had made his brother-in-law. He ban-

ished all the Christians from his house, re-established the worship of idols, and abandoned himself to all the abominations that are the natural fruits of idolatry. His insatiable passion for pleasures revived. He gave himself up to all manner of debauchery, and that with so little reserve or restraint that ladies of the highest rank were compelled to submit to his infamous and brutal advances.

Constantia grieved in secret at her husband's course of life, but to no purpose; for neither her remonstrances nor entreaties, nor the charms of her person, which pleaded with so much eloquence, were strong enough to produce any good effects upon him, who was such a slave to his passions that he scrupled at nothing that could contribute to their gratification. He was not content with having dishonoured the most illustrious families, but was earnestly bent upon corrupting a young lady in the Empress's suite, whose virtue recommended her to Constantia infinitely more than her beauty, though she had a great share of the latter.

The Court was then at Nicomedia, which was, without dispute, the most agreeable town in Bithynia, where Diocletian had built a magnificent palace, which was the ordinary residence of the Emperors. It was then that the famous Eusebius became known to the Empress, who introduced him to Licinius, and on her solicitation he was made bishop of Nicomedia.

Constantia loved Glaphyra most of all the ladies at Court. She was a young person of incomparable beauty and virtue. The Emperor was captivated with her charms, and, not being a man to deny his inclinations, used all the means he could think of to seduce her; but knowing of what importance it was to his design to go artfully to work and not to alarm the Empress, who was very watchful over the conduct of her ladies, he employed Benignus, captain of his guards, to negotiate the affair.

Princes, more than all others, are so unfortunate as to meet with people who are ever ready to sacrifice honour and conscience to please them. Benignus informed Glaphyra of the impression that her beauty had made on the Emperor, and what Licinius expected from her. He did not fail to exaggerate the advantages she might reckon upon if she yielded upon this occasion, the influence it would procure her at Court, and the respect that would be shown her by all the empire as soon as it should be known that she was mistress of the Emperor's affections. He put in operation all that cunning and artifice with which those who undertake that sort of infamous commerce are so well acquainted.

Glaphyra, who was not only a Christian, but with great strictness lived up to the religion she professed, was much surprised at these words, and, far from congratulating herself upon the conquest, she was extremely afflicted. She foresaw at once all she had to suffer from a prince of his violent passions, who stuck at nothing to gratify them. This speech of Benignus made her so confused that it sufficiently demonstrated how greatly she was embarrassed at a declaration which she neither expected nor desired; she gave the captain of the guard such an answer as was consistent with her usual virtue and discretion, and then went to communicate this to the Empress, and consult with her how she was to behave. Constantia well knew that Licinius was not easily dissuaded from anything he had resolved upon; on the contrary, the more obstacles he met with, the more obstinate he was; and, as she acted in everything with great prudence, she did not think fit to expose Glaphyra's chastity to the powerful attempts of Licinius, nor to provoke him by reproaches, which are more apt to augment the evil than cure it; but, after considering in her mind what was most proper to be done, she at last determined that Glaphyra should be disguised in male attire. She ordered magnificent apparel to be provided for her with the greatest expedition, gave her a splendid equipage, and a large sum of money, and committing her to the care of people whose virtue she could depend upon, ordered them to conduct her to a place of safety.

Glaphyra, thus disguised, quitted Nicomedia, and set out on her travels; she everywhere passed for a young military tribune, who was charged with some secret orders from the Court, till she arrived at Amasia, the capital of Pontus in Asia. Quintius, the most important person in the city, taking Glaphyra for a young nobleman who was honoured with the Emperor's particular confidence, paid him a visit, and even offered him his house. The pretended tribune yielded to the civility of Quintius, and was prevailed on to accept an apartment in his palace; he enquired into the state of the Christian religion at Amasia, and had the satisfaction of being informed that the Christians were under the direction of a bishop, who was remarkable for his zeal, piety, and eloquence.

It would have been almost impossible for Glaphyra not to confide her secret and the reason of her journey to somebody or other, as she foresaw that a stranger who had the appearance of a person of distinction would be narrowly observed. She thought she could not do better than make a confidant of this good bishop, and put herself under his protection. Besides, she was persuaded that it was her duty to open her heart to some discreet person, who might give her the consolation and assistance she stood in need of.

The bishop's name was Basil, a prelate of a most exemplary life, and to him Glaphyra communicated the secret of her journey, and the danger to which she must have been exposed if she had not fled in disguise. Basil commended the innocent artifice she had made use of to preserve her honour, comforted her with good advice, and confirmed her in her generous resolution to die rather than submit to the infamous desires of Licinius. He instructed her how she should conduct herself during the stay she should be obliged to make at Amasia, and, above all, recommended her to be exceedingly careful not to mention this affair to any other person for fear the governor of the town should come to hear of it.

She followed carefully the counsel that Basil had given her, and informed the Empress of the charitable care the bishop of Amasia took of her, together with her resolution of continuing in that place under the guidance of a prelate, who was both able and willing to assist her.

Constantia was rejoiced to hear of her being safe, and sent her from time to time considerable sums of money, which Glaphyra applied to pious uses. She gave the greatest part of it to the bishop, who, taking advantage of the tranquillity the Christians enjoyed at that time, made use of it for the construction of a church, which his small funds would by no means have enabled him to build; so that the Empress's liberality to Glaphyra was a very seasonable aid. Constantia being informed by Glaphyra that the bishop had occasion for money to finish the building, made him a handsome present for that purpose.

Glaphyra's flight made a great noise at Court, and Licinius, who did not, without the utmost vexation, see the prey delivered out of his clutches, ordered that the strictest search should be made in every place that he imagined she was likely to have retired to, but in vain; Glaphyra, in Amasia, was secure against the indignation and power of the tyrant.

The Empress had frequently the pleasure of receiving letters from her favourite, but unluckily, Benignus, the Emperor's confidant, intercepted one of them, by which accident he discovered the whole secret, and informed Licinius of it. This put the Emperor in such a rage that he thought of no less than sacrificing Glaphyra and Basil to his fury. In fact, he directed the Governor of Amasia, who was a Pagan, to send him Glaphyra and the bishop in irons.

Licinius, however, had not the satisfaction of being revenged on Glaphyra, for it pleased Providence to recompense her virtue by delivering her from this world; so that, when the Emperor's orders arrived at Amasia, she was already dead. Basil was conducted to Nicomedia, where he received the crown of martyrdom for having protected the honour and chastity of this holy virgin.

The cruelty of Licinius towards the Christians much offended Constantine. That pious Emperor, who was as zealous for the Church as his colleague was attached to heathen superstitions, could not with indifference see

Licinius violating the most essential condition of their treaty, by which he had bound himself to permit the Christians in the East to practice their religion in perfect liberty. Constantia, who was a true Christian herself, informed her brother secretly of everything that passed at Licinius's Court that was prejudicial to the Church. It is true that when, by her remonstrances, she imagined she had inspired her husband with more human sentiments, she interceded on his behalf with her brother; and the Emperor, who was extremely fond of his sister, dissembled the reason he had to complain of Licinius, and even pardoned his revolts; but Licinius was only the more ungrateful. That perfidious dissembler was secretly hatching treason against Constantine at the very time when he himself enjoyed the empire, merely because Constantine would not deprive him of it.

Constantia thought this monstrous ingratitude was unworthy of pardon, and would no longer intercede with her brother for Licinius, who was not to be influenced either by threats or kindness. Constantine, therefore, finding that he could never be secure against the plots and conspiracies of Licinius if he did not put it out of his power to injure him, declared war against him, and obtained a complete victory, which Constantia heard of with pleasure. She knew that Licinius was a declared enemy to Christianity, and that the interests of her family were not to be put before her religion: that her husband was incapable of being ever induced to abandon his idols, after all the arguments and means she had made use of to procure his conversion, but without success. Besides, she had reason to apprehend that some time or other Licinius might get the better of her brother, either by force or treachery, and then she could expect nothing but that she herself would fall a sacrifice to the advantages her brother had gained over her husband. She was of opinion that, after having so often interested herself for him and employed all the influence she had with her brother to procure forgiveness for Licinius, who was ever ungrateful and rebellious, it was no longer her duty to show so much affection and zeal for a husband who was by no means deserving of it, especially since by continuing to do so she might give just grounds to her brother to suspect her of being his enemy; therefore, when Licinius was defeated, she brought his imperial robe to her brother, to show that she did not intend to espouse his cause or concern herself any longer about him.

Constantine, however, had so much regard for his sister as to grant Licinius his life, and assign him a revenue suitable to his rank, but he, whose turbulent and unquiet temper was never at rest, could not forbear forming parties, and intriguing with factious and seditious people against Constantine, so he was at last put to death.

Constantia resided in her brother's Court, together with young Licinius, her son. This prince was very handsome, and had a great deal of vivacity in his countenance, but, at the same time, a haughtiness in his air and carriage that was not agreeable. His father had brought him up a pagan, and though Constantia had prevailed on him to turn Christian in appearance, it was very easy to perceive that in reality he was as much a heathen as ever. Constantine, to comfort his sister for the loss of her husband, and to demonstrate to the whole empire that he had been compelled to put Licinius to death for his repeated treasons, declared the young prince consul, which office he exercised with so much pride and ostentation that he sufficiently showed he had ambition enough to aspire to a higher position. Fausta was jealous of this, and feared that in Licinius her children would one day find a dangerous competitor, and that he would revenge upon them the death of his father. Constantine, who foresaw things long beforehand, made the same reflections, which did not a little contribute to determine him to put young Licinius to death.

Constantia was infinitely afflicted at the loss of her son, but in a great measure dissembled her grief rather than occasion any uneasiness to her brother, for whom her interest as well as her duty obliged her to have great regard. He, indeed, had so extraordinary an affection for her that he gave her a power equal to his own, which was increased by the death of the Empress Helena, for whom Constantine had always the greatest regard.

Constantia, who was widow of one Emperor and sister of another, succeeded to the influence that Helena had enjoyed at Court. All favours passed through her hands. Her brother's affection for her procured her the esteem and respect of the whole empire.

Eusebius, whom Constantia had made bishop of Nicomedia, cultivated with great assiduity his acquaintance with her, for that prelate, being of a supple, complaisant disposition, excelled in the art of paying court, so that nobody was better received by the Empress than the bishop of Nicomedia. This gave him considerable influence at the Emperor's palace, and as he knew so well how to put in practice everything that could contribute to his advancement, he soon insinuated himself into the good graces of Constantine, and became very powerful, though he had secretly favoured the party of Licinius against the Emperor, and even against Christians in general, in order to secure to himself a favourable reception in whichever of the Courts should get the better of the other. He did not at all scruple to make religion subservient to his temporal interests and ambition. As soon as Arius had broached his new doctrine, and had drawn upon himself an excommunication from the bishop of Alexandria, Eusebius, who was tainted with the same doctrines, undertook to defend him. He introduced him at Court, and took no small pains to convert the Empress Constantia to those tenets, in which he succeeded only too well, for she swallowed with greediness the fatal poison of heresy. Arius had an imposing exterior, a grave and devout air, a polite and insinuating conversation, and so much the appearance of a virtuous and religious man that the Empress was deceived by it, and looked upon him as a person of rare and uncommon talents, who knew better than the rest of mankind how to treat of divine matters and the mysteries of religion. It was after this manner, says St. Jerome, that Arius, being resolved to propagate his heresy, began by seducing the Emperor's sister; and as he further observes, it has always been a maxim of those deceivers to lay their snares for women in the first place, as the serpent began by seducing Eve.

It is certain that Arianism could not possibly have met with a more powerful protectress than Constantia, so it is not to be wondered at if it spread prodigiously, and caused great disorders in the Church. To put a stop to this, Constantine assembled the famous Council of Nicaea, at which the errors of Arius were condemned. Eusebius was deposed, and the Emperor would have banished him if the prelate, who was extremely loth to quit the Court, had not pretended to renounce Arianism, and signed the condemnation of that heresy, against which the Council had thundered out its anathemas.

After this he found no great difficulty in reinstating himself in the good graces of Constantine by the help of his friends, especially by the Empress's interest. As he was still an Arian at heart, he laboured incessantly to promote that doctrine, which the Council had exploded, and to invent calumnies against Athanasius, who had been made bishop of Alexandria, and was the greatest opposer of Arius. Eusebius's cunning and artifices at first met with all the success he could desire. He accused Athanasius of a thousand crimes, and of treason among the rest, and so cleverly disguised his imposture with an appearance of truth that the Emperor looked upon Athanasius as a very dangerous and seditious person. But the good patriarch, having been cited before Constantine, so clearly proved the falsehood of those slanders that the Emperor was convinced of his innocence, conceived a greater esteem for him than ever, and determined to banish his accusers.

This was a thunderbolt to Eusebius, who did not expect so unlucky a turn of fortune. Constantia was extremely afflicted at his disgrace, but knowing that her brother was highly exasperated against him, and that her interceding for him at that time would make Constantine suspect that she held the same opinions, she

thought it best not to employ her influence in his behalf
till a more favourable opportunity.

This she thought she had found soon after, on the
dedication of the town of Constantinople, which was
called after the Emperor, and which he made the seat of
the empire. Constantine at the same time celebrated the
twenty-fifth year of his reign, and the fifth year since
his son Constantius was created Cæsar, which greatly
added to the magnificence of the ceremony. Constantia
concluded that there could not possibly be a more convenient time than this to solicit the return of Eusebius,
whose absence she could not bear. She made use of
all her influence with her brother to obtain this favour,
and also set her nephew Constantius to work for the
same end, who joined his entreaties to those of Constantia. The Emperor, not being able to resist these importunities, consented that the prelate should return.

Constantia could not have done a greater disservice to
the Church; for Eusebius was more to be feared than
Arius himself, who would not have been able to propagate his tenets without the assistance of Eusebius and
some other bishops. This justice must, however, be done
to the Empress, that she did not believe that Eusebius
was heretically inclined, but rather imagined that he was
unreasonably persecuted by those who were jealous of
his superior merit and learning. This princess was
persuaded that his opinions were very innocent, and
being desirous to distinguish herself from other people,
pretended to greater knowledge in divine mysteries than
the rest of her sex, and so drank deep of the poison of
Arianism, and, not thinking there was the least harm in
it, became the protectress of its most zealous champion.

What was still worse, she persisted in this error till her death, for to her last moment she continued in her endeavours to recommend to Constantine's favour and friendship the most dangerous enemy of the Church. This person was a priest, entirely devoted to the Arians, and more zealous for that doctrine than Arius himself. He concealed his true sentiments under the appearance of extraordinary piety, which deceived those who were not intimately acquainted with him. Eusebius, the bishop of Nicomedia, put the greatest confidence in this hypocrite, and trusted him with his most important secrets. He introduced him to the Empress Constantia as a man of consummate virtue. This priest, by his devout air, his infatuating conversation, and external sanctity, maintained the character that was given of him to the Empress, and gained such an ascendency over her that he could manage her as he pleased. Constantia did nothing without his advice; and, as she affected to practise a devotion that was out of the common track and different from other people's, she listened to nobody but this artful deceiver, who, under pretence of conducting her to perfection by such sublime methods as were far above the capacity of inferior geniuses, infected her with the most dangerous heresy, which was prepared with the greatest art and cunning.

As soon as this dissembler perceived that the Empress placed entire confidence in him, he consulted with his patron Eusebius about the means of getting Arius recalled, and how to interest the Empress in his favour. They felt that it would be very difficult to procure his pardon if they did not take the greatest precautions; for Constantine was extremely zealous for the opinions upheld at the Council of Nicaea, and consequently was no friend of those who were accused of differing from them. This priest, therefore, while with the Empress, artfully turned the conversation upon Arius, and, affecting to sigh and look very melancholy, the Empress asked him the reason of it. The priest answered, with an air of affliction, that he could not help being grieved when he thought of the sad condition of one of the best of men, who was cruelly oppressed by those who envied the sublime talents and extraordinary gifts with which Providence had blessed him. "Arius," said he, "is unfortunate only because he is the worthiest and greatest ecclesiastic the Church can boast of; his merit and virtue are his only crimes. This divine man is fallen under the displeasure of the patriarch Alexander, and is become the object of his persecution. He cannot endure a person whose profound doctrine is universally esteemed, and who has acquired such knowledge of the mysteries of religion as few have attained to. The patriarch has done his utmost to banish from Alexandria this person of uncommon parts and learning, merely because he has been eclipsed by him; and has caused him to be condemned in the Council by imputing to him doctrines and opinions that he never entertained. The whole population of Alexandria is witness of this great man's innocence, for he has for many years past preached with such general applause, that it is acknowledged by everybody that none before him has ever shown such noble and sublime sentiments in religious matters. This man, however, so much favoured and enlightened by Heaven, and who deserves the highest dignities in the Church, is fallen a sacrifice to the blackest malice and envy, banished from his country, driven shamefully out of the Church, and treated with greater hatred than if he were a declared enemy to religion."

Constantia listened with great attention to her director, whom she little suspected of any intention to deceive her. She did not doubt that all he had said of Arius, and the persecutions he had undergone, was literally true. From that time Constantia looked upon Arius as the greatest man in the Church, being persuaded that he who had spoken so much in his behalf was the person in the world the most capable of judging of true merit. She dared not, however, at that time intercede for him with her brother, knowing him to be very averse to Arianism. It was for all that a great advantage to Arius and his disciples to have prepossessed the Empress in his behalf, for they knew so well how to make the most of her sentiments towards him that they never rested till they had gained their point, and secured his recall from banishment.

Matters were in this state when Constantia fell dangerously ill, and during her sickness Constantine visited her every day. He gave her undoubted tokens of the sincere love and affection he bore her, and of his ardent desire to do everything in his power to aid her recovery; but her disease could not be cured by all the remedies that could be thought of, so that Constantia knew she was near her end. The Emperor was in the utmost affliction, when he was informed by the physicians that he was to lose the person in the world he loved best. The Empress, finding that death was approaching very fast, and seeing her brother at her bed's foot overwhelmed with sorrow, took him by the hand, and with dying looks, "My dear brother," said she, in a weak voice, "I have received from you an infinite number of favours and kindnesses, which you have conferred upon me with so much generosity that I cannot doubt you will grant that which I am now to ask. It is indeed the last request I shall ever trouble you with, but more valuable than all the rest. It is that you will give me leave, in return for all your goodness, to make you such a present as will, above all things, show my sincere affection and gratitude. Princes are surrounded by courtiers and sycophants, who are zealous enough for their own interests to promote their temporal honour and grandeur, but they are so unfortunate as to have but few real friends about them who are solicitous for their eternal salvation. See here," said she, "a man whose virtue, merit, and fidelity I am well acquainted with," presenting to him her director; "he will inspire you with those exalted sentiments which he has received from the Almighty, and which he has been so good as to impart to me. He will be always inviolably attached to your spiritual interests, and will conduct you to perfection by such ways as Providence has communicated to no other but himself. Your future happiness will be safe in his hands, so I can safely affirm that I give you an inestimable treasure. I beseech you to put entire confidence in him, and to be ever mindful that he was given you by a sister who has nothing to wish for but your everlasting happiness. I will now confess to you that it has not been without the most sensible grief and concern that I have seen you so apt to be deceived by those who have made an ill use of the trust you have placed in them, and have prevailed on you to persecute, very unjustly, the most deserving of the clergy, who have, by their instigation, been shamefully driven from the Church. Take care that that unreasonable severity does not draw upon you some dreadful punishment. This is the last petition of a sister who, you may be assured, is now solicitous for nothing but your true interest, and who must leave you in a few moments."

She had great difficulty in uttering these words. The agony of death seized her, and she expired in the presence of her brother, who was inconsolable, and upon whom her words made great impression.

Thus Constantia employed the last moments of her life in recommending to Constantine's protection Arius and his followers, who knew but too well how to take advantage of the indulgence that was procured them by Constantia's dying request, which sunk deep into the heart of the Emperor.

INDEX

A

ACTE, Nero enamoured of, 233. Aspires to the throne, 234. Resolves to marry her, 236. Trumps up a fictitious genealogy in her favour, 237. Grows cool to her, 240. Parts with her, 264.

Agrippa (Son of Julia), his character, 74. Adopted by Augustus, 74. Suspected by the Emperor, and why, 74. Banished, 74. Visited in his banishment by Augustus, 75. Augustus presents him with his signet, 97. Envied by Marcellus on that account, 97. Murdered, 78.

Agrippa (Vipsanius), his descent, 104. In the confidence of Augustus, 104. Repudiates Marcella, and marries Julia, 105. His issue, 105. His magnificence, 94. Builds the Pantheon, 94. His death, 107.

Agrippina, wife of Germanicus, her character and family, 83. Hated by Livia, and why, 84. Brings the ashes of her husband to Rome, 85.

Agrippina, wife of Claudius, her character, etc., 177. Guilty of incest, 178, 179. Marries Ahenobarbus, 179. Her intrigues discovered, 180. Banished, 181 and seq. Recalled, 181. Endeavours to entice her uncle Claudius, 181. Married to Crispus Passienus, 182. Proposed as a wife for Claudius, 184. Married to him, 185 and seq. Begins her reign with a good action, 185. Governs the Emperor, 186, 194. Becomes imperious and cruel, 186. Comparison between her and Messalina, 187. Her efforts for the advancement of her son Nero, 188. Prediction of à Chaldæan regarding him, ibid. Gratifies her vengeance and avarice, 188. Favours Vitellius, 190. Forms a design of having her son adopted by the Emperor Claudius, 191. Honoured with the title of August, ibid. Her boundless ambition, 193. Presents sent her from all nations, 194. Causes many dignities to be conferred on Nero, 194 and seq. Her aversion to Narcissus, and for what, 196. Attempts his destruction, 197. Meditates the murder of her husband, 199. Accomplishes it, 200. Keeps his death secret, and with what view, 201. Determines to sacrifice Domitia Lepida, 200. Falls furiously on such as opposed her, 202 and seq. Destroys Silanus,

C

H

L

cutes, and at length puts to death, Prisca and Valeria, 787 and seq. Conspires against Constantine, 802. Put to death, 803.

Livia Drusilla, her character, 28. Her person and endowments, 29. Married to T. Claudius Nero, 30. Proves with child, 30. Desirous of a son, 30. Method taken by her to discover if she was with child of a boy, 30. Delivered of Tiberius, 31. Undergoes great hardship, and upon what account, 45. Augustus becomes enamoured of her, 47. Obliges Nero to resign her, 49. Delivered of Drusus, 50. Declared sacred, 54. Temples erected in honour of her, 59. Suspected of poisoning Marcellus, 65, 69. Of the murder of Gaius and Lucius Cæsar, 73 and seq. Of causing Agrippa to be murdered, 78. Of poisoning the Emperor, 77. Her influence over Augustus, an instance of it, 66. Procures many honours for her son Tiberius, 70. Her resentment on the subject of Augustus's visiting Agrippa, 75. Affects inconsolable sorrow for the death of Augustus, 78. Causes him to be immortalised, 78. Consecrated a priestess in the temple of Augustus, 78. Mortified at the ingratitude of Tiberius, 79. Defends Plancina, 85. Uncommon privileges and honours conferred on her, 86. Her death, 88.

Lollia Paulina, her descent, 129. Marries Memmius Regulus, 131. Yielded up to Caligula by Memmius, 131. Divorced, 131. Her attempt to captivate the Emperor Claudius, 132 and seq. Callistus speaks in her favour, 133. Accused, 135. Banished, 136.

Lucilla, her descent, 459. Her character, 458. Person, 461. Married to Verus, 466. To Pompeianus, 471. Her lewdness, 472. Her intrigue with Quadratus, 472 and seq. Her incest, 473. Her jealousy of Crispina, 473. Determines to dethrone the Emperor, 474. Persuades her gallant Quadratus to join her, 474. Discovered, 476. Banished, and afterwards put to death, 476.

Lucius Cæsar, his descent, 105 and seq. His death, 73.

M

Macrinus, his character, etc., 598. Marries Celsa, 599. Raised to the greatest employments by her means, 600. Præfect of the Prætorian Guards, 601. Made Emperor, 601. Makes peace with the Persians, 602. Makes his son partner in the empire, 603. Makes wholesome laws, 604. Defeated by the army of Heliogabalus, 611. Killed, ib.

Mæsa, conducts Heliogabalus, her grandson, to Antioch, 612. Her advice to him, 615. Is admitted to the Senate, 616. Reviews the Prætorian cohorts, 618. Endeavours to procure the empire for her grandson, Alexianus, 632. Succeeds, 633. Her death, 644.

Magnia Urbica, consort of the Emperor Carus, 751.

P

Z

THE END